MW00791673

The Handbook of
financial
instruments

THE FRANK J. FABOZZI SERIES

The Handbook of
financial
instruments

FRANK J. FABOZZI

EDITOR

John Wiley & Sons, Inc.

Published by John Wiley & Sons, Inc., Hoboken, New Jersey
Published simultaneously in Canada

For general information on our other products and services, or technical support, please contact our Customer Care Department within the United States at 800-762-2974, outside the United States at 317-572-3993 or fax 317-572-4002.

Wiley also publishes its books in a variety of electronic formats. Some content that appears in print may not be available in electronic books.

ISBN: 0-471-22092-2

Printed in the United States of America

10 9 8 7 6 5 4 3 2 1

contents

preface

One of the most important investment decisions that an investor encounters is the allocation of funds among the wide range of financial instruments. That decision requires an understanding of the investment characteristics of all asset classes. The objective of *The Handbook of Financial Instruments* is to explain financial instruments and their characteristics.

In Chapter 1, financial assets and financial markets are defined. Also explained in the chapter are the general characteristics of common stock and fixed-income securities, the properties of financial markets, the general principles of valuation, the principles of leverage, mechanisms for borrowing funds in the market using securities as collateral, and the role of derivative products.

Chapter 2 provides the fundamentals of investing. This is done in terms of the phases of the investment management process. The topics included in the chapter are traditional and alternative asset classes, how asset classes are determined, various types of risk, active versus passive portfolio management, and active versus indexed portfolio construction.

Chapter 3 explains the proper methodology for computing investment returns. Complications associated with calculating investment returns include selection of the appropriate inputs in the calculation, treatment of client contributions and withdrawals from an investment account, the timing of contributions and withdrawals, the difference between return earned by the investment manager on the funds invested and the return earned by the client, and how to determine annual returns from subperiod returns (e.g., different methods for averaging).

Equity, more popularly referred to as common stock, is the subject of Chapters 4 and 5. Chapter 4 describes the markets where common stock is traded, the types of trades that can be executed by retail and institutional investors (e.g., block trades and program trades), transaction costs, stock market indicators, the pricing efficiency of the equity market, common stock portfolio management, active portfolio management (e.g., top-down versus bottom-up approaches, fundamental versus technical analysis, popular active stock market strategies, and equity style management).

Where an investor can obtain information about the issuers of common stock and the type of information available is the subject of Chapter 5.

Chapters 6 through 20 cover fixed income products—money market instruments, Treasury securities (fixed principal and inflation indexed securities), federal agency securities, municipal securities, corporate bonds, preferred stock, emerging market debt, leveraged loans, and structured products. Structured products covered include agency mortgage-backed securities, nonagency mortgage-backed securities, real estate-backed asset-backed securities (e.g., home equity loan-backed securities and manufactured home loan-backed securities), commercial mortgage-backed securities, non-real estate-backed securities (e.g., credit card receivable-backed securities, auto loan-backed securities, Small Business Administration loan-backed securities, student loan-backed securities, aircraft lease-backed securities, and rate reduction bonds), and collateralized debt obligations.

Chapter 21 provides comprehensive coverage of investment companies, more popularly referred to as mutual funds. Topics covered are the types of investment companies, fund sales charges and annual operating expenses, multiple share classes, types of funds by investment objective, regulation of funds, the advantages and disadvantages of mutual funds, and alternatives to mutual funds. One alternative to a mutual fund is an exchange-traded fund. The advantages of an exchange-traded fund are explained Chapter 22, which also covers competitor products.

Stable value products are covered in Chapter 23. These products provide for a guaranteed return of principal at a contractually specified rate, the guarantee being only as good as the issuer of the contract. Examples include fixed annuities and traditional guaranteed investment contracts (GICs), separate account GICs, and bank investment contracts. Comprehensive coverage of investment-oriented life insurance products is provided in Chapter 24. These products include cash value life insurance (variable life, universal life, and variable universal life) and annuities (variable, fixed, and GICs). General account versus separate account products and the taxability of life insurance products are also discussed in the chapter.

Two major alternative asset classes are hedge funds and private equity. They are the subject of Chapters 25 and 26, respectively. The coverage of hedge funds includes regulation, strategies employed by hedge funds (e.g., long/short hedge funds, global macro hedge fund, short selling hedge funds, arbitrage hedge funds, and market neutral hedge funds), evidence on performance persistence, selecting a hedge fund manager, and the various aspects of due diligence. Private equity includes four strategies for private investing—venture capital (i.e., financing of start-up companies), leverage buyouts, mezzanine financing (hybrid of private debt and private equity), and distressed debt investing. Each of these strategies is reviewed in Chapter 26.

Real estate investment is covered in Chapter 27. The topics covered include the distinguishing features of real estate investments, the nature of the investors, components of the real estate investment universe (private equity, private debt, commercial mortgage-backed securities, and public equity) and their risk/return characteristics, the primary reasons to consider real estate in an investment portfolio, and how to bring real estate into a portfolio (i.e., execution).

Derivative instruments are covered in Chapters 28–31—futures/forward contracts, options, futures options, swaps, caps, and floors. The focus is on how these instruments can be employed to control risk. Chapter 28 covers equity derivatives and describes the fundamentals of pricing stock index futures and options on individual stocks. Chapter 29 is devoted to interest rate derivatives and how they are employed to control interest rate risk. Because of the unique investment characteristics of mortgage-backed securities, instruments are available that can be used by institutional investors to control the interest rate and prepayment risks associated with these securities and to obtain exposure to the market on a leveraged basis. These products, mortgage swaps, are described in Chapter 30. In addition to controlling interest rate risk, investors are concerned with credit risk. Instruments for controlling this risk, credit derivatives, are explained in Chapter 31.

Managed futures, an alternative asset class, is the subject of Chapter 32. The term managed futures refers to the active trading of futures and forward contracts. The underlying for the futures/forward contracts traded can be financial instruments (stock indexes or bonds), commodities, or currencies (i.e., foreign exchange).

The Handbook of Financial Instruments provides the most comprehensive coverage of financial instruments that has ever been assembled in a single volume. I thank all of the contributors to this book for their willingness to take the time from their busy schedules to contribute.

Frank J. Fabozzi

contributing authors

William J. Adams	Massachusetts Financial Services
Mark J. P. Anson	CalPERS
John B. Brynjolfsson	PIMCO Real Return Bond Fund
John R. Caswell	Galliard Capital Management
Moorad Choudhry	City University Business School
Bruce M.Collins	QuantCast
Joseph F. DeMichele	Delaware Investments
John Dunlevy	Beacon Hill Asset Management
Frank J. Fabozzi	Yale University
Bruce Feibel	Eagle Investment Systems
Michael J. Fleming	Federal Reserve Bank of New York
Gary L. Gastineau	ETF Advisors, LLC
Laurie S. Goodman	UBS Warburg
Duane C. Hewlett	Delaware Investments
Susan Hudson-Wilson	Property & Portfolio Research, LLC
Robert R. Johnson	Association for Investment Management and Research
Frank J. Jones	The Guardian Life Insurance Company of America
George P. Kegler	Cassian Market Consultants
Maria Mednikov Loucks	UBS Asset Management
Steven V. Mann	University of South Carolina
John N. McElravey	Banc One Capital Markets, Inc.
Steven Miller	Standard & Poor's
John A. Penicook, Jr.	UBS Asset Management
Pamela P. Peterson	Florida State University
Uwe Schillhorn	UBS Asset Management
Karl P. Tourville	Galliard Capital Management
David Yuen	Franklin Templeton Investments
Thomas A. Zimmerman	UBS Warburg

CHAPTER 1

Overview of Financial Instruments

Frank J. Fabozzi, Ph.D., CFA
Adjunct Professor of Finance
School of Management
Yale University

Broadly speaking, an asset is any possession that has value in an exchange. Assets can be classified as tangible or intangible. A tangible asset is one whose value depends on particular physical properties—examples are buildings, land, or machinery. Intangible assets, by contrast, represent legal claims to some future benefit. Their value bears no relation to the form, physical or otherwise, in which these claims are recorded. Financial assets are intangible assets. For financial assets, the typical benefit or value is a claim to future cash. This book deals with the various types of *financial assets* or *financial instruments*.

The entity that has agreed to make future cash payments is called the *issuer* of the financial instrument; the owner of the financial instrument is referred to as the *investor*. Here are seven examples of financial instruments:

- A loan by Fleet Bank (investor/commercial bank) to an individual (issuer/borrower) to purchase a car
- A bond issued by the U.S. Department of the Treasury
- A bond issued by Ford Motor Company
- A bond issued by the city of Philadelphia
- A bond issued by the government of France

1

- A share of common stock issued by Microsoft Corporation, an American company
- A share of common stock issued by Toyota Motor Corporation, a Japanese company

In the case of the car loan by Fleet Bank, the terms of the loan establish that the borrower must make specified payments to the commercial bank over time. The payments include repayment of the amount borrowed plus interest. The cash flow for this asset is made up of the specified payments that the borrower must make.

In the case of a U.S. Treasury bond, the U.S. government (the issuer) agrees to pay the holder or the investor the interest payments every six months until the bond matures, then at the maturity date repay the amount borrowed. The same is true for the bonds issued by Ford Motor Company, the city of Philadelphia, and the government of France. In the case of Ford Motor Company, the issuer is a corporation, not a government entity. In the case of the city of Philadelphia, the issuer is a municipal government. The issuer of the French government bond is a central government entity.

The common stock of Microsoft entitles the investor to receive dividends distributed by the company. The investor in this case also has a claim to a pro rata share of the net asset value of the company in case of liquidation of the company. The same is true of the common stock of Toyota Motor Corporation.

DEBT VERSUS EQUITY INSTRUMENTS

Financial instruments can be classified by the type of claim that the holder has on the issuer. When the claim is for a fixed dollar amount, the financial instrument is said to be a *debt instrument*. The car loan, the U.S. Treasury bond, the Ford Motor Company bond, the city of Philadelphia bond, and the French government bond are examples of debt instruments requiring fixed payments.

In contrast to a debt obligation, an *equity instrument* obligates the issuer of the financial instrument to pay the holder an amount based on earnings, if any, after the holders of debt instruments have been paid. Common stock is an example of an equity claim. A partnership share in a business is another example.

Some securities fall into both categories in terms of their attributes. Preferred stock, for example, is an equity instrument that entitles the investor to receive a fixed amount. This payment is contingent, however, and due only after payments to debt instrument holders are made.

Another "combination" instrument is a convertible bond, which allows the investor to convert debt into equity under certain circumstances. Both debt instruments and preferred stock that pay fixed dollar amounts are called *fixed-income instruments*.

CHARACTERISTICS OF DEBT INSTRUMENTS

As will become apparent, there are a good number of debt instruments available to investors. Debt instruments include loans, money market instruments, bonds, mortgage-backed securities, and asset-backed securities. In the chapters that follow, each will be described. There are features of debt instruments that are common to all debt instruments and they are described below. In later chapters, there will be a further discussion of these features as they pertain to debt instruments of particular issuers.

Maturity

The term to maturity of a debt obligation is the number of years over which the issuer has promised to meet the conditions of the obligation. At the maturity date, the issuer will pay off any amount of the debt obligation outstanding. The convention is to refer to the "term to maturity" as simply its "maturity" or "term." As we explain later, there may be provisions that allow either the issuer or holder of the debt instrument to alter the term to maturity.

The market for debt instruments is classified in terms of the time remaining to its maturity. A *money market instrument* is a debt instrument which has one year or less remaining to maturity. Debt instruments with a maturity greater than one year are referred to as a *capital market debt instrument*.

Par Value

The *par value* of a bond is the amount that the issuer agrees to repay the holder of the debt instrument by the maturity date. This amount is also referred to as the *principal, face value, redemption value*, or *maturity value*. Bonds can have any par value.

Because debt instruments can have a different par value, the practice is to quote the price of a debt instrument as a percentage of its par value. A value of 100 means 100% of par value. So, for example, if a debt instrument has a par value of $1,000 and is selling for $900, it would be said to be selling at 90. If a debt instrument with a par value of $5,000 is selling for $5,500, it is said to be selling for 110. The reason why a debt instrument sells above or below its par value is explained in Chapter 2.

Coupon Rate

The *coupon rate*, also called the *nominal rate* or the *contract rate*, is the interest rate that the issuer/borrower agrees to pay each year. The dollar amount of the payment, referred to as the *coupon interest payment* or simply *interest payment*, is determined by multiplying the coupon rate by the par value of the debt instrument. For example, the interest payment for a debt instrument with a 7% coupon rate and a par value of $1,000 is $70 (7% times $1,000).

The frequency of interest payments varies by the type of debt instrument. In the United States, the usual practice for bonds is for the issuer to pay the coupon in two semiannual installments. Mortgage-backed securities and asset-backed securities typically pay interest monthly. For bonds issued in some markets outside the United States, coupon payments are made only once per year. Loan interest payments can be customized in any manner.

Zero-Coupon Bonds

Not all debt obligations make periodic coupon interest payments. Debt instruments that are not contracted to make periodic coupon payments are called *zero-coupon instruments*. The holder of a zero-coupon instrument realizes interest income by buying it substantially below its par value. Interest then is paid at the maturity date, with the interest earned by the investor being the difference between the par value and the price paid for the debt instrument. So, for example, if an investor purchases a zero-coupon instrument for 70, the interest realized at the maturity date is 30. This is the difference between the par value (100) and the price paid (70).

There are bonds that are issued as zero-coupon instruments. Moreover, in the money market there are several types of debt instruments that are issued as discount instruments. These are discussed in Chapter 6.

There is another type of debt obligation that does not pay interest until the maturity date. This type has contractual coupon payments, but those payments are accrued and distributed along with the maturity value at the maturity date. These instruments are called *accrued coupon instruments* or *accrual securities* or *compound interest securities*.

Floating-Rate Securities

The coupon rate on a debt instrument need not be fixed over its lifetime. *Floating-rate securities*, sometimes called *floaters* or *variable-rate securities*, have coupon payments that reset periodically according to some reference rate. The typical formula for the coupon rate on the dates when the coupon rate is reset is:

$$\text{Reference rate} \pm \text{Quoted margin}$$

The quoted margin is the additional amount that the issuer agrees to pay above the reference rate (if the quoted margin is positive) or the amount less than the reference rate (if the quoted margin is negative). The quoted margin is expressed in terms of *basis points*. A basis point is equal to 0.0001 or 0.01%. Thus, 100 basis points are equal to 1%.

To illustrate a coupon reset formula, suppose that the reference rate is the 1-month London interbank offered rate (LIBOR)—an interest rate described in Chapter 6. Suppose that the quoted margin is 150 basis points. Then the coupon reset formula is:

1-month LIBOR + 150 basis points

So, if 1-month LIBOR on the coupon reset date is 5.5%, the coupon rate is reset for that period at 7% (5% plus 200 basis points).

The reference rate for most floating-rate securities is an interest rate or an interest rate index. There are some issues where this is not the case. Instead, the reference rate is the rate of return on some financial index such as one of the stock market indexes discussed in Chapter 4. There are debt obligations whose coupon reset formula is tied to an inflation index. These instruments are described in Chapter 8.

Typically, the coupon reset formula on floating-rate securities is such that the coupon rate increases when the reference rate increases, and decreases when the reference rate decreases. There are issues whose coupon rate moves in the opposite direction from the change in the reference rate. Such issues are called *inverse floaters* or *reverse floaters* .

A floating-rate debt instrument may have a restriction on the maximum coupon rate that will be paid at a reset date. The maximum coupon rate is called a *cap*.

Because a cap restricts the coupon rate from increasing, a cap is an unattractive feature for the investor. In contrast, there could be a minimum coupon rate specified for a floating-rate security. The minimum coupon rate is called a *floor*. If the coupon reset formula produces a coupon rate that is below the floor, the floor is paid instead. Thus, a floor is an attractive feature for the investor.

Provisions for Paying off Debt Instruments

The issuer/borrower of a debt instrument agrees to repay the principal by the stated maturity date. The issuer/borrower can agree to repay the entire amount borrowed in one lump sum payment at the maturity date. That is, the issuer/borrower is not required to make any principal repayments prior to the maturity date. Such bonds are said to have a *bullet maturity*. An issuer may be required to retire a specified portion of an issue each year. This is referred to as a *sinking fund requirement*.

There are loans, mortgage-backed securities, and asset-backed securities pools of loans that have a schedule of principal repayments that are made prior to the final maturity of the instrument. Such debt instruments are said to be *amortizing instruments.*

There are debt instruments that have a *call provision.* This provision grants the issuer/borrower an option to retire all or part of the issue prior to the stated maturity date. Some issues specify that the issuer must retire a predetermined amount of the issue periodically. Various types of call provisions are discussed below.

Call and Refunding Provisions

A borrower generally wants the right to retire a debt instrument prior to the stated maturity date because it recognizes that at some time in the future the general level of interest rates may fall sufficiently below the coupon rate so that redeeming the issue and replacing it with another debt instrument with a lower coupon rate would be economically beneficial. This right is a disadvantage to the investor since proceeds received must be reinvested at a lower interest rate. As a result, a borrower who wants to include this right as part of a debt instrument must compensate the investor when the issue is sold by offering a higher coupon rate.

The right of the borrower to retire the issue prior to the stated maturity date is referred to as a "call option." If the borrower exercises this right, the issuer is said to "call" the debt instrument. The price that the borrower must pay to retire the issue is referred to as the *call price.*

When a debt instrument is issued, typically the borrower may not call it for a number of years. That is, the issue is said to have a *deferred call.* The date at which the debt instrument may first be called is referred to as the *first call date.*

If a bond issue does not have any protection against early call, then it is said to be a *currently callable issue.* But most new bond issues, even if currently callable, usually have some restrictions against certain types of early redemption. The most common restriction is prohibiting the refunding of the bonds for a certain number of years. *Refunding* a bond issue means redeeming bonds with funds obtained through the sale of a new bond issue.

Many investors are confused by the terms noncallable and nonrefundable. Call protection is much more absolute than refunding protection. While there may be certain exceptions to absolute or complete call protection in some cases, it still provides greater assurance against premature and unwanted redemption than does refunding protection. Refunding prohibition merely prevents redemption only from certain sources of funds, namely the proceeds of other debt issues sold at a lower cost of money. The bondholder is only protected if interest rates decline, and the borrower can obtain lower-cost money to pay off the debt.

Prepayments

For amortizing instruments—such as loans and securities that are backed by loans—there is a schedule of principal repayments but individual borrowers typically have the option to pay off all or part of their loan prior to the scheduled date. Any principal repayment prior to the scheduled date is called a *prepayment*. The right of borrowers to prepay is called the prepayment option. Basically, the prepayment option is the same as a call option.

Options Granted to Bondholders

There are provisions in debt instruments that give either the investor and/or the issuer an option to take some action against the other party. The most common type of embedded option is a call feature, which was discussed earlier. This option is granted to the issuer. There are two options that can be granted to the owner of the debt instrument: the right to put the issue and the right to convert the issue.

A debt instrument with a *put provision* grants the investor the right to sell it back to the borrower at a specified price on designated dates. The specified price is called the *put price*. The advantage of the put provision to the investor is that if after the issuance date of the debt instrument market interest rates rise above the debt instrument's coupon rate, the investor can force the borrower to redeem the bond at the put price and then reinvest the proceeds at the prevailing higher rate.

A convertible debt instrument is one that grants the investor the right to convert or exchange the debt instrument for a specified number of shares of common stock. Such a feature allows the investor to take advantage of favorable movements in the price of the borrower's common stock or equity.

VALUATION OF A FINANCIAL INSTRUMENT

Valuation is the process of determining the fair value of a financial instrument. Valuation is also referred to as "pricing" a financial instrument. Once this process is complete, we can compare a financial instrument's computed fair value as determined by the valuation process to the price at which it is trading for in the market (i.e., the market price). Based on this comparison, an investor will be able to assess the investment merit of a financial instrument.

There are three possibilities summarized below along with their investment implications.

Market Price versus Fair Value	Investment Implications
Market price equal to fair value	Financial instrument is fairly priced
Market price is less than fair value	Financial instrument is undervalued
Market price is greater than fair value	Financial instrument is overvalued

A financial instrument that is undervalued is said to be "trading cheap" and is a candidate for purchase. If a financial instrument is overvalued, it is said to be "trading rich." In this case, an investor should sell the financial instrument if he or she already owns it. Or, if the financial instrument is not owned, it is possible for the investor to sell it anyway. Selling a financial instrument that is not owned is a common practice in some markets. This market practice is referred to as "selling short." We will discuss the mechanics of selling short in Chapter 4. The two reasons why we say that it is possible for an investor to sell short are (1) the investor must be permitted or authorized to do so and (2) the market for the financial instrument must have a mechanism for short selling.

FINANCIAL MARKETS

A financial market is a market where financial instruments are exchanged (i.e., traded). Although the existence of a financial market is not a necessary condition for the creation and exchange of a financial instrument, in most economies financial instruments are created and subsequently traded in some type of financial market. The market in which a financial asset trades for immediate delivery is called the *spot market* or *cash market*.

Role of Financial Markets

Financial markets provide three major economic functions. First, the interactions of buyers and sellers in a financial market determine the price of the traded asset. Or, equivalently, they determine the required return on a financial instrument. Because the inducement for firms to acquire funds depends on the required return that investors demand, it is this feature of financial markets that signals how the funds in the financial market should be allocated among financial instruments. This is called the *price discovery process*.

Second, financial markets provide a mechanism for an investor to sell a financial instrument. Because of this feature, it is said that a financial market offers "liquidity," an attractive feature when circumstances either force or motivate an investor to sell. If there were not liquidity, the owner would be forced to hold a financial instrument until the issuer initially contracted to make the final payment (i.e., until the debt instrument matures) and an equity instrument until the company is either voluntarily or involuntarily liquidated. While all financial markets provide some form of liquidity, the degree of liquidity is one of the factors that characterize different markets.

The third economic function of a financial market is that it reduces the cost of transacting. There are two costs associated with transacting: search costs and information costs. *Search costs* represent explicit costs, such as the money spent to advertise one's intention to sell or purchase a financial instrument, and implicit costs, such as the value of time spent in locating a counterparty. The presence of some form of organized financial market reduces search costs. *Information costs* are costs associated with assessing the investment merits of a financial instrument, that is, the amount and the likelihood of the cash flow expected to be generated. In a price efficient market, prices reflect the aggregate information collected by all market participants.

Classification of Financial Markets

There are many ways to classify financial markets. One way is by the type of financial claim, such as debt markets and equity markets. Another is by the maturity of the claim. For example, the money market is a financial market for short-term debt instruments; the market for debt instruments with a maturity greater than one year and equity instruments is called the *capital market.*

Financial markets can be categorized as those dealing with financial claims that are newly issued, called the *primary market*, and those for exchanging financial claims previously issued, called the *secondary market* or the market for seasoned instruments.

Markets are classified as either *cash markets* or *derivative markets*. The latter is described later in this chapter. A market can be classified by its organizational structure: It may be an *auction market* or an *over-the-counter market*. We describe these organizational structures when we discuss the market for common stocks in Chapter 4.

BORROWING FUNDS TO PURCHASE FINANCIAL INSTRUMENTS

Some investors follow a policy of borrowing a portion or all of the funds to buy financial instruments. By doing so an investor is creating *financial leverage* or simply leverage. We first describe the principle of leverage and then explain how an investor can create a leveraged position in financial markets.

Principles of Leverage

The objective in leveraging is to earn a higher return on the funds borrowed than it cost to borrow those funds. The disadvantage is that if the funds borrowed earn less than the cost of the borrowed funds, then the investor would have been better off without borrowing.

Here is a simple example. Suppose an investor can invest $100,000 today in a financial instrument. The investor puts up his own funds to purchase the financial instrument and this amount is referred to as the *investor's equity*. Suppose that the financial instrument at the end of one year provides a cash payment to the investor of $5,000. Also assume that the value of the financial instrument has appreciated from $100,000 to $110,000. Thus, the investor's return is $5,000 in the form of a cash payment plus capital appreciation of $10,000 for a total of $15,000. The return this investor realized is 15% on the $100,000 investment. Instead of an appreciation in price for the financial instrument, suppose its value declined to $97,000. Then the investor's return would be $2,000 ($5,000 cash payment less the depreciation in the value of the financial instrument of $3,000) or a 2% return.

Now let's see where leverage comes in. Suppose that our investor can borrow another $100,000 to purchase an additional amount of the financial instrument. Consequently, $200,000 is invested, $100,000 of which is the investor's equity and $100,000 of which is borrowed funds. Let's suppose that the cost of borrowing the $100,000 is 7%. In the case where the financial instrument appreciated, the investor's return on equity is summarized below:

Investment in financial instrument   = $200,000
Cash payment   = $10,000
Values of financial instrument at end of year = $220,000
Appreciation in value of financial instrument = $20,000
Cost of borrowed funds = $7,000 (7% × $100,000)
Dollar return = $10,000 + $20,000 − $7,000 = $23,000
Return on investor's equity = 23% (= $23,000/$100,000)

Thus the investor increased the return on equity from 15% (when no funds were borrowed) to 23% (when $100,000 was borrowed). The reason should be obvious. The investor borrowed $100,000 at a cost of 7% and then earned on the $100,000 borrowed 15%. The difference of 8% between the return earned on the money borrowed and the cost of the money borrowed accrued to the benefit of the investor in terms of increasing the return on equity.

Let's try this one more time assuming that the investor borrowed $200,000 at a cost of 7% and the value of the financial instruments increased. The results are summarized below:

Investment in financial instrument = $300,000
Cash payment = $15,000
Value of financial instrument at end of year = $330,000
Appreciation in value of financial instrument = $30,000
Cost of borrowed funds = $14,000 (7% × $200,000)
Dollar return = $15,000 + $30,000 − $14,000 = $31,000
Return on investor's equity = 31% (= $31,000/$100,000)

By borrowing $200,000, the investor has increased the return on equity compared to the case of no borrowing or borrowing just $100,000.

That is the good news and occurs if the return earned on the borrowed funds exceeds the cost of borrowing. But there is a risk that this will not occur. For example, take the case where the investor borrows $100,000 but the financial instrument's value declines. Then we have the following situation:

Investment in financial instrument = $200,000
Cash payment = $10,000
Value of financial instrument at end of year = $194,000
Depreciation in value of financial instrument = $6,000
Cost of borrowed funds = $7,000 (7% × $100,000)
Dollar return = $10,000 − 6,000 − $7,000 = −$3,000
Return on investor's equity = −3% (= −$3,000/$100,000)

The return on investor's equity in this case is −3%. This is less than the investor would have realized if no funds were borrowed (2%). The reason is that the investor earned 2% on the $100,000 borrowed and had to pay 7% to borrow the funds. The difference of 5% between the cost of borrowing and the return on the $100,000 borrowed works against the investor in terms of reducing the return on the investor's equity.

It is easy to see why the more borrowed in this scenario, the more it would have decreased the return on investor's equity.

Collateralized Borrowing in the Financial Markets

How does an investor create leverage? One obvious way is to take out a loan from a financial institution. However, there is a standard mechanism in most sectors of the financial market that allows an investor to create leverage. The investor can use the financial instrument purchased with the borrowed funds as collateral for the loan.

In the stock market, the form of collateralized borrowing is referred to as "buying on margin." This will be explained in Chapter 4. In the bond market, there are various forms of collateralized borrowing. For individual investors, typically the mechanism is buying on margin. For institutional investors, a repurchase agreement is used. This agreement will be explained in Chapter 6. It is actually a short-term investment to the entity that wants to lend funds (hence it is called a money market instrument) and a source of funds for an investor who wants a collateralized loan.

There is a specialized type of repurchase agreement in the mortgage-backed securities market called a dollar roll. This will be explained in Chapter 14.

DERIVATIVE MARKETS

So far we have focused on the cash market for financial instruments. With some financial instruments, the contract holder has either the obligation or the choice to buy or sell a financial instrument at some future time. The price of any such contract derives its value from the value of the underlying financial instrument, financial index, or interest rate. Consequently, these contracts are called *derivative instruments*.

The primary role of derivative instruments is to provide investors with an inexpensive way of controlling some of the major risks that we will describe in this book. We will take a closer look at this in Chapter 28. Unfortunately, derivative instruments are too often viewed by the general public—and sometimes regulators and legislative bodies—as vehicles for pure speculation (that is, legalized gambling). Without derivative instruments and the markets in which they trade, the financial systems throughout the world would not be as efficient or integrated as they are today.[1]

---

[1] A May 1994 report published by the U.S. General Accounting Office (GAO) titled *Financial Derivatives: Actions Needed to Protect the Financial System* recognized the importance of derivatives for market participants. Page 6 of the report states:

> Derivatives serve an important function of the global financial market-place, providing end-users with opportunities to better manage financial risks associated with their business transactions. The rapid growth and increasing complexity of derivatives reflect both the increased demand from end-users for better ways to manage their financial risks and the innovative capacity of the financial services industry to respond to market demands.

Types of Derivative Instruments

The two basic types of derivative instruments are futures/forward contracts and options contracts. A *futures contract* or *forward contract* is an agreement whereby two parties agree to transact with respect to some financial instrument at a predetermined price at a specified future date. One party agrees to buy the financial instrument; the other agrees to sell the financial instrument. Both parties are obligated to perform, and neither party charges a fee. The distinction between a futures and forward contract is explained in Chapter 29.

An *option contract* gives the owner of the contract the right, but not the obligation, to buy (or sell) a financial instrument at a specified price from (or to) another party. The buyer of the contract must pay the seller a fee, which is called the *option price*. When the option grants the owner of the option the right to buy a financial instrument from the other party, the option is called a call option. If, instead, the option grants the owner of the option the right to sell a financial instrument to the other party, the option is called a put option. Options are more fully explained in Chapter 28.

Derivative instruments are not limited to financial instruments. In this book we will describe derivative instruments where the underlying asset is a financial asset, or some financial benchmark such as a stock index or an interest rate, or a credit spread. Moreover, there are other types of derivative instruments that are basically "packages" of either forward contracts or option contracts. These include swaps, caps, and floors, all of which are discussed in Chapter 29).

CHAPTER 2

Fundamentals of Investing

Frank J. Fabozzi, Ph.D., CFA
Adjunct Professor of Finance
School of Management
Yale University

In this chapter the fundamentals of investing will be reviewed. We will explain these fundamentals in terms of the phases that are involved in investing. These phases include: setting investment objectives, establishing an investment policy, selecting a portfolio strategy, constructing a portfolio, and evaluating performance.

SETTING INVESTMENT OBJECTIVES

The investment process begins with a thorough analysis of the investment objectives of the entity whose funds are being invested. These entities can be classified as *individual investors* and *institutional investors*.

The objectives of an individual investor may be to accumulate funds to purchase a home or other major acquisition, to have sufficient funds to be able to retire at a specified age, or to accumulate funds to pay for college tuition for children.

Institutional investors include

- Pension funds
- Depository institutions (commercial banks, savings and loan associations, and credit unions)
- Insurance companies (life insurance companies, property and casualty insurance companies, and health insurance companies)

15

■ Regulated investment companies (mutual funds)
■ Endowments and foundations
■ Treasury departments of corporations, municipal governments, and government agencies

In general we can classify institutional investors into two broad categories—those that must meet contractually specified liabilities and those that do not. We refer to those in the first category as institutions with "liability-driven objectives" and those in the second category as institutions with "non–liability-driven objectives." Some institutions have a wide range of investment products that they offer investors, some of which are liability-driven and others that are non-liability driven.

ESTABLISHING AN INVESTMENT POLICY

Once the investment objectives are identified, an investor must then establish policy guidelines to satisfy the investment objectives. Setting policy begins with the *asset allocation decision*. That is, a decision must be made as to how the investor's funds should be distributed among asset classes. In making the asset allocation decision, investors will look at the risk and return characteristics of the asset classes in which they may invest and the correlation between the returns of each asset class. We define what is meant by an asset class and the notion of risk in the sections to follow.

The asset allocation will take into consideration any investment constraints or restrictions. Asset allocation models are commercially available for assisting those individuals responsible for making this decision.

In the development of investment policies, the following factors must be considered:

■ Client constraints
■ Regulatory constraints
■ Accounting and tax issues

Asset Classes

From the perspective of a U.S. investor, the convention today is to refer to the following as *traditional asset classes*:

U.S. common stocks
Non-U.S. (or foreign) common stocks
U.S. bonds
Non-U.S. (or foreign) bonds

Cash equivalents
Real estate

Cash equivalents are defined as short-term debt obligations that have little price volatility and are discussed in Chapter 6.

Common stock and bonds are further divided into other asset classes. For U.S. common stocks, the following are classified as asset classes:

Large capitalization stocks
Mid capitalization stocks
Small capitalization stocks
Growth stocks
Value stocks

"Capitalization" means the market capitalization of the company's common stock. It is equal to the total market value of all of the common stock outstanding for that company. For example, suppose that a company has 100 million shares of common stock outstanding and each share has a market value of $10. Then the capitalization of this company is $1 billion (100 million shares times $10 per share). The market capitalization of a company is commonly referred to as its "market cap" or simply "cap."

While the market cap of a company is easy to determine given the market price per share and the number of shares outstanding, how does one define "value" and "growth" stocks? We'll see how that is done in Chapter 4.

For U.S. bonds, the following are classified as asset classes:

U.S. government bonds
Investment-grade corporate bonds
High-yield corporate bonds
U.S. municipal bonds (i.e., state and local bonds)
Mortgage-backed securities
Asset-backed securities

All of these securities are described in later chapters, where what is meant by "investment grade" and "high yield" is also explained. Sometimes, the first three bond asset classes listed above are further divided into "long term" and "short term."

The following asset classes are classified for the non-U.S. common stock and bond asset classes:

Developed market foreign stocks
Emerging market foreign stocks
Developed market foreign bonds
Emerging market foreign bonds

In addition to the traditional asset classes listed above, there are asset classes commonly referred to as *alternative asset classes*. Some of the more popular ones include:

Hedge funds
Private equity
Venture capital
Managed futures

These four asset classes are discussed in Chapters 25, 26, and 32.

How does one define an asset class? One highly respected investment manager, Mark Kritzman, describes how this is done as follows:[1]

> . . . some investments take on the status of an asset class simply because the managers of these assets promote them as an asset class. They believe that investors will be more inclined to allocate funds to their products if they are viewed as an asset class rather than merely as an investment strategy.

He then goes on to propose criteria determining asset class status, although we won't review the criteria he proposed here.

Along with the designation of an investment as an asset class comes a barometer to be able to quantify performance—the risk, return, and the correlation of the return of the asset class with that of other asset classes. The barometer is called a "benchmark index" or simply "index." Listed in Exhibit 2.1 are benchmark indexes for the various asset classes that cover common stocks.

If an investor wants exposure to a particular asset class, he or she must be able to buy a sufficient number of the individual securities comprising the asset class. Equivalently, the investor has to buy a sufficient number of individual securities comprising the index representing that asset class. This means that if an investor wants exposure to the U.S. large cap equity market and the S&P 500 is the index (consisting of 500 companies) representing that asset class, then the investor cannot simply buy the shares of a handful of companies and hope to acquire the expected exposure to that asset class. For institutional investors, acquiring a sufficient number of individual securities comprising an asset class is often not a problem. However, for individual investors, obtaining exposure to an asset class by buying a sufficient number of individual securities is not simple. How can individual investors accomplish this?

---

[1] Mark Kritzman, "Toward Defining an Asset Class," *The Journal of Alternative Investments* (Summer 1999), p. 79.

EXHIBIT 2.1   Benchmark Indexes for Common Stock Asset Classes

Asset Class	Benchmark Index
19	19
U.S. Large Cap Equity	Standard & Poor's (S&P) 500
U.S. Large Cap Value	Frank Russell 1000 Value, S&P/Barra 500 Value
U.S. Large Cap Growth	Frank Russell 1000 Growth, S&P/Barra 500 Growth
U.S. Mid Cap Equity	Frank Russell Mid Cap
U.S. Small Cap Equity	Frank Russell 2000
U.S. Small Cap Value	Frank Russell 2000 Value
U.S. Small Cap Growth	Frank Russell 2000 Growth
International Equity	Morgan Stanley Capital International (MSCI) EAFE, Salomon Smith Barney International, MSCI All Country World (ACWI) ex U.S.
Emerging Markets	MSCI Emerging Markets

Fortunately, there is an investment vehicle that can be used to obtain exposure to asset classes in a cost-effective manner. The vehicle is an investment company, more popularly referred to as a *mutual fund*. This investment vehicle is the subject of Chapter 21. For now, what is important to understand is that there are mutual funds that invest primarily in specific asset classes. Such mutual funds offer investors the opportunity to gain exposure to asset classes without having expertise in the management of the individual securities in that asset class and by investing a sum of money that, in the absence of a mutual fund, would not allow the investor to acquire a sufficient number of individual assets to obtain the desired exposure.

Risks Associated with Investing

There are various measures of risk. We will describe each of them here.

Total Risk

The dictionary defines risk as "hazard, peril, exposure to loss or injury." With respect to investments, investors have used a variety of definitions to describe risk. Today, the most commonly accepted definition of risk is one that involves a well-known statistical measure known as the variance. Specifically, investors quantify risk in terms of the variance of an asset's expected return. The variance of a random variable is a measure of the dispersion of the possible outcomes around the expected value. In the case of an asset's return, the variance is a measure of the dispersion of the possible outcomes for the return around the expected return.

There are two criticisms of the use of the variance as a measure of risk. The first criticism is that since the variance measures the dispersion of an asset's return around its expected value, it considers the possibility of returns above the expected return and below the expected return. Investors, however, do not view possible returns above the expected return as an unfavorable outcome. In fact, such outcomes are favorable. Because of this, some researchers have argued that measures of risk should not consider the possible returns above the expected return. Various measures of downside risk, such as risk of loss and value at risk, are currently being used by practitioners. The second criticism is that the variance is only one measure of how the returns vary around the expected return. When a probability distribution is not symmetrical around its expected return, then a statistical measure of the skewness of a distribution should be used in addition to the variance.

One way of reducing the risk associated with holding an individual security is by diversifying. Often, one hears investors talking about diversifying their portfolio. By this an investor means constructing a portfolio in such a way as to reduce portfolio risk without sacrificing return. This is certainly a goal that investors should seek. However, the question is, how does one do this in practice?

Some investors would say that a portfolio can be diversified by including assets across all asset classes. For example, one investor might argue that a portfolio should be diversified by investing in stocks, bonds, and real estate. While that might be reasonable, two questions must be addressed in order to construct a diversified portfolio. First, how much should be invested in each asset class? Should 40% of the portfolio be in stocks, 50% in bonds, and 10% in real estate, or is some other allocation more appropriate? Second, given the allocation, which specific stocks, bonds, and real estate should the investor select?

Some investors who focus only on one asset class such as common stock argue that such portfolios should also be diversified. By this they mean that an investor should not place all funds in the stock of one company, but rather should include stocks of many companies. Here, too, several questions must be answered in order to construct a diversified portfolio. First, which companies should be represented in the portfolio? Second, how much of the portfolio should be allocated to the stocks of each company?

Prior to development of portfolio theory by Dr. Harry Markowitz,[2] while investors often talked about diversification in these general terms, they never provided the analytical tools by which to answer the ques-

---

[2] Harry M. Markowitz, "Portfolio Selection," *Journal of Finance* (March 1952), pp. 77–91.

tions posed here. Dr. Markowitz demonstrated that a diversification strategy should take into account the degree of covariance or correlation between asset returns in a portfolio. (The covariance or correlation of asset returns is a measure of the degree to which the returns on two assets vary or change together.) Indeed a key contribution of what is now popularly referred to as "Markowitz diversification" or "mean-variance diversification" is the formulation of a security's risk in terms of a portfolio of securities, rather than the risk of an individual security. Markowitz diversification seeks to combine securities in a portfolio with returns that are less than perfectly positively correlated in an effort to lower portfolio risk (variance) without sacrificing return. It is the concern for maintaining return, while lowering risk through an analysis of the covariance between security returns, that separates Markowitz diversification from other approaches suggested for diversification and makes it more effective.

The principle of Markowitz diversification states that as the correlation (covariance) between the returns for assets that are combined in a portfolio decreases, so does the variance of the return for that portfolio. The good news is that investors can maintain expected portfolio return and lower portfolio risk by combining assets with lower (and preferably negative) correlations. However, the bad news is that very few assets have small to negative correlations with other assets. The problem, then, becomes one of searching among a large number of assets in an effort to discover the portfolio with the minimum risk at a given level of expected return or, equivalently, the highest expected return at a given level of risk.

Systematic versus Unsystematic Risk   The total risk of an asset or a portfolio can be divided into two types of risk: systematic risk and unsystematic risk. Professor William Sharpe defined *systematic risk* as the portion of an asset's variability that can be attributed to a common factor.[3] It is also sometimes called *undiversifiable risk* or *market risk*. Systematic risk is the minimum level of risk that can be attained for a portfolio by means of diversification across a large number of randomly chosen assets. As such, systematic risk is that which results from general market and economic conditions that cannot be diversified away.

Sharpe defined the portion of an asset's variability that can be diversified away as *unsystematic risk*. It is also sometimes called *diversifiable risk, unique risk, residual risk, idiosyncratic risk*, or *company-specific risk*. This is the risk that is unique to a company, such as a strike, the outcome of unfavorable litigation, or a natural catastrophe.

---

[3] William F. Sharpe, "A Simplified Model for Portfolio Analysis," *Management Science* (January 1963), pp. 277–299.

EXHIBIT 2.2   The Capital Market Line

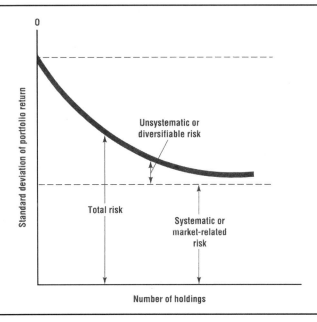

How diversification reduces unsystematic risk for portfolios is illustrated in Exhibit 2.2. The vertical axis shows the variance of a portfolio return. The variance of the portfolio return represents the total risk for the portfolio (systematic plus unsystematic). The horizontal axis shows the number of holdings of different assets (e.g., the number of common stock held of different issuers). As can be seen, as the number of asset holdings increases, the level of unsystematic risk is almost completely eliminated (i.e., diversified away). Studies of different asset classes support this. For example, for common stock, several studies suggest that a portfolio size of about 20 randomly selected companies will completely eliminate unsystematic risk leaving only systematic risk.[4] In the case of corporate bonds, generally less than 40 corporate issues are needed to eliminate unsystematic risk.

The relationship between the movement in the price of an asset and the market can be estimated statistically. There are two products of the estimated relationship that investors use. The first is the *beta* of an asset. Beta measures the sensitivity of an asset's return to changes in the market's return. Hence, beta is referred to as an *index of systematic risk* due

---

[4] The first empirical study of this type was by Wayne H. Wagner and Sheila Lau, "The Effect of Diversification on Risks," *Financial Analysts Journal* (November–December 1971), p. 50.

to general market conditions that cannot be diversified away. For example, if an asset has a beta of 1.5, it means that, on average, if the market's changes by 1%, the asset's return changes by 1.5%. The beta for the market is 1. A beta greater than 1 means that the systematic risk is greater than that of the market; a beta less than 1 means that the systematic risk is less than that of the market. Brokerage firms, vendors such as Bloomberg, and online internet services provide information on beta for common stock.

The second product is the ratio of the amount of systematic risk relative to the total risk. This ratio is called the *coefficient of determination* or *R-squared*. This ratio varies from 0 to 1. A value of 0.8 for a portfolio means that 80% of the variation in the return of the portfolio is explained by movements in the market. For individual assets, this ratio is typically low because there is a good deal of unsystematic risk. However, through diversification the ratio increases as unsystematic risk is reduced (see Exhibit 2.2).

Inflation or Purchasing Power Risk

Inflation risk or *purchasing power risk* arises because of the variation in the value of an asset's cash flows due to inflation, as measured in terms of purchasing power. For example, if an investor purchases an asset that produces an annual return of 5% and the rate of inflation is 3%, the purchasing power of the investor has not increased by 5%. Instead, the investor's purchasing power has increased by 2%. Inflation risk is the risk that the investor's return from the investment in an asset will be less than the rate of inflation.

Common stock is viewed as having little inflation risk. For all but inflation protection bonds, an investor is exposed to inflation risk by investing in fixed-rate bonds because the interest rate the issuer promises to make is fixed for the life of the issue.

Credit Risk

An investor who purchases a security not guaranteed by the U.S. government is viewed as being exposed to credit risk. This risk is defined as the risk that the issuer will fail to satisfy the terms of the obligation with respect to the timely payment of interest and repayment of the amount borrowed thereby forcing the issuer into bankruptcy. All investors in a bankrupt entity (common stockholders and bondholders) will realize a decline in the value of their security as a result of bankruptcy.

In the case of bonds, investors gauge the credit risk of an entity by looking at the credit ratings assigned to issues by rating companies, popularly referred to as *rating agencies*. There are three rating agencies in the United States: Moody's Investors Service, Inc., Standard & Poor's Corporation, and Fitch. These ratings are discussed in Chapter 11.

Liquidity Risk

When an investor wants to sell an asset, he or she is concerned whether the price that can be obtained from dealers is close to the true value of the asset. For example, if recent trades in the market for a particular asset have been between $40 and $40.50 and market conditions have not changed, an investor would expect to sell the asset in that range.

Liquidity risk is the risk that the investor will have to sell an asset below its true value where the true value is indicated by a recent transaction. The primary measure of liquidity is the size of the spread between the bid price (the price at which a dealer is willing to buy an asset) and the ask price (the price at which a dealer is willing to sell an asset). The wider the bid-ask spread, the greater the liquidity risk.

Liquidity risk is also important for portfolio managers that must mark to market positions periodically. For example, the manager of a mutual fund is required to report the market value of each holding at the end of each business day. This means accurate price information must be available. Some assets do not trade frequently and are therefore difficult to price.

Exchange Rate or Currency Risk

An asset whose payments are not in the domestic currency of the investor has unknown cash flows in the domestic currency. The cash flows in the investor's domestic currency are dependent on the exchange rate at the time the payments are received from the asset. For example, suppose an investor's domestic currency is the U.S. dollar and that the investor purchases an asset whose payments are in euros. If the euro depreciates relative to the U.S. dollar at the time a euro payment is received, then fewer U.S. dollars will be received.

The risk of receiving less of the domestic currency than is expected at the time of purchase when an asset makes payments in a currency other than the investor's domestic currency is called *exchange rate risk* or *currency risk*.

Risks for Bonds

There are systematic risks that affect bond returns in addition to those described above. They include interest rate risk, call/prepayment risk, and reinvestment risk.

Interest Rate Risk The price of a bond changes as interest rates change. Specifically, price moves in the opposite direction to the change in interest rates. That is, if interest rates increase, the price of a bond will decline; if interest rates decrease, the price of a bond will increase. This is the reason a bond will sell above its par value (i.e., sell at a premium) or below its par value (i.e., sell at a discount). The risk that the price of a bond or bond portfolio will decline when interest rates increase is called *interest rate risk*.

The sensitivity of the price of a bond to changes in interest rates depends on the following factors:

- The bond's coupon rate
- The bond's maturity
- The level of interest rates

Specifically, the following relationships hold:

- All other factors being constant, the lower the coupon rate, the greater the price sensitivity of a bond for a given change in interest rates.
- All other factors being constant, the longer the maturity, the greater the price sensitivity of a bond for a given change in interest rates.
- All other factors being constant, the lower the level of interest rates, the greater the price volatility of a bond for a given change in interest rates.

Consequently, the price of a zero-coupon bond with a long maturity is highly sensitive to changes in interest rates. The price sensitivity is even greater in a low interest rate environment than in a high interest rate environment. For money market instruments, since their maturity is less than one year, the price is not very sensitive to changes in interest rates.

The price sensitivity of a bond to changes in interest rates can be estimated. This measure is called the *duration* of a bond. Duration is the approximate percentage change in the price of a bond for a 100-basis-point change in interest rates. For example, if a bond has a duration of 8, this means that for a 100-basis-point change in interest rates, the price will change by approximately 8%. For a 50-basis-point change in interest rates, the price of this bond would change by approximately 4%.

Given the price of a bond and its duration, the dollar price change can be estimated. For example if our bond with a duration of 8 has a price of $90,000, the price will change by about 8% for a 100-basis-point change in interest rates and therefore dollar price change will be about $7,200 (8% times $90,000). For a 50-basis-point change, the price would change by about $3,600.

The concept of duration applies to a bond portfolio also. For example, if an investor has a bond portfolio with a duration of 6 and the market value of the portfolio is $1 million, this means that a change in interest rates of 100 basis points will change the value of the portfolio by approximately 6% and therefore the value of the portfolio will change by approximately $60,000. For a 25-basis-point change in interest rates, the portfolio's value will change by approximately 1.5% and the portfolio's value will change by approximately $15,000.

How is duration computed? First, two prices are computed. One is based on an increase in interest rates and the second is based on a decrease in interest rates. Duration is then computed as follows:

$$\text{Duration} = \frac{\text{Price if rates decrease} - \text{Price if rates increase}}{2 \times \text{Initial price} \times \text{Change in rates in decimal form}}$$

Typically, interest rates fluctuate up and down by an amount less than 50 basis points. But regardless of the rate change used, the interpretation is still that it is the approximate percentage price change for a 100-basis-point change in rates.

There are limitations of duration that the investor should recognize. First, in calculating duration or using the duration provided by financial consultants or fund managers, it is assumed that the prices calculated in the numerator are done properly. This is not a problem for simple bonds. However, there are bonds where if interest rates are changed the estimated price must be estimated by complex pricing models. In turn, those models are based on several assumptions. So, for example, it is not surprising that two brokers providing information on duration for a complex bond could have materially different estimates. One broker could report a duration of 4 while another a duration of 6! Moreover, mutual fund managers who manage a portfolio containing a large allocation to complex bonds could report a duration that is significantly different than the true price sensitivity of the fund to changes in interest rates due to improperly calculating the duration of the complex bonds.

The second limitation of duration is that it is a good approximation for small changes in interest rates (e.g., 50-basis-point change in rates) but the approximation is poorer for a larger change in interest rates. This does not mean that it is not useful for giving the investor a feel for the price sensitivity of a bond or a portfolio.

The third limitation has to do with the duration of a portfolio. In computing the duration of the portfolio, first the duration of each bond in the portfolio is computed. Then a weighted average of the duration of the bonds in the portfolio is computed to get the portfolio duration. The limitation comes about because it is assumed that the interest rate for all maturities change by the same number of basis points. So, if a portfolio has a 2-year, a 10-year, and a 20-year bond, when using a portfolio's duration it is assumed that the 2-year, 10-year, and 20-year bonds change by the same number of basis points. This assumption is commonly referred to as the "parallel yield curve assumption."

Call/Prepayment Risk   A bond may include a provision that allows the issuer to retire or call all or part of the issue before the maturity date. From the investor's perspective, there are three disadvantages to call provisions. First, the cash flow pattern of a callable bond is not known with certainty because it is not known when the bond will be called. Second, because the issuer is likely to call the bonds when interest rates have dropped below the bond's coupon rate, the investor is exposed to *reinvestment risk*; this is risk that the investor will have to reinvest the proceeds when the bond is called at interest rates lower than the bond's coupon rate. Finally, the price appreciation potential of a bond will be reduced relative to an otherwise comparable bond without a call provision. Because of these three disadvantages faced by the investor, a callable bond is said to expose the investor to *call risk*. The same disadvantages apply to mortgage-backed and asset-backed securities where the borrower can prepay. In this case the risk is referred to as *prepayment risk*.

Reinvestment Risk   Reinvestment risk is the risk that proceeds available for reinvestment must be reinvested at a lower interest rate than the instrument that generated the proceeds. In addition to reinvestment risk when investing in a callable or prepayable bond, reinvestment risk occurs when an investor purchases a bond and relies on the yield of that bond as a measure of return potential. This point we be discussed later.

SELECTING A PORTFOLIO STRATEGY

Given the investment objectives and the investment policy, the investor must then develop a portfolio strategy. Portfolio strategies can be classified as either active or passive.

An *active portfolio strategy* uses available information and forecasting techniques to seek a better performance than a portfolio that is simply diversified broadly. Essential to all active strategies are expectations about the factors that influence the performance of an asset class. For example, with active common stock strategies this may include forecasts of future earnings, dividends, or price-earnings ratios. With bond portfolios that are actively managed, expectations may involve forecasts of future interest rates and sector spreads. Active portfolio strategies involving foreign securities may require forecasts of local interest rates and exchange rates.

A *passive portfolio strategy* involves minimal expectational input, and instead relies on diversification to match the performance of some index. In effect, a passive strategy assumes that the marketplace will reflect all available information in the price paid for securities. Between these extremes of active and passive strategies, new strategies have sprung up that have elements of both. For example, the core of a portfolio may be passively managed with the balance actively managed.

Given the choice among active or passive management, which should be selected? The answer depends on the investor's view of how "price-efficient" the market is and the investor's risk tolerance. By marketplace price efficiency we mean how difficult it would be to earn a greater return than passive management after adjusting for the risk associated with a strategy and the transaction costs associated with implementing that strategy. If an asset class is highly price efficient, the investor would want to pursue a passive strategy.

The most common passive strategy is indexing. In indexing, the investor designs a portfolio so that it will replicate the performance of the index.

CONSTRUCTING THE PORTFOLIO

Once a portfolio strategy is selected, the next step is to select the specific financial instruments to be included in the portfolio. In the discussion to follow, we will refer to financial instruments as "securities." This requires an evaluation of each security and the creation of an efficient portfolio. An *efficient portfolio* is one that provides the greatest expected return for a given level of risk, or equivalently, the lowest risk for a given expected return.

Constructing an Indexed Portfolio

As just mentioned, an investor who pursues the most popular form of a passive strategy, indexing, will assemble a portfolio that attempts to match the performance of the index. In theory, it is quite simple to do. An investor can purchase every security in the index. The amount purchased of a particular security should be equal to the percentage of that security in the index.

For example, consider the S&P 500. As the name indicates, there are 500 companies whose stock (the security) is in included in the index. Two of the stocks are Microsoft and Johnson & Johnson. On February 28, 2002, Microsoft's market capitalization was $315,924 million and Johnson & Johnson's market capitalization was $186,798 million. The market capitalization of all 500 companies on that same day was $10,079 billion. Therefore, the percentage of the portfolio that would be allocated to these two companies in a portfolio indexed to the S&P 500 would have been:

$$\text{Microsoft} = \frac{\$315,924}{\$10,079,000} = 3.13\%$$

$$\text{Johnson \& Johnson} = \frac{\$186,798}{\$10,079,000} = 1.85\%$$

Suppose an investor had $10 million to invest on February 28, 2002. The dollar amount invested in Microsoft and Johnson & Johnson to match the index would have been $315,000 and $185,000, respectively.

From a practical perspective, it may be difficult to buy all the securities comprising an index for several reasons. First, transaction costs from buying and rebalancing the indexed portfolio may be too expensive, resulting in the underperformance of the indexed portfolio relative to the index. Second, the amount to be invested may be such that all of the securities comprising the index cannot be acquired. For example, if an investor has $10,000 to invest in the stock market, the stock of only a few companies could be acquired. Finally, in some indexes not all of the securities can be acquired without great difficulty. For example, in the case of indexing to match the performance of a bond index, some of the bond issues included in the index may not trade frequently and are difficult to acquire.

For individuals, index replication is typically not accomplished by buying individual securities. Rather, if available, a mutual fund that has as its objective the creation of a portfolio to replicate an index is purchased. This overcomes the problems of the individual investor creating the indexed portfolio. Managers of mutual funds have a larger amount to invest and therefore can acquire a large number of securities in the index and can do so minimizing transaction costs. A good example is the common stock indexed mutual funds.

For institutional investors, even with a large amount of funds to invest, the portfolio manager still faces the problem of transaction costs and unavailability of certain securities. There are trading arrangements that have been developed in some markets that allow for more efficient execution of trades so as to minimize transaction costs and therefore the likelihood that the indexed portfolio will underperform the index. For common stock, these trading arrangements are described in Chapter 4. In the case of unavailable securities or a universe of securities so large that it is impractical to acquire all the securities in the index, there are methodologies that can be used to minimize the risk of not matching the index. We'll discuss this further below.

Constructing an Active Portfolio

In an active strategy, an investor is seeking to outperform the index or, in the case of liability-driven institutional investors, earn a higher return than a liability that it must pay. The construction of an active portfolio begins with an analysis of the factors that have historically determined the return on the index. Once these factors are identified, then the index can be decomposed into these factors or, more specifically, a risk profile of the index can be identified based on these factors.

Active management involves a deliberate decision by the portfolio manager to create a portfolio that departs from the risk profile of the index by accepting a larger or smaller exposure to one or more factors. Departures from the risk profile of the index represents bets on these factors. For example, consider common stock. One of the important factors that determines the risk profile of a common stock index such as the S&P 500 is the composition of the index in terms of industry sectors. Suppose that a portfolio manager believes that he or she can select industry sectors that can outperform and underperform. Then the portfolio manager will deliberately overweight the industry sectors that are expected to outperform and underweight those that are expected to underperform.

For an indexing strategy, in contrast, this approach involves creating a portfolio with a profile that matches the risk profile (i.e., matching the factors) of the index. This mitigates the problem mentioned earlier of having to buy all the securities in the index.

Techniques for Selecting Securities in an Active Strategy

Portfolio construction involves assessing the exposure of individual securities to the factors. In addition, an expected return is required to construct a portfolio. The expected return can be obtained subjectively without any formal analysis (a "hunch"), by using technical analysis, or by using financial models. Technical analysis is explained in Chapter 4. Here we will discuss financial models. These include:

Discounted cash flow models
Capital asset pricing model
Multi-factor asset pricing model

Discounted Cash Flow Models   Discounted cash flow models begin by projecting the cash flow of a security over the security's expected life. Then, the discounted value (or present value) of each cash flow is obtained by using an appropriate discount rate. The sum of all the expected cash flows is the theoretical value of the security. In the case of common stock, discounted cash flow models are called *dividend discount models* because the cash flow is based on projected dividends.

It is the theoretical value that is then compared to the market price to identify securities that are fairly priced (theoretical value equal to the market price), rich (theoretical value less than the market price), or cheap (theoretical value greater than the market price). Cheap securities are primary candidates for acquisition and rich securities are to be avoided or shorted if allowed by investment guidelines.

The discounted cash flow models can be used to calculate the expected return rather than the theoretical value. This is done by beginning with the market price and the expected cash flows. The expected return is then the interest rate that will make the present value of the expected cash flow equal to the market price. A more commonly used name for the expected return is the *internal rate of return* (IRR) or *yield*. The procedure for computing the IRR involves iterating through different interest rates until finding the one that makes the present value of the expected cash flows equal to the market price.

In the case of bonds, the term yield is more commonly used than IRR. For bonds, several yield measures are calculated. For all bonds, a yield based on the expected cash flows to the maturity date is computed. This yield is called the *yield to maturity*. For a bond that is callable, a call date is assumed and the expected cash flows are determined up to that assumed call date. The yield then calculated is called the *yield to call*. Typically for a callable bond, an investor calculates the yield to maturity and yield to call and refers to the smaller of the two values as the *yield to worst*.

For asset-backed and mortgage-backed securities, prepayments affect the expected cash flows. Based on some assumed prepayment rate, the expected cash flows can be computed. Given the market price and the expected cash flows, the IRR can be calculated and is referred to as the *cash flow yield*.

Yield measures suffer from three major problems as a measure of a security's expected return. First, a yield measure assumes that the expected cash flows will be realized. If the model for projecting the future cash flows is poor, the resulting expected return will not be a good estimate. This is also true for the theoretical value. Second, the assumption in a yield calculation is that the investor will hold the security until the last cash flow is received. Consequently, for an investor who buys a security with the intent of holding it for a time period that is less than the security's expected life, the yield will not be a good measure of expected return. Finally, a property of any yield measure is that it assumes that any cash flows received from the security can be reinvested at the computed yield. For example, if an investor is considering investing in private equity and the computed yield is 20%, the assumption is that all interim cash flows received can be reinvested from the time of receipt until the end of the expected life of that investment at a rate of 20%. The risk that the investor will have to reinvest at a lower rate is what we referred to earlier in this chapter as reinvestment risk.

Capital Asset Pricing Model   The *capital asset pricing model* (CAPM) is an economic model that shows the relationship between the expected return of an asset and risk. The risk in this model is market risk. CAPM asserts that the expected return for a security is equal to the risk-free rate available in the market plus a risk premium demanded by the market. The risk premium is determined by the risk measure. We introduced this risk measure earlier. It is the beta of an asset—that is, the sensitivity of the asset's return to changes in the overall market. In the CAPM, the risk premium is

$$\text{Beta} \times (\text{Expected return on the market} - \text{Risk-free rate})$$

Therefore, the expected return for a security according to the CAPM is

$$\begin{aligned} &\text{Expected return} \\ &= \text{Risk-free rate} + \text{Beta} \times (\text{Expected return on the market} - \text{Risk-free rate}) \end{aligned}$$

The CAPM has been the cornerstone of financial theory since the mid 1960s.[5] However, there have been many criticisms of the CAPM. The major one has been that the only risk that affects the expected return is market risk.

Multi-Factor Asset Pricing Models   Multi-factor asset pricing models are models that assert that the expected return for a security is based on the factors that empirically have been found to affect the return on all securities. The expected return in such models is equal to the risk-free rate plus a risk premium. The risk premium, in turn, depends on the exposure of the security to the factors. The exposure of a security to a factor is called the "factor beta."

---

[5] The CAPM was introduced by William Sharpe in 1964 in William F. Sharpe, "Capital Asset Prices," *Journal of Finance* (September 1964), pp. 425–442.

For each risk factor a market price is estimated. The product of the factor beta and the market price of risk for that factor summed over all the factors is then the risk premium. The expected return is then equal to the risk-free rate plus the risk premium.

EVALUATING PERFORMANCE

Periodically the investor must assess the performance of the portfolio and therefore the portfolio strategy. This process begins with calculating the return realized over the investment period. The procedure for calculating the realized return is described in Chapter 3. The realized return is then compared to the return on the benchmark. The benchmark can be a market index or a minimum return established by a liability. The comparison will allow the investor to determine whether the portfolio outperformed, matched, or underperformed the benchmark.

However, the process does not stop there. It is common to compare the performance relative to the risk accepted—a reward-to-risk ratio. The most common measure used is the *Sharpe ratio*. The numerator of the Sharpe ratio is the return over the risk-free rate. The risk of the portfolio is measured by the standard deviation of the portfolio. The Sharpe ratio is thus:

$$\frac{\text{Portfolio return} - \text{Risk-free rate}}{\text{Standard deviation of portfolio}}$$

The Sharpe ratio is therefore is a measure of the excess return relative to the total variability of the portfolio.

For institutional investors, more elaborate techniques to assess performance are employed. The most common is the use of multi-factor asset pricing models. While these models can be used to construct a portfolio, they can also be used to identify the reasons for underperformance or outperformance. These models do so by allowing the investor to determine the factor exposures that resulted in better or worse performance than the benchmark index.

CHAPTER 3

Calculating Investment Returns

Bruce Feibel
Director
Performance Measurement Technology
Eagle Investment Systems

After investment objectives have been set, strategy determined, assets allocated, and trades are made, the next task is to value the portfolio and begin the process of performance measurement. Whether an investor makes his own investing decisions or delegates this duty to advisors, all parties are interested in calculating and weighing the results. The first stage in the performance measurement process is to compute a *return*, which is the income and profit earned on the capital that the investor places at risk in the investment.

Suppose $100 is invested in a fund and the fund subsequently increases in value such that the investor receives $130 back. What was the return on this investment? The investor gained $30. Taking this *dollar return* and dividing it by the $100 invested, and multiplying the decimal result 0.3 by 100 gives us the return expressed as a percentage; that is, 30%.

A *rate of return* is the gain received from an investment over a period of time expressed as a percentage. Returns are a ratio relating how much was gained given how much was risked. We interpret a 30% return as a gain over the period equal to almost 1/3 of the original $100 invested.

Although it appears that no special knowledge of investments is required to calculate and interpret rates of return, several complications make the subject worthy of further investigation:

- Selection of the proper inputs to the return calculation
- Treatment of additional client contributions and withdrawals to and from the investment account

■ Adjusting the return to reflect the timing of these contributions and
  withdrawals
■ Differentiating between the return produced by the investment man-
  ager and the return experienced by the investor
■ Computing returns spanning multiple valuation periods
■ Averaging periodic rates of return

These are the issues that we will address in this chapter. In it, we summarize what has evolved to be the investment industry standard approach
to calculating and reporting portfolio rates of return. Individual and
institutional investors, investing via separate and commingled accounts,
using a myriad of strategies and asset classes, use the methodology presented in this chapter to calculate the returns earned by their investment
portfolios. The tools covered here are relevant whether you are an individual monitoring the performance of your own personal brokerage
account, a financial planner providing advice to many individuals, the
manager of a mutual fund, or a plan sponsor overseeing dozens of specialist investment managers. In the illustrations that are used to explain
the various concepts presented in the chapter, a spreadsheet format is
used so that it is easier for the reader to replicate the calculations.

SINGLE PERIOD RATE OF RETURN

Why do we compute rates of return to describe the performance of an
investment when we could simply judge our performance by the absolute
dollars gained over time? After all, there is no better judge than money in
the bank! There are several reasons that returns have emerged as the preferred statistic for summarizing investment performance:

■ The rate of return concentrates a lot of information into a single statistic. Individual data points about the beginning and ending market values, income earned, cash contributions and withdrawals, and trades for
  all of the holdings in the portfolio are compressed into a single number.
■ This single number, the return, is a ratio. It is faster for an investor to
  analyze proportions than absolute numbers. For example, if an investor is told she earned an 8% rate of return, she can instantly begin to
  judge whether she is happy with this result, compared to the need to
  pore over valuation and transaction statements first.
■ Returns are comparable even if the underlying figures are not. An
  investor can compare returns even when the portfolios have different
  base currencies or have different sizes. For example, if an investor puts

$100 to work and gains $10, she has earned the same return as an investor who put $1 million to work and ended up with $1.1 million.

■ Returns calculated for different periods are comparable; that is, an investor can compare this year's return to last year's.

■ The interpretation of the rate of return is intuitive. Return is the value reconciling the beginning investment value to the ending value over the time period we are measuring. An investor can take a reported return and use it to determine the amount of money he would have at the end of the period given the amount invested.

$$MVE = MVB \times (1 + \text{Decimal return})$$

where

$$MVE = \text{market value at the end of the period}$$
$$MVB = \text{market value at the start of the period}$$

For example, if we were to invest $100 at a return of 40%, we would have $140 at the end of the period: $100 × (1.40) = $140. Adding one to the decimal return before multiplying gives a result equal to the beginning value plus the gain/loss over the period. Multiplying by the return of 0.4 gives the gain/loss over the period ($40).

Let's look closer at the calculation of return. In our introductory example we earned a $30 gain on an investment of $100. By dividing the gain by the amount invested we derive the 30% return using

$$\text{Return in percent} = \left(\frac{\text{Gain or Loss}}{\text{Investment made}} \right) \times 100$$

Suppose that instead of investing and then getting our money back within a single period, we held an investment worth $100 at the beginning of the period and continued to hold it at the end of the period when it was valued at $130. Multiplying the first ratio by 100 transforms the decimal fraction into a percentage gain; 30% in our example (0.3 × 100 = 30%).

The same return can be calculated whether an investor buys and then liquidates an investment within a period or carries it over from a prior period and holds on to it. When we measure the return on an investment that we buy and hold across periods, we treat the beginning market value as if it were a new investment made during the period, and the ending market value as if it were the proceeds from the sale of the investment at the end of the period.

We have used two forms of the return calculation so far. It does not matter which one we use. The two methods are equivalent.

$$\left(\frac{\text{Gain or Loss}}{\text{Investment made}}\right) \times 100 = \left[\left(\frac{\text{Current value}}{\text{Investment made}}\right) - 1\right] \times 100$$

We can demonstrate that the two forms are same by deriving the second form of the calculation from the first.

$$\left(\frac{\text{MVE} - \text{MVB}}{\text{MVB}}\right) \times 100 \rightarrow \left(\frac{\text{MVE}}{\text{MVB}} - \frac{\text{MVB}}{\text{MVB}}\right) \times 100 \rightarrow \left(\frac{\text{MVE}}{\text{MVB}} - 1\right) \times 100$$

Using the first form, the numerator of the rate of return calculation is the *unrealized gain or loss:* the difference between the starting and ending market value. If there were income earned during the period, we also add it into the numerator, making the numerator more properly the market value plus accrued income. In either form of the calculation the denominator is the *investment made*. The number we select for the denominator represents the *money at risk* during the period. For the first measurement period, the investment made is equal to the amount originally invested in the portfolio. In subsequent periods, it is equal to the ending market value of the previous period. The calculation of a return where we invested $100 at the end of December and it rises to $110 in January and then $120 in February is provided in the following spreadsheet.

	A	B	C	D
1	Month End	Market Value	Dollar Return	Percent Return
2	31-Dec-2000	100		
3	31-Jan-2000	110	10	10.00
4	28-Feb-2000	120	10	9.09
5				
6			=B4-B3	=((C4/B3)*100)

Notice that even though we earned the same $10 dollar return in January and February, the percent return is higher in January (10/100 = 10.00%) than it was in February (10/110 = 9.09%). The reason for the lower February return is that the money at risk in the fund for February equals not only the original investment of $100 but also the $10 gained in January. With more money put at risk, the same dollar gain results in a lower return to the investment.

By using the *market value* of the investment to calculate returns, we recognize a gain on the investment even though it is not actually *realized* by selling it at the end of the period. To calculate returns that include unrealized gains, we value the portfolio at the end of each measurement period. These dates are the periodic *valuation dates*. A return calculated between two valuation dates is called a *single period, holding period,* or *periodic* return. The periodicity of single period returns is related to the frequency of portfolio valuation. For example, single period returns can be calculated on a daily basis for mutual funds which are valued at the close of the market each night, but may be calculated only monthly for institutional separate accounts, or quarterly for a share in a real estate partnership, as these types of holdings are not valued as frequently. Valuations are performed at least as often as participants are allowed to move money into or out of a commingled fund.

Components of Single Period Returns

When there are no transactions into or out of an investment account and no income earned, to calculate a single period return, we simply divide the ending market value by the beginning market value. Total portfolio market values are derived by summing up the values of the underlying investments within the fund. If we are calculating the return earned on our share of a commingled portfolio, such as a mutual fund, the market value equals the sum of the shares we own multiplied by the unit value of each share on the valuation date. Unit values are calculated by dividing the sum of the individual security market values that comprise the fund by the number of shares outstanding. Portfolio holdings are determined on a trade date basis. With *trade date accounting* we include securities in the portfolio valuation on the day the manager agrees to buy or sell the securities, as opposed to waiting for the day the trades are settled with the broker.

The *market value* of each security is the amount we would expect to receive if the investment were sold on the valuation date. It is calculated using observed market prices and exchange rates wherever possible. Determining market value is easy for instruments like exchange-traded equities, but we need to estimate the current value of other investment types. For example, bonds that do not trade often are marked to market by reference to the price of similar bonds that did trade that day. Although it is possible, say for liquidity reasons, that we could not actually realize the observed market closing price used in the valuation if we were to actually sell the investment, this method avoids introducing subjective estimates of trading impact into return calculations. If the fund holds cash, it too is included in the valuation of the fund.

The individual security market values include a measure of income earned or *accrued income* on the investment. Accrued income is income earned but not yet received. For example, if an investor sells a bond between coupon dates, the investor sells the interest accrued from the last payment date to the buyer of the bond. Because the interest sold would be part of the proceeds if the security were sold on the valuation date, we also include it in the calculation of market value. Returns that reflect both the change in market value and the income earned during the period are called *total returns*. In a similar manner, the total portfolio market value is adjusted for accrued receivables and payables to and from the fund. For example, the accrued management fee payable to the investment manager is subtracted from the total market value.

While it is outside the scope of this chapter to itemize the finer points of valuing every type of security the fund could invest in, the principles of market quote driven, trade date, accrual based valuation are used to judge the worth of each security in the portfolio, which are then summed to the portfolio level and result in the single period return calculation formula:

Percent Rate of Return

$$= \left[\left(\frac{\text{Ending Market Value} + \text{Ending Accrued Income}}{\text{Beginning Market Value} + \text{Beginning Accrued Income}} \right) - 1 \right] \times 100$$

It is worthwhile to note what factors we do not explicitly include in the return calculation. The *cost of investments* is *not* considered in performance measurement after the first period's return calculation (except for securities that are valued at their amortized cost). For each subsequent period, the ending market value for the previous period is used as the beginning market value for the next period. The justification for this practice is that we assume that the investment cycle begins afresh with each valuation period, and it is the current market value, and not the original cost, that is invested, or put at risk again, in the next period.

The return calculation makes no reference to gains *realized* in the course of security sales during the period. In fact the portfolio beginning and ending market values include both *unrealized* and *realized capital appreciation* generated by trading within the portfolio during the period. Consider a portfolio with this sequence of activity:

December 31, 2000
  ■ Holds 100 shares Stock A priced at $1 per share = $100 MVB

January 31, 2001
  ■ Stock A valued at $110 for a (10/100 = 10%) return in January

February 28, 2001
  ■ Stock A valued at $115 for a (5/110 = 4.55%) return in February

March 1, 2001
  ■ 50 shares of Stock A are sold for $1.15 per share, netting $57.50
  ■ The realized gain on the sale is $7.50 ($57.50 − $50 = $7.50)
  ■ 10 Shares of Stock B at $5.75 a share are purchased with the proceeds

March 31, 2001
  ■ Stock A valued at (50 shares × $1 = $50)

- Stock B valued at (10 shares × $5 = $50)
- The total portfolio is worth $100, for a (−15/115 = −13.04%) loss in March

The spreadsheet below shows that we do not explicitly use the realized gain of $7.50 in the return calculation for March.

	A	B	C	D	E	F
1	Date	MV Stock A	MV Stock B	Total MV	Gain/Loss	% Return
2	31-Dec-2000	100.00	0.00	100.00		
3	31-Jan-2001	110.00	0.00	110.00	10.00	10.00
4	28-Feb-2001	115.00	0.00	115.00	5.00	4.55
5	01-Mar-2001	57.50	57.50	115.00		
6	31-Mar-2001	50.00	50.00	100.00	-15.00	-13.04
7						
8					=D6-D5	=((E6/D5)*100)

The realized gain on the sale of Stock A was committed to the purchase of Stock B, which was then marked to market at the end of the March. We explicitly calculate the unrealized market value change during the period (−15.00), and this market value change implicitly includes any realized gains/losses on securities sold during the period.

It is possible that the manager might not reinvest the sale proceeds via the purchase of another security. In this case, we still do not explicitly include the realized gain in the calculation of return. Instead, we include the cash received on the sale in the total fund market value. The following spreadsheet illustrates the fact that we do not need to know about the transactions *within* the portfolio during the valuation period in order to calculate portfolio level performance.

	A	B	C	D	E	F
1	Date	MV Stock A	Cash	Total MV	Gain/Loss	% Return
2	31-Dec-2000	100.00	0.00	100.00		
3	31-Jan-2001	110.00	0.00	110.00	10.00	10.00
4	28-Feb-2001	115.00	0.00	115.00	5.00	4.55
5	01-Mar-2001	57.50	57.50	115.00		
6	31-Mar-2001	50.00	57.90	107.90	-7.10	-6.17
7						
8					=D6-D5	=((E6/D5)*100)

Transactions within the portfolio during the period do not affect the total fund level return calculation because they have an equal and opposite impact on performance—a purchase of one security is a sale of another (cash). This is also true of income received during the period. Income received on a security is an outflow from that security but an inflow of cash. To calculate portfolio level performance when there are no additional contributions and withdrawals, we only need to calculate the market value of all of the securities in the fund and cash balances at the beginning and end of the holding period.

EXHIBIT 3.1   Cash Flows

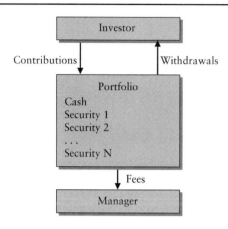

Return on Investment (ROI)

So far we have looked at the calculation of a single period return for situations where the market value of our holdings is made available for investment at the start of the next period. Individual and institutional investors also make periodic additional investments, or *contributions* to, and *withdrawals* from investment accounts. These net contributions to the fund are *not* included as a component of investment return; they represent an increase of capital at risk but not a capital gain on our investment. For this reason, when a fund receives new money, it is not possible to measure performance by simply observing the change in market value.

These asset transfers into and out of the fund are sometimes called *cash flows*. Cash flow is a generic term for different transaction types. For a defined benefit pension plan, the cash flows include periodic corporate contributions to fund the plan and withdrawals to service retirees. For a mutual fund, cash flows include purchases or liquidations of fund shares and exchanges of shares between funds. Exhibit 3.1 shows the generic transactional relationships between the investor, the manager, and the portfolio.

The value of the cash flow is the amount of money deposited or withdrawn. A positive cash flow is a flow into the fund. A negative cash flow is a flow out of the fund. Sometimes contributions are made in securities and not cash; this occurs, for example, when a portfolio is transitioned to a new investment manager. The monetary value of these "in-kind" contributions is measured by the current value of the assets transferred at the time of the contribution. In these situations it is important to use the current market value rather than the original cost.

If the original cost were used, the return calculation for the first period after the contribution would credit the entire return to date as earned in the first period after the transfer.

When there are cash flows, we need to adjust the calculation of gain/ loss in the numerator of the return calculation to account for the fact that the increase in market value was not entirely due to investment earnings. For example, suppose we have a portfolio with an MVB of 100 and a MVE of 130. What is the gain if we invested an additional $10 during the period? We started off with $100 and ended up with $130. We subtract out the additional investment before calculating the gain.

$$\text{Gain/Loss} = (\text{Current Value} - \text{Original Investment} - \text{Net Cash Inflows} + \text{Net Cash Outflows})$$

The gain in this case is $20 (130 − 100 − 10 + 0). The $20 gain/loss during the period combines two amounts—the gain on the original $100 and the gain on the additional $10 invested. If instead of a net inflow, we had a net outflow because we took money out of the portfolio during the period, the second component would be the gain earned up until the money was withdrawn.

When there are cash flows, in addition to modifying the numerator, we need to modify the denominator of the return calculation to account for additional capital invested or withdrawn during the measurement period. We can modify the rate of return calculation to account for additional investment or withdrawals. The result is the *return on investment* (ROI) formula. ROI is the gain or loss generated by an investment expressed as a percentage of the amount invested, adjusted for contributions and withdrawals.

$$\text{ROI in percent} = \left(\frac{(\text{EMV} + \text{NOF}) - (\text{BMV} + \text{NIF})}{\text{BMV} + \text{NIF}} \right) \times 100$$

where NIF are the net inflows and NOF are the net outflows. The following spreadsheet shows the calculation of the ROI.

	A	B	C	D	E
1	MVB	In Flows	Out Flows	MVE	Return on Investment %
2	100.00	10.00	0.00	130.00	18.18
3		=(((D2+C2)-(A2+B2))/(A2+B2))*100			
4					

The first expression in the numerator (EMV + NOF) replaces the EMV used in the ROR calculation. We adjust the ending market value for any withdrawals from the portfolio. Notice that this increases the numerator and the resulting return. Withdrawals are treated as a *benefit* to performance. In the second expression, we are subtracting the amount invested in order to calculate the gain. The inflows are treated as an investment, which reduces the gain. Contributions are treated as a *cost* to performance. The total amount invested (BMV + NIF) is the ROI denominator. By adding the contributions to the BMV we reduce the return, because we are dividing the same gain by a larger number.

Is 18.18% a fair return to account for the case where BMV = 100, EMV = 130, and there was a NIF = 10? The answer is: it depends. Note that there is an implicit assumption that the NIF was available for investing, or at risk, for the complete period. If the additional inflow was put into the fund at the beginning of the period, the investor did not have use of the money for the entire period. The investor would expect a higher fund return to compensate for this as compared to his keeping the money and investing in the fund only at the end of the period. So, returns should take into account the timing of the additional cash flows. If the investment were made sometime during the period, the investor did have use of the capital for some part of the period. For example, if the measurement period was a month and the $10 contribution came midway through the month, the fund had $100 of invested capital for the first half of the month and $110 for the second half. The gain of $20 was made on a smaller invested balance; therefore the return credited to the account should be *higher* than 18.18%.

While ROI adjusts for portfolio contributions and withdrawals, it does not adjust for the *timing* of these cash flows. Because of the assumption that contributions were available for the whole period, ROI will give the same return no matter when in the period the flows occur. Another drawback of the ROI as a measure of investment performance is that it does not adjust for the *length* of the holding period. The ROI calculation gives the same result whether the gain was earned over a day, a year, or 10 years. For these reasons, we need a measure of return that reflects both the timing of cash flows and the length of the period for which the assets were at risk. Both adjustments are derived from concepts related to the time value of money, which we review next.

Time Value of Money

Returns can be equated to the interest rates used in the calculation of the future value of a fixed income investment. However, unlike returns, interest rates are known ahead of time, so we can project the future value at the beginning of the period. The future value of an investment equals the present value plus the interest and other gains earned over the period.

$$FV = PV \times (1 + R)^N$$

where

FV = value at end of period
PV = current value of the investment
R   = rate of income earned per period
N   = number of valuation periods

In return calculations, it is the R that is unknown. We calculate this rate R using observations of the beginning and ending market values. To derive the equivalent of the future value, which is the MVE of an investment during a single period, we multiply the MVB by 1 plus the interest rate.

Ending Market Value = Beginning Market Value × (1 + Interest Rate)

The difference between the ending and beginning market values is the income earned. *Compounding* is the reinvestment of income to earn more income in subsequent periods. In a *simple interest* scenario, the income earned is not reinvested in order for it to compound in the following periods. For example, if a MVB = 1000 is put to work for a period of 4 months at an interest rate = 5% per month, we calculate an ending value of 1200.

Ending market value
= Beginning market value
  × [1 + (Rate in percent/100) × No. of time periods invested]
= 1,000 × [1 + (5%/100) × 4] = 1,200

We use the simple interest calculation if the investor withdraws the income earned at the end of each period. In this example, the total gain over the four months is 200. Dividing by the $1,000 invested gives a 20% return for the four-month period. This equals the monthly periodic dollar return multiplied by four.

If the income and gains are retained within the investment vehicle or *reinvested*, they will accumulate and increase the starting balance for each subsequent period's income calculation. For example, $100 invested at 7% for 10 years, assuming yearly compounding, produces an ending value of $196.72.

	A	B	C	D	E	F	G	H
1	Year	BMV	Interest Rate	EMV	Principal	Interest	Interest on Interest	% of Value
2	0			100.00	100.00			
3	1	100.00	0.07	107.00	100.00	7.00	0.00	
4	2	107.00	0.07	114.49	100.00	14.00	0.49	0%
5	3	114.49	0.07	122.50	100.00	21.00	1.50	1%
6	4	122.50	0.07	131.08	100.00	28.00	3.08	2%
7	5	131.08	0.07	140.26	100.00	35.00	5.26	4%
8	6	140.26	0.07	150.07	100.00	42.00	8.07	5%
9	7	150.07	0.07	160.58	100.00	49.00	11.58	7%
10	8	160.58	0.07	171.82	100.00	56.00	15.82	9%
11	9	171.82	0.07	183.85	100.00	63.00	20.85	11%
12	10	183.85	0.07	196.72	100.00	70.00	26.72	14%
13								
14				=B12*(1+C12)		=C12*B3*A12	=D12-(E12+F12)	=G12/D12

Unfortunately, the reinvestment assumption is not realistic for all investors. For example, any taxable investor investing outside a vehicle shielded from taxes, such as a qualified retirement account, will have to pay taxes on income earned. The taxes reduce the income available for reinvestment in the next period. Given this fact, one of the trends in performance measurement is the incorporation of taxes into the return calculation.

The reinvestment assumption is important because the power of investing lies in the *compound interest*, the interest on the interest earned in prior periods. Given the 10-year investment earning a 7% yearly return, the interest on interest component comprises 14% of the terminal value. With a 30-year investment at 7%, the interest on interest will approach 60% of the ending value.

When interest earnings are withdrawn after each period, the simple interest calculation is a better measure of the situation. If income is left to earn more income, then compound interest is the better measure. Compound interest is assumed in almost all investment applications. With interest rates, we usually assume that interest is reinvested at the same interest rate for subsequent periods. The difference between working with returns instead of interest rates is that in return calculations, while we also assume that the income is reinvested, we recognize that the periodic returns fluctuate over time.

While we understand that earning a higher return over the holding period will increase the ending investment value, the frequency of compounding also impacts the ending value. As shown in the spreadsheet that follows, an investment that has the same return has a higher value if the income is compounded more frequently

	A	B	C	D	E
1	Frequency	MVB	Periods	Return	MVE
2	Yearly	1000.00	1.00	0.07	1070.00
3	Monthly	1000.00	12.00	0.07	1072.29
4	Daily	1000.00	365.25	0.07	1072.50
5			=FV(D4/C4,C4,0,B4*-1)		
6					

Interest rates are usually quoted on a yearly or *annual* basis. We can adjust the quoted annual interest rate to account for more frequent compounding:

$$ MVE = MVB \times \left(1 + \frac{r_{period} \times m}{m} \right)^{m \times periods} $$

where

r = the periodic interest rate

m = times per period that interest is paid, or compounds

For example, if a $100 investment yielded 3% for 6 months (i.e., MVB = 100 and MVE = 103), the value at the end of one year, assuming semiannual compounding and reinvestment of the interest, is $106.09:

$$106.09 \ = \ 100 \times \left(1 + \frac{(0.03 \times 2)}{2}\right)^{2 \times 1 \text{ (year)}}$$

Returns that Take Time Into Account

Given the fact that money has a time value, let's return to a question that we considered earlier: What is the proper holding period return to attribute to a fund where the MVB equals $100, we invest an additional $10 during the period, and the MVE = $130?

No matter when in the period the investment was made, the dollar gain is $20 ($130 − $100 − $10) for the period. The return over the period depends on the timing of the additional investment. The return could be as low as 18.18% or as high as 20%. If the $10 were invested at the *beginning of the period*, capital employed equals the original investment of $100 plus the additional investment of $10.

$$\left(\frac{130 - 100 - 10}{100 + 10}\right) \times 100 \rightarrow \left(\frac{130 - 110}{110}\right) \times 100 \rightarrow \left(\frac{20}{110}\right) \times 100 \ = \ 18.18\%$$

If instead the additional investment were made precisely at the *end of the period*, the capital employed during the period is just $100, so the return is 20%.

$$\left(\frac{130 - 100 - 10}{100}\right) \times 100 \rightarrow \left(\frac{130 - 110}{100}\right) \times 100 \rightarrow \left(\frac{20}{100}\right) \times 100 \ = \ 20\%$$

Given the same dollar gain, we should credit the overall investment with a higher return as the contribution is made closer to the end of the period. If the investment is made at the end of the period, the additional contribution is not included in the denominator. The same numerator divided by a smaller denominator leads to the higher return. The higher return is justified when the contribution is made at the end of the period because the capital at risk during the period was lower yet we earned the same dollar gain.

This example shows that it is important to track the time when contributions or withdrawals are made into an investment account in order to accurately determine returns. We always adjust the numerator for the additional contributions or withdrawals during the period. We either include the full amount of the contribution in the denominator, none of it, or a partial amount, depending on the timing of the cash flow. When the denominator of a return calculation is adjusted for contributions or withdrawals we refer to the denominator as the *average capital employed* or the *average invested balance*.

PERFORMANCE OF AN INVESTMENT: MONEY WEIGHTED RETURNS

In this section we establish the need to recognize the effects of both investor and manager decisions when calculating the return earned by the investor, but isolating the effects of investor decisions when calculating the return to be attributed to the manager. The dollar, or money weighted return (MWR) is the performance of the investment portfolio and incorporates the effects of both decisions.

Timing of Investor Decisions

In addition to the time value of money, the *market timing* of the investor contributions and withdrawals will affect realized returns. The capital markets provide us with positive long-term returns but volatile periodic returns. Market timing is a term that relates the time an investor makes his investment to the market cycle—that is, is the investor buying low and selling high.

For example, suppose we are investing via a mutual fund—an investment vehicle described in Chapter 21—and during the month the fund's net asset value per share (NAV) varied between 10.00 and 12.00 and there were no distributions.

Date	NAV per share
5/31	10.00
6/10	12.00
6/20	10.00
6/30	11.00

The monthly return that will be published for this fund is (11/10 = 10%). The following spreadsheet shows the calculation of various holding period returns for the month.

	A	B	C	D	E	F
1	Period	Return From	Calculated As	Return	% Return	
2	1	5/31 – 6/10	((12 / 10) – 1) x 100	0.20	20.00	
3	2	5/31 – 6/20	((10 / 10) –1) x 100	0.00	0.00	Published Return
4	3	5/31 – 6/30	((11 / 10) – 1) x 100	0.10	10.00	
5	4	6/10 – 6/20	((10 / 12) –1) x 100	-0.17	-16.67	
6	5	6/10 – 6/30	((11 / 12) – 1) x100	0.09	9.09	
7	6	6/20 – 6/30	((11 / 10) – 1 x 100	0.10	10.00	

The investor with perfect foresight, or luck, invested on 5/31 and withdrew on 6/10 to earn a 20% return. The investor with poor timing, who bought at the high on 6/10 and sold at the bottom on 6/20, had a – 16.67% return. This spread of 36.67% represents the return differential due to the timing of the cash flows. The important point for investment performance measurement is that these cash flows were at the *discretion of the investor*, not the manager. Actions of the investment manager would have had no impact on this differential return; the manager would have put the money to work according to his mandate.

Commingled funds have many investors. Some pursue a buy and hold strategy, some are trading in and out of the fund, and others have a regular program of buying or selling new shares. In a time when the market moved up, down, and back up, the returns earned by different investors could be quite different depending on the cash flows and return volatility. Admittedly, the returns in this example are artificially volatile. The point is that the actual returns experienced by the investor vary depending on their own investment timing decisions.

In the previous example, the advertised return for the period would be the 10% return, which was measured from the start of the monthly period to the end. Even though different investors experienced different returns, the investment manager for the mutual fund had no control over these timing decisions; therefore 10% is an accurate representation of his performance. It is the appropriate return to use when comparing the performance to a peer group average or to a benchmark.

Timing of Investment Manager Decisions

When we calculate returns, we can also consider the timing of decisions that are the responsibility of the manager. Consider two managers starting with the same $100 portfolio at the beginning of the month. Both receive $10 client contributions. Their strategies differ only in that Manager 1 attempts to time the market as shown in this example. Assume that the market moves down 10% during the month. Manager 1 leaves the contribution in cash. The following spreadsheet shows that Manager 1's return is –9.05%.

	A	B	C	D
1	Segment	MVB	Percent Return	MVE
2	Cash	10	0.01	10.05
3	Equity	100	-0.10	90.00
4	Total	110	-9.05	100.05
5			↑	
6			=((D4/B4)-1)*100	

The following spreadsheet shows that Manager 2 invests the contribution in equities at the beginning of the month and realizes a –10.00% return.

	A	B	C	D
1	Segment	MVB	Percent Return	MVE
2	Cash	0.00	0.01	0.00
3	Equity	110.00	-0.10	99.00
4	Total	110.00	-10.00	99
5			↑	
6			=((D4/B4)-1)*100	

Despite the negative returns, Manager 1 earned 95 basis points [–9.05% – (–10%)] in *value added* over Manager 2 due to the beneficial decision to leave the contribution in the relatively higher yielding cash segment during the month.

Segregating Investor and Manager Timing Decisions

It is often the case that the manager and the investor are two different people. The preceding sections illustrate a performance measurement problem: Decisions made by the investor and the investment manager must be segregated in order to properly calculate returns that reflect their respective responsibilities.

The ideal performance statistic for measuring the return experienced by the investor would include effects of both:

■ The timing of investor decisions to make an investment into the portfolio
■ The decisions made by the manager to allocate assets and select securities within the portfolio

The first effect is purely attributable to decisions made by the investor. The second also can be considered attributable to the investor because he made the decision to hire the manager. The actual returns experienced by the investor are affected by the combination of the two effects. The ideal statistic for measuring the return produced by the manager neutralizes the timing effect because he (usually) has no control over the timing of external cash flows. Because of this need to isolate the timing of investor decisions, we need two different measures of return.

The *money weighted return* (MWR) is used when we need to measure the performance as experienced by the investor. MWR is a performance statistic reflecting how much money was earned during the measurement period. This amount is influenced by the timing of decisions to contribute or withdraw money from a portfolio, as well as the decisions made by the manager of the portfolio. The MWR is contrasted with the performance statistic used to measure manager performance, the *time weighted returns* (TWR), which is discussed later. As we will see, the MWR is important even if we are interested only in evaluating manager performance, because it is sometimes used in the estimation of the TWR.

MWR is the return an investor actually experiences after making an investment. It reconciles the beginning market value and additional cash flows into the portfolio to the ending market value. The timing and size of the cash flows have an impact on the ending market value:

Transaction	Before Market	Effect on Performance
Contribute	Goes Up	Positive
Contribute	Goes Down	Negative
Withdraw	Goes Up	Negative
Withdraw	Goes Down	Positive

To accurately reflect these transactions, the MWR takes into account not only the amount of the flows but also the timing of the cash flows. Different investors into a portfolio will invest different amounts and make their investment on different dates. Because of the differences in cash flow timing and magnitude, it is not appropriate to compare the MWR calculated for two different investors.

When there are no cash flows, the return is calculated as the ending market value over the beginning market value. If there were a cash flow, we need to take into account the amount and the timing of the flow. To account for the timing of the flow, we calculate a weighting adjustment, which will be used to adjust the cash flow for the portion of the period that the cash flow was invested. The spreadsheet below shows that if we are calculating a MWR for a 1-year period and there are two cash flows, the first at the end of January and the second at the end of February, the flows will be weighted by 0.92 for the January month end flow (the flow will be available to be invested for 92% of the year) and 0.83 for the February month end flow (the flow will be available to be invested for 83% of the year).

	A	B	C	D
1	Date	Time into Total Period	Months Invested	Period Weight
2	31-Dec-2000	0	12	1.00
3	31-Jan-2001	1	11	0.92
4	28-Feb-2001	2	10	0.83
5			↑	
6			=12-B4	=C4/12

Internal Rate of Return (IRR)

Suppose we invest $100 at the beginning of the year and end up with $140 at the end of the year. We made cash flows of $10 each at the end of January and February. What is the MWR return for this situation? The MWR we are looking for will be the value that solves this equation:

$$100 \times (1 + \text{MWR}) + 10 \times (1 + \text{MWR})^{0.92} + 10 \times (1 + \text{MVR})^{0.83} = 140$$

The return that reconciles the beginning value and intermediate cash flows to the ending value is the *internal rate of return* or *IRR*. The return is the value that solves for IRR in this equation:

$$\text{MVE} = \text{MVB} \times (1 + \text{IRR}) + \text{CF}_1 \times (1 + \text{IRR})^1 \ldots \text{CF}_N \times (1 + \text{IRR})^N$$

where

CF = amount of the cash flow in or out of the portfolio

N = percentage of the period that the CF was available for investment

The IRR is the rate implied by the observed market values and cash flows. For all but the simplest case, we cannot solve for the IRR directly. Unfortunately, we cannot use algebra to rearrange the terms of the equation to derive the solution. The IRR is calculated using a trial and error process where we make an initial guess and then iteratively try successive values informed by how close we were to the solution in the last try, until we solve the problem.

Techniques have been developed to perform the iteration efficiently and converge on a solution quickly. The following spreadsheet shows the calculation of the IRR using the Excel solver utility:

	A	B	C	D	E	F
1	Date	Months Invested	Period Weight	Value	Future Value of Flow	
2	Dec-31-2000	12	1.00	100	117.05	=D2*((1+E8)^C2)
3	Jan-31-2001	11	0.92	10	11.55	=D3*((1+E8)^C3)
4	Feb-28-2001	10	0.83	10	11.40	=D4*((1+E8)^C4)
5	Dec-31-2001			140	140.00	=SUM(E2:E4)
6						
7		IRR calculated using solver		Difference:	0.00	=D5-E5
8				IRR:	0.1705	
9				Percent Return:	17.05	=E8*100

Here, we set the difference between the ending market value in cell D5 equal to the sum of the future values in cell E5. We then solved for the IRR in cell E8. The IRR is 17.05% because, as demonstrated below, it is the interest rate that resolves the flows to the ending market value.

$$100 \times (1 + 0.1705) + 10 \times (1 + 0.1705)^{0.92} + 10 \times (1 + 0.1705)^{0.83} = 140$$

Notice that there is an assumption embedded in the IRR formula: the rate of return is assumed to be constant within the period. In this example, each cash flow is compounded at 17.05% for the complete portion of the year invested.

We can calculate an IRR for periods that are less than a year. The period weight used for each of the cash flows is the percentage of the total period under consideration. For example, a cash flow on the 10th of a 31-day month would be weighted at $[31 - 10)/31)] = 0.7097$ of the month. (This assumes that the contribution was made at the beginning of the day on the 10th, subtract a day if we assume cash flows occur at the end of the day.) The results of IRR calculations done for less than a year are interpreted as an IRR over the period measured. The following spreadsheet shows the calculation of the monthly IRR where MVB = 1,000 on December 31, 2000, MVE = 1,200 on January 31, 2001, and there were two cash flows, $400 into the portfolio on January 10, 2001, and $100 out of the portfolio on January 20, 2001.

	A	B	C	D	E	F
1	Date	Days Invested	Period Weight	Value	Future Value of Flow	
2	31-Dec-2000	31	1.00	1000	919.85	=D2*((1+E8)^C2)
3	10-Jan-2001	22	0.71	400	376.97	=D3*((1+E8)^C3)
4	20-Jan-2001	12	0.39	-100	-96.82	=D4*((1+E8)^C4)
5	31-Jan-2001			1200	1200.00	=SUM(E2:E4)
6						
7				Difference:	0.00	=D5-E5
8				IRR:	-0.08	
9				Percent Return:	-8.02	=E8*100

When we have withdrawals from the account, we make the cash flow adjustments used in the IRR negative. The one-month IRR for this pattern of cash flows is –8.02%

Problems with the IRR

We classify the IRR as a MWR because it takes into account both the timing and size of cash flows into the portfolio. It is an appropriate measure of the performance of the investment as experienced by the investor. The fact that the IRR needs to be calculated via iteration used to make the IRR an expensive calculation, because of the computer time used by the iteration algorithm. This is not a problem today. But, the historical problem led to the development of various creative methods to cheaply estimate the IRR. One of these methods, the Modified Dietz method, is still the most common method used by analysts to compute MWRs and, as we will see, estimate returns between valuation dates when we are calculating a TWR.

Modified Dietz Return

The *Modified Dietz return* is a simple interest estimate of the MWR. The Modified Dietz calculation is the same as the ROI calculation, except the cash flows added to the beginning market value are adjusted according to the time they were invested in the portfolio.

$$\text{Modified Dietz Return} = \frac{\text{MVE} - \text{MVB} - \text{CF}}{\text{MVB} + \{[(\text{CD} - C_i)/\text{CD}] \times \text{CF}_i\}} \times 100$$

where

CF $\;=\;$ net amount of the cash flows for the period
CD $\;=\;$ total days in the period
C_i $\;=\;$ the day of the cash flow
CF_i $\;=\;$ the amount of the net cash flow on C_i

The calculation is named for the developer, Peter Dietz, who was associated with the Frank Russell pension consulting company. The original Dietz method, not currently used, makes the assumption that cash flows occurred midway through the period.

To illustrate the calculation of a Modified Dietz return, consider the following situation.

Begin Market Value + Accrued Income   MVB   100
End Market Value + Accrued Income   MVE   120
Sum (Client Contribution/Withdrawal)   CF   10 on the 20th of a
                                                                  30-day month

To calculate the Modified Dietz return as shown, first we calculate the *adjustment factor*, which is 0.33, assuming that the flow occurs at the end of the day on the 20th.

$$\frac{30 - 20}{30} = 0.33$$

Then we adjust the cash flow by multiplying the amount by the adjustment factor: $0.33 \times \$10 = \$3.33$. We then add the modified flow to the beginning market value in the denominator, and calculate the Modified Dietz return, 9.68%.

$$9.68\% = \frac{120 - 100 - 10}{100 + 3.33} \times 100$$

Both the IRR and Modified Dietz formulas are money weighted returns. MWR results *are* affected by the timing and magnitude of the cash flows during the period. The return statistics that completely eliminate the impact of investor cash flows are time weighted returns.

PERFORMANCE OF THE INVESTMENT MANAGER: TIME WEIGHTED RETURNS

A rate of return is the percentage change in the value of an asset over some period of time. Total returns are calculated by dividing the capital gain/loss and income earned by the value of the investment at the beginning of the period. As we saw earlier in this chapter, investors experience different returns investing in the same fund depending on the timing and magnitude of their cash flows into and out of the portfolio. Returns are used in evaluating the performance of an investment manager, but he or she (usually) has no control over the timing and amount of investor flows, so we need a performance measure that negates the effect of these cash flows. The desired return would judge the manager by the return on money invested over the whole period and eliminate the effect of client cash flows.

Time Weighted Return

The *time weighted return* (TWR) is a form of total return that measures the performance of a dollar invested in the fund over the complete measurement period. The TWR eliminates the timing effect that external portfolio cash flows have on performance, leaving only the effects of the market and manager decisions.

To calculate a time weighted return, we break the period of interest into subperiods, calculate the returns earned during the subperiods, and then compound these subperiod returns to derive the TWR for the whole period. The subperiod boundaries are the dates of each cash flow. Specifically, the steps to calculate a TWR are as follows.

1. Begin with the market value at the beginning of the period.
2. Move forward through time toward the end of the period.
3. Note the value of the portfolio immediately before a cash flow into or out of the portfolio.
4. Calculate a *subperiod return* for the period between the valuation dates.
5. Repeat 3 and 4 for each cash flow encountered.
6. When there are no more cash flows, calculate a subperiod return for the last period using the end of period market value.
7. Compound the subperiod returns by taking the product of (1 + the subperiod returns).

The last step is called *geometric linking,* or *chain linking,* of the returns. Chain linking has the same function as compounding in the future value calculation. We employ chain linking instead of the future value formula when the periodic returns change from subperiod to subperiod.

$$\text{Time Weighted Return} = [(1 + R_1) \times (1 + R_2) \times \ldots (1 + R_N) - 1] \times 100$$

where R_N are the subperiod returns.

The TWR assumes compounding and reinvestment of the gains earned in the previous subperiods. The expression (1 + the subperiod return) is called a *wealth relative* or *growth rate*, which represents the increase in capital over the subperiod. For example, if a portfolio is worth $100 at the beginning of the subperiod, and $105 at the end of the subperiod before the next cash flow, the subperiod return is 5% and the growth rate for the subperiod equals 1.05.

Below we will illustrate the steps to calculate a TWR. We calculate the TWR for a month where fund market values were:

Date	End of Day Valuation
5/31	1000
6/9	1100
6/19	1200
6/30	1200

And there were two cash flows during the month:

Date	Cash Flow
6/10	200
6/20	−100

Divide the Period into Subperiods

The first step in the TWR calculation is to divide the period we are interested in into subperiods, where the subperiods are segregated by the cash flow dates. The next step is to note the value the portfolio before each cash flow. If we are working with a beginning of day cash flow assumption, we use the valuation performed on the night prior to the cash flow.

Date	Beginning of Day Valuation	Cash Flow	End of Day Valuation
5/31			1000
6/9			1100
6/10	1100	200	
6/19			1200
6/20	1200	−100	
6/30	1200		1200

We have two cash flows and three subperiods.

1. 5/31 to the end of day 6/9
2. 6/10 to the end of day 6/19
3. 6/20 to the end of day 6/30

Note that there are (1 + the number of cash flow dates) subperiods.

Calculate Subperiod Returns

Next we calculate a single period return for each subperiod. The time of day assumption governs the treatment of the cash flows in the subperiod return formula. Here we assume that cash flows occur at the beginning of the day. With a beginning of day assumption, we add the cash flow to the beginning day market value to form the denominator of the return. Cash flows into the portfolio are added to the denominator, cash flows out of the portfolio are subtracted. If there is more than one cash flow during the day we net the flows together.

$$\text{Subperiod Return (start of day flow assumption)} = \frac{\text{MVE}}{\text{MVB} + \text{Net Cash Inflows}}$$

If we are calculating performance for a unitized product such as a mutual fund, the inputs to the subperiod return formula are the net asset value per share and dividend distributions. The effect of the cash flow adjustment is to negate the effect of the contributions/withdrawals from the return calculation. The calculation of the three subperiod returns, 10.00%, −7.69%, and 9.09%, is shown in the following spreadsheet.

	A	B	C	D	E	F	G
1	Subperiod	Return From	BMV	CF	EMV	Percent Return	Growth Rate
2	1	5/31 − 6/10	1000	0	1100	10.00	1.10
3	2	6/10 − 6/20	1100	200	1200	−7.69	0.92
4	3	6/20 − 6/30	1200	−100	1200	9.09	1.09
5					=((E4/(C4 + D4))−1)*100		=1+(F4/100)
6							

EXHIBIT 3.2 Time Weighted Return

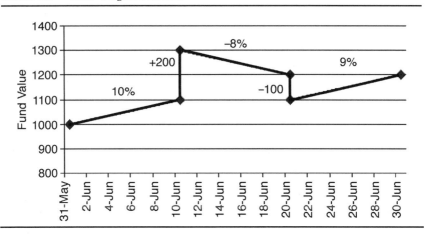

Calculate Multiple Period Returns

The percentage return for the month is calculated by chain linking the subperiod returns.

$$[(1.1000) \times (0.9231) \times (1.0909) - 1] \times 100 = 10.77\%$$

By calculating the return in this way, we have completely eliminated from the return the impact of the cash flows into and out of the portfolio. Exhibit 3.2 provides a way to visualize how the TWR eliminates cash flow effects from the return calculation.

There are some exceptions to the general rule that TWR is the appropriate measure of manager performance. In some situations, the portfolio manager does have discretion over the timing of cash flows. For example, in the management of private equity funds (an investment vehicle discussed in Chapter 26), the general partner draws down the capital committed when he wants to invest it. However, in most performance measurement applications, the TWR is the appropriate measure of manager performance.

Estimating the Time Weighted Return

There is a potential hurdle to implementing this methodology. TWR requires a valuation of the portfolio before each cash flow. Unfortunately, these periodic valuations are not always available. For example, many institutional separate accounts are valued on a monthly frequency, but the client may deposit or withdraw from the account at any time during the month. While industry trends lean in the direction of daily valuations, until these are available for all investment vehicles, we need a way of estimating the true TWR when contributions and withdrawals are made in between valuation dates.

We can approximate a TWR by calculating a MWR for each subperiod between valuation dates and compounding them over longer periods using the chain linking method used to link subperiod returns into a TWR. This linked MWR estimate of TWR provides a reliable approximation of the TWR in situations where the cash flows are small relative to the portfolio size and there is low return volatility within the subperiod. If the cash flows are large and the market is volatile during the period, the MWR estimate of TWR will be inaccurate. So it is important to note that the linked MWR is an *estimate* of the TWR over the longer period. While the cash flows are weighted within the subperiod, the cash flows are still influencing the returns. The linking process does not remove the effect of the cash flows from the cumulative return calculation. A compromise solution to calculating a TWR is to perform a special valuation whenever there are large cash flows and then link the subperiod MWR.

Exhibit 3.3 summarizes the differences between the money and time weighted returns.

EXHIBIT 3.3

	Money Weighted Returns	Time Weighted Returns
Measures	The average growth rate of all dollars invested over the period	The growth rate of a single dollar invested over the period
Usage in analyzing investment results	Appropriate measure of investor or fund performance	Appropriate for measuring performance of vehicle or manager Appropriate for market comparison Appropriate for comparing managers
Effect of external cash flows	Reflects both the timing and amount of dollars at work over the period	Eliminates the effect of both timing and amount of money at work
Statistic represents	The return that reconciles MVB, CF, and MVE	The return of $1 invested in the portfolio from beginning to end
Calculation drawbacks	Iteration required for IRR calculation	A valuation is required before each flow.

MULTIPLE PERIOD RETURN CALCULATION

We can compute rates of return over multiple periods by compounding the single period returns. We are often interested in an average of the periodic returns that reflects the compounding function. The average returns are often restated to an annual average basis. These topics are covered in this section.

Cumulative Returns

We saw the compounding process at work when we employed subperiod returns in the chain linking process to create a multiperiod TWR. In this same way, we can derive cumulative returns for any period of interest, such as month-to-date, year-to-date, first quarter of the year, 1-year, 3-year, and since-account-inception. To compound the returns, we multiply (1 + decimal return) for each period.

$$\text{Cumulative Return} = [(\text{Growth Rate}_1) \times (\text{Growth Rate}_2) \ldots - 1] \times 100$$

The following spreadsheet shows the calculation of a cumulative 5-year return given the series of yearly returns 9%, 6%, –2%, 8%, and –4%.

	A	B	C	D	E
1				Growth Rates	
2	Year	Return	Single Period	Compounded	Cumulative %
3	1	0.09	1.09	1.09	
4	2	0.06	1.06	1.16	
5	3	–0.02	0.98	1.13	=PRODUCT(C3:C7)
6	4	0.08	1.08	1.22	
7	5	–0.04	0.96	1.17	17.40
8				=(D7–1)*100	
9					

By compounding the returns we find that the cumulative 5-year return is 17.40%.

Since we often are interested in the performance of an investment over time, we can maintain *cumulative growth rates*. Cumulative growth rates are useful for quickly calculating the cumulative return over multiple periods because we do not need to reference the intermediate returns or growth rates. Cumulative growth rates are calculated by taking the previous period ending cumulative growth rate and multiplying by (1 + current period return). We can use cumulative growth rates to calculate the expected value of an investment by multiplying it by the cumulative growth factor. For example, $100 invested into a fund with a compound 5-year growth rate of 1.2568 will result in an ending value of $125.68.

$$100 \times (1.2568) = 125.68$$

Growth rates also can be used to derive the return between any two dates.

$$\text{Return} = \left[\left(\frac{\text{End Period Growth Rate}}{\text{Begin Period Growth Rate}} \right) - 1 \right] \times 100$$

We calculate cumulative returns when we are interested in the performance of investments over long-term periods. Note that cumulative returns incorporate the assumption that investment gains are reinvested into the fund and compounded over time. The appreciation at the end of each period, as measured by the return, is treated as if it is income that is reinvested into the portfolio in the next period.

Compressing Periods

Single period returns are usually calculated on a daily or monthly periodic frequency. The single period returns can be compressed into longer-term returns by compounding. For example, the daily returns calculated over the course of a month can be compressed, or "rolled up," into a monthly return. Compounding 12 monthly periodic returns will give the same result as if the underlying daily returns were used. In a similar fashion, monthly returns can be compressed into yearly returns for purposes of calculating multiyear returns. In our previous calculation to illustrate cumulative returns, we used five yearly frequency returns to derive the 5-year cumulative return. If the yearly returns were actually calculated using a daily frequency, we could have chain linked the approximately 1,250 (250 trading days × 5 years) daily returns and derived the same result. It is easier to work with the compressed monthly, quarterly, or yearly returns, even if they were originally calculated on a daily basis.

Arithmetic Mean Return

Often, we are interested in calculating average, or mean, investment returns. Average returns can be used to compare the performance of investment managers or funds over time. There are two methods for calculating the average of a series of returns: the arithmetic and geometric methods. As a measure of the average return, a mean return can be calculated by adding the periodic returns together and dividing by the number of returns.

$$\text{Arithmetic Mean Return} = \frac{\text{Sum (Periodic Returns)}}{\text{Count of Returns}}$$

The periodicity of the returns must be the same for each of the returns (i.e., all of the returns must be daily, monthly, or yearly returns). The arithmetic mean return cannot be used in all applications. For example, we may want to use an average yearly return to project the future value of an investment. One problem with using arithmetic mean returns is that they do not take into account the compounding of returns over time. For example, if we have two yearly returns:

Year	Return
1	10%
2	20%

The arithmetic mean return is 15% [(20 + 10)/2]. The compound 2-year return is 32%.

$$[(1.10) \times (1.20) - 1] \times 100 = 32.00\%$$

If we take the arithmetic mean return and plug it into the compounding formula we will get a higher result than we did using the actual periodic returns.

$$[(1.15) \times (1.15) - 1] \times 100 = 32.25\%$$

Use of the arithmetic mean return to reconcile the beginning to ending investment value overstates the ending value. The average return we use in this application should be lower than the arithmetic mean return in order to account for the compounding process.

Geometric Mean Return

When we multiply the average yearly return by the total number of years, it does not equal the compounded return because it does not take into account the income earned by reinvesting the prior period income. In the previous example, the 20% return in Year 2 was earned by reinvesting the 10% Year 1 return, but that is not accounted for in the arithmetic average. To fix this, instead of taking the arithmetic mean return we calculate the geometric mean return. The *geometric mean return* is the nth root of the compound return, where n is the number of periods used to calculate the compound cumulative return. That is:

$$\text{Geometric Mean Return} = [\sqrt[N]{(1 + \text{Cumulative Return})} - 1] \times 100$$

(Note that finding the root is the inverse of multiplying the growth rates.)

The following spreadsheet shows that the geometric average yearly return derived from a two-year compound return of 32% equals 14.89%.

	A	B	C	D	E
1				Growth Rates	
2	Year	Return	Single Period	Compounded	Cumulative %
3	1	0.10	1.10	1.10	
4	2	0.20	1.20	1.32	32.00
5		=PRODUCT(C3:C4)			
6			Arithmetic yearly average:	15.00	
7			Geometric yearly average:	14.89	
8			=((D4^(1/2))-1)*100		
9					

In Excel, to take the nth root, we raise the compound growth rate to the $(1/N)$ power.

$$(\sqrt[2]{1.32} - 1) \times 100 \to (1.1489 - 1) \times 100 = 14.89\%$$

Plugging the geometric mean return into the compound growth formula yields the compound return for the period.

$$\text{Compound Return} = \{[1 + (\text{Geometric Mean Return}/100)]^N - 1\} \times 100$$

We can back into the 32% compound return for two months using the geometric average return of 14.89%.

$$\{[1 + (14.89/100)]^2 - 1\} \times 100 \to [(1.1489)^2 - 1] \times 100$$
$$\to (1.32 - 1) \times 100 \to 32\%$$

or

$$\{[(1.1489) \times (1.1489)] - 1\} \times 100 = 32\%$$

Column C in the spreadsheet that follows shows that one advantage of using average returns is that we do not need to know the actual periodic returns in order to calculate a future value:

	A	B	C	D	E
1	Year	Actual Return	Geometric Average Return		
2	1	0.15	0.0534	=((1+(B6/100))^(1/3))-1	
3	2	0.07	0.0534	=C2	
4	3	-0.05	0.0534	=C2	
5					
6	Year 1-3 in %	16.90	16.90	=((1+C2)*(1+C3)*(1+C4)-1)*100	
7		=((1+B2)*(1+B3)*(1+B4)-1)*100			
8					

Annualizing Returns Less than a Year

No matter how short or long the actual investment period, returns are typically presented on a yearly, or *annual basis*. We do this because it is easier to compare investment returns if the time periods over which each investment has been made are put on an equivalent basis. The geometric mean return when calculated for a 1-year period is called an *average annual return, compound annual return*, or *annualized return*.

Interest rates are typically quoted on an annualized basis. If we have a return for a period less than a year and we need to turn it into an annual return, we can compound it by raising the holding period return to the power equal to the number of periods in the year:

$$\{[(1 + \text{Period rate})^{\#\text{ of periods}}] - 1\} \times 100$$

In this case, we would need to continue to reinvest at the single-period rate to produce the annual return. For this reason, returns that are annualized based on a cumulative period of less than a year are *hypothetical* projections of the annual return. As an extreme example of the problem of using annual returns calculated in this way, suppose the market had a great month and is up 20%. Conversion to an annual basis results in a 792% compounded annual return

An annualized return calculated for a holding period of less than a year would be interpreted as the return for a year *if* performance for the rest of the year is equal to that actually experienced so far in the year.

Annualizing Returns Greater than a Year

If the multiperiod compound return that we are annualizing was calculated for a period greater than a year, the rate is restated to an annual basis using the inverse of the compounding formula. The inverse of taking a number and raising it to a power n is to take the nth root of the number.

$$\{[\sqrt[\#\text{ of years}]{(1 + \text{Period rate})}] - 1\} \times 100$$

For example, if an investment earned 19.1% over a 3-year period, the return can be quoted as an annual average return of 6% by finding the third root of the cumulative growth rate.

$$\{[\sqrt[3]{(1.19102)}] - 1\} \times 100 = 6.00$$

Notice that we calculate the annualized return by first taking the root of the cumulative growth rate as opposed to taking the *n*th root of the cumulative return. The *n*th root of the growth rate is the geometric average growth rate. To transform the average growth rate into a geometric average return we subtract 1 and multiply by 100.

We usually need to calculate an annualized return for cumulative periods that are not exact multiples of a year. To calculate annualized returns for such odd periods, we can calculate the actual number of calendar days in the cumulative period and divide by 365.25 to calculate an annualized equivalent.

$$\text{Annualized Return} = \left[\left(\sqrt[\frac{\text{Number of Days}}{365.25}]{\text{Linked Growth Rates}}\right) - 1\right] \times 100$$

For example, the annualized equivalent of a 14% return earned over 16 months is equal to 10.37%.

Compound Annual Internal Rate of Return

If we are working with a dollar weighted IRR calculated over periods longer than a year, we can also calculate an annual equivalent. To do this, we adjust the weights used to reconcile the cash flows to the ending market value so that they are multiples of a year. The calculation of an annual equivalent of a 5-year IRR equal to 10.00% is shown in the following spreadsheet:

	A	B	C	D	E	F	G
1	Year	Days	Flow	Value	Weight	FV	
2	0	0	400	0	5.00	440	=FV(F9,E2,0,-C2,0)
3	1	365	100		4.00	110	=FV(F9,E2,0,-C3,0)
4	2	730	100		3.00	110	=FV(F9,E2,0,-C4,0)
5	3	1095	(50)		2.00	(55)	=FV(F9,E2,0,-C5,0)
6	4	1460	(50)		1.00	(55)	=FV(F9,E2,0,-C6,0)
7	5	1825		550		550	→
8							
9					Difference:	(0)	=F7-D7
10	Total Days:	1825			*Annual Return:	0.02	
11					Annual % Return:	1.93	=F10*100
12					Growth Rate:	1.01926	=1+F10
13					Years:	5.00	=((B7-0)/365.25)
14					Compound Return:	10.00	=((F12^F13)-1)*100

This is equivalent to an annualized IRR of 1.93%. Notice that we weighted the beginning investment balance by 5 years, the first cash flow by 4 years, and so on.

SUMMARY

In this chapter we outlined the procedures for calculating and interpreting the meaning of investment returns. Periodic portfolio valuation and cash flow figures are transformed into single period returns. Time weighted returns measure the results attributable to the investment manager. Dollar weighted returns reflect both the performance of the manager and the timing of investor transactions.

Rates of return are a description of one facet of investment performance. Performance measurement is also concerned with measuring the risks taken to earn these returns, and the attribution of returns to market activity and active management. As the investment cycle turns, the return, risk, and attribution statistics we calculate in performance measurement are the inputs to the next round of asset allocation and security selection decisions.

CHAPTER 4

Common Stock

Frank J. Fabozzi, Ph.D., CFA
Adjunct Professor of Finance
School of Management
Yale University

Frank J. Jones, Ph.D.
Chief Investment Officer
The Guardian Life Insurance Company of America

Robert R. Johnson, Ph.D., CFA
Senior Vice President
Association for Investment Management and Research

In this chapter we will discuss the investment characteristics of common stock, explain the markets where common stock is traded, the arrangements made for the trading of common stock by retail (i.e., individual) and institutional investors, and review common stock portfolio strategies.

COMMON STOCK VERSUS PREFERRED STOCK

Common stocks are also called *equity securities* . Equity securities represent an ownership interest in a corporation. Holders of equity securities are entitled to the earnings of the corporation when those earnings are distributed in the form of *dividends* ; they are also entitled to a pro rata share of the remaining equity in case of liquidation.

Common stock is only one type of equity security. Another type is preferred stock. The key distinction between the two forms of equity securities is the degree to which their holders may participate in any distribution of earnings and capital and the priority given to each class in the distribution of earnings. Typically, preferred stockholders are entitled to a fixed dividend, which they receive before common stockholders may receive any dividends. Therefore, we refer to preferred stock as a senior corporate security, in the sense that preferred stock interests are senior to the interests of common stockholders. Preferred stock is discussed Chapter 12.

WHERE STOCK TRADING OCCURS

It is in the market for common stock through the trades they make that investors express their opinions about the economic prospects of a company. The aggregate of these trades provides the market consensus opinion about the price of the stock.

In the United States, secondary market trading in common stocks has occurred in two different ways. The first is on organized exchanges, which are specific geographical locations called trading floors, where representatives of buyers and sellers physically meet. The trading mechanism on exchanges is the auction system, which results from the presence of many competing buyers and sellers assembled in one place.

The second type is via over-the-counter (OTC) trading, which results from geographically dispersed traders or market-makers linked to one another via telecommunication systems. That is, there is no trading floor. This trading mechanism is a negotiated system whereby individual buyers negotiate with individual sellers.

Exchange markets are called central auction specialist systems and OTC markets are called multiple market maker systems. In recent years a new method of trading common stocks via independently owned and operated electronic communications networks (ECNs) has developed and is growing quickly.

In the United States there are two national stock exchanges: (1) the New York Stock Exchange (NYSE), commonly called the "Big Board," and (2) the American Stock Exchange (AMEX or ASE), also called the "Curb." National stock exchanges trade stocks of not only U.S. corporations but also non-U.S. corporations. In addition to the national exchanges, there are regional stock exchanges in Boston, Chicago (called the Midwest Exchange), Cincinnati, San Francisco (called the Pacific

Coast Exchange) and Philadelphia. Regional exchanges primarily trade stocks from corporations based within their region.

The major OTC market in the U.S. is NASDAQ (the National Association of Securities Dealers Automated Quotation System), which is owned and operated by the NASD (the National Association of Securities Dealers), although it is in the process of becoming independent. The NASD is a securities industry self-regulatory organization (SRO) that operates subject to the oversight of the Securities and Exchange Commission (SEC). NASDAQ is a national market. During 1998, NASDAQ and AMEX merged to form the NASDAQ-AMEX Market Group, Inc.

The NYSE is the largest exchange in the U.S. with the shares of approximately 3,000 companies listed. The AMEX is the second largest national stock exchange in the U.S., with over 750 issues listed for trading. NASDAQ has a greater number of listed stocks but with much less market capitalization than the NYSE.

According to the Securities Act of 1934, there are two categories of traded stocks. The first is exchange traded stocks (also called "listed" stocks). The second is OTC stocks which are also non-exchange traded stocks and are, thus, by inference, "non-listed." However, as we will describe later in this chapter, NASDAQ stocks have listing requirements (the NASDAQ National Market and the NASDAQ Small Capitalization Market). Thus, a more useful and practical categorization is as follows:

1. Exchange listed stocks (national and regional exchanges)
2. NASDAQ listed OTC stocks
3. Non-NASDAQ OTC stocks

We will focus on each of these markets later in this section.

The four major types of markets on which stocks are traded are referred to as follows:

- First Market—trading on exchanges of stocks listed on an exchange
- Second Market—trading in the OTC market of stocks not listed on an exchange
- Third Market—trading in the OTC market of stocks listed on an exchange
- Fourth Market—private transactions between institutional investors who deal directly with each other without utilizing the services of a broker-dealer intermediary

These types of markets are discussed in the following sections.

Exchanges

Stock exchanges are formal organizations, approved and regulated by the SEC. They are comprised of "members" that use the exchange facilities and systems to exchange or trade "listed" stocks. These exchanges are physical locations where members assemble to trade. Stocks that are traded on an exchange are said to be *listed stocks* . That is, these stocks are individually approved for trading on the exchange by the exchange. To be listed, a company must apply and satisfy requirements established by the exchange for minimum capitalization, shareholder equity, average closing share price, and other criteria. Even after being listed, exchanges may delist a company's stock if it no longer meets the exchange requirements.

To have the right to trade securities or make markets on an exchange floor, firms or individuals must become a *member* of the exchange, which is accomplished by buying a *seat* on the exchange. The number of seats is fixed by the exchange and the cost of a seat is determined by supply and demand by those who want to sell or buy seats.

There are two kinds of stocks listed on the five regional stock exchanges:

1. Stocks of companies that either could not qualify for listing on one of the major national exchanges or could qualify for listing but chose not to list
2. Stocks that are also listed on one of the major national exchanges

The second group of stocks are called *dually listed stocks*. The motivation of a company for dual listing is that a local brokerage firm that purchases a membership on a regional exchange can trade their listed stocks without having to purchase a considerably more expensive membership on the national stock exchange where the stock is also listed. Alternatively, a local brokerage firm could use the services of a member of a major national stock exchange to execute an order, but in this case it would have to give up part of its commission.

The regional stock exchanges compete with the NYSE for the execution of smaller trades. Major national brokerage firms have in recent years routed such orders to regional exchanges because of the lower cost they charge for executing orders or the better prices received.

The NYSE

The NYSE is conducted as a centralized continuous auction market at a designated location on the trading floor, called a "post," with brokers representing their customers' buy and sell orders. A single *specialist* is the market maker for each stock. A member firm may be designated as a specialist for the common stock of more than one company, that is, several stocks can trade at the same post. But only one specialist is designated for the common stock of each listed company.

A specialist for each stock stands at a trading position around one of the 17 NYSE "posts." Each post is essentially an auction site where orders, bids, and offers arrive. Most orders arrive from floor brokers via an electronic delivery system called the SuperDot (Super Designated Order Turnaround). SuperDot is an electronic order routing and reporting system linking member firms electronically worldwide directly to the specialist's post on the trading floor of the NYSE. The majority of NYSE orders are processed electronically through SuperDot.

In addition to the single specialist market-maker on an exchange, other firms that are members of an exchange can trade for themselves or on behalf of their customers. NYSE member firms, which are broker-dealer organizations that serve the investing public, are represented on the trading floor by brokers who serve as fiduciaries in the execution of customer orders.

The largest membership category on the NYSE is that of the *commission broker*. A commission broker is an employee of one of the nearly 500 securities houses ("stockbrokers" or "wirehouses") devoted to handling business on the exchange. Commission brokers execute orders for their firm on behalf of their customers at agreed commission rates. These houses may deal for their own account as well as on behalf of their clients.

Other transactors on the exchange floor include the following categories. *Independent floor brokers* work on the exchange floor and execute orders for other exchange members who have more orders than they can handle alone or who require assistance in carrying out large orders. Floor brokers take a share in the commission received by the firm they are assisting. *Registered traders* are individual members who buy and sell for their own account. Alternatively, they may be trustees who maintain membership for the convenience of dealing and to save fees.

As explained earlier, *specialists* are dealers or market makers assigned by the NYSE to conduct the auction process and to maintain an orderly market in one or more designated stocks. Specialists may act as both a broker (agent) and a dealer (principal). In their role as a broker or agent, specialists represent customer orders in their assigned stocks, which arrive at their post electronically or are entrusted to them by a floor broker to be executed if and when a stock reaches a price specified by a customer (limit or stop order). As a dealer or principal, specialists buy and sell shares in their assigned stocks for their own account as necessary to maintain an orderly market. Specialists must always give precedence to public orders over trading for their own account.

In general, public orders for stocks traded on the NYSE, if they are not sent to the specialist's post via SuperDot, are sent from the member firm's office to its representative on the exchange floor, who attempts to execute the order in the trading crowd. Later in this chapter we discuss the various types of orders that an investor can ask a broker to execute. There are certain types of orders where the order will not be executed immediately on the trading floors. These are limit orders and stop orders. If the order is a limit order or a stop order and the member firm's floor broker cannot transact the order immediately, they can wait in the trading crowd or give the order to the specialist in the stock, who will enter the order in that specialist's *limit order book* (or simply, *book*) for later execution based on the relationship between the market price and the price specified in the limit or stop order. The book is the list in which specialists keep the limit and stop orders given to them, arranged by size, from near the current market price to further away from it. While the book was formerly an actual physical paper book, it is now maintained electronically. Only the specialist can view the orders in the book for their stock. This exclusivity with respect to the limit order book is obviously an advantage to the specialist, which to some degree offsets their obligation to make fair and orderly markets. At the time of this writing, however, the NYSE was planning to make the specialists' book available to investors electronically.

A significant advantage of the NYSE market is its diversity of participants. At the exchange, public orders meet each other often with minimal dealer intervention, contributing to an efficient mechanism for achieving fair securities prices. The liquidity provided by the NYSE market stems from the active involvement of the following principal groups: the individual investor; the institutional investor; the member firm acting as both agent and dealer; the member-firm broker on the trading floor acting as agent, representing the firm's customer orders; the independent broker on the trading floor acting as agent and handling customer orders on behalf of other member firms; and the specialist, with assigned responsibility in individual securities on the trading floor. Together these groups provide depth and diversity to the market.

NYSE-assigned specialists have four major roles:

1. As dealers, they trade for their own accounts when there is a temporary absence of public buyers or sellers, and only after the public orders in their possession have been satisfied at a specified price.
2. As agents, they execute market orders entrusted to them by brokers, as well as orders awaiting a specific market price.
3. As catalysts, they help to bring buyers and sellers together.
4. As auctioneers, they quote current bid/asked prices that reflect total supply and demand for each of the stocks assigned to them.

In carrying out their duties, specialists may, as indicated, act as either an agent or a principal. When acting as an *agent*, the specialist simply fills customer market orders, limit or stop orders (either new orders or orders from their book) by opposite orders (buy or sell). When acting as a *principal*, the specialist is charged with the responsibility of maintaining a *fair and orderly market*. Specialists are prohibited from engaging in transactions in securities in which they are registered unless such transactions are necessary to maintain a fair and orderly market. Specialists profit only from those trades in which they are involved; that is, they realize no revenue for trades in which they are an agent.

The term "fair and orderly market" means a market in which there is price continuity and reasonable depth. Thus, specialists are required to maintain a reasonable spread between bids and offers and small changes in price between transactions. Specialists are expected to bid and offer for their own account if necessary to promote such a fair and orderly market. They cannot put their own interests ahead of public orders and are obliged to trade on their own accounts against the market trend to help maintain liquidity and continuity as the price of a stock goes up or down. They may purchase stock for their investment account only if such purchases are necessary to create a fair and orderly market.

Specialists are responsible for balancing buy and sell orders at the opening of the trading day in order to arrange an equitable opening price for the stock. Specialists are expected to participate in the opening of the market only to the extent necessary to balance supply and demand for the security to effect a reasonable opening price. While trading throughout the day is via a continuous auction-based system, the opening is conducted via a single-price call auction system. The specialists conduct the call and determine the single price.

If there is an *imbalance* between buy and sell orders either at the opening or during the trading day and the specialist cannot maintain a fair and orderly market, then they may, under restricted conditions, close the market in that stock (that is, discontinue trading) until they are able to determine a price at which there is a balance of buy and sell orders. Such closes of trading can occur either during the trading day or at the opening, which is more common, and can last for minutes or days. Closings of a day or more may occur when, for example, there is an acquisition of one firm by another or when there is an extreme announcement by the corporation (for this reason, many announcements are after the close of trading).

The Over-the-Counter Market

The OTC market is called the market for "unlisted stocks." As explained earlier, while there are listing requirements for exchanges, there are also "listing requirements" for the NASDAQ National and Small Capitalization OTC markets, which are discussed in the following section. Nevertheless, exchange traded stocks are called "listed," and stocks traded on the OTC markets are called "unlisted."

There are three parts of the OTC market—two under the aegis of NASD (the NASDAQ markets) and a third market for truly unlisted stocks, the non-NASDAQ OTC markets.

NASDAQ Stock Market

Established in 1971, the NASDAQ stock market was developed as a wholly-owned subsidiary of the NASD. The NASD is the National Association of Securities Dealers, a self-regulatory organization (SRO) subject to oversight by the SEC. NASD, a private organization, represents and regulates the dealers in the OTC market.

NASDAQ is essentially a telecommunications network that links thousands of geographically-dispersed market making participants. NASDAQ is an electronic quotation system that provides price quotations to market participants on NASDAQ listed stocks. While there is no central trading floor, NASDAQ has become an electronic "virtual trading floor." There are more than 4,700 common stocks included in the NASDAQ system with a total market value of over $3.5 trillion. Some 535 dealers, known as market makers, representing some of the world's largest securities firms, provide competing bids to buy and offers to sell NASDAQ stocks to investors.

The NASDAQ stock market has two broad tiers of securities: (1) the NASDAQ National Market (NNM) and the Small Capitalization Market. Newspapers have separate sections for these two tiers of stocks (sections labeled the "NASDAQ National Market" and the "NASDAQ Small Capitalization Market"). The NASDAQ NMS is the dominant OTC market in the United States.

As of December 2000, there were approximately 3,800 stocks on the NASDAQ NNM system and 900 on the Small Cap Market. The Small Cap Market is smaller in terms of number of companies, trading volume (both share and dollar amount), and market value of companies

Securities are actually "listed" on both tiers of NASDAQ, that is they must meet fairly stringent listing requirements for size, issuer profitability, trading volume, governance, public disclosure, and other factors. Securities traded on these NASDAQ tiers must meet specified minimum standards for both initial listing and continued listing. The financial criteria for listing in the Small Cap Market are not as stringent as in the NNM system. Small Cap companies often grow and move up to the NNM market. The NNM issues are more widely known, have more trading volume, and have more market makers.

There are also differences in the listing requirements for the NYSE and NASDAQ (NNM). One difference is that profitability is required for companies listed on NYSE but not on NASDAQ. The requirement for market capitalization also differs.

Many stocks that qualify for listing on the NYSE remain on NAS-DAQ, including Microsoft and Intel at the end of 2000. Occasionally companies switch from NASDAQ to the NYSE. However, only one has switched from the NYSE to NASDAQ since 1970 (Aeroflex, Inc.).

The main responsibility of a NASDAQ NNM market maker is to post continuous two-sided quotes (bid and ask), which consist of a price and a size. Between 9:30 a.m. and 4:00 p.m. Eastern time, these quotes must be firm, which means that if any NASD member presents an order to a market maker, the market maker is obligated to trade at terms no worse than its quotes. Failure to do so constitutes "backing away," which can be subject to regulatory sanction.[1]

Other OTC Markets

While the NASDAQ stock markets are the major parts of the U.S. OTC markets, the vast majority of the OTC issues (about 8,000) do not trade on either of the two NASDAQ systems. There are two types of markets for these stocks. The securities traded on these markets are not listed, that is have no listing requirements. Thus, these two OTC markets are not "issuer services." Rather, they are "subscriber services"—that is, subscribers can make bids and offers for any stock not listed on exchanges or NASDAQ.

The first of these two non-NASDAQ OTC markets is the OTC Bulletin Board (OTCBB), sometimes called simply the "Bulletin Board." OTCBB is owned and operated by NASDAQ and regulated by NASD. The OTCBB displays real-time quotes, last-sale prices and volume information for approximately 5,500 securities. It includes stocks not traded on NYSE, Amex, or NASDAQ.

The second non-NASDAQ OTC market is the "Pink Sheets," which is owned and operated by the National Quotation Bureau. Prior to the creation of NASDAQ in 1971, dealer quotations were disseminated by paper copy only. These copies were printed on pink paper for which rea-

---

[1] More specifically, NASDAQ NNM market makers must (1) continuously post these firm two-sided quotes good for 1,000 shares (for most stocks), (2) report trades promptly, (3) be subject to automatic execution against their quotes via the Small Order Execution System (SOES), (4) integrate customer limit orders into their proprietary quotes, and (5) give precedence to customer limit orders; not place a quote on any system that is different than their NASDAQ quote unless that system is linked back into NASDAQ. Market makers must report price and volume in NMS issues to the NASD through their NASDAQ terminals within 90 seconds of the trade.

son these OTC securities were called "pink sheet stocks." The Pink Sheets are still published weekly. In addition, an electronic version of the Pink Sheets is updated daily and disseminated over market data vendor terminals. In order to provide greater visibility to these issues, many of which are low priced and thinly traded, transactions in pink sheet issues are subject to price and volume reporting under NASD Schedule D. These pink sheet securities are often pejoratively called "penny stocks."

These two markets are subscriber markets only—that is, any subscriber can enter quotes for securities on the systems. However, the trades on these markets are executed not on these systems but via the telephone. If the trades are conducted by NASD members, which is usually the case, they are reported to NASD and disseminated by ACT (the NASDAQ trade reporting system).

The OTCBB, however, tends to trade more active stocks than the Pink Sheets. OTCBB trades approximately the most active 4,000 stocks.

The Third Market

A stock may be both listed on an exchange and also traded in the OTC market, called the *third market*. Like NASDAQ, the third market is a network of broker-dealers that aggregates quotation information and provides inter-participant order routing tools, but leaves order execution to market participants. Dealers that make markets in the third market operate under the regulatory jurisdiction of the NASD. While the third market is not owned by the NASD, market makers in the third market use some of the facilities provided by NASDAQ. When the NASD created NASDAQ in 1971, it included substantially similar functionality for third market listed trading, including the CQS (Consolidated Quotations Service) for third market quotes, and CTS for third market trades, which are discussed below.

Alternative Trading Systems—The Fourth Market

It is not necessary for two parties involved in a transaction to use an intermediary. That is, the services of a broker or a dealer are not required to execute a trade. The direct trading of stocks between two customers without the use of a broker is called the *fourth market* . This market grew for the same reasons as the third market—the excessively high minimum commissions established by the exchanges.

A number of proprietary alternative trading systems (ATSs), which comprise the fourth market, are operated by the NASD members or member affiliates. These fourth market ATSs are for-profit "broker's brokers" that match investor orders and report trading activity to the marketplace via NASDAQ or the third market. In a sense, ATSs are similar to exchanges because they are designed to allow two participants to meet directly on the system and are maintained by a third party who also serves a limited regulatory function by imposing requirements on each subscriber.

Broadly, there are two types of ATSs: electronic communications networks and crossing networks.

Electronic Communications Networks

Electronic communications networks (ECNs) are privately owned broker/dealers that operate as market participants within the NASDAQ system. They display quotes that reflect actual orders and provide institutions and NASDAQ market makers with an anonymous way to enter orders. Essentially, an ECN is a limit order book that is widely disseminated and open for continuous trading to subscribers who may enter and access orders displayed on the ECN. ECNs offer transparency, anonymity, automated service, and reduced prices, and are therefore effective for handling small orders. ECNs are used to disseminate firm commitments to trade (firm bids or offers) to participants, or subscribers, which have typically either purchased or leased hardware for the operation of the ECN or have built a custom connection to the ECN. ECNs may also be linked into the NASDAQ marketplace via a quotation representing the ECN's best buy and sell quote. In general, ECNs use the internet to link buyers and sellers, bypassing brokers and trading floors.

Since ECNs are part of the NASDAQ execution, their volume is counted as part of the NASDAQ volume. ECNs account for over 30% of NASDAQ trading in exchange trading.

Instinet (Institutional Networks Corporation), the first ECN, began operating in 1969, and continues to be a very large ECN in terms of activity. Instinet was acquired by Reuters Holdings in 1987. Instinet is an NASD member broker-dealer and trades both NASDAQ and exchange-listed stocks. Instinet was originally intended as a system through which institutional investors could cross trades, that is, a crossing network. However, market makers are now significant participants in Instinet. Instinet usage for NASDAQ securities, that is usage as an ECN, began to grow in the mid-1980s when market makers were allowed to subscribe.

Since 1969, nine additional ECNs have been created: Island, Archipelago, REDI Book, Bloomberg Tradebook, BRASS Utility, Strike, Attain, NexTrade, and Market XT. Two of the ECNs, Archipelago and Island, have applied to the SEC to become exchanges.

Crossing Networks

Systems have been developed that allow institutional investors to "cross" trades—that is, match buyers and sellers directly—typically via computer. Crossing networks are batch processes that aggregate orders for execution at prespecified times. Crossing networks provide anonymity and reduced cost, and are specifically designed to minimize a trading cost that we will describe later (market impact cost). They vary considerably in their approach to market structure, including the type of order information that can be entered by the subscriber and the amount of pre-trade transparency that is available to participants.

At present, there are three major crossing networks: ITG Posit, the Arizona Stock Exchange (AZX), and Optimark. Instinet, the original crossing network, operates a fourth crossing network in addition to its current ECN offering.

Instinet is an interactive *hit-and-take* system, which means that participants search for buyers or sellers electronically, and negotiate and execute trades. It is a computerized execution service, registered with the SEC. The service permits subscribers to search for the opposite side of a trade without the cost of brokerage during Instinet's evening crossing network. Many mutual funds and other institutional investors use Instinet.

ITG Posit is more than a simple order-matching system. Rather, it matches the purchase and sale of portfolios in a way that optimizes the liquidity of the system. ITG's hourly POSIT operates only during the trading day.

The AZX in Phoenix, which commenced trading in March 1992, has been an after-hours electronic marketplace where anonymous participants trade stocks via personal computers. This exchange provides a call auction market which accumulates bids and offers for a security and, at designated times, derives a single price that maximizes the number of shares to be traded. It now conducts call auctions at 9:30 a.m., 10:30 a.m., 12:30 p.m., 2:30 p.m., and 4:30 p.m. EST.[2]

TRADING MECHANICS

Next we describe the key features involved in trading stocks. Later in the chapter, we discuss trading arrangements (block trades and program trades) that developed specifically for coping with the trading needs of institutional investors.

Types of Orders and Trading Priority Rules

When an investor wants to buy or sell a share of common stock, the price and conditions under which the order is to be executed must be communicated to a broker. The simplest type of order is the market order, an order

---

[2] For a discussion of the concepts underlying the Arizona Stock Exchange, see the AZX website www.azx.com.

to be executed at the best price available in the market. If the stock is listed and traded on an organized exchange, the best price is assured by the exchange rule that when more than one order on the same side of the buy/sell transaction reaches the market at the same time, the order with the best price is given priority. Thus, buyers offering a higher price are given priority over those offering a lower price; sellers asking a lower price are given priority over those asking a higher price.

Another priority rule of exchange trading is needed to handle receipt of more than one order at the same price. Most often, the priority in executing such orders is based on the time of arrival of the order—the first orders in are the first orders executed—although there may be a rule that gives higher priority to certain types of market participants over other types of market participants who are seeking to transact at the same price. For example, on exchanges orders can be classified as either *public orders* or orders of those member firms dealing for their own account (both non-specialists and specialists). Exchange rules require that public orders be given priority over orders of member firms dealing for their own account.

The danger of a market order is that an adverse move may take place between the time the investor places the order and the time the order is executed. To avoid this danger, the investor can place a *limit order* that designates a price threshold for the execution of the trade. A *buy limit order* indicates that the stock may be purchased only at the designated price or lower. A *sell limit order* indicates that the stock may be sold at the designated price or higher. The key disadvantage of a limit order is that there is no guarantee that it will be executed at all; the designated price may simply not be obtainable. A limit order that is not executable at the time it reaches the market is recorded in the limit order book that we mentioned earlier in this chapter.

The limit order is a *conditional order*: It is executed only if the limit price or a better price can be obtained. Another type of conditional order is the *stop order*, which specifies that the order is not to be executed until the market moves to a designated price, at which time it becomes a market order. A *buy stop order* specifies that the order is not to be executed until the market rises to a designated price, that is, until it trades at or above, or is bid at or above, the designated price. A *sell stop order* specifies that the order is not to be executed until the market price falls below a designated price—that is, until it trades at or below, or is offered at or below, the designated price. A stop order is useful when an investor cannot watch the market constantly. Profits can be preserved or losses minimized on a stock position by allowing market movements to trigger a trade. In a sell (buy) stop order, the designated price is lower (higher) than the current market price of the stock. In a sell (buy) limit order, the designated price is higher (lower) than the current market price of the stock.

The relationships between the two types of conditional orders, and the market movements which trigger them, appear in Exhibit 4.1.

There are two dangers associated with stop orders. Stock prices sometimes exhibit abrupt price changes, so the direction of a change in a stock price may be quite temporary, resulting in the premature trading of a stock. Also, once the designated price is reached, the stop order becomes a market order and is subject to the uncertainty of the execution price noted earlier for market orders.

A *stop-limit order*, a hybrid of a stop order and a limit order, is a stop order that designates a price limit. In contrast to the stop order, which becomes a market order if the stop is reached, the stop-limit order becomes a limit order if the stop is reached. The stop-limit order can be used to cushion the market impact of a stop order. The investor may limit the possible execution price after the activation of the stop. As with a limit order, the limit price may never be reached after the order is activated, which therefore defeats one purpose of the stop order—to protect a profit or limit a loss.

EXHIBIT 4.1   Conditional Orders and the Direction of Triggering Security Price Movements

Price of Security	Limit Order	Market if touched order	Stop limit order	Stop order
Higher price	Price specified for a *sell limit order*	Price specified for a *sell market if touched order*	Price specified for a limit *buy stop order*	Price specified for a *buy stop order*
Current Price	—	—	—	—
Lower Price	Price specified for a *buy limit order*	Price specified for a *buy market if touched order*	Price specified for a *sell stop limit order*	Price specified for a *sell stop order*
Comment	Can be filled only at price or better (that is, does not become a market order when price is reached)	Becomes market order when price is reached	Does not become a market order when price is reached; can be executed only at price or better	Becomes market order when price is reached

An investor may also enter a *market if touched order*. This order becomes a market order if a designated price is reached. A market if touched order to buy becomes a market order if the market falls to a given price, while a stop order to buy becomes a market order if the market rises to a given price. Similarly, a market if touched order to sell becomes a market order if the market rises to a specified price, while the stop order to sell becomes a market order if the market falls to a given price. We can think of the stop order as an order designed to get out of an existing position at an acceptable price (without specifying the exact price), and the market if touched order as an order designed to get into a position at an acceptable price (also without specifying the exact price).

Orders may be placed to buy or sell at the open or the close of trading for the day. An opening order indicates a trade to be executed only in the opening range for the day, and a closing order indicates a trade is to be executed only within the closing range for the day.

An investor may enter orders that contain order cancellation provisions. A *fill or kill order* must be executed as soon as it reaches the trading floor or it is immediately canceled. Orders may designate the time period for which the order is effective—a day, week, or month, or perhaps by a given time within the day. An *open* order, or *good till canceled* order, is good until the investor specifically terminates the order.

Orders are also classified by their size. One *round lot* is typically 100 shares of a stock. An *odd lot* is defined as less than a round lot. For example, an order of 75 shares of Digital Equipment Corporation (DEC) is an odd lot order. An order of 350 shares of DEC includes an odd lot portion of 50 shares. A block trade is defined on the NYSE as an order of 10,000 shares of a given stock or a total market value of $200,000 or more.

Both the major national stock exchanges and the regional stock exchanges have systems for routing orders of a specified size (that are submitted by brokers) through a computer directly to the specialists' posts where the orders can be executed. On the NYSE, this system is the Super-Dot system. The AMEX's Post Execution Reporting system allows orders up to 2,000 shares to be routed directly to specialists. The regional stock exchanges have computerized systems for routing small orders to specialists. The Small Order Execution system of the NASDAQ routes and executes orders up to 1,000 shares of a given stock.

Short Selling

Short selling involves the sale of a security not owned by the investor at the time of sale. The investor can arrange to have her broker borrow the stock from someone else, and the borrowed stock is delivered to implement the sale. To cover her short position, the investor must subsequently purchase the stock and return it to the party that lent the stock.

Let us look at an example of how this is done in the stock market. Suppose Ms. Stokes believes that Wilson Steel common stock is overpriced at $20 per share and wants to be in a position to benefit if her assessment is correct. Ms. Stokes calls her broker, Mr. Yats, indicating that she wants to sell 100 shares of Wilson Steel. Mr. Yats will do two things: (1) sell 100 shares of Wilson Steel on behalf of Ms. Stokes, and (2) arrange to borrow 100 shares of that stock to deliver to the buyer. Suppose that Mr. Yats is able to sell the stock for $20 per share and borrows the stock from Mr. Jordan. The shares borrowed from Mr. Jordan will be delivered to the buyer of the 100 shares. The proceeds from the sale (ignoring commissions) will be $2,000. However, the proceeds do not go to Ms. Stokes because she has not given her broker the 100 shares. Thus, Ms. Stokes is said to be "short 100 shares."

Now, let's suppose one week later the price of Wilson Steel stock declines to $15 per share. Ms. Stokes may instruct her broker to buy 100 shares of Wilson Steel. The cost of buying the shares (once again ignoring commissions) is $1,500. The shares purchased are then delivered to Mr. Jordan, who lent 100 shares to Ms. Stokes. At this point, Ms. Stokes has sold 100 shares and bought 100 shares. So, she no longer has any obligation to her broker or to Mr. Jordan—she has covered her short position. She is entitled to the funds in her account that were generated by the selling and buying activity. She sold the stock for $2,000 and bought it for $1,500. Thus, she realizes a profit before commissions of $500. From this amount, commissions are subtracted.

Two more costs will reduce the profit further. First, a fee will be charged by the lender of the stock. Second, if there are any dividends paid by Wilson Steel while the stock is borrowed, Ms. Stokes must compensate Mr. Jordan for the dividends he would have been entitled to.

If, instead of falling, the price of Wilson Steel stock rises, Ms. Stokes will realize a loss if she is forced to cover her short position. For example, if the price rises to $27, Ms. Stokes will lose $700, to which must be added commissions and the cost of borrowing the stock (and possibly dividends).

Exchanges impose restrictions as to when a short sale may be executed; these so-called *tick-test rules* are intended to prevent investors from destabilizing the price of a stock when the market price is falling. A short sale can be made only when either (1) the sale price of the particular stock is higher than the last trade price (referred to as an *uptick trade*), or (2) if there is no change in the last trade price of the particular stock (referred to as a *zero uptick*), the previous trade price must be higher than the trade price that preceded it. For example, if Ms. Stokes wanted to short Wilson Steel at a price of $20, and the two previous trade prices were $20⅛, and then $20, she could not do so at this time because of the uptick trade rule. If the previous trade prices were $19⅞, $19⅞, and then $20, she could short the stock at $20 because of the uptick trade rule. Suppose that the sequence of the last three trades is: $19⅞, $20, and $20. Ms. Stokes could short the stock at $20 because of the zero uptick rule.

Margin Transactions

Investors can borrow cash to buy securities and use the securities themselves as collateral. For example, suppose Mr. Boxer has $10,000 to invest and is considering buying Wilson Steel, which is currently selling for $20 per share. With his $10,000, Mr. Boxer can buy 500 shares. Suppose his broker can arrange for him to borrow an additional $10,000 so that Mr. Boxer can buy an additional 500 shares. Thus, with a $20,000 investment, he can purchase a total of 1,000 shares. The 1,000 shares will be used as collateral for the $10,000 borrowed, and Mr. Boxer will have to pay interest on the amount borrowed.

A transaction in which an investor borrows to buy shares using the shares themselves as collateral is called buying on margin. By borrowing funds, an investor creates financial leverage. Note that Mr. Boxer, for a $10,000 investment, realizes the consequences associated with a price change of 1,000 shares rather than 500 shares. He will benefit if the price rises but be worse off if the price falls (compared to borrowing no funds).

To illustrate, we now look at what happens if the price subsequently changes. If the price of Wilson Steel rises to $29 per share, ignoring commissions and the cost of borrowing, Mr. Boxer will realize a profit of $9 per share on 1,000 shares, or $9,000. Had Mr. Boxer not borrowed $10,000 to buy the additional 500 shares, his profit would be only $4,500. Suppose, instead, the price of Wilson Steel stock decreases to $13 per share. Then, by borrowing to buy 500 additional shares, he lost $7 per share on 1,000 shares instead of $7 per share on just 500 shares.

The funds borrowed to buy the additional stock will be provided by the broker, and the broker gets the money from a bank. The interest rate that banks charge brokers for these funds is the *call money rate* (also labeled the *broker loan rate*). The broker charges the borrowing investor the call money rate plus a service charge.

Margin Requirements

The brokerage firm is not free to lend as much as it wishes to the investor to buy securities. The Securities Exchange Act of 1934 prohibits brokers from lending more than a specified percentage of the market value of the securities. The *initial margin requirement* is the proportion of the total market value of the securities that the investor must pay as an equity share, and the remainder is borrowed from the broker. The 1934 act gives the Board of Governors of the Federal Reserve (the Fed) the responsibility to set initial margin requirements. The initial margin requirement has been below 40%, and is 50% as of this writing.

The Fed also establishes a maintenance margin requirement. This is the minimum proportion of (1) the equity in the investor's margin account to (2) the total market value. If the investor's margin account falls below the minimum maintenance margin (which would happen if the share price fell), the investor is required to put up additional cash. The investor receives a margin call from the broker specifying the additional cash to be put into the investor's margin account. If the investor fails to put up the additional cash, the broker has the authority to sell the securities in the investor's account.

Let us illustrate a maintenance margin. Assume an investor buys 100 shares of stock at $60 per share for $6,000 on 50% margin and the maintenance margin is 25%. By purchasing $6,000 of stock on 50% margin, the investor must put up $3,000 of cash (or other equity) and, thus, borrows $3,000 (referred to as the debit balance).The investor, however, must maintain 25% of margin. To what level must the stock price decline to hit the maintenance margin level? The price is $40. At this price, the stock position has a value of $4,000 ($40 × 100 shares). With a loan of $3,000, the equity in the account is $1,000 ($4,000 − $3,000), or 25% of the account value ($1,000/$4,000 = 25%). If the price of the stock decreases below $40, the investor must deposit more equity to bring the equity level up to 25%. In general, if the maintenance margin is 25%, the account level has to decrease to 4/3 times the amount borrowed (the debit balance) to reach the minimum maintenance margin level.

There are also margin requirements for short selling. Consider a similar margin example for a short position. An investor shorts (borrows and sells) 100 shares of stock at $60 for total stock value of $6,000.With an initial margin of 50%, the investor must deposit $3,000 (in addition to leaving the $6,000 from the sale in the account).This leaves the investor with a *credit balance* of $9,000 (which does not change with the stock price since it is in cash). However, the investor owes 100 shares of the stock at the current market price. To what level must the stock price increase to hit the maintenance margin level, assumed to be 30% (which is the equity in the account as a percentage of the market value of the stock)? The answer is $69.23, for a total stock value of $6,923. If the stock is worth $6,923, there is $2,077 of equity in the account ($9,000 − $6,923),which represents 30% of the market value of the stock ($2,077/ $6,923 = 30%). If the maintenance margin is 30%, the value of the stock which triggers the maintenance level is calculated by multiplying the credit balance by 10/13 (10/13 × $9,000 = $6,923).

A summary of the long and short margin requirements is provided below:

Margin	Long	Short
Initial	50%	50%
Maintenance	25%	30%
Multiple of debit (long) or credit (short) balance to require maintenance	4/3	10/13

TRADING COSTS

An important aspect of an investment strategy is controlling the trading costs necessary to implement the strategy. The measurement of trading costs is, while important, very difficult.

We begin by defining trading costs. Trading costs can be decomposed into two major components: *explicit costs* and *implicit costs*. Explicit costs are the direct costs of trading, such as broker commissions, fees, and taxes. Implicit costs represent such indirect costs as the price impact of the trade and the opportunity costs of failing to execute in a timely manner or at all. Whereas explicit costs are associated with identifiable accounting charges, no such reporting of implicit costs occurs.

Explicit Costs

The main explicit cost is the commission paid to the broker for execution. Commission costs are fully negotiable and vary systematically by broker type and market mechanism. The commission may depend on both the price per share and the number of shares in the transaction.[3] In addition to commissions, there may be other explicit costs. These explicit costs include custodial fees (the fees charged by an institution that holds securities in safekeeping for an investor) and transfer fees (the fees associated from transferring an asset from one owner to another).

Since the introduction of negotiated commissions in May 1975, the opportunity has arisen for the development of discount brokers. These brokers charge commissions at rates much less than those charged by other brokers, but offer little or no advice or any other service apart from execution of the transaction.

---

[3] For more on this point, see Bruce M. Collins and Frank J. Fabozzi, "A Methodology for Measuring Transactions Costs," *Financial Analysts Journal* (March–April 1991), pp. 27–36.

In general, commissions began a downward trend in 1975 which continued through 1996, when they reached 4.5¢ per share. Based on a study by the Plexus Group, after increasing during 1997, commissions reached 4.5¢ per share again in the first quarter of 1999. Only small, easily traded orders have become cheaper, not the larger and more difficult trades. Commissions for larger trades (over 10,000 shares) have been relatively stable at about 4.8¢ per share. Commissions for trades under 10,000 shares on the other hand, have declined to 2.8¢ per share.[4]

The Plexus Group study also found that the commissions on capital committing trades—trades that require a commitment of the dealer's own capital to accomplish the trade rather than simply executing the trade by matching two customer orders on an agency basis—are higher and have not declined. Investors should expect to pay for the use of the dealer's capital and the associated risk. Similarly, soft dollar trades, discussed below, have high and stable commissions. Consequently, investors may be penalized for not being able to "shop around" for lower commissions. Overall, it is the commissions on agency trades (trades on which the dealer need not commit capital) and non-soft dollar trades (for which the customer can shop around) that are the lowest and have declined the most.

There are also two other issues that relate to transactions costs— "soft dollars" and "payment for order flow." These issues are discussed in the following sections.

Soft Dollars

Investors often choose their broker/dealer based on who will give them the best execution at the lowest transaction cost on a specific transaction, and also based on who will provide complementary services (such as research) over a period of time. Order flow can also be "purchased" by a broker/dealer from an investor with "soft dollars." In this case, the broker/dealer provides the investor, without explicit charge, services such as research or electronic services, typically from a third party for which the investor would otherwise have had to pay "hard dollars" to the third party, in exchange for the investor's order flow. Of course, the investor pays the broker/dealer for the execution service.

According to such a relationship, the investor preferentially routes their order to the broker/dealer specified in the soft dollar relationship and does not have to pay "hard dollars," or real money, for the research or other services. This practice is called paying "soft dollars" (i.e., directing their order flow) for the ancillary research. For example, client A preferentially directs his order flow to broker/dealer B (often a specified

---

[4] Plexus Group, "Withering Commissions, Winning Brokers: Who Will Survive?" unpublished study, December 1999.

amount of order flow over a specified period, such as a month or year) and pays the broker/dealer for these execution services. In turn, broker/dealer B pays for some research services provided to client A. Very often the research provider is a separate firm, say, firm C. Thus, soft dollars refer to money paid by an investor to a broker/dealer or a third party through commission revenue rather than by direct payments.

The disadvantage to the broker/dealer is that they have to pay hard dollars (to the research provider) for the client's order flow. The disadvantage to the client is that they are not free to "shop around" for the best bid or best offer, net of commissions, for all their transactions, but have to do an agreed amount of transaction volume with the specific broker/dealer. In addition, the research provider may give a preferential price to the broker/dealer. Thus, each of these participants in the soft dollar relationship experiences some advantage, but also an offsetting disadvantage.

The SEC has imposed formal and informal limitations on the type and amount of soft dollar business institutional investors can conduct. For example, while an institutional investor can accept research in a soft dollar relationship, they cannot accept furniture or vacations. SEC disclosure rules, passed in 1995, require investment advisors to disclose, among other things, the details on any product or services received through soft dollars.

Payment for Order Flow

In payment for order flow arrangements, an OTC market maker may offer a cash payment to other brokerage firms which have customer order flow in exchange for the right to execute the broker's order flow, thus providing a reason for the broker preferencing trades to certain market makers for each stock. Such payment for order flow has occurred mainly on NASDAQ on which there are several market makers for each stock. Rebates are typically on a per-share basis and have historically been about 2¢ a share.

The reasons for payment for order flow remain controversial. One possible reason is that it is a device for price discrimination based on the information content of the order. Specifically, market makers may pay for orders that are placed by "uninformed traders," and hence are more profitable to execute; but they may not pay for orders placed by "informed traders," which are less profitable. In general, retail order flow is considered to be uninformed, and institutional and professional order flow to be informed. In fact, most payment for order flow arrangements are with retail brokerage houses and the average size of purchased orders is significantly below the overall average trade size. Obviously small retail trades are preferred by the market makers who pay for order flow and are considered uninformed order flow. The data appear to be consistent with the uniformed/informed trader hypothesis.

Inter-market market-maker competition and inter-exchange competition via payment for order flow remains controversial.[5] The relevant policy question is whether retail broker/dealers are diverted from sending their retail orders to the best markets, thereby disadvantaging their customers, or whether a portion of the payment accrues to the customer, thereby benefiting the customer. The advent of decimalization during 2000, discussed later, has permitted smaller bid/offer spreads and has reduced the degree of payment for order flow. Overall, both soft dollars and payment for order flow remain controversial.

Implicit Costs

Implicit trading costs include impact costs, timing costs, and opportunity costs.

Impact Costs

The *impact cost* of a transaction is the change in market price due to supply/demand imbalances as a result of the trade. Bid-ask spread estimates, although informative, fail to capture the fact that large trades—those that exceed the number of shares the market maker is willing to trade at the quoted bid and ask prices—may move prices in the direction of the trade. That is, large trades may increase the price for buy orders and decrease the price for sell orders. The resulting market impact or price impact of the transaction can be thought of as the deviation of the transaction price from the "unperturbed price" that would have prevailed had the trade not occurred. As discussed above, crossing networks are designed to minimize impact costs.

Timing Cost

The *timing cost* is measured as the price change between the time the parties to the implementation process assume responsibility for the trade and the time they complete the responsibility. Timing costs occur when orders are on the trading desk of a buy side firm (e.g., an investment management firm), but have not been released to the broker because the trader fears that the trade may swamp the market.

Opportunity Costs

The *opportunity cost* is the "cost" of securities not traded. This cost results from missed or only partially completed trades. These costs are the natural consequence of the release delays. For example, if the price moves too much before the trade can be completed, the manager will not make the trade. In practice, this cost is measured on shares not traded based on

---

[5] Floyd Norris, "Wall St. Said to Gain Most in Policy Shift," *New York Times* (Dec. 20, 2000), pp. C1, C6.

the difference between the market price at the time of decision and the closing price 30 days later.

While commissions and impact costs are actual and visible out-of-pocket costs, opportunity costs and timing costs are the costs of foregone opportunities and are invisible. Opportunity costs can arise for two reasons. First, some orders are executed with a delay, during which the price may move against the investor. Second, some orders incur an opportunity cost because they are only partially filled or are not executed at all.

Classification of Trading Costs

We have thus far classified four main trading costs—commissions, impact costs, timing costs, and opportunity costs—as explicit or implicit trading costs. This categorization is based on whether or not the costs are identifiable accounting costs. Another categorization of these costs is execution costs versus opportunity costs. This categorization is based on whether or not the trades are completed. A schematic diagram of trading costs using this categorization is shown in Exhibit 4.2.

The categorization of the four costs according to the two criteria is as follows.

Explicit versus Implicit	Execution versus Opportunity
Explicit	*Execution*
Commission	Commission
	Impact
Implicit	*Opportunity*
Impact	Timing
Timing	Opportunity
Opportunity	

EXHIBIT 4.2   Diagram of Types of Trading Costs

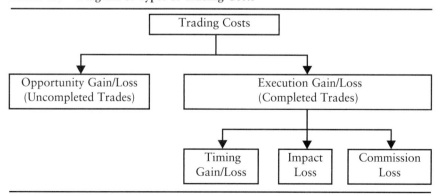

Source: "Alpha Capture," *Plexus Group*, Second Quarter, 1999.

Research on Transaction Costs

Overall, while the trading commission is the most obvious, measurable, and discussed trading cost, it is only one of the four types of trading costs and, in fact, as discussed below, may be the smallest. The implicit trading costs are much more difficult to measure.

Recent studies in transactions costs allow several conclusions. They are:

1. Although considerable debate still surrounds how to measure trading costs, the consensus is that implicit trading costs are economically significant relative to explicit costs (and also relative to realized portfolio returns).
2. Equity trading costs vary systematically with trade difficulty and order-placement strategy.
3. Differences in market design, investment style, trading ability, and reputation are important determinants of trading costs.
4. Even after researchers control for trade complexity and trade venue, trading costs are found to vary considerably among managers.
5. Accurate prediction of trading costs requires more detailed data on the entire order-submission process than are generally available, especially information on pre-trade decision variables.

These findings suggest that the concept of "best execution" for institutional traders is difficult to measure and hence to enforce.[6]

TRADING ARRANGEMENTS FOR RETAIL AND INSTITUTIONAL INVESTORS

Trades are executed by both individuals, called retail investors, and institutions. There are several differences in the way each group trades. The first is size: institutions typically transact much larger orders than individuals. The second is commissions: consistent with their larger size, institutions typically pay lower commissions than individuals. While institutional commissions have declined since 1975, some retail commissions have also declined significantly recently as a result of the advent of discount brokers, as discussed in the next section.

The third difference is the method of order execution. While both an individual and an institution may trade through a broker/dealer, the manner in which their orders are entered and executed may be considerably different, even if the trades are through the same broker/dealer. An

[6] Donald B. Keim and Ananth Madhavan, "The Cost of Institutional Equity Trades," *Financial Analysts Journal* (July/August 1998), pp.50–59.

individual trading through a broker/dealer typically goes through a stockbroker (financial consultant). These orders go to a retail exchange execution desk and from there to the NYSE (usually through SuperDot) or to the OTC execution desk where it will be transacted with another market maker on NASDAQ.

Retail investors receive a "confirm" (confirmation) of the trade, typically in the mail. Institutional investors generally give their order directly to the institutional broker/dealer execution desk for both exchange and OTC orders. Exchange orders may be sent to the broker/dealer's floor broker, and OTC orders may be transacted with another broker/dealer or internalized at a competitive bid/offer. Competing bids or offers are typically obtained in all cases.

Retail Stock Trading

Historically, there has been a decline in the direct household ownership of common stocks. This decline does not necessarily lead to the conclusion that households have decreased their common stock holdings. Rather, it means that households are holding more of their common stock through intermediaries such as mutual funds rather than directly in the form of common stock. While households hold more total common stock than before, they hold less common stock directly, and thus, increasingly the stock executions are done by institutions, such as mutual funds, rather than by individuals.

One of the reasons for individuals owning stocks through mutual funds rather than directly involves transaction costs; that is, institutions can transact stocks more cheaply than individuals.While this advantage for institutions remains, transaction costs for individuals have declined significantly during the last decade.

Since May Day 1975, stock trading commissions have declined both for institutions and individuals. However, prior to 1990, individuals traded stocks mainly through so-called "full service brokers," where commissions reflected not only the stock trade execution, but also the counsel of a stockbroker and perhaps research. The largest full-service broker/dealers are also known as "wirehouses." These firms typically do institutional trading and investment banking as well as retail business. The commissions for these full service brokers have declined since 1975.

However, in addition, a "discount broker" industry developed in which the stockbroker provided no advice and no research. Individuals entered their orders via a telephone. More recently, individuals could enter their orders via their personal computer—these are called "online" or "Web based" brokerage firms. Consistent with the lower provision of service by discount brokers and online brokers, stock trading commissions decreased significantly. Thus, individuals could trade and own stocks more efficiently.

To remain competitive to a wide range of clients in this environment, the traditional full service brokerage firms responded by offering customers alternative means of transacting common stock. For example, many full service brokerage firms offer the traditional services of a stockbroker and research at a high commission, and, in addition, offer direct order entry only at a lower commission. On the other hand, some discount brokers have begun to offer more service at a higher commission.

Thus, there continue to be ebbs and flows in the balance between more service and low commissions in the retail trading of common stock. Both online brokers, who offer no service and low commissions, and managers of segregated accounts, who offer enhanced services for a large fee, are growing along with full service stock brokerages and mutual funds.

Despite paying higher commissions than institutions, individual investors may have some advantages over institutions. Because individuals usually transact smaller orders, they will incur smaller impact costs. In addition, if individual investors transact online, they may have shorter time lags. It is for these and other reasons that "packaged products" of individual stocks such as "folios" are becoming more attractive.

Institutional Trading

With the increase in trading by institutional investors, trading arrangements more suitable to these investors were developed. Institutional needs included trading in large size and trading groups of stocks, both at a low commission and with low market impact. This has resulted in the evolution of special arrangements for the execution of certain types of orders commonly sought by institutional investors: (1) orders requiring the execution of a trade of a large number of shares of a given stock and (2) orders requiring the execution of trades in a large number of different stocks at as near the same time as possible. The former types of trades are called *block trades*; the latter are called *program trades*. An example of a block trade would be a mutual fund seeking to buy 15,000 shares of IBM stock. An example of a program trade would be a pension fund wanting to buy shares of 200 names (companies) at the end of a trading day ("at the close").

The institutional arrangement that has evolved to accommodate these two types of institutional trades is the development of a network of trading desks of the major securities firms and other institutional investors that communicate with each other by means of electronic display systems and telephones. This network is referred to as the upstairs market. Participants in the upstairs market play a key role by (1) providing liquidity to the market so that such institutional trades can be executed, and (2) by arbitrage activities that help to integrate the fragmented stock market.

Block Trades

On the NYSE, block trades are defined as either trades of at least 10,000 shares of a given stock, or trades of shares with a market value of at least $200,000, whichever is less. Since the execution of large numbers of block orders places strains on the specialist system in the NYSE, special procedures have been developed to handle them. Typically, an institutional customer contacts its salesperson at a brokerage firm, indicating that it wishes to place a block order. The salesperson then gives the order to the block execution department of the brokerage firm. Note that the salesperson does not submit the order to be executed to the exchange where the stock might be traded or, in the case of an unlisted stock, try to execute the order on the NASDAQ system. The sales traders in the block execution department contact other institutions to attempt to find one or more institutions that would be willing to take the other side of the order. That is, they use the upstairs market in their search to fill the block trade order. If this can be accomplished, the execution of the order is completed.

If the sales traders cannot find enough institutions to take the entire block (for example, if the block trade order is for 40,000 shares of IBM, but only 25,000 can be "crossed" with other institutions), then the balance of the block trade order is given to the firm's market maker. The market maker must then make a decision as to how to handle the balance of the block trade order. There are two choices. First, the brokerage firm may take a position in the stock and buy the shares for its own account. Second, the unfilled order may be executed by using the services of competing market makers. In the former case, the brokerage firm is committing its own capital.

NYSE Rule 127 states that if a member firm receives an order for a large block of stock that might not be readily absorbed by the market, the member firm should nevertheless explore the market on the floor, including, where appropriate, consulting with the specialist as to his interest in the security. If a member firm intends to cross a large block of stock for a public account at a price that is outside of the current quote, it should inform the specialist of its intention.

Program Trades

Program trades involve the buying and/or selling of a large number of names simultaneously. Such trades are also called basket trades because effectively a "basket" of stocks is being traded. The NYSE defines a program trade as any trade involving the purchase or sale of a basket of at least 15 stocks with a total value of $1 million or more.

The two major applications of program trades are asset allocation and index arbitrage. With respect to asset allocation trades, some examples of why an institutional investor may want to use a program trade are deployment of new cash into the stock market; implementation of a decision to move funds invested in the bond market to the stock market (or vice versa); and rebalancing the composition of a stock portfolio because of a change in investment strategy. A mutual fund money manager can, for example, move funds quickly into or out of the stock market for an entire portfolio of stocks through a single program trade. All these strategies are related to asset allocation.

The growth of mutual fund sales and massive equity investments by pension funds and insurance companies during the 1990s have all given an impetus to such methods to trade baskets or bundles of stocks efficiently. Other reasons for which an institutional investor may have a need to execute a program trade should be apparent later when we discuss an investment strategy called indexing.

There are several commission arrangements available to an institution for a program trade, and each arrangement has numerous variants. Considerations in selecting one (in addition to commission costs) are the risk of failing to realize the best execution price, and the risk that the brokerage firms to be solicited about executing the program trade will use their knowledge of the program trade to benefit from the anticipated price movement that might result—in other words, that they will frontrun the transaction (for example, buying a stock for their own account before filling the customer buy order).

From a dealer's perspective, program trades can be conducted in two ways, namely on an agency basis and on a principal basis. An intermediate type of program trade, the agency incentive arrangement, is an additional alternative. A program trade executed on an agency basis involves the selection by the investor of a brokerage firm solely on the basis of commission bids (cents per share) submitted by various brokerage firms. The brokerage firm selected uses its best efforts as an agent of the institution to obtain the best price. Such trades have low explicit commissions. To the investor, the disadvantage of the agency program trade is that, while commissions may be the lowest, the execution price may not be the best because of impact costs and the potential frontrunning by the brokerage firms solicited to submit a commission bid. The investor knows in advance the commission paid, but does not know the price at which the trades will be executed. Another disadvantage is that there is increased risk of adverse selection of the counter-party in the execution process.

Related to the agency basis is an *agency incentive arrangement*, in which a benchmark portfolio value is established for the group of stocks in the program trade. The price for each "name" (i.e., specific stock) in the program trade is determined as either the price at the end of the previous day or the average price of the previous day. If the brokerage firm can execute the trade on the next trading day such that a better-than-benchmark portfolio value results—a higher value in the case of a program trade involving selling, or a lower value in the case of a program trade involving buying—then the brokerage firm receives the specified commission plus some predetermined additional compensation. In this case the investor does not know in advance the commission or the execution price precisely, but has a reasonable expectation that the price will be better than a threshold level.

What if the brokerage firm does not achieve the benchmark portfolio value? It is in such a case that the variants come into play. One arrangement may call for the brokerage firm to receive only the previously agreed-upon commission. Other arrangements may involve sharing the risk of not realizing the benchmark portfolio value with the brokerage firm. That is, if the brokerage firm falls short of the benchmark portfolio value, it must absorb a portion of the shortfall. In these risk-sharing arrangements, the brokerage firm is risking its own capital. The greater the risk sharing the brokerage firm must accept, the higher the commission it will charge.

The brokerage firm can also choose to execute the trade on a principal basis. In this case, the dealer would commit its own capital to buy or sell the portfolio and complete the investor's transaction immediately. Since the dealer incurs market risk, it would also charge higher commissions. The key factors in pricing principal trades are: liquidity characteristics, absolute dollar value, nature of the trade, customer profile, and market volatility. In this case, the investor knows the trade execution price in advance, but pays a higher commission.

To minimize frontrunning, institutions often use other types of program trade arrangements. They call for brokerage firms to receive, not specific names and quantities of stocks, but only aggregate statistical information about key portfolio parameters. Several brokerage firms then bid on a cents per share basis on the entire portfolio (also called "blind baskets"), guaranteeing execution at either closing price (termed "market-at-close") or a particular intra-day price to the customer. Note that this is a principal trade. Since mutual fund net asset values are calculated using closing prices, a mutual fund that follows an indexing strategy (i.e., an index fund), for instance, would want guaranteed market-at-close execution to minimize the risk of not performing as well as the stock index. When the winning bidder has been selected, it receives the details of the portfolio. While the commission in this type of transaction is higher, this procedure increases the risk to the brokerage firm of successfully executing the program trade. However, the brokerage firm can use stock index futures to protect itself from market-wide movements if the characteristics of the portfolio in the program trade are similar to the index underlying the stock index futures contract.

PRICE LIMITS AND COLLARS

Trading or price limits specify a minimum price limit below which the market price index level may not decline due to an institutionally mandated termination of trading, at least at prices below the specified price (the price limit) for a specified period of time. For example, if the Dow Jones Industrial Average (DJIA) was trading at 11,000 and its price limit was 500 points below that, then no trades could occur below 10,500. This pause in trading is intended to "give the market a breather" to at least calm emotions. Trading limits had previously been used in the futures markets but not in the stock market.

These price limits have been modified several times since their implementation soon after the stock market crash of 1987. Two different types of price limits are discussed below.

Rule 80B or "Circuit Breakers"

On April 15, 1998, the NYSE implemented new regulations to increase and widen thresholds at which trading is halted for single-day declines in the DJIA. The point levels are set quarterly at 10%, 20%, and 30% of the DJIA by using the DJIA average closing value of the previous month, rounded to the nearest 50 points. Point levels are adjusted on January 1, April 1, July 1, and October 1.

Rule 80A or "Trading Collar"

Another type of trading restriction applies to index arbitrage trading whereby, for example, a basket of S&P 500 stocks is bought (sold) against the sale (purchase) of an S&P 500 futures contract. On February 16, 1999, following approval by the SEC, the NYSE implemented revisions to Rule 80A, which restricts index arbitrage trading. Specifically, the set 50-point collar was eliminated and the trigger level was allowed to track the DJIA. The revised collar is calculated quarterly as 2% of the average closing value of the DJIA for the last month of the previous quarter, rounded down to the nearest 10 points and is currently implemented as follows:

- A decline in the DJIA of 210 points or more requires all index arbitrage sell orders of the S&P 500 stocks to be stabilizing, or "sell plus," for the remainder of the day, unless on the same trading day, the DJIA advances to a value of 100 points or less below its previous close.

■ An advance in the DJIA of 210 points requires all index arbitrage buy orders of the S&P 500 stocks to be stabilizing, or "buy minus," for the remainder of the day, unless the DJIA retreats to 100 points or less above its previous close.

■ The restrictions will be reimposed each time the DJIA advances or declines the predetermined amount.

STOCK MARKET INDICATORS

Stock market indicators have come to perform a variety of functions, from serving as benchmarks for evaluating the performance of professional money managers to answering the question "How did the market do today?" Thus, stock market indicators (indexes or averages) have become a part of everyday life. Even though many of the stock market indicators are used interchangeably, it is important to realize that each indicator applies to, and measures, a different facet of the stock market.

The most commonly quoted stock market indicator is the DJIA. Other popular stock market indicators cited in the financial press are the Standard & Poor's 500 Composite (S&P 500), the New York Stock Exchange Composite Index (NYSE Composite), the NASDAQ Composite Index, and the Value Line Composite Average (VLCA). There are a myriad of other stock market indicators such as the Wilshire stock indexes and the Russell stock indexes, which are followed primarily by institutional money managers.

In general, market indexes rise and fall in fairly similar patterns. Although the correlations among indexes are high, the indexes do not move in exactly the same way at all times. The differences in movement reflect the different manner in which the indexes are constructed. Three factors enter into that construction: the universe of stocks represented by the sample underlying the index, the relative weights assigned to the stocks included in the index, and the method of averaging across all the stocks.

Some indexes represent only stocks listed on an exchange. Examples are the DJIA and the NYSE Composite, which represent only stocks listed on the NYSE or Big Board. By contrast, the NASDAQ includes only stocks traded over the counter. A favorite of professionals is the S&P 500 because it is a broader index containing both NYSE-listed and OTC-traded shares. Each index relies on a sample of stocks from its universe, and that sample may be small or quite large. The DJIA uses only 30 of the NYSE-traded shares, while the NYSE Composite includes every one of the listed shares. The NASDAQ also includes all shares in its universe, while the S&P 500 has a sample that contains only 500 of the more than 8,000 shares in the universe it represents.

The stocks included in a stock market index must be combined in certain proportions, and each stock must be given a weight. The three main approaches to weighting are: (1) weighting by the market capitalization, which is the value of the number of shares times price per share; (2) weighting by the price of the stock; and (3) equal weighting for each stock, regardless of its price or its firm's market value. With the exception of the Dow Jones averages (such as the DJIA) and the VLCA, nearly all of the most widely used indexes are market-value weighted. The DJIA is a price-weighted average, and the VLCA is an equally weighted index.

Stock market indicators can be classified into three groups: (1) those produced by stock exchanges based on all stocks traded on the exchanges; (2) those produced by organizations that subjectively select the stocks to be included in indexes; and (3) those where stock selection is based on an objective measure, such as the market capitalization of the company. The first group includes the New York Stock Exchange Composite Index, which reflects the market value of all stocks traded on the NYSE. While it is not an exchange, the NASDAQ Composite Index falls into this category because the index represents all stocks traded on the NASDAQ system.

The three most popular stock market indicators in the second group are the Dow Jones Industrial Average, the Standard & Poor's 500, and the Value Line Composite Average. The DJIA is constructed from 30 of the largest blue-chip industrial companies traded on the NYSE. The companies included in the average are those selected by Dow Jones & Company, publisher of the *Wall Street Journal*. The S&P 500 represents stocks chosen from the two major national stock exchanges and the over-the-counter market. The stocks in the index at any given time are determined by a committee of Standard & Poor's Corporation, which may occasionally add or delete individual stocks or the stocks of entire industry groups. The aim of the committee is to capture present overall stock market conditions as reflected in a very broad range of economic indicators. The VLCA, produced by Value Line Inc., covers a broad range of widely held and actively traded NYSE, AMEX, and OTC issues selected by Value Line.

In the third group we have the Wilshire indexes produced by Wilshire Associates (Santa Monica, California) and Russell indexes produced by the Frank Russell Company (Tacoma, Washington), a consultant to pension funds and other institutional investors. The criterion for inclusion in each of these indexes is solely a firm's market capitalization. The most comprehensive index is the Wilshire 5000, which actually includes more than 6,700 stocks now, up from 5,000 at its inception. The Wilshire 4500 includes all stocks in the Wilshire 5000 except for those in the S&P 500. Thus, the shares in the Wilshire 4500 have smaller capitalization than those in the Wilshire 5000. The Russell 3000 encompasses the 3,000 largest companies in terms of their market capitalization. The Russell 1000 is limited to the largest 1,000 of those, and the Russell 2000 has the remaining smaller firms.

Two methods of averaging may be used. The first and most common is the arithmetic average. An arithmetic mean is just a simple average of the stocks, calculated by summing them (after weighting, if appropriate) and dividing by the sum of the weights. The second method is the geometric mean, which involves multiplication of the components, after which the product is raised to the power of 1 divided by the number of components.

PRICING EFFICIENCY OF THE STOCK MARKET

A price efficient market is one in which security prices at all times fully reflect all available information that is relevant to their valuation. When a market is price efficient, investment strategies pursued to outperform a broad-based stock market index will not consistently produce superior returns after adjusting for (1) risk and (2) transaction costs.

Numerous studies have examined the pricing efficiency of the stock market. While it is not our intent in this chapter to provide a comprehensive review of these studies, we can summarize the basic findings and implications for investment strategies.

Forms of Efficiency

There are three different forms of pricing efficiency: (1) weak form, (2) semistrong form, and (3) strong form.[7] The distinctions among these forms rests in the relevant information that is believed to be taken into consideration in the price of the security at all times. *Weak-form efficiency* means that the price of the security reflects the past price and trading history of the security. *Semistrong-form efficiency* means that the price of the security fully reflects all public information (which, of course, includes but is not limited to, historical price and trading patterns). *Strong-form efficiency* exists in a market where the price of a security reflects all information, whether it is publicly available or known only to insiders such as the firm's managers or directors.

The preponderance of empirical evidence supports the claim that developed common stock markets are efficient in the weak form. The evidence emerges from numerous sophisticated tests that explore whether or

---

[7] Eugene F. Fama, "Efficient Capital Markets: A Review of Theory and Empirical Work," *Journal of Finance* (May 1970), pp. 383–417.

not historical price movements can be used to project future prices in such a way as to produce returns above what one would expect from market movements and the risk class of the security. Such returns are known as *positive abnormal returns*. The implications are that investors who follow a strategy of selecting stocks solely on the basis of price patterns or trading volume—such investors are referred to as *technical analysts* or *chartists*—should not expect to do better than the market. In fact, they may fare worse because of the higher transaction costs associated with frequent buying and selling of stocks.

Evidence on price efficiency in the semi-strong form is mixed. Some studies support the proposition of efficiency when they suggest that investors who select stocks on the basis of *fundamental security analysis*— which consists of analyzing financial statements, the quality of management, and the economic environment of a company—will not outperform the market. This result is certainly reasonable. There are so many analysts using the same approach, with the same publicly available data, that the price of the stock remains in line with all the relevant factors that determine value. On the other hand, a sizable number of studies have produced evidence indicating that there have been instances and patterns of pricing inefficiency in the stock market over long periods of time. Economists and financial analysts often label these examples of inefficient pricing as *anomalies in the market*, that is, phenomena that cannot be easily explained by accepted theory.

Empirical tests of strong form pricing efficiency fall into two groups: (1) studies of the performance of professional money managers, and (2) studies of the activities of insiders (individuals who are either company directors, major officers, or major stockholders). Studying the performance of professional money managers to test the strong form of pricing efficiency has been based on the belief that professional managers have access to better information than the general public. Whether or not this is true is moot because the empirical evidence suggests professional managers have been unable to outperform the market consistently. In contrast, evidence based on the activities of insiders has generally revealed that this group often achieves higher risk-adjusted returns than the stock market. Of course, insiders could not consistently earn those high abnormal returns if the stock prices fully reflected all relevant information about the values of the firms. Thus, the empirical evidence on insiders argues against the notion that the market is efficient in the strong-form sense.

Implications for Investing in Common Stock

Common stock investment strategies can be classified into two general categories: active strategies and passive strategies. *Active strategies* are those that attempt to outperform the market by one or more of the following: (1) timing the selection of transactions, such as in the case of technical analysis, (2) identifying undervalued or overvalued stocks using fundamental security analysis, or (3) selecting stocks according to one of the market anomalies. Obviously, the decision to pursue an active strategy must be based on the belief that there is some type of gain from such costly efforts, but gains are possible only if pricing inefficiencies exist. The particular strategy chosen depends on why the investor believes this is the case.

Investors who believe that the market prices stocks efficiently should accept the implication that attempts to outperform the market cannot be systematically successful, except by luck. This implication does not mean that investors should shun the stock market, but rather that they should pursue a *passive strategy*, one that does not attempt to outperform the market. Is there an optimal investment strategy for someone who holds this belief in the pricing efficiency of the stock market? Indeed there is. The theoretical basis rests on modern portfolio theory and capital market theory. According to modern portfolio theory, the market portfolio offers the highest level of return per unit of risk in a market that is price efficient. A portfolio of financial assets with characteristics similar to those of a portfolio consisting of the entire market—the market portfolio—will capture the pricing efficiency of the market.

But how can such a passive strategy be implemented? More specifically, what is meant by a *market portfolio*, and how should that portfolio be constructed? In theory, the market portfolio consists of all financial assets, not just common stock. The reason is that investors compare all investment opportunities, not just stock, when committing their capital. Thus, our principles of investing must be based on capital market theory, not just stock market theory. When the theory is applied to the stock market, the market portfolio has been defined as consisting of a large universe of common stocks. But how much of each common stock should be purchased when constructing the market portfolio? Theory states that the chosen portfolio should be an appropriate fraction of the market portfolio; hence, the weighting of each stock in the market portfolio should be based on its relative market capitalization. Thus, if the aggregate market capitalization of all stocks included in the market portfolio is $T and the market capitalization of one of these stocks is $A, then the fraction of this stock that should be held in the market portfolio is $A/$T.

The passive strategy that we have just described is called *indexing*. As pension fund sponsors in the 1990s increasingly came to believe that money managers were unable to outperform the stock market, the amount of funds managed using an indexing strategy has grown substantially.

OVERVIEW OF COMMON STOCK PORTFOLIO MANAGEMENT

In this section we provide an overview of common stock portfolio management and then describe the various strategies pursued by money managers and the evidence on the performance of such strategies. Basically, these strategies can be classified into one of two types: active and passive. The selection of a strategy depends on two factors. The first is the risk tolerance of the investor. The second is the investor's view of the efficiency of the stock market. If an investor believes the stock market is efficient, he would tend to favor a passive strategy; an investor who believes the stock market is inefficient will embrace an active strategy.

Overview of Active Portfolio Management

A useful way of thinking about active versus passive management is in terms of the following three activities performed by investors: (1) portfolio construction (deciding on the stocks to buy and sell), (2) trading of securities, and (3) portfolio monitoring.[8] Generally, investors pursuing active strategies devote the majority of their time to portfolio construction. In contrast, with passive strategies such as indexing (discussed later), investors devote less time to this activity.

Top-Down versus Bottom-Up Approaches

An investor who pursues active management may follow either a top-down or bottom-up approach. With a *top-down approach*, an investor begins by assessing the macroeconomic environment and forecasting its near-term outlook. Based on this assessment and forecast, an investor decides on how much of the portfolio's funds to allocate among the different sectors of the common stock market and how much to allocate to cash equivalents (i.e., short-term money market instruments). The sectors of the common stock market can be classified as follows: basic materials, communications, consumer staples, financials, technology, utilities, capital goods, consumer cyclicals, energy, health care, and transportation. Industry classifications give a finer breakdown and include, for example, aluminum, paper, international oil, beverages, electric utilities, telephone and telegraph, and so forth.

In making the allocation decision, an investor who follows a top-down approach relies on an analysis of the common stock market to identify those sectors and industries that will benefit the most on a relative

---

[8] Jeffrey L. Skelton, "Investment Opportunities with Indexing," in Katrina F. Sherrerd (ed.), *Equity Markets and Valuation Methods* (Charlottesville, VA: The Institute of Chartered Financial Analysts, 1988).

basis from the anticipated economic forecast. Once the amount to be allocated to each sector and industry is made, the investor then looks for the individual stocks to include in the portfolio.

In contrast to the top-down approach, an investor who follows a *bottom-up approach* focuses on the analysis of individual stocks and gives little weight to the significance of economic and market cycles. The primary tool of the investor who pursues a bottom-up approach is *fundamental security analysis*. The product of the analysis is a set of potential stocks to purchase that have certain characteristics that the manager views as being attractive. For example, these characteristics can be a low price-earnings ratio or small market capitalization.

Within the top-down and bottom-up approaches there are different strategies pursued by active equity managers. These strategies are often referred to as "equity styles" which we describe later when we discuss equity style management.

Fundamental versus Technical Analysis

Also within the top-down and bottom-up approaches to active management are two camps as to what information is useful in the selection of stocks and the timing of the purchase of stocks. These two camps are the fundamental analysis camp and the technical analysis camp.

Traditional fundamental analysis involves the analysis of a company's operations to assess its economic prospects. The analysis begins with the financial statements of the company in order to investigate the earnings, cash flow, profitability, and debt burden. The fundamental analyst will look at the major product lines, the economic outlook for the products (including existing and potential competitors), and the industries in which the company operates. The results of this analysis will be an assessment of the growth prospects of earnings. Based on the growth prospects of earnings, a fundamental analyst attempts to determine the fair value of the stock using one or more common stock valuation models (i.e., dividend discount models and asset pricing models which we discussed in Chapter 2). The estimated fair value is then compared to the market price to determine if the stock is fairly priced in the market, cheap (a market price below the estimated fair value), or rich (a market price above the estimated fair value).[9]

---

[9] The father of traditional fundamental analysis is Benjamin Graham who espoused this analysis in his classic book *Security Analysis*. There have been several editions of this book. The first edition was printed in 1934 and coauthored with Sidney Cottle. A more readily available edition is a coauthored version with Sidney Cottle, Roger F. Murray, and Frank E. Block, *Security Analysis*, Fifth Edition (New York: McGraw-Hill, 1988).

Technical analysis ignores company information regarding the economics of the firm. Instead, technical analysis focuses on price and/or trading volume of individual stocks, groups of stocks, and the market overall resulting from shifting supply and demand. This type of analysis is not only used for the analysis of common stock, but it is also a tool used in the trading of commodities, bonds, and futures contracts.

Fundamental analysis and technical analysis can be integrated within a strategy. Specifically, an investor can use fundamental analysis to identify stocks that are candidates for purchase or sale and employ technical analysis to time the purchase or sale.

Popular Active Stock Market Strategies

Throughout the history of the stock market there have been numerous strategies suggested about how to "beat the market." Below we describe several popular stock market strategies.

Strategies Based on Technical Analysis

Various common stock strategies that involve only historical price movement, trading volume, and other technical indicators have been suggested since the beginning of stock trading in the United States, as well as in commodity and other markets throughout the world. Many of these strategies involve investigating patterns based on historical trading data (past price data and trading volume) to forecast the future movement of individual stocks or the market as a whole. Based on observed patterns, mechanical trading rules indicating when a stock should be bought, sold, or sold short are developed. Thus, no consideration is given to any factor other than the specified technical indicators. As we explained earlier in this chapter, this approach to active management is called technical analysis. Because some of these strategies involve the analysis of charts that plot price and/or volume movements, investors who follow a technical analysis approach are sometimes called *chartists*. The overlying principle of these strategies is to detect changes in the supply of and demand for a stock and capitalize on the expected changes.

Dow Theory The grandfather of the technical analysis school is Charles Dow. During his tenure as editor of the *Wall Street Journal* , his editorials theorized about the future direction of the stock market. This body of writing is now referred to as the *Dow Theory*.[10] This theory rests on two basic assumptions. First, according to Charles Dow, "The averages in their day-

---

[10] The father of modern technical analysis is Charles Dow, a founder of the *Wall Street Journal* and its first editor from July 1889 to December 1902.

to-day fluctuations discount everything known, everything foreseeable, and every condition which can affect the supply of or the demand for corporate securities." This assumption sounds very much like the efficient market theory. But there's more. The second basic assumption is that the stock market moves in trends—up and down—over periods of time. According to Charles Dow, it is possible to identify these stock price trends and predict their future movement.

According to the Dow Theory, there are three types of trends or market cycles. The *primary trend* is the long-term movement in the market. Primary trends are basically four-year trends in the market. From the primary trend, a trend line showing where the market is heading can be derived. The secondary trend represents short-run departures of stock prices from the trend line. The third trend is short-term fluctuations in stock prices. Charles Dow believed that upward movements in the stock market were tempered by fallbacks that lost a portion of the previous gain. A market turn occurred when the upward movement was not greater than the last gain. In assessing whether or not a gain did in fact occur, he suggested examining the comovements in different stock market indexes such as the Dow Jones Industrial Average and the Dow Jones Transportation Average. One of the averages is selected as the primary index and the other as the confirming index. If the primary index reaches a high above its previous high, the increase is expected to continue if it is confirmed by the other index also reaching a high above its previous high.

Simple Filter Rules The simplest type of technical strategy is to buy and sell on the basis of a predetermined movement in the price of a stock; the rule is basically if the stock increases by a certain percentage, the stock is purchased and held until the price declines by a certain percentage, at which time the stock is sold. The percentage by which the price must change is called the *filter*. Every investor pursuing this technical strategy decides his or her own filter.

Moving Averages Some technical analysts make decisions to buy or sell a stock based on the movement of a stock over an extended period of time (for example, 200 days). An average of the price over the time period is computed, and a rule is specified that if the price is greater than some percentage of the average, the stock should be purchased; if the price is less than some percentage of the average, the stock should be sold. The simplest way to calculate the average is to calculate a simple moving average. Assuming that the time period selected by the technical analyst is 200 days, then the average price over the 200 days is determined. A more complex moving average can be calculated by giving greater weight to more recent prices.

Advance/Decline Line   On each trading day, some stocks will increase in price or "advance" from the closing price on the previous trading day, while other stocks will decrease in price or decline from the closing price on the previous trading day. It has been suggested by some market observers that the cumulative number of advances over a certain number of days minus the cumulative number of declines over the same number of days can be used as an indicator of short-term movements in the stock market.

Relative Strength   The relative strength of a stock is measured by the ratio of the stock price to some price index. The ratio indicates the relative movement of the stock to the index. The price index can be the index of the price of stocks in a given industry or a broad-based index of all stocks. If the ratio rises, it is presumed that the stock is in an uptrend relative to the index; if the ratio falls, it is presumed that the stock is in a downtrend relative to the index. Similarly, a relative strength measure can be calculated for an industry group relative to a broad-based index. Relative strength is also referred to as price momentum or price persistence.

Price and Trading Relationship   One popular Wall Street adage is that "It takes volume to make price move." This suggests a price-volume relationship as a signal for detecting the price movement of a stock used in some technical analyses. The argument put forth by technical analysts is that a rise in both trading volume and price signals investor interest in the stock, and this interest should be sustained. In contrast, a rise in price accompanied by a decline in trading volume signals a subsequent decline in the price of the stock.

Short Interest Ratio   Some technical analysts believe that the ratio of the number of shares sold short relative to the average daily trading volume is a technical signal that is valuable in forecasting the market. This ratio is called the short ratio. However, the economic link between this ratio and stock price movements can be interpreted in two ways. On one hand, some market observers believe that if this ratio is high, this is a signal that the market will advance. The argument is that short sellers will have to eventually cover their short position by buying the stocks they have shorted and, as a result, market prices will increase. On the other hand, there are some market observers who believe this a bearish signal being sent by market participants who have shorted stocks in anticipation of a declining market.

Nonlinear Dynamic Models   Some market observers believe that the patterns of stock price behavior are so complex that simple mathematical models are insufficient for detecting historical price patterns and for forecasting future price movements. Thus, while stock prices may appear to change randomly, there may be a pattern that simple mathematical tools cannot describe. Scientists have developed complex mathematical models for detecting patterns from observations of some phenomenon that appear to be random. Generically, these models are called nonlinear dynamic models because the mathematical equations used to detect any structure in a pattern are nonlinear equations and there is a complex system of such equations.

Nonlinear dynamic models have been suggested for analyzing stock price patterns. There have been several empirical studies that suggest that stock prices exhibit the characteristics of a nonlinear dynamic model. The particular form of nonlinear dynamic model that has been suggested is *chaos theory*. At this stage, the major insight provided by chaos theory is that stock price movements that may appear to be random may in fact have a structure that can be used to generate abnormal returns. However, the actual application has fallen far short of the mark. Interviews with market players by Sergio Focardi and Caroline Jonas in 1996 found that "chaos theory is conceptually too complex to find much application in finance today."[11]

Market Overreaction To benefit from favorable news or to reduce the adverse effect of unfavorable news, investors must react quickly to new information.[12] Cognitive psychologists have shed some light on how people react to extreme events. In general, people tend to overreact to extreme events. People tend to react more strongly to recent information and they tend to heavily discount older information.

The question is, do investors follow the same pattern? That is, do investors overreact to extreme events? The overreaction hypothesis suggests that when investors react to unanticipated news that will benefit a company's stock, the price rise will be greater than it should be given that information, resulting in a subsequent decline in the price of the stock. In contrast, the overreaction to unanticipated news that is expected to adversely affect the economic well-being of a company will force the price down too much, followed by a subsequent correction that will increase the price.

If, in fact, the market does overreact, investors may be able to exploit this to realize positive abnormal returns if they can (1) identify an

[11] Sergio Focardi and Caroline Jonas, *Modeling the Market: New Theories and Techniques* (New Hope, PA: Frank J. Fabozzi Associates), p. 14.
[12] Werner DeBondt and Richard Thaler, "Does the Market Overreact?" *Journal of Finance* (July 1985), pp. 793–805.

extreme event and (2) determine when the effect of the overreaction has been impounded in the market price and is ready to reverse. Investors who are capable of doing this will pursue the following strategies. When positive news is identified, investors will buy the stock and sell it before the correction to the overreaction. In the case of negative news, investors will short the stock and then buy it back to cover the short position before the correction to the overreaction.

Strategies Based on Fundamental Analysis

As explained earlier, fundamental analysis involves an economic analysis of a firm with respect to earnings growth prospects, ability to meet debt obligations, competitive environment, and the like. We discuss a few of these strategies later where we discuss equity style management.

Proponents of semistrong market efficiency argue that strategies based on fundamental analysis will not produce abnormal returns. The reason is simply that there are many analysts undertaking basically the same sort of analysis, with the same publicly available data, so that the price of the stock reflects all the relevant factors that determine value.

The focus of strategies based on fundamental analysis is on the earnings of a company and the expected change in earnings. In fact, a study by Chugh and Meador found that two of the most important measures used by analysts are short-term and long-term changes in earnings.[13]

In the 1980s, the firm of Stern Stewart developed and trademarked a measure of profitability called economic value added (EVA®). This measure is the difference between a company's operating profit and the dollar cost of capital. That is, unlike the conventional method for computing profit which fails to give recognition to the cost of equity capital, EVA deducts this cost. EVA then measures the value added by corporate management to profits after the equity funds that management used in generating operating income is taken into consideration as a cost.[14]

Earnings Surprises Studies have found that it not merely the change in earnings that is important. The reason is that analysts have a consensus forecast of a company's expected earnings. What might be expected to generate abnormal returns is the extent to which the market's forecast of future earnings differs from actual earnings that are subsequently announced. The divergence between the forecasted earnings by the mar-

---

[13] Lal Chugh and Joseph Meador, "The Stock Valuation Process: The Analysts' View," *Financial Analysts Journal* (November–December 1984), pp. 41–48.

[14] For a discussion of EVA and its implications for portfolio managers, see James L. Grant, *Foundations of Economic Value Added* (New Hope, PA: Frank J. Fabozzi Associates, 1997).

ket and the actual earnings announced is called an earnings surprise. When the actual earnings exceed the market's forecast, then this is a positive earnings surprise; a negative earnings surprise arises when the actual earnings are less than the market's forecast.

There have been numerous studies of earnings surprises. These studies seem to suggest that identifying stocks that may have positive earnings surprises and purchasing them may generate abnormal returns. Of course, the difficulty is identifying such stocks.

Low Price-Earnings Ratio   The legendary Benjamin Graham proposed a classic investment model in 1949 for the "defensive investor"—one without the time, expertise, or temperament for aggressive investment. The model was updated in each subsequent edition of his book, *The Intelligent Investor*.[15] Some of the basic investment criteria outlined in the 1973 edition are representative of the approach:

1. A company must have paid a dividend in each of the last 20 years.
2. Minimum size of a company is $100 million in annual sales for an industrial company and $50 million for a public utility.
3. Positive earnings must have been achieved in each of the last 10 years.
4. Current price should not be more than 1½ times the latest book value.
5. Market price should not exceed 15 times the average earnings for the past three years.

Graham considered the P/E ratio as a measure of the price paid for value received. He viewed high P/Es with skepticism and as representing a large premium for difficult-to-forecast future earnings growth. Hence, lower-P/E, higher-quality companies were viewed favorably as having less potential for earnings disappointments and the resulting downward revision in price.

While originally intended for the defensive investor, numerous variations of Graham's low-P/E approach are currently followed by a number of professional investment advisors.

Market Neutral Long-Short Strategy   An active strategy that seeks to capitalize on the ability of a manager to select stocks is a market neutral long-short strategy. The basic idea of this strategy is as follows. First, using the models described in later chapters, a manager analyzes the expected return of individual stocks within a universe of stocks. Based on this analysis, the manager can classify those stocks as either "high-expected return stocks"

---

[15] This model is fully described in Benjamin Graham, *The Intelligent Investor*, Fourth rev. ed. (New York: Harper & Row, 1973), Chapter 14.

or "low-expected return stocks." A manager could then do one of the following: (1) purchase only high-expected return stocks, (2) short low-expected return stocks, or (3) simultaneously purchase high-expected return stocks and short low-expected return stocks.

The problem with the first two strategies is that general movements in the market can have an adverse affect. For example, suppose a manager selects high-expected return stocks and the market declines. Because of the positive correlation between the return on all stocks and the market, the drop in the market will produce a negative return even though the manager may have indeed been able to identify high-expected return stocks. Similarly, if a manager shorts low-expected return stocks and the market rallies, the portfolio will realize a negative return. This is because a rise in the market means that the manager must likely cover the short position of each stock at a higher price than which a stock was sold.

Let's look at the third alternative—simultaneously purchasing stocks with high-expected returns and shorting those stocks with low-expected returns. Consider what happens to the long and the short positions when the market in general moves. A drop in the market will hurt the long position but benefit the short position. A market rally will hurt the short position but benefit the long position. Consequently, the long and short positions provide a hedge against each other.

While the long-short position provides a hedge against general market movements, the degree to which one position moves relative to the other is not controlled by simply going long the high-expected return stocks and going short the low-expected return stocks. That is, the two positions do not neutralize the risk against general market movements. However, the long and short positions can be created with a market exposure that neutralizes any market movement. Specifically, long and short positions can be constructed to have the same beta and, as a result, the beta of the collective long-short position is zero. For this reason, this strategy is called a market neutral long-short strategy. If, indeed, a manager is capable of identifying high- and low-expected return stocks, then neutralizing the portfolio against market movements will produce a positive return whether the market rises or falls.

Here is how a market neutral long-short portfolio is created. It begins with a list of stocks that fall into the high-expected return stocks and low-expected return stocks categories. (In fact, we classify this strategy as a fundamental analysis strategy because fundamental analysis is used to identify the stocks that fall into the high- and low-expected return stock categories.) The high-expected return stocks are referred to as "winners" and are candidates to be included in the long portfolio; the low-expected return stocks are referred to as "losers" and are candidates to be included in the short portfolio.

Suppose a client allocates $10 million to a manager to implement a market neutral long-short strategy.[16] Suppose further that the manager (with the approval of the client) uses the $10 million to buy securities on margin. As explained earlier in this chapter, the investor can borrow up to 50% of the market value of the margined securities. This means that the manager has $20 million to invest—$10 million in the long position and $10 million in the short position.

When buying securities on margin, the manager must be prepared for a margin call. Thus, a prudent policy with respect to managing the risk of a margin call is not to invest the entire amount. Instead, a liquidity buffer of about 10% of the equity capital is typically maintained. This amount is invested in high-quality short-term money market instruments. The portion held in these instruments is said to be held in "cash." In our illustration, since the equity capital is $10 million, $1 million is held in cash, leaving $9 million to be invested in the long position, therefore, $9 is million is shorted. The portfolio then looks as follows: $1 million cash, $9 million long, and $9 million short.

Market Anomaly Strategies

While there are managers who are skeptical about technical analysis and others who are skeptical about fundamental analysis, some managers believe that there are pockets of pricing inefficiency in the stock market. That is, there are some investment strategies that have historically produced statistically significant positive abnormal returns. These market anomalies are referred to as the small-firm effect, the low-price-earnings-ratio effect, the neglected-firm effect, and various calendar effects. There is also a strategy that involves following the trading transactions of the insiders of a company.

Some of these anomalies are a challenge to the semistrong form of pricing efficiency since they use the financial data of a company. This would include the small-firm effect and the low price-earnings effect. The calendar effects are a challenge to the weak form of pricing efficiency. Following insider activities with regard to buying and selling the stock of their company is a challenge to both the weak and strong forms of pricing efficiency. The challenge to the former is that, as will be explained shortly, information on insider activity is publicly available and, in fact, has been suggested as a technical indicator in popular television programs such as "Wall Street Week." Thus, the question is whether "outsiders" can use information about trading activity by insiders to generate abnormal returns. The challenge to the strong form

---

[16] This illustration is from Bruce I. Jacobs and Kenneth N. Levy, "The Long and Short on Long-Short," *Journal of Investing* (Spring 1997), pp. 78–88.

of pricing efficiency is that insiders are viewed as having special information and therefore they may be able to generate abnormal returns using information acquired from their special relationship with the firm.

Small-Firm Effect The small-firm effect emerges in several studies that have shown that portfolios of small firms (in terms of total market capitalization) have outperformed the stock market (consisting of both large and small firms). Because of these findings, there has been increased interest in stock market indicators that monitor small-capitalization firms. We will describe this more fully when we discuss equity style management.

Low P/E Effect Earlier we discussed Benjamin Graham's strategy for defensive investors based on low price-earnings ratios. The low price-earnings-ratio effect is supported by several studies showing that portfolios consisting of stocks with a low price-earnings ratio have outperformed portfolios consisting of stocks with a high price-earnings ratio. However, there have been studies that found after adjusting for transaction costs necessary to rebalance a portfolio as prices and earnings change over time, the superior performance of portfolios of low-price-earnings-ratio stocks no longer holds. An explanation for the presumably superior performance is that stocks trade at low price-earnings ratios because they are temporarily out of favor with market participants. As fads do change, companies not currently in vogue will rebound at some indeterminate time in the future.

Neglected Firm Effect Not all firms receive the same degree of attention from security analysts, and one school of thought is that firms that are neglected by security analysts will outperform firms that are the subject of considerable attention. One study has found that an investment strategy based on the level of attention devoted by security analysts to different stocks may lead to positive abnormal returns. This market anomaly is referred to as the *neglected firm effect*.

Calendar Effects While some empirical work focuses on selected firms according to some criterion such as market capitalization, price-earnings ratio, or degree of analysts' attention, the calendar effect looks at the best time to implement strategies. Examples of anomalies are the January effect, month-of-the-year effect, day-of-the-week effect, and holiday effect. It seems from the empirical evidence that there are times when the implementation of a strategy will, on average, provide a superior performance relative to other calendar time periods.

Following Insider Activity   While the SEC has a more comprehensive definition of an insider, we can think of insiders of a corporation as the corporate officers, directors, and holders of large amounts of a company's
common stock. The SEC requires that all trading activity by insiders be
reported by the 10th of the month following the trade. The SEC then
releases this information in a report called the *SEC Insider Transaction
Report*. Thus, after a time lag, the information is made publicly available. Studies have found that insiders have been able to generate abnormal returns using their privileged position. However, when outsiders use
this information, one study found that after controlling for the other
anomalies discussed above and transaction costs, outsiders cannot benefit from this information. In other words, insider activity information
published by the SEC is not a useful technical indicator for generating
abnormal returns.

One of the difficulties with assessing all of the strategies described
here is that the factors that are believed to give rise to market anomalies
are interrelated. For example, small firms may be those that are not
given much attention by security analysts and that trade at a low price-
earnings ratio. Even a study of insider activity must carefully separate
abnormal profits that may be the result of a market anomaly having
nothing to do with insider activity. For example, one study that found
no abnormal returns from following insiders also found that if there are
any abnormal returns they are due to the size and low price-earnings
effects. There have been many attempts to disentangle these effects.[17]

Equity Style Management

Several academic studies found that there were categories of stocks that
had similar characteristics and performance patterns. Moreover, the
returns of these stock categories performed differently than other categories of stocks. That is, the returns of stocks within a category were
highly correlated and the returns between categories of stocks were relatively uncorrelated. The first such study was by James Farrell who called
these categories of stocks "clusters."[18] He found that for stocks there
were at least four such categories or clusters—growth, cyclical, stable,
and energy. In the later half of the 1970s, there were studies that suggested even a simpler categorization by size (as measured by total capitalization) produced different performance patterns.

---

[17] See Bruce I. Jacobs and Kenneth N. Levy, "Investment Analysis: Profiting from a
Complex Equity Market," Chapter 2 in Frank J. Fabozzi (ed.), *Active Equity Portfolio Management* (New Hope, PA: Frank J. Fabozzi Associates, 1998).
[18] James L. Farrell, Jr., "Homogenous Stock Groupings: Implications for Portfolio
Management," *Financial Analysts Journal* (May–June 1975), pp. 50–62.

Practitioners began to view these categories or clusters of stocks with similar performance as a "style" of investing. Some managers, for example, held themselves out as "growth stock managers" and others as "cyclical stock managers." Using size as a basis for categorizing style, some managers became "large cap" investors while others "small cap" investors. ("Cap" means market capitalization.) Moreover, there was a commonly held belief that a manager could shift "styles" to enhance performance return.

Today, the notion of an equity investment style is widely accepted in the investment community. Next we look at the popular style types and the difficulties of classifying stocks according to style.

Types of Equity Styles

Stocks can be classified by style in many ways. The most common is in terms of one or more measures of "growth" and "value." Within a growth and value style there is a substyle based on some measure of size. The most plain vanilla classification of styles is as follows: (1) large value, (2) large growth, (3) small value, and (4) small growth.

The motivation for the value/growth style categories can be explained in terms of the most common measure for classifying stocks as growth or value—the price-to-book value per share (P/B) ratio. Earnings growth will increase the book value per share. Assuming no change in the P/B ratio, a stock's price will increase if earnings grow. A manager who is growth oriented is concerned with earnings growth and seeks those stocks from a universe of stocks that have higher relative earnings growth. The growth manager's risks are that growth in earnings will not materialize and/or that the P/B ratio will decline.

For a value manager, concern is with the price component rather than with the future earnings growth. Stocks would be classified as value stocks within a universe of stocks if they are viewed as cheap in terms of their P/B ratio. By cheap it is meant that the P/B ratio is low relative to the universe of stocks. The expectation of the manager who follows a value style is that the P/B ratio will return to some normal level and thus even with book value per share constant, the price will rise. The risk is that the P/B ratio will not increase.

Within the value and growth categories there are substyles. In the value category, there are three substyles: low price-to-earnings (P/E) ratio, contrarian, and yield.[19] The low-P/E manager concentrates on

---

[19] Jon A. Christopherson and C. Nola Williams, "Equity Style: What It Is and Why It Matters," Chapter 1 in T. Daniel Coggin, Frank J. Fabozzi, and Robert D. Arnott (eds.), *The Handbook of Equity Style Management: Second Edition* (New Hope, PA: Frank J. Fabozzi Associates, 1997).

companies trading at low prices to their earnings. The P/E ratio can be defined as the current P/E, a normalized P/E, or a discounted future earnings. The contrarian manager looks at the book value of a company and focuses on those companies that are selling at a low valuation relative to book value. The companies that fall into this category are typically depressed cyclical stocks or companies that have little or no current earnings or dividend yields. The expectation is that the stock is on a cyclical rebound or that the company's earnings will turn around. Both these occurrences are expected to lead to substantial price appreciation. The most conservative value managers are those that focus on companies with above average dividend yields and are expected to be capable of increasing, or at least maintaining, those yields. This style is followed by a manager who is referred to as a yield manager.

Growth managers seek companies with above average growth prospects. In the growth manager style category, there tends to be two major substyles. The first is a growth manager who focuses on high-quality companies with consistent growth. A manager who follows this substyle is referred to as a consistent growth manager. The second growth substyle is followed by an earnings momentum growth manager. In contrast to a growth manager, an earnings momentum growth manager prefers companies with more volatile, above-average growth. Such a manager seeks to buy companies in expectation of an acceleration of earnings.

There are some managers who follow both a growth and value investing style but have a bias (or tilt) in favor of one of the styles. The bias is not sufficiently identifiable to categorize the manager as a solely growth or value manager. Most managers who fall into this hybrid style are described as growth at a price managers or growth at a reasonable price managers (often referred to as "GARP"). These managers look for companies that are forecasted to have above-average growth potential selling at a reasonable value.

Style Classification Systems

Now that we have a general idea of the two main style categories, growth and value, and the further refinement by size, let's see how an investment manager goes about classifying stocks into the categories. We call the methodology for classifying stocks into style categories a style classification system. Vendors of style indexes have provided direction for developing a style classification system. However, managers often develop their own system.

Developing such a system is not a simple task. To see why, let's take a simple style classification system where we just categorize stocks into value and growth using one measure, the price-to-book value ratio. The lower the P/B ratio, the more the stock looks like a value stock. The style classification system would then be as follows:

Step 1: Select a universe of stocks.
Step 2: Calculate the total market capitalization of all the stocks in the universe.
Step 3: Calculate the P/B ratio for each stock in the universe.
Step 4: Sort the stocks from the lowest P/B ratio to the highest P/B ratio.
Step 5: Calculate the accumulated market capitalization starting from the lowest P/B ratio stock to the highest P/B ratio stock.
Step 6: Select the lowest P/B stocks up to the point where one-half the total market capitalization computed in Step 2 is found.
Step 7: Classify the stocks found in Step 6 as value stocks.
Step 8: Classify the remaining stocks from the universe as growth stocks.

While this style classification system is simple, it has both theoretical and practical problems. First, from a theoretical point of view, there is very little distinguishing the last stock on the list that is classified as value and the first stock on the list classified as growth. From a practical point of view, the transaction costs are higher for implementing a style using this classification system. The reason is that the classification is at a given point in time based on the prevailing P/B ratio and market capitalizations. At a future date, P/B ratios and market capitalizations change, resulting in a different classification of some of the stocks. This is often the case for those stocks on the border between value and growth that could jump over to the other category. This is sometimes called "style jitter." As a result, the manager will have to rebalance the portfolio and sell off stocks that are not within the style classification sought.

There are two refinements that have been made to style classification systems in an attempt to overcome these two problems. First, more than one categorization variable has been used in a style classification system. Categorization variables that have been used based on historical and/or expectational data include dividend/price ratio (i.e., dividend yield), cash flow/price ratio (i.e., cash flow yield), return on equity, earnings variability, and earnings growth. As an example of this refinement, consider the style classification system developed by one firm, Frank Russell, for the Frank Russell style indices. The universe of stocks included (either 1,000 for the Russell 1000 index or 2,000 for the Russell 2000 index) were classified as part of their value index or growth index using two categorization variables. The two variables are the P/B ratio and a long-term growth forecast.

The second refinement has been to develop better procedures for making the cut between growth and value. This involves not classifying every stock into one category or the other. Instead, stocks may be classified into three groups: "pure value," "pure growth," and "middle-of-the-road" stocks. The three groups would be such that they each had one third of the total market capitalization. The two extreme groups, pure value and pure growth, are not likely to face any significant style jitter. The middle-of-the road stocks are assigned a probability of being value or growth. This style classification system is used by Frank Russell.

Thus far our focus has been on style classification in terms of value and growth. As we noted earlier, sub-style classifications are possible in terms of size. Within a value and growth classification, there can be a model determining large value and small value stocks, and large growth and small growth stocks. The variable most used for classification of size is a company's market capitalization. To determine large and small, the total market capitalization of all the stocks in the universe considered is first calculated. The cutoff between large and small is the stock that will provide an equal market capitalization to each group.

CHAPTER 5

Sources of Information for Investing in Common Stock

Pamela P. Peterson, Ph.D., CFA
Professor of Finance
Florida State University

Frank J. Fabozzi, Ph.D., CFA
Adjunct Professor of Finance
School of Management
Yale University

There is a wealth of financial information about companies available to financial analysts and investors. The popularity of the Internet as a means of delivery has made vast amounts of information available to everyone, displacing print and fax as a means of communication. Consider the amount of information available about Microsoft Corporation. Not only can investors find annual reports, quarterly reports, press releases, and links to the company's filings with regulators on Microsoft's web site, anyone can download data for analysis and listen-in on Microsoft's conversations with analysts.

A key source of information in analyzing the earnings of a company as well as its economic well-being is provided in various financial reports required to be published by the company. In this chapter we look at these reports and other sources of information.

SOURCES OF FINANCIAL INFORMATION

There are many sources of information available to analysts. One source of information is the company itself, preparing documents for regulators and distribution to shareholders. Another source is information prepared by government agencies that compile and report information about industries and the economy. Still another source is information prepared by financial service firms that compile, analyze, and report financial and other information about the company, the industry, and the economy.

The basic information about a company can be gleaned from publication (both print and Internet), annual reports, and sources such as the federal government and commercial financial information providers. The basic information about a company consists of the following:

- Type of business (e.g., manufacturer, retailer, service, utility)
- Primary products
- Strategic objectives
- Financial condition and operating performance
- Major competitors (domestic and foreign)
- Competitiveness of the industry (domestic and foreign)
- Position of the company in the industry (e.g., market share)
- Industry trends (domestic and foreign)
- Regulatory issues (if applicable)
- Economic environment

A thorough financial analysis of a company requires examining events that help explain the firm's present condition and effect on its future prospects. For example, did the firm recently incur some extraordinary losses? Is the firm developing a new product, or acquiring another firm? Current events can provide useful information to the financial analyst. A good place to start is with the company itself and the disclosures that it makes—both financial and otherwise.

Most of the company-specific information can be picked up through company annual reports, press releases, and other information that the company provides to inform investors and customers about itself. Information about competitors and the markets for the company's products must be determined through familiarity with the products of the company and its competitors. Information about the economic environment can be found in many available sources. We will take a brief look at the different types of information in the remainder of this chapter.

EXHIBIT 5.1   Federal Regulation of Securities and Markets in the United States

Law	Description
Securities Act of 1933	Regulates new offerings of securities to the public; requires the filing of a registration statement containing specific information about the issuing corporation and prohibits fraudulent and deceptive practices related to security offers.
Securities and Exchange Act of 1934	Establishes the Securities and Exchange Commission (SEC) to enforce securities regulations and extends regulation to the secondary markets.
Investment Company Act of 1940	Gives the SEC regulatory authority over publicly held companies that are in the business of investing and trading in securities.
Investment Advisers Act of 1940	Requires registration of investment advisors and regulates their activities.
Federal Securities Act of 1964	Extends the regulatory authority of the SEC to include the over-the-counter securities markets.

INFORMATION PREPARED BY THE COMPANY

Documents prepared by a company can be divided into two groups:

1. Disclosures required by regulatory authorities, including documents that a corporation prepares and files with the Securities and Exchange Commission (SEC), and
2. Documents that a corporation prepares and distributes to shareholders.

Though both types of documents provide financial and related information about the company, the documents prepared for regulators differ from those prepared for shareholders in terms of the depth of information and form of presentation.

Disclosures Required by Regulatory Authorities

Companies whose stock is traded in public markets are subject to a number of securities laws that require specific disclosures. Several of these securities laws are described briefly in Exhibit 5.1. Publicly traded companies are required by securities laws to disclose information through filings with the SEC. The SEC, a federal agency that administers federal securities laws, established by the Securities and Exchange Act of 1934, carries out the following activities:

- Issues rules that clarify securities laws or trading procedure issues
- Requires disclosure of specific information
- Makes public statements on current issues
- Oversees the self-regulation of the securities industry by the stock exchanges and professional groups such as the National Association of Securities Dealers

The publicly traded company must make a number of periodic and occasional filings with the SEC. In addition, major shareholders and executives must make periodic and occasional filings. A number of these filings are described in Exhibit 5.2 and in more detail in the following sections.

10-K and 10-Q Filings

The 10-K is an annual report required by Section 13 of the Securities and Exchange Act of 1934. The 10-K filing contains the information provided in the annual report plus additional requirements, such as the management discussion and analysis (MDA), and must be filed within 90 days after close of a corporation's fiscal year.

The 10-K comprises five parts:

Part I.   Covers business, properties, legal proceedings, principal security holders, and security holdings of management

Part II. Covers selected financial data, management's discussion and analysis of financial conditions and results of operations, financial statements, and supplementary data

Part III. Covers directors and executive officers and remuneration of directors and officers

Part IV. Provides complete, audited annual financial information

Part V.   Schedule of various items provided

The MDA is required by the SEC Regulation S-K, Item 303. This regulation requires information and discussion regarding:

EXHIBIT 5.2 Filings of Publicly Traded Companies and Their Owners and Executives

Statement	Purpose	Information
Proxy statement (Schedule 14A)[a]	Issued by the company pertaining to issues to be put to a vote by shareholders; complies with Regulation 14A; circumstances that are required for a vote are determined by state law	Description of issues to be put to a vote; management's recommendations regarding these issues; compensation of senior management; shareholdings of officers and directors
8-K filing	Filed to report unscheduled, material events or events that may be considered of importance to shareholders of the SEC	Description of significant events that are of interest to investors and are filed as these events occur
10-K report	Annual disclosure of financial information required of all publicly traded companies; due 90 days following the company's fiscal year-end	Description of the company's business, financial statement data found in the company's annual report, notes to the financial statements, and additional disclosures including a management discussion and analysis
10-Q report	Quarterly disclosure by publicly-traded companies; required 45 days following the end of each of the company's first three fiscal quarters	A brief presentation of quarterly financial statements, notes, and management's discussion and analysis
Prospectus	Filing made by a company intending to issue securities; registration statement complying with the Securities Act of 1933.	Basic company and financial information of the issuing company
Registration statements (e.g., S-1, S-2, F-1)	A registration statement is a filing made by a company issuing securities to the public; required by the 1933 Act	Financial statement information as well as information that describes the business and management of the firm
Schedule 13D	Filing made by a person reporting beneficial ownership of shares of common stock of a publicly traded company such that the filer's beneficial ownership is more than 5% of a class of registered stock; filed within 10 days of the shares' acquisition	Report of an acquisition of shares, including information on the identity of the acquiring party, the source and amount of funds used to make the purchase, and the purpose of the purchase
Schedule 14D-1	Filing for a tender offer by someone other than the issuer such that the filer's beneficial ownership is more than 5% of a class of registered stock	Report of an offer to buy shares including information on the identity of the acquiring party, the source and amount of funds used to make the purchase, and the purpose of the purchase, and the terms of the offer

[a] There are different types of proxy statements: preliminary, confidential, and definitive. The most common is the definitive proxy, generally indicated with the abbreviation DEF (e.g., DEF 14A).

Type of Information	Disclosures
Liquidity	• Trends and commitments, events and uncertainties that are likely to affect the company's liquid resources
Capital resources	• Commitments for capital expenditures • Trends in capital resources • Changes in debt, equity, and off-balance sheet financing
Results of operations	• Significant economic events, changes, or uncertainties that likely affect income from operations • Significant revenues or expenses • Detail increases in revenues regarding price and quantities of goods sold • Impact of inflation on revenues and income from continuing operations

In addition to the specific information, the MDA should include any other information that is necessary to understand a company's operating results, financial condition, and changes in financial condition.

The MDA provides a discussion of risks, trends, and uncertainties that pertain to the company and is a useful device for management to explain the financial results in terms of the company's strategies, recent actions (e.g., mergers), and the company's competitors. The MDA also provides information that may help reconcile previous years' financial results with the current year's. Form 10-Q must be filed within 45 days after close of a corporation's fiscal quarter. This filing is similar to the 10-K, yet there is much less detailed information.

Proxy Statements

In addition to the financial statement and management discussion information available in the periodic 10-Q and 10-K filings, useful non-financial information is available in proxy statements. The proxy statement notifies designated classes of shareholders of matters to be voted upon at a shareholders' meeting. The proxy statement provides an array of information on issues such as:

■ The reappointment of the independent auditor
■ Compensation (salary, bonus, and options) of the top five executives
■ Stock ownership of executives and directors

Some of this information is innocuous (e.g., reappointment of the auditor), yet some raises a "red flag" suggesting a significant financial problem or situation. Red flags include:

- Compensation committee interlocks (i.e., member of management is a member of the board of director's compensation committee)
- Self-dealing (i.e., the company is doing business with other companies for which a member of the company's management has a financial interest)
- A change in auditors
- Transactions with related parties (e.g., look for family members who are managers of subsidiaries or divisions)
- Anti-takeover provisions (often referred to as "shareholders' rights plans")
- Management compensation that continues to increase even though the company's performance has declined
- Three or more different types of compensation plans for the same managers
- A board of directors that consists of a majority of inside and affiliated directors. *Inside directors* are current employees of the company. *Affiliated directors* are either former employees or are employees of firms that do business with the company (e.g., the company's banker).

Also, the information can sometimes reveal rather interesting (and perhaps unusual) information about the company's management and their decisions. Consider a few examples from proxy statements:

- The $195,000 expenditure in 1990 by Occidental Petroleum to finance a book about Armand Hammer, its chairman at the time.[1]
- In 1990, an Executive Vice-President of W. R. Grace and Chief Executive Officer of the subsidiary, National Medical Care, consented to the entry of a misdemeanor finding and to the payment of a fine for his importation of skins of endangered species in violation of federal law.[2]
- Mr. Goldston, the president and chief executive officer and a director of the Einstein Noah Bagel Corporation was also employed by Boston Chicken "to undertake various special projects for Boston Chicken." Following this arrangement, Mr. Goldston became Vice Chairman of the Board and a director of Boston Chicken. It is comforting that "Boston Chicken has agreed to structure Mr. Goldston's future projects so that his employment with Boston Chicken will not interfere with his duties" with Einstein Noah Bagel.[3]

---

[1] Though the book was cancelled after the death of Armand Hammer. (Earl C. Gottschalk Jr. "Proxy Statements Offer Juicy Tip-offs at Some Firms," *Wall Street Journal* (April 17, 1991), p. c1, c17.
[2] W. R. Grace Form 14A proxy statement dated April 10, 1995.
[3] Einstein Noah Bagel Company, Form 14A proxy statement dated April 1, 1997.

8-K Filing

The 8-K statement is an occasional filing that provides useful information about the company that is not generally found in the financial statements. The 8-K statement is filed by a company if there is a significant event. The specific events that require filing this statement are:

- A change in control of the company
- An acquisition or disposition of a significant amount of assets
- The bankruptcy or receivership of the company
- A change in the company's auditing firm
- A resignation of a member of the board of directors because of a disagreement with the company's operations, policies, or practices

For example, in Discovery Zone's June 3, 1996 8-K filing, they reported information regarding their auditors that provides a "red flag."

> On June 3, 1996, Discovery Zone, Inc. (the "Registrant") was informed by its independent accountants, Price Waterhouse LLP ("PW"), that PW declined to stand for re-election as the Registrant's independent accountants for the year ending December 31, 1996. The Board of Directors of the Registrant did not recommend or approve the change in independent accountants.

In addition, any other event that the company deems important to shareholders may be reported using an 8-K filing. Because 8-K filings are triggered by major company events, it is useful for the analyst to keep abreast of any such filings for the companies that they follow.

Registration Statement and Prospectus

When a corporation offers a new security to the public, the SEC requires that the corporation prepare and file a registration statement. The registration statement presents financial statement data, along with detailed information about the new security. A condensed version of this statement, called a *prospectus*, is made available to potential investors.

Documents Distributed to Shareholders

The objective of financial reporting is to "provide information that is useful to present and potential investors and creditors and other users in making rational investment, credit, and similar decisions."[4] With that objective in mind, the financial reports prepared and distributed by the

---

[4] Financial Accounting Concept 1, *Objectives of Financial Reporting by Business Enterprises* (Stamford: Financial Accounting Standards Board).

company should assist users in assessing "the amounts, timing and uncertainty of prospective net cash inflows of the enterprise."[5] Therefore, the financial reports to shareholders are not simply a presentation of the basic financial statements—the balance sheet, the income statement, and the statement of cash flows—but also communicate additional non-financial information, such as information about the relevant risks and uncertainties of the company. To that end, recent changes in accounting standards have broadened the extent and type of the information presented within the financial statements and in notes to the financial statements. For example, companies are now required to disclose risks and uncertainties related to their operations, how they use estimates in the preparation of financial statements, and the vulnerability of the company to geographic and customer concentrations.[6]

The annual report is the principal document used by corporations to communicate with shareholders. It is not an official SEC filing; consequently, companies have significant discretion in deciding on what types of information are reported and the way it is presented. The annual report presents the financial statements (the income statement, the balance sheet, and the statement of cash flows), notes to these statements, a discussion of the company by management, the report of the independent accountants, and, for fiscal years beginning after December 15, 1997, financial information on operating segments, product and services, geographical areas, and major customers.[7] Along with this basic information, annual reports may present 5- or 10-year summaries of key financial data, quarterly data, and other descriptions of the business or its products.

Because of the wide latitude that companies have in presenting the information to shareholders, the reports range from the austere to the lavish (e.g., Walt Disney Company's 1997 report, with its 8-page letter from CEO Michael Eisner and 44 pages describing its products). Some are straightforward (e.g., Berkshire Hathaway) and some are just silly (e.g., Gulf Canada Resources Ltd.'s depiction of its CEO as a "secret agent").[8] Quarterly reports to shareholders provide limited financial

---

[5] Financial Accounting Concept 1, *Objectives of Financial Reporting by Business Enterprises*.

[6] Statement of Position 94-6 *Disclosure of Significant Risks and Uncertainties* (Accounting Standards Executive Committee, 1994), effective for fiscal years beginning after December 15, 1995.

[7] Statement of Financial Accounting Standards, No. 131 *Disclosures about Segments of an Enterprise and Related Information* (Stamford: Financial Accounting Standards Board, June 1997).

[8] Jeanne Moos, "Annual Reports to Remember" [http://www.cnnfn.com/hotstories/, December 24, 1997].

information on operations. These reports are simpler and more compact in presentation than their annual counterparts.

In addition to the annual and quarterly reports, companies provide information through press releases using commercial wire services such as PR Newswire (www.prnewswire.com), Business Wire (www.businesswire.com), First Call (www.firstcall.com), or Dow Jones (bis.dowjones.com). The wire services then distribute this information to print and Internet mediums. The information provided in press releases includes earnings, dividend, new product, and acquisition announcements.

Letter to Shareholders

The letter to shareholders included in the annual and quarterly reports is sometimes dismissed by analysts and investors as unimportant because the management discussion analysis in the 10-K and shareholder report provides more detailed information. Moreover, management has less flexibility in preparing the MDA. If management is found to materially mislead investors in the MDA, SEC action can be taken. In contrast, no action will be taken by the SEC if the chief executive officer's letter to shareholders—typically prepared by the firm's investor relations or public relations staff—is optimistic despite the financial difficulties currently facing the firm.

It is because of the flexibility that management has in preparing the letter to shareholders that there may be a material difference between the statements made in the MDA and the letter to shareholders. Thornton O'Glove, former publisher of the *Quality of Earnings Report*, refers to this as *differential disclosure*.[9] O'Glove provides the following example of differential disclosure.[10] While the example is now 15 years old, the principle still holds.

In the early 1980s one of hottest microcomputer stocks was that of Convergent Technologies (CVGT). The key to the company's future prospects rested with a few key products it had developed. In 1983, this company reported earnings of $0.40 a share compared to $0.42 in 1982. The letter to shareholders in the 1983 annual report was quite optimistic and began by noting that "1983 was a year of progress and challenge for Convergent Technologies." The balance of the letter to shareholders was relatively upbeat, but there were exceptions. The letter noted, for example, that shipment of one of its key product, NGEN, was below expectations and costs were above expectations. The reason given in the letter was: "Slow manufacturing start-up and disappointing

---

[9] Thornton L. O'Glove (with Robert Sobel), *Quality of Earnings* (New York, NY: The Free Press, 1987), p. 44.
[10] O'Glove, *Quality of Earnings*, pp. 46–49.

performance by some suppliers." The letter also praised another product, WorkSlate (a powerful portable microcomputer which can also function as a terminal) and stated that: "These machines were sent as 'high tech stocking stuffers' to initial customers ordering through the American Express Christmas catalog," with a good reception.

The financial data showed that revenues rose from $96.4 million to $163.5 million, net income went from $11.9 million to $14.9 million, but CVGT earned only $0.40 per share compared with $0.42 in 1982 due to a substantial increase in the number of shares outstanding. In spite of these performance results, the letter ended on this note: "Upon reflection, 1983 was a year of investment and a year of rewards. . . We have retained our tough operating culture and entrepreneurial spirit, and will continue to set demanding goals for ourselves."

Now let's look at what was said in the MDA in the 1983 10-K for this company. The reader is told that there was only one supplier for one of its main products, a microprocessor, and only one supplier for the disk drives. The MDA stated that: "To date the disk drives have been manufactured in limited quantities and the microprocessor is on allocation from its manufacturer." The MDA claimed that this had no material impact upon the business. However, later in the 10-K the following was stated: "with the increased demand for certain components in the computer system industry the Company believes that there is a greater likelihood that the Company will experience such delays." Further, "some of these new components have yet to be manufactured in volume by their suppliers. The Company's ability to manufacture these products may be adversely affected by the inability of the Company's vendors to supply high quality components in adequate quantities." For another key product of the company, a similar situation existed.

For a more recent example, consider the perspectives on operating profit used in PepsiCo. Inc.'s 1997 annual report and 10-K. Factually correct data can be presented in both the annual report and the 10-K, but interpreted with different emphasis. In PepsiCo Inc.'s annual report's *Letter from the Chairman,*

> "In snacks and beverages—called 'continuing operations in the financial pages'—our operating profit grew 30% and earnings per share grew 62%. Operating profit margins improved by almost three percentage points."

A 30% increase in operating profits is quite impressive. In the MDA of the 10-K, a slightly different—and slightly less "rosy"—reading of the data is presented, with the 30% increase in *reported* profit and only a 13% increase in *ongoing* operations' profit:

	Operating Profit ($ in millions)			% Growth Rates	
	1997	1996	1995	1997	1996
Reported	$2,662	$2,040	$2,606	30	(22)
Ongoing*	$2,952	$2,616	$2,672	13	(2)

* Ongoing excludes the effect of the unusual items (see Note 2).

In 1997, reported operating profit increased $622 million. Ongoing operating profit increased $336 million reflecting segment operating profit growth of $392 million or 14%, partially offset by a $56 million or 32% increase in unallocated expenses. The increase in segment operating profit primarily reflects the volume gains and lower raw material costs in worldwide Beverages. The increase in unallocated expenses relates to higher corporate expenses and foreign exchange losses in 1997 compared to gains in 1996." (PepsiCo Inc. 1997 10-K, p. 13)

And although the operating profit margin improved from 10.0% to 12.7% (the "almost three percentage points"), using data that is presented in both the annual report and the 10-K, the analyst can calculate that 1997's margin was lower than 1995's margin of 13.7%.[11]

The point is that the analyst may find the letter to shareholders interesting. However, the MDA may identify where potential problems may exist, while the letter to shareholders may present a more rosy picture of the future prospects of the firm.

Issues in Using Financial Statement Data

There are a number of issues that should be considered in using the financial statement data provided in company and quarterly reports. We will look at these issues in the chapters to follow. For now, here are just three such issues:

- The restatement of prior years' data
- The different accounting standards used by non U.S. companies
- Possible "off-balance sheet" activity

---

[11] In fact, 1997's operating profit margin is less than the 1994 margin of 13.9% and the 1993 margin of 13.6%, as well. In other words, 1996 was a particularly poor year and the 1997 results suggest a partial recovery of margins—but look good when compared to 1996.

EXHIBIT 5.3   Selected Financial Data for Harnischfeger Industries, Inc., 1991

Dollar Amounts in Thousands Except Per Share Amounts	As Reported in 1991	As Restated for 1991 in 1995
Net sales	$1,584,114	$1,863,703
Operating income	$120,920	$194,682
Net income	$64,610	$79,966
Total assets	$1,506,882	$2,135,627
Earnings per share	$2.08	$1.90
Book value per share	$19.82	$11.98
Number of employees	11,600	17,100

Source: Harnischfeger Industries, Inc., 1991 Annual Report, pp. 34–35, and Harnischfeger Industries, Inc., 1995 Annual Report, pp. 46–47.

The Restatement of Prior Years' Data

When a company reports financial data for more than one year, which is often the case, previous years' financial data are restated to reflect any changes in accounting methods or acquisitions that have taken place since the previous data had been reported. Consider the case of Harnischfeger Industries, Inc. shown in Exhibit 5.3. The originally reported data for 1991 are shown alongside the restated 1991 data reported in the 1995 financial statements. So which data are correct? Both. The 1991 data has simply been restated in 1995 to reflect accounting changes and acquisitions since 1991 to make the data comparable to the current 1995 data. Therefore, the analyst must consider which data are most appropriate to use in the analysis.[12] If, for example, the analyst is looking at Harnischfeger and its competitive position in 1991, the analyst would want to use the as-reported 1991 data. If, on the other hand, the analyst is looking at trends in some of the data in an effort to forecast future operating performance or financial condition, the restated 1991 data are more appropriate.

There Are Different Accounting Standards Used by Non-U.S. Companies

Another concern is dealing with financial statements of non-U.S. reporting entities. There are several reasons for this concern. First, as of this

---

[12] In academic studies that examine the relation between stock prices and accounting information, the "as originally reported" data are most often the relevant data to use because the researcher is examining the market's reaction to the accounting information as it is released. It is reasonable to assume that investors use all currently available information, but it is not reasonable to assume that investors are psychic and therefore know what the information will be restated as in future years.

writing, there are no internationally acceptable standards of financial reporting. This includes not only the accounting methods that are acceptable for handling certain economic transactions and the degree of disclosure, but other issues. Specifically, there is no uniform treatment of the frequency of disclosure. Some countries require only annual or semiannual reporting rather than quarterly as in the United States. Moreover, there is a major concern with non-U.S. auditors. The enhancement role played by auditors in some countries is far from ideal, with little emphasis on the independence of the auditor and the reporting entity. In fact, in some countries, the nation's securities laws may require that the auditor be a member of the governing board of the reporting entity. Even where there is an independent auditor, the education and training of auditors may be inadequate. And some blame lax accounting standards for the problems in the Asian, Russian, and Latin American markets, where the poor quality of financial information make it difficult for investors to assess companies' operating performance and risk.[13] The International Accounting Standards Committee (IASC) has attempted to resolve many of these concerns. However, at this time, an analyst should look extremely closely at non-U.S. financial reports, particularly for issuers in emerging markets.

There May Be "Off-Balance Sheet" Activity

There have always been some corporate investing or financing activities that simply do not show up in financial statements. Though there have been improvements in accounting standards that have moved much of this activity to the financial statements (e.g., leases, pension benefits, post-retirement benefits), opportunities remain to conduct business that is not represented adequately in the financial statements. An example is the case of joint ventures. As long as the investing corporation does not have a controlling interest in the joint venture, the assets and financing of the venture can remain off the balance sheet. Limited information is provided in footnotes to the statements, but this information is insufficient to judge the performance and risks of the joint venture. The opportunity to keep some information from the financial statements places a greater burden on the financial analyst to dig deep into the company's notes to the financial statements, filings with the SEC, and the financial press.

---

[13] Nanette Byrnes, "Needed: Accounting the World Can Trust," *Business Week* (October 12, 1998), p. 46.

INTERVIEWING COMPANY REPRESENTATIVES

Interviewing representatives of a company may produce additional information and insight into the company's business. The starting place for the interview is the company's investors' relations (IR) office, which is generally well-prepared to address the analyst's questions.

The key is for the analyst to prepare before meeting with the IR officer so that the interview questions can be well focused. This preparation includes understanding the company's business, its products, the industry in which it operates, and its recent financial disclosures. The analyst must understand the industry-specific terminology and any industry-specific accounting methods. In the telecommunications industry, for example, the analyst must understand measures such as gigahertz and minutes-in-use, and such terms as bandwidth, point-of-presence, and spectrum.[14] As another example, an analyst for the oil and gas industry should understand that a degree day is a measure of temperature variation from a reference temperature.

The analyst must keep in mind that the IR officer has an obligation to treat all investors in a fair manner, which means that the IR officer cannot give a financial analyst material information that is not also available to others. There is also information that the IR officer cannot give the analyst. For example, in a very competitive industry it may not be appropriate to give monthly sales figures for specific products. The analyst must understand the competitive nature of the industry and understand what information is typically not revealed in the industry.

Because the analyst comes armed with knowledge of the company's financial statements, the questions should focus on taking a closer look at the information provided by these disclosures:

■ Extraordinary or unusual revenues and expenses
■ Large differences between earnings from cash flows
■ Changes in how data is reported
■ Explanations for deviations from consensus earnings expectations
■ How the company values itself versus the market's valuation
■ Sales to major customers

An analyst that uses a statistical model to develop forecasts for the company or its industry may, of course, require very specific data that may not be readily available in the financial statements.

---

[14] *The Telecommunications Industry* (Charlottesville, VA: Association for Investment Management and Research, 1994), pp. 108–110.

It is sometimes useful to determine what the company expects to earn in the future. Though companies may be reluctant to provide a specific earnings forecast, they will sometimes respond to a query regarding analysts' consensus earnings forecasts. In their response about analysts' forecasts, the company may reveal its own forecast. If a company provides a forecast of its earnings, the analyst must consider the forecast in light of the company's previous forecasting; for example, some companies may consistently underestimate future earnings in order to avoid a negative earnings surprise. Further, the company's forecast or response to a consensus forecast may be accompanied by significant defensive disclosures that concern the risks that the company may not meet projected earnings.

INFORMATION PREPARED BY GOVERNMENT AGENCIES

Federal and state governmental agencies provide a wealth of information that may be useful in analyzing a company, its industry, or the economic environment.

Company-Specific Information
One of the most prominent innovations in the delivery of company information is the Securities and Exchange Commission's *Electronic Data Gathering and Retrieval* (EDGAR) system that is available on the Internet (www.sec.gov). The EDGAR system provides on-line access to most SEC filings for all public domestic companies from 1994 forward. The primary financial statement filings, such as the 10-K and 10-Q, are required EDGAR filings, though some filings (e.g., insider security ownership and 10-K filings of foreign corporations) are optional. The EDGAR system provides access within 24 hours of filing, providing up-to-date information that is accessible to everyone.

In addition to the EDGAR system at the SEC site, several financial service companies provide free or fee access to the information in the EDGAR system in different database forms that assist in searching or database creation tasks.[15]

Industry Data
The analysis of a company requires that the analyst look at the other firms that operate in the same line of business. The purpose of examining these other companies is to get an idea of the market in which the com-

---

[15] These services include EDGAR On-line (www.edgar-online.com) and EDGAR from Compustat (www.compustat.com).

pany's products are sold: What is the degree of competition? What are the trends? What is the financial condition of the company's competitors?

Several government agencies provide information that is useful in an analysis of an industry. The primary governmental providers of industry data are the U.S. Bureau of the Census and the Bureau of Economic Analysis, an agency of the U.S. Department of Commerce. A recent innovation is the creation of Stat-USA, a fee-based collection of governmental data. Stat-USA is an electronic provider of industry and sector data that is produced by the U.S. Department of Commerce. The available data provided for different industries include gross domestic product, shipments of products, inventories, orders, and plant capacity utilization.[16]

The government classification of businesses into industries is based on the North American Industry Classification System (NAICS).[17] NAICS is a recently adopted system of industry identification, replacing the Standard Industrial Classification (SIC) system in 1997.[18] The NAICS is a 6-digit system that classifies businesses using 350 different classes. The broadest classification comprises the first two digits of the 6-digit code. These are listed in Exhibit 5.4. The NAICS is now the basis for the classification of industry-specific data produced by governmental agencies. Like the SIC system before it, the NAICS will, over time, become the basis for the classification of companies for industry-specific data used by non-governmental information providers as well.

Economic Data

Another source of information for financial analysis is economic data, such as the gross domestic product and consumer price index, which may be useful in assessing the recent performance or future prospects of a firm or industry. For example, suppose an analyst is evaluating a firm that owns a chain of retail outlets. What information will the analyst need to judge the firm's performance and financial condition? The analyst needs financial data, but they do not tell the whole story. The analyst also needs information on consumer spending, producer prices, and consumer prices. These economic data are readily available from government sources, a few of which are listed in Exhibit 5.5.

---

[16] Web access to this data is available through the Department of Commerce site (www.doc.gov), Stat-USA (eee.sstat-USA.gov), and the Census Bureau (www.census.gov).
[17] This classification system is the result of the joint efforts of the U.S. Bureau of Economic Analysis (BEA), the U.S. Bureau of Labor Statistics, the U.S. Census Bureau, Statistics Canada, and Mexico's Instituto Nacional de Estadistica, Geografia e Informatica (INEGI).
[18] The SIC system was developed by the Office of Management and Budget and had been in use since the 1930s.

EXHIBIT 5.4 North American Industry Classification System Sector Codes

Code	NAICS Sectors
11	Agriculture, Forestry, Fishing and Hunting
21	Mining
22	Utilities
23	Construction
31-33	Manufacturing
42	Wholesale Trade
44-45	Retail Trade
48-49	Transportation and Warehousing
51	Information
52	Finance and Insurance
53	Real Estate and Rental and Leasing
54	Professional, Scientific, and Technical Services
55	Management of Companies and Enterprises
56	Administrative and Support, Waste Management and Remediation Services
61	Education Services
62	Health Care and Social Assistance
71	Arts, Entertainment, and Recreation
72	Accommodation and Foodservices
81	Other Services (except Public Administration)
92	Public Administration

Source: http://www.census.gov/epcd/www/naics.html

EXHIBIT 5.5 Examples of Government Sources of Economic Data

Publisher	Web sources	Print or CD-Rom Product
Board of Governors of the Federal Reserve System	www.bog.frb.fed.us	Federal Reserve Bulletin
Bureau of Economic Analysis	www.bea.doc.gov	National Product Accounts Business Inventories Gross Product by Industry
Stat-USA	www.stat-usa.gov	National Trade Data Bank
U.S. Census Bureau	www.census.gov	CenStats
U.S. Department of Commerce	www.doc.gov	Survey of Current Business

INFORMATION PREPARED BY FINANCIAL SERVICE COMPANIES

A whole industry exists to provide financial and related information about individual companies, industries, and the economy. The ease and low cost of providing such data on the Internet has fostered a proliferation of information providers. However, the prominent providers in today's Internet-based world are some of the same providers that were prominent in the print medium.

Company-Specific Information

Information about an individual company is available from a vast number of sources, including the company itself through its own web pages. In addition to relaying the company's financial information that is presented by the company through its communication with shareholders and regulators, there are many financial service firms that compile the financial data and present analyses.

Several sources of data on individual companies are listed in Exhibit 5.6. This is by no means an exhaustive listing because of the large and growing number of information providers. The providers distinguish themselves in the market for information through the breadth of coverage (in terms of the number of companies in their database), the depth of coverage (in terms of the extensive nature of their data for individual companies), or their specialty (e.g., the collection of analyst recommendations and forecasts).

Industry Data

The first step in analyzing the industry is to define the company's industry. The NAICS and its predecessor, the SIC, are systems of classification of companies, yet they do not classify companies—they simply set up a coding system that once the company's productive activities are identified by the analyst, a company can then be classified into a specific, coded industry. Though it may seem a simple task, the fact that most companies operate in more than one line of business complicates the definition of the industry and the analysis process. Consider RJR Nabisco which operates in both the tobacco and the food industries, contributing 49% and 51% of net sales, respectively.[19] Because it operates in two different industries, it is difficult to classify RJR Nabisco into one or another NAICS code. As a result of its operating significantly in two industries, the financial analyst must analyze both of these industries.

---

[19] RJR Nabisco Holdings, 10-K, note 15 "Segment Information."

EXHIBIT 5.6   Sources of Individual Company Financial Data

Financial Reporting Service	Product	Brief Description
Disclosure www.disclosure.com	Global Access	Electronic database of companies' financial statements and financial analyst forecasts
Dun & Bradstreet www.dnb.com	Principal International Businesses	Electronic database of selected information on 50,000 companies in 140 countries
Fitch IBCA www.fitchibca.com	BankScope	Comprehensive database of financials on 10,000 international banks
	CreditDisk	International bank rating service on CD-ROM
	Fitch IBCA Research	In-depth research on U.S. corporations
	International Bank Rating Review	Ratings, key financial statistics, background, and one-page credit assessments of 650 banks around the world
Moody's Investor Services www.moodys.com	Company Data Direct	An online database of information on a companies' history, financial statements, and long-term debts
	Company Data with EDGAR	An electronic database consisting of company SEC filings
Standard and Poor's, McGraw-Hill, Inc. www.standardpoor.com	Compustat	Electronic database of annual and quarterly financial statement and market data coverage for over 18,000 North American and 11,000 global companies
	Market Insight	Web-based access to individual company financial statement data on the Standard & Poor's universe of companies
	EDGAR from Compustat	A searchable electronic database consisting of company 10-K and 10-Q filings
Value Line, Inc. www.valueline.com	DataFile	Electronic database with annual and quarterly financial statement and monthly market price data for over 5,000 securities on an "as reported" basis since 1955
	Estimates & Projections File	Electronic data with Value Line's proprietary estimates of earnings and dividends for the 1,700 companies
Zacks Investment Research www.zacks.com	Zacks Historical Data	Electronic database comprised of financial statement data, analyst forecasts, earnings surprises and stock recommendations
	Zacks Research System (ZRA)	An electronic database that includes financial statement, price, and earnings data for over 6,000 companies

The classification of companies into industries is based on judgment and different financial reporting services and different analysts may classify the same company into different industries. One provider may classify a company based on the line of business that generates the largest percentage of sales, whereas another provider may classify a company according to the largest percentage of assets in that industry. The analyst must be aware of how the reporting service classifies companies into industries when using industry data.

In addition to the classification problem, another problem arises in the calculation of industry statistics that may be used as inputs into the analysis. Consider an industry comprised of the following four companies:

Company	Return on Assets
A	23%
B	20%
C	15%
D	10%

What is this industry's return on assets? Is it the arithmetic average of 17%? That's one way of looking at it. But what if the companies are quite different in terms of size? If company A has $10 million in assets and companies B, C, and D each have only $1 million, the simple average of 17% does not appear to adequately represent the industry's return. It seems reasonable that some type of weighting be applied to reflect the difference in size, though the choice of weights is left to the judgment of the analyst. If the analyst is using industry averages that are prepared by someone else, it is important for the analyst to understand how the average is derived.

Aside from the financial statement data, the analyst may need to collect additional information about a company and industry that is industry-specific. For example, in analyzing the airline industry, the load factor (the percentage of seats sold) is an indicator of activity that is related to an airline's performance. Additional examples of industry-specific factors are described in Exhibit 5.7. It is important for the analyst to understand the type of information that is relevant for an analysis.

A number of financial information providers offer industry-specific data and compile financial data by industry. Some services, such as Standard & Poor's Compustat and Value Line, provide industry data based on their large universe of stocks covered in their database of individual company financial data.

EXHIBIT 5.7 Examples of Industry-Specific Factors

Industry	Factor	Explanation
Advertising	Gross billings	Total dollar amount of revenues from advertising
Air transport	Load factor	Percentage of seats sold
Aircraft manufacturer	Backlog	Number of aircraft ordered for production that are not completed
Banking/Credit	Loan origination	Dollar amount of loans made
	Loan loss provision	Percentage of loans considered to be bad debt
	Cards in force	Number of credit cards outstanding
Electric Utility	Load factor	Average of the percentage of total capacity used
Retail	Same-store sales	Revenues of the same store in a previous period
Savings and Loan	Interest cost to gross income	Percentage of interest paid on deposits to total gross income
Semi-conductor	Book-to-bill ratio	Ratio of orders to completed orders
Telecommunications	Cost per access line	Ratio of operating cost to number of lines of service

Economic Data

Much of the economic data that is used in financial analysis is taken from government sources, though some information is independently produced through surveys and research. There are many commercial services that collect and disseminate this and other information. These services include AP Business News (www.ap.org), Bridge (www.bridge.com), and Business Wire (www.businesswire.com). Financial publications, such as the *Wall Street Journal* (www.wsj.com), *Investors Business Daily* (www.investors.com), and the *Financial Times* (www.ft.com), provide economic data in both in print and electronic forms. In addition, databases, such as McGraw-Hill's DRI U.S. Central Data Base (USCEN), collect and market historical series of U.S. economic and financial data.

SUMMARY

Companies prepare and distribute information for regulators and shareholders. This information includes annual and quarterly financial reports (e.g., 10-K, 10-Q). Additional information may be gathered through interviewing a company's representatives. Effective use of the interview as a source of company information requires extensive preparation and knowledge of the company by the analyst. Government agencies and commercial services prepare and disseminate information about individual companies, industries, and the economy.

CHAPTER 6

Money Market Instruments

Frank J. Fabozzi, Ph.D., CFA
Adjunct Professor of Finance
School of Management
Yale University

Steven V. Mann, Ph.D.
Professor of Finance
The Moore School of Business
University of South Carolina

Moorad Choudhry
Senior Fellow
Centre for Mathematical Trading and Finance
City University Business School

The money market is the market for financial instruments that have a maturity of one year or less. The financial instruments traded in this market include securities issued by the U.S. Department of the Treasury (specifically, Treasury bills), U.S. federal agency securities (discount note and various "bill" products), depository institutions (negotiable certificates of deposit, federal funds, and bankers acceptances), insurance companies (funding agreements), commercial paper, medium-term notes, repurchase agreements, short-term municipal securities, short-term mortgage-backed securities, and asset-backed securities. In this chapter we cover all but the last three financial instruments.

U.S. TREASURY BILLS

The U.S. Treasury is the largest single borrower in the world. Treasury bills are short-term discount instruments with original maturities of less than one year. All Treasury securities are backed by the full faith and credit of the U.S. government. This fact, combined with their volume (in terms of dollars outstanding) and liquidity, afford Treasury bills a central place in the money market. Indeed, interest rates on Treasury bills serve as benchmark short-term rates throughout the U.S. economy as well as in international money markets.

Treasury bills are issued at a discount to par value, have no coupon rate, and mature at par value. The Treasury currently issues on a regular basis bills with original maturities of 4 weeks, 13 weeks (3 months) and 26 weeks (6 months), as well as cash-management bills with various maturities.

Cash management bills are offered from time to time with various maturities. The time between the announcement of an issue, auction, and issuance is usually a week or less. Cash management bills are issued to bridge seasonal fluctuations in the Treasury's cash position. Owing to their variable issuance and maturity, cash management bills can mature on any business day.

All Treasury securities are sold and transferable in increments of $1,000. Previously, Treasury bills were available in minimum purchase amounts of $10,000. Treasury bills are issued in book-entry form. This means that the investor receives only a receipt as evidence of ownership instead of a paper certificate. The primary advantage of book entry is ease in transferring ownership of the security. Interest income from Treasury securities is subject to federal income taxes but is exempt from state and local income taxes.

The U.S. Department of the Treasury maintains a regular and predictable schedule for their security offerings. The current auction cycle for Treasury bills is weekly. With the exception of holidays and special circumstances, the offering is announced on Thursday and is auctioned the following Monday. The issue/settlement day is the Thursday following the auction. Because of holidays, the maturities may be either longer or shorter by one day. The auction process and the determination of the winning bidders is explained in Chapter 7.

Between the auction's announcement and the actual issuance of the securities, trading of bills takes place in the *when-issued* or *wi market*. Essentially, this when-issued market is nothing more than an active forward market in the bills. Many dealers enter a Treasury bill auction with large short positions and hope to cover these positions with bills obtained at the auction. Dealers make commitments with their customers and other dealers to make/take delivery of bills for an agreed upon price with settlement occurring after the bills are issued. In fact, all deliveries on when-issued trades occur on the issue day of the security traded. When-issued yields serve as important indicators for yields that will prevail at the auction.

Price Quotes for Treasury Bills

The convention for quoting bids and offers in the secondary market is different for Treasury bills and Treasury coupon securities. Bids/offers on bills are quoted in a special way. Unlike bonds that pay coupon interest, Treasury bill values are quoted on a bank discount basis, not on a price basis. The yield on a bank discount basis is computed as follows:

$$Y_d = \frac{D}{F} \times \frac{360}{t}$$

where:

Y_d = annualized yield on a bank discount basis (expressed as a decimal)

D = dollar discount, which is equal to the difference between the face value and the price

F = face value

t = number of days remaining to maturity

For example, Exhibit 6.1 presents the PX1 Governments screen from Bloomberg. Data for the most recently issued bills appear in the upper lefthand corner. The first and second columns indicate the security and its maturity date. In the third column, there is an arrow indicating an up or down tick for the last trade. The fourth column indicates the current bid/ask rates. A bond-equivalent yield (discussed later) using the ask yield/price is contained in column 5. The last column contains the change in bank discount yields based on the previous day's closing rates as of the time posted.

Exhibit 6.2 presents the same information for all outstanding bills (page PX2). Other important market indicators are contained in the lower left-hand corner of the screen.

As an example using the information in Exhibit 6.1, consider a Treasury bill with 91 days to maturity and a face value of $1,000. Suppose this bill is trading at 995.854444. The dollar discount, D, is computed as follows:

$$D = \$1,000 - 995.854444 = \$4.145556$$

EXHIBIT 6.1   Bloomberg PX1 Screen

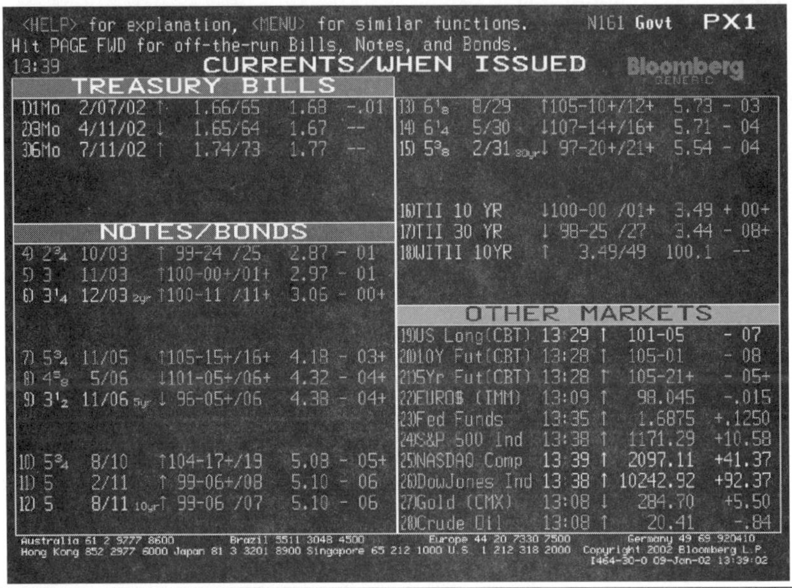

Source: Bloomberg Financial Markets

EXHIBIT 6.2   Bloomberg PX2 Screen

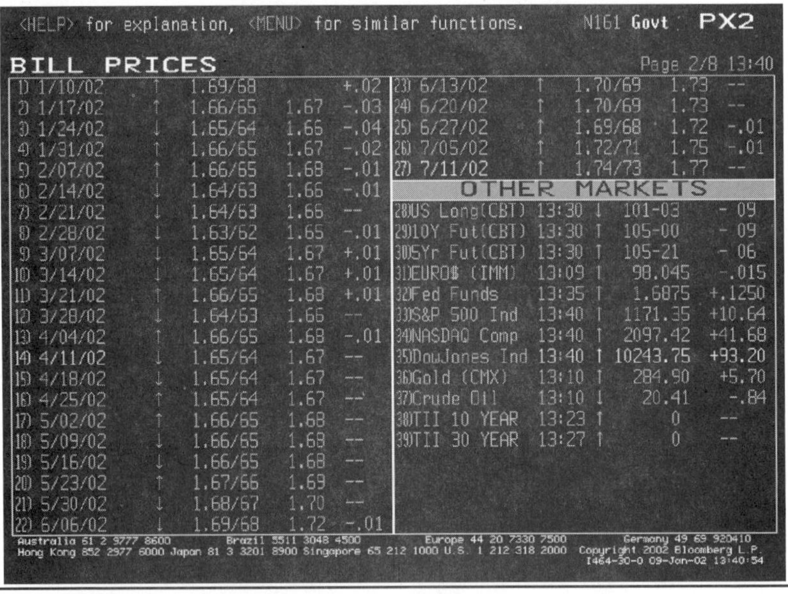

Source: Bloomberg Financial Markets

Therefore,

$$Y_d = \frac{\$4.145556}{\$1,000} \times \frac{360}{91} = 1.64\%$$

Given the yield on a bank discount basis, the price of a Treasury bill is found by first solving the formula for Y_d given the dollar discount (D), as follows:

$$D = Y_d \times F \times (t/360)$$

The price is then

$$price = F - D$$

Using the information in Exhibit 6.1, for the current 91-day bill with a face value of $1,000, if the yield on bank discount basis is quoted as 1.64%, D is equal to

$$D = 0.0164 \times \$1,000 \times 91/360 = \$4.14556$$

Therefore,

$$price = \$1,000 - \$4.145556 = \$995.854444$$

The quoted yield on a bank discount basis is not a meaningful measure of the return from holding a Treasury bill, for two reasons. First, the measure is based on a face-value investment rather than on the actual dollar amount invested. Second, the yield is annualized according to a 360-day rather than a 365-day year, making it difficult to compare Treasury bill yields with Treasury notes and bonds, which pay interest on a 365-day basis. The use of 360 days for a year is a money market convention for some money market instruments, however. Despite its shortcomings as a measure of return, this is the method that dealers have adopted to quote Treasury bills. Many dealer quote sheets and some other reporting services provide two other yield measures that attempt to make the quoted yield comparable to that for a coupon bond and other money market instruments.

CD Equivalent Yield

The CD *equivalent yield* (also called the *money market equivalent yield*) makes the quoted yield on a Treasury bill more comparable to yield quotations on other money market instruments that pay interest on a 360-day basis. It does this by taking into consideration the price of the Treasury bill (i.e., the amount invested) rather than its face value. The formula for the CD equivalent yield is

$$\text{CD equivalent yield} = \frac{360\,Y_d}{360 - t(Y_d)}$$

For example, using the data from Exhibit 6.1 for the 91-day bill that matured on April 11, 2002, the ask rate on a bank discount basis is 1.64%. The CD equivalent yield is computed as follows:

$$\text{CD equivalent yield} = \frac{360(0.0164)}{360 - 91(0.0164)} = 0.01647 = 1.647\%$$

Bond-Equivalent Yield

The measure that seeks to make the Treasury bill quote comparable to coupon Treasuries is called the *bond-equivalent yield* . This yield measure makes the quoted yield on a Treasury bill more comparable to yields on Treasury notes and bonds that use an actual/actual day count convention. In order to convert the yield on a bank discount to a bond-equivalent yield, the following formula is used:

$$\text{Bond-equivalent yield} = \frac{T(Y_d)}{360 - t(Y_d)}$$

where T is the actual number of days in the calendar year (i.e., 365 or 366).

As an example, using the same Treasury bill with 91 days to maturity and a face value of $1,000 that would be quoted at 1.64% on a bank discount basis, the bond-equivalent yield is calculated as follows:

$$\text{Bond-equivalent yield} = \frac{365(0.0164)}{360 - 91(0.0164)} = 0.0167 = 1.67\%$$

This number matches the bond-equivalent yield given by the Bloomberg screen in Exhibit 6.1.

GOVERNMENT SPONSORED AGENCY INSTRUMENTS

U.S. government agency securities can be classified by the type of issuer— those issued by federal agencies and those issued by government sponsored enterprises. Federal agencies are fully owned by the U.S. government and have been authorized to issue securities directly in the marketplace. They include the Export-Import Bank of the United States, the Tennessee Valley Authority (TVA), the Commodity Credit Corporation, the Farmers Housing Administration, the General Services Administration, the Government National Mortgage Association, the Maritime Administration, the Private Export Funding Corporation, the Rural Electrification Administration, the Rural Telephone Bank, the Small Business Administration, and the Washington Metropolitan Area Transit Authority. The only federal agency that is an active issuer of short-term debt obligations is the TVA. With the exception of securities of the Tennessee Valley Authority and the Private Export Funding Corporation, the securities are backed by the full faith and credit of the United States government. Interest income on securities issued by federally related institutions is exempt from state and local income taxes.

Government sponsored enterprises (GSEs) are privately owned, publicly chartered entities. They were created by Congress to reduce the cost of capital for certain borrowing sectors of the economy deemed to be important enough to warrant assistance. The entities in these privileged sectors include farmers, homeowners, and students. GSEs issue securities directly in the marketplace. Today there are six GSEs that currently issue debentures: Federal National Mortgage Association, Federal Home Loan Mortgage Corporation, Federal Agricultural Mortgage Corporation, Federal Farm Credit System, Federal Home Loan Bank System, and Student Loan Marketing Association. The interest earned on obligations of the Federal Home Loan Bank System, the Federal Farm Credit System, and the Student Loan Marketing Association are exempt from state and local income taxes.

Although there are differences between federal agencies and GSEs, it is common to refer to the securities issued by these entities as U.S. agency securities or, simply, agency securities. In this chapter we will discuss the short-term debt obligations issued by the six GSEs and the TVA. Chapter 9 provides information about each of these agencies and other securities that are covered. All of the securities issued by these entities expose an investor to credit risk. Consequently, agency securities offer a higher yield than comparable maturity Treasury securities.

Fannie Mae

Fannie Mae issues short-term debt in the form of discount notes. Discount notes are unsecured general obligations issued at a discount from their face value and mature at their face value. They are issued in book-entry form through the Federal Reserve banks and have original maturities that range from overnight to 360 days with the exception of 3-month,

6-month, and 1-year maturities. These maturities are available through Fannie Mae's Benchmark Bills program, discussed shortly.

Discount notes are offered every business day via daily posting by Fannie Mae's selling group of discount note dealers. These dealer firms make a market in these discount notes and the secondary market is well-developed. Investors may choose among cash-, regular-, or skip-day settlements.

Fannie Mae introduced the Benchmark Bills program in early November 1999 as an important component of its discount note program. Benchmark Bills, like discount notes, are unsecured general obligations issued in book-entry form as discount instruments and are payable at par on their maturity date. However, unlike discount notes, Benchmark Bills are issued at regularly scheduled weekly auctions where the size of the issuance is announced in advance. When the program was launched, Benchmark Bills were issued in two maturities—3-month and 6-month. In October 2000, Fannie Mae introduced a 1-year (360 days) that are auctioned every two weeks.

Fannie Mae announces the size of each weekly auction on Tuesday sometime during mid-morning Eastern time. Exhibit 6.3 presents a Bloomberg news report from September 18, 2001 of a Fannie Mae auction announcement of 3- and 6-month Benchmark Bills. The auction itself is conducted on Wednesdays. Fannie Mae accepts bids from a subset of eight of the dealers from its Selling Group of Discount Note Dealers. These eight dealers (called ACCESS dealers) can submit bids on their own account or on behalf of their customers. The bids may be either competitive or non-competitive. The minimum bid size is $50,000 with additional increments of $1,000. Moreover, bidding dealers are subject to a 35% takedown rule. A takedown rule limits the amount a single buyer can bid on or hold to 35% of the total auction amount.

Bids are submitted in the form of yields on a bank discount basis out to three decimal points and are accepted between 8:30 a.m. and 9:30 a.m Eastern time. The submitted bids are ranked from lowest to the highest. As noted previously, this is equivalent to arranging the bids from highest price to the lowest price. Starting from the lowest yield bid, all competitive bids are accepted until the amount to be distributed to the competitive bidders is completely allocated. The highest accepted bid is called the *stop out discount rate* and all accepted bids are filled at this price (i.e., a single price auction). Exhibit 6.4 presents a Bloomberg news report of the results of a September 19, 2001 auction of 3-month and 6-month Benchmark Bills. Non-competitive bids are also executed at the stop out discount rate and are allocated on the basis of when the bids were received (i.e., first-come, first-served). The minimum face value is $1,000. The day count convention—like virtually every security discussed in this chapter—is Actual/360.

EXHIBIT 6.3 Bloomberg Announcement for a Fannie Mae Benchmark Bill Auction

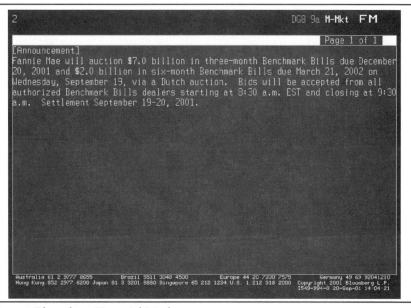

Source: Bloomberg Financial Markets

EXHIBIT 6.4 Bloomberg Announcement of Fannie Mae Benchmark Bill Auction Results

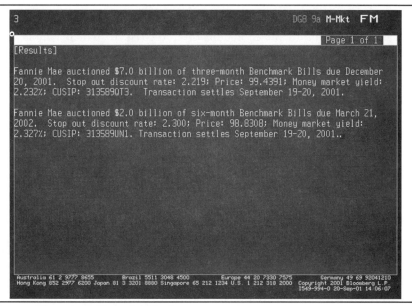

Source: Bloomberg Financial Markets

EXHIBIT 6.5 Summary Statistics of the Yield Between Benchmark Bills versus U.S. Treasury Bill Yields

Statistic	3-Month Yield Spread	6-Month Yield Spread	1-Year Yield Spread
Mean	31.307	26.984	37.528
Standard Deviation	13.627	9.626	10.381
Minimum	2.036	6.731	16.552
Maximum	98.504	58.709	77.686

Source: Fannie Mae

Although the Benchmark Bills program is a subset of their well-established discount notes program, Fannie Mae has taken steps such that the two programs do not interfere with one another. Specifically, Fannie Mae does not issue discount notes in any given week with a maturity date within one week on either side of a Benchmark Bill's maturity date. For example, in a particular week, Fannie Mae will not issue a discount note with a maturity between two months, three weeks to three months, or one week. The maturity lockout is in effect for 6-month and 1-year Benchmark Bills as well. However, the two programs are also complementary in that a 3-month Benchmark Bill with two months until maturity may be "reopened" as a 2-month discount note with the same maturity date and CUSIP as the bill.

Benchmark Bills trade at a spread over comparable maturity U.S. Treasury Bills due to the modicum of credit risk to which Fannie Mae debt investors are exposed. Exhibit 6.5 presents some summary statistics of daily 3-month, 6-month, and 1-year Benchmark Bill yield spreads versus comparable maturity U.S. Treasury Bills for the period August 1, 2000 through July 20, 2001.

Federal Home Loan Mortgage Corporation

Federal Home Loan Mortgage Corporation (Freddie Mac) issues discount notes and Reference Bills. While at issuance discount notes can range in maturity from overnight to 365 days, half of these notes have maturities of three days or less. The most popular maturities are one month and three months. Freddie Mac discount notes are offered for sale continuously with rates posted 24 hours a day (business days) through a group of investment banks that belong to the Freddie Mac dealer group. These notes are issued in book entry form through the Federal Reserve Bank of New York and have a minimum face value of $1,000 with increments of $1,000 thereafter. The pricing conventions are the same as U.S. Treasury bills.

Freddie Mac's Reference Bills program is similar in structure to Fannie Mae's Benchmark Bills. One important difference between the two is that Reference Bills are offered in more maturities namely, one month (28 days), two months (56 days), three months (91 days), six months (182 days), and one year (364 days).

Like U.S. Treasury bills and Benchmark Bills, Reference Bills are sold weekly using a Dutch auction. 1-month and 2-month Reference Bills are auctioned each week on Monday, while 3-month maturities are auctioned weekly on Tuesday. The 6-month and 1-year Reference Bills are auctioned every four weeks on Tuesday on an alternating schedule such that every two weeks either a 6-month or a 1-year maturity will be auctioned. In order to give their investors flexibility, Freddie Mac offers multiple settlement dates. For Reference bills auctioned on Mondays, investors may choose between cash and regular settlement dates. For those auctioned on Tuesdays, investors may choose between cash, regular, and skip-day settlement dates. Auctions of Reference Bills are announced on Thursday for the following week and have a minimum size of $1 billion.

Federal Home Loan Bank System

The Federal Home Loan Bank System ("FHLBank System") issues discount notes. Like the other discount notes discussed earlier, these securities are unsecured general obligations sold at a discount from par and mature at their face value. Minimum face values are $100,000 with additional increments of $1,000. The maturities range from overnight to 360 days. FHLBank System discount notes are generally offered for sale on a continuous basis generally by one or more of the following ways: (1) auction; (2) sale to dealers as principal; and (3) allocation to selected dealers as agent in accordance with FHLBank System procedures for reoffering the notes to investors.

Federal Farm Credit System

The Federal Farm Credit System (FFCS) issues discount notes that are unsecured, joint obligations of the FFCS. Maturities range from overnight to 365 days with the majority having maturities of less than 90 days. Minimum face values are $5,000 and with $1,000 increments. All discount notes have cash settlement.

The FFCS also issues short-term securities with maturities less than one year that are issued at par and pay interest at maturity. Exhibit 6.6 presents a Bloomberg DES (Security Description) screen for an interest at maturity security that looks much like the certificates of deposits discussed later in this chapter. This security was issued by the FFCS on August 1, 2001 and matured on November 1, 2001. Note that *unlike* most of securities in the money market, the day count convention is 30/360.

EXHIBIT 6.6 Bloomberg Security Description Screen of a Federal Farm Credit System Security

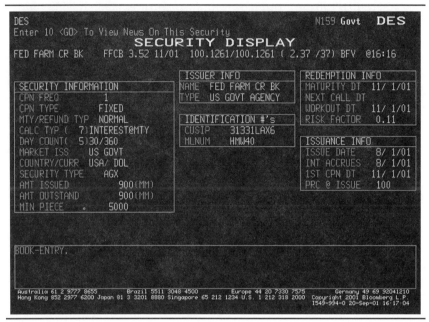

Source: Bloomberg Financial Markets

On the issuance date of August 1, 2001, the yield on this security was 3.52% as can be seen from the upper left-hand side of the screen. Accordingly, the interest at maturity is determined by multiplying the face value, the yield at issuance, and the fraction of a year using a 30/360 day count convention. With the 30/360 day count, all months are assumed to have 30 days and all years are assumed to have 360 days. There are 90 days between August 1, 2001 and November 1, 2001 using a 30/360 day count convention.

The interest at maturity is computed as follows assuming a $1 million face value:

$$\$1,000,000 \times 0.0352 \times (90/360) = \$8,800$$

Exhibit 6.7 presents a Bloomberg Yield Analysis (YA) screen for this security. Suppose a $1,000,000 face value is purchased with a settlement day of September 21, 2001 for the full price (i.e., flat price plus accrued interest) of $1,006,150.03 as can be seen from the "PAYMENT INVOICE" box on the right-hand side of the screen. We know the investor receives $1,008,800 at maturity, so the if buyer holds the security until maturity, she will receive the difference of $2,649.97. This calculation agrees with the "GROSS PROFIT" on the right-hand side of the screen.

A yield calculation which may require some explanation is labeled "DISCOUNT EQUIVALENT" in Exhibit 6.7. This security is similar to a discount security in that the security does not pay a cash flow until maturity. The discount equivalent yield puts discount notes which are quoted on a bank discount basis and interest at maturity securities on the same basis. Namely, suppose the face value of the security is $1,008,800 and the security full price's is $1,006,150.03, what is the yield on the bank discount basis? To see this, recall the formula for the dollar discount (D):

$$D = Y_d \times F \times (t/360)$$

where

Y_d = discount yield
F = face value
t = number of days until maturity

EXHIBIT 6.7   Bloomberg Yield Analysis Screen of a Federal Farm Credit System Security

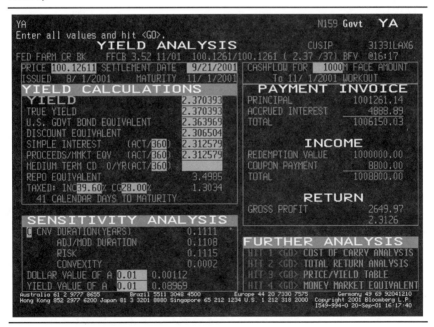

Source: Bloomberg Financial Markets

EXHIBIT 6.8　Bloomberg Security Description Screen of a Farmer Mac Discount Note

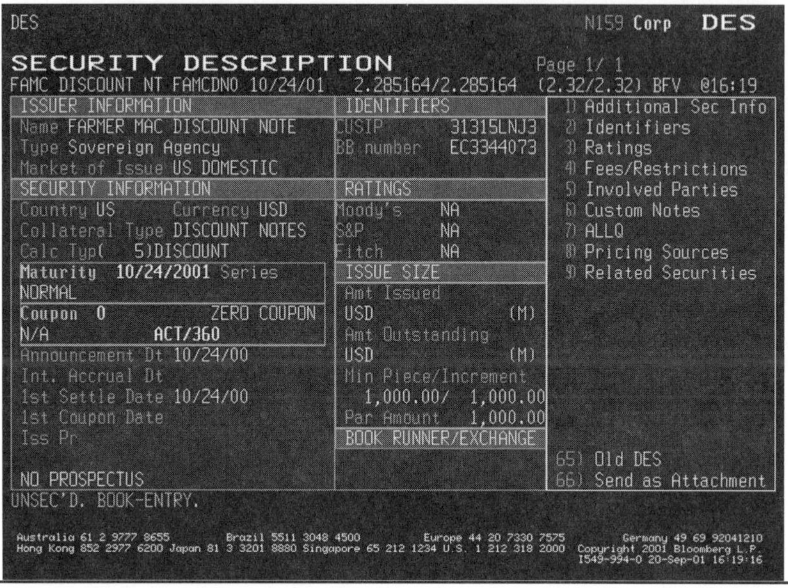

Source: Bloomberg Financial Markets

In this case, the face value is $1,008,800, the dollar discount is $2,649.97, and the actual number of days until maturity is 41 since discount securities use an Actual/360 day count convention. Inserting these numbers into the formula gives us:

$$\$2,649.97 = Y_d \times \$1,008,800 \times (41/360)$$

Solving for Y_d gives us:

$$Y_d = 0.02306504 = 2.306504\%$$

The calculation agrees with the yield calculation displayed in the "YIELD CALCULATIONS" box on the left-hand side of the screen in Exhibit 6.7.

Federal Agricultural Mortgage Corporation

The Federal Agricultural Mortgage Corporation ("Farmer Mac") issues discount notes with maturities that range from overnight to 365 days and are offered on a continuous basis. Farmer Mac discount notes are available with cash-, regular-, and skip-day settlement dates. Exhibit 6.8 presents a Bloomberg DES (Security Description) for a Farmer Mac discount note that was issued on October 24, 2000 and matures on October 24, 2001. The maturity for Farmer Mac discount notes will always fall on a business day. As can be seen in the "ISSUE SIZE" box in bottom center of the screen, the minimum face value is $1,000 with additional increments of $1,000 thereafter.

Exhibit 6.9 is a Bloomberg YA (Yield Analysis) screen for the same Farmer Mac discount note. From this screen, we see that the discount yield is 2.28516% that corresponds to a price of 99.784179 (per $100 of face value) with settlement on September 20, 2001. From the "CASH-FLOW ANALYSIS" box on the right-hand side of the screen, it can be seen that an investor can purchase a $1 million face value package of notes that mature on October 24, 2001 for $997,841.79. The interest income of $2,158.21 is fully taxable at the federal, state, and local levels.

Student Loan Marketing Association

The Student Loan Marketing Association ("Sallie Mae") issues floating-rate debt either tied to the 91-day U.S. Treasury bill rate or, to a lesser extent, 3-month LIBOR, discount notes, and short-term interest at maturity securities that are callable. Exhibit 6.10 presents a Bloomberg DES screen for a Sallie Mae interest at maturity security that was issued on August 2, 2001 and matures on July 23, 2002. The security is callable at par on October 23, 2001, approximately three months after issuance.

EXHIBIT 6.9 Bloomberg Yield Analysis Screen of a Farmer Mac Discount Note

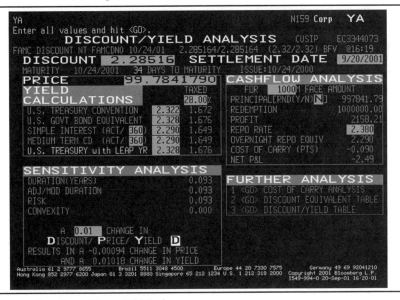

Source: Bloomberg Financial Markets

EXHIBIT 6.10   Bloomberg Security Description Screen of a Sallie Mae Callable
Security

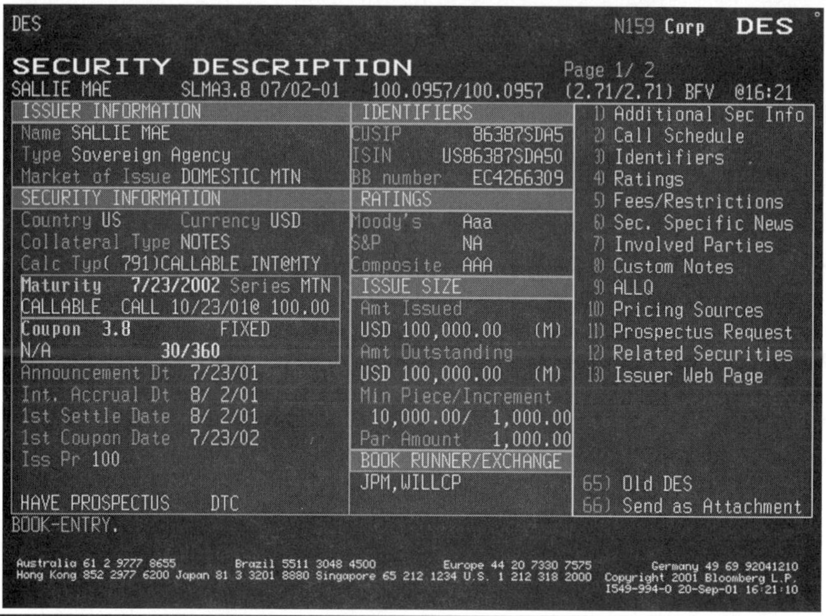

```
DES                                                 N159 Corp   DES °
SECURITY DESCRIPTION                         Page 1/ 2
SALLIE MAE        SLMA3.8 07/02-01   100.0957/100.0957  (2.71/2.71) BFV  @16:21
┌ISSUER INFORMATION─────────┬IDENTIFIERS────────────┐ 1) Additional Sec Info
│Name SALLIE MAE            │CUSIP        86387SDA5  │ 2) Call Schedule
│Type Sovereign Agency      │ISIN      US86387SDA50  │ 3) Identifiers
│Market of Issue DOMESTIC MTN│BB number   EC4266309  │ 4) Ratings
├SECURITY INFORMATION───────┼RATINGS─────────────────┤ 5) Fees/Restrictions
│Country US      Currency USD│Moody's     Aaa        │ 6) Sec. Specific News
│Collateral Type NOTES      │S&P         NA          │ 7) Involved Parties
│Calc Typ( 791)CALLABLE INT@MTY│Composite AAA        │ 8) Custom Notes
│Maturity   7/23/2002 Series MTN├ISSUE SIZE───────────┤ 9) ALLQ
│CALLABLE  CALL 10/23/01@ 100.00│Amt Issued          │ 10) Pricing Sources
│Coupon  3.8          FIXED  │USD 100,000.00   (M)   │ 11) Prospectus Request
│N/A          30/360        │Amt Outstanding        │ 12) Related Securities
│Announcement Dt  7/23/01   │USD 100,000.00   (M)   │ 13) Issuer Web Page
│Int. Accrual Dt  8/ 2/01   │Min Piece/Increment     │
│1st Settle Date  8/ 2/01   │  10,000.00/  1,000.00  │
│1st Coupon Date  7/23/02   │Par Amount    1,000.00  │
│Iss Pr 100                 ├BOOK RUNNER/EXCHANGE─────┤
│                           │JPM,WILLCP             │ 65) Old DES
│HAVE PROSPECTUS    DTC     │                       │ 66) Send as Attachment
│BOOK-ENTRY.                │                       │
└───────────────────────────┴───────────────────────┘
Australia 61 2 9777 8655      Brazil 5511 3048 4500      Europe 44 20 7330 7575      Germany 49 69 92041210
Hong Kong 852 2977 6200 Japan 81 3 3201 8880 Singapore 65 212 1234 U.S. 1 212 318 2000 Copyright 2001 Bloomberg L.P.
                                                                          I549-994-0 20-Sep-01 16:21:10
```

Source: Bloomberg Financial Markets

Tennessee Valley Authority

The Tennessee Valley Authority's discount note program is structured similarly to those described previously. There are two differences nonetheless. First, the face value of TVA's discount notes is $100,000 with additional increments of $1,000 thereafter. Second, interest on these securities is exempt from state and local taxes except estate, inheritance, and gift taxes.

COMMERCIAL PAPER

Commercial paper is a short-term promissory note issued in the open market as an obligation of the issuing entity. Commercial paper is sold at a discount and pays face value at maturity. The discount represents interest to the investor in the period to maturity. Although some issues are in registered form, commercial paper is typically issued in bearer form. Commercial paper is the largest segment of money market exceeding even U.S. Treasury bills with just over $1.5 billion in commercial paper outstanding at the end of April 2001.

The maturity of commercial paper is typically less than 270 days; a typical issue matures in less than 45 days. Naturally, there are reasons for this. First, the Securities and Exchange Act of 1933 requires that securities be registered with the Securities and Exchange Commission (SEC). Special provisions in the 1933 act exempt commercial paper from these registration requirements so long as the maturity does not exceed 270 days. To avoid the costs associated with registering issues with the SEC, issuers rarely issue commercial paper with a maturity exceeding 270 days. In Europe, commercial paper maturities range between 2–365 days. To pay off holders of maturing paper, issuers generally "rollover" outstanding issues; that is, they issue new paper to pay off maturing paper.

Another consideration in determining the maturity is whether the paper would be eligible collateral by a bank if it wanted to borrow from the Federal Reserve Bank's discount window. In order to be eligible, the paper's maturity may not exceed 90 days. Because eligible paper trades at a lower cost than paper that is ineligible, issuers prefer to sell paper whose maturity does not exceed 90 days.

The combination of its short maturity and low credit risk make commercial paper an ideal investment vehicle for short-term funds. Most investors in commercial paper are institutional investors. Money market mutual funds are the largest single investor of commercial paper. Pension funds, commercial bank trust departments, state and local governments, and nonfinancial corporations seeking short-term investments comprise most of the balance.

The market for commercial paper is a wholesale market and transactions are typically sizeable. The minimum round-lot transaction is $100,000. Some issuers will sell commercial paper in denominations of $25,000.

Although commercial paper is the largest sector of the money market, there is relatively little trading in the secondary market, the reason being that most investors in commercial paper follow a "buy and hold" strategy. This is to be expected because investors purchase commercial paper that matches their specific maturity requirements. Any secondary market trading is usually concentrated among institutional investors in a few large, highly rated issues. If investors wish to sell their commercial paper, they can usually sell it back to the original seller—either the dealer or the issuer.

Direct Paper versus Dealer Paper

Commercial paper is classified as either direct paper or dealer paper. *Direct paper* is sold by an issuing firm directly to investors without using a securities dealer as an intermediary. The vast majority of the issuers of direct paper are financial firms. Because financial firms require a continuous source of funds in order to provide loans to customers, they find it cost effective to have a sales force to sell their commercial paper directly to investors. Direct issuers post rates at which they are willing to sell commercial paper with financial information vendors such as Bloomberg, Reuters, and Telerate.

Although commercial paper is a short-term security, it is issued within a longer term program, usually for three to five years for European firms: U.S. commercial paper programs are often open-ended. For example, a company might establish a 5-year commercial paper program with a limit of $100 million. Once the program is established, the company can issue commercial paper up to this amount. The program is continuous and new paper can be issued at any time, daily if required.

In the case of dealer placed commercial paper, the issuer uses the services of a securities firm to sell its paper. Commercial paper sold in this manner is referred to as *dealer paper*.

Commercial Paper Credit Ratings

All investors in commercial paper are exposed to credit risk. Credit risk is the possibility the investor will not receive the timely payment of interest and principal at maturity. While some institutional investors do their own credit analysis, most investors assess a commercial paper's credit risk using ratings by nationally recognized statistical rating organizations (NRSROs). The SEC currently designates only Fitch, Moody's, and Standard & Poor's as NRSROs for rating U.S. corporate debt obligations. Exhibit 6.11 presents the commercial paper ratings from the NRSROs.

The risk that the investor faces is that the borrower will be unable to issue new paper at maturity. This risk is referred to as rollover risk. As a safeguard against rollover risk, commercial paper issuers secure backup lines of credit sometimes called "liquidity enhancement." Most commercial issuers maintain 100% backing because the NRSROs that rate commercial paper usually require a bank line of credit as a precondition for a rating. However, some large issues carry less than 100% backing. Backup lines of credit typically contain a "material adverse change" provision that allows the bank to cancel the credit line if the financial condition of the issuing firm deteriorates substantially.

EXHIBIT 6.11 Ratings of Commercial Paper

	Fitch	Moody's	S&P
Superior	F1+/F1	P1	A1+/A1
Satisfactory	F2	P2	A2
Adequate	F3	P3	A3
Speculative	F4	NP	B, C
Defaulted	F5	NP	D

EXHIBIT 6.12   Bloomberg Direct Issuer Program Description Screen for GE Capital
Commercial Paper

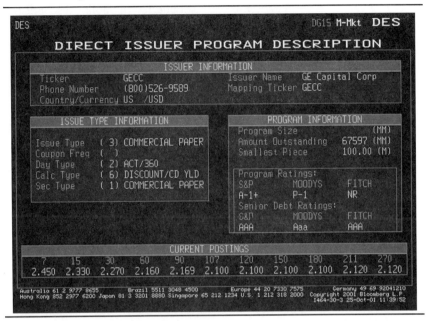

Source: Bloomberg Financial Markets

The commercial paper market is divided into tiers according to credit risk ratings. The "top top tier" consists of paper rated A1+/P1/F1+. "Top tier" is paper rated A1/P1, F1. Next, "split tier" issues are rated either A1/P2 or A2/P1. The "second tier" issues are rated A2/P2/F2. Finally, "third tier" issues are rated A3/P3/F3.

Yields on Commercial Paper

Like Treasury bills, commercial paper is a discount instrument. In other words, it is sold at a price less than its maturity value. The difference between the maturity value and the price paid is the interest earned by the investor, although some commercial paper is issued as an interest-bearing instrument.

As an example, consider some commercial paper issued by GE Capital. Exhibit 6.12 presents Bloomberg's Money Market Security screen for this security that was issued on October 25, 2001 that matures in 45 days. From Bloomberg's Yield Analysis (YA) screen in Exhibit 6.13, we see that commercial paper has a discount yield of 2.27% at the upper left-hand side of the screen. The day count convention in the United States and most European commercial paper markets is Actual/360 with the notable exception being the UK which uses Actual/365. Given the yield on a bank discount basis, the price is found the same way as the price of a Treasury bill described earlier in this chapter, by first solving for the dollar discount (D) as follows:

$$D = Y_d \times F \times (t/360)$$

where

Y_d = discount yield
F = face value
t = number of days until maturity

The price is then

$$\text{price} = F - D$$

With a settlement day of October 25, 2001, the GE Capital commercial paper has 45 days to maturity. Assuming a face value of $100 and a yield on a bank discount basis of 2.27%, D is equal to

$$D = 0.0227 \times \$100 \times 45/360 = \$0.28375$$

EXHIBIT 6.13 Bloomberg Yield Analysis Screen for GE Capital Commercial Paper

```
YA                                                                DG15 M-Mkt  YA
Enter all values and hit <GO>.
                              YIELD ANALYSIS

GECC    GE Capital Corp    COMMERCIAL PAPER    12/09/01 - 10/25/01

                       SETTLEMENT DATE  10/25/01

        DISCOUNT              2.270000      OVERNIGHT REPO EQUIV.   2.276
        PRICE                99.71625       REPO RATE               2.510
        US TREASURY YIELD     2.308
        US GOVT BOND EQUIVALENT 2.314       COST OF CARRY (PTS.)   -0.234
        ANNUAL CD--ACT 360    2.276         ACTUAL DAYS TO MATURITY  45
        S/A CD--ACT 360       2.276

        AFTER TAX YIELD    (TAX 28.00 %)    TREASURY  1.662    CD  1.639
        YIELD VALUE OF AN      0.010        TREASURY  0.01020  CD  0.01006

        NUMBER OF SECURITIES   1000
        PRINCIPAL          997162.50
        REDEMPTION VALUE  1000000.00
        PROFIT                2837.50       COC (PER DAY)         -6.47

Australia 61 2 9777 8655      Brazil 5511 3048 4500    Europe 44 20 7330 7575    Germany 49 69 92041210
Hong Kong 852 2977 6200 Japan 81 3 3201 8880 Singapore 65 212 1234 U.S. 1 212 318 2000  Copyright 2001 Bloomberg L.P.
                                                                    1464-30-3 25-Oct-01 11:41:43
```

Source: Bloomberg Financial Markets

Therefore,

$$\text{price} = \$100 - \$0.28375 = \$99.71625$$

This calculation agrees with the price displayed in the box on the upper left-hand side of the screen in Exhibit 6.13.

The yield on commercial paper is higher than that on Treasury bill yields. There are three reasons for this relationship. First, the investor in commercial paper is exposed to credit risk. Second, interest earned from investing in Treasury bills is exempt from state and local income taxes. As a result, commercial paper has to offer a higher yield to offset this tax advantage offered by Treasury bills. Finally, commercial paper is far less liquid than Treasury bills. The liquidity premium demanded is probably small, however, because commercial paper investors typically follow a buy-and-hold strategy and so are usually less concerned with liquidity.

ASSET-BACKED COMMERCIAL PAPER

Asset-backed securities are discussed in several chapters in this book. Here we will briefly describe asset-backed commercial paper (hereafter, "ABC paper") which is commercial paper issued by either corporations or large financial institutions through a bankruptcy-remote special purpose corporation.

ABC paper is usually issued to finance the purchase of receivables and other similar assets. Some examples of assets underlying these securities include trade receivables (i.e., business-to-business receivables), credit card receivables, equipment loans, automobile loans, health care receivables, tax liens, consumer loans, and manufacturing-housing loans.

According to Moody's, an investor in ABC paper is exposed to three major risks.[1] First, the investor is exposed to credit risk because some portion of the receivables being financed through the issue of ABC paper will default, resulting in losses. Obviously, there will always be defaults so the risk faced by investors is that the losses will be in excess of the credit enhancement. Second is liquidity risk which is the risk that collections on the receivables will not occur quickly enough to make principal and interest payments to investors. Finally, there is structural risk that involves the possibility that the ABC paper conduit may become embroiled in a bankruptcy proceeding, which disrupts payments on maturing commercial paper.

---

[1] Mark H. Adelson, "Asset-Backed Commercial Paper: Understanding the Risks," Moody's Investor Services, April 1993.

MEDIUM-TERM NOTES

A medium-term note (MTN) is a corporate debt instrument with a characteristic akin to commercial paper in that notes are offered continuously to investors by an agent of the issuer. Investors can select from several maturity ranges: 9 months to 1 year, more than 1 year to 18 months, more than 18 months to 2 years, and so on up to any number of years. Medium-term notes issued in the United States are registered with the Securities and Exchange Commission under Rule 415 (i.e., the shelf registration rule) which gives a corporation the maximum flexibility for issuing securities on a continuous basis. MTNs are also issued by non-U.S. corporations, federal agencies, supranational institutions, and sovereign governments. The MTN market is primarily institutional with individual investors being of little import.

The label "medium-term note" is a misnomer. Traditionally, the term "note" or "medium-term" was used to refer to debt issues with a maturity greater than 1 year but less than 15 years. Certainly this is not descriptive of MTNs since they have been issued with maturities from 9 months to 30 years, and even longer. The focus here is on short-term MTNs with maturities of one year or less. MTNs are discussed further in Chapter 11.

Borrowers have flexibility in designing MTNs to satisfy their own needs. They can issue fixed- or floating-rate debt. The coupon payments for MTNs can be denominated in U.S. dollars or in another currency.

A corporation that desires an MTN program will file a shelf registration with the SEC for the offering of securities. While the SEC registration for MTN offerings are between $100 million and $1 billion, once the total is sold, the issuer can file another shelf registration. The registration will include a list of the investment banking firms, usually two to four, that the corporation has arranged to act as agents to distribute the MTNs. The large New York-based investment banking firms dominate the distribution market for MTNs. As an illustration, Exhibit 6.14 presents a Bloomberg Money Market Program Description screen for Amgen Inc. MTN program. There are three things to note. First, across the bottom of the screen, it indicates this a $400 million program. Second, as listed on the left-hand side of the screen, the MTNs issued under this program are denominated in multiple currencies. Third, as can be seen at the bottom of the "PROGRAM INFORMATION" box, two investment banking firms—Bear Stearns (BEAR) and Goldman Sachs (GS)—will distribute the issue. Not all MTNs are sold on an agency basis; some have been underwritten.

EXHIBIT 6.14   Bloomberg Money Market Program Description Screen for an Amgen Medium-Term Note Program

```
DES                                            DG15 M-Mkt  DES
Tab into field and hit <GO> to create a MMKT security
        MONEY MARKET PROGRAM DESCRIPTION
  ISSUER INFORMATION            SECURITY INFORMATION     Options
  Name   AMGEN INC              Maturity        /  /    2)Credit Profile
  Industry  Medical-Biomedical/Gene  Issue date  10/25/01 3)Issuer Info
  PROGRAM INFORMATION           Coupon                   4)Related Security
  Ticker (Issuer )AMGN   Series:   1st Coupon Date 6/ 1/02 5)Related Programs
  Program Type (MTN )Med Term Note                        6)Custom Notes
  Reg Type        o             ID:                       7)Drawdown
  Coupon Freq ( 2)SEMI-ANNUAL                            8)Involved Parties
  Day Type   ( 5) 30/360                                  9)Company News
  Calc Type ( 13)ODD CPN METHOD  Min Piece/Increment    10)Issuer Web Page
  Coupon Dates  6/ 1 12/ 1        1000.00/   1000.00    11)Prospectus
  Country/Curr  US  /MULT        Base CUSIP
  Program Size       400(MM)     03116J
  Guarantor
  Type                           Delivery DTC
  LOC Amount         (M) Exp:
  Paying Agent   CITI            RATING: Long    Short    Program
  Dealer  BEAR   GS              S&P    A        A-1      A
                                 MOODY  A2       P-1      A2
                                 FITCH  NR       NR       NR
 ISSUED UNDER A 400mm US$ PROGRAMME DUE 9 MONTHS OR MORE FROM DATE OF ISSUE.
 Australia 61 2 9777 8655    Brazil 5511 3048 4500    Europe 44 20 7330 75/5   Germany 49 69 92041210
 Hong Kong 852 2977 6200 Japan 81 3 3201 8900 Singapore 65 212 1234 U.S. 1 212 318 2000 Copyright 2001 Bloomberg L.P.
                                                                      1464-30-3 25-Oct-01 15:59:58
```

Source: Bloomberg Financial Markets

An issuer with an active MTN program will post rates for the maturity ranges it wishes to sell. Fixed-rate interest payments are typically on a semiannual basis with the same interest payment dates applicable to all of the notes of a particular series of an issuer. Of course, the final interest payment is made at maturity. Floating-rate MTNs may have more frequent coupon payments. If interest rates are volatile, posted rates may change, sometimes more than once per day. The notes are priced at par which appeals to many investors because they do not have to be concerned with either amortizing premiums or accreting discounts. Any change in new rates will not affect the rates on previously issued notes.

The purchaser may usually set the maturity as any business day with the offered maturity range, subject to the borrower's approval. This is a very important benefit of MTNs as it enables a lender to match maturities with its very own specific requirements. As they are continuously offered, an investor can enter the market when portfolio needs require and will usually find suitable investment opportunities. With underwritten issues, the available supply—both in the new issue and secondary markets—might be unsatisfactory for the portfolio's needs. A particular series of MTNs may have many different maturities but all will be issued under the same indenture. The bulk of the notes sold have maturities of less than five years.

LARGE-DENOMINATION NEGOTIABLE CDS

A certificate of deposit (CD) is a financial asset issued by a depository institution that indicates a specified sum of money that has been deposited with them. Depository institutions issue CDs to raise funds for financing their business activities. A CD bears a maturity date and a specified interest rate or floating-rate formula. While CDs can be issued in any denomination, only CDs in amounts of $100,000 or less are insured by the Federal Deposit Insurance Corporation. There is no limit on the maximum maturity but Federal Reserve regulations stipulate that CDs cannot have a maturity of less than seven days.

A CD may be either nonnegotiable or negotiable. If nonnegotiable, the initial depositor must wait until the CD's maturity date for the return of their deposits plus interest. An early withdrawal penalty is imposed if the depositor chooses to withdraw the funds prior to the maturity date. In contrast, a negotiable CD allows the initial depositor (or any subsequent owner of the CD) to sell the CD in the open market prior to the maturity date.

There are two types of negotiable CDs. The first is the large-denomination CD, usually issued in denominations of $1 million or more. The second type is the small-denomination CD (less than $100,000) which is a retail-oriented product. Our focus here is on the large-denomination negotiable CD with maturities of one year or less and we refer to them as simply CDs throughout the chapter.

CD Issuers

CDs whose cash flows are denominated in U.S. dollars can be classified into four types according to the issuing institution. First are the CDs issued by domestic banks. Second are CDs that are denominated in U.S. dollars but are issued outside the United States. These CDs are called *Eurodollar CDs* or *Euro CDs*. A third type of CD is called a *Yankee CD* which is a CD denominated in U.S. dollars and issued by a non-U.S. bank with a branch in the United States. Finally, thrift CDs are those issued by savings and loans and savings banks.

Money center banks and large regional banks are the primary issuers of domestic CDs. Most CDs are issued with a maturity of less than one year. Those issued with a maturity greater than one year are called *term CDs*.

Unlike the discount instruments discussed in this chapter, yields on domestic CDs are quoted on an interest-bearing basis. CDs with a maturity of one year or less pay interest at maturity (i.e., simple interest). The day count convention is Actual/360. Domestic CDs issued in the United Kingdom denominated in pounds sterling are quoted the same way except the day count convention is Actual/365.

Eurodollar CDs are U.S. dollar-denominated CDs issued primarily in London by U.S., Canadian, European, and Japanese banks. The CDs earn a fixed rate of interest related to dollar LIBOR. The term LIBOR comes from the *London Interbank Offered Rate* and is the interest rate at which one London bank offers funds to another London bank of acceptable credit quality in the form of a cash deposit. The rate is "fixed" by the British Bankers Association every business morning by the average of the rates supplied by member banks. The LIBID is the market's "bid" rate—the rate at which banks pay for funds in the London market. The quote spread for a selected maturity is therefore the difference between LIBOR and LIBID.

CD Yields

The yield quoted on a CD is a function of the credit quality of the issuing bank, its expected liquidity level in the market, and of course the CD's maturity as this will be considered relative to the money market yield curve. As CDs are issued by depository institutions as part of their short-term funding and liquidity requirement, issue volumes are driven by the demand for loans and availability of alternative sources for potential borrowers. However, the credit quality of the issuing bank is the primary consideration. In the U.S. market, "prime" CDs—issued by highly rated domestic banks—trade at a lower yield than "non-prime" CDs. Similarly, in the U.K. market, the lowest yield is paid by "clearer" CDs which are issued by the clearing banks (e.g., RBS NatWest plc, HSBC and Barclays plc). In both markets, CDs issued by foreign financial institutions such as French or Japanese banks will trade at higher yields.

CD yields are higher than yields on Treasury securities of like maturity. The spread is due primarily to the credit risk that a CD investor is exposed to and the fact that CDs offer less liquidity. The spread due to credit risk will vary with both economic conditions in general and confidence in the banking system in particular, increasing in times when the market's risk aversion is high or when there is a crisis in the banking system.

Eurodollar CDs offer a higher yield than U.S. domestic CDs on average. There are three reasons that account for this. First, there are reserve requirements imposed by the Federal Reserve on CDs issued by U.S. banks in the United States that do not apply to issuers of Eurodollar CDs. The reserve requirement effectively raises the cost of funds to the issuing bank because it cannot invest all the proceeds it receives from the issuance of the CD and the amount that must be kept as reserves will not earn a return for the bank. Because it will earn less on funds raised by selling domestic CDs, the domestic issuing bank will pay less on its domestic CD than on a Euro CD. Second, the bank issuing the CD must pay an insurance premium to the FDIC, which again raises the cost of funds. Finally, Euro CDs are dollar obligations that are payable by an entity operating under a foreign jurisdiction, exposing the holders to a risk (called sovereign risk) that their claim may not be enforced by the foreign jurisdiction. As a result, a portion of the spread between the yield offered on Euro CDs and domestic CDs reflects what can be thought of as a sovereign risk premium. This premium varies with the degree of confidence in the international banking system.

FEDERAL FUNDS

Depository institutions are required to hold reserves to meet their reserve requirements. The level of the reserves that a depository institution must maintain is based on its average daily deposits over the previous 14 days. To meet these requirements, depository institutions hold reserves at their district Federal Reserve Bank. These reserves are called *federal funds* .

Because no interest is earned on federal funds, a depository institution that maintains federal funds in excess of the amount required incurs an opportunity cost of the interest forgone on the excess reserves. Correspondingly, there are also depository institutions whose federal funds are short of the amount required. The federal funds market is where depository institutions buy and sell federal funds to address this imbalance. Typically, smaller depository institutions (e.g., smaller commercial banks, some thrifts, and credit unions) almost always have excess reserves while money center banks usually find themselves short of reserves and must make up the deficit. The supply of federal funds is controlled by the Federal Reserve through its daily open market operations.

Most transactions involving federal funds last for only one night; that is, a depository institution with insufficient reserves that borrows excess reserves from another financial institution will typically do so for the period of one full day. Because these reserves are loaned for only a short time, federal funds are often referred to as "overnight money."

One way that depository institutions with a required reserves deficit can bring reserves to the required level is to enter into a repurchase agreement (as described later) with a counterparty other than a financial institution. The repurchase agreement (which consists of the sale of a security and an agreement to repurchase it later) will provide funds for a short period of time, after which the bank buys back the security as previously agreed. Of course, an alternative to the repo is for the bank to borrow federal funds from a depository institution that holds excess reserves.

Thus, depository institutions view the repo market and the federal funds market as close substitutes.

Federal Funds Rate

The interest rate at which federal funds are bought (borrowed) by depository institutions that need these funds and sold (lent) by depository institutions that have excess federal funds is called the federal funds rate. The federal funds is a benchmark short-term interest rate. Indeed, other short-term interest rates (e.,g, Treasury bills) often move in tandem with movements in the federal funds rate. The rate most often cited for the federal funds market is known as the *effective federal funds rate* . The daily effective federal funds rate is a volume-weighted average of rates for federal fund trades arranged through the major New York brokers.

Although the term of most federal funds transactions is overnight, there are longer-term transactions that range from one week to one year. Trading typically takes place directly between buyer and seller, usually between a large bank and one of its correspondent banks. Some federal funds transactions require the use of a broker. The broker stays in constant touch with prospective buyers/sellers, arranging deals between them for a commission. Brokers provide another service to this market in (normally) unsecured loans because they often can give lenders credit analyses of borrowers if the lenders have not done business with them previously.

BANKERS ACCEPTANCES

A *bankers acceptance* is a written promise issued by a borrower to a bank to repay borrowed funds. The lending bank lends funds and in return accepts the ultimate responsibility to repay the loan to its holder, hence the name—bankers acceptance. The acceptance is negotiable and can be sold in the secondary market. The investor who buys the acceptance can collect the loan on the day repayment is due. If the borrower defaults, the investor has legal recourse to the bank that made the first acceptance. Bankers acceptances are also known as bills of exchange, bank bills, trade bills, or commercial bills.

Essentially, bankers acceptances are instruments created to facilitate commercial trade transactions. The use of bankers acceptances to finance commercial transactions is known as acceptance financing. The transactions in which acceptances are created include the import and export of goods, the storage and shipping of goods between two overseas countries where neither the importer nor the exporter is based in the home country, and the storage and shipping of goods between two entities based at home.

Bankers acceptances are sold on a discounted basis just like Treasury bills and commercial paper. The rate that a bank charges a customer for issuing a bankers acceptance is a function of the rate at which the bank believes it will be able to sell it in the secondary market. A commission is added to this rate. The major investors in bankers acceptances are money market mutual funds and municipal entities.

Bankers acceptances have declined in importance in recent years in favor of other forms of financing. There are several reasons that account for this decline. First, the rise in financial disintermediation has reduced corporations' dependence on bank financing in that they now have access to a wider range of funding options (e.g., commercial paper). Second is the vicious circle of low liquidity which leads to less issuance and so on. Third, in July 1984, the Federal Reserve discontinued the use of bankers acceptances as collateral for repurchase agreements when conducting open market operations.

The Creation of a Bankers Acceptance

The most efficient way to explain the creation of a bankers acceptance is by an illustration. The following fictitious parties are involved in this process:

- PCs For Less plc, a firm in London that sells a wide variety of information appliances;
- Kameto Ltd., a manufacturer of personal computers based in Japan
- ABC Bank plc, a clearing bank based in London
- Samurai Bank, a bank based in Japan
- Palmerston Bank plc, another bank based in London
- Adam Smith Investors plc, a money market fund based in Edinburgh

PCs For Less and Kameto Ltd. are preparing to enter into a deal in which PCs For Less will import a consignment of personal computers (PCs) with a transaction value of £1 million. However, Kameto Ltd. is concerned about the ability of PCs For Less to make payment on the PCs when they are delivered. To circumvent this uncertainty, both parties decided to fund the transaction using bankers acceptance financing. The terms of the transaction are that payment must be made by PCs For Less within 60 days after the PCs have been shipped to the United Kingdom. In determining whether it is willing to accept the £1 million, Kameto Ltd. must calculate the present value of the amount because it will not be receiving this sum until 60 days after shipment. Therefore, both parties agree to the following terms:

- PCs For Less arranges with its banker, ABC Bank plc, to issue a letter of credit (LOC, also known as a time draft). The LOC states that ABC Bank plc will guarantee the payment of £1 million that PCs For Less must make to Kameto 60 days from shipment. The LOC is sent by

ABC Bank to Kameto's bankers who are Samurai Bank. On the receipt of the LOC, Samurai Bank notifies Kameto, who will then ship the PCs. After the PCs are shipped, Kameto presents the shipping documents to Samurai and receives the present value of £1 million. This completes the transaction for Kameto Ltd.

■ Samurai Bank presents the LOC and the shipping documents to ABC Bank plc. The latter will stamp the LOC as "accepted", thus creating a bankers acceptance. This means that ABC Bank plc agrees to pay the holder of the bankers acceptance the sum of £1 million on the acceptance's maturity date. PCs For Less will receive the shipping documents so that it can then take delivery of the PCs once it signs a note or some other financing arrangement with ABC Bank plc.

At this point, the holder of the bankers acceptance is Samurai Bank and it has the following two choices available: (1) the bank may retain the bankers acceptance in its loan portfolio or (2) it may request that ABC Bank plc make a payment of the present value of £1 million. Let's assume that Samurai Bank elects to request payment of the present value of £1 million. Now the holder of the bankers acceptance is ABC Bank plc. It also has two choices that it can make: (1) it may retain the bankers acceptance as an investment or (2) it may sell it to another investor. Once again, assume it chooses the latter, and one of its clients, Adam Smith Investors, is interested in a high-quality security with same maturity as the bankers acceptance. Accordingly, ABC Bank plc sells the acceptance to Adam Smith Investors at the present value of £1 million calculated using the relevant discount rate for paper of that maturity and credit quality. Alternatively, it may have sold the acceptance to another bank, such as Palmerston Bank plc that also creates bankers acceptances. In either case, on the maturity of the bankers acceptance, its holder presents it to ABC Bank plc and receives the maturity value of £1 million, which the bank in turn recovers from PCs For Less plc.

The holder of the bankers acceptance is exposed to credit risk on two fronts: the risk that the original borrower is unable to pay the face value of the acceptance and the risk that the accepting bank will not be able to redeem the paper. For this reason, the rate paid on a bankers acceptance will trade at a spread over the comparable maturity risk-free benchmark security (e.g., U.S. Treasury bills). Investors in acceptances will need to know the identity and credit risk of the original borrower as well as the accepting bank.

Eligible Bankers Acceptances

An accepting bank that chooses to retain a bankers acceptance in its portfolio may be able to use it as collateral for a loan obtained from the central bank during open market operations, for example, the Federal Reserve in the United States and the Bank of England in the United Kingdom. Not all acceptances are eligible to be used as collateral in this manner, as the acceptances must meet certain criteria as specified by the central bank. The main requirements for eligibility are that the acceptance's maturity must not exceed a certain maturity (a maximum of six months in the United States and three months in the United Kingdom) and that it must have been created to finance a self-liquidating commercial transaction. In the United States, eligibility is also important because the Federal Reserve imposes a reserve requirement on funds raised via bankers acceptances that are ineligible. Bankers acceptances sold by an accepting bank are potential liabilities of the bank but reserve requirements impose a limit on the amount of eligible bankers acceptances that a bank may issue. Acceptances eligible for deposit at a central bank offer a lower discount rate than ineligible ones and also act as a benchmark for prices in the secondary market.

FUNDING AGREEMENTS

Funding agreements (FAs) are short-term debt instruments issued by insurance companies. Specifically, a funding agreement is a contract issued by an insurance company that provides the policyholder the right to receive the coupon payments as scheduled and the principal on the maturity date. These contracts are guaranteed by the insurer's general account or a separate account. FAs are not publicly traded and therefore are less liquid than other money market instruments such as commercial paper. In recent years, medium-term notes (U.S. MTNs and Global MTNs) have become increasingly popular. These are securitizations whose cash flows are backed by a portfolio of FAs.

Coupon rates may be either fixed or floating. Reference rates have included U.S. Treasury rates, LIBOR, commercial paper rates, the federal funds rate, and the prime rate. The unique feature of FAs is that the holder of this security has an embedded put option with a 7-, 30-, 90-, 180-day or 1-year expiration. Therefore, FAs are putable back to the issuer at par. Yields offered on FAs depend on the credit quality of issuing insurer, the structure of the embedded put option, and the term to maturity.

The major investors in FAs are money market mutual funds. Short-dated putable FAs are structured to qualify as *2a-7* eligible money market mutual fund investments because they are illiquid investments since, as we noted earlier, they are not publicly traded.[2] A study by Moody's inves-

---

[2] Information in this paragraph was obtained from "Update on Short-Term Puttable Funding Agreements," Moody's Investors Service, October 2001, p. 9.

tigated the reasons why money market mutual funds invest in FAs. The following reasons were cited:

1. FAs are attractive short-term investments.
2. FAs are highly rated and are "stable value"-type products
3. Investors like FAs as an established product.

REPURCHASE AGREEMENTS

One of the largest segments of the money markets worldwide is the market in repurchase agreements or repo. A most efficient mechanism by which to finance bond positions, repo transactions enable market makers to take long and short positions in a flexible manner, buying and selling according to customer demand on a relatively small capital base. Repo is also a flexible and relatively safe investment opportunity for short-term investors.

A repurchase agreement or "repo" is the sale of security with a commitment by the seller to buy the same security back from the purchaser at a specified price at a designated future date. For example, a dealer who owns a 10-year U.S. Treasury note might agree to sell this security (the "seller") to a mutual fund (the "buyer") for cash today while simultaneously agreeing to buy the same 10-year note back at a certain date in the future (or in some cases on demand) for a predetermined price. The price at which the seller must subsequently repurchase the security is called the repurchase price and the date that the security must be repurchased is called the repurchase date. Simply put, a repurchase agreement is a collateralized loan where the collateral is the security that is sold and subsequently repurchased. One party (the "seller") is borrowing money and providing collateral for the loan; the other party (the 'buyer') is lending money and accepting a security as collateral for the loan. To the borrower, the advantage of a repurchase agreement is that the short-term borrowing rate is lower than the cost of bank financing, as we will see shortly. To the lender, the repo market offers an attractive yield on a short-term secured transaction that is highly liquid. This latter aspect is the focus of the discussion to come. In particular, we will focus on the U.S. repo market.[3]

---

[3] For a discussion of the U.K. repo market, see Chapter 9 in Frank J. Fabozzi, Steven V. Mann, and Moorad Choudhry, *Global Money Markets* (New York, NY: John Wiley & Sons, 2002).

The Basics

Suppose a government securities dealer purchases a 5% coupon Treasury note that matures on August 15, 2011 with a settlement date of Thursday, November 15, 2001. The face amount of the position is $1 million and the note's full price (i.e., flat price plus accrued interest) is $1,044,843.75. Further, suppose the dealer wants to hold the position until the end of the next business day which is Thursday, November 16, 2001. Where does the dealer obtain the funds to finance this position?

Of course, the dealer can finance the position with its own funds or by borrowing from a bank. Typically, the dealer uses a repurchase agreement or "repo" market to obtain financing. In the repo market, the dealer can use the purchased Treasury note as collateral for a loan. The term of the loan and the interest rate a dealer agrees to pay are specified. The interest rate is called the repo rate. When the term of a repo is one day, it is called an overnight repo. Conversely, a loan for more than one day is called a term repo. The transaction is referred to as a repurchase agreement because it calls for the security's sale and its repurchase at a future date. Both the sale price and the purchase price are specified in the agreement. The difference between the purchase (repurchase) price and the sale price is the loan's dollar interest cost.

Let us return now to the dealer who needs to finance the Treasury note that it purchased and plans to hold it overnight. We will illustrate this transaction using Bloomberg's Repo/Reverse Repo Analysis screen (RRRA) that appears in Exhibit 6.15. The settlement date is the day that the collateral must be delivered and the money lent to initiate the transaction. Likewise, the termination date of the repo agreement is November 16, 2001 and appears in the lower left-hand corner. At this point we need to ask, who is the dealer's counterparty (i.e., the lender of funds)? Suppose that one of the dealer's customers has excess funds in the amount of $1,044,843.75 called the "SETTLEMENT MONEY" and is the amount of money loaned in the repo agreement. On November 15, 2001, the dealer would agree to deliver ("sell") $1,044,843.75 worth of Treasury notes to the customer and buy the same Treasury security for an amount determined by the repo rate the next day on November 16, 2001.

Suppose the repo rate in this transaction is 1.83%—see the upper right-hand corner of the screen. Then, as will be explained shortly, the dealer would agree to deliver the Treasury notes for $1,044,843.75 and repurchase the same securities for $1,044,896.86 the next day. The $53.11 difference between the "sale" price of $1,044,843.75 and the repurchase price of $1,044,896.86 is the dollar interest on the financing.

EXHIBIT 6.15   Bloomberg Repo/Reverse Repo Analysis Screen

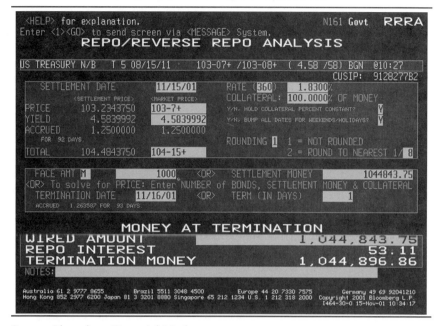

Source: Bloomberg Financial Markets

Repo Interest

The following formula is used to calculate the dollar interest on a repo transaction:

dollar interest = (dollar principal) × (repo rate) × (repo term/360)

Notice that the interest is computed using a day count convention of Actual/360 like most money market instruments. In our illustration, using a repo rate of 1.83% and a repo term of one day, the dollar interest is $53.11 as shown below:

$$\$53.11 = \$1,044,843.75 \times 0.0183 \times (1/360)$$

This calculation agrees with repo interest as calculated in the lower right-hand corner of Exhibit 6.15.

The advantage to the dealer of using the repo market for borrowing on a short-term basis is that the rate is lower than the cost of bank financing for reasons explained shortly. From the customer's perspective (i.e., the lender), the repo market offers an attractive yield on a short-term secured transaction that is highly liquid.

Reverse Repo and Market Jargon

In the illustration presented above, the dealer is using the repo market to obtain financing for a long position. Dealers can also use the repo market to cover a short position. For example, suppose a government dealer established a short position in the 30-year Treasury bond three days ago and must now cover the position—namely, deliver the securities. The dealer accomplishes this task by engaging in a reverse repo. In a reverse repo, the dealer agrees to buy securities at a specified price with a commitment to sell them back at a later date for another specified price. In this case, the dealer is making collateralized loan to its customer. The customer is lending securities and borrowing funds obtained from the collateralized loan to create leverage.

There is a great deal of Wall Street jargon surrounding repo transactions. In order to decipher the terminology, remember that one party is lending money and accepting a security as collateral for the loan; the other party is borrowing money and providing collateral to borrow the money. By convention, whether the transaction is called a repo or a reverse repo is determined by viewing the transaction from the dealer's perspective. If the dealer is borrowing money from a customer and providing securities as collateral, the transaction is called a repo. If the dealer is borrowing securities (which serve as collateral) and lends money to a customer, the transaction is called a reverse repo.

Types of Collateral

While in our illustration, we use a Treasury security as collateral, the collateral in a repo is not limited to government securities. Money market instruments, federal agency securities, and mortgage-backed securities are also used. In some specialized markets, even whole loans are used as collateral.

Documentation

Most repo market participants in the United States use the Master Repurchase Agreement published by the Bond Market Association (BMA). In Europe, the Global Master Repurchase Agreement published by the BMA and the International Securities Market Association has become widely accepted.[4]

Credit Risks

Just as in any borrowing/lending agreement, both parties in a repo transaction are exposed to credit risk. This is true even though there may be high-quality collateral underlying the repo transaction. Consider our initial

---

[4] The agreements may be downloaded from www.isma.org.

example in Exhibit 6.15 where the dealer uses U.S. Treasuries as collateral to borrow funds. Let us examine under which circumstances each counterparty is exposed to credit risk.

Suppose the dealer (i.e., the borrower) defaults such that the Treasuries are not repurchased on the repurchase date. The investor gains control over the collateral and retains any income owed to the borrower. The risk is that Treasury yields have risen subsequent to the repo transaction such that the market value of the collateral is worth less than the unpaid repurchase price. Conversely, suppose the investor (i.e., the lender) defaults such that the investor fails to deliver the Treasuries on the repurchase date. The risk is that Treasury yields have fallen over the agreement's life such the dealer now holds an amount of dollars worth less than the market value of the collateral. In this instance, the investor is liable for any excess of the price paid by the dealer for replacement securities over the repurchase price.

Repo Margin

While both parties are exposed to credit risk in a repo transaction, the lender of funds is usually in the more vulnerable position. Accordingly, the repo is structured to reduce the lender's credit risk. Specifically, the amount lent should be less than the market value of the security used as collateral, thereby providing the lender some cushion should the collateral's market value decline. The amount by which the market value of the security used as collateral exceeds the value of the loan is called *repo margin* or "haircut." Repo margins vary from transaction to transaction and are negotiated between the counterparties based on factors such as the following: term of the repo agreement, quality of the collateral, creditworthiness of the counterparties, and the availability of the collateral. Minimum repo margins are set differently across firms and are based on models and/or guidelines created by their credit departments. Repo margin is generally between 1% and 3%. For borrowers of lower credit worthiness and/or when less liquid securities are used as collateral, the repo margin can be 10% or more.[5]

To illustrate the role of a haircut in a repurchase agreement, let us once again return to the government securities dealer who purchases a 5% coupon, 10-year Treasury note and needs financing overnight. Recall, the face amount of the position is $1 million and the note's full price (i.e., flat price plus accrued interest) is $1,044,843.75. As before, we will use Bloomberg's RRRA screen to illustrate the transaction in Exhibit 6.16.

---

[5] At the time of this writing, the Basel Committee on Banking Supervision is proposing standards for repo margins for capital-market driven transactions (i.e., repo/reverse repos, securities borrowing/lending, derivatives transactions, and margin lending). These standards would only apply to banks.

EXHIBIT 6.16   Bloomberg Repo/Reverse Repo Analysis Screen

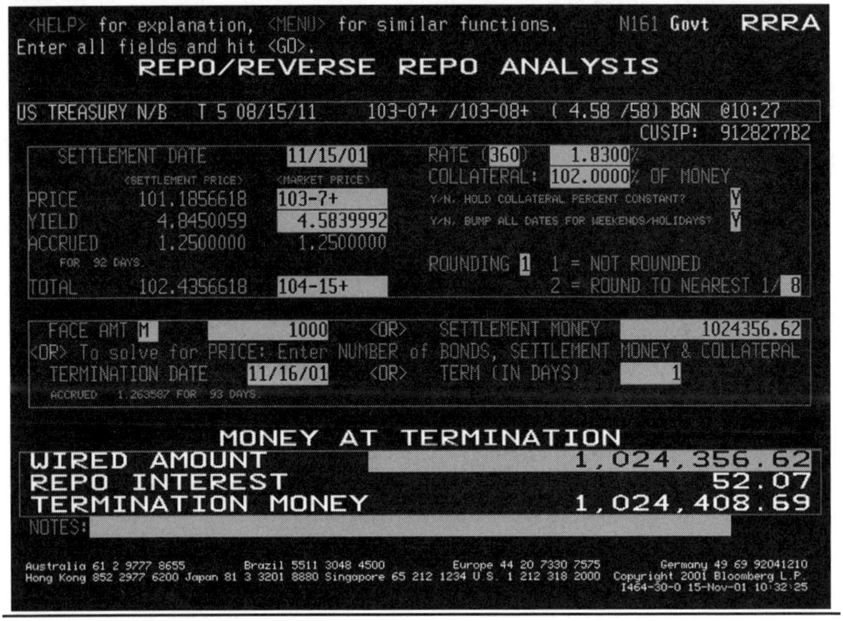

Source: Bloomberg Financial Markets

When a haircut is included, the amount the customer is willing to lend is reduced by a given percentage of the security's market value. In this case, the collateral is 102% of the amount being lent. This percentage appears in the box labeled "COLLATERAL" in the upper left-hand corner of the screen. Accordingly, to determine the amount being lent, we divide the note's full price of $1,044,843.75 by 1.02 to obtain $1,024,356.62 which is labeled "SETTLEMENT MONEY" located on the right-hand side of the screen. Suppose the repo rate in this transaction is 1.83%. Then, the dealer would agree to deliver the Treasury notes for $1,024,356.62 and repurchase the same securities for $1,024,408.69 the next day. The $52.07 difference between the "sale" price of $1,024,356.62 and the repurchase price of $1,024,408.69 is the dollar interest on the financing. Using a repo rate of 1.83% and a repo term of 1 day, the dollar interest is calculated as shown below:

$$\$52.07 = \$1,024,356.62 \times 0.0183 \times (1/360)$$

This calculation agrees with the repo interest as calculated in the lower right-hand corner of Exhibit 6.16.

Marking the Collateral to Market

Another practice to limit credit risk is to mark the collateral to market on a regular basis. Marking a position to market means simply recording the position's value at its market value. When the market value changes by a certain percentage, the repo position is adjusted accordingly. The decline in market value below a specified amount will result in a margin deficit. The Master Repurchase Agreement gives the "seller" (the dealer/borrower in our example) the option to remedy the margin deficit by either providing additional cash or by transferring additional securities that are reasonably acceptable to the buyer (the investor/lender in our example). Conversely, if the market value rises above the amount required by margin, this results in margin excess. If this occurs, the "buyer" will remedy the excess by either transferring cash equal to the amount of the excess or returning a portion of the collateral to the "seller."

Delivery of the Collateral

One concern in structuring a repurchase agreement is delivery of the collateral to the lender. The most obvious procedure is for the borrower to actually deliver the collateral to the lender or to the cash lender's clearing agent. If this procedure is followed, the collateral is said to be "delivered out." At the end of the repo term, the lender returns collateral to the borrower in exchange for the repurchase price (i.e., the amount borrowed plus interest).

The drawback of this procedure is that it may be too expensive, particularly for short-term repos (e.g., overnight) owing to the costs associated with delivering the collateral. Indeed, the cost of delivery is factored into the repo rate of the transaction in that if delivery is required this translates into a lower repo rate paid by the borrower. If delivery of collateral is not required, an otherwise higher repo rate is paid. The risk to the lender of not taking actual possession of the collateral is that the borrower may sell the security or use the same security as collateral for a repo with another counterparty.

As an alternative to delivering out the collateral, the lender may agree to allow the borrower to hold the security in a segregated customer account. The lender still must bear the risk that the borrower may use the collateral fraudulently by offering it as collateral for another repo transaction. If the borrower of the cash does not deliver out the collateral, but instead holds it, then the transaction is called a *hold-in-custody repo* (HIC repo). Despite the credit risk associated with a HIC repo, it is used in some transactions when the collateral is difficult to deliver (e.g., whole loans) or the transaction amount is relatively small and the lender of the funds is comfortable with the borrower's reputation.

Investors participating in a HIC repo must ensure: (1) they transact only with dealers of good credit quality since a HIC repo may be perceived as an unsecured transaction and (2) the investor (i.e., the lender of cash) receives a higher rate in order to compensate them for the higher credit risk involved. In the U.S. market, there have been cases where dealer firms that went into bankruptcy and defaulted on loans were found to have pledged the same collateral for multiple HIC transactions.

Another method for handling the collateral is for the borrower to deliver the collateral to the lender's custodial account at the borrower's clearing bank. The custodian then has possession of the collateral that it holds on the lender's behalf. This method reduces the cost of delivery because it is merely a transfer within the borrower's clearing bank. If, for example, a dealer enters into an overnight repo with Customer A, the next day the collateral is transferred back to the dealer. The dealer can then enter into a repo with Customer B for, say, five days without having to redeliver the collateral. The clearing bank simply establishes a custodian account for Customer B and holds the collateral in that account. In this type of repo transaction, the clearing bank is an agent to both parties. This specialized type of repo arrangement is called a *tri-party repo* .

Determinants of the Repo Rate

Just as there is no single interest rate, there is not one repo rate. The repo rate varies from transaction to transaction depending on a number of factors: quality of the collateral, term of the repo, delivery requirement, availability of the collateral, and the prevailing federal funds rate. Panel A of Exhibit 6.17 presents a Bloomberg screen (MMR) that contains repo and reverse repo rates for maturities of 1 day, 1 week, 2 weeks, 3 weeks, 1 month, 2 months, and 3 months using U.S. Treasuries as collateral on November 15, 2001. Panel B presents repo and reverse repo rates with agency securities as collateral. Note how the rates differ by maturity and type of collateral. For example, the repo rates are higher when agency securities are used as collateral versus governments. Moreover, the rates generally decrease with maturity that mirrors the inverted Treasury yield curve on that date.

Another pattern evident in these data is that repo rates are lower than the reverse repo rates when matched by collateral type and maturity. These repo (reverse repo) rates can be viewed as the rates at which the dealer will borrow (lend) funds. Alternatively, repo (reverse repo) rates are prices at which dealers are willing to buy (sell) collateral. While a dealer firm primarily uses the repo market as a vehicle for financing its inventory and covering short positions, it will also use the repo market to run a "matched book." A dealer runs a matched book by simultaneously entering into a repo and a reverse repo for the same collateral with the same maturity. The dealer does so to capture the spread at which it enters into a repurchase agreement (i.e., an agreement to borrow funds) and a reverse repurchase agreement (i.e., an agreement to lend funds). For example, suppose that a dealer enters into a term repo for one month with a money market mutual fund and a reverse repo with a corporate credit union for one month for which the collateral is identical. In this arrangement, the dealer is borrowing funds from the money market mutual fund and lending funds to the corporate credit union. From Panel A in Exhibit 6.17, we find that the repo rate for a one-month repurchase agreement is 1.90% and repo rate for a one-month reverse repurchase agreement is 1.97%. If these two positions are established simultaneously, then the dealer is borrowing at 1.90% and lending at 1.97% thereby locking in a spread of seven basis points. The term matched book is something of a misnomer in that most matched books are deliberately mismatched to take advantage of a trader's expectation of the short-term yield curve. Traders engage in positions to take advantage of (1) short-term interest rate movements and (2) anticipated demand and supply in the underlying bond.

The delivery requirement for collateral also affects the level of the repo rate. If delivery of the collateral to the lender is required, the repo rate will be lower. Conversely, if the collateral can be deposited with the bank of the borrower, a higher repo rate will be paid. For example, on November 15, 2001, Bloomberg reports that the general collateral rate (repos backed by non-specific collateral) is 2.10% if delivery of the collateral is required. For a tri-party repo discussed earlier, the general collateral rate is 2.13%.

The more difficult it is to obtain the collateral, the lower the repo rate. To understand why this is so, remember that the borrower (or equivalently the seller of the collateral) has a security that lenders of cash want for whatever reason. Such collateral is said to be "on special." Collateral that does not share this characteristic is referred to as "general collateral." The party that needs collateral that is "on special" will be willing to lend funds at a lower repo rate in order to obtain the collateral. For example, on November 14, 2001, Bloomberg reports the on-the-run 5-year Treasury note (3.5% coupon maturing November 15, 2006) was "on special" such that the overnight repo rate was 0.65%. At the time, the general collateral rate was 2.13%.

While these factors determine the repo rate on a particular transaction, the federal funds rate discussed earlier determines the general level of repo rates. The repo rate generally will trade lower than the federal funds rate, because a repo involves collateralized borrowing while a federal funds transaction is unsecured borrowing. For example, for the period October 2, 2000 to April 6, 2001 (129 observations) the overnight repo rate was, on average, 8.17 basis points below the federal funds rate.

EXHIBIT 6.17   Bloomberg Screens Presenting Repo and Reverse Repo Rates for Various Maturities and Collateral
Panel A: U.S. Treasuries

```
 Press 98<GO> to make a copy, 99<GO> to clear news alerts.      M-Mkt  MMR
 10:35      REPO/REVERSE  RP  O/N & TERM        Page 1 / 3
 94<GO> View News.
  SECURITY        | TIME  | LAST  | CHANGE | OPEN  | HIGH  | LOW   | CLOSE
 GOVERNMENT
 Repo
 Dealer pays int
  4)RPGT01D        10:05    2.11    +.04    2.11    2.11    2.11    2.07
  5)RPGT01W        10:05    1.95    -.02    1.95    1.95    1.95    1.97
  6)RPGT02W        10:05    1.93    -.05    1.93    1.93    1.93    1.98
  7)RPGT03W        10:05    1.98    -.02    1.98    1.98    1.98    2.00
  8)RPGT01M        10:05    1.90    -.05    1.90    1.90    1.90    1.95
  9)RPGT02M        10:05    1.90    --      1.90    1.90    1.90    1.90
 10)RPGT03M        10:05    1.83    -.05    1.83    1.83    1.83    1.88
 Reverse Repo
 Dealer earns int
 13)RVGT01D        10:05    2.15    +.05    2.15    2.15    2.15    2.10
 14)RVGT01W        10:05    2.10    +.07    2.10    2.10    2.10    2.03
 15)RVGT02W        10:05    2.00    -.03    2.00    2.00    2.00    2.03
 16)RVGT03W        10:05    2.05    --      2.05    2.05    2.05    2.05
 17)RVGT01M        10:05    1.97    -.04    1.97    1.97    1.97    2.01
 18)RVGT02M        10:05    1.95    --      1.95    1.95    1.95    1.95
 19)RVGT03M        10:05    1.95    +.04    1.95    1.95    1.95    1.91
 PAGE FOR MTGE REPO
 Australia 61 2 9777 8655    Brazil 5511 3048 4500    Europe 44 20 7330 7575   Germany 49 69 92041210
 Hong Kong 852 2977 6200 Japan 81 3 3201 8880 Singapore 65 212 1234 U.S. 1 212 318 2000  Copyright 2001 Bloomberg L.P.
                                                                      1464-30-0 15-Nov-01 10:35:24
```

Panel B: Agency Securities

```
 Press 98<GO> to make a copy, 99<GO> to clear news alerts.      M-Mkt  MMR
 10:36      REPO/REVERSE  RP  O/N & TERM        Page 3 / 3
 94<GO> View News.
  SECURITY        | TIME  | LAST  | CHANGE | OPEN  | HIGH  | LOW   | CLOSE
 AGENCY
 Repo
  3)RPAG01D        10:05    2.15    +.05    2.15    2.15    2.15    2.10
  4)RPAG01W        n.a.      .00    n.a.    n.a.    n.a.     .00    n.a.
  5)RPAG03W        10:05    2.05    +.01    2.05    2.05    2.05    2.04
  6)RPAG01M        n.a.      .00    n.a.    n.a.    n.a.     .00    n.a.
  7)RPAG02M        10:05    2.00    +.01    2.00    2.00    2.00    1.99
  8)RPAG03M        10:05    1.85    -.09    1.85    1.85    1.85    1.94

 Reverse Repo
 11)RVAG01D        10:05    2.22    +.08    2.22    2.22    2.22    2.14
 12)RVAG01W        10:05    2.10    +.02    2.10    2.10    2.10    2.08
 13)RVAG02W        10:05    2.09    +.01    2.09    2.09    2.09    2.08
 14)RVAG03W        10:05    2.10    --      2.10    2.10    2.10    2.10
 15)RVAG01M        10:05    2.05    -.01    2.05    2.05    2.05    2.06
 16)RVAG02M        10:05    2.05    --      2.05    2.05    2.05    2.05
 17)RVAG03M        10:05    2.00    +.01    2.00    2.00    2.00    1.99
 Australia 61 2 9777 8655    Brazil 5511 3048 4500    Europe 44 20 7330 7575   Germany 49 69 92041210
 Hong Kong 852 2977 6200 Japan 81 3 3201 8880 Singapore 65 212 1234 U.S. 1 212 318 2000  Copyright 2001 Bloomberg L.P.
                                                                      1464-30-0 15-Nov-01 10:36:05
```

Source: Bloomberg Financial Markets

Callable Repo

In a callable repo arrangement, the lender of cash in a term fixed-rate repo has the option to terminate the repo early. In other words, the repo transaction has an embedded interest rate option which benefits the lender of cash if rates rise during the repo's term. If rates rise, the lender may exercise his or her option to call back the cash and reinvest at a higher rate. For this reason, a callable repo will trade at a lower repo rate than an otherwise identical conventional repo.

CHAPTER 7

U.S. Treasury Securities

Frank J. Fabozzi, Ph.D., CFA
Adjunct Professor of Finance
School of Management
Yale University

Michael J. Fleming, Ph.D.*
Senior Economist
Federal Reserve Bank of New York

United States Treasury securities are direct obligations of the U.S. government issued by the Department of the Treasury. They are backed by the full faith and credit of the U.S. government and are therefore considered to be free of credit risk. Issuance to pay off maturing debt and raise needed cash has created a stock of marketable Treasuries that totaled $2.8 trillion on June 30, 2001.[1] Treasuries trade in a highly liquid round-the-clock secondary market with high levels of trading activity and narrow bid-ask spreads. Despite the absence of credit risk and the high level of liquidity, an investor in a Treasury security is still subject to interest

---

[1] The stock of nonmarketable Treasury securities on the same date totaled $2.9 trillion. Of this, $2.4 trillion was non-public debt (held in government accounts), $0.2 trillion was held by private investors in the form of U.S. savings bonds, and $0.2 trillion was held in a special series by state and local governments (Monthly Statement of the Public Debt, www.publicdebt.ustreas.gov/opd/opddload.htm). This chapter focuses on marketable Treasury securities.

---

*The views expressed in this chapter are those of the authors' and not necessarily those of the Federal Reserve Bank of New York or the Federal Reserve System. The research assistance of April Bang is gratefully acknowledged.

185

rate risk and non-U.S. investors who seek to convert payments from U.S. dollars to their local currency are exposed to currency risk. As will be explained, there are Treasury securities that are available that eliminate inflation risk and reinvestment risk.

Treasury securities serve several important purposes in financial markets. Due to their liquidity and well-developed derivatives markets, Treasuries are used extensively to price, as well as hedge positions in, other fixed-income securities. Exemption of interest income from state and local taxes also helps make Treasuries a popular investment asset to institutions and individuals. Moreover, by virtue of their creditworthiness and vast supply, Treasuries are a key reserve asset of central banks and other financial institutions.

TYPES OF SECURITIES

Treasuries are issued as either discount or coupon securities. Discount securities pay a fixed amount at maturity, called face value or par value, with no intervening interest payments. Discount securities are so called because they are issued at a price below face value with the return to the investor being the difference between the face value and the issue price. Coupon securities are issued with a stated rate of interest, pay interest every six months, and are redeemed at par value (or principal value) at maturity. Coupon securities are issued at a price close to par value with the return to the investor being primarily the coupon payments received over the security's life.

The Treasury issues securities with original maturities of one year or less as discount securities. These securities are called Treasury bills. The Treasury currently issues bills with original maturities of 13 weeks (3 months) and 26 weeks (6 months), as well as cash-management bills with various maturities. The Treasury announced in July 2001 that it would start issuing bills with 4-week maturities. On June 30, 2001, Treasury bills accounted for $620 billion (22%) of the $2.8 trillion in outstanding marketable Treasury securities. Because their maturity is less than one year, Treasury bills are viewed as part of the money market and were discussed in Chapter 6.

Securities with original maturities of more than 1 year are issued as coupon securities. Coupon securities with original maturities of more than 1 year but not more than 10 years are called *Treasury notes*. Coupon securities with original maturities of more than 10 years are called *Treasury bonds*. The Treasury currently issues notes with maturities of 2 years, 5 years, and 10 years. In October 2001, the Treasury suspended issuance of 30-year Treasury bonds. While a few issues of the outstanding bonds are callable, the Treasury has not issued new callable Treasury securities since 1984. On June 30, 2001 Treasury notes accounted for $1.5 trillion (52%) of the outstanding marketable Treasury securities and Treasury bonds accounted for $617 billion (22%).

In January 1997, the Treasury began selling inflation-indexed securities. The principal of these securities is adjusted for inflation using the consumer price index for urban consumers. Semiannual interest payments are a fixed percentage of the inflation-adjusted principal and the inflation-adjusted principal is paid at maturity. On June 30, 2001, Treasury inflation-indexed notes and bonds accounted for $129 billion (5%) of the outstanding marketable Treasury securities. As these securities are discussed in detail in Chapter 8, the remainder of this chapter focuses on nominal (or fixed-rate) Treasuries.

THE PRIMARY MARKET

Marketable Treasuries are sold in the primary market through sealed-bid, single-price (or uniform price) auctions. Each auction is announced several days in advance by means of a Treasury Department press release or press conference. The announcement provides details of the offering, including the offering amount and the term and type of security being offered, and describes some of the auction rules and procedures. Exhibit 7.1 shows the August 1, 2001 announcement by the Department of the Treasury of the August 2001 auctioning of a 10-year note.

Treasury auctions are open to all entities. Bids must be made in multiples of $1,000 (with a $1,000 minimum) and submitted to a Federal Reserve Bank (or branch) or to the Treasury's Bureau of the Public Debt. Competitive bids must be made in terms of yield and must typically be submitted by 1:00 p.m. eastern time on auction day. Noncompetitive bids must typically be submitted by noon on auction day. While most tenders (or formal offers to buy) are submitted electronically, both competitive and noncompetitive tenders can be made on paper.[2]

All noncompetitive bids from the public up to $1 million for bills and $5 million for coupon securities are accepted. The lowest yield (i.e., highest price) competitive bids are then accepted up to the yield required to cover the amount offered (less the amount of noncompetitive bids). The

---

[2] Commercial bidders, such as broker/dealers and depository institutions, are encouraged to submit tenders electronically by computer, although paper tenders are accepted. Non-commercial bidders are encouraged to submit tenders electronically by phone or Internet, although mailed-in paper tenders are accepted. Bidding procedures are described in detail on the Bureau of the Public Debt's website at www.publicdebt.ustreas.gov.

highest yield accepted is called the *stop-out yield*. All accepted tenders (competitive and noncompetitive) are awarded at the stop-out yield. There is no maximum acceptable yield, and the Treasury does not add to or reduce the size of the offering according to the strength of the bids.

EXHIBIT 7.1   Treasury Announcement of an Auction

DEPARTMENT OF THE TREASURY

TREASURY NEWS

OFFICE OF PUBLIC AFFAIRS • 1500 PENNSYLVANIA AVENUE, N.W. • WASHINGTON, D.C. • 20220 • (202) 622-2960

```
FOR RELEASE WHEN AUTHORIZED AT PRESS CONFERENCE  CONTACT:  Office of Financing
August 1, 2001                                             202/691-3550
                        TREASURY AUGUST QUARTERLY FINANCING
     The Treasury will auction $11,000 million of 4-3/4-year 4-5/8% notes,
$11,000 million of 10-year notes, and $5,000 million of 29-1/2-year 5-3/8%
bonds to refund $11,885 million of publicly held securities maturing
August 15, 2001, and to raise about $15,115 million of new cash.
     In addition to the public holdings, Federal Reserve Banks hold $2,207
million of the maturing securities for their own accounts, which may be
refunded by issuing additional amounts of the new securities.
     Up to $1,000 million in noncompetitive bids from Foreign and Inter-
national Monetary Authority (FIMA) accounts bidding through the Federal
Reserve Bank of New York will be included within the offering amount of
each auction.  These noncompetitive bids will have a limit of $200 million
per account and will be accepted in the order of smallest to largest, up
to the aggregate award limit of $1,000 million.
     TreasuryDirect customers requested that we reinvest their maturing
holdings of approximately $37 million into the 4-3/4-year note, $11 million
into the 10-year note, and $1 million into the 29-1/2-year bond.
     All of the auctions being announced today will be conducted in the
single-price auction format.  All competitive and noncompetitive awards will
be at the highest yield of accepted competitive tenders.  The allocation
percentage applied to bids awarded at the highest yield will be rounded up to
the next hundredth of a whole percentage point, e.g., 17.13%.
     NOTE:  The net long position reporting threshold amount for only the
29-1/2-year bond is $1 billion.
     All of the securities being offered today are eligible for the STRIPS
program.
     This offering of Treasury securities is governed by the terms and con-
ditions set forth in the Uniform Offering Circular for the Sale and Issue
of Marketable Book-Entry Treasury Bills, Notes, and Bonds (31 CFR Part 356,
as amended).
     Details about the notes and bond are given in the attached offering
highlights.
                                  oOo
Attachment
```

For press releases, speeches, public schedules and official biographies, call our 24-hour fax line at (202) 622-2040

EXHIBIT 7.1 (Continued)

HIGHLIGHTS OF TREASURY OFFERINGS TO THE PUBLIC
AUGUST 2001 QUARTERLY FINANCING

August 1, 2001

Offering Amount	$11,000 million	$11,000 million	$5,000 million
Public Offering	Offering amount less the amount awarded to FIMA accounts		

Description of Offering:

Term and type of security	4-3/4-year notes (reopening)	10-year notes	29-1/2-year bonds (reopening)
Series	E-2006	C-2011	Bonds of February 2031
CUSIP number	912827 6X 5	912827 7B 2	912810 FP 8
Auction date	August 7, 2001	August 8, 2001	August 9, 2001
Issue date	August 15, 2001	August 15, 2001	August 15, 2001
Dated date	May 15, 2001	August 15, 2001	February 15, 2001
Maturity date	May 15, 2006	August 15, 2011	February 15, 2031
Interest rate	4-5/8%	Determined based on the highest accepted competitive bid	5-3/8%
Amount currently outstanding	$16,181 million	Not applicable	$10,887 million
Yield	Determined at auction	Determined at auction	Determined at auction
Interest payment dates	November 15 and May 15	February 15 and August 15	February 15 and August 15
Minimum bid amount and multiples	$1,000	$1,000	$1,000
Accrued interest payable by investor	$11.56250 per $1,000 (from May 15 to August 15, 2001)	None	None
Premium or discount	Determined at auction	Determined at auction	Determined at auction

STRIPS Information:

Minimum amount required	$1,000	$1,000	$1,000
Corpus CUSIP number	912820 GG 6	912820 GL 5	912803 CK 7
Due date(s) and CUSIP number(s) for additional TINT(s)	Not applicable	Not applicable	Not applicable

The following rules apply to all securities mentioned above:

Submission of Bids:

Noncompetitive bids: Accepted in full up to $5,000,000 at the highest accepted yield.

Foreign and International Monetary Authority (FIMA) bids: Noncompetitive bids submitted through the Federal Reserve Banks as agents for FIMA accounts. Accepted in order of size from smallest to largest with no more than $200 million awarded per account. The total noncompetitive amount awarded to Federal Reserve Banks as agents for FIMA accounts will not exceed $1,000 million. A single bid that would cause the limit to be exceeded will be partially accepted in the amount that brings the aggregate award total to the $1,000 million limit. However, if there are two or more bids of equal amounts that would cause the limit to be exceeded, each will be prorated to avoid exceeding the limit.

Competitive bids:

(1) Must be expressed as a yield with three decimals, e.g., 7.123%.

(2) Net long position for each bidder must be reported when the sum of the total bid amount, at all yields, and the net long position is $2 billion or greater for each of the notes and $1 billion or greater for the bond.

(3) Net long position must be determined as of one half-hour prior to the closing time for receipt of competitive tenders.

Maximum Recognized Bid at a Single Yield: 35% of public offering

Maximum Award: 35% of public offering

Receipt of Tenders: Noncompetitive tenders: Prior to 12:00 noon eastern daylight saving time on auction day
Competitive tenders: Prior to 1:00 p.m. eastern daylight saving time on auction day

Payment Terms: By charge to a funds account at a Federal Reserve Bank on issue date, or payment of full par amount with tender. TreasuryDirect customers can use the Pay Direct feature which authorizes a charge to their account of record at their financial institution on issue date.

189

Historically, the Treasury auctioned securities through multiple-price (or discriminatory) auctions. With multiple-price auctions, the Treasury still accepted the lowest-yielding bids up to the yield required to sell the amount offered (less the amount of noncompetitive bids). However, accepted bids were awarded at the particular yields bid, rather than at the stop-out yield. Noncompetitive bids were awarded at the weighted-average yield of the accepted competitive bids rather than at the stop-out yield.[3]

Within an hour following the 1:00 p.m. auction deadline, the Treasury announces the auction results. Announced results include the stop-out yield, the associated price, and the proportion of securities awarded to those investors who bid exactly the stop-out yield. Also announced is the quantity of noncompetitive tenders, the median-yield bid, and the *bid-to-cover ratio*. The bid-to-cover ratio is the ratio of the total amount bid for by the public to the amount awarded to the public. For notes and bonds, the announcement includes the coupon rate of the new security. The coupon rate is set to be that rate (in increments of ⅛ of 1%) that produces the price closest to, but not above, par when evaluated at the yield awarded to successful bidders.

Exhibit 7.2 shows the results of the 10-year note auction. Note the following:

- The high yield or stop yield was 5.078% and this was the yield at which all winning bidders were awarded.
- The coupon rate on the issue was set at 5%.
- Given the yield of 5.078%, the coupon rate of 5%, and the maturity of 10 years, the price that all winning bidders paid was $99.394 (per $100 par value).
- Those bidders who bid the high yield of 5.078 were allocated 63.7% of the amount that they bid.
- Since the total amount of bids by both competitive and noncompetitive bidders was $31,352,037,000 and the total amount awarded was $11,000,055,000, the bid-to-cover ratio was 2.85 (= $31,352,037,000/ $11,000,055,000).

Accepted bidders make payment on issue date through a Federal Reserve account or account at their financial institution, or they provide payment in full with their tender. Marketable Treasury securities are issued in book-entry form and held in the commercial book-entry system operated by the Federal Reserve Banks or in the Bureau of the Public Debt's Treasury Direct book-entry system.

---

[3] In September 1992 the Treasury started conducting single-price auctions for the 2- and 5-year notes. In November 1998 the Treasury adopted the single-price method for all auctions.

EXHIBIT 7.2   Results of a 10-Year Note Auction

PUBLIC DEBT NEWS

Department of the Treasury • Bureau of the Public Debt • Washington, DC 20239

```
                       TREASURY SECURITY AUCTION RESULTS
                      BUREAU OF THE PUBLIC DEBT - WASHINGTON DC

FOR IMMEDIATE RELEASE                        CONTACT:      Office of Financing
August 08, 2001                                            202-691-3550

            RESULTS OF TREASURY'S AUCTION OF 10-YEAR NOTES

Interest Rate:  5%                   Issue Date:     August 15, 2001
Series:         C-2011               Dated Date:     August 15, 2001
CUSIP No:       9128277B2            Maturity Date:  August 15, 2011


            High Yield:   5.078%    Price:  99.394

   All noncompetitive and successful competitive bidders were awarded
securities at the high yield.  Tenders at the high yield were
allotted  63.72%.  All tenders at lower yields were accepted in full.

            AMOUNTS TENDERED AND ACCEPTED (in thousands)
```

Tender Type	Tendered	Accepted
Competitive	$ 31,244,345	$ 10,892,363
Noncompetitive	107,692	107,692
SUBTOTAL	31,352,037	11,000,055 1/
Federal Reserve	1,043,030	1,043,030
TOTAL	$ 32,395,067	$ 12,043,085

```
   Median yield   5.070%:  50% of the amount of accepted competitive tenders
was tendered at or below that rate.  Low yield   5.030%:  5% of the amount
of accepted competitive tenders was tendered at or below that rate.

BID-TO-COVER RATIO = 31,352,037 / 11,000,055 = 2.85
NO FIMA NONCOMPETITIVE BIDS WERE TENDERED IN TODAY'S AUCTION.  THE STRIPS
MINIMUM IS $1,000.

1/ Awards to TREASURY DIRECT = $69,605,000
```

http://www.publicdebt.treas.gov

Primary Dealers

While the primary market is open to all investors, the primary government securities dealers play a special role. Primary dealers are firms with which the Federal Reserve Bank of New York interacts directly in the course of its open market operations. They include large diversified securities firms, money center banks, and specialized securities firms, and are foreign- as well as U.S.-owned. Among their responsibilities, primary dealers are expected to participate meaningfully in Treasury auctions, make reasonably good markets to the Federal Reserve Bank of New York's trading desk, and supply market information and commentary to the Fed. The dealers must also maintain certain designated capital standards. The 25 primary dealers as of July 2, 2001 are listed in Exhibit 7.3.

EXHIBIT 7.3   Primary Government Securities Dealers as of July 2, 2001

ABN AMRO Incorporated	Fuji Securities Inc.
BMO Nesbitt Burns Corp.	Goldman, Sachs & Co.
BNP Paribas Securities Corp.	Greenwich Capital Markets, Inc.
Banc of America Securities LLC	HSBC Securities (USA) Inc.
Banc One Capital Markets, Inc.	J. P. Morgan Securities, Inc.
Barclays Capital Inc.	Lehman Brothers Inc.
Bear, Stearns & Co., Inc.	Merrill Lynch Government
CIBC World Markets Corp.	Securities Inc.
Credit Suisse First Boston	Morgan Stanley & Co. Inc.
Corporation	Nomura Securities International, Inc.
Daiwa Securities America Inc.	SG Cowen Securities Corporation
Deutsche Banc Alex. Brown Inc.	Salomon Smith Barney Inc.
Dresdner Kleinwort Wasserstein	UBS Warburg LLC.
Securities LLC	Zions First National Bank

Source: Federal Reserve Bank of New York (www.newyorkfed.org/pihome/news/opnmktops/).

Historically, Treasury auction rules tended to facilitate bidding by the primary dealers. Rule changes enacted in 1991, however, allowed any government securities broker or dealer to submit bids on behalf of customers and facilitated competitive bidding by non-primary dealers.[4]

Auction Schedule

To minimize uncertainty surrounding auctions, and thereby reduce borrowing costs, the Treasury offers securities on a regular, predictable schedule as shown in Exhibit 7.4. Two-year notes are offered every month. They are announced for auction on a Wednesday, auctioned on the following Wednesday, and issued on the last day of the month (or the first day of the following month).

The remaining coupon securities are issued as a part of the Treasury's Quarterly Refunding in February, May, August, and November. The Trea-

---

[4] The rule changes followed Salomon Brothers Inc. admission in August 1991 of deliberate and repeated violations of auction rules. While the rules preclude any bidder from being awarded more than 35% of any issue, Salomon amassed significantly larger positions by making unauthorized bids on behalf of their customers. For the 5-year note auctioned on February 21, 1991, for example, Salomon bid for 105% of the issue (including two unauthorized customer bids) and was awarded 57% of the issue. For further information on the auction violations and subsequent rule changes, see the *Joint Report on the Government Securities Market*, published by the Department of the Treasury, the Securities and Exchange Commission, and the Board of Governors of the Federal Reserve System in January 1992.

sury holds a press conference on the first Wednesday of the refunding months (or on the last Wednesday of the preceding months) at which it announces details of the upcoming auctions. The auctions then take place on the following Tuesday (5-year) and Wednesday (10-year), with issuance on the 15th of the refunding month.

While the Treasury seeks to maintain a regular issuance cycle, its borrowing needs change over time. Most recently, the improved fiscal situation has reduced the Treasury's borrowing needs resulting in decreased issuance and a declining stock of outstanding Treasury securities.[5] To maintain large, liquid issues, the Treasury eliminated regular issuance of the 3-year note in 1998 and the 52-week bill in 2001. It also reduced issuance of the 5-year note from monthly to quarterly in 1998.

In addition to maintaining a regular issuance cycle, the Treasury tries to maintain a constant issue size for securities of a given maturity. As shown in Exhibit 7.4, typical public issue sizes as of June 2001 were $10–11 billion for the 2 year note, $11 13 billion for the 5 year note, and $9 11 billion for the 10-year note.[6] Issue sizes have also changed in recent years in response to the government's decreased funding needs. Issue sizes for 2-year notes, for example, were $15 billion as recently as 1999, $4–5 billion larger than issue sizes in the first half of 2001.

EXHIBIT 7.4 Auction Schedule for U.S. Treasury Securities
Issue frequency and typical issue sizes as of June 2001 are reported for the six regularly issued Treasury securities. Public issue sizes exclude amounts issued to refund maturing securities of Federal Reserve Banks.

Issue	Issue Frequency	Public Issue Size
13-week bill	weekly	$12.5–15.0 billion
26-week bill	weekly	$10.5–12.0 billion
2-year note	monthly	$10.0–11.0 billion
5-year note	quarterly	$11.0–13.0 billion
10-year note	quarterly	$9.0–11.0 billion
30-year bond	semiannually	$10.0 billion

Source: Bloomberg for issue sizes.

---

[5] Gross Treasury issuance fell from $2.5 trillion in 1996 to $2.0 trillion in 2000 (Bond Market Association, www.bondmarkets.com/research/tsyiss.shtml) and the stock of marketable Treasuries fell from $3.5 trillion in March 1997 (at its peak) to $2.8 trillion in June 2001 (Monthly Statement of the Public Debt, www.publicdebt.ustreas.gov/opd/opddload.htm).
[6] Public issue sizes exclude amounts issued to refund maturing securities of Federal Reserve Banks.

Reopenings

While the Treasury regularly offers new securities at auction, it often offers additional amounts of outstanding securities. In February 2000, the Treasury instituted a regular schedule of reopenings for its longer-term debt, whereby it offers additional amounts of outstanding securities at every other auction of its 5-, 10-, and, prior to October 2001, 30-year securities. New 10-year notes, for example, are offered in February and August, with smaller reopenings in May and November.

Exhibit 7.1 shows the August 1, 2001 announcement of two reopenings: a 4¾-year note and a 29½-year bond. The 4¾-year note was originally a 5-year note (issued in May 2001) and the 29½-year bond was originally a 30-year bond (issued in February 2001). For this reason, the coupon rate was provided for each issue. Exhibit 7.5 shows the auction results for the 29½-year Treasury bond. Recall that this was a reopened issue. The coupon rate was already set at 5⅜%. The high yield or stop yield was 5.520%. Given the coupon rate of 5⅜%, the yield of 5.520%, and the maturity of 29½ years, the price that winning bidders paid was $97.900 (per $100 of par value).

Buybacks

To maintain the sizes of its new issues and help manage the maturity of its debt, the Treasury launched a debt buyback program in January 2000. Under the program, the Treasury redeems outstanding unmatured Treasury securities by purchasing them in the secondary market through reverse auctions. The redemption operations are typically announced on the third and fourth Wednesdays of each month and conducted the next day. Each announcement contains details of the operation, including the operation size, the eligible securities, and some of the operation rules and procedures.

The Treasury conducted 20 buyback operations in 2000 (the first in March), and 12 in the first half of 2001. Operations sizes ranged from $750 million par to $3 billion par over this period, with all but two between $1 and $2 billion. The number of eligible securities in the operations ranged from 6 to 26, but was more typically in the 10 to 12 range. Eligible securities were limited to those with original maturities of 30 years, consistent with the Treasury's goal of using buybacks to prevent an increase in the average maturity of the public debt.

THE SECONDARY MARKET

Secondary trading in Treasury securities occurs in a multiple-dealer over-the-counter market rather than through an organized exchange. Trading takes place around the clock during the week, from the three main trading centers of Tokyo, London, and New York. The vast majority of trading takes place during New York trading hours, roughly 7:30 a.m. to 5:00 p.m. eastern time. The primary dealers are the principal market makers, buying and selling securities from customers for their own accounts at their quoted bid and ask prices. For the first half of 2001, primary dealers reported daily trading activity in the secondary market that averaged $296 billion per day.[7]

EXHIBIT 7.5   Results of a 29½-Year Auction

PUBLIC DEBT NEWS

Department of the Treasury • Bureau of the Public Debt • Washington, DC 20239

```
               TREASURY SECURITY AUCTION RESULTS
            BUREAU OF THE PUBLIC DEBT - WASHINGTON DC

FOR IMMEDIATE RELEASE                    CONTACT:   Office of Financing
August 09, 2001                                     202-691-3550

         RESULTS OF TREASURY'S AUCTION OF 29-1/2-YEAR BONDS

   This issue is a reopening of a bond originally issued February 15, 2001.

Interest Rate:  5 3/8%            Issue Date:    August 15, 2001
Series:                          Dated Date:    August 15, 2001
CUSIP No:       912810FP8         Maturity Date: February 15, 2031
STRIPS Minimum: $1,000

            High Yield:  5.520%     Price:  97.900

   All noncompetitive and successful competitive bidders were awarded
securities at the high yield.  Tenders at the high yield were
allotted   7.10%.  All tenders at lower yields were accepted in full.

         AMOUNTS TENDERED AND ACCEPTED (in thousands)

     Tender Type                   Tendered            Accepted
     -----------                 -------------       -------------
     Competitive           $      10,772,512    $      4,967,684
     Noncompetitive                   32,343              32,343
                                 -------------       -------------
       SUBTOTAL                   10,804,855           5,000,027 1/

     Federal Reserve                 540,230             540,230
                                 -------------       -------------
       TOTAL              $       11,345,085    $      5,540,257

   Median yield   5.472%:  50% of the amount of accepted competitive tenders
was tendered at or below that rate.  Low yield   5.400%:  5% of the amount
of accepted competitive tenders was tendered at or below that rate.

BID-TO-COVER RATIO = 10,804,855 / 5,000,027 = 2.16
NO FIMA NONCOMPETITIVE BIDS WERE TENDERED IN TODAY'S AUCTION.

1/ Awards to TREASURY DIRECT = $21,301,000
```

http://www.publicdebt.treas.gov

[7] Federal Reserve Bank of New York (www.ny.frb.org/pihome/statistics/). As the data is collected from all of the primary dealers but no other entities, trades between primary dealers are counted twice, and trades between non-primary dealers are not counted at all. The figure excludes financing transactions, such as repurchase agreements and reverse repurchase agreements.

Interdealer Brokers

In addition to trading with their customers, the dealers trade among themselves through interdealer brokers. The brokers provide the dealers with proprietary electronic screens that post the best bid and offer prices called in by the dealers, along with the associated quantities bid or offered (minimums are $5 million for bills and $1 million for notes and bonds). The dealers execute trades by calling the brokers, who post the resulting trade price and size on their screens. The dealer who initiates a trade by "hitting" a bid or "taking" an offer pays the broker a small fee.

Interdealer brokers thus facilitate information flows in the market while providing anonymity to the trading dealers. For the most part, the brokers act only as agents and serve only the primary dealers and a number of non-primary dealers. The brokers include BrokerTec, Cantor Fitzgerald/eSpeed, Garban-Intercapital, Hilliard Farber, and Tullett & Tokyo Liberty.

Federal Reserve

The Federal Reserve is another important participant in the secondary market for Treasury securities by virtue of its Treasury holdings, open market operations, and surveillance activities. The Federal Reserve Banks held $535 billion in Treasuries as of June 30, 2001, or 16% of the publicly held stock. The Federal Reserve Bank of New York buys and sells Treasuries through open market operations as one of the tools used to implement the monetary policy directives of the Federal Open Market Committee (FOMC). Finally, the New York Fed follows and analyzes the Treasury market and communicates market developments to other government agencies, including the Federal Reserve Board and the U.S. Treasury.

Market Transparency

Despite the huge volume of trading in the secondary market for government securities, the transparency of the market is nowhere near the level of that for common stocks. However, there have been some major strides in the reporting of government securities transactions since 1990. The most prominent example is GovPX, Inc., a private firm created in 1990 by the primary dealers and the interdealer brokers. GovPX provides 24-hour, worldwide distribution of government securities information as transacted by market participants through interdealer brokers. The information reported by GovPX includes the price and size of the best bid and best offer, trade prices and sizes, total volume (aggregate daily volume per issue and aggregate volume across all issues), and current rates and volume (intra-day updates) for repo transactions. The information reported by GovPX is distributed through Bloomberg Financial Markets, Reuters, and Bridge to 50,000 global users.

Trading Activity

While the Treasury market is extremely active and liquid, much of the activity is concentrated in a small number of the roughly 200 issues outstanding. The most recently auctioned securities of a given maturity, called *on-the-run* or *current securities*, are particularly active. Analysis of data from GovPX shows that on-the-run issues accounted for 64% of trading activity in 1999. Older issues of a given maturity are called *off-the-run securities*. While nearly all Treasury securities are off-the-run, they accounted for only 29% of interdealer trading in 1999.

The remaining 7% of interdealer trading in 1999 occurred in when-issued securities. When-issued securities are securities that have been announced for auction but not yet issued. When-issued trading facilitates price discovery for new issues and can serve to reduce uncertainty about bidding levels surrounding auctions. The when-issued market also enables dealers to sell securities to their customers in advance of the auctions, and thereby bid competitively with relatively little risk. While most Treasury market trades settle the following day, trades in the when-issued market settle on the issue date of the new security.

There are also notable differences in trading activity by issue type. According to 1999 data from GovPX, the on-the-run Treasury notes are the most actively traded securities, with average daily trading of $6.4 billion for the 2-year, $4.0 billion for the 5-year, and $2.7 billion for the 10-year.[8] Trading activity in when-issued securities is concentrated in the shorter-term issues, with the most active securities being the 2-year note ($1.5 billion), the 13-week bill ($883 million), and the 26-week bill ($651 million). Off-the-run trading is similarly concentrated, with the most active being the 3-month bill ($157 million per issue), the 2-year note ($86 million per issue), and the 26-week bill ($63 million per issue). Trading in longer-term off-the-run securities is extremely thin, with mean daily per-issue trading of just $20 million for the 5-year note and $10 million for the 10-year note.

Quoting Conventions for Treasury Coupon Securities

In contrast to quoting conventions for Treasury bills, discussed in Chapter 6, Treasury notes and bonds are quoted in the secondary market on a price basis in points where one point equals 1% of par.[9] The points are

---

[8] GovPX tracks trading activity among several of the interdealer brokers and thus covers much, but not all, of the interdealer market. Total interdealer trading volume therefore exceeds the figures given in the text (particularly for longer-term securities).

[9] Notes and bonds are quoted in yield terms in when-issued trading because coupon rates for new notes and bonds are not set until after these securities are auctioned.

split into units of *32nds*, so that a price of 96-14, for example, refers to a price of 96 and 14 *32nds* or 96.4375 per 100 of par value. Following are other examples of converting a quote to a price per $100 of par value:

Quote	No. of 32nd	Price per $100 par
91-19	19	91.59375
107-22	22	107.6875
109-06	6	109.1875

The 32nds are themselves often split by the addition of a plus sign or a number. A plus sign indicates that half a *32nd* (or a *64th*) is added to the price, and a number indicates how many eighths of 32nds (or 256ths) are added to the price. A price of 96-14+ therefore refers to a price of 96 plus 14 32nds plus 1 64th or 96.453125, and a price of 96-142 refers to a price of 96 plus 14 *32nds* plus 2 *256ths* or 96.4453125. Following are other examples of converting a quote to a price per $100 of par value:

Quote	No. of 32nds	No. of 64ths	No. of 256ths	Price per $100 par
91-19+	19	1		91.609375
107-222	22		2	107.6953125
109-066	6		6	109.2109375

In addition to price, the yield to maturity is typically reported alongside the price.

Typical bid-ask spreads in the interdealer market for the on-the-run coupon issues range from $\frac{1}{128}$ point for the 2-year note to $\frac{3}{64}$ point for the 30-year bond, as shown in Exhibit 7.6. A 2-year note might therefore be quoted as 99-082/99-08+ whereas a 30-year bond might be quoted as 95-23/95-24+. Bid-ask spreads vary with market conditions, and are usually wider outside of the interdealer market and for less active issues.

ZERO-COUPON TREASURY SECURITIES

The Treasury does not issue zero-coupon notes or bonds. These securities are created from existing Treasury notes and bonds through coupon stripping. Coupon stripping is the process of separating the coupon payments of a security from the principal and from one another. After stripping, each piece of the original security can trade by itself, entitling its holder to a particular payment on a particular date. A newly issued 10-year Treasury note, for example, can be split into its 20 semi-annual coupon payments and its principal payment, resulting in 21 individual securities. As the components of stripped Treasuries consist of single payments (with no intermediate coupon payments), they are referred to as *Treasury zero coupons* or *Treasury zeros* or *Treasury strips*.

On quote sheets and vendor screens Treasury strips are identified by whether the cash flow is created from the coupon (denoted "ci"), principal from a Treasury bond (denoted "bp"), or principal from a Treasury note (denoted "np"). Strips created from coupon payments are called *coupon strips* and those created from the principal are called *principal strips*. The reason why a distinction is made between coupon strips and principal strips has to do with the tax treatment by non-U.S. entities as discussed below.

As they make no intermediate payments, strips sell at discounts to their face value, and frequently at deep discounts due to their oftentimes long maturities. On June 29, 2001, for example, the closing bid price for the February 2031 principal strip was just $19.41 (per $100 face value).

Zero-coupon instruments such as Treasury strips eliminate reinvestment risk. Consequently, the yield at the time of purchase on strips is the pre-tax return that will be realized if an issue is held to maturity. Strips enable investors to closely match their liabilities with Treasury cash flows, and are thus popular with pension funds and insurance companies. Strips also appeal to speculators as their prices are more sensitive to changes in interest rates than coupon securities with the same maturity date.

EXHIBIT 7.6 Bid-Ask Spreads for U.S. Treasury Securities
Statistics for the spread between the best bid and the best offer in the interdealer market are reported for the on-the-run securities of each issue. Bill spreads are reported in yield terms in basis points and coupon spreads are reported in price terms in points.

Issue	Median Spread	95% Range
13-week bill	0.5 basis points	0–2.5 basis points
26-week bill	0.5 basis points	0–2.5 basis points
2-year note	$\frac{1}{128}$ point	0–$\frac{1}{64}$ point
5-year note	$\frac{1}{64}$ point	0–$\frac{1}{32}$ point
10-year note	$\frac{1}{32}$ point	0–$\frac{2}{32}$ point
30-year bond	$\frac{3}{64}$ point	0–$\frac{6}{32}$ point

Source: Authors' calculations, based on 1999 data from GovPX, Inc.

The Treasury introduced its Separate Trading of Registered Interest and Principal Securities (STRIPS) program in February 1985 to improve the liquidity of the zero-coupon market. The program allows the individual components of eligible Treasury securities to be held separately in the Federal Reserve's book entry system. Institutions with book-entry accounts can request that a security be stripped into its separate components by sending instructions to a Federal Reserve Bank. Each stripped component receives its own CUSIP (or identification) number and can then be traded and registered separately. The components of stripped Treasuries remain direct obligations of the U.S. government. The STRIPS program was originally limited to new coupon security issues with maturities of 10 years or longer, but was expanded to include all new coupon issues in September 1997.[10]

Reconstitution

Since May 1987, the Treasury has also allowed the components of a stripped Treasury security to be reassembled into their fully constituted form. An institution with a book-entry account assembles the principal component and all remaining interest components of a given security and then sends instructions to a Federal Reserve Bank requesting the reconstitution.

Tax Treatment

A disadvantage of a taxable entity investing in stripped Treasury securities is that accrued interest is taxed each year even though interest is not paid. Since tax payments must be made on interest earned but not received, these instruments are negative cash flow instruments until the maturity date.

One reason strips are identified on quote sheets and vendor screens by whether the cash flow is created from the coupon or the principal is that some foreign buyers have a preference for the strips created from the principal. This preference is due to the tax treatment of interest in their home country. Some countries' tax laws treat the interest as a capital gain—which receives a preferential tax treatment (i.e., lower tax rate) compared

---

[10] As of June 30, 2001, $174 billion of fixed-rate Treasury notes and bonds were held in stripped form, representing 9% of the $2.0 trillion in eligible fixed-rate coupon securities. There is wide variation across issue types and across issues of a particular type in the rate of stripping. As of June 30, 28% of eligible bonds were stripped but only 2% of eligible notes were stripped. Among the notes, one issue was 41% stripped on June 30, while 30 eligible note issues were not stripped at all. On a flow basis, securities were stripped at a rate of $17.3 billion per month in the first half of 2001, and reconstituted at a rate of $17.0 billion per month.

to ordinary interest income—if the stripped security was created from the principal.

SUMMARY

U.S. Treasury securities are obligations of the U.S. government issued by the Department of the Treasury. They play several important roles in financial markets, serving as a pricing benchmark, hedging instrument, reserve asset, and investment asset.

Investors in Treasury securities are perceived not to be exposed to credit risk. However, investors in Treasuries are exposed to interest rate risk and reinvestment risk, and investors in fixed-rate Treasuries are exposed to inflation risk. By investing in Treasury strips (i.e., Treasury zero-coupon securities), an investor eliminates reinvestment risk.

The regular and predictable issuance of Treasuries has been disrupted in recent years by the government's decreased funding needs. Recent debt-management changes include the suspension of issuance of the 52-week bill and the 30-year bond and the introduction of a debt buyback program.

CHAPTER 8

Inflation-Indexed Bonds

John B. Brynjolfsson, CFA
Executive Vice President and Manager
PIMCO Real Return Bond Fund

Historically, the greatest financial risk savers have faced has been inflation. During periods when too much money is chasing too few goods,
savers' financial needs inflate as the cost of living rises and their financial
resources shrink as asset valuations are debased. In particular, rising inflation hits equities with a one-two punch, as higher input prices put downward pressure on earnings, and higher interest rates put downward
pressure on price-to-earnings ratios. Meanwhile savers' fixed income
portfolios also suffer as rising market yields drive bond prices down,
while accelerating inflation tends to make the inflation adjusted yield on
cash instruments fall, or even become what turns out to be negative, when
examined in retrospect.

There is good news however. Investors have a tool that mitigates the
corrosive impact that inflation would otherwise have on their financial
plans. That tool is Treasury Inflation Protection Securities (TIPS).[1]

TIPS are bonds that are contractually guaranteed to protect and
grow purchasing power. The U.S. Treasury adjusts TIPS' principal based
upon changes in the consumer price index (CPI) daily so that upon
maturity investors maintain their original purchasing power.[2] In addi-

---

[1] Treasury Secretary Robert Rubin coined the term TIPS in 1996, before the official
launch of "Treasury Inflation-Indexed Securities" (TIIS) in January 1997. Market participants have gravitated to a generic use of the acronym TIPS and also use it to refer
to all forms of inflation-indexed bonds. Other terms sometimes used for them include
"IPBS," "TIIS," "Inflation-Linked Bonds," "Linkers," and "Real Return Bonds."
[2] The CPI series used to calculate TIPS is the non-seasonally adjusted Consumer Price
Index for all Urban Consumers (CPI-U). See CPI section later in this chapter.

tion, the Treasury calculates the semiannual coupon payments based upon this indexed principal amount so that investors also maintain the purchasing power of the income their assets generate.

The Treasury launched the TIPS program in 1997, and through the end of 2001 has issued over $145 billion of the securities. According to Federal Reserve Bank statistics, on a typical day more than $2 billion dollars trade in the secondary market. Since the 1940s, more than 15 governments and numerous corporations have issued similarly structured securities. In the U.K., inflation-indexed securities account for more than 20% of government bonds outstanding.

TIPS are best known as a defensive hedge against the fear of inflation, but they offer tactical and strategic advantages as well. Tactically, investors are attracted to the opportunity TIPS afford to speculate on changes in inflation and real interest rates. Strategically, individual and institutional investors with long-term objectives are attracted to TIPS' high real yield, their muted price volatility, and their low, or negative, correlation with other asset classes. They have found TIPS help them achieve their long-term investment goals, and reduce risk in the process.

The unique characteristics of TIPS qualify them as a fundamental asset class, as are equities, traditional bonds, and cash.

This chapter covers various aspects of TIPS, focusing on the U.S. Treasury TIPS but introducing substantive differences of other TIPS where appropriate. We begin with the mechanics of TIPS' cash flows. We then explore real yield and real duration—two measures that are analogous to a nominal bonds' yield to maturity and effective duration. The valuation and performance section presents a framework, and evaluates the TIPS market in the context of that framework.

MECHANICS AND MEASUREMENT

The merit of TIPS is that the principal and interest repaid to investors fluctuates based on the level of the CPI such that the *purchasing power* of each payment is fixed. As a consequence, the *real yield* of TIPS (the growth in purchasing power that a hold-to-maturity investor will earn) is fixed.

How TIPS Work

An illustration will be used to demonstrate how TIPS work. Exhibit 8.1 provides the data for the illustration. The following assumptions are made:

EXHIBIT 8.1 Stylized Cash Flow of TIPS

	Purchase	First Annual Coupon	Interim Annual Coupon	Last Annual Coupon	Principal	Return (per annum)
Date	1/15/02	1/15/03	1/15/07	1/15/12	1/15/12	1/15/12
Real $ Cash Flow	(1,000)	30.00	30.00	30.00	1,000	3.00
CPI (Base = 200)	200.0	204.0	220.8	243.8	243.8	2.00
Indexed Principal	1,000	1,020	1,104	1,219	1,219	(na)
Nominal $ Cash Flow	(1,000)	30.60	33.12	36.57	1,218.99	5.06%

Source: Pacific Investment Management Company

- issuance date of 1/15/02
- issuance price of $100.00 per $100.00 of face[3]
- 10-year maturity
- 3% real coupon paid annually
- 2% annualized inflation rate
- original principal amount of $1,000

If the CPI for the TIPS issuance date is 200.00 and the CPI for a coupon date one year later is 204.00, year-over-year inflation would be reported as 2.00%. Then the TIPS' adjusted principal would be 1.02 times its original value, or $1,020 per $1,000 of face. This ratio of CPI for a given date to the CPI for a TIPS issue date is termed the "index ratio." It forms the basis for TIPS' indexation.

In particular, this indexed principal is used to calculate the coupon paid; and the Treasury calculates the amount of each coupon payment, *after the principal has been adjusted for inflation.*[4] Exhibit 8.1 shows that the compounding effect of a 3% real coupon with a 2% inflation rate results in a *nominal* cash flow annualized return of 5.06%.

The calculations of actual Treasury TIPS cash flows and returns are only somewhat more complicated. TIPS pay interest semiannually at one-half their stated annual coupon rate. The inflation-indexed principal is accrued daily, based on an interpolation between the two monthly CPI figures reported immediately prior to the settlement month. And lastly, the U.S. Treasury uses an intricate rounding and truncating procedure for interim and final calculations (included in Bloomberg analytics). (See Exhibit 8.2.)

---

[3] Face, or face value, is also known as original principal and par value.
[4] Typically investors are not treated this generously. For example "simple" interest, periodically compounded interest, and even continuously compounded interest do not calculate interest on an end-of-period growing balance.

EXHIBIT 8.2 Bloomberg Screen Illustrating Actual Settlement Calculations

```
1                                                    DG48 Govt   YA
Bond Matures on a HOLIDAY
          INFLATION-INDEXED   YIELD   ANALYSIS
TSY INFL IX N/B   TII3 ³₈ 01/15/07 102-9+  /102-11   ( 2.93 /92) BGN  @16:59
PRICE  [102 ½]              CUSIP 9128272M    REAL COUPON  3 ³₈
SETTLEMENT DATE  [5/ 9/2001]    REAL CPN ACCRUED INT   1.062845
┌─YIELD─────────────MATURITY──┐ ┌──ECONOMIC  FACTORS──┐
│CALCULATIONS       1/15/2007 │ │BASE CPI VALUE  1/15/1997 158.43548│
│STREET REAL YIELD      [2.924]│ │                              │
│TREASURY YIELD EQUIVALENT [2.923]│ │REFERENCE CPI    5/ 9/2001 175.90323│
│                             │ │CPURNSA <INDEX>    3/01   176.20000│
│                             │ │CPURNSA <INDEX>    2/01   175.80000│
│INFLATION ASSUMPTION [3.4352]%│ │CPI @ LAST CPN DATE      174.04516│
│YIELD W/INFLATION ASSUMPTION [6.370]│ │FLAT INDEX RATIO          1.09852│
│YIELD WITHOUT INFLATION [2.915]│ │ACCRUED RATIO GROWTH      0.01173│
└─────────────────────────────┘ │INDEX RATIO               1.11025│
       Personal default Yield Betas now available. Type COVR<GO>.
┌─SENSITIVITY  ANALYSIS──┐ ┌──PAYMENT   INVOICE──┐
│ FOR VARIOUS  REAL vs NOMINAL │ │                    FACE [1000]M│
│   YIELD BETA ASSUMPTIONS ( SEE <HELP> )│ │FLAT            1124266.56│
│YIELD-BETA ASSUMPTION [0.000][0.500][1.000]│ │INFLATION ACCRUAL  12004.92│
│EFFECTIVE DURATION   0.000  2.507  5.015│ │GROSS AMOUNT    1136271.48│
│RISK                 0.000  2.879  5.757│ │CPN ACCR. 114  DAYS 11800.24│
│CONVEXITY            0.000  0.073  0.292│ │NET AMOUNT      1148071.72│
                                          Inflation Compensation  110250.00
Copyright 2001 BLOOMBERG L.P.  Frankfurt:69-920410  Hong Kong:2-977-6000  London:207-330-7500  New York:212-318-2000
Princeton:609-279-3000   Singapore:65-212-1000   Sydney:2-9777-8686   Tokyo:3-3201-8900   Sao Paulo:11-3048-4500
                                                                    I644-1012-0 08-May-01 17:35:29
```

Source: Bloomberg Financial Markets

The Consumer Price Index

The specific consumer price index (CPI) series used for TIPS indexation is the "Non-Seasonally Adjusted, All-Urban Consumer Price Index" (NSA CPI-U). It is reported monthly. Unlike the seasonally-adjusted series, the NSA CPI-U is not subject to revision. One consequence of utilizing the NSA CPI-U is that the series includes predictable seasonal fluctuations in inflation. For example, in December of most years inflation is muted by year-end price-cutting and inventory liquidations. As a result the Non-Seasonally Adjusted CPI-U index tends to fall slightly below its trend. In certain other months it tends to rise slightly above the underlying trend.

The CPI report that surveys the price level in a given month and is therefore named for that month, for example May, is typically reported on or near the 15th of the following month, in this example June. There is then an additional two-week delay between this reporting date, and the subsequent first of the month, upon which TIPS literally begin accruing the reported inflation. This two-week accrual cushion allows for potential delays in the official release date of CPI or other disruptions, and eliminates the need to calculate day-counts across month-ends. The last daily accrual of the May CPI report then occurs on July 31, about 7 weeks after the CPI figure is first reported; and therefore, the May CPI is fully incorporated into the August 1 TIPS principal.

This relatively quick two-week turnaround of CPI reports into TIPS' indexation is described as a 3-month lag because the May (month 5) CPI is fully incorporated into all TIPS by August 1 (month 8). Indexation for dates other than the first are calculated by linear interpolation.

So, to calculate the TIPS principal for any settlement date, for example August 10, the procedure is as follows:

1. Find the TIPS principal that applies to August 1: this is based on the May NSA CPI-U report (month 8 minus 3 = month 5).
2. Find the TIPS principal that applies to September 1: this is based on the June NSA CPI-U report (month 9 minus 3 = month 6).
3. Divide 9, the number of days of accrual (the 10th day of the month minus the 1st day of the month) by 31 (the number of days in that month).
4. Linearly interpolate by adding 9/31 of the difference between the August 1 and September 1 TIPS principal values to the August 1 value.

Real Yield and Nominal Yield

The real yield of a TIPS bond represents the annualized growth rate of purchasing power earned when holding the security to maturity. TIPS' real yield can easily be calculated on a standard bond calculator by entering the TIPS quoted market price, coupon rate, and maturity date. The calculator does not know the bond is a TIPS, or that the quoted price and coupon rate are *real*. So it is therefore user's responsibility to interpret the numerical result as the "real yield."[5]

The *real* yield of a *nominal* bond is more difficult to calculate, as it can only be precisely determined with the benefit of hindsight. In practice, when analysts speak of a nominal bond's "real yield" they may be:

■ Referring to its "current" real yield (approximated by subtracting the current year-over-year inflation rate from the bond's nominal yield),
■ Forecasting the nominal bond's future real yield based on their expectation, or other forecasts, of future inflation, or
■ Speaking of historical realized real returns on bonds that have matured.

Put another way, TIPS' real yields are easy to calculate and well defined, whereas nominal bonds' real yields are not.

---

[5] Two phenomena that could cause a minor difference in TIPS quoted real yield from the "TIPS realized real yield" equation are: (1) real reinvestment rate of coupon cash flows; and, (2) the time-lag between the "applicable" date for the CPI and the applicable date for TIPS indexing.

The opposite situation occurs with nominal yields. While the nominal yield of a conventional bond is easily determined, the nominal yield of TIPS is more difficult to pin down. The nominal yield realized by holding TIPS to maturity depends upon the average level and trajectory of inflation over the bond's lifetime. The realized nominal yield of a TIPS can be approximated as:

TIPS realized nominal yield = (1 + real yield) × (1 + inflation) − 1

Break-Even Inflation Rate

The break-even inflation rate is the rate that results in the hold-to-maturity investor in TIPS "breaking even" with the hold-to-maturity investor in a comparable maturity nominal bond. Using the above equation, the nominal yield of the TIPS can be set to equal the nominal yield of the conventional bond. Solving the equation for the break-even inflation rate:

$$\text{Break-even inflation rate} = \frac{(1 + \text{conventional nominal yield})}{(1 + \text{TIPS real yield})} - 1$$

If the conventional bond's nominal yield is 5% and the TIPS real yield is 3% (both expressed in simple annualized terms), the break-even inflation rate is 1.94%. For most purposes approximating the above equation as the simple difference between the two bonds' yields (2.00%) is appropriate—and general industry practice.

Exhibit 8.3 plots nominal yields, real yields, and their differences over a period including the fall of 1998. This period was notably marked by a significant deflationary scare. An astute investor might have construed the dramatic decline of the break-even inflation rate to below 1% as unduly pessimistic, and therefore a trading opportunity.

Although the break-even inflation rate may be useful to assess market inflation expectations or to gauge break-even requirements for narrowly constrained fixed-income investors, it generally overstates the *risk-adjusted* break-even inflation rate appropriate for long-term investors. In particular, the riskier nominal bonds embody inflation risk premiums. Researchers have estimated the embedded inflation risk premium in nominal bonds to be between 0.50% and 1.0%.[6]

---

[6] Gerald Lucas and Timothy Quek, "Valuing and Trading TIPS," *Handbook of Inflation-Indexed Bonds* (New Hope, PA: Frank J. Fabozzi Associates, 1999). In that chapter, the authors suggest that a part of (or the entire) "inflation-risk premium" may be offset, citing the tremendous supply of TIPS, the illiquidity of TIPS, and the substantial exposure that TIPS have to changes in real interest rates. For a more detailed discussion of implied break-evens and risk-premiums, see the seminal work on expectations and markets by M. Harrison and D. Kreps, "Martingales and Multiperiod Securities Markets," *Journal of Economic Theory* (1979), pp. 381–408.

EXHIBIT 8.3　　Bloomberg Screen Showing Break-Even Inflation Rates

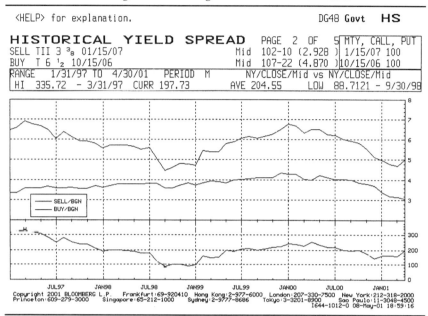

Source: Bloomberg Financial Markets

Because TIPS are indexed to CPI, exhibit low volatility, and have a low correlation to other assets, an inflation risk premium should not be embodied in TIPS yields. Therefore, the risk-adjusted break-even inflation rate for TIPS equals the calculated break-even inflation rate MINUS the inflation risk premium. This means an investor can advantageously use TIPS even when his expected inflation rate equals the break-even inflation rate naively calculated by simply substituting TIPS yields from nominal bonds' yield. Such an investor will gain by lowering overall portfolio risk, or from reallocating the risk capacity created.

DURATION

Duration is the measure of a bond's market value sensitivity to changes in *specified* yields—real *or* nominal. The earlier discussion of real and nominal yields is pivotal to any discussion of duration.

Real Duration

By definition, the *real* duration of TIPS is the percentage change in its market value associated with a 100-basis-point change in its *real* yield. For example, if the market value of TIPS is $1,000 and the market values associated with a 50-basis-point decrease and a 50-basis-point increase in the TIPS real yield are $1,051 and $951 respectively, the TIPS real duration is 10. In order to center the calculation at current yield levels, the 100-basis-point change in the definition is applied equally, as a 50-basis-point decrease and a 50-basis-point increase in yield.

Algebraically, the formula for TIPS real duration is:

$$100 \times [\text{MV(real yield} + 0.50\%) - \text{MV(real yield} - 0.50\%)]/\text{MV(real yield)}$$

where MV = market value.

Not surprisingly, the TIPS real duration formula is identical to the formula for a nominal bond's nominal duration. It follows that TIPS real duration can be calculated using a standard bond calculator that reports duration based on the user keying in details including the bond's coupon and maturity. As with the calculation for real yield, it is the user's responsibility to remember that the result is the TIPS' *real* duration.

Real duration is highly relevant to TIPS portfolio managers. It is an unambiguous metric that allows a managed portfolio of TIPS to be compared to a benchmark portfolio of TIPS. However its application is limited, as real duration dramatically overstates the exposure of TIPS to changes in nominal yields, and does not quantify the risk impact of adding TIPS to a portfolio of nominal bonds. There are a number of reasons for this. First, real yields tend to be significantly less volatile than nominal yields—so a portfolio of all TIPS with a given real duration typically will be less volatile than a portfolio of all nominal bonds with a numerically identical nominal duration. Second, the correlation of real yields with nominal yields tends to be quite low—so even adjusting real durations for the lower real yield price volatility would tend to overstate duration. In particular, when TIPS with substantial real durations are introduced to replace a fraction of bond portfolios with comparable volatility, much of the substituted risk is diversified away, and overall portfolio volatility falls rather than remaining unchanged.

Effective Duration

To explore the risk impact of tactically adding TIPS to a conventional portfolio, a manager needs a measure of TIPS' sensitivity to changes in *nominal* interest rates. This measure is known as *effective duration* . The limitation is that since one must infer a change in real yield from the given change in nominal yield, the measure is conjectural rather than deterministic.

Initially this dilemma caused more than a few managers to conclude that the risk exposure of TIPS could not be managed within the context of a conventional fixed-income portfolio.[7] Although crude, the best metric we have found for converting TIPS real yield into "effective duration" is to apply a 20% to 50% multiplicative factor to TIPS real durations. This factor is often described as a "yield beta"—a reference to the second coefficient (beta) of a linear regression of change in real yield against a change in nominal yield. TIPS effective duration should only be used as a loose metric for nominal interest rate exposure because substantial risk (basis risk) remains.

Occasionally, nominal yields fall and TIPS real yields rise, meaning that retrospectively TIPS experience negative effective durations. Conversely, occasionally nominal yields rise, and real yields rise even more, meaning TIPS experience capital losses larger than *ex ante* effective durations predict. It is incumbent that managers who use TIPS manage the basis risk that TIPS embody beyond their modest effective duration.

Exhibit 8.4 plots the weekly change in TIPS 2007 real yield on the vertical axis as a scatter, with the corresponding weekly change in nominal yield on the horizontal axis. The slope of the "best-fit" regression line shows that historically the "yield beta" over that period, at 17%, has been somewhat lower than the 20% to 50% that we use. The regression result will vary (as a function of the time period chosen to calculate the individual change), the time period included in the study, the securities chosen, and perhaps most importantly, the economic environment.

TIPS real duration measures risk as it relates to change in real yield and TIPS effective duration measures risk as it relates to changes in nominal yield. Another measure of TIPS risk is volatility. Volatility is simply the standard deviation of TIPS prices (or returns). It varies over time and across maturities as a function of the calculation period and measurement interval. Exhibit 8.5 graphs the historical price volatility of the first Treasury 10-year TIPS issued.

---

[7] However, this challenge is not novel. In the 1980s managers of mortgage-backed securities overcame similar concerns. The calculation of effective duration for mortgages calls for an inference that a change in nominal Treasury yield will result in a change in the underlying yield of mortgage cash flows and mortgage payments. Similar to TIPS, yields underlying mortgage pricing are not perfectly correlated with Treasury yields. In fact, during the deflationary scare in the summer of 1998, mortgage prices dramatically underperformed what naïve calculations of mortgage effective durations would have predicted. For a brief period, as Treasury yields fell mortgage yields actually rose. Nonetheless, effective duration is broadly used to determine fluctuations in mortgages as a function of fluctuations in nominal yields. It is incumbent upon fixed-income managers to manage the basis risk remaining.

EXHIBIT 8.4   Bloomberg Screen—Historical Regression Analysis—Weekly Yield Changes of 2007 TIPS versus Yield Changes of 2006 Treasury

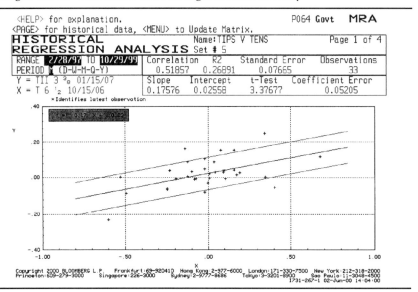

Source: Bloomberg Financial Markets

EXHIBIT 8.5   Bloomberg Graph of TIPS Bond's 26-Week Rolling Price Volatility

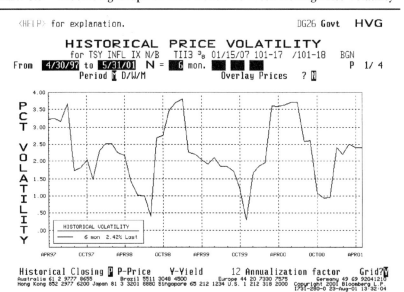

Source: Bloomberg Financial Markets

QUOTATION AND SETTLEMENT

In the United States, TIPS are quoted on a "real-clean" basis—as distinguished from a "nominal-dirty" basis. Fractions of a dollar are quoted as units of $\frac{1}{32}$.

In this instance, "real" means that U.S. TIPS prices are quoted on the basis of 100 inflation-adjusted units of principal. For example (see Example 2), the quoted price 102-11 can be interpreted as 102 and $\frac{11}{32}$ real dollars, meaning the investor is paying 102.3438% of the indexed principal amount, for the principal of the bond. So if the bond's principal has grown from $1,000 per bond to $1,102.50 per bond, the price paid for the principal will be $1,136.27. While this may seem intuitive, it is not the only way to quote TIPS prices. If prices were quoted on a nominal basis, as they are in the U.K. Linker market, this same purchase would be quoted as 113.63 (102.3438 × 1.1025 = the real price times the index ratio). Similarly, to convert the real price quoted on U.S. TIPS to a nominal price for the bond, which necessarily is paid in "nominal dollars" upon settlement, one must multiply the real price by the index ratio.

Clean means the quoted TIPS price does not include the accrued-interest amount that the buyer of a TIPS bond owes the seller. Just as with nominal bonds, the TIPS buyer must compensate the seller for coupon income that has been earned since the last coupon payment. Parties, therefore, can calculate the settlement proceeds by multiplying real accrued interest by the index ratio and adding the result to the clean settlement price. In practice, a computer algorithm as shown in Exhibit 8.2 is used to incorporate rounding procedures prescribed by the Treasury.

In the U.K. Linker market, quotes are on a "nominal clean price" basis, and therefore some of their linkers trade at prices above $200 per $100 original face. This is because the country's Retail Price Index (RPI) has more than doubled since the Bank of England began issuing these bonds in the early 1980s, so some of the index ratios are above 2.0.

In Australia and New Zealand, Inflation-Indexed Bonds (IIBs) typically are quoted and traded on a "real yield" basis. This means that the traders are quoting the most intuitive of all measures, real yield, and settlement computers are therefore performing the multistep calculations needed to convert this to settlement proceeds suitable for wire transfer.

In the Canadian and French markets, TIPS are quoted similarly to U.S. TIPS, except of course local inflation indexes are referenced.

CHAPTER 9

Federal Agency Securities

Frank J. Fabozzi, Ph.D., CFA
Adjunct Professor of Finance
School of Management
Yale University

George P. Kegler
President
Cassian Market Consultants

Federal agency securities can be classified by the type of issuer—federally related institutions and government-sponsored enterprises. Federal agencies that provide credit for certain sectors of the credit market issue two types of securities: debentures and mortgage-backed/asset-backed securities. Our focus here is on the former securities.

FEDERALLY RELATED INSTITUTIONS

Federally related institutions are arms of the federal government and generally do not issue securities directly in the marketplace. Federally related institutions include the Export-Import Bank of the United States, the Tennessee Valley Authority, the Commodity Credit Corporation, the Farmers Housing Administration, the General Services Administration, the Government National Mortgage Association, the Maritime Administration, the Private Export Funding Corporation, the Rural Electrification Administration, the Rural Telephone Bank, the Small Business Administration, and the Washington Metropolitan Area Transit Authority.

All federally related institutions are exempt from SEC registration. With the exception of securities of the Tennessee Valley Authority and the Private Export Funding Corporation, the securities are backed by the full faith and credit of the U.S. government. Interest income on securities issued by federally related institutions is exempt from state and local income taxes.

Since the federally related institution that has issued securities in recent years is the Tennessee Valley Authority (TVA), we discuss these securities.

Tennessee Valley Authority

Established by Congress in 1933 primarily to provide flood control, navigation, and agricultural and industrial development, and to promote the use of electric power in the Tennessee Valley region, the TVA is the largest public power system in the United States. The TVA primarily finances its capital requirements through internally generated funds and by issuing debt. The TVA issues a variety of debt securities in U.S. dollars and other currencies (British pounds and Euros). The debt obligations issued by the TVA may be issued only to provide capital for its power program or to refund outstanding debt obligations.

TVA debt obligations are not guaranteed by the U.S. government. However, the securities are rated triple A by Moody's and Standard and Poor's. The rating is based on the TVA's status as a wholly owned corporate agency of the U.S. government and the view of the rating agencies of the TVA's financial strengths. These strengths include (1) the requirements that bondholders of power bonds are given a first pledge of payment from net power proceeds, and (2) electricity rates charged by the TVA are sufficient to ensure both the full payment of annual debt service and operating and capital costs.

According to the TVA's annual report, as of September 30, 2000, TVA had 36 long-term public debt issues outstanding, totaling $24 billion. There are issues targeted to individual investors (retail debt offerings) and institutional investors (nonretail offerings).

For retail offerings, there are standard callable bonds (2000 Series A through Series E and 1998 Series A Estate Features), with one interesting investment feature. There is an "estate feature" that allows the bonds to be redeemed at par value plus accrued interest upon the death of the bondholder. The Putable Automatic Rate Reset Securities (PARRS) bonds (1999 Series A and 1998 Series D) are noncallable but have two interesting features. First, they have a fixed coupon rate for the first 5 years. Then there is an annual reset provision that provides for a reduction in the issue's coupon rate under certain conditions. The reduction is tied to the 30-year Treasury Constant Maturity (CMT). Second, the bondholder has the right to put the bond at par value plus accrued interest if and when the coupon rate is reduced. More recently, the TVA has issued "electronotes." The retail bonds (as well as electronotes) just described are referred to as "power bonds." There are retail bonds that are "subordinated debt." That is, they are subordinated to the power bonds. The only outstanding issue is the 1996 Series A Quarterly Income Debt Securities (QIDS).

For institutional investors, the TVA has global bonds outstanding (e.g., 2001 Series A, 2001 Series C, 2000 Series G, 1999 Series B, 1998 Series G, 1998 Series C, 1995 Series E and 1995 Series A) that are noncallable and issued in U.S. dollars. There are two global issues denominated in British pounds that are noncallable (1998 Series H & 2001 Series B) and a deal (1996 Series Global) initially issued in German Marks, now denominated in Euros. There are putable issues that may not be called (2000 Series F Put, 1997 Series C Exchange, and 1996 Series A Double Put). There is even one issue that is inflation indexed (1997 Series A Inflation-Indexed VIPS).

GOVERNMENT-SPONSORED ENTERPRISES

Government-sponsored enterprises (GSEs) are privately owned, publicly chartered entities. They were created by Congress to reduce the cost of capital for certain borrowing sectors of the economy deemed to be important enough to warrant assistance. The entities in these sectors include farmers, homeowners, and students. The enabling legislation dealing with a GSE is reviewed periodically. GSEs issue securities directly in the marketplace. The market for these securities, while smaller than that of Treasury securities, has in recent years become an active and important sector of the bond market. Since 1998, a number of the GSEs have initiated programmatic debt issuance platforms, which will be discussed in more detail, in addition to more traditional funding methodologies. GSEs are also issuers of foreign currency denominated and U.S. dollar global bonds.

There are six GSEs that currently issue debentures: Federal National Mortgage Association, Federal Home Loan Mortgage Corporation, Federal Agricultural Mortgage Corporation, Federal Farm Credit System, Federal Home Loan Bank System, and Student Loan Marketing Association. The Federal National Mortgage Association, Federal Home Loan Mortgage Corporation, and Federal Home Loan Bank are responsible for providing credit to the housing sectors. The Federal Agricultural

Mortgage Corporation provides the same function for agricultural mortgage loans. The Federal Farm Credit Bank System is responsible for the credit market in the agricultural sector of the economy. The Student Loan Marketing Association provides funds to support higher education.

The interest earned on obligations of the Federal Home Loan Bank System, the Federal Farm Credit System, and the Student Loan Marketing Association are exempt from state and local income taxes. In addition to the debt obligations issued by these six GSEs, there are issues outstanding by one-time GSE issuers that have been dismantled. These GSEs include the Financing Corporation, Resolution Trust Corporation, and the Farm Credit Assistance Corporation.

The price quotation conventions for GSE securities will vary between types of debt. Short term GSE discount notes are quoted on a yield basis, the same as for Treasury Bills. The most liquid programmatic GSE issues are generally quoted on two primary bases. One is a price basis, like Treasury securites. That is, the bid and ask price quotations are expressed as a percentage of par plus fractional 32nds of a point. Two is a spread basis, as an indicated yield spread in basis points, off a choice of proxy curves or issue. The Treasury market is the most popular bellwether proxy from which most GSE debt is quoted. The less liquid GSE securities types, such as callable debt, that contain some form of optionality, may be quoted on a yield spread basis off either Treasuries, U.S. dollar interest rate swaps curve (the interest rate swap market is described in detail in Chapter 29), or a yield curve referencing GSE debt or a particular GSE issue.

A third quotation convention was introduced to the GSE debt market in 2001, when Freddie Mac began its Reference Note auctions. In pre-auction trading the issues have been quoted on a 'When Issued' (WI)[1] basis, a straight yield basis, such as used in trading Treasury WI issues. This quotation convention is used until the issue is priced at auction, at which point the price quotes usually return to a yield spread basis. Some GSE issues trade with almost the same liquidity as Treasury securities. Other issues that are supported only by a few dealers trade much like off-the-run corporate bonds.

Types and Features of GSE Securities

In general, GSEs issue two types of debt: debentures and discount notes. Debentures can be either notes or bonds. GSE issued notes, with minor exceptions, have 1 to 20 year maturities and bonds have maturities longer than 20 years. There are issues with bullet maturities and those with call

---

[1] See, *The Bond Market Association's Practice Guidelines for When Issued Trading in GSE Auctioned Securities*, January, 2001.

provisions. GSEs also issue structured notes. The variety of notes issued by the GSEs will be discussed in greater detail later in this chapter.

Discount notes are short-term obligations with maturities ranging from overnight to 360 days. As with Treasury bills, no coupon interest is paid. Instead, the investor earns interest by buying the note at a discount.

Programmatic GSE Issuance Platforms

In 1998, the Federal National Mortgage Association (Fannie Mae) and the Federal Home Loan Mortgage Corporation (Freddie Mac) began issuing respectively, Benchmark and Reference Notes and Bonds. These programmatic platforms incorporated pre-announced funding calendars and large minimum sized issues to introduce greater transparency in their funding programs and to promote greater liquidity for the issued debt. In 1999, both GSEs included Benchmark Bills and Reference Bills, respectively, in weekly auction formats to augment their short-term discount note funding programs. Subsequently, the Federal Home Loan Banks and the Federal Farm Credit Banks, through their respective funding entities, the Federal Home Loan Banks Office of Finance and the Federal Farm Credit Funding Corporation, initiated programmatic debt platforms. Federal Home Loan Banks issue Federal Home Loan TAPs and Federal Farm Credit Banks issue Farm Credit Designated Notes. Whereas the funding needs of Freddie Mac and Fannie Mae are derived from single corporate entities, which allows for more exact issuance calendar announcements, the demands of funding separate bank balance sheets within the Federal Home Loan Bank and Federal Farm Credit Bank systems has limited the amount of programmatic funding for these GSEs. Freddie Mac, Fannie Mae, and the Federal Home Loan Banks utilize auctions when issuing most of their short-term debt. Though varying in size and scope between the GSEs, the auctioned maturities include regular 1-, 2-, 3-, 6-, and 12-month maturities. Freddie Mac has also incorporated auctions in the issuance of 2-, 3-, and 5-year Reference Notes. This has allowed the "When Issued" (WI) trading of GSE coupon debt for the first time, a significant milestone in the transparency and liquidity of the GSE securities market.

Both Freddie Mac and Fannie Mae will periodically announce repurchase and/or exchange transactions involving their programmatic issued securities.

Description of GSEs and Securities Issued

The six GSEs that currently issue securities and the three GSEs that have outstanding issues can be briefly described as follows.

Federal National Mortgage Association (Fannie Mae)

The residential mortgage debt market in the United States represents the largest mortgage debt market in the world. The problem the U.S. government faces is to attract investors to invest in residential mortgages. At one time, savings and loan associations were the primary investors, especially with special inducements the government provided. But since there was not an active market where these debt instruments traded, mortgages were illiquid and financial institutions that invested in them were exposed to liquidity risk.

In the 1930s, Congress figured out a way to handle this problem. It created a federally related institution, the Federal National Mortgage Association, popularly known as "Fannie Mae," which was charged with the responsibility to create a liquid secondary market for mortgages. Fannie Mae was to accomplish this objective by buying and selling mortgages. Fannie Mae needed a funding source in case it faced a liquidity squeeze. Congress provided this by giving Fannie Mae a credit line with the Treasury.

Despite the presence of Fannie Mae, the secondary mortgage market did not develop to any significant extent. During periods of tight money, Fannie Mae could do little to mitigate a housing crisis. In 1968, Congress divided Fannie Mae into two entities: (1) the current Fannie Mae and (2) the Government National Mortgage Association (popularly known as "Ginnie Mae"). Ginnie Mae's function is to use the "full faith and credit of the U.S. government" to support the market for government-insured mortgages. (The mortgage-backed securities guaranteed by Ginnie Mae are discussed in Chapter 14.) While starting out as a federally related institution, today Fannie Mae is a GSE.

Fannie Mae issues Benchmark Bills, Benchmark Notes and Benchmark Bonds, Callable Benchmark Notes, Subordinated Benchmark Notes, Investment Notes, callable securities, and structured notes. Benchmark Notes and Benchmark Bonds are noncallable instruments. The minimum issue size is $4 billion for Benchmark Notes and $2 billion for Benchmark Bonds. Issued quarterly are 2-year or 3-year, 5-year, 10-year, and 30-year maturities.

Federal Home Loan Mortgage Corporation (Freddie Mac)

In 1970, two years after Congress divided Fannie Mae into the now current Fannie Mae and Ginnie Mae, Congress created the Federal Home Loan Mortgage Corporation (Freddie Mac). The reason for the creation of Freddie Mac was to provide support for conventional mortgages. These mortgages are not guaranteed by the U.S. government.

Freddie Mac issues Reference Bills, discount notes, medium-term notes, Reference Notes and Bonds, Callable Reference Notes, Euro Reference Notes (debt denominated in Euros) and global bonds. Reference Bills and discount notes are issued with maturities of 1 year or less. Reference Notes and Bonds have maturities of 2 to 30 years and Callable Reference Notes have maturities of 2 to 10 years. Freddie Mac will issue and/or reopen Reference Bills, Reference Notes, 30-year Reference Bonds, and Euro Reference Notes according to a published issuance calendar and within minimum issue size guidelines. Freddie Mac Reference Notes and Reference Bonds are eligible for stripping.

Both Freddie Mac and Fannie Mae issue bullet and callable medium term notes (MTNs) and structured notes, which are customized based on demand (reverse inquiry) from institutional investors. The structured notes issued have been various floating-rate, zero-coupon, and step-up securities. There are securities denominated in U.S. dollars as well as issues denominated in a wide range of foreign currencies.

Freddie Mac and Fannie Mae issue subordinated securities, in the form of Freddie SUBS and Fannie Mae Subordinated Benchmark Notes, respectively. These are unsecured subordinated obligations of the separate corporations that rank junior in right of payment to all of Freddie Mac's and Fannie Mae's existing and future obligations. The payment structure is as follows. Separately the effected corporation must defer payment of interest on all outstanding subordinated debt if certain conditions are realized. Deferral of interest is not permitted for more than five consecutive years nor beyond the maturity date. Accrual of interest is compounded at the issue's coupon rate. During any deferral period, the effected GSE may not declare or pay dividends on, or redeem, purchase, or acquire its common stock or its preferred stock. The first separate offerings of Freddie Mac and Fannie Mae subordinated debt issues were in 2001, both receiving an Aa2 from Moody's Investors Service and AA– from Standard & Poor's.

Federal Home Loan Bank System (FHL Banks)

The Federal Home Loan Bank System (FHLBanks) consists of the 12 district Federal Home Loan Banks and their member banks. The Federal Home Loan Bank Board was originally responsible for regulating all federally chartered savings and loan associations and savings banks, as well as state-chartered institutions insured by the Federal Savings and Loan Insurance Corporation. These responsibilities have been curtailed since 1989.

The major source of debt funding for the Federal Home Loan Banks is the issuance of consolidated debt obligations, which are joint and several obligations of the 12 Federal Home Loan Banks. Consolidated FHLBank discount notes with maturities from 1 to 360 days are issued daily. Discount notes are also auctioned twice weekly in 4-, 9-, 13-, and 26-week maturities. Because FHLBank bond issuance is directly related to member bank needs, there is no debt calendar in the traditional sense. Bullets, callables, and floaters are issued on a daily basis. The FHL-Banks have several Programs to facilitate the issuance of certain bond types. The TAP Issue program was launched in 1999. This program aggregates FHLBank demand for six common (1.5-, 2-, 3-, 5-, 7-, and 10-year) bullet maturities, and then offers them daily through competitive auctions. These issues feature standardized terms and are reopened via auction for 3-month periods, enabling them to reach multibillion dollar size. TAP Issues can also be reopened as they roll down the curve. Callable bonds are issued daily, primarily as customized issues from reverse inquiry of institutional investors. The FHLBank Global Bond Program will periodically offer larger sized ($1 billion minimum for callable and $3 billion minimum for bullet maturities) with standardized term and are targeted to foreign investors in either U.S. dollars or other currencies.

The Federal Agricultural Mortgage Corporation (Farmer Mac)

The Federal Agricultural Mortgage Corporation (Farmer Mac) provides a secondary market for first mortgage agricultural real estate loans. It was created by Congress in 1998 to improve the availability of mortgage credit to farmers, ranchers, and rural homeowners, businesses, and communities. It does so by purchasing qualified loans from lenders in the same way as Freddie Mac and Fannie Mae.

Farmer Mac raises funds by selling debentures and mortgage-backed securities backed by the loans purchased. The latter securities are called agricultural mortgage-backed securities (AMBS). The debentures that are issued include discount notes and medium-term notes.

Federal Farm Credit Bank System (Farm Credit)

The purpose of the Federal Farm Credit Bank System (FFCBS) is to facilitate adequate, dependable credit and related services to the agricultural sector of the economy. The Farm Credit System consists of three entities: the Federal Land Banks, Federal Intermediate Credit Banks, and Banks for Cooperatives. Before 1979, each entity issued securities in its own name. Starting in 1979, they began to issue debt on a consolidated basis as "joint and several obligations" of the FFCBS. All financing for the FFCBS is arranged through the Federal Farm Credit Banks Funding Corporation (FFCBFC), which issues consolidated obligations.

The FFCBFC issues debt through five formats. Discount notes are offered daily through posted rates. Calendar Bonds of 3- and 6-month maturities are offered monthly. Designated Bonds of typically 2-year maturities can be offered twice monthly as either a new issue ($1 billion minimum) or reopening ($100 million minimum). Unscheduled bonds are issued throughout the month in varying sizes and structures either by competitive bidding or negotiated reverse inquiry by institutional investors. FFCB Master Notes are issued as individually tailored daily investment agreements usually designed for a single investor.

Student Loan Marketing Association (Sallie Mae)

Popularly known as "Sallie Mae," the Student Loan Marketing Association provides liquidity for private lenders participating in the Federal Guaranteed Student Loan Program, the Health Education Assistance Loan Program, and the PLUS loan program (a program that provides loans to the parents of undergraduate students). Sallie Mae issues unsecured debt in the form of discount notes, monthly floating-rate notes that mature in 6 months, longer term bullet and callable fixed rate notes, and zero-coupon bonds. In addition, it issues longer-term floating-rate bonds. In 1995, Sallie Mae began issuing floating-rate notes backed by student loans. These securities are called asset-backed securities. In Chapter 17, we describe asset-backed securities issued by Sallie Mae. In 1997 Sallie Mae began a process to unwind its status as a GSE. Until this multiyear process is completed, all debt issued under its GSE s status will be "grandfathered" as GSE debt until maturity.

Financing Corporation (FICO)

The deposits of savings and loans were once insured by the Federal Savings and Loan Insurance Corporation (FSLIC), overseen by the Federal Home Loan Bank Board. When difficulties encountered in the savings and loan industry raised concerns about FSLIC's ability to meet its responsibility to insure deposits, Congress passed the Competitive Equality and Banking Act in 1987. This legislation included provisions to recapitalize FSLIC and establish a new government-sponsored agency, the Financing Corporation (FICO), to issue debt in order to provide funding for FICO. FICO issued its first bonds in September 1987—a 30-year non-callable $500 million issue. The principal of these bonds is backed by zero-coupon Treasury securities. The legislation permitted FICO to issue up to $10.825 billion but not more than $3.75 billion in any 1 year. FICO was legislated to be dismantled in 2026, or after all securities have matured, whichever came sooner.

Resolution Trust Corporation (REFCORP)

The 1987 legislation that created FICO did not go far enough to resolve the problems facing the beleaguered savings and loan industry. In 1989, Congress passed more comprehensive legislation, the Financial Institutions Reform, Recovery and Enforcement Act (FIRREA). This legislation had three key elements. First, it transferred supervision of savings and loans to a newly created Office of Thrift Supervision. Second, it shifted the FSLIC insurance function to a Savings Association Insurance Fund, placed under the supervision of the Federal Deposit Insurance Corporation. Third, it established the Resolution Trust Corporation (RTC) as a GSE charged with the responsibility of liquidating or bailing out insolvent savings and loan institutions. The RTC obtained its funding from the Resolution Funding Corporation (REFCORP), which was authorized to issue up to $40 billion of long-term bonds. The principal of this debt is backed by zero-coupon Treasury bonds. REFCORP has issued both 30-year and 40-year bonds.

Farm Credit Financial Assistance Corporation (FACO)

In the 1980s, the FFCBS faced financial difficulties because of defaults on loans made to farmers. The defaults were caused largely by high interest rates in the late 1970s and early 1980s and by depressed prices on agricultural products. To recapitalize the Federal Farm Credit Bank System, Congress created the Farm Credit Financial Assistance Corporation (FACO) in 1987. This federally sponsored agency was authorized to issue debt to assist the FFCBS. FACO bonds, unlike the debt of other GSEs, are backed by the Treasury.

GSE Futures Market

In 2000, Agency futures contracts were listed on both the Chicago Merchantile Exchange (CME) and the Chicago Board of Trade (CBT). The contracts have essentially the same maturity and delivery specifications, modeled after the contracts for U.S. Treasury securities. The pool of deliverable issues is made up of qualifying Fannie Mae Benchmark and Freddie Mac Reference securities as both securities have similar credit, issuance, and tax characteristics. Currently 5- and 10-year maturity contracts are listed on the CBT. Futures contracts are described in more detail Chapter 29.

Repo Transactions Market in GSE Debt Collateral

Due to the high credit characteristics (all senior debt issued by the GSEs is rated Aaa by Moody's) discussed in more detail below and the steady increase in secondary trading activity, an active "repo" market has developed in GSE debt. Based on data published by The Bond Market Association[2] for the first six months of 2001, of all the repurchase transactions cleared through the Government Securities Clearing Corporation, 12.1% involved GSE debt collateral. For the like period in 2000, GSE collateral was used in 7.6% of total repurchase transactions. GSE debt is also accepted collateral for monetary policy related temporary reserve operations conducted by the Federal Reserve Bank of New York's "Open Market" desk. GSE collateral will typically have a 2% "haircut"[3] when used in securities repurchase transactions as compared to 5–7% haircuts on investment rated corporate debt.

Credit Risk

With the exception of the securities issued by the Farm Credit Financial Assistance Corporation, GSE securities are not backed by the full faith and credit of the U.S. government, as is the case with Treasury securities. Consequently, investors purchasing GSEs are exposed to credit risk. The yield spread between these securities and Treasury securities of comparable maturity reflects differences in perceived credit risk and liquidity. The spread attributable to credit risk reflects any financial difficulty faced by the issuing GSEs and the likelihood that the federal government will allow the GSE to default on its outstanding obligations.

Two examples will illustrate this point. In late 1981 and early 1982, the net income of the Federal National Mortgage Association weakened, causing analysts to report that the securities of this GSE carried greater credit risk than previously perceived. As a result, the yield spread over Treasuries on its debt rose from 91 basis points (on average) in 1981 to as high as 150 basis points. In subsequent years, the Federal National Mortgage Association's net income improved, and its yield spread to Treasuries narrowed. As another example, in 1985 the yield spread on securities of the Farm Credit Bank System rose substantially above those on comparable-maturity Treasuries because of this GSE's financial difficulties. The spread between 1985 and 1986 varied with the prospects of Congressional approval of a bailout measure for the system.

Yield Spreads

Because of credit risk and liquidity, GSEs will trade at a yield premium to comparable-maturity Treasury securities. The yield spread will differ

---

[2] The Bond Market Association's *Quarterly Review* , August 2001.
[3] A haircut is the extra percent of margin required for repo or reverse repo transactions involving any type of security. Haircut schedules will vary depending on credit, maturity, and type of security used.

for each issuing entity, the maturity of the issue, and the call feature. Exhibit 9.1 shows the yield spread for noncallable GSEs by maturity on July 13, 2001, as reported by Lehman Brothers. To see how the spread can vary over time, the last four columns show the spread for high, low, average, and standard deviation for the prior 12 months. Also shown in the exhibit are the spreads by maturity for the Fannie Mae Benchmarks and Freddie Mac Reference Notes.

EXHIBIT 9.1   GSE Spreads versus Benchmark Treasury (July 13, 2001)

		Last 12 Months			
	Current	High	Low	Avg.	St. Dev.
Noncallable					
2-yr	47.0	61.0	38.0	53.0	4.7
3-yr	93.0	93.0	48.0	61.8	8.1
5-yr	75.0	92.0	60.0	79.2	6.5
7-yr	108.0	108.0	85.0	92.4	4.2
10-yr	90.0	126.0	77.0	104.6	13.9
30-yr	95.0	135.0	74.0	108.6	18.0
FNMA Benchmarks					
2-yr	33.5	57.0	28.5	42.8	6.8
3-yr	75.5	76.0	44.5	57.7	8.1
5-yr	67.0	83.5	51.5	70.7	9.6
7-yr	86.0	97.0	55.0	83.9	7.8
10-yr	79.0	114.5	67.0	87.1	13.0
30-yr	83.0	125.0	62.0	88.7	16.0
FHLMC Reference Notes					
2-yr	37.5	56.0	—	38.5	15.2
3-yr	81.5	93.0	44.5	61.0	12.2
5-yr	69.5	84.5	51.5	71.2	9.9
10-yr	80.0	116.5	67.5	88.3	13.1
30-yr	84.0	127.0	64.0	90.2	16.1
Callable					
3-yr/nc 1	80.0	105.0	68.0	93.9	8.7
5-yr/nc 1	99.0	147.0	84.0	133.6	15.3
5-yr/nc 2	91.0	129.0	76.0	115.3	12.5
5-yr/nc 3	84.0	112.0	67.0	98.9	9.9
10-yr/nc 3	138.0	177.0	83.0	153.3	20.0
10-yr/nc 5	121.0	159.0	70.0	129.4	18.4

EXHIBIT 9.1   (Continued)

	Current	Last 12 Months			
		High	Low	Avg.	St. Dev.
Callable OAS					
3-yr/nc 1	60.0	70.0	45.0	61.9	5.4
5-yr/nc 1	80.0	85.0	65.0	76.5	4.7
5-yr/nc 2	80.0	85.0	65.0	76.5	4.7
5-yr/nc 3	80.0	85.0	65.0	76.5	4.8
10-yr/nc 3	95.0	153.0	70.0	109.6	14.1
FNMA Callable Benchmarks					
5-yr/nc2	87.0	—	—	—	—
10-yr/nc3	117.0	—	—	—	—

Source: Lehman Brothers, *Global Relative Value*, Fixed Income Research, July 16, 2001, p. 120.

Callable GSE securities will trade at a higher spread than noncallable securities. This can be seen in Exhibit 9.1 (see "Callable"). Look at the three 5-year callable securities—5-year/nc 1, 5-year/nc 3, and 5-year/nc 3. The longer the time before an issue can be called, the less valuable the embedded option. As a result, the longer the noncall period, the lower the spread.

Trading Volume

Exhibit 9.2 (on the following page) displays the average daily Primary Dealers reported volume, in quarterly increments, for the basic types of Treasury, GSE, and MBS securities. The growth in GSE securities issuance and the initiation of programmatic debt platforms is clearly reflected in the primary dealer trading activity over this 3-year period.

EXHIBIT 9.2   Comparative Trading Volumes for Treasury/GSE/MBS
(In billions of $)

Date	Treasury Bills	Treasury Coupons	GSE Discount Notes	GSE Coupons	MBS
1/15/98	40,433.5	181,795.3			55,003.8
4/16/98	39,048.9	203,730			67,647.2
7/16/98	34,957.1	189,217.2	38,383.4	5,253.3	67,258.7
10/15/98	31,278.1	192,956.2	40,509.8	8,572.3	74,399.3
1/14/99	31,807.9	177,715.8	42,649.6	8,261.9	73,182.6
4/15/99	32,867	168,454.9	41,365.1	12,035.1	76,031.8
7/15/99	29,241.8	162,577.6	41,337.3	11,621.4	72,127
10/14/99	25,872.6	150,775.5	45,006.5	10,699.2	66,243
1/20/00	29,538.4	144,233.7	46,040.5	10,069.7	54,623
4/20/00	30,765.6	178,058.9	52,234	16,650.1	63,466.9
7/20/00	24,130.4	176,732.8	57,875.4	17,761.1	66,853
10/26/00	20,607.4	160,924.9	52,714.7	18,782.4	69,677.9
2/1/01	30,876.6	203,114.4	52,993.8	23,256.9	81,224
7/19/01	27,257.1	255,000.1	58,586.7	28,560.7	101,618

Data Source: Federal Reserve Bank of New York.

CHAPTER 10

Municipal Securities

Frank J. Fabozzi, Ph.D., CFA
Adjunct Professor of Finance
School of Management
Yale University

Debt obligations are issued by state and local governments and by entities that they establish. Local government units include municipalities, counties, towns and townships, school districts, and special service system districts. Included in the category of municipalities are cities, villages, boroughs, and incorporated towns that received a special state charter. Counties are geographical subdivisions of states whose functions are law enforcement, judicial administration, and construction and maintenance of roads. As with counties, towns and townships are geographical subdivisions of states and perform similar functions as counties. A special-purpose service system district, or simply special district, is a political subdivision created to foster economic development or related services to a geographical area. Special districts provide public utility services (water, sewers, and drainage) and fire protection services. Public agencies or instrumentalities include authorities and commissions.

The number of municipal bond issuers is remarkable. One broker/ dealer's estimate places the total at 60,055. Also, Bloomberg Financial Markets' (Bloomberg) database contains 55,000 active issuers. Even more noteworthy is the number of different issues. Interactive Data, a company that provides pricing information for institutional investors, claims that it provides daily prices for more than 1.2 million individual issues in its database. Bloomberg's database contains 1.7 million issues with complete description pages.

In this chapter, we discuss the types of debt obligations issued by states, municipal governments, and public agencies and their instrumentalities. These securities are popularly referred to as *municipal securities*, although they are also issued by states and public agencies and their instruments.

TAX-EXEMPT AND TAXABLE MUNICIPAL SECURITIES

There are both tax-exempt and taxable municipal securities. "Tax-exempt" means that interest on a municipal security is exempt from federal income taxation. The tax-exemption of municipal securities applies to interest income, not capital gains. The exemption may or may not extend to taxation at the state and local levels.

The state tax treatment depends on (1) whether the issue from which the interest income is received is an "in-state issue" or an "out-of-state issue," and (2) whether the investor is an individual or a corporation. The treatment of interest income at the state level will be one of the following:

■ taxation of interest from municipal issues regardless of whether the issuer is in-state or out-of-state
■ exemption of interest from all municipal issues regardless of whether the issuer is in-state or out-of-state
■ exemption of interest from municipal issues that are in-state but some form of taxation where the source of interest is an out-of-state issuer.

For individuals, for those states that have a state income tax, only the following states tax interest income from in-state issuers (although there may be some exceptions for certain out-of-state issues): Illinois, Iowa, Kansas, Oklahoma, and Wisconsin. Exhibit 10.1 identifies those states for which out-of-state issues are exempt from taxation. This exhibit also shows the maximum state tax rate on municipals and the effective state tax rate on municipals. (We'll see what the last three column in Exhibit 10.1 mean later in this chapter.)

Most municipal securities that have been issued are tax-exempt. Municipal securities are commonly referred to as tax-exempt securities although taxable municipal securities have been issued and are traded in the market. Municipalities issue taxable municipal bonds to finance projects that do not qualify for financing with tax-exempt bonds. An example is a sports stadium. The most common types of taxable municipal bonds are industrial revenue bonds and economic development bonds. Since there are federally mandated restrictions on the amount of tax-exempt bonds that can be issued, a municipality will issue taxable bonds when the maximum is reached. There are some issuers who have issued taxable bonds in order to take advantage of demand outside of the United States.

EXHIBIT 10.1   Tax Treatment for Out-of State Issuer Interest Income for Individuals as of April 2, 2002 (1)

State	Max. State Tax on Muni.	Effective State Tax	Basis Point Reduction for a Bond Yielding...		
			3.00%	5.00%	6.00%
Alabama	5.00%	3.07%	9	15	18
Alaska (1)	0.00%	0.00%	0	0	0
Arizona	7.00%	4.30%	12	21	25
Arkansas	7.00%	4.30%	12	21	25
California	9.30%	5.71%	17	28	34
Colorado	4.63%	2.84%	8	14	17
Connecticut	4.50%	2.76%	8	13	16
Delaware	5.95%	3.65%	10	18	21
D.C. (2)	0.00%	0.00%	0	0	0
Florida (3)	0.00%	0.00%	0	0	0
Georgia	6.00%	3.68%	11	18	22
Hawaii	8.50%	5.22%	15	26	31
Idaho	8.20%	5.03%	15	25	30
Illinois (4)	3.00%	1.84%	5	9	11
Indiana (2)	0.00%	0.00%	0	0	0
Iowa (4)	8.98%	5.51%	16	27	33
Kansas	6.45%	3.96%	11	19	23
Kentucky	6.00%	3.68%	11	18	22
Louisiana	6.00%	3.68%	11	18	22
Maine	8.50%	5.22%	15	26	31
Maryland (5)	7.60%	4.67%	13	23	27
Massachusetts	5.60%	3.44%	10	17	20
Michigan	4.20%	2.58%	7	21	15
Minnesota	7.85%	4.82%	14	24	28
Mississippi	5.00%	3.07%	9	15	18
Missouri	6.00%	3.68%	11	18	22
Montana	11.00%	6.75%	20	33	40
Nebraska	6.68%	4.10%	12	20	24
Nevada(2)	0.00%	0.00%	0	0	0
New Hampshire	5.00%	3.07%	9	15	16

EXHIBIT 10.1   (Continued)

State	Max State Tax on Muni	Effective State Tax	Basis Point Reduction for a Bond Yielding...		
			3.00%	5.00%	6.00%
New Jersey	6.37%	3.91%	11	19	23
New Mexico	8.20%	5.03%	15	25	30
New York	6.85%	4.21%	12	21	25
New York City (7)	10.67%	6.55%	19	32	39
North Carolina	7.75%	4.76%	14	23	28
North Dakota	0.00%	0.00%	0	0	0
Ohio	6.98%	4.29%	12	21	25
Oklahoma (4)	6.75%	4.14%	12	20	24
Oregon	9.00%	5.53%	16	27	33
Pennsylvania (3)	2.80%	1.72%	5	8	10
Rhode Island (6)	10.10%	6.20%	18	31	37
South Carolina	7.00%	4.30%	12	21	25
South Dakota (2)	0.00%	0.00%	0	0	0
Tennessee	6.00%	3.68%	11	18	22
Texas	0.00%	0.00%	0	0	0
Utah (2)	0.00%	0.00%	0	0	0
Vermont	9.50%	5.83%	17	29	34
Virginia	5.75%	3.53%	10	17	21
Washington(2)	0.00%	0.00%	0	0	0
West Virginia	6.50%	3.99%	11	19	23
Wisconsin (4)	6.75%	4.14%	12	20	24
Wyoming (2)	0.00%	0.00%	0	0	0

Notes:
(1) Calculations assume a federal tax rate of 38.6% and 100% state tax deduction
(2) Out-of-state bonds are exempt from taxation
(3) Out-of-state bonds may be subject to person property tax
(4) Certain state and local bond issues are exempt from state taxation
(5) Counties may levy an income tax that ranges from 20% to 60% of the state income tax, depending on the county
(6) State tax rate is equal to 25. 5% of the federal tax rate
(7) New York State tax plus New York City tax
Derived from information published in *The Bond Buyer Notes* .
Source: "How Much Does it Take to 'Buy Out of State'?" Morgan Stanley Dean Witter. Text provided by John M. Dillon, FVP, Senior Municipal Analyst. Chart provided by Adam Topalian, Principal, Private Wealth Management, Market Strategist. Morgan Stanley Dean Witter is not a tax advisor. Investors should consult their tax advisor before making any tax-related investment decisions.

There are other types of tax-exempt bonds. These include bonds issued by nonprofit organizations. Such organizations are structured so that none of the income from the operations of the organization benefit an individual or private shareholder. The designation of a nonprofit organization must be obtained from the Internal Revenue Service. Since the tax-exempt designation is provided pursuant to Section 501(c)(3) of the Internal Revenue Code, the tax-exempt bonds issued by such organizations are referred to as *501(c)(3) obligations*. Museums and foundations fall into this category. Tax-exempt obligations also include bonds issued by the District of Columbia and any possession of the United States—Puerto Rico, the U.S. Virgin Islands, Guam, American Samoa, and the Northern Mariana Islands. The interest income from securities issued by U.S. territories and possessions is exempt from federal, state, and local income taxes in all 50 states.

TAX PROVISIONS AFFECTING MUNICIPALS

Federal tax rates and the treatment of municipal interest at the state and local levels affect municipal security values and strategies employed by investors. There are provisions in the Internal Revenue Code that investors in municipal securities should recognize. These provisions deal with original issue discounts, the alternative minimum tax, and the deductibility of interest expense incurred to acquire municipal securities.

Treatment of Original-Issue Discount

If at the time of issuance the original-issue price is less than its maturity value, the bond is said to be an *original-issue discount* (OID) *bond*. The difference between the par value and the original-issue price represents tax-exempt interest that the investor realizes by holding the issue to maturity.

For municipal bonds there is a complex treatment that few investors recognize when purchasing OID municipal bonds. The Revenue Reconciliation Act of 1993 specifies that any capital appreciation from the sale of a municipal bond that was purchased in the secondary market after April 30, 1993 could be either (1) free from any federal income taxes, (2) taxed at the capital gains rate, (3) taxed at the ordinary income rate, or (4) taxed at a combination of the two rates.

The key to the tax treatment is the *rule of de minimis* for any type of bond. The rule states that a bond is to be discounted up to 0.25% from the par value for each remaining year of a bond's life before it is affected by ordinary income taxes. The discounted price based on this rule is called the *market discount cutoff price*. The relationship between the market price at which an investor purchases a bond, the market discount cutoff price, and the tax treatment of the capital appreciation realized from a sale is as follows. If the bond is purchased at a market discount, but the price is higher than the market discount cutoff price, then any capital appreciation realized from a sale will be taxed at the capital gains rate. If the purchase price is lower than the market discount cutoff price, then any capital appreciation realized from a sale may be taxed as ordinary income or a combination of the ordinary income rate and the capital gains rate. (Several factors determine what the exact tax rate will be in this case.)

The market discount cutoff price changes over time because of the *rule of de minimis*. The price is revised. An investor must be aware of the revised price when purchasing a municipal bond because this price is used to determine the tax treatment.

Alternative Minimum Tax

Alternative minimum taxable income (AMTI) is a taxpayer's taxable income with certain adjustments for specified tax preferences designed to cause AMTI to approximate economic income. For both individuals and corporations, a taxpayer's liability is the greater of (1) the tax computed at regular tax rates on taxable income and (2) the tax computed at a lower rate on AMTI. This parallel tax system, the *alternative minimum tax* (AMT), is designed to prevent taxpayers from avoiding significant tax liability as a result of taking advantage of exclusions from gross income, deductions, and tax credits otherwise allowed under the Internal Revenue Code.

One of the tax preference items that must be included is certain tax-exempt municipal interest. As a result of AMT, the value of the tax-exempt feature is reduced. However, the interest of not all municipal issues is subject to the AMT. Under the current tax code, tax-exempt interest earned on all private activity bonds issued after August 7, 1986 must be included in AMTI. There are two exceptions. First, interest from bonds that are issued by 501(c)(3) organizations (i.e., not-for-profit organizations) is not subject to AMTI. The second exception is interest from bonds issued for the purpose of refunding if the original bonds were issued before August 7, 1986. The AMT does not apply to interest on governmental or nonprivate activity municipal bonds. An implication is that those issues that are subject to the AMT will trade at a higher yield than those exempt from AMT.

Deductibility of Interest Expense Incurred to Acquire Municipals

Ordinarily, the interest expense on borrowed funds to purchase or carry investment securities is tax deductible. There is one exception that is relevant to investors in municipal bonds. The Internal Revenue Code specifies that interest paid or accrued on "indebtedness incurred or continued to purchase or carry obligations, the interest on which is wholly exempt from taxes," is not tax deductible. It does not make any difference if any tax-exempt interest is actually received by the taxpayer in the taxable year. In other words, interest is not deductible on funds borrowed to purchase or carry tax-exempt securities.[1]

TYPES OF MUNICIPAL SECURITIES

Municipal securities are issued for various purposes. Short-term notes typically are sold in anticipation of the receipt of funds from taxes or receipt of proceeds from the sale of a bond issue, for example. Proceeds from the sale of short-term notes permit the issuing municipality to cover seasonal and temporary imbalances between outlays for expenditures and inflows from taxes. Municipalities issue long-term bonds as the principal means for financing both (1) long-term capital projects such as schools, bridges, roads, and airports, and (2) long-term budget deficits that arise from current operations.

An *official statement* describing the issue and the issuer is prepared for new offerings. Municipal securities have legal opinions that are summarized in the official statement. The importance of the legal opinion is twofold. First, bond counsel determines if the issue is indeed legally able to issue the securities. Second, bond counsel verifies that the issuer has properly prepared for the bond sale by having enacted various required ordinances, resolutions, and trust indentures and without violating any other laws and regulations.

---

[1] Special rules apply to commercial banks. At one time, banks were permitted to deduct all the interest expense incurred to purchase or carry municipal securities. Tax legislation subsequently limited the deduction first to 85% of the interest expense and then to 80%. The 1986 tax law eliminated the deductibility of the interest expense for bonds acquired after August 6, 1986. The exception to this nondeductibility of interest expense rule is for *bank-qualified issues*. These are tax-exempt obligations sold by small issuers after August 6, 1986 and purchased by the bank for its investment portfolio.

An issue is bank qualified if (1) it is a tax-exempt issue other than private activity bonds, but including any bonds issued by 501(c)3 organizations, and (2) it is designated by the issuer as bank qualified and the issuer or its subordinate entities reasonably do not intend to issue more than $10 million of such bonds. A nationally recognized and experienced bond attorney should include in the opinion letter for the specific bond issue that the bonds are bank qualified.

There are basically two types of municipal security structures: tax-backed debt and revenue bonds. We describe each type as follows, as well as variants.

Tax-Backed Debt

Tax-backed debt obligations are instruments issued by states, counties, special districts, cities, towns, and school districts that are secured by some form of tax revenue. Tax-backed debt includes general obligation debt, appropriation-backed obligations, debt obligations supported by public credit enhancement programs, and short-term debt instruments. We discuss each type as follows.

General Obligation Debt

The broadest type of tax-backed debt is *general obligation debt.* There are two types of general obligation pledges: unlimited and limited. An *unlimited tax general obligation debt* (also called an *ad valorem property tax debt*) is the stronger form of general obligation pledge because it is secured by the issuer's unlimited taxing power. The tax revenue sources include corporate and individual income taxes, sales taxes, and property taxes. Unlimited tax general obligation debt is said to be secured by the *full faith and credit of the issuer.* A limited tax general obligation debt (also called a *limited ad valorem tax debt*) is a limited tax pledge because for such debt there is a statutory limit on tax rates that the issuer may levy to service the debt.

Certain general obligation bonds are secured not only by the issuer's general taxing powers to create revenues accumulated in a general fund, but also by certain identified fees, grants, and special charges, which provide additional revenues from outside the general fund. Such bonds are known as *double-barreled* in security because of the dual nature of the revenue sources. For example, the debt obligations issued by special-purpose service systems may be secured by a pledge of property taxes, a pledge of special fees/operating revenue from the service provided, or a pledge of both property taxes and special fees/operating revenues. In the last case, they are double-barreled.

Appropriation-Backed Obligations

Agencies or authorities of several states have issued bonds that carry a potential state liability for making up shortfalls in the issuing entity's obligation. The appropriation of funds from the state's general tax revenue must be approved by the state legislature. However, the state's pledge is not binding. Debt obligations with this nonbinding pledge of tax revenue are called *moral obligation bonds.* Because a moral obligation bond requires legislative approval to appropriate the funds, it is classified as an *appropriation-backed obligation.*

An example of the legal language describing the procedure for a moral obligation bond that is enacted into legislation is as follows:

> In order to further assure the maintenance of each such debt reserve fund, there shall be annually apportioned and paid to the agency for deposit in each debt reserve fund such sum, if any, as shall be certified by the chairman of the agency to the governor and director of the budget as necessary to restore such reserve fund to an amount equal to the debt reserve fund requirement. The chairman of the agency shall annually, on or before December 1, make and deliver to the governor and director of the budget his certificate stating the sum or sums, if any, required to restore each such debt reserve fund to the amount aforesaid, and the sum so certified, if any, shall be apportioned and paid to the agency during the then current state fiscal year.

The purpose of the moral obligation pledge is to enhance the creditworthiness of the issuing entity. The first moral obligation bond was issued by the Housing Finance Agency of the state of New York. Historically, most moral obligation debt has been self-supporting; that is, it has not been necessary for the state of the issuing entity to make an appropriation. In those cases in which state legislatures have been called on to make an appropriation, they have. For example, the states of New York and Pennsylvania did this for bonds issued by their Housing Finance Agency; the state of New Jersey did this for bonds issued by the Southern Jersey Port Authority.

Another type of appropriation-backed obligation is lease-backed debt. There are two types of leases. One type is basically a secured long-term loan disguised as lease. The "leased" asset is the security for the loan. In the case of a bankruptcy, the court would probably rule such an obligation as the property of the user of the leased asset and the debt obligation of the user. In contrast, the second type of lease is a true lease in which the user of the leased asset (called the *lessee*) makes periodic payments to the leased asset's owner (called the *lessor*) for the right to use the leased asset. For true leases, there must be an annual appropriation by the municipality to continue making the lease payments.

Dedicated Tax-Backed Obligations

In recent years, states and local governments have issued increasing amounts of bonds where the debt service is to be paid from so-called dedicated revenues such as sales taxes, tobacco settlement payments, fees, and penalty payments. Many are structured to mimic asset-backed securities.

Debt Obligations Supported by Public Credit Enhancement Programs

While a moral obligation is a form of credit enhancement provided by a state, it is not a legally enforceable or legally binding obligation of the state. There are entities that have issued debt that carries some form of public credit enhancement that is legally enforceable. This occurs when there is a guarantee by the state or a federal agency or when there is an obligation to automatically withhold and deploy state aid to pay any defaulted debt service by the issuing entity. Typically, the latter form of public credit enhancement is used for debt obligations of a state's school systems.

Here are some examples of state credit enhancement programs. Virginia's bond guarantee program authorizes the governor to withhold state aid payments to a municipality and divert those funds to pay principal and interest to a municipality's general obligation holders in the event of a default. South Carolina's constitution requires mandatory withholding of state aid by the state treasurer if a school district is not capable of meeting its general obligation debt. Texas created the Permanent School Fund to guarantee the timely payment of principal and interest of the debt obligations of qualified school districts. The fund's income is obtained from land and mineral rights owned by the state of Texas.

Short-Term Debt Instruments

Short-term debt instruments include municipal notes, commercial paper, variable-rate demand obligations, and a hybrid of the last two products.

Municipal Notes   Usually, municipal notes are issued for a period of 12 months, although it is not uncommon for such notes to be issued for periods as short as 3 months and for as long as 3 years. Municipal notes include *bond anticipation notes* (BANs) and *cash flow notes*. BANs are issued in anticipation of the sale of long-term bonds. The issuing entity must obtain funds in the capital market to pay off the obligation.

Cash flow notes include *tax anticipation notes* (TANs) and *revenue anticipation notes* (RANs). TANs and RANs (also known as TRANs) are issued in anticipation of the collection of taxes or other expected revenues. These are borrowings to even out irregular flows into the treasury of the issuing entity. The pledge for cash flow notes can be either a broad general obligation pledge of the issuer or a pledge from a specific revenue source. The lien position of cash flow noteholders relative to other general obligation debt that has been pledged the same revenue can be either (1) a first lien on all pledged revenue, thereby having priority over general obligation debt that has been pledged the same revenue, (2) a lien that is in parity with general obligation debt that has been pledged the same revenue, or (3) a lien that is subordinate to the lien of general obligation debt that has been pledged the same revenue.

Commercial Paper   In Chapter 6, we discuss commercial paper issued by corporations. Commercial paper is also used by municipalities to raise funds on a short-term basis ranging from 1 day to 270 days. There are two types of commercial paper issued, unenhanced and enhanced. *Unenhanced commercial paper* is a debt obligation issued based solely on the issuer's credit quality and liquidity capability. *Enhanced commercial paper* is a debt obligation that is credit enhanced with bank liquidity facilities (e.g., a letter of credit), insurance, or a bond purchase agreement. The role of the enhancement is to reduce the risk of nonrepayment of the maturing commercial paper by providing a source of liquidity for payment of that debt in the event no other funds of the issuer are currently available.

Provisions in the 1986 tax act restricted the issuance of tax-exempt commercial paper. Specifically, the act limited the new issuance of municipal obligations that are tax exempt, and as a result, every maturity of a tax-exempt municipal issuance is considered a new debt issuance. Consequently, very limited issuance of tax-exempt commercial paper exists. Instead, issuers use one of the next two products to raise short-term funds.

Variable-Rate Demand Obligations   Variable-rate demand obligations (VRDOs) are floating-rate obligations that have a nominal long-term maturity but have a coupon rate that is reset either daily or every 7 days. The investor has an option to put the issue back to the trustee at any time with 7 days notice. The put price is par plus accrued interest. There are unenhanced and enhanced VRDOs.

Commercial Paper/VRDO Hybrid   The commercial paper/VRDO hybrid is customized to meet the cash flow needs of an investor. As with tax-exempt commercial paper, there is flexibility in structuring the maturity because a remarketing agent establishes interest rates for a range of maturities. Although the instrument may have a long nominal maturity, there is a put provision as with a VRDO. Put periods can range from 1 day to more than 360 days. On the put date, the investor can put back the bonds, receiving principal and interest, or the investor can elect to extend the maturity at the new interest rate and put date posted by the remarketing agent at that time. Thus the investor has two choices when initially purchasing this instrument: the interest rate and the put date. Interest is generally paid on the put date if the date is within 180 days. If the put date is more than 180 days forward, interest is paid semiannually.

Commercial paper dealers market these products under a proprietary name. For example, the Merrill Lynch product is called Unit Priced Demand Adjustable Tax-Exempt Securities, or UPDATES. Lehman Brothers markets these simply as money market municipals and Goldman Sachs refers to these securities as flexible rate notes.

Revenue Bonds [2]

The second basic type of security structure is found in a revenue bond. Revenue bonds are issued for enterprise financings that are secured by the revenues generated by the completed projects themselves, or for general public-purpose financings in which the issuers pledge to the bondholders the tax and revenue resources that were previously part of the general fund. This latter type of revenue bond is usually created to allow issuers to raise debt outside general obligation debt limits and without voter approval.

Revenue bonds can be classified by the type of financing. These include utility revenue bonds, transportation revenue bonds, housing revenue bonds, higher education revenue bonds, health care revenue bonds, seaport revenue bonds, sports complex and convention center revenue bonds, and industrial development revenue bonds. We discuss these revenue bonds as follows. Revenue bonds are also issued by Section 501(c)3 entities (museums and foundations).

Utility Revenue Bonds

Utility revenue bonds include water, sewer, and electric revenue bonds. Water revenue bonds are issued to finance the construction of water treatment plants, pumping stations, collection facilities, and distribution systems. Revenues usually come from connection fees and charges paid by the users of the water systems. Electric utility revenue bonds are secured by revenues produced from electrical operating plants. Some bonds are for a single issuer who constructs and operates power plants and then sells the electricity. Other electric utility revenue bonds are issued by groups of public and private investor-owned utilities for the joint financing of the construction of one or more power plants.

---

[2] The descriptions of revenue bonds, special bonds, and municipal derivative securities are adapted from my various writings with Sylvan G. Feldstein of The Guardian Life Insurance Company.

Also included as part of utility revenue bonds are resource recovery revenue bonds. A resource recovery facility converts refuse (solid waste) into commercially saleable energy, recoverable products, and residue to be landfilled. The major revenues securing these bonds usually are (1) fees paid by those who deliver the waste to the facility for disposal, (2) revenues from steam, electricity, or refuse-derived fuel sold to either an electric power company or another energy user, and (3) revenues from the sale of recoverable materials such as aluminum and steel scrap.

Transportation Revenue Bonds

Included in the category of transportation revenue bonds are toll road revenue bonds, highway user tax revenue bonds, airport revenue bonds, and mass transit bonds secured by farebox revenues. For toll road revenue bonds, bond proceeds are used to build specific revenue-producing facilities such as toll roads, bridges, and tunnels. The pledged revenues are the monies collected through tolls. For highway-user tax revenue bonds, the bondholders are paid by earmarked revenues outside of toll collections, such as gasoline taxes, automobile registration payments, and driver's license fees. The revenues securing airport revenue bonds usually come from either traffic-generated sources—such as landing fees, concession fees, and airline fueling fees—or lease revenues from one or more airlines for the use of a specific facility such as a terminal or hangar.

Housing Revenue Bonds

There are two types of housing revenue bonds: *single-family mortgage revenue bonds* and *multifamily housing revenue bonds*. The former revenue bonds are secured by the mortgages and loan repayments on 1-to-4-single-family homes. Security features vary but can include Federal Housing Administration (FHA), Veterans Administration (VA), or private mortgage insurance. Multifamily revenue bonds are usually issued for multifamily housing projects for senior citizens and low-income families. Some housing revenue bonds are secured by mortgages that are federally insured; others receive federal government operating subsidies or interest-cost subsidies. Still others receive only local property tax reductions as subsidies.

Higher Education Revenue Bonds

There are two types of higher education revenue bonds: college and university revenue bonds and student loan revenue bonds. The revenues securing public and private college and university revenue bonds usually include dormitory room rental fees, tuition payments, and sometimes the general assets of the college or university. For student loan revenue bonds, student loan repayments are sometimes 100% guaranteed either directly by the federal government or by a state guaranty agency.

Health Care Revenue Bonds

Health care revenue bonds are issued by private, not-for-profit hospitals (including rehabilitation centers, children's hospitals, and psychiatric institutions) and other health care providers such as health maintenance organizations (HMOs), continuing care retirement communities and nursing homes, cancer centers, university faculty practice plans, and medical specialty practices. The revenue for health care revenue bonds usually depends on federal and state reimbursement programs (such as Medicaid and Medicare), third-party commercial payers (such as Blue Cross, HMOs, and private insurance), and individual patient payments.

Seaport Revenue Bonds

The security for seaport revenue bonds can include specific lease agreements with the benefiting companies or pledged marine terminal and cargo tonnage fees.

Special Bond Structures

Some municipal securities have special security structures. These include insured bonds, bank-backed municipal bonds, and refunded bonds. We describe these three special security structures as follows.

Insured Bonds

Insured bonds, in addition to being secured by the issuer's revenue, are also backed by insurance policies written by commercial insurance companies. Insurance on a municipal bond is an agreement by an insurance company to pay the bondholder any bond principal and/or coupon interest that is due on a stated maturity date but that has not been paid by the bond issuer. The payment by the bond insurer is not an advance payment of the principal to pay off the issue and interest. Rather, the payments are made according the original schedule of payments that the issuer would have had to make.

Once issued, municipal bond insurance usually extends for the term of the bond issue, and it cannot be canceled by the insurance company. Because bond insurance is an unconditional promise by the insurer to meet the principal and interest payment obligations of the issuer, should the issuer be unable to do so for the life of the bond issue, it is different from credit enhancement in the form of a letter of credit, described later.

Because municipal bond insurance reduces credit risk for the investor, the marketability of certain municipal bonds can be greatly expanded. Municipal bonds that benefit most from the insurance would include lower-quality bonds, bonds issued by smaller governmental units not widely known in the financial community, bonds that have a sound though complex and confusing security structure, and bonds issued by infrequent local-government borrowers that do not have a general market following among investors.

There are two major groups of municipal bond insurers. The first includes the "monoline" companies that are primarily in the business of insuring municipal bonds. Almost all of the companies that are now insuring municipal bonds can be characterized as monoline in structure. The second group of municipal bond insurers includes the "multiline" property and casualty companies that usually have a wide base of business, including insurance for fires, collisions, hurricanes, and health problems. Most new issues in the municipal bond market today are insured by the following monoline insurers: AMBAC Indemnity Corporation (AMBAC); Financial Guaranty Insurance Company (FGIC); Financial Security Assurance, Inc. (FSA); and Municipal Bond Investors Assurance Corporation (MBIA Corp.). State insurance commissions regulate bond insurance companies. In addition, bond insurance companies are rated by credit rating agencies.

The credit quality considerations of bond insurers in evaluating whether or not to insure an issue are more stringent than that used by a rating agency in assigning a rating to an issue. This is because the bond insurer is making a commitment for the life of the issue. In contrast, a rating agency assigns a rating that would be expected to change in the future if there is credit deterioration of the issuer. That is, a rating agency can change a rating but an insurer cannot change its obligation. Consequently, bond insurers typically insure bonds that would have received an investment grade rating (at least triple B) in the absence of any insurance. Depending on competitive conditions and insurer costs, the premium charged for bond insurance typically ranges from 0.1% to 2% of the combined principal and interest payable over the issue's life.

Bank-Backed Municipal Bonds

Since the 1980s, municipal obligations have been increasingly supported by various types of credit facilities provided by commercial banks. The support is in addition to the issuer's cash flow revenues. There are three basic types of bank support: letter of credit, irrevocable line of credit, and revolving line of credit.

A *letter of credit* is the strongest type of support available from a commercial bank. Under this arrangement, the bank is required to advance funds to the trustee if a default has occurred. An *irrevocable line of credit* is not a guarantee of the bond issue, though it does provide a level of security. A *revolving line of credit* is a liquidity-type credit facility that provides a source of liquidity for payment of maturing debt in the event no other funds of the issuer are currently available. Because a bank can cancel a revolving line of credit without notice if the issuer fails to meet certain covenants, bond security depends entirely on the creditworthiness of the municipal issuer.

Refunded Bonds

Although originally issued as either revenue or general obligation bonds, municipal bonds are sometimes refunded. A refunding usually occurs when the original bonds are escrowed or collateralized by direct obligations guaranteed by the U.S. government. By this it is meant that a portfolio of securities guaranteed by the U.S. government are placed in a trust. The portfolio of securities is assembled such that the cash flows from the securities match the obligations that the issuer must pay. For example, suppose that a municipality has a 7% $100 million issue with 12 years remaining to maturity. The municipality's obligation is to make payments of $3.5 million every 6 months for the next 12 years and $100 million 12 years from now. If the issuer wants to refund this issue, a portfolio of U.S. government obligations can be purchased that has a cash flow of $3.5 million every 6 months for the next 12 years and $100 million 12 years from now.

Once this portfolio of securities whose cash flows match those of the municipality's obligation is in place, the refunded bonds are no longer general obligation or revenue bonds. The bonds are now supported by the cash flows from the portfolio of securities held in an escrow fund. Such bonds, if escrowed with securities guaranteed by the U.S. government, have little, if any, credit risk. They are the safest municipal bonds available.

The escrow fund for a refunded municipal bond can be structured so that the refunded bonds are to be called at the first possible call date or a subsequent call date established in the original bond indenture. Such bonds are known as *prerefunded municipal bonds*. While refunded bonds are usually retired at their first or subsequent call date, some are structured to match the debt obligation to the retirement date. Such bonds are known as *escrowed-to-maturity bonds*.

Municipal Derivative Securities

In recent years, a number of municipal products have been created from the basic fixed-rate municipal bonds. This has been done by splitting up cash flows of newly issued bonds as well as bonds existing in the secondary markets. These products have been created by dividing the coupon interest payments and principal payments into two or more bond classes, or *tranches*. The resulting bond classes may have far different yield and price volatility characteristics than the underlying fixed-rate municipal bond from which they were created.

The name derivative securities has been attributed to these bond classes because they derive their value from the underlying fixed-rate municipal bond. Two examples are municipal strip obligations and inverse floaters.

Municipal strip obligations are created when a municipal bond's cash flows are used to back zero-coupon instruments. The maturity value of each zero-coupon bond represents a cash flow of the underlying security. These are similar to the strips that are created in the Treasury market that are described in Chapter 7.

The primary vehicle to create inverse floaters is the Tender Offer Bond (TOB) programs. TOBs feature a liquidity facility, which makes these floating-rate derivatives putable and therefore eligible for money market funds. These liquidity facilities typically last 364 days and are provided by highly rated banks or broker-dealers. Several proprietary programs have been developed to market and sell plain-vanilla TOBs, which are used by mutual bond funds and insurance companies. Additionally, TOBs are used in more exotic combination trades by a few Wall Street structured products areas. Salomon Smith Barney's proprietary program is called "ROCs & ROLs." The short-term certificates are called ROCs or Residual Option Certificates. The inverse floaters are called the "ROLs" or Residual Option Longs. Lehman's is called RIBS and Trust Receipts, and Morgan Stanley's proprietary program is called municipal trust certificates.

DEBT RETIREMENT STRUCTURE

Municipal securities are issued with one of two debt retirement structures or a combination of both. Either a bond has a *serial maturity structure* or a *term maturity structure*. A serial maturity structure requires a portion of the debt obligation to be retired each year. A term maturity structure provides for the debt obligation to be repaid on a final date.

The various provisions explained in Chapter 1 for paying off an issue prior to maturity—call provisions and sinking fund provisions—are also found in municipal securities. In revenue bonds there is a *catastrophe call provision* that requires the issuer to call the entire issue if the facility is destroyed.

For housing revenue bonds, the repayment of principal is made with each payment by the borrower. More specifically, there is a schedule of principal repayments. We will explain this when we cover mortgage-backed securities in later chapters. Moreover, as will be explained, a borrower has the right to pay off a mortgage prior to the maturity date. Any principal repayment in excess of the scheduled principal repayment is called a prepayment.

CREDIT RISK

Investors rely on the credit ratings that are assigned by the nationally recognized statistical rating organizations, or simply rating companies. While there are three commercial rating companies, the two dominant companies with respect to rating municipal debt obligations are Standard & Poor's and Moody's. We discuss these ratings when we cover corporate debt obligations in Chapter 11. The factors that should be considered in assessing the credit risk of an issue are summarized next.

In assessing the credit risk of tax-backed debt, four basic categories are considered. The first category includes information on the issuer's debt structure to determine the overall debt burden. The second category relates to the issuer's ability and political discipline to maintain sound budgetary policy. The third category involves determining the specific local taxes and intergovernmental revenues available to the issuer, as well as obtaining historical information both on tax collection rates, which are important when looking at property tax levies, and on the dependence of local budgets on specific revenue sources. The final category of information is an assessment of the issuer's overall socioeconomic environment. The major factors here include trends of local employment distribution and composition, population growth, real estate property valuation, and personal income.

Revenue bonds are issued for either project or enterprise financings where the bond issuers pledge to the bondholders the revenues generated by the operating projects financed, or for general public-purpose financings in which the issuers pledge to the bondholders the tax and revenue resources that were previously part of the general fund. While there are numerous security structures for revenue bonds, the underlying principle in assessing the credit risk is whether the project being financed will generate sufficient cash flows to satisfy the obligations due bondholders.

The trust indenture and legal opinion should explain what are the revenues for the bonds and how they realistically may be limited by federal, state, and local laws and procedures. The importance of this is that although most revenue bonds are structured and appear to be supported by identifiable revenue streams, those revenues sometimes can be negatively affected directly by other levels of government.

Flow-of-Funds Structure for Revenue Bonds

For a revenue bond, the revenue of the enterprise is pledged to service the debt of the issue. The details of how revenue received by the enterprise will be disbursed are set forth in the trust indenture. Typically, the flow of funds for a revenue bond is as follows. First, all revenues from the enterprise are put into a revenue fund. From the revenue fund, disbursements for expenses are made to the following funds: *operation and maintenance fund*, *sinking fund*, *debt service reserve fund*, *renewal and replacement fund*, *reserve maintenance fund*, and *surplus fund*.[3]

TAX RISK

The investor in municipal securities is exposed to *tax risk*. There are two types of tax risk to which tax-exempt municipal security investors are exposed. The first is the risk that the federal income tax rate will be reduced. The higher the marginal tax rate, the greater the value of the tax-exemption feature. As the marginal tax rate declines, the price of a tax-exempt municipal security will decline.

The second type of tax risk is that a municipal bond issued as a tax-exempt issue may be eventually declared by the Internal Revenue Service to be taxable. This may occur because many municipal revenue bonds have elaborate security structures that could be subject to future adverse congressional action and IRS interpretation. A loss of the tax-exemption feature will cause the municipal bond to decline in value in order to provide a yield comparable to similar taxable bonds.

SECONDARY MARKET

Municipal bonds are traded in the over-the-counter market supported by municipal bond dealers across the country. Markets are maintained on smaller issuers (referred to as "local credits") by regional brokerage

---

[3] There are structures in which it is legally permissible for others to tap the revenues of the enterprise prior to the disbursement set forth in the flow-of-funds structure just described. For example, it is possible that the revenue bond could be structured such that the revenue is first applied to the general obligation of the municipality that has issued the bond.

firms, local banks, and by some of the larger Wall Street firms. Larger issuers (referred to as "general market names") are supported by the larger brokerage firms and banks, many of whom have investment banking relationships with these issuers. There are brokers who serve as intermediaries in the sale of large blocks of municipal bonds among dealers and large institutional investors. Some municipal bonds are traded via the Internet.

In the municipal bond markets, an odd lot of bonds is $25,000 or less in par value for retail investors. For institutions, anything less than $100,000 in par value is considered an odd lot. Dealer spreads depend on several factors. For the retail investor, the spread can range from as low as one-quarter of one point ($12.50 per $5,000 par value) on large blocks of actively traded bonds to four points ($200 per $5,000 of par value) for odd lot sales of an inactive issue. For institutional investors, the dealer spread rarely exceeds one-half of one point ($25 per $5,000 of par value).

The convention for both corporate and Treasury bonds is to quote prices as a percentage of par value with 100 equal to par. Municipal bonds, however, generally are traded and quoted in terms of yield (yield to maturity or yield to call). The price of the bond in this case is called a *basis price*. The exception is certain long-maturity revenue bonds. A bond traded and quoted in dollar prices (actually, as a percentage of par value) is called a *dollar bond*.

Actual price and trade information for specific municipal bonds is available on a daily basis at no charge via the Internet at *www.investing inbonds.com*. This is the homepage of the Bond Market Association. The trade information provided is from the Municipal Securities Rulemaking Board and Standard & Poor's J.J. Kenny. The original source of the trades reported are dealer-to-dealer transactions and dealer-to-institutional customer and retail (individual investor) transactions.

YIELDS ON MUNICIPAL BONDS

Because of the tax-exempt feature of municipal bonds, the yield on municipal bonds is less than that on Treasuries with the same maturity. Exhibit 10.2 demonstrates this point.

Shown in the exhibit is the yield on AAA general obligation municipal bonds and the yield on same-maturity U.S. Treasuries. The *yield ratio* is the ratio of the municipal yield to the yield of a same-maturity Treasury security. Notice that the yield ratio increases with maturity. The ratio has changed over time. The higher the tax rate, the more attractive the tax-exempt feature and the lower the yield ratio.

EXHIBIT 10.2   Yield Ratio AAA General Obligation Municipal Bonds to U.S. Treasuries of the Same Maturity (February 12, 2002)

Maturity	Yield on AAA General Obligation (%)	Yield on U.S. Treasury (%)	Yield Ratio
3 months	1.29	1.72	0.75
6 months	1.41	1.84	0.77
1 year	1.69	2.16	0.78
2 years	2.20	3.02	0.73
3 years	2.68	3.68	0.73
4 years	3.09	4.13	0.75
5 years	3.42	4.42	0.77
7 years	3.86	4.84	0.80
10 years	4.25	4.95	0.86
15 years	4.73	5.78	0.82
20 years	4.90	5.85	0.84
30 years	4.95	5.50	0.90

Source: Bloomberg Financial Markets

A common yield measure used to compare the yield on a tax-exempt municipal bond with a comparable taxable bond is the *equivalent taxable yield*. The equivalent taxable yield is computed as follows:

$$\text{Equivalent taxable yield} = \frac{\text{Tax-exempt yield}}{1 - \text{Marginal tax rate}}$$

For example, suppose an investor in the 40% marginal tax bracket is considering the acquisition of a tax-exempt municipal bond that offers a yield of 3.0%. The equivalent taxable yield is 5%, as shown below:

$$\text{Equivalent taxable yield} = \frac{0.03}{(1 - 0.40)} = 0.05 = 5\%$$

When computing the equivalent taxable yield, the traditionally computed yield to maturity is not the tax-exempt yield if the issue is selling at a discount because only the coupon interest is exempt from federal income taxes. Instead, the yield to maturity after an assumed tax rate on the capital gain is computed and used in the numerator of the formula above. The yield to maturity after an assumed tax on the capital gain is calculated.

Yield Spread Relationships within the Municipal Market

Yield spreads within the municipal bond market are attributable to various factors. Unlike the taxable fixed income market, there is no risk-free interest rate benchmark. Instead, the benchmark interest rate is for a generic triple-A rated general obligation bond or a revenue bond. Thus, the benchmark triple-A rated issue or index is the base rate used in the municipal bond market.

Tax Treatment at the State and Local Levels

State and local governments may tax interest income on municipal issues that are exempt from federal income taxes. Earlier in this chapter we discussed that a state can either tax or exempt the interest depending on whether the source of the interest is from an in-state or out-of-state issuer. The implication is that two municipal securities with the same credit rating and the same maturity may trade at some spread because of the relative demand for bonds of municipalities in different states. For example, in high-income-tax states such as New York and California, the demand for bonds of municipalities will drive down their yield relative to municipalities in a low-income-tax state such as Florida.

Since there is an advantage of buying in-state issues rather than out-of-state issues for individual investors in states that tax interest income on out-of-state issues, the question is: What is the yield given up? The last three columns in Exhibit 10.1, labeled "Basis Point Reduction," can be used by an individual investor to answer that question. It shows for in-state yield levels of 3%, 5%, and 6%, approximately how much must be deducted from the out-of-state issue to obtain the same in-state yield. Take for example, an investor in Oregon who is considering an in-state issue offering a 3% yield. From the exhibit, the basis point reduction can be seen to be 16. This means that if a municipal issuer outside of Oregon is offering a yield of 3.17% (assuming the same credit rating), then this would be the same as investing in a municipal issue in Oregon offering a yield of 3%.

CHAPTER 11

Corporate Bonds

Frank J. Fabozzi, Ph.D., CFA
Adjunct Professor of Finance
School of Management
Yale University

C orporations issue various types of financial instruments to raise funds. In general, corporate financial instruments can be classified as either a debt obligation or equity. In turn, equity can be classified as either common stock or preferred stock. In Chapter 4, common stock is covered. In Chapter 12, preferred stock is explained. Basically, the common stockholders are the residual owners of the firm. Preferred stockholders have priority over common stockholders in the case of distribution of dividends and proceeds in the case of liquidation of the firm.

The debt obligations of a corporation include bonds, medium-term notes, asset-backed securities, commercial paper, and bank loans. The key feature of corporate debt obligations is that they have a priority over the claims of equity holders in the case of bankruptcy. In this chapter we will focus on corporate bonds and medium-term notes. Other than the way in which they are issued, there is no difference between corporate bonds and medium-terms notes. Asset-backed securities, commercial paper, and banks loans are covered in Chapters 17, 6, and 19, respectively.

CORPORATE BANKRUPTCY AND CREDITOR RIGHTS

The holder of a corporate debt instrument has priority over the equity owners in a bankruptcy proceeding. Moreover, there are creditors who have priority over other creditors. The law governing bankruptcy in the United States is the Bankruptcy Reform Act of 1978.

One purpose of the act is to set forth the rules for a corporation to be either liquidated or reorganized. The liquidation of a corporation means that all the assets will be distributed to the holders of claims of the corporation and no corporate entity will survive. In a reorganization, a new corporate entity will result. Some security holders of the bankrupt corporation will receive cash in exchange for their claims, others may receive new securities in the corporation that results from the reorganization, and others may receive a combination of both cash and new securities in the resulting corporation.

Another purpose of the bankruptcy act is to give a corporation time to decide whether to reorganize or liquidate and then the necessary time to formulate a plan to accomplish either a reorganization or liquidation. This is achieved because when a corporation files for bankruptcy, the act grants the corporation protection from creditors who seek to collect their claims. The petition for bankruptcy can be filed either by the company itself, in which case it is called a *voluntary bankruptcy*, or by its creditors, in which case it is called an *involuntary bankruptcy*. A company that files for protection under the bankruptcy act generally becomes a "debtor-in-possession," and continues to operate its business under the supervision of the court.

The bankruptcy act comprises 15 chapters, each chapter covering a particular type of bankruptcy. Chapter 7 deals with the liquidation of a company; Chapter 11 deals with the reorganization of a company. When a company is liquidated, creditors receive distributions based on the "absolute priority rule" to the extent assets are available. The absolute priority rule is the principle that senior creditors are paid in full before junior creditors are paid anything. For secured and unsecured creditors, the absolute priority rule guarantees their seniority to equity-holders.

The Rights of Creditors: Theory versus Practice

What actually occurs in a bankruptcy? That is, does the absolute priority rule hold in a liquidation and a reorganization? In liquidations, the absolute priority rule generally holds. In contrast, studies of actual reorganizations under Chapter 11 have found that the violation of absolute priority is the rule rather than the exception.

There are several possible explanations suggested as to why in a reorganization the distribution made to claimholders will diverge from that required by the absolute priority principle. The first explanation is that the longer the negotiation process among the parties, the greater the bankruptcy costs and the smaller the amount to be distributed to all parties. This is because the longer the negotiation process among the parties, the more likely that the company will be operated in a manner that is not in the best interest of the creditors and, as a result, the smaller the amount remaining for distribution. Since all impaired classes including equityholders generally must approve the plan of reorganization, creditors often convince equityholders to accept the plan by offering to distribute some value to them.

A second explanation is that the violation of absolute priority reflects a recontracting process between stockholders and senior creditors that gives recognition to the ability of management to preserve value on behalf of stockholders. According to this view, creditors are less informed than management about the true economic operating conditions of the firm. Because the distribution to creditors in the plan of reorganization is based on the valuation by the firm, creditors without perfect information easily suffer the loss. Managers generally have a better understanding than creditors or stockholders about a firm's internal operations, while creditors and stockholders can have better information about industry trends. Management may therefore use its superior knowledge to present the data in a manner that reinforces its position.

The essence of another explanation is that the increasing complexity of firms that declare bankruptcy will accentuate the negotiating process and result in an even higher incidence of violation of the absolute priority rule. The likely outcome is further supported by the increased number of official committees in the reorganization process, as well as the increased number of financial and legal advisors.

There are some who argue that creditors will receive a higher value in reorganization than they would in liquidation in part because of the costs associated with liquidation. These additional costs include commissions and Chapter 7-specific costs. The commissions associated with liquidation can be significant. The commission charged on the sale of a particular asset could be as high as 20% of the gross proceeds from the asset. Total liquidation costs can be significant.

Finally, the lack of symmetry in the tax system (negative taxes are not permitted, although loss deductions may be carried forward) results in situations in which the only way to use all current loss deductions is to merge. The tax system may encourage continuance or merger and discourage bankruptcy.

SECURED DEBT[1]

A corporate debt issue can be secured or unsecured. Here we look at secured debt. By secured debt it is meant that some form of collateral is pledged to ensure repayment of the debt.

Utility Mortgage Bonds

Debt secured by real property such as plant and equipment is called *mortgage debt*. The largest issuers of mortgage debt are the electric utility companies. Other utilities, such as telephone companies and gas pipeline and distribution firms, have also used mortgage debt as sources of capital, but generally to a lesser extent than electrics.

Most electric utility bond indentures do not limit the total amount of bonds that may be issued. This is called an *open-ended mortgage*. The mortgage generally is a first lien on the company's real estate, fixed property, and franchises, subject to certain exceptions or permitted encumbrances owned at the time of the execution of the indenture or its supplement. The *after-acquired property clause* also subjects to the mortgage property that is acquired by the company after the filing of the original or supplemental indenture.

To provide for proper maintenance of the property and replacement of worn-out plant, maintenance fund, maintenance and replacement fund, or renewal and replacement fund, provisions are placed in indentures. These clauses stipulate that the issuer spend a certain amount of money for these purposes. Depending on the company, the required sums may be around 15% of operating revenues. As defined in other cases, the figure is based on a percentage of the depreciable property or amount of bonds outstanding.

Another provision for bondholder security is the *release and substitution of property clause*. If the company releases property from the mortgage lien (such as through a sale of a plant or other property that may have become obsolete or no longer necessary for use in the business, or through the state's power of eminent domain), it must substitute other property or cash and securities to be held by the trustee, usually in an amount equal to the released property's fair value. It may use the proceeds or cash held by the trustee to retire outstanding bonded debt. Certainly, a bondholder would not let go of the mortgaged property without substitution of satisfactory new collateral or adjustment in the amount of the debt because the bondholder should want to maintain the

---

[1] This section and the two that follow are adapted from Richard S. Wilson and Frank J. Fabozzi, *Corporate Bonds: Structure and Analysis* (Frank J. Fabozzi Associates, 1996).

value of the security behind the bond. In some cases the company may waive the right to issue additional bonds.

Although the typical electric utility mortgage does not limit the total amount of bonds that may be issued, certain issuance tests or bases usually have to be satisfied before the company can sell more bonds. New bonds are often restricted to no more than 60% to 66⅔% of the value of net bondable property. A further earnings test found often in utility indentures requires interest charges to be covered by pretax income available for interest charges of at least two times.

Mortgage bonds go by many different names. The most common of the senior lien issues are *first mortgage bonds* , *first refunding mortgage bonds* , *first and refunding mortgage bonds,* and *first and general mortgage bonds* .

There are instances when a company might have two or more layers of mortgage debt outstanding with different priorities. This situation usually occurs because companies cannot issue additional first mortgage debt (or the equivalent) under the existing indentures. Often this secondary debt level is called *general and refunding mortgage bonds* (G&R). In reality, this is mostly second mortgage debt.

Other Mortgage Debt

Nonutility companies do not offer much mortgage debt nowadays; the preferred form of debt financing is unsecured. In the past, railroad operating companies were frequent issuers of mortgage debt. In many cases, a wide variety of secured debt might be found in a company's capitalization. One issue may have a first lien on a certain portion of the right of way and a second mortgage on another portion of the trackage, as well as a lien on the railroad's equipment, subject to the prior lien of existing equipment obligations. Certain railroad properties are not subject to such a lien. Railroad mortgages are often much more complex and confusing to bond investors than other types of mortgage debt.

In the broad classification of industrial companies, only a few have first mortgage bonds outstanding. Mortgages may also contain maintenance and repair provisions, earnings tests for the issuance of additional debt, release and substitution of property clauses, and limited after-acquired property provisions. In some cases, shares of subsidiaries might also be pledged as part of the lien. Some mortgage bonds are secured by a lien on a specific property rather than on most of a company's property, as in the case of an electric utility.

Other Secured Debt

Debt can be secured by many different assets. Collateral trust debentures, bonds, and notes are secured by financial assets such as cash, receivables, other notes, debentures, or bonds, and not by real property. Collateral trust notes and debentures have been issued by companies engaged in vehicle leasing. The eligible collateral is held by a trustee and periodically marked to market to ensure that the market value has a liquidation value in excess of the amount needed to repay the entire outstanding bonds and accrued interest. If the collateral is insufficient, the issuer must bring the value of the collateral up to the required amount by a designated date. If the issuer is unable to do so, the trustee would then sell collateral and redeem bonds.

Another collateralized structure allows for the defeasance or "mandatory collateral substitution," which provides the investor assurance that it will continue to receive the same interest payments until maturity. Instead of redeeming the bonds with the proceeds of the collateral sale, the proceeds are used to purchase a portfolio of U.S. government securities in such an amount that the cash flow is sufficient to meet the principal and interest payments on the bond. Because of the structure of these issues, the rating agencies (discussed below) have assigned such issues their highest credit rating. The rating is based on the strength of the collateral and the issue's structure, not on the issuer's credit standing.

Equipment Trust Financing: Railroads

Railroads and airlines have financed much of their rolling stock and aircraft with secured debt. The securities go by various names such as *equipment trust certificates* (ETCs), in the case of railroads, and secured equipment certificates, guaranteed loan certificates, and loan certificates in the case of airlines. Railroads probably comprise the largest and oldest group of issuers of secured equipment financing.

The credit ratings for equipment trust certificates are higher than on the same company's mortgage debt or other public debt securities. This is due primarily to the collateral value of the equipment, its superior standing in bankruptcy compared with other claims, and the instrument's generally self-liquidating nature. The railroad's actual creditworthiness may mean less for some equipment trust investors than for investors in other railroad securities or, for that matter, other corporate debt obligations.

Equipment trust certificates are issued under agreements that provide a trust for the benefit of the investors. Each certificate represents an interest in the trust equal to its principal amount and bears the railroad's unconditional guarantee of prompt payment, when due, of the principal and dividends (the term dividends is used because the payments represent income from a trust and not interest on a loan). The trustee holds the title to the equipment, which when the certificates are retired, passes to, or vests in, the railroad, but the railroad has all other ownership rights. It can take the depreciation and can utilize any tax benefits on the subject equipment. The railroad agrees to pay the trustee sufficient rental for the principal payments and the dividends due on the certificates, together with expenses of the trust and certain other charges. The railroad uses the equipment in its normal operations and is required to maintain it in good operating order and repair (at its own expense). If the equipment is destroyed, lost, or becomes worn out or unsuitable for use (i.e., suffers a "casualty occurrence"), the company must substitute the fair market value of that equipment in the form of either cash or additional equipment. Cash may be used to acquire additional equipment unless the agreement states otherwise. The trust equipment is usually clearly marked that it is not the railroad's property.

Immediately after the issuance of an ETC, the railroad has an equity interest in the equipment that provides a margin of safety for the investor. Normally, the ETC investor finances no more than 80% of the cost of the equipment and the railroad the remaining 20%. Although modern equipment is longer-lived than that of many years ago, the ETC's length of maturity is still generally the standard 15 years (there are some exceptions).

The structure of the financing usually provides for periodic retirement of the outstanding certificates. The most common form of ETC is the serial variety. It is usually issued in 15 equal maturities, each one coming due annually in years 1 through 15. There are also sinking fund equipment trust certificates where the ETCs are retired through the operation of a normal sinking fund, one-fifteenth of the original amount issued per year.

The standing of railroad or common carrier ETCs in bankruptcy is of vital importance to the investor. Because the equipment is needed for operations, the bankrupt railroad's management will more than likely reaffirm the lease of the equipment because, without rolling stock, it is out of business. Cases of disaffirmation of equipment obligations are very rare indeed, but if equipment debt were to be disaffirmed, the trustee could repossess and then try to release or sell it to others. Any deficiency due the equipment debtholders would still be an unsecured claim against the bankrupt railway company. Standard-gauge, nonspecialized equipment should not be difficult to release to another railroad.

The Bankruptcy Reform Act of 1978 provides specifically that railroads be reorganized, not liquidated, and subchapter IV of Chapter 11 grants them special treatment and protection. One very important feature found in Section 77(j) of the preceding Bankruptcy Act was carried over to the new law. Section 1168 states that Section 362 (the automatic stay provision) and Section 363 (the use, sale, or lease of property section) are not applicable in railroad bankruptcies. It protects the rights of

the equipment lenders while giving the trustee the chance to cure any
defaults. Railroad bankruptcies usually do not occur overnight but
creep up gradually as the result of steady deterioration over the years.
New equipment financing capability becomes restrained. The outstanding equipment debt at the time of bankruptcy often is not substantial
and usually has a good equity cushion built in. Equipment debt of non-
common carriers such as private car leasing lines does not enjoy this
special protection under the Bankruptcy Act.

Airline Equipment Debt

Airline equipment debt has some of the special status that is held by
railroad equipment trust certificates. Like railroad equipment obligations, certain equipment debt of certified airlines, under Section 1110 of
the Bankruptcy Reform Act of 1978, is not subject to Sections 362 and
363 of the Act, namely the automatic stay and the power of the court to
prohibit the repossession of the equipment. The creditor must be a lessor, a conditional vendor, or hold a purchase money security interest
with respect to the aircraft and related equipment. The secured equipment must be new, not used. It gives the airline 60 days in which to
decide to cancel the lease or debt and to return the equipment to the
trustee. If the reorganization trustee decides to reaffirm the lease in
order to continue using the equipment, it must perform or assume the
debtor's obligations, which become due or payable after that date, and
cure all existing defaults other than those resulting solely from the
financial condition, bankruptcy, insolvency, or reorganization of the airline. Payments resume, including those that were due during the delayed
period. Thus, the creditor will get either the payments due according to
the terms of the contract or the equipment.

The equipment is an important factor. If the airplanes are of recent
vintage, well-maintained, fuel efficient, and relatively economical to operate, it is more likely that a company in distress and seeking to reorganize
would assume the equipment lease. However, if the outlook for reorganization appears dim from the outset and the airplanes are older and less
economical, the airline could very well disaffirm the lease. In this case,
releasing the aircraft or selling it at rents and prices sufficient to continue
the original payments and terms to the security holders might be difficult. Of course, the resale market for aircraft is on a plane-by-plane basis
and highly subject to supply and demand factors. Multimillion-dollar
airplanes have a somewhat more limited market than do boxcars and
hopper cars worth only a fraction of the value of an airplane.

The lease agreement required the airline to pay a rental sufficient to
cover the interest, amortization of principal, and a return to the equity

participant. The airline was responsible for maintaining and operating the aircraft, as well as providing for adequate insurance. It must also keep the equipment registered and record the ETC and lease under the Federal Aviation Act of 1958. In the event of a loss or destruction of the equipment, the company may substitute similar equipment of equal value and in as good operating condition and repair and as airworthy as that which was lost or destroyed. It also has the option to redeem the outstanding certificates with the insurance proceeds.

Do not be misled by the title of the issue just because the words "secured" or "equipment trust" appear. Investors should look at the collateral and its estimated value based on the studies of recognized appraisers compared with the amount of equipment debt outstanding. Is the equipment new or used? Do the creditors benefit from Section 1110 of the Bankruptcy Reform Act? Because the equipment is a depreciable item and subject to wear, tear, and obsolescence, a sinking fund starting within several years of the initial offering date should be provided if the debt is not issued in serial form. Of course, the ownership of the aircraft is important as just noted. Obviously, one must review the obligor's financials because the investor's first line of defense depends on the airline's ability to service the lease rental payments.

UNSECURED DEBT

We have discussed many of the features common to secured debt. Take away the collateral and we have unsecured debt.

Unsecured debt, like secured debt, comes in several different layers or levels of claim against the corporation's assets. But in the case of unsecured debt, the nomenclature attached to the debt issues sounds less substantial. For example, "general and refunding mortgage bonds" may sound more important than "subordinated debentures," even though both are basically second claims on the corporate body. In addition to the normal debentures and notes, there are junior issues; for example, General Motors Acceptance Corporation, in addition to senior unsecured debt, had public issues designated as "senior subordinated" and "junior subordinated notes," representing the secondary and tertiary levels of the capital structure. The difference in a high-grade issuer may be considered insignificant as long as the issuer maintains its quality. But in cases of financial distress, the junior issues usually fare worse than the senior issues. Only in cases of very well-protected junior issues will investors come out whole— in which case, so would the holders of senior indebtedness. Thus, many investors are more than willing to take junior debt of high-grade companies; the minor additional risk, compared to that of the senior debt of lower-rated issuers, may well be worth the incremental income.

Subordination of the debt instrument might not be apparent from the issue's name. This is often the case with bank and bank-related securities. For example, the term "capital notes" would not sound like a subordinated debt instrument to most inexperienced investors unfamiliar with the jargon of the debt world. Yet capital notes are junior securities.

Credit Enhancements

Some debt issuers have other companies guarantee their loans. This is normally done when a subsidiary issues debt and the investors want the added protection of a third-party guarantee. The use of guarantees makes it easier and more convenient to finance special projects and affiliates, although guarantees are extended to operating company debt.

There are also other types of third-party credit enhancements. Some captive finance subsidiaries of industrial companies enter into agreements requiring them to maintain fixed charge coverage at such a level so that the securities meet the eligibility standards for investment by insurance companies under New York State law. The required coverage levels are maintained by adjusting the prices at which the finance company buys its receivables from the parent company or through special payments from the parent company. These supplemental income maintenance agreements, while usually not part of indentures, are very important considerations for bond buyers.

Another credit-enhancing feature is the *letter of credit* (LOC) issued by a bank. A LOC requires the bank to make payments to the trustee when requested so that monies will be available for the bond issuer to meet its interest and principal payments when due. Thus the credit of the bank under the LOC is substituted for that of the debt issuer. Insurance companies also lend their credit standing to corporate debt, both new issues and outstanding secondary market issues, a common practice for municipal bonds.

While a guarantee or other type of credit enhancement may add some measure of protection to a debtholder, caution should not be thrown to the wind. In effect, an investor's job may become even more complex because an analysis of both the issuer and the guarantor should be performed. In many cases, only the latter is needed if the issuer is merely a financing conduit without any operations of its own. However, if both concerns are operating companies, it may very well be necessary to analyze both because the timely payment of principal and interest ultimately will depend on the stronger party. A downgrade of the enhancer's claims-paying ability reduces the value of the bonds.

Negative Pledge Clause

One of the important protective provisions for unsecured debtholders is the *negative pledge clause*. This provision, found in most senior unsecured debt issues and a few subordinated issues, prohibits a company from creating or assuming any lien to secure a debt issue without equally securing the subject debt issue(s) (with certain exceptions). Designed to prevent other creditors from obtaining a senior position at the expense of existing creditors, "it is not intended to prevent other creditors from sharing in the position of debenture holders."[2] Again, it is not necessary to have such a clause unless the issuer runs into trouble. But like insurance, it is not needed until the time that no one wants arrives.

Negative pledge clauses are not just boiler plate material added to indentures and loan agreements to give lawyers extra work. They have provided additional security for debtholders when the prognosis for corporate survival was bleak.

INDENTURES

As we have seen, corporate debt securities come with an infinite variety of features, yet we have just scratched the surface. While prospectuses may provide most of the needed information, the indenture is the more important document. The indenture sets forth in great detail the promises of the issuer. Here we will look at what indentures of corporate debt issues contain. For corporate debt securities to be publicly sold, they must (with some permitted exceptions) be issued in conformity with the Trust Indenture Act of 1939. This act requires that debt issues subject to regulation by the Securities and Exchange Commission (SEC) have a trustee. Also, the trustee's duties and powers must be spelled out in the indenture.

Some corporate debt issues are issued under a *blanket indenture* or *open-ended indenture*; for others a new indenture must be written each time a new series of debt is sold. A blanket indenture is often used by electric utility companies and other issuers of general mortgage bonds, but it is also found in unsecured debt. The initial or basic indenture may have been entered into 30 or more years ago, but as each new series of debt is created, a supplemental indenture is written.

---

[2] *Commentaries on Model Debenture Indenture Provisions 1965 Model All Registered Issues 1967 and Certain Negotiable Provisions Which May Be Included in a Particular Incorporating Indenture* (Chicago, IL: American Bar Foundation, 1971), p. 350.

Covenants

Certain limitations and restrictions on the borrower's activities are set forth in the indenture. Some covenants are common to all indentures, such as to pay interest, principal, and premium, if any, on a timely basis, to pay all taxes and other claims when due unless contested in good faith, and to maintain all properties used and useful in the borrower's business in good condition and working order. These are often called affirmative covenants since they call upon the debtor to make promises to do certain things.

Negative covenants require the borrower not to take certain actions. Borrowers want the least restrictive loan agreement available, while lenders should want the most restrictive, consistent with sound business practices. A company might be willing to include additional restrictions (up to a point) if it can get a lower interest rate on the loan. When companies seek to weaken restrictions in their favor, they are often willing to pay more interest or give other consideration.

An infinite variety of restrictive covenants can be placed on borrowers, depending on the type of debt issue, the economics of the industry and the nature of the business, and the lenders' desires. Some of the more common restrictive covenants include various limitations on the company's ability to incur debt, since unrestricted borrowing can lead a company and its debtholders to ruin. Thus, debt restrictions may include limits on the absolute dollar amount of debt that may be outstanding or may require a ratio test (e.g., debt may be limited to no more than 60% of total capitalization or that it cannot exceed a certain percentage of net tangible assets).

There may be an *interest coverage test* or *fixed-charge coverage test* of which there are two types. One, a *maintenance test,* requires the borrower's ratio of earnings available for interest or fixed charges to be at least a certain minimum figure on each required reporting date (such as quarterly or annually) for a certain preceding period. The other type, a *debt incurrence test,* only comes into play when the company wishes to do additional borrowing. In order to take on additional debt, the required interest or fixed-charge coverage figure adjusted for the new debt must be at a certain minimum level for the required period prior to the financing. Incurrence tests are generally considered less stringent than maintenance provisions. There could also be cash flow tests or requirements and working capital maintenance provisions.

CORPORATE BOND RATINGS

Many large institutional investors and many investment banking firms have their own credit analysis departments. Few individual investors and institutional bond investors, though, do their own analysis. Instead, they rely primarily on nationally recognized statistical rating organizations that perform credit analyses and issue their conclusions in the form of ratings. The three commercial rating companies are Moody's Investors Service, Standard & Poor's Corporation, and Fitch.

Rating Symbols

The rating systems use similar symbols, as shown in Exhibit 11.1. In all systems the term *high grade* means low credit risk, or conversely, high probability of future payments. The highest-grade bonds are designated by Moody's by the symbol Aaa, and by the other two rating systems by the symbol AAA. The next highest grade is denoted by the symbol Aa (Moody's) or AA (the other two rating systems); for the third grade all rating systems use A. The next three grades are Baa or BBB, Ba or BB, and B, respectively. There are also C grades.

Bonds rated triple A (AAA or Aaa) are said to be *prime*; double A (AA or Aa) are of *high quality*; single A issues are called *upper medium grade*; and triple B are *medium grade*. Lower-rated bonds are said to have speculative elements or be distinctly speculative.

All rating agencies use rating modifiers to provide a narrower credit quality breakdown within each rating category. S&P and Fitch use a rating modifier of plus and minus. Moody's uses 1, 2, and 3 as its rating modifiers.

Bond issues that are assigned a rating in the top four categories are referred to as *investment-grade bonds*. Issues that carry a rating below the top four categories are referred to as *noninvestment-grade bonds* or *speculative bonds*, or more popularly as *high-yield bonds* or *junk bonds*. Thus, the corporate bond market can be divided into two sectors: the investment-grade and noninvestment-grade markets.

A bond issue may be assigned a "dual" rating if there is a feature of the bond that rating agencies believe would alter the credit risk. For example, Standard & Poor's assigns a dual rating to putable bonds. The first rating is the normal rating based on the likelihood of repayment of principal and interest as due in the absence of the put feature. The second rating reflects the ability of the issuer to repay the principal at the put date if the bondholder exercises the put option.

The Rating Process

The rating process involves the analysis of a multitude of quantitative and qualitative factors over the past, present, and future. Ratings should be prospective because future operations should provide the wherewithal to repay the debt. The ratings apply to the particular issue, not the issuer. While bond analysts rely on numbers and calculate many ratios to get a picture of the company's debt-servicing capacity, a rating is only an opinion or judgment of an issuer's ability to meet all of its obligations when due, whether during prosperity or during times of stress. The purpose of ratings is to rank issues in terms of the probability of default, taking into account the special features of the issue, the relationship to other obligations of the issuer, and current and prospective financial conditions, and operating performance.

EXHIBIT 11.1 Summary of Corporate Bond Rating Systems and Symbols

Fitch	Moody's	S&P	Summary Description
Investment Grade — High Creditworthiness			
AAA	Aaa	AAA	Gilt edge, prime, maximum safety
AA+	Aa1	AA+	
AA	Aa2	AA	High-grade, high-credit quality
AA–	Aa3	AA–	
A+	A1	A+	
A	A2	A	Upper-medium grade
A–	A3	A–	
BBB+	Baa1	BBB+	
BBB	Baa2	BBB	Lower-medium grade
Speculative — Lower Creditworthiness			
BB+	Ba1	BB+	
BB	Ba2	BB	Low grade, speculative
BB–	Ba3	BB–	
B+	B1		
B	B2	B	Highly speculative
B–	B3		
Predominantly Speculative, Substantial Risk, or in Default			
CCC+		CCC+	
CCC	Caa	CCC	Substantial risk, in poor standing
CC	Ca	CC	May be in default, very speculative
C	C	C	Extremely speculative
		CI	Income bonds—no interest being paid
DDD			
DD			Default
D		D	

In conducting its examination, the rating agencies consider the four Cs of credit—character, capacity, collateral, and covenants. The first of the Cs stands for *character of management*, the foundation of sound credit. In assessing management quality, the analysts at Moody's, for example, try to understand the business strategies and policies formulated by management. Following are factors that are considered: strategic direction, financial philosophy, conservatism, track record, succession planning, and control systems.

The next C is *capacity* or the ability of an issuer to repay its obligations. In assessing the ability of an issuer to pay, an analysis of the financial statements is undertaken. In addition to management quality, the factors examined by Moody's, for example, are industry trends, the regulatory environment, basic operating and competitive position, financial position and sources of liquidity, company structure (including structural subordination and priority of claim), and parent company support agreements.

The third C, *collateral*, is looked at not only in the traditional sense of assets pledged to secure the debt, but also to the quality and value of those unpledged assets controlled by the issuer. In both senses the collateral is capable of supplying additional aid, comfort, and support to the debt and the debtholder. Assets form the basis for the generation of cash flow that services the debt in good times as well as bad.

The final C is for *covenants*, the terms and conditions of the lending agreement. As discussed earlier, covenants lay down restrictions on how management operates the company and conducts its financial affairs.

Ratings of bonds change over time. Issuers are *upgraded* when their likelihood of default (as assessed by the rating company) decreases, and *downgraded* when their likelihood of default (as assessed by the rating company) increases. The rating companies publish the issues that they are reviewing for possible rating change.

To help investors understand how ratings change over time, the rating agencies publish this information periodically in the form of a table. This table is called a *rating transition matrix*. The table is useful for investors to assess potential downgrades and upgrades. A rating transition matrix is available for different holding periods. Typically these tables show that for investment-grade bonds, the probability of a downgrade is much higher than for an upgrade. Second, the longer the transition period, the lower the probability that an issue will retain its original rating.

SPECULATIVE-GRADE BONDS

Speculative-grade bonds are those rated below investment grade by the rating agencies (i.e., BB+ and lower by Fitch and S&P, and Ba1 and less by Moody's). They may also be unrated, but not all unrated debt is speculative. Also known as junk bonds, promoters have given these securities other euphemisms such as high-interest bonds, high-opportunity debt, and high-yield securities. While some of these terms may be misleading to the uninitiated, they are used throughout the investment world, with "junk" and "high yield" the most popular. We will also use "junk" and "high yield" in this chapter.

Speculative-grade bonds may not be high-yielders at all because they may not be paying any interest, and there may be little hope for the resumption of interest payments; even the return expected from a reorganization or liquidation may be low. Some high-yield instruments may not be speculative-grade at all because they may carry investment-grade ratings. The higher yields may be due to fears of premature redemption of high-coupon bonds in a lower interest rate environment. The higher yields may be caused by a sharp decline in the securities markets, which has driven down the prices of all issues, including those with investment merit.

While the term "junk" tarnishes the entire less-than-investment-grade spectrum, it is applicable to some specific situations. Junk bonds are not useless stuff, trash, or rubbish as the term would imply. At times, investors overpay for their speculative-grade securities so they feel that they may have purchased junk or worthless garbage. But this is also the case when they have overpaid for high-grade securities. There are other times when profits may be made from buying junk bonds; certainly then, these bonds are not junk but something that may be quite attractive. Also, not all securities in this low-grade sector of the market are on the verge of default or bankruptcy. Many issuers might be on the fringe of the investment-grade sector. Market participants should be discriminating in the choice of their terminology.

Types of Issuers

Several types of issuers fall into the less-than-investment-grade high-yield category. These include original issuers, fallen angels, and restructuring and leveraged buyouts.

Original issuers may be young, growing corporations lacking the stronger balance sheet and income statement profile of many established corporations, but often with lots of promise. Also called venture capital situations or growth or emerging market companies, the debt is often sold with a story projecting future financial strength. From this we get the term "story bond." There are also the established operating firms with financials neither measuring up to the strengths of investment-grade corporations nor possessing the weaknesses of companies on the verge of bankruptcy.

Fallen angels are formerly companies with investment-grade-rated debt that have come upon hard times with deteriorating balance sheet and income statement financial parameters.[3] They may be in default or near bankruptcy. In these cases, investors are interested in the workout value of the debt in a reorganization or liquidation, whether within or outside of the bankruptcy courts. Some refer to these issues as "special situations."

Restructurings and leveraged buyouts are companies that have deliberately increased their debt burden with a view toward maximizing shareholder value. The shareholders may be the existing public group to which the company pays a special extraordinary dividend, with the funds coming from borrowings and the sale of assets. Cash is paid out, net worth decreased and leverage increased, and ratings drop on existing debt. Newly issued debt gets junk bond status because of the company's weakened financial condition.

In a leveraged buyout (LBO), a new and private shareholder group owns and manages the company.[4] The debt issue's purpose may be to retire other debt from commercial and investment banks and institutional investors incurred to finance the LBO. The debt to be retired is called "bridge financing" because it provides a bridge between the initial LBO activity and the more permanent financing.

Unique Features of Some Issues

Often actions taken by management that result in the assignment of a noninvestment-grade bond rating result in a heavy interest payment burden. This places severe cash flow constraints on the firm. To reduce this burden, firms involved with heavy debt burdens have issued bonds with *deferred coupon structures* that permit the issuer to avoid using cash to make interest payments for a period of 3 to 7 years. There are three types of deferred coupon structures: (1) deferred-interest bonds, (2) step-up bonds, and (3) payment-in-kind bonds.

Deferred-interest bonds are the most common type of deferred coupon structure. These bonds sell at a deep discount and do not pay interest for an initial period, typically from 3 to 7 years. (Because no interest is paid for the initial period, these bonds are sometimes referred to as zero-coupon bonds.) *Step-up bonds* do pay coupon interest, but the coupon rate is low for an initial period and then increases ("steps up") to a higher coupon rate. Finally, *payment-in-kind* (PIK) *bonds* give the issuer an option to pay cash at a coupon payment date or give the bondholder

---

[3] Companies that have been upgraded to investment-grade status are referred to as rising stars.

[4] For a further discussion, see Chapter 26.

a similar bond (i.e., a bond with the same coupon rate and a par value equal to the amount of the coupon payment that would have been paid). The period during which the issuer can make this choice varies from 5 to 10 years.

An *extendible reset bond* is a bond structure that allows the issuer to reset the coupon rate so that the bond will trade at a predetermined price. The coupon rate may reset annually or even more frequently, or reset only one time over the life of the bond. Generally, the coupon rate at the reset date will be the average of rates suggested by two investment banking firms. The new rate will then reflect (1) the level of interest rates at the reset date and (2) the credit spread the market wants on the issue at the reset date. The difference between an extendible reset bond and a floating-rate bond is that for the latter the coupon rate resets according to a fixed spread over the reference rate, with the index spread specified in the indenture. The amount of the index spread reflects market conditions at the time the issue is offered. The coupon rate on an extendible reset bond, in contrast, is reset based on market conditions (as suggested by several investment banking firms) at the time of the reset date. Moreover, the new coupon rate reflects the new level of interest rates and the new spread that investors seek.

The advantage to investors of extendible reset bonds is that the coupon rate will reset to the market rate—both the level of interest rates and the credit spread—in principle keeping the issue at par value. In fact, experience with extendible reset bonds has not been favorable during the recent period of difficulties in the high-yield bond market.

"Clawback provisions" in speculative-grade bond issues grant the issuer a limited right to redeem a portion of the bonds during the non-call period if the proceeds are from an initial public stock offering. The disadvantage of a clawback provision for the investor is that the bonds can be called at a point in time just when the issuer's finances have been strengthened through access to the equity market.

Default and Recovery Statistics

We conclude our discussion of high-yield corporate bonds with a discussion of default and recovery statistics. From an investment perspective, default rates by themselves are not of paramount significance: it is perfectly possible for a portfolio of high-yield corporate bonds to suffer defaults and to outperform Treasuries at the same time, provided the yield spread of the portfolio is sufficiently high to offset the losses from default.

Furthermore, because holders of defaulted bonds typically recover a percentage of the face amount of their investment, the default loss rate can be substantially lower than the default rate. The *default loss rate* is defined as follows:

default loss rate = default rate × recovery rate

For example, a default rate of 5% and a recovery rate of 30% means a default loss rate of only 3.5% (70% of 5%).

Therefore, focusing exclusively on default rates merely highlights the worst possible outcome that a diversified portfolio of high-yield corporate bonds would suffer, assuming all defaulted bonds would be totally worthless.

In their 1987 study, Altman and Nammacher found that the annual default rate for low-rated corporate debt was 2.15%, a figure that Altman has updated since to 2.40%.[5] The firm of Drexel Burnham Lambert (DBL), a major issuer of high-yield bonds at one time, also estimated default rates of about 2.40% per year.[6] Asquith, Mullins, and Wolff, however, found that nearly one out of every three high-yield corporate bonds defaults.[7] The large discrepancy arises because the studies use three different definitions of "default rate"; even if applied to the same universe of bonds (which they are not), all three results could be valid simultaneously.

Altman and Nammacher define the default rate as the par value of all high-yield bonds that defaulted in a given calendar year, divided by the total par value outstanding during the year. Their estimates (2.15% and 2.40%) are simple averages of the annual default rates over a number of years. DBL took the cumulative dollar value of all defaulted high-yield bonds, divided by the cumulative dollar value of all high-yield issuance, and further divided by the weighted average number of years outstanding to obtain an average annual default rate. Asquith, Mullins, and Wolff use a cumulative default statistic. For all bonds issued in a given year, the default rate is the total par value of defaulted issues as of the date of their study, divided by the total par amount originally issued to obtain a cumulative default rate. Their result (that about one in three high-yield bonds default) is not normalized by the number of years outstanding.

---

[5] Edward I. Altman and Scott A. Nammacher, *Investing in Junk Bonds* (New York: John Wiley, 1987) and Edward I. Altman, "Research Update: Mortality Rates and Losses, Bond Rating Drift," unpublished study prepared for a workshop sponsored by Merrill Lynch Merchant Banking Group, High Yield Sales and Trading, 1989.

[6] 1984–1989 issues of *High Yield Market Report: Financing America's Futures* (New York and Beverly Hills: Drexel Burnham Lambert, Incorporated).

[7] Paul Asquith, David W. Mullins, Jr., and Eric D. Wolff, "Original Issue High Yield Bonds: Aging Analysis of Defaults, Exchanges, and Calls," *Journal of Finance* (September 1989), pp. 923–952.

Although all three measures are useful indicators of bond default propensity, they are not directly comparable. Even when restated on an annualized basis, they do not all measure the same quantity. The default statistics from all studies, however, are surprisingly similar once cumulative rates have been annualized. Altman and Kishore find for the period 1971 to 1997 that the arithmetic average default rate for the entire period was 2.6%, and the weighted average default rate (i.e., weighted by the par value of the amount outstanding for each year) was 3.3%. For a more recent time period, 1985 to 1997, the arithmetic average default rate was higher, 3.7%.[8]

Next let's look at the historical loss rate realized by investors in high-yield corporate bonds. Just as with default rates, there are different methodologies that can be used to compute recovery rates. For example, the methodology for computing the default loss rate by Altman and Kishore is as follows.[9] First, the default loss of principal is computed by multiplying the default rate for the year by the average loss of principal. The average loss of principal is computed by first determining the recovery per $100 of par value. They quantify the recovery per $100 of par value using the weighted average price of all issues after default. The difference between par value of 100 and the recovery of principal is the default loss of principal.

Several studies have found that the recovery rate is closely related to the bond's seniority. Altman and Kishore computed the weighted average recovery rate for 777 bond issues that defaulted between 1978 and 1997 for the following bond classes: (1) senior-secured, (2) senior-unsecured, (3) senior-subordinated, (4) subordinated, and (5) discount and zero-coupon. The recovery rate for senior-secured bonds averaged 59% of face value, compared with 49% for senior-unsecured, 35% for senior-subordinated, and 32% for subordinated bonds.

CORPORATE BOND INDEXES

The three broad-based U.S. bond market indexes are the Lehman Brothers U.S. Aggregate Index, the Salomon Smith Barney (SSB) Broad Investment-Grade Bond Index (BIG), and the Merrill Lynch Domestic Market Index. The three broad-based U.S. bond market indexes are computed daily and are "market-value weighted." This means that for each issue, the ratio of

---

[8] See Exhibits 5 and 6 in Edward I. Altman and Vellore M. Kishore, "Defaults and Returns on High Yield Bonds," Chapter 14 in Frank J. Fabozzi (ed.), *The Handbook of Corporate Debt Instruments* (New Hope, PA: Frank J. Fabozzi Associates, 1998).
[9] See Exhibits 5 and 6 in Altman and Kishore, "Defaults and Returns on High Yield Bonds."

the market value of an issue relative to the market value of all issues in the index is used as the weight of the issue in all calculations.

Each index is broken into sectors. The Lehman index, for example, is divided into the following six sectors: (1) Treasury sector, (2) agency sector, (3) mortgage passthrough sector, (4) commercial mortgage-backed securities sector, (5) asset-backed securities sector, and (6) credit sector. The credit sector in the Lehman Brothers index includes corporate issues. In all three indexes, the only issues that are included are investment-grade issues.

The three investment banking firms that created the broad-based bond market indexes have also created separate high-yield indexes. In addition, the firms of CS First Boston and Donaldson Lufkin and Jenrette have created indexes for this sector. The number of issues included in each high-yield index varies from index to index. The types of issues permitted (e.g., convertible, floating-rate, payment-in-kind) also varies.

MEDIUM-TERM NOTES

Medium-term notes (MTNs) are debt instruments with the unique characteristic that they are offered continuously to investors by an agent of the issuer. Investors can select from several maturity ranges: 9 months to 1 year, more than 1 year to 18 months, more than 18 months to 2 years, and so on up to any number of years. MTNs are registered with the Securities and Exchange Commission under Rule 415 (the "shelf registration rule"), which gives a corporation the maximum flexibility for issuing securities on a continuous basis. MTNs are also issued by foreign corporations, federal agencies, supranational institutions, and foreign countries. The MTN market is primarily institutional, with individual investors being of little import.

The term "medium-term note" to describe this corporate debt instrument is misleading. Traditionally, the term "note" or "medium-term" was used to refer to debt issues with a maturity greater than 1 year but less than 15 years. Certainly this is not a characteristic of MTNs since they have been sold with maturities from 9 months to 30 years, and even longer. For example, in July 1993, Walt Disney Corporation issued a security with a 100-year maturity off its medium-term note shelf registration.

Borrowers have flexibility in designing MTNs to satisfy their own needs. They can issue fixed- or floating-rate debt. The coupon payments can be denominated in U.S. dollars or in a foreign currency.

An issuer with an active MTN program will post the rates for the maturity ranges it wishes to sell. The purchaser may usually set the maturity as any business day within the offered maturity range, subject to the borrower's approval. This is a very important benefit of MTNs because it enables a lender to match maturities with its own specific requirements. As they are continuously offered, an investor can enter the market when portfolio needs require and will usually find suitable investment opportunities.

There are issuers of MTNs that couple their offerings with transactions in the derivative markets (options, futures/forwards, swaps, caps, and floors) to create debt obligations with more interesting risk/return features than are available in the corporate bond market. These are called *structured notes*. Structured notes allow institutional investors who are restricted to investing in investment-grade debt issues the opportunity to participate in other asset classes to make a market play. For example, an investor who buys an MTN whose coupon rate is tied to the performance of the S&P 500 is participating in the equity market without owning common stock. If the coupon rate is tied to a foreign stock index, the investor is participating in the equity market of a foreign country without owning foreign common stocks.

YIELD AND YIELD SPREADS

Corporate bond yields trade at a spread (i.e., a higher yield) over Treasury securities with the same maturity (or duration). The spread reflects the credit risk and liquidity risk associated with corporate bonds relative to Treasury securities. The size of the spread varies over time depending on the market's expectation regarding the concerns with defaults. For example, yield spreads for corporates tend to widen (i.e., increase) in recessions and narrow (i.e., decrease) in prosperous economic periods. At a given point in time, the spread varies with the credit rating. Specifically, the lower the credit rating of a corporate bond, the greater the spread. So, for example, a double A rated corporate bond will offer a lower spread than a single A rated corporate bond.

For corporate bonds that are callable, a portion of the spread reflects the call risk associated with holding a callable corporate bond relative to a Treasury security with a comparable maturity. The measure commonly used for a spread that adjusts for the risks associated with a bond being called is the *option-adjusted spread*.

Exhibit 11.2 shows the spread over Treasuries for corporate bonds issued by industrial, utility, finance, and bank entities as reported by Lehman Brothers. The spreads are for bullet issues (i.e., issues that are noncallable for life) and are reported by maturity and credit rating. The exhibit shows the 90-day high, low, and average for the week ending

September 7, 2001. Basically, it is a term structure of credit spreads. For callable and putable securities, an option-adjusted spread is calculated. Exhibit 11.3 shows the estimated spread for the 20 largest issuers in the credit sector of the Lehman Brothers Index on September 7, 2001. Exhibit 11.4 shows the approximate spreads for the largest issues in the Lehman High Yield Index on the same date.

Within the corporate bond market there is a spread based on maturity for issues of the same credit quality. For example, 1-year single A corporate bonds will offer a different spread than 10-year single A corporate bonds. In the Treasury securities market we saw this type of relationship between yield and maturity which in graphical form is called the Treasury yield curve. There are corporate yield curves by credit rating. That is, there is a AAA corporate yield curve and a BBB corporate yield curve. Typically credit spread increases with maturity. In addition, the shape of the yield curve is not the same for all credit ratings. The lower the credit rating, typically, the steeper the yield curve. For each corporate yield curve, a corporate yield spread curve by credit rating can be obtained by simply subtracting the corresponding yield on the Treasury yield curve.

CONVERTIBLE BONDS

A convertible bond is a corporate bond issue that can be converted into common stock at the option of the bondholder. We conclude this chapter with a description of the basic features of convertible bonds and their investment characteristics.

Basic Features of Convertible Bonds

The conversion provision of a bond grants the bondholder the right to convert the security into a predetermined number of shares of common stock of the issuer. An *exchangeable bond* grants the bondholder the right to exchange the security for the common stock of a firm other than the issuer of the security. In our discussion, we use the term convertible bond to refer to both convertible and exchangeable bonds.

Conversion Ratio

The number of shares of common stock that the bondholder will receive from exercising the call option of a convertible bond is called the *conversion ratio*. The conversion privilege may extend for all or only some portion of the bond's life, and the stated conversion ratio may change over time. It is always adjusted proportionately for stock splits and stock dividends.

EXHIBIT 11.2 Secondary Market Bullet Bid Spreads for 90 Days (in Basis Points) for Corporate Bonds (September 7, 2001)

Maturity	AA Sprd./1-wk. Chg.	AA 90-day High	AA Low	AA Avg.	A Sprd./1-wk. Chg.	A 90-day High	A Low	A Avg.	BBB Sprd./1-wk. Chg.	BBB 90-day High	BBB Low	BBB Avg.
Industrials												
5	79/+1	80	65	76	108/+5	108	96	102	143/+2	155	140	148
10	103/+4	103	94	98	149/+5	149	124	132	169/+5	170	157	165
30	116/+4	116	107	112	166/+5	166	144	152	185/+5	188	174	182
Utilities												
5	97/+2	110	90	98	128/0	135	125	132	167/+4	173	157	167
10	115/0	130	110	117	143/0	150	140	147	195/+3	200	185	193
30	125/0	145	120	127	157/0	165	153	160	215/+3	222	205	215
Finance												
3	82/+2	88	80	83	123/+1	123	97	110				
5	96/+2	109	91	100	150/+9	150	122	136				
10	129/+2	136	118	126	186/+9	186	149	165				
Banks												
3	70/0	79	70	73	82/0	88	80	84				
5	98/0	107	90	100	112/+3	117	101	111				
10	130/+4	132	119	125	151/+4	151	138	144				
	BB				**B**							
High Yield												
10	378/−21	433	329	377	712/−15	825	703	743				

Source: Lehman Brothers, *Global Relative Value*, Fixed Income Research, September 10, 2001, p. 144.

274

EXHIBIT 11.3 Approximate Benchmark Spreads of the 20 Largest Issuers in the Credit Sector of the Lehman Brothers Index (September 7, 2001)

	2-yr.	5-yr.	10-yr.	30-yr.
Ford/Ford Motor Credit (A2/A)	120	165	202	215
CitiGroup/Citicorp (Aa2/AA–)	65	99	124	130
GM/GMAC (A2/A)	115	165	197	190
Worldcom, Inc. (A3/BBB+)	170	195	260	275
BankAmerica Corp. (Aa3/A)	70	115	148	155
GE (Aaa/AAA)	52	66	97	n/a
IBRD (Aaa/AAA)	15	48	65	62
Mexico (Baa3/BB+)	150	250	322	330
Verizon Communications (A1/A+)	80	115	145	165
AT&T/TCI Communications (A2/A)	125	160	195	220
Tyco International (Baa1/A)	107	130	167	180
IADB (Aaa/AAA)	20	50	73	76
Household Finance (A2/A)	75	118	160	n/a
Wells Fargo (Aa3/A)	65	96	135	n/a
Qwest Communications Intl. (Baa1/BBB+)	155	195	235	245
Morgan Stanley Dean Witter & Co. (Aa3/AA–)	75	120	160	n/a
DaimlerChrysler (A3/A–)	110	158	195	215
Lehman Brothers (A2/A)	80	130	165	n/a
AOL Time Warner (Baa1/BBB+)	100	122	165	188
JP Morgan Chase & Co. (A1/A)	70	110	150	n/a
Average 9/7/01	91	130	168	189
Change vs. 8/31/01	1	3	6	9
Year-to-date change	–37	–40	–36	–41

Source: Lehman Brothers, *Global Relative Value*, Fixed Income Research, September 10, 2001, p. 145.

For example, suppose that the Izzobaf Corporation issued a convertible bond with a conversion ratio of 25.32 shares. This means that for each $1,000 of par value of this issue the bondholder exchanges for Izzobaf's common stock, he will receive 25.32 shares.

At the time of issuance of a convertible bond, the issuer effectively grants the bondholder the right to purchase the common stock at a price equal to:

$$\frac{\text{Par value of convertible bond}}{\text{Conversion ratio}}$$

EXHIBIT 11.4 Approximate Benchmark Spreads of the Largest Issues in the Lehman High Yield Index (September 7, 2001)

	Coupon	Maturity	Rating	Bid Spread (bp) Current	1-wk. Chg.
Nextel Communications, Inc.	9.375	11/15/09	B1/B	1,081	140
Allied Waste North America	10.000	8/1/09	B2/B+	443	10
Level 3 Communications	9.13	5/1/08	B3/CCC+	2,161	−3
Nextel Communications, Inc.	0.000	2/15/08	B1/B	176	0
Echostar DBS Corporation	9.375	2/1/09	B1/B	389	−7
Telewest Communications PLC	11.00	10/1/07	B2/B	1,200	57
Calpine Canada Energy Fin.	8.500	5/1/08	BA1/BB+	345	0
Williams Communications Group, Inc.	10.875	10/1/09	B2/B+	2,378	−5
Charter Communications Hlds, LLC	8.63	4/1/09	B2/B+	423	−30
Charter Communications Hlds, LLC	0.000	4/1/11	B2/B+	617	−42
Average				921	12

Source: Lehman Brothers, *Global Relative Value*, Fixed Income Research, September 10, 2001, p. 145.

This price is referred to in the prospectus as the *stated conversion price*. Sometimes the issue price of a convertible bond may not be equal to par. In such cases, the stated conversion price at issuance is usually determined by the issue price.

The stated conversion price for the Izzobaf convertible issue is:

$$\text{Stated conversion price} = \frac{\$1,000}{25.32} = \$39.49$$

Call Provisions

Almost all convertible issues are callable by the issuer. Typically there is a noncall period (i.e., a time period from the time of issuance that the convertible bond may not be called). Some issues have a provisional call feature that allows the issuer to call the issue during the noncall period if the stock reaches a certain price.

Put Provision

A put option grants the bondholder the right to require the issuer to redeem the issue at designated dates for a predetermined price. Some convertible bonds are putable. Put options can be classified as "hard" puts and "soft" puts. A hard put is one in which the convertible bond must be redeemed by the issuer only for cash. In the case of a soft put, the issuer has the option to redeem the convertible bond for cash, common stock, subordinated notes, or a combination of the three.

Traditional Analysis of Convertible Bonds

There have been sophisticated models for valuing corporate bonds using option pricing theory since a convertible bond has several embedded options—the right to convert by the bondholder, the right to call by the issuer, and, if the issue is putable, the right to put the issue by the bondholder. In this section we discuss the traditional analysis used to analyze convertible bonds so that their investment characteristics can be appreciated.

Minimum Value of a Convertible Bond

The *conversion value* or *parity value* of a convertible bond is the value of the security if it is converted immediately. That is,

Conversion value = Market price of common stock × Conversion ratio

The minimum price of a convertible bond is the greater of

1. Its conversion value, or
2. Its value as a security without the conversion option—that is, based on the convertible bond's cash flows if not converted. This value is called its *straight value* or *investment value* .

If the convertible bond does not sell for the greater of these two values, arbitrage profits could be realized. For example, suppose the conversion value is greater than the straight value, and the convertible bond is selling at its straight value. An investor can buy the convertible bond at the straight value and convert it. By doing so, the investor realizes a gain equal to the difference between the conversion value and the straight value. Suppose, instead, the straight value is greater than the conversion value, and the convertible bond is selling at its conversion value. By buying the convertible bond at the conversion value, the investor will realize a higher yield than a comparable straight security.

To illustrate, assuming that the market price per share of Izzobaf's common stock is currently $33, then for Izzobaf's convertible issue the conversion value per $1,000 of par value is equal to:

$$\text{Conversion value} = \$33 \times 25.32 = \$835.56$$

Therefore, the conversion value per $100 of par value is $83.556.

Suppose that given the appropriate yield for a straight bond issued by Izzobaf's convertible would result in a straight price of $98.19 per $100 par value. Since the minimum value of the Izzobaf convertible bond is the greater of the conversion value and the straight value, the minimum value is $98.19.

Market Conversion Price

The price that an investor effectively pays for the common stock if the convertible bond is purchased and then converted into the common stock is called the *market conversion price* or *conversion parity price*. It is found as follows:

$$\text{Market conversion price} = \frac{\text{Market price of convertible bond}}{\text{Conversion ratio}}$$

The market conversion price is a useful benchmark because once the actual market price of the stock rises above the market conversion price, any further stock price increase is certain to increase the value of the convertible bond by at least the same percentage. Therefore, the market conversion price can be viewed as a breakeven price.

An investor who purchases a convertible bond rather than the underlying stock pays a premium over the current market price of the stock. This premium per share is equal to the difference between the market conversion price and the current market price of the common stock. That is,

Market conversion premium per share
= Market conversion price − Current market price

The market conversion premium per share is usually expressed as a percentage of the current market price as follows:

$$\text{Market conversion premium ratio} = \frac{\text{Market conversion premium per share}}{\text{Market price of common stock}}$$

Why would someone be willing to pay a premium to buy the stock? Recall that the minimum price of a convertible bond is the greater of its conversion value or its straight value. Thus, as the common stock price declines, the price of the convertible bond will not fall below its straight value. The straight value therefore acts as a floor for the convertible bond's price. The straight value at some future date, however, is unknown; the value will change as interest rates in the market change.

Assuming the following for the Izzobaf convertible bond:

Market price per $1,000 of par value = $1,065.00
Conversion ratio = 25.32

Then the calculation of the market conversion price, market conversion premium per share, and market conversion premium ratio for the Izzobaf convertible bond is shown below:

$$\text{Market conversion price} = \frac{\$1,065}{25.32} = \$42.06$$

$$\text{Market conversion premium per share} = \$42.06 - \$33 = \$9.06$$

$$\text{Market conversion premium ratio} = \frac{\$9.06}{\$33} = 0.275 \text{ or } 27.5\%$$

Current Income of Convertible Bond versus Common Stock

As an offset to the market conversion premium per share, investing in the convertible bond rather than buying the stock directly generally means that the investor realizes higher current income from the coupon interest paid than would be received as common stock dividends paid on the number of shares equal to the conversion ratio. Investors evaluating a convertible bond typically compute the time it takes to recover the premium per share by computing the premium payback period (which is also known as the breakeven time). This is computed as follows:

$$\frac{\text{Market conversion premium per share}}{\text{Favorable income differential per share}}$$

where the favorable income differential per share is equal to the following for a convertible bond:

$$\frac{\text{Coupon interest} - (\text{Conversion ratio} \times \text{Common stock dividend per share})}{\text{Conversion ratio}}$$

The premium payback period does not take into account the time value of money.

Assume for the Izzobaf convertible bond, the coupon rate is 5.75%. We know that the market conversion premium per share is $9.06. The favorable income differential per share is found as follows:

Coupon interest from bond = 0.0575 × $1,000 = $57.50

Conversion ratio × Dividend per share = 25.32 × $0.90 = $22.79
Therefore,

$$\text{Favorable income differential per share} = \frac{\$57.50 - \$22.79}{25.32} = \$1.37$$

and

$$\text{Premium payback period} = \frac{\$9.06}{\$1.37} = 6.6 \text{ years}$$

Without considering the time value of money, the investor would recover the market conversion premium per share in about 7 years.

Downside Risk with a Convertible Bond

Investors usually use the straight value as a measure of the downside risk of a convertible bond because the price of the convertible bond cannot fall below this value. Thus, the straight value acts as the current floor for the price of the convertible bond. The downside risk is measured as a percentage of the straight value and computed as follows:

$$\text{Premuim over straight value} = \frac{\text{Market price of the convertible bond}}{\text{Straight value}} - 1$$

The higher the premium over straight value, all other factors constant, the less attractive the convertible bond.

Despite its use in practice, this measure of downside risk is flawed because the straight value (the floor) changes as interest rates change. If interest rates rise, the straight value falls, making the floor fall. Therefore, the downside risk changes as interest rates change.

For our hypothetical convertible bond, the Izzobaf bond, since the market price of the convertible bond is $106.5 and the straight value is $98.19, the premium over straight value is:

$$\text{Premuim over straight value} = \frac{\$106.5}{\$98.19} - 1 = 0.085 \text{ or } 8.5\%$$

The Upside Potential of a Convertible Bond

The evaluation of the upside potential of a convertible bond depends on the prospects for the underlying common stock. Thus, the techniques for analyzing common stocks on equity analysis should be employed.

Investment Characteristics of a Convertible Bond

The investment characteristics of a convertible bond depend on the common stock price. If the price is low, so that the straight value is considerably higher than the conversion value, the security will trade much like a straight bond. The convertible bond in such instances is referred to as a *bond equivalent* or a *busted convertible*.

When the price of the stock is such that the conversion value is considerably higher than the straight value, then the convertible bond will trade as if it were an equity instrument; in this case it is said to be a *common stock equivalent*. In such cases, the market conversion premium per share will be small.

Between these two cases, bond equivalent and common stock equivalent, the convertible bond trades as a hybrid security, having the characteristics of both a bond and common stock.

The Risk/Return Profile of a Convertible Bond

Let's use the Izzobaf convertible bond to compare the risk/return profile from investing in a convertible bond or the underlying common stock. The stock can be purchased in the market for $33. By buying the convertible bond, the investor is effectively purchasing the stock for $42.06 (the market conversion price per share). Let's look at the potential profit and loss, assuming that Izzobaf's stock price rises to $50 and a scenario in which the stock price falls to $25.

If the stock price rises to $50, the direct purchase of the stock would generate a profit of $17 per share ($50 – $33), or a return of 34%. If the convertible bond is purchased, the conversion value is $1,266 per $1,000 of par value (conversion ratio of 25.32 times $50). Assuming that the straight value per $1,000 of par value is unchanged at $981.90, the minimum value for the convertible bond is $1,266. Since the initial price of the convertible bond per $1,000 of par value is $1,065, the profit is $201, and the return is 18.9% ($201/$1,065). The lower return by buying the convertible bond rather than the stock is because a higher price was effectively paid for the stock. Specifically, by buying the convertible bond, a per share price of $42.06 was paid. The profit per share is then $7.94, which produces the return of 18.9% ($7.94/$42.06).

Now let's look at what would happen if Izzobaf's stock price declines to $25. If the stock is purchased, there would be a loss of $8 per share or, equivalently, a return of −24%. For the convertible bond, the conversion value would be $633 (conversion ratio of 25.3 times $25). However, the convertible bond's minimum price is the greater of the convertible bond value and the straight value. Assuming the straight value stays at $981.90, this would be the value of the convertible bond. The loss on the convertible bond is therefore $83.10 or 7.8% ($83.10/$1,065).

One of the critical assumptions in this analysis is that the straight value does not change except for the passage of time. If interest rates rise, the straight value will decline. Even if interest rates do not rise, the perceived creditworthiness of the issuer may deteriorate, causing investors to demand a higher yield.

The scenario clearly demonstrates that there are benefits and drawbacks to investing in convertible bonds. The disadvantage is the upside potential given up because a premium per share must be paid. An advantage is the reduction in downside risk (as determined by the straight value).

CHAPTER 12

Preferred Stock

Steven V. Mann, Ph.D.
Professor of Finance
The Moore School of Business
University of South Carolina

Frank J. Fabozzi, Ph.D., CFA
Adjunct Professor of Finance
School of Management
Yale University

Preferred stock is an equity security, not a debt instrument, but it combines features of both common stock and debt. The preferred stockholder is entitled to cash dividends paid by the issuing corporation. Unlike the cash dividends paid to common shareholders, however, cash dividends paid to preferred shareholders are fixed by contract, usually at a specified dollar amount or percentage of their par or face value. So, in its most basic form, a share of preferred stock can be thought of as a perpetuity—an endless stream of cash dividends. The specified percentage is called the *dividend rate*; it need not be fixed, but may float over the life of the issue.

Almost all preferred stock limits the payments to be received by the security holder to a specified amount. Historically, there have been issues entitling the preferred stockholder to participate in earnings distribution beyond the specified amount (based on some formula). For instance, a preferred stock may pay additional cash dividends after all common dividends have been paid. A preferred stock with this feature is referred to as *participating* preferred stock. However, most preferred stock issued today is *nonparticipating* in that the cash flows received will never exceed those specified in the contract and may be less.

Failure to make preferred stock dividend payments cannot force the issuer into bankruptcy. Should the issuer not make the preferred stock dividend payment, usually made quarterly, one of two things can happen, depending on the terms of the issue. The dividend payment can accrue until it is fully paid. Preferred stock with this feature is called *cumulative* preferred stock. If a dividend payment is missed and the security holder must forgo the payment, the preferred stock is said to be *noncumulative* preferred stock. Failure to make dividend payments may result in the imposition of certain restrictions on management. For example, if dividend payments are in arrears, preferred stockholders might be granted voting rights and elect some number of directors. This is called *contingent voting* because their preferred shareholders' right to vote is contingent on their dividends not being paid.

Preferred stock has some important similarities with debt, particularly in the case of cumulative preferred stock: (1) the returns to preferred stockholders promised by the issuer are fixed, and (2) preferred stockholders have priority over common stockholders with respect to dividend payments and distribution of assets in the case of bankruptcy. (The position of noncumulative preferred stock is considerably weaker.) Because of this second feature, preferred stock is called a "senior security" in that it is senior to common stock. On a balance sheet, preferred stock is classified as equity. It is important to note that the claim of preferred shareholders to the issuer's assets in the event of bankruptcy differs when there is more than one class of preferred stock outstanding. For instance, *first* preferred stock's claim to dividends and assets has priority over other preferred stock. Correspondingly, *second* preferred stock ranks below at least one other issue of preferred stock.

Almost all preferred stock has a *sinking fund* provision and these are structured similarly to those associated with debt issues. A sinking fund is a provision allowing for a preferred stock's periodic retirement over its life span. Most sinking funds require a specific number of shares or a certain percentage of the original issue to be retired periodically, usually annually. Sinking fund payments can be satisfied by either paying cash and calling the required number of shares, usually at par, or delivering shares purchased in the open market. Most sinking funds give the issuer a noncumulative option to retire an additional amount of preferred stock equal to the mandatory requirement. This is called a "double-up" option. Preferred shares acquired to satisfy a sinking fund requirement are usually called "by lot." This is, essentially, the random selection of preferred shares with computer programs.

EXHIBIT 12.1   Total Amount of Preferred Stock, Corporate Debt, and
Common Stock Issued in U.S. (1999–2001)

Year	U.S. Preferred Stock (000s $)	U.S. Corporate Debt (000s $)	U.S. Common Equity (000s $)
1999	25,194,063	868,348,969	173,998,791
2000	8,535,606	839,746,371	213,446,398
2001	33,634,742	1,004,705,535	136,506,464

Source: Bloomberg Financial Markets

PREFERRED STOCK ISSUANCE

Of the three major types of securities used by corporations to finance
their operations (common stock, debt, and preferred stock), preferred
stock runs a distant third in terms of total dollars issued. Exhibit 12.1
presents the total amount (in thousands of dollars) in the United States
of preferred stock, corporate debt, and common stock issued annually
for the years 1999–2001. In Exhibit 12.2, we present the top 25 underwriters of preferred stock for 2001 and give the amount issued by each
as well as the number of deals underwritten.

Since the early 1980s, there have been two fundamental shifts in the
issuance pattern of preferred stock. First, historically, utilities have been
the major issuers of preferred stock, accounting for more than half of each
year's issuance. Since 1985, major issuers have become financially oriented companies—finance companies, banks, thrifts, and insurance companies. Utilities now account for less than 30% of annual preferred stock
issuance. Second, in the past, all preferred stock paid a fixed dividend.
Today, the majority of preferred stock issued carries an adjustable-rate
dividend.

Types of Preferred Stock

There are three types of preferred stock: (1) fixed-rate preferred stock,
(2) adjustable-rate preferred stock, and (3) auction and remarketed preferred stock.

Fixed-Rate Preferred Stock

With fixed-rate preferred stock, the dividend rate is fixed as long as the
issue is outstanding. Prior to 1982, all publicly issued preferred stock
was *fixed-rate preferred stock.* As an illustration of this type, Exhibit
12.3 presents a Bloomberg "Preferred Security Display" screen of a Fan-

nie Mae fixed-rate preferred stock. These shares were issued on September 30, 1998 with an issue price of $50 per share and carry a 5.25% dividend that is delivered quarterly or $0.65625 per share. Exhibit 12.4 presents the "Call Schedule" for this issue that indicates it can be called in whole or in part at any time on or after September 30, 1999 at a price of $50 per share. Fannie Mae must give notice of at least 30 days prior to a call.

EXHIBIT 12.2   Top 25 Underwriters of Preferred Stock for 2001

	Underwriter	Amount (000s $)	Deal Count
1	Salomon Smith Barney	11, 931,655	62
2	Morgan Stanley	7,676,900	36
3	Merrill Lynch & Co.	4,664,583	38
4	Lehman Brothers	2,852,250	20
5	UBS Warburg	1,916,687	22
6	Bear Stearns & Co., Inc.	762,500	3
7	Bank of America	575,000	1
8	Goldman Sachs & Co.	564,583	5
9	J. P. Morgan	350,000	2
10	Bank One	250,000	1
11	Stifel, Nicolaus & Co., Inc.	234,700	7
12	Wachovia Corp.	208,750	4
13	Credit Suisse First Boston	207,188	3
14	Legg Mason Wood Walker	170,500	5
15	FleetBoston Corp.	125,000	1
16	Ferris, Baker Watts, Inc.	119,500	2
17	Advest, Inc.	103,500	1
18	A. G. Edwards & Sons, Inc.	100,521	5
19	First Tennessee Bank	100,000	1
20	Sandler O'Neil & Partners	100,000	1
21	Wells Fargo Bank	100,000	1
22	Janney Montgomery Scott	100,000	1
23	Howe Barnes Investments, Inc.	91,475	6
24	Banco Bilbao Vizcaya Argentaria	80,000	1
25	Ryan Beck & Co.	60,000	1

Source: Bloomberg Financial Markets

EXHIBIT 12.3   Bloomberg's Preferred Security Display for
Fannie Mae Preferred Stock

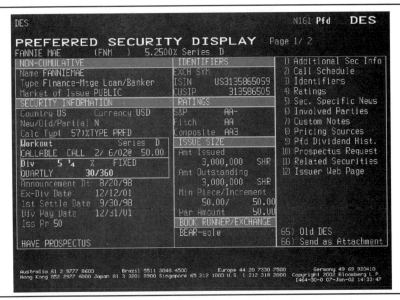

Source: Bloomberg Financial Markets

EXHIBIT 12.4   Bloomberg's Call Schedule for Fannie Mae Preferred Stock

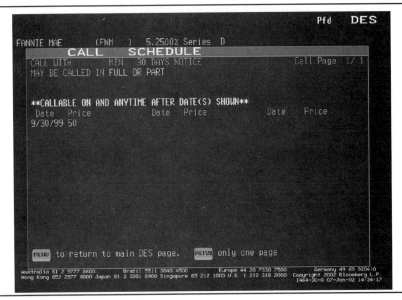

Source: Bloomberg Financial Markets

Adjustable-Rate Preferred Stock

For *adjustable-rate preferred stock* (ARPS), the dividend rate is reset quarterly based on a predetermined spread from the highest of three points on the Treasury yield curve. The predetermined spread is called the *dividend reset spread*. The three points on the yield curve (called the *benchmark rate*) to which the dividend reset spread is either added to or subtracted from is the highest of (1) the 3-month Treasury bill rate, (2) the 10-year constant maturity rate, or (3) a 10-year or 30-year constant maturity rate. Correspondingly, the dividend reset spread may be expressed as a certain percentage of the benchmark rate. As an example, Citigroup has preferred stock outstanding issued in August 1994 where the dividend rate is 84% of the highest of the 3-month U.S. Treasury bill rate, the 10-year CMT, and the 30-year CMT. This issue is callable at the issue price of $25. The motivation for linking the dividend rate to the highest of the three points on the Treasury yield curve is to provide the investor with protection against unfavorable shifts in the yield curve. However, since the U.S. Treasury yield curve is upward-sloping most of the time, the dividend rate is effectively tied to the long-term Treasury rate.

Auction Rate and Remarketed Preferred Stock

Most ARPS are perpetual, with a floor and ceiling imposed on the dividend rate of most issues. Because most ARPS are not putable, however, ARPS can trade below par if after issuance the spread demanded by the market to reflect the issuer's credit risk is greater than the dividend reset spread. The popularity of ARPS declined when instruments began to trade below their par value because the dividend reset rate is determined at the time of issuance, not by market forces. In particular, if an issuer's credit risk deteriorates, the dividend rate formula remains unchanged and the value of the preferred stock will decline. In 1984, a new type of preferred stock, *auction rate preferred stock*, was designed to overcome this problem, particularly for corporate treasurers who sought tax-advantaged short-term instruments to invest excess funds. The dividend rate on auction rate preferred is reset periodically, as with ARPS, but the dividend rate is established through a Dutch auction process.[1] Participants in the auction consist of current holders and potential buyers. The dividend rate that participants are willing to accept reflects current market conditions as well as commercial paper rates that typically serve as benchmarks. Auction rate preferred stock's dividend rate is reset every 28 or 49 days.

---

[1] This type of preferred stock is also called Dutch auction preferred stock.

EXHIBIT 12.5 Bloomberg's Preferred Security Display for
GE Capital Auction Rate Preferred Stock

Source: Bloomberg Financial Markets

As an illustration, GE Capital issued some auction rate preferred stock in December 1990. Exhibit 12.5 presents the Bloomberg "Preferred Security Display" screen for this issue. Exhibit 12.6 presents the Bloomberg "Auction Rate Preferred History" screen. We see at the top of the screen that the benchmark rate is the 60-day commercial paper rate and the reset frequency is 49 days. The bottom portion of the screen presents the dividend history.

In the case of *remarketed* preferred stock, the dividend rate is determined periodically by a remarketing agent who resets the dividend rate so that any preferred stock can be tendered at par and can be resold (remarketed) at the original offering price. An investor has the choice of dividend resets every 7 days or every 49 days. As an example, Exhibit 12.7 presents a Preferred Security Display screen for some remarketed preferred stock issued by a closed-end fund of Duff and Phelps in November 1988. Note three things about the issue. First, the dividend reset is every 49 days. Second, there is a mandatory redemption date of November 28, 2012. Third, the issue is callable on any payment date at par (i.e., $100,000) plus accrued dividends.

EXHIBIT 12.6 Bloomberg's Auction Rate Preferred History for GE Capital Auction Rate Preferred Stock

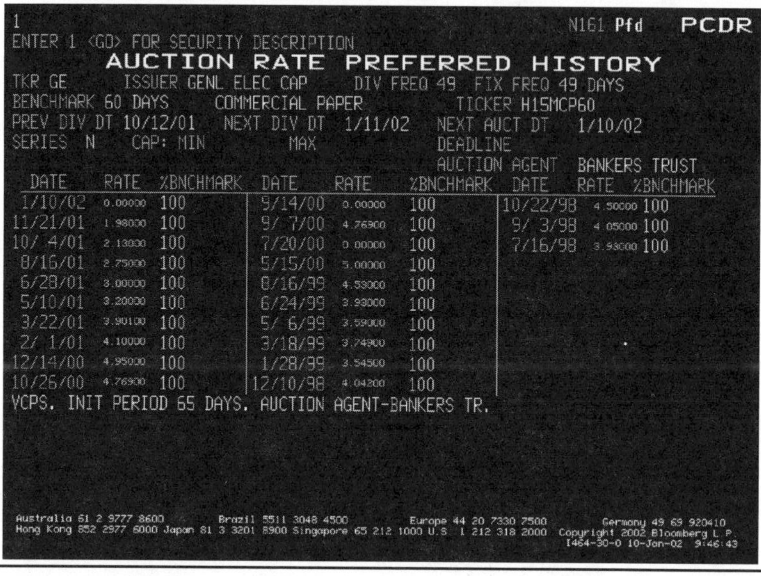

1 N161 Pfd PCDR
ENTER 1 <GO> FOR SECURITY DESCRIPTION

AUCTION RATE PREFERRED HISTORY

TKR GE ISSUER GENL ELEC CAP DIV FREQ 49 FIX FREQ 49 DAYS
BENCHMARK 60 DAYS COMMERCIAL PAPER TICKER H15MCP60
PREV DIV DT 10/12/01 NEXT DIV DT 1/11/02 NEXT AUCT DT 1/10/02
SERIES N CAP: MIN MAX DEADLINE
AUCTION AGENT BANKERS TRUST

DATE	RATE	%BNCHMARK	DATE	RATE	%BNCHMARK	DATE	RATE	%BNCHMARK
1/10/02	0.00000	100	9/14/00	0.00000	100	10/22/98	4.50000	100
11/21/01	1.98000	100	9/ 7/00	4.76900	100	9/ 3/98	4.05000	100
10/ 4/01	2.13000	100	7/20/00	0.00000	100	7/16/98	3.93000	100
8/16/01	2.75000	100	5/15/00	5.00000	100			
6/28/01	3.00000	100	8/16/99	4.53000	100			
5/10/01	3.20000	100	6/24/99	3.93000	100			
3/22/01	3.90100	100	5/ 6/99	3.59000	100			
2/ 1/01	4.10000	100	3/18/99	3.74900	100			
12/14/00	4.95000	100	1/28/99	3.54500	100			
10/26/00	4.76900	100	12/10/98	4.04200	100			

VCPS. INIT PERIOD 65 DAYS. AUCTION AGENT-BANKERS TR.

Australia 61 2 9777 8600 Brazil 5511 3048 4500 Europe 44 20 7330 7500 Germany 49 69 920410
Hong Kong 852 2977 6000 Japan 81 3 3201 8900 Singapore 65 212 1000 U.S. 1 212 318 2000 Copyright 2002 Bloomberg L.P.
I464-30-0 10-Jan-02 9:46:43

Source: Bloomberg Financial Markets

EXHIBIT 12.7 Bloomberg's Preferred Security Display for Duff & Phelps Remarketed Preferred Stock

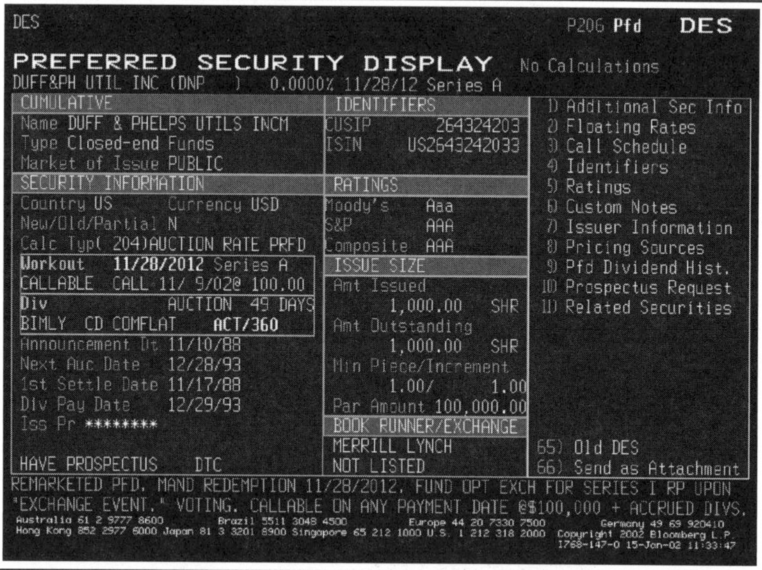

DES P206 Pfd DES

PREFERRED SECURITY DISPLAY No Calculations

DUFF&PH UTIL INC (DNP) 0.0000% 11/28/12 Series A

CUMULATIVE
Name DUFF & PHELPS UTILS INCM
Type Closed-end Funds
Market of Issue PUBLIC

SECURITY INFORMATION
Country US Currency USD
New/Old/Partial N
Calc Typ(204)AUCTION RATE PRFD
Workout 11/28/2012 Series A
CALLABLE CALL 11/ 9/02@ 100.00
Div AUCTION 49 DAYS
BIMLY CD COMFLAT ACT/360
Announcement Dt 11/10/88
Next Auc Date 12/28/93
1st Settle Date 11/17/88
Div Pay Date 12/29/93
Iss Pr ********
HAVE PROSPECTUS DTC

IDENTIFIERS
CUSIP 264324203
ISIN US2643242033

RATINGS
Moody's Aaa
S&P AAA
Composite AAA

ISSUE SIZE
Amt Issued
1,000.00 SHR
Amt Outstanding
1,000.00 SHR
Min Piece/Increment
1.00/ 1.00
Par Amount 100,000.00

BOOK RUNNER/EXCHANGE
MERRILL LYNCH
NOT LISTED

1) Additional Sec Info
2) Floating Rates
3) Call Schedule
4) Identifiers
5) Ratings
6) Custom Notes
7) Issuer Information
8) Pricing Sources
9) Pfd Dividend Hist.
10) Prospectus Request
11) Related Securities
65) Old DES
66) Send as Attachment

REMARKETED PFD. MAND REDEMPTION 11/28/2012. FUND OPT EXCH FOR SERIES I RP UPON "EXCHANGE EVENT." VOTING. CALLABLE ON ANY PAYMENT DATE @$100,000 + ACCRUED DIVS.

Australia 61 2 9777 8600 Brazil 5511 3048 4500 Europe 44 20 7330 7500 Germany 49 69 920410
Hong Kong 852 2977 6000 Japan 81 3 3201 8900 Singapore 65 212 1000 U.S. 1 212 318 2000 Copyright 2002 Bloomberg L.P.
1768-147-0 15-Jan-02 11:33:47

Source: Bloomberg Financial Markets

PREFERRED STOCK RATINGS

As with corporate debt instruments, preferred stock is rated. A preferred stock rating is an assessment of the issuer's ability to make timely dividend payments and fulfill any other contractually specified obligations (e.g., sinking fund payments). The three nationally recognized statistical rating organizations (NRSROs) that rate corporate bonds also rate preferred stock—Fitch, Moody's Investors Service, Inc., and Standard & Poor's Ratings Group.

Symbols used by the NRSROs for rating preferred stock are the same as those used for rating long-term debt. However, it is important to note the rating applies to the security issue in question and not to the issuer per se. As such, two different securities issued by the same firm could have different ratings. Panels A and B of Exhibit 12.8 show a Bloomberg screen with the S&P's preferred stock rating definitions. At the bottom of Panel B, it indicates that S&P attaches "+"s and " "s which are called "notches" to denote an issue's relative standing within the major ratings categories. Moody's attaches "1"s, "2"s, and "3"s to indicate the same information.

EXHIBIT 12.8 Panel A: Standard & Poor's Preferred Stock Ratings Definitions

Page N161n **Pfd** **RATD**

Standard & Poor's
Preferred Stock Ratings
Page 2/3

AAA This is the highest rating that may be assigned by Standard & Poor's to a preferred stock issue and indicates an extremely strong capacity to pay the preferred stock obligations.

AA A preferred stock issue rated 'AA' also qualifies as a high-quality, fixed-income security. The capacity to pay preferred stock obligations is very strong, although not as overwhelming as for issues rated 'AAA'.

A An issue rated 'A' is backed by a sound capacity to pay the preferred stock obligations, although it is somewhat more susceptible to the adverse effects of changes in circumstances and economic conditions.

BBB An issue rated 'BBB' is regarded as backed by an adequate capacity to pay the preferred stock obligations. Whereas it normally exhibits adequate protection parameters, adverse economic conditions or changing circumstances are more likely to lead to a weakened capacity to make payments for a preferred stock in this category than for issues in the 'A' category.

EXHIBIT 12.8 (Continued)
Panel B: Standard & Poor's Preferred Stock Ratings Definitions

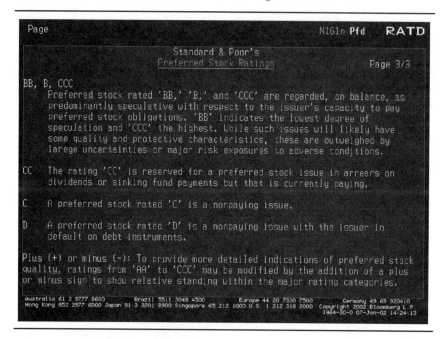

Source: Bloomberg Financial Markets

Tax Treatment of Dividends

Unlike debt, payments made to preferred stockholders are treated as a distribution of earnings. This means that they are not tax deductible to the corporation under the current tax code.[2] Interest payments are tax deductible, not dividend payments. While this raises the after-tax cost of funds if a corporation issues preferred stock rather than borrowing, there is a factor that reduces the cost differential: a provision in the tax code exempts 70% of qualified dividends from federal income taxation if the recipient is a qualified corporation. For example, if Corporation A owns the preferred stock of Corporation B, for each $100 of dividends received by A, only $30 will be taxed at A's marginal tax rate. The purpose of this provision is to mitigate the effect of double taxation of corporate earnings.

There are two implications of this tax treatment of preferred stock dividends. First, the major buyers of preferred stock are corporations

---

[2] An exception is Trust-Originated Preferred Securities, discussed later.

seeking tax-advantaged investments. Second, the cost of preferred stock issuance is lower than it would be in the absence of the tax provision because the tax benefits are passed through to the issuer by the willingness of corporate investors to accept a lower dividend rate.

CONVERTIBLE PREFERRED STOCK

Some preferred stock is convertible into the common stock of the issuer. The conversion feature grants the preferred shareholder the right to convert a share of preferred stock into a predetermined amount of common stock of the issuer. A convertible preferred stock is preferred stock with an embedded call option on the common stock. However, most convertible preferred stock issues are also callable which, in essence, allows the issuer to force the preferred shareholders to either convert their preferred stock into common stock or redeem their shares for cash.

To understand the preferred stockholder's decision when their shares are called, we must define some terms. First, the preferred stock's *conversion value* is the number of common shares into which one share of a preferred stock can be converted multiplied by the current share of the common stock. Second, the *effective call price* is the sum of the nominal call price applicable at the time of the call plus any accrued dividends.[3] Given this backdrop, if a convertible issue is called, the preferred shareholder's decision is generally straightforward. If the effective call price is greater than the conversion value, the preferred shareholder will surrender the security in exchange for its redemption value. If the conversion value is greater than the effective call price, the preferred shareholder will convert the shares into common stock. Firms usually call preferred stock issues when they are "in-the-money" (i.e., the conversion value exceeds the call price). Thus, a call of an "in-the-money" preferred stock is known as a "conversion-forcing-call."

As an illustration of callable and convertible preferred stock, consider a preferred stock issued by Western Gas Resources which has an annual cash dividend of $2.6250 per share, payable quarterly. Exhibit 12.9 presents the Bloomberg Preferred Security Display screen for this issue. Each of these preferred shares is convertible until December 31, 2049 into 1.2579 common shares at any time. The preferred shares were callable at a price of $50.79. The parity price is the conversion value that is the market price of the common stock ($30.61) multiplied by the

---

[3] Convertible preferred stock investors should carefully read the prospectus because many issues contain a so-called "screw clause" which means if the issue is called, the investor does not receive the accrued dividends from the last payment date.

number of common shares into which a preferred share can be converted (1.2579). Correspondingly, the premium is the ratio of the preferred stock's market value divided by the conversion value expressed as a percentage. Investors pay a premium to buy the common shares via the convertible preferred stock because the conversion feature represents an embedded call option on the common stock that need only be converted when it is in the best interest of the convertible preferred investor. The investor's downside risk is limited to the straight value of the preferred stock (i.e., the value of the convertible preferred stock without the conversion feature).

Convertible Preferred Stock with Special Features

The mid-1990s witnessed an explosion of innovations in convertible preferred shares with special features. In this last section of the chapter, we sketch some of the major types.

EXHIBIT 12.9   Bloomberg's Preferred Security Display for Western Gas Resources Convertible Preferred Stock

```
DES                                        P206 Pfd    DES
PREFERRED SECURITY DISPLAY  Page 1/ 3
WESTERN GAS RES  (WGR   ) $ 2.6250  Series             [EXCH]
CONVERTIBLE INFORMATION      IDENTIFIERS        1) Additional Sec Info
CONV TO        1.2579 SHARES  EXCH SYM WGR A    2) Call Schedule
WGR   (US ) $30.61 ( 0.20)   ISIN   US9582593011  3) Convertible Info.
CONVERTIBLE UNTIL 12/31/49   CUSIP     958259301  4) Identifiers
PARITY   38.50 PREMIUM  20.77% RATINGS          5) Ratings
CUMULATIVE                    Moody's    B1      6) Sec. Specific News
Name WESTERN GAS RESOURCES   S&P        B+      7) Custom Notes
Market of Issue PUBLIC       Fitch      BB      8) Issuer Information
SECURITY INFORMATION         ISSUE SIZE         9) Pricing Sources
Country US     Currency USD   Amt Issued         10) Pfd Dividend Hist.
Div    $2 5/8       FIXED        2,760,000  SHR  11) Prospectus Request
QUARTLY      30/360          Amt Outstanding     12) Related Securities
Workout         Series          2,760,000  SHR  13) Issuer Web Page
CONV/CALL    2/12/020  50.79  Min Piece/Increment
1st Settle Date 2/25/94       100.00/  100.00
Div Pay Date   11/12/01      Par Amount   50.00
Ex-Div Date     9/26/01      BOOK RUNNER/EXCHANGE
Calc Typ (  56)FIXED TYPE PRFD  MORGAN STANLEY   65) Old DES
HAVE PROSPECTUS              NEW YORK            66) Send as Attachment
INIT CV PREMIUM 25%. TRANS AGT: CHEMICAL SHAREHLDER SVC. INIT DVD: $.576/SH.
O/S 2/01.
Australia 61 2 9777 8600     Brazil 5511 3048 4500    Europe 44 20 7330 7500    Germany 49 69 920410
Hong Kong 852 2977 6000 Japan 81 3 3201 8900 Singapore 65 212 1000 U.S. 1 212 318 2000  Copyright 2002 Bloomberg L.P.
                                                          I768-147-0 15-Jun-02 11:10:51
```

Source: Bloomberg Financial Markets

Trust Originated Preferred Securities

Trust Originated Preferred Securities (TOPrS) are convertible preferred securities that differ from the convertible preferred shares just described in that the issuer may deduct the cash dividends for tax purposes yet still receive partial equity credit from the rating agencies. The primary issuer sets up a Delaware statutory business trust to issue the securities to the investing public but the securities are guaranteed by the primary issuer. TOPrS' dividend payments are not subject to the 70% dividend exclusion and the issuer may defer dividends up to 20 quarters (5 years). However, if the dividends are deferred, the primary issuer may not pay dividends to common or preferred shareholders and TOPrS dividends accrue and compound quarterly. TOPrS are usually callable beginning 3 to 5 years from the date of issuance and usually mature in 20-30 years. Due to their tax treatment and the possibility of dividend deferrals, TOPrS carry a relatively higher dividend yield than other preferred stock.

A Miscellany of Acronyms

There are a host of convertible preferred products that provide investors with higher dividend yields and limited participation in the upside potential of common stock underlying the convertible. Dividend Enhanced Convertible Stocks (DECS) created by Salomon Smith Barney and Preferred Redeemable Increased Dividends Equity Securities (PRIDES) created by Merrill Lynch are two prominent examples. These convertible preferred securities offer high dividend yields, mandatory conversion at maturity (usually 3 to 4 years), and conversion ratios that adjust downward as the underlying common stock appreciates, thereby limiting the upside potential.

Another similar type of convertible preferred security is Preferred Equity Redemption Cumulative Stock (PERCS) which was created by Merrill Lynch. PERCS also offer a high dividend yield and require mandatory conversion at maturity, but cap the investor's upside potential by adjusting the conversion ratio at maturity so that the investor receives a fixed dollar amount of common stock.[4]

---

[4] For a detailed discussion of these securities, see T. Anne Cox, "Convertible Structures: Evolution Continues," Chapter 2 in Izzy Nelken (ed.) *Handbook of Hybrid Instruments* (New York: John Wiley & Sons, 2000).

CHAPTER 13

Emerging Markets Debt

Maria Mednikov Loucks, CFA
Director, Emerging Markets Debt Portfolio Manager
UBS Asset Management

John A. Penicook, Jr., CFA, CPA
Managing Director, Emerging Markets and High Yield Debt
UBS Asset Management

Uwe Schillhorn, CFA*
Director, Emerging Markets Debt Portfolio Manager
UBS Asset Management

Emerging markets debt (EMD) warrants consideration in diversified portfolios based upon its normal return potential, risk characteristics, and portfolio diversification benefits. Fundamental investment analysis of this market requires an understanding of sovereign credit risk and the compositional complexities of the emerging market bonds themselves. The normal return potential of the market, in conjunction with its low correlation to other bond and equity markets, offers the opportunity to improve a portfolio's risk/reward profile.

In the broadest sense, the group of emerging countries includes all nations not considered industrialized or already "developed." Since the

* The authors gratefully acknowledge comments and input from their colleagues at UBS Asset Management—Stefano Cavaglia, YuChen Lin, Derek Sasveld, Eriks Smidchens, and Stuart Waugh.

latter group has only two dozen or so members, the emerging country universe encompasses most of the world's population and geography. However, because most emerging countries have no investable debt securities, only a subset of these countries comprises the emerging markets debt universe. Hence, the more precise terminology is emerging market, rather than emerging country.

While convention and market terminology lump all of these countries into one market, there are profound, fundamental differences among them. Many Latin American countries have a history of poor macroeconomic management and suffer from deep social inequality, but their recent economic performances have largely improved. Eastern Europe is recovering from decades of central planning, but some countries have pre-war histories of success with capitalism. Opening these markets up to the rest of the world has the potential of producing large growth rates. Africa is generally income-poor, but commodity-rich. Finally, a number of Southeastern Asian countries have very high savings rates, resulting in exportation rather than importation of capital. As more emerging countries develop sovereign bond markets, inter-regional and inter-country differences will expand diversification opportunities, improving the risk/return profile of the asset class.

Emerging market issuers rely on international investors for capital. Emerging markets cannot finance their fiscal deficits domestically because domestic capital markets are poorly developed and local investors are unable or unwilling to lend to the government. Although emerging market issuers differ greatly in terms of credit risk, dependence on foreign capital is the most basic characteristic of the asset class. After the Asian crisis in 1997, investors realized that even investment-grade sovereign issuers can run into problems when access to foreign capital is constrained.

The growth of emerging market economies and the greater reliance of emerging markets on bond financing lead to an increase in importance of developing countries' debt securities in the international marketplace. While still small in comparison to that of industrialized country debt, the overall size of the market (see Exhibit 13.1) has expanded from 1.4% of the World Bond Market in 1993 to 4.8% in 2000, making it an important sector of the global capital market.[1] From 1992 to 2000, total trading volume of EMD securities has quadrupled (see Exhibit 13.2). In this chapter we review EMD generally, examine different security structures, and provide some perspective on the long-term and current attractiveness of this asset class.

---

[1] Domestic debt includes local currency and hard currency-denominated bonds issued under domestic law.

EXHIBIT 13.1 Emerging Markets Debt Universe Market Capitalization as of December 2000

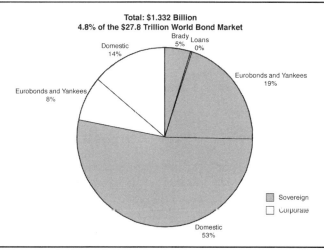

Source: Bank of International Settlements, J.P. Morgan, Merrill Lynch

EXHIBIT 13.2 Emerging Markets Debt Trading Volume

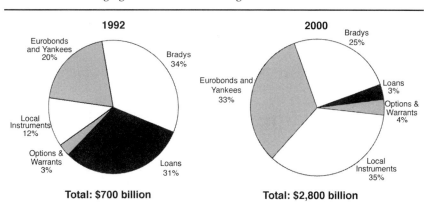

Source: Emerging Markets Trader's Association

EMERGING MARKETS DEBT INSTRUMENTS

Sovereign EMD instruments can be divided into three segments: Brady bonds, Eurobonds, and local issues. The characteristics and histories of these market segments are examined in this section. This section also discusses emerging market corporate bonds and popular index alternatives.

Most emerging market bonds are denominated in U.S. dollars. However, Euro-denominated issuance has grown from 17% of total EMD issuance in 1997 to 31% of total issuance in 2000.[2] Euro-denominated EMD securities are typically held in retail accounts, have lower issuance size and are less liquid than comparable U.S. dollar-denominated bonds.

Due to relative illiquidity and less attractive spreads of Euro-denominated EMD, U.S.-based emerging markets debt investors hold the bulk of their assets in U.S. dollar-denominated securities. Unlike emerging market equity and developed foreign bond markets, direct currency risk (i.e., the risk of foreign exchange losses) is not a major consideration for a U.S.-based investor. U.S. interest rate risk, however, is important to the sovereign market just as it is to the U.S. high yield and corporate bond markets. Trading occurs primarily in New York and secondarily in London. Most issues settle via the ordinary Euroclear mechanism; costly local custody arrangements are unnecessary. So while the sovereign market has several characteristics in common with traditional U.S. bond markets, it remains unique in nature due to sovereign default risk.

The Brady Plan and Resulting Bonds

Narrowly defined, the *Brady Plan* refers to an innovative debt renegotiation format, whereby defaulted sovereign bank loans were written down and converted into bonds; the bonds themselves also have unique structures. Mexico was the first Brady Plan participant in 1989.[3] More broadly, the Brady Plan encompasses the entire set of economic policy prescriptions that developing countries adopted in order to receive additional international aid. This aid allowed them to meet their responsibilities under the Brady Plan.

The Brady Plan differed from previous approaches in a number of respects. For the first time, underlying structural problems of the debtor countries were addressed (such as protected markets and controlled prices). Typically, the principal amount of the defaulted loans was effectively reduced by 35% to 50%; sometimes interest and interest arrears were also reduced. This principal forgiveness had the effect of both raising the loans' value in the secondary market and lowering the borrowers' debt burden. Further, the commercial banks' loans to private and sovereign entities were transformed into sovereign bonds, thus enhancing their appeal to investors. Exhibit 13.3 shows the debt reduction obtained by some countries that participated in a Brady Plan restructuring.

---

[2] Darrell Tonge, "The Risk-Return Properties of Euro-Denominated Emerging Market Debt," Salomon Smith Barney (May 2001).

[3] Former U.S. Treasury Secretary Nicholas Brady was credited with this approach.

EXHIBIT 13.3 Debt Reduction Achieved through Brady Plan
(In U.S. Dollars, Billions)

Country	Debt Pre-Brady[1]	Effective Debt Reduction
Argentina	29.9	35%
Brazil	45.6	35%
Bulgaria	8.1	50%
Ecuador	8.0	45%
Mexico	33.0	35%
Nigeria	5.8	35%
Panama	3.5	31%
Peru	10.6	54%
Philippines	4.5	35%
Poland	14.0	45%
Venezuela	19.3	35%

[1] Pre-Brady Plan debt figures equal face amount plus interest arrears.

Source: Salomon Brothers, ANZ, J.P. Morgan

The features of Brady bonds vary. Most were issued with a final maturity between 10 and 30 years and have semiannual coupons; many Brady bonds have amortizing principal payments. Coupons may be fixed, floating, step-up or a hybrid combination. Unique features such as principal collateral, rolling interest guarantees, and value recovery rights were added to Brady bonds in order to improve creditworthiness and attract investors.

U.S. Treasury zero-coupon securities were purchased to serve as collateral for a bond's principal payment. High quality money market instruments were purchased to serve as collateral for the rolling interest guarantee. Rolling interest guarantees cover either two or three coupon payments; after a coupon payment is made, the guarantee rolls to cover the next set of coupon payments. If the collateral is used, the issuer has no obligation to replace it. Due to collateralization, Brady bonds require special analytical methods to calculate basic bond statistics; these methods are discussed later in this chapter.

Value recovery rights provide the investor with additional upside if the debt service capacity of the debtor improves. Some value recovery rights are known as oil warrants because their value is linked to a country's oil export receipts. Large oil exporters (Mexico, Nigeria, Venezuela) attached oil warrants to some of their Brady bonds. Other countries, such as Bulgaria, enhanced some Brady bonds with value recovery rights whose value was linked to GDP growth.

EXHIBIT 13.4 Typical Brady Plan Alternative—Bond Formats[1]

Discount Bonds

- Original loans reduced by 35% to 50% of face value. 30-year bullet amortization.
- Coupon floats at a spread over LIBOR.
- Principal collateralized with U.S. Treasury "zeros" and rolling interest guarantee.

Par Bonds

- Debt exchanged at par. 30-year bullet amortization.
- Coupon fixed at below market rate.
- Principal collateralized with U.S. Treasury "zeros" and rolling interest guarantee.

Debt Conversion Bonds (DCB) and New Money Bonds (NMB)

- Exchange of old bank loans (DCB) contingent upon "new money" bonds (NMB).
- DCB matures in 18 years. NMB matures in 15 years. Both bonds amortize principal.
- DCB and NMB coupons float at a spread over LIBOR.
- No collateral; pure sovereign risk.

Front Loaded Interest Reduction Bonds (FLIRB)

- FLIRB matures in 18 years and amortizes principal.
- Coupon initially set below market rates and is later replaced with a coupon that floats over LIBOR.
- Rolling interest guarantee available for first 5 or 6 years after bond issuance.

Past Due Interest (PDI), Interest Arrearage Bond (IAB), Floating-Rate Bond (FRB), and Eligible Interest (EI)

- Issued in exchange for interest arrearage. Principal is amortized.
- Coupons float at a spread over LIBOR.
- No collateral; pure sovereign risk.

[1] Many Brady bonds are callable at 100 on any payment date for face value plus accrued interest.

Exhibit 13.4 describes the most common types of Brady bonds. Brady bonds still command a large portion of EMD trading volume. However, since new debt is raised in the Eurobond format, the relative importance of Brady bonds will decline over time.

The Brady Plan is generally associated with overall economic improvement in the participating countries, but it is not clear that the Plan caused this improvement. Perhaps alternative debt resolutions would also have led to economic gains, or perhaps positive global economic trends were more important than the Plan itself. While the economic ramifications of the Brady Plan may be debated, it was instrumental in launching a new debt market.

Eurobonds

Eurobonds are internationally issued securities denominated in hard currencies. Most Eurobonds have a fixed coupon and a bullet maturity.

As a portion of trading volume, Eurobonds now make up the largest portion of the emerging debt market. The importance of Eurobonds will continue to increase because new debt is raised in the Eurobond format and countries opportunistically exchange Brady debt for Eurobonds. Exchanging Brady bonds for Eurobonds is attractive if a country can issue Eurobonds for lower yields than existing Brady bonds. In some cases, countries have chosen to exchange Brady bonds for Eurobonds in order to receive cash flow savings through lower coupons/amortizations or to release the treasury collateral backing certain Bradys.

Eurobonds were serviced during the 1980s bank loan crisis. A possible motivation behind such an admirable repayment history may have been that these obligations were small compared to bank debt, so that defaulting on them was much less economical. A second possible motivation may derive from the unique nature of bonds relative to loans. Debt restructuring negotiations of loans are easier because loans involve a small, easily identified and relatively homogeneous group of creditors, i.e., banks. It is difficult for a bank to not restructure its loan to a country and to free-ride on other banks' willingness to do so. By contrast, bond holders are a large and diverse group with no incentives to stay on good terms with the country. This makes broad approval of a bond restructuring more difficult.

Both Eurobonds and Brady bonds are held by a diverse group of creditors, however there is a market perception that distressed sovereign issuers could try to selectively default on Bradys while they continue to service Eurobonds. Since Eurobonds represent the structure of future issuance, a selective default will allow a sovereign to maintain some type of reputation in the capital markets.

The recent growth of the Eurobond market makes future preferential treatment less likely. Since Eurobonds are now a larger portion of a sovereign's total debt, future restructurings are likely to include Eurobonds in order to meaningfully decrease a country's debt burden. The recent restructuring of Ecuadorian bonds (Eurobonds and Bradys) took approximately a year from the time of default suggesting that sovereign restructurings are possible despite a diverse group of bond holders. In addition,

Ecuador was unable to selectively default on its Bradys; it restructured both Eurobonds and Brady bonds.

Local Issues

Several developing countries have functioning and relatively liquid domestic debt markets. Local issues are issued under local law. The bulk of local issues are denominated in local currencies, but a large portion is denominated in major currencies (USD, Euro, Yen) or linked to a major currency. Because of historically high and variable inflation rates and volatile exchange rates, most emerging market, local currency-denominated bonds are short-term instruments. Besides evaluating direct currency risk, international investors need to be compensated for the lack of protection offered by local laws and potential settlement difficulties. Foreign investor interest may grow as governance of local financial markets improves, but the 1998 Russian Treasury bill (GKO) default will be a reminder that hinders investor enthusiasm.

Corporate Bonds

The risk analysis of an EMD corporation hinges on its ownership type and its sensitivity to domestic economy. EMD corporations may be owned by the sovereign, an established multinational or have local ownership. A corporation may sell its product domestically (e.g., a cable operator) or it may earn hard-currency by exporting its product (e.g., an oil company).[4]

Rating agencies have historically limited a corporation's debt rating to its country's sovereign credit rating because corporate debt manifests specific corporate business risk in addition to the sovereign risk of its government. In effect, a *sovereign ceiling* limited a corporation's credit ratings. The theory behind the sovereign ceiling is that the sovereign entity ultimately controls the corporation's access to foreign currency and its tax burden. Essentially, the corporation depends on a benevolent legal and institutional framework from the sovereign government and, therefore, is never a better credit risk than the sovereign itself.

Recently, both Standard and Poor's and Moody's have weakened the sovereign ceiling by allowing certain corporates to receive ratings above their sovereign ceiling. Standard and Poor's sometimes rates corporations above their respective sovereign ceiling if they operate in highly dollarized economies, if they are geographically diversified, or if they have offshore parent support or structural enhancements. Moody's allows corporates to be rated above the sovereign ceiling if there are external support mechanisms (i.e., support from a multinational parent), if there is a low chance

---

[4] Sovereign owned corporations are often referred to as quasi-sovereign.

of a moratorium in the event of a sovereign default, and if the borrower has access to foreign exchange.

In the debt crises of the 1980s, Latin countries imposed a blanket debt moratorium on all foreign currency borrowers, many of which were corporations and banks. In recent sovereign defaults (Ecuador, Pakistan, Russia, and Ukraine), corporate access to foreign currency was not restricted by the government, but there were few corporate foreign currency borrowers. Because every sovereign default is different, is difficult to predict how future distressed sovereigns will act.

With the exception of a few foreign-owned exporters, there remain strong arguments in support of the sovereign ceiling. Some argue that a particular international corporation, like a government-owned oil company, may be so vital to the country's access to foreign currency, that the corporation's credit reputation may supersede the country's ability to access international capital markets. However, while a nationally vital corporation may receive government assistance, it does not follow that its bondholders in general will prosper. Thus, one would expect most corporate issues to offer higher yields than their sovereign counterparts.

Although corporate debt has grown as a percentage of total emerging markets debt, most EMD corporate debt lacks the liquidity to facilitate active institutional investing. In many cases, market segmentation due to retail investing and liquidity constraints leads to relative prices of EMD corporate bonds versus sovereign bonds that are not justified, given the additional risks.

Emerging Markets Debt Indices

The J.P. Morgan Emerging Markets Bond Index Global (EMBI Global) is currently the most widely used benchmark by EMD investors (Exhibit 13.5). The EMBI Global consists of only U.S. dollar-denominated, sovereign bonds and does not use ratings as an inclusion criterion for issuers. The EMBI Global contains countries with investment-grade long-term foreign-currency ratings such as China, non-rated issuers such as Nigeria, and defaulted issuers such as Ivory Coast. As of December 31, 2000, there were 27 issuers in the EMBI Global.

In order for a country to be included in the EMBI Global it must meet either an *income per capita criterion* or a *debt restructuring criterion*. Countries that meet the *income per capita criterion* are classified in the lower or medium income per capita tier by the World Bank (income per capita less than $9,635). Countries that meet the *debt restructuring criterion* have restructured their external or local debt within the last 10 years. Popular emerging markets equity indices also use income per capita to classify countries for inclusion.

EXHIBIT 13.5 Emerging Markets Bond Index Global (J.P. Morgan) as of December 29, 2000

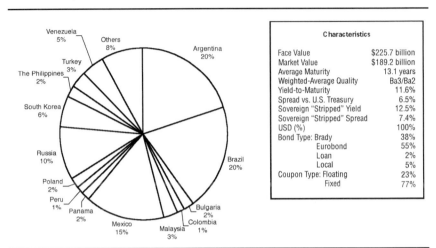

Characteristics	
Face Value	$225.7 billion
Market Value	$189.2 billion
Average Maturity	13.1 years
Weighted-Average Quality	Ba3/Ba2
Yield-to-Maturity	11.6%
Spread vs. U.S. Treasury	6.5%
Sovereign "Stripped" Yield	12.5%
Sovereign "Stripped" Spread	7.4%
USD (%)	100%
Bond Type: Brady	38%
Eurobond	55%
Loan	2%
Local	5%
Coupon Type: Floating	23%
Fixed	77%

Once a country meets the criteria to be included in the EMBI Global, a particular bond must meet certain liquidity requirements. The liquidity requirements used by EMD indices are stringent in comparison to those used by other bond indices. In order to be included in the EMBI Global, a bond must have at least $500 million face amount outstanding, at least 2.5 years to maturity, verifiable prices, and verifiable cash flows.[5] The liquid nature of the EMBI Global Index facilitates the trading of index swaps and allows investors to quickly implement top-down strategy changes.

As of December 31, 2000, the market capitalization of the EMBI Global was $189 billion and had the following instrument composition: Brady bonds (38%), Eurobonds (55%), local issues (5%), and loans (2%).

Lack of diversification is the greatest concern voiced by investors regarding the EMD asset class in general and about EMD indices in particular. EMD indices have historically had high exposure to a small number of large individual issuers, such as Argentina, Brazil, and Mexico and to the Latin American region overall.

Index providers have responded to investor concerns by switching from ratings-based to GDP/capita-based country inclusion criteria (thus including higher-rated sovereigns) and by lowering liquidity requirements. From December 1995 to December 2000, the proportion of Latin

---

[5] As of 12/31/2000, the minimum face outstanding for the Lehman Investment Grade Corporate Index and the Merrill Lynch High Yield Index was $150 million and $100 million, respectively.

American issuers in J.P. Morgan's EMD indices fell from 88% to 66% and the number of issuers increased from 9 to 27.[6]

The EMBI Global has poor issuer diversification when compared to U.S. high-yield and U.S. investment-grade credit indices. While most U.S. high-yield and U.S. investment grade credit indices have hundreds of issuers, the EMBI Global only contains 27 sovereign issuers. Three issuers in the EMBI Global have a market weight in the index that is over 10%: Argentina (20%), Brazil (20%), and Mexico (15%). However, since an EMD portfolio is usually a small piece of an institutional investor's portfolio, issuer diversification should be less of a concern.

Lehman Brothers and Merrill Lynch calculate EMD indices that are broader than the EMBI Global; these indices are part of larger index mappings for global high-yield and U.S. bond plus strategies.[7] Lehman and Merrill indices include EMD corporates and non-dollar EMD securities. J.P. Morgan introduced a Euro-denominated EMD benchmark in May 2001; at inception, the index contained 15 countries and had a market cap of Euro 43.2 billion.

ANALYTICS/MARKET CONVENTIONS

The myriad of bond types in the Brady market: fixed-rate, floating, step-up-to-fixed, step-up-to-floating coupons, together with different collateralization structures and amortization schedules make standard yield calculations and comparisons inapplicable. For example, comparing the yield on a collateralized bond of country A to the yield on an uncollateralized bond of country B does not provide information as to the yield on the risky sovereign cash flows, which is important to the investor. As a result, a number of conventions have been established by market participants in order to facilitate relative value comparisons among the different developing country bonds and between these bonds and other fixed income securities. Indeed, a new vocabulary has been created for the developing country debt market. The purpose of these analytical tools is to evaluate the sovereign portion of the bond independent of the collateral.

---

[6] Compares the J.P. Morgan EMBI in 1995 with the J.P. Morgan EMBI Global in 2000. The J.P. Morgan EMBI was a predecessor to the J.P. Morgan EMBI Global.

[7] Global high yield includes three components: U.S. High Yield, Euro High Yield and EMD. U.S. bond plus is an investment-grade portfolio that allows the portfolio manager to take opportunistic non-index exposure to U.S. High Yield, EMD, and non-dollar bonds.

Stripped Yield and Stripped Spread

Brady bonds are unique in that for a number (but not all) of these bonds, two (or more) semiannual coupon payments are collateralized with money market securities, while the principal payment at maturity is collateralized with U.S. Treasury zero-coupon bonds. A purchase of this type of Brady bond is effectively an investment in a combination of AA money market securities, a U.S. zero-coupon government bond, and a series of sovereign payments. Yield to maturity, if calculated in the standard way, is thus a weighted average of the riskless yields of the collateral and the risky yields of the sovereign payments. "Stripped yield" avoids this averaging by solving for the interest rate that the market applies solely to those cash flows which are sensitive to the sovereign credit risk. For example, on December 29, 2000, the Brazilian Par Brady bond had a yield to maturity of 9.18% and a stripped yield of 14.65%.

The correct analytical procedure is to value the collateral by discounting the collateral cash flows at the appropriate spot interest rate and to subtract this collateral value from the bond's market price; the remainder is the price of the sovereign cash flows. Given the sovereign cash flows and their derived price, the yield to maturity can then be calculated. In short, the bond is separated into collateral and sovereign components.

The term "stripped yield" is used because the collateral is stripped away from the Brady bond for analytical purposes, indicating the interest rate the market applies to the sovereign's credit. Stripped yield, sovereign yield, and sovereign stripped yield are interchangeable terms. The "stripped spread" is simply the stripped yield less the equivalent Treasury yield. Exhibit 13.6 illustrates the valuation process for a hypothetical Brady bond. Collateral cash flows are discounted at U.S. Treasury rates while sovereign cash flows are priced at Treasury rates plus a sovereign credit spread.

The coupon collateral is a contingent, or rolling, interest guarantee. If the sovereign borrower makes its coupon payment, the collateral remains in place and rolls forward to cover the next scheduled coupon payment. In the event of default, interest collateral would be paid to the bondholder in lieu of the sovereign's payments. Market participants disagree on the exact valuation methodology for the interest guarantee because of differing opinions on contingent valuations. Some use probability models to estimate the timing of the contingent guarantee, others assume that the immediate coupon payments are riskless, and yet others ignore the rolling interest guarantee altogether for yield calculations. Stripped spread comparisons of various Brady issues are only meaningful in the context of a particular model.

EXHIBIT 13.6   Brady Bonds Valuation — An Illustration

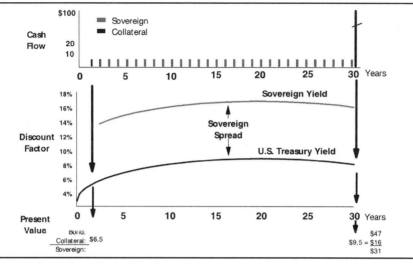

Note: Valuing the collateral by discounting the collateral cash flows at the approximate U.S. "spot" interest rate, allows the present value of the collateral ($16) to be subtracted from the market price of the bond ($47) to derive the present value of the sovereign cash flows ($31). Given the timing of these sovereign cash flows, a yield to maturity on the stripped sovereign portion can then be calculated.

Risk Measures

In addition to yield calculations, market participants have adapted traditional price sensitivity measures to the special features of Brady bonds. Interest rate duration estimates a bond's price responsiveness to changes in U.S. interest rates—all cash flows are revalued given changes in the U.S. yield curve. A bond is less sensitive to changes in U.S. interest rates if the bond's coupons are floating (i.e., reset at a spread above Treasury yields). The investor is also concerned with isolating the bond's price response to a change in creditworthiness. Since only a portion of the bond's cash flows are exposed to sovereign credit risk (in some cases as little as 50%), a change in stripped spread will result in the repricing of only a subset of the cash flows (the sovereign cash flows).

Thus, in addition to the standard interest rate duration measure, "spread duration" measures the bond's price responsiveness to movements in the stripped spread. If an overall widening of credit spreads is expected, the portfolio manager now has the tool to estimate which bonds will be more or less adversely affected. A Brady bond's spread duration is a function of the collateralization level, stripped yield level, and cash flow timing. Exhibit 13.7 compares spread and interest rate durations for various bonds in Brazil.

EXHIBIT 13.7   Spread and Interest Rate Durations: Brazilian Bonds as of December 29, 2000

Bond	Maturity	Type	Coupon	Principal	Interest Rate Duration	Spread Duration
Republic 14.5% due 2009	10/15/09	Eurobond	Fixed	Bullet	4.96	4.96
Republic 11% due 2040	8/17/40	Eurobond	Fixed	Bullet	7.06	6.97
EI	4/15/06	Brady	Floating	Amortizing	0.16	2.29
FLIRB	4/15/09	Brady	Floating	Amortizing	−0.28	3.91
DCB	4/15/12	Brady	Floating	Amortizing	−0.75	4.86
C	4/15/14	Brady	Fixed[1]*	Amortizing	5.09	5.08
Par	4/15/24	Brady	Step-Up	Collateralized	12.50	3.04
Discount	4/15/24	Brady	Floating	Collateralized	3.85	3.22

[1] The coupon of the Brazilian C bond partially capitalized until April 2000.

The high spread volatility of EMD bonds makes accurate risk measurement a necessity. Exhibit 13.8 compares the historical volatilities of various countries in the EMD Index. While the volatility of EMD Index stripped spread changes is approximately 50%, volatility of individual countries varies from 35% in South Africa to 92% in Russia. Exhibit 13.8 also shows that EMD spread volatility is much higher than the volatility of U.S. Treasury yields, so that most of the risk in an EMD portfolio comes from credit selection rather than U.S. yield curve exposure.

Since volatility of EMD bonds varies significantly from country to country, portfolio managers are using more advanced techniques to measure a portfolio's risk exposure. One technique is to adjust bond spread durations by a sensitivity measure that adjusts for volatility and correlation with the overall market.

Attribution of Returns

As previously noted, sovereign bonds are issued in a myriad of formats (various combinations of floating/fixed rate and collateralized/uncollateralized). The characteristics of one country's bonds may differ greatly from another country's because of aforementioned differences in collateralization level, stripped yields, and maturity. In short, investors should be careful when comparing total returns across countries because of the significantly different bond formats. Because investors can manage or hedge general U.S. interest rate exposure outside of the sovereign market, a sovereign bond's total return can most usefully be separately attributed to U.S. interest rate exposure and to sovereign spread performance.

EXHIBIT 13.8 Emerging Markets Bond Index Plus "Stripped" Spread History (through December 2000)

Index	Index Start Date	Stripped Spread Volatility[1]	Maximum Spread	Minimum Spread	Average Spread	12/31/00 Stripped Spread
EMD Index	12/31/90	50%	15.6%	3.5%	7.9%	7.3%
Argentina	4/30/93	67%	16.3%	2.9%	7.2%	7.7%
Brazil	12/31/90	59%	15.1%	3.6%	8.3%	7.5%
Bulgaria	11/30/94	61%	21.5%	4.6%	10.4%	7.7%
Columbia	5/28/99	43%	8.2%	4.2%	6.6%	7.6%
Ecuador	6/30/95	76%	47.6%	5.0%	16.9%	14.1%
Korea	4/30/98	74%	9.7%	1.4%	3.0%	2.6%
Mexico	12/31/90	54%	16.4%	2.7%	6.1%	3.9%
Morocco	3/31/96	87%	15.2%	2.5%	5.6%	5.8%
Nigeria	1/31/92	65%	31.6%	4.3%	15.3%	18.1%
Panama	7/31/96	54%	6.8%	2.2%	4.1%	5.0%
Peru	3/31/97	66%	9.4%	3.4%	5.4%	6.9%
Philippines	6/30/91	60%	9.6%	1.6%	5.2%	6.4%
Poland	11/30/94	54%	8.6%	1.5%	3.1%	2.4%
South Africa	3/31/96	35%	4.2%	1.0%	2.2%	4.2%
Russia	7/31/97	92%	57.1%	4.6%	22.6%	11.7%
Turkey	7/30/99	44%	8.7%	3.8%	5.2%	8.0%
Venezuela	12/31/90	65%	25.8%	3.1%	9.9%	9.6%

[1] Annualized standard deviation of monthly stripped spread or yield changes, logarithmic basis.

U.S. Treasury Strips	Start Date	Yield Volatility	Maximum Yield	Minimum Yield	Average Yield
1-Year	12/31/90	18%	7.1%	3.1%	5.2%
10-Year	12/31/90	14%	8.6%	4.4%	6.6%
30-Year	12/31/90	10%	8.7%	5.0%	7.0%

To illustrate these distinct effects, Exhibit 13.9 reviews December 2000 EMBI Global returns. The returns are divided into a U.S. Yield Factor and a Spread Factor. In December, U.S. interest rates declined by 35 basis points for 10-year bonds and 18 basis points for 30-year bonds. The impact of U.S. interest rate changes varied across countries. Bulgaria, which has predominantly floating-rate issues, had a slightly negative U.S. Yield Curve Factor, while the bulk of Chile's return came from the U.S. Yield Curve Factor (Chile has a fixed-rate 10-year bond in the Index).

EXHIBIT 13.9   Emerging Markets Bond Index Global Factor Returns—
December 2000

Spread Factor[1]		U.S. Yield Curve Factor		Total Return	
Nigeria	9.49%	Poland	2.74%	Nigeria	11.65%
Ukraine	7.47%	Chile	2.72%	Ukraine	9.70%
Bulgaria	7.21%	South Africa	2.61%	Peru	7.62%
Peru	6.25%	Philippines	2.46%	Argentina	6.71%
Argentina	5.03%	Thailand	2.39%	Colombia	6.63%
Brazil	4.58%	Cote d'Ivoire	2.37%	Bulgaria	6.56%
Colombia	4.35%	Colombia	2.28%	Brazil	5.95%
Turkey	3.71%	Mexico	2.28%	Turkey	5.84%
Philippines	3.11%	Malaysia	2.27%	Philippines	5.57%
EMBI Global	2.63%	Ukraine	2.23%	Poland	4.70%
Poland	1.96%	Ecuador	2.18%	EMBI Global	4.41%
Croatia	1.76%	Nigeria	2.16%	Ecuador	3.88%
Ecuador	1.69%	Turkey	2.13%	Chile	3.73%
Chile	1.00%	China	2.13%	Malaysia	3.14%
Russia	0.99%	Russia	2.12%	Russia	3.11%
Malaysia	0.87%	Korea	1.89%	Korea	2.48%
Korea	0.59%	EMBI Global	1.78%	Mexico	2.43%
Morocco	0.47%	Argentina	1.69%	South Africa	2.27%
Panama	0.46%	Venezuela	1.47%	Thailand	2.06%
Mexico	0.15%	Lebanon	1.38%	Croatia	1.99%
Hungary	0.04%	Brazil	1.37%	Hungary	1.40%
Thailand	−0.33%	Peru	1.37%	Panama	1.30%
South Africa	−0.34%	Hungary	1.36%	China	1.29%
Lebanon	−0.68%	Panama	0.85%	Morocco	0.73%
Algeria	−0.77%	Morocco	0.26%	Lebanon	0.70%
China	−0.83%	Croatia	0.23%	Venezuela	−0.25%
Venezuela	−1.72%	Algeria	0.02%	Algeria	−0.75%
Cote d'Ivoire	−10.07%	Bulgaria	−0.66%	Cote d'Ivoire	−7.70%

[1] Sovereign credit spread (incremental income) plus spread change effect (principal).

Evolving assessments of creditworthiness had very differing return impacts as shown in the spread factor. Credit risk declined in Nigeria after the government reached a tentative agreement with the Paris Club to reschedule $23 billion dollars of principal and interest payments.[8] Contrary to earlier speculation, private bondholders were not forced to

[8] The Paris Club represents bilateral creditors. Nigeria's rescheduling was contingent on Nigeria's adherence to an IMF program.

restructure their claims. In contrast, Cote d'Ivoire credit risk increased as the country continued to spiral towards political and economic collapse.

SOVEREIGN CREDIT ANALYSIS

A country's bond spreads are related to its willingness and capacity to repay its debt. The latter depends directly on the amount of obligations coming due at a point in time and the foreign exchange resources and refinancing opportunities available at that time. Both economic and political factors should be considered when analyzing the resources available for a sovereign.

Economic Considerations

Many economic measures are relevant to assessing the credit risk of a developing country. One manner of organizing economic and financial considerations is to compartmentalize measures into three categories: structural, solvency, and serviceability. In addition to making the analysis more manageable by removing redundancies, this categorization produces a term structure of credit risk, akin to the well-known notion of the term structure of interest rates. An understanding of individual country politics, as well as the role of various international agencies, is also an essential part of sovereign credit analysis.

Structural

Measures belonging to this category describe the long-term fundamental health of the country. They include economic variables such as reliance on a particular commodity for export earnings, welfare indicators such as per capita GNP, and social/economic measures such as income distribution. These variables generally are not directly linked to default, but countries with poor structural fundamentals are likely to develop economic problems. Further, given two countries that are similar in other respects, the one with the inferior structural measures will have a lower capacity to tolerate adverse economic shocks.

Solvency

In contrast to the structural variables, the solvency class contains intermediate term measures of a country's economic health. In particular, these variables should reflect the country's ability, over time, to meet its central government debt obligations. Both internal and external debt are included. Countries with inferior solvency measures, all else being equal, have higher default risk because international debt service competes with local economic constituencies for resources.

Serviceability

The factors in this category are of short-term, if not immediate, concern. They reflect the country's foreign exchange reserve position relative to its obligations (and are therefore usually presented in ratio form). Some examples include: debt service (% exports) and external debt (% GDP). Despite good or improving fundamentals and strong solvency measures, a developing country may be forced into a crisis if its reserves are (or will become) deficient, or if alternative reserve sources, such as the International Monetary Fund, are circumscribed. Recent experience suggests that serviceability, or liquidity, is a paramount concern.[9]

Political Considerations

Peculiar to analyzing developing country investments are certain critical political issues such as international aid and policy instability. The United States and multilateral agencies such as the World Bank and IMF have invested a great deal of political and financial capital in the recovery of developing countries and their return to the global marketplace. Therefore, an event which would ordinarily raise the likelihood of default may actually induce international organizations to assist the emerging country and reduce the probability of default. Alternatively, the movement to representative government and open markets is a recent phenomenon, and in many developing countries, there are few institutions in place to serve as anchors to these policies. The resignation or death of one key policy maker may be enough to alter economic policy. In sum, political factors can cut both ways: the politics of individual countries are often fragile, but international politics often have acted as counterbalances in the past.

In recent years, multilateral organizations have launched a debate and an initiative to make financial aid conditional on bondholder participation in providing financial relief to distressed sovereigns.[10] In 1999, Romania withstood an initiative from the IMF to default on its Eurobond payments and did not restructure its Eurobonds. At this stage, it is unclear if multilateral agencies are willing or able to influence a sovereign's relationship with its bondholders. However, it is likely that sovereign bondholders will take a more active roll in resolving financial crises in emerging markets.

While nascent representative governments may suffer from institutional instability, it is important to recognize that these countries have undergone profound political change in a short time. Most countries have

---

[9] Christopher Mahoney, "What Have We Learned? Explaining the World Financial Crisis," Moody's Investor Service (March 1999).

[10] This is commonly referred to as "bailing in" bondholders.

moved from military rule to competitive, multiparty democracies within the decade. For example, in 1982, approximately 80% of the emerging market countries' populations were under communist or military rule; now approximately 97% are governed by democratic rule.

Willingness to Pay

Some argue that sovereign risk analysis is doomed to failure because, notwithstanding the ability to pay, a country may be unwilling to make good on its debt obligations. Distinguishing sovereign risk from corporate or municipal credit risk on this basis alone exposes a deficient understanding of default risk. Borrowers default when their competing economic interests override the damage done by default. Default is never a casual decision. Issuers wait until they are completely destitute to make this decision. Corporations and municipalities are faced with the same decision as sovereign borrowers: at what point are you willing to capitulate and damage your reputation?

For example, in 1991, Columbia Gas Systems found the burden of high-priced, long-term gas supply contracts of the energy shortage era so damaging to its future that management declared bankruptcy and forced its suppliers to renegotiate the supply contracts to lower prices. Similarly, Orange County, California viewed the financial implications of their failed investment scheme so negatively that they too declared bankruptcy. Orange County taxpayers perceived little ownership of the problem because of the obscure nature of the investment scheme and its genitor. Most important, both borrowers were willing to default even though the debtors had substantial resources available to pay creditors and suppliers. The point is that economic strain creates a willingness issue for borrowers of all types.[11]

Sovereign Credit Perspective

Exhibit 13.10 provides some perspective on the economic performance and financial measures of the primary EMD countries relative to developed countries. The figure compares statistics for the 10 largest emerging market debtors with G7 statistics. Developing countries' inflation performance is clearly inferior, but savings rates and central government debt measures compare favorably with those for industrialized countries and the Maastricht hurdles related to European Monetary Union. In particular, the average developing country central government debt/GDP ratio of 50% compares well to the 80% average debt/GDP ratio for the industrialized countries.

---

[11] Vincent Truglia, "Sovereign Risk: Bank Deposits versus Bonds," Moody's Investor Service (October 1995).

EXHIBIT 13.10   Sovereign Credit Perspective 2000

	Central Govt. Debt/GDP	Total External Debt/GDP[1]	Budget/ GDP	GDP Growth Current	GDP Growth 5 year	Annual Savings/ GDP	Inflation Current[2]	Inflation 5 year
Argentina	47%[3]	52%	−3.7%	−0.5%	2.7%	13%	−1%	0%
Brazil	50%	41%	−4.6%	4.0%	2.2%	21%	6%	7%
Malaysia	37%	46%	−2.8%	8.3%	4.8%	10%	2%	3%
Mexico	43%	28%	−1.1%	6.9%	5.4%	10%	9%	18%
Philippines	95%	78%	−3.3%	3.4%	3.6%	13%	7%	7%
Poland	38%	42%	−2.4%	4.1%	5.0%	20%	10%	12%
Russia	66%	57%	1.0%	7.3%	0.0%	16%	21%	33%
Korea	39%	27%	1.1%	9.0%	4.8%	28%	2%	4%
Turkey	59%	60%	−17.8%	7.2%	3.9%	22%	55%	55%
Venezuela	25%	28%	3.2%	3.2%	0.7%	34%	16%	37%
Canada	104%	28%	1.4%	4.6%	5.9%	5%	3%	2%
France	64%	11%	−1.2%	3.1%	4.8%	8%	2%	1%
Germany	61%	4%	1.3%	2.9%	3.1%	7%	2%	1%
Italy	111%	2%	−0.3%	2.9%	2.9%	7%	3%	2%
Japan	109%	−20%	−6.3%	1.5%	−0.1%	15%	−1%	0%
U.K.	55%	43%	2.1%	3.0%	3.9%	8%	3%	3%
U.S.	58%	14%	2.4%	4.9%	6.7%	7%	3%	2%
Maastricht[4]	60%		−3.0%					

[1] Total external debt is equal to net external debt for developed economies and gross external debt for emerging economies.
[2] Average annual basis. Maastricht: Not more than 1.5% above the average of the three lowest inflation rate EU members.
[3] 1999 data.
[4] Maastricht Hurdles for European Economic and Monetary Union.

Sources: International Monetary Fund, International Institute of Finance, J.P. Morgan, OECD, and Salomon Smith Barney

This juxtaposition highlights the fact that the major risk in emerging economies is often not the government's debt load on the economy, but access to foreign exchange. Because of previous poor policy management, weak banking systems, and ineffective leadership, many emerging countries are forced to borrow in foreign currency (usually U.S. dollars). Developing countries access foreign currency through foreign direct investment, exports, portfolio investment, and official loans, all of which depend upon sound economic management and stable political leadership. This access to dollars, which is a serviceability issue, can largely be a matter of investor confidence in policy makers and is a unique risk to this market. Total external debt (public and private foreign currency denominated debt) relative to GDP for emerging countries is not significantly different from that of developed countries, but, in some cases, these developing countries have difficulty accessing foreign currency through exports or through foreign direct investment.

This additional risk aside, three macro trends may lead investors to be optimistic that emerging countries will continue their economic development process and eventually become better credit risks. First, the retreat of communism and the Soviet State signal an end to dismal economic incentives for much of the world. Second, the movement to more democratic forms of government should, in the long run, stimulate a more competitive marketplace of ideas and policies. Lastly, the high rate of integration (trade, tourism, information technology, etc.) and the rapid pace of technological change make economic isolation more costly and less acceptable to the populace.

The current economic position of emerging countries is in some ways not radically different from their developed counterparts. What differentiates them is that emerging market borrowers have less institutional stability, less demonstrated commitment to free market principles, and less reliable access to foreign exchange. These problems lead primarily to a weaker serviceability measure, but do not necessarily imply structural infirmity or insolvency.

PORTFOLIO CONSIDERATIONS

Since the beginning of 1991 when Brady bonds became viable assets for institutional investors, the EMD Index has outperformed the broad global and U.S. bond markets by a wide margin. Exhibit 13.11 displays EMD Index return premia (defined as total return less U.S. cash return) along with return premia for other market indices. Of course, given the nature of the risk inherent in these bonds and the immaturity of the market, volatility is also greater. The portfolio benefits of EMD are illustrated in Exhibit 13.12, which shows a simplified efficient frontier, including Emerging Debt Markets. The efficient frontier including Emerging Debt Markets has dominated the Developed Markets alternative since 1990. Other major indices are also plotted for comparative purposes.

Correlations

An attractive feature of the emerging sovereign market is its low correlation to other asset classes, including other U.S. bond markets, as illustrated in Exhibit 13.13. Emerging market spreads also have no historic correlation with U.S. Treasury yields. Sometimes, EMD spreads have declined following a monetary easing in the U.S. Other times, investors shift from risk assets, such as EMD, to low risk assets causing Treasury yields and EMD spreads to move in opposite directions. Low correlation to other fixed income assets makes EMD an attractive addition to a diversified portfolio.

EXHIBIT 13.11   Market Indices Return Premia and Volatility
(December 31, 1990–December 31, 2000)

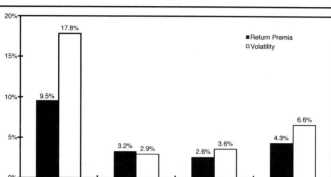

EMD–EMD Index, merged data histories from J.P. Morgan Indices; BIG–Broad Investment Grade Index, Salomon Brothers; WGBI–World Government Bond Index, Salomon Brothers; GIM–Global Investable Market Index (contains equity and debt), Brinson Partners. Return Premia equals total return less cash return calculated on a logarithmic basis in U.S. dollars. Volatility equals annualized standard deviation based on monthly return premia.

EXHIBIT 13.12   Efficient Frontier Full Period (December 1990–December 2000)

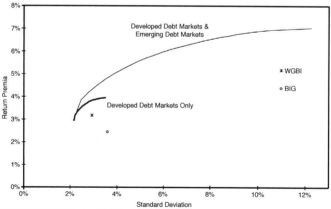

Developed Debt Markets and Emerging Debt Markets include 14 DMs, 12 EMs and the components of BIG. Developed Debt Markets only frontier includes Australia, Austria, Belgium, Canada, Denmark, France, Germany, Italy, Japan, Netherlands, Spain, Sweden, Switzerland, U.K. and the components of BIG. Frontiers based on monthly logarithmic return premia from December 1990, or index inception, to December 2000. Countries with less than 2 years of data are excluded. Frontier percentage constrained at 25% maximum for Australia, Canada, France, Germany, Japan, Switzerland, U.K. and the components of BIG.

EXHIBIT 13.13   Market Indices Return Premia—Correlation Matrix
December 31, 1990–December 29, 2000

	EMD	WGBI	BIG	GIM
EMD	1.00			
WGBI	0.18	1.00		
BIG	0.21	0.85	1.00	
GIM	0.61	0.38	0.40	1.00

EMD–EMD Index, merged data histories from J.P. Morgan Indices; BIG–Broad Investment Grade Index, Salomon Brothers; WGBI–World Government Bond Index, Salomon Brothers; GIM–Global Investable Market Index (contains equity and debt), Brinson Partners. Return premia equals total return less cash return calculated on a logarithmic basis in U.S. dollars. Correlations based on monthly return premia.

EXHIBIT 13.14   Emerging Markets Bond Index Plus Conditional Annualized
Volatility (December 1990–December 2000)

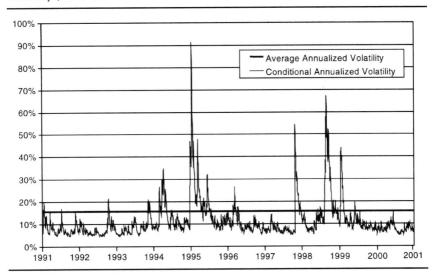

Return Volatility

Exhibit 13.14 provides a perspective on return premia volatility. The average annualized return volatility between December 1990 and December 2000 is 15.6%. The conditional annualized volatility, which measures short-term volatility, shows dramatic volatility spikes.[12] Returns are vola-

---

[12] Conditional annualized volatility calculated from daily returns by using generalized autoregressive conditional heteroscedasticity (GARCH).

tile for two distinct reasons. First, the economic development process in these countries is inherently volatile. These countries are attempting to abandon long-ingrained social, economic, and political structures in a very short period of time. Second, return volatility often has less to do with the credit risk of the borrowers than the perspective of the investors. A casual observer of this market's return pattern might draw the conclusion that sovereign credit risk itself fluctuates wildly. A closer examination would reveal the scarcity of long-term investors, despite the inappropriateness of this sector for those with brief time horizons and high liquidity needs. As a result, much of the historical volatility was driven by liquidity considerations and speculation. Fundamentals did not change as rapidly as market price fluctuations would imply.

Events in the winter of 1994/1995 in the emerging debt market resembled the precipitous price declines in the U.S. high-yield bond market in 1989 and the mortgage market in 1994. In both cases, investors had taken on more risk than they understood or appreciated (corporate credit risk and interest rate option risk, respectively) and had enjoyed very good absolute returns for a significant period of time. Moreover, these securities were particularly ill-suited for their respective owners. In the case of high-yield bonds, the investment horizon of retail mutual fund investors was a poor match for this illiquid and volatile market. In the case of the mortgage market, portfolio managers of retail-oriented, short-term government bond funds (and others) were heavily invested in securities with extreme prepayment sensitivity. When interest rates began to rise, reversing a three-year trend, homeowner prepayments slowed abruptly. The value of many sensitive securities declined precipitously as prepayment assumptions were reassessed.

The emerging debt market mirrored these examples in two respects: (1) it produced uniformly stellar returns over a preceding 3-year period and (2) mutual fund managers placed billions of dollars of these securities in retail-oriented mutual funds that had liquidity and risk tolerances inconsistent with the nature of the securities. The panic liquidation of these investments after the Mexican peso devaluation caused tremendous illiquidity in the market, pushing prices down well below fundamental value.

EMD prices declined precipitously again in August 1998 during Russia's financial crisis. Once again, three prior years of uninterrupted, high returns had caused investors to become complacent regarding sovereign credit risk. In the Russian case, many leveraged foreign investors speculated in local currency Treasury Bills (GKOs) which went into default with an approximate 90% loss. The losses in the GKO market damaged the U.S. dollar-denominated sovereign debt market as leveraged investors liquidated their positions and other participants reassessed their assumptions.

EXHIBIT 13.15   Comparison of the Four Major International Debt Crises

	1820s	1870s	1930s	1980s
Countries of Major Private Creditors	Britain	Britain France Germany	USA Britain Netherlands Switzerland	USA European Countries Japan Canada
Major Defaulters	Latin America Greece	Egypt Turkey Spain Latin America	Germany Eastern Europe Latin America	Latin America Eastern Europe Africa
Systemic Factors	• Lending to belligerents • Lack of lending experience and information	• Lending to belligerents or profligate rulers • Strong political influence	• Worldwide depression • Trade wars • Poor economic management	• Oil and interest rate shocks • Worldwide recession
Main Instrument	Bonds	Bonds	Bonds	Bank loans
Settlement Process	Private Negotiations	Private Bondholders' Councils	Private Bondholders' Councils	IMF Paris Club Bank committees Brady Plan

Source: John F.H. Purcell and Jeffrey A. Kaufman, "The Risks of Sovereign Lending: Lessons from History," Salomon Brothers, September 1993, p. 9.

Long-term investors such as mutual funds, pension funds, and insurance companies have gradually replaced banks, flight capital, and hedge funds as the primary holders of EMD bonds. As the investor base evolves, volatility due to liquidity panics should lessen.

Expected Return

The long-term expected return on the sovereign, or risky, cash flows is a function of yield, default probability, and recovery value.

Default probability is crucial to expected returns, yet is a very difficult decision area. International bond defaults have occurred since the 1820s (including U.S. borrowers). Other major default episodes occurred in the 1870s, 1930s, and 1980s. Generally, past crises were due to poor use of loaned funds or worldwide economic depression or recession. Exhibit 13.15 reviews the circumstances of previous debt crises.

In this light, certain developments have improved the EMD credit environment. As more investment is being privately channeled, such as FDI, rather than publicly placed, borrowers are no longer wasting resources on armaments or huge white elephants. Currency and bond markets provide emerging market politicians with constant feedback about the appropriateness of their policies. Moreover, as the number of EMD issuers expands, the probability of simultaneous economic difficulties should diminish.

If investors are willing to expose their portfolios to implicit sovereign risk through multinational equity commitments, they would be well served to consider the pricing of explicit sovereign risk. If the optimistic economic assumptions girding the emerging markets earnings estimates of multinational corporations are reasonable, then implicit sovereign default expectations appear too high. In short, if equity investors prosper through international expansion into emerging economies, host country defaults are unlikely.

The restructuring of Russia's defaulted Soviet debt and Ecuador's Brady Bonds in 2000 suggest that EMD recovery rates may be higher than U.S. corporate recovery rates. Before restructuring, Russian and Ecuadorian bonds traded at 33 and 36, respectively. Prior to credit deterioration and subsequent default, these bonds traded at approximately 50. The exact recovery amount for these bonds is difficult to calculate because, being themselves the result of a former debt restructuring, they were not issued at par and traded immediately at deep discounts. But investors that bought these bonds in the secondary market prior to credit deterioration/default realized recovery values even higher than the historical corporate bond recovery rate (48% of original face).

In the short run, the discount rates applied to bond cash flows will drive prices and returns; but in the long run, the cash flows themselves determine returns. Presuming that debt relief would be sufficient to resume debt repayments, cash flows can then be estimated by projecting the probability and timing of any future default/renegotiation. Holding the discount rate constant, a cash flow reduction roughly translates into a proportional return reduction. Thus, if a debtor immediately reduced its coupon payments on a 30-year obligation by 40% (and then made all future payments), the expected holding period return would decrease by approximately 45%. If the stated cash flows were priced to return 14%, the 40% coupon reduction would drop expected returns to approximately 7.8%. Each year that passes without a default significantly boosts returns; the expected return climbs to 10.8% if rescheduling does not occur until year seven.

Exhibit 13.16 examines return scenarios given varying recovery rates and varying pricing yields. (The pricing yield is simply the yield to maturity given the price of the cash flows.) The top graph illustrates that at the currently high pricing yields, holding period returns climb rapidly as default is avoided. Also, after ten years of payments, returns are relatively insensitive to recovery assumptions, due to high compounding rates. The bottom graph indicates that for a given principal recovery assumption of 60%, returns are more variable at higher pricing yields.

EXHIBIT 13.16   Long-Term Return Scenarios Varying Rate of Recovery—40%, 50%, 60%
Pricing Yield 16%

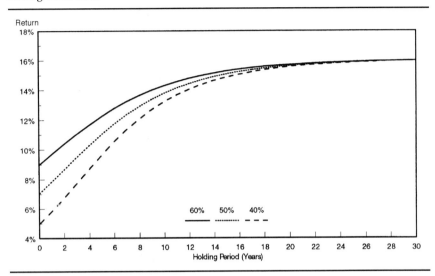

Varying Rate of Recovery—10%, 14%, 18% Yield Environment
Rate of Recovery 60%

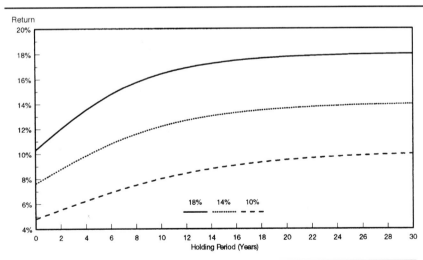

EXHIBIT 13.17   Conditional Default Probability versus Return Recovering Rate
Assumption = 60% (Varying Price Yield)

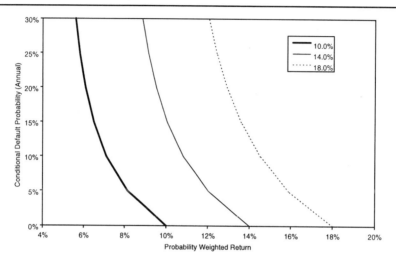

Another manner of assessing prospective returns is to consider the
implied conditional probability of default (conditional upon no previous default and equally probable in any year). That is, given market
pricing, recovery estimates, and required return, what is the implied
annual probability of default? Exhibit 13.17 plots annual default probability (for three pricing scenarios) versus probability-weighted return,
assuming a 60% recovery value. For example, if the sovereign cash flow
is priced to yield 14%, the recovery assumption in the event of default is
60%, and the required return is 10%, then the implied annual conditional default probability is approximately 15%. Framed in this manner,
the investor can judge the reasonableness of this default assumption in
light of intermediate global economic trends and portfolio diversification effects.

In summary, sovereign default episodes are relatively rare and no
easier to anticipate than large macroeconomic shifts. Pricing yields,
recovery value assumptions, and default probabilities determine expected
returns.

Asset Allocation

Exhibit 13.18 highlights the equilibrium risk/reward position of emerging
markets debt as a class relative to other financial markets (risk defined as
beta: the asset class volatility relative to that of a globally diversified portfolio). The risk/reward position is much closer to traditional equity markets

than other bond markets. The forward looking estimates of 16% annual-ized standard deviation of return premia and 0.46 correlation to the global market translate into an estimated beta of 1.12, given a 6.6% global market risk assumption. In light of these portfolio characteristics, limited performance history and judgments regarding liquidity and sovereign risks, risk premium in equilibrium is estimated at 3.6% per year (i.e. the incremental return over cash required by a globally diversified investor). Consequently, despite the high estimate of volatility, Emerging Markets Debt as an asset class provides an attractive portfolio risk/reward trade-off in equilibrium. One manner of framing this trade-off is the Treynor ratio, or risk premium relative to beta; from this viewpoint, Emerging Markets Debt compares favorably to other asset classes.

Exhibit 13.19 shows the differences in spreads between emerging market bonds and similarly rated U.S. corporates. As of December 2000, BBB- and BB-rated emerging market bonds had spreads that were 99 and 257 basis points higher than similarly rated U.S. corporate spreads, while B-rated emerging market bonds had spreads that were 13 basis points lower than B-rated U.S. corporate spreads. The spread difference between BBB-rated EMD and U.S. corporate bonds has historically shown little volatility. In contrast, the difference between EMD and corporate spreads for B-rated bonds has varied significantly.

EXHIBIT 13.18 Equilibrium Risk/Reward[1]
Global Market Beta as Equilibrium Risk Premium

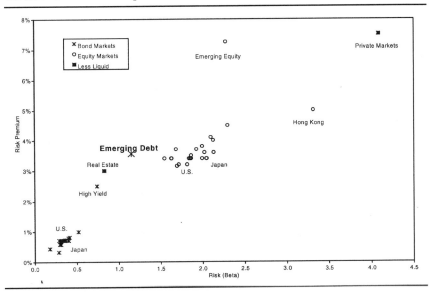

[1] Based on forward-looking estimates.

EXHIBIT 13.19   Emerging Markets Debt versus U.S. High-Yield Stripped Spread by Rating (December 1997 through December 2000)

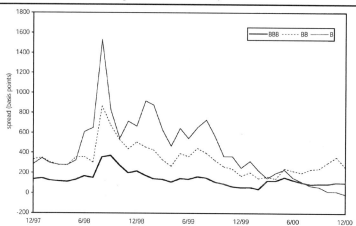

Sources: Emerging Market Debt spread information from J.P.Morgan. U.S. corporate spread information from Merrill Lynch.

In December 2000, U.S. High-Yield (B– and BB– rated bonds) spreads were at relatively low levels compared to EMD spreads due to the recent difficulties in the technology and telecommunications sectors. At the end of 2000, Moody's U.S. high-yield default rate stood at 5.6% and was expected to increase to levels last seen in 1991.

ACTIVE MANAGEMENT OPPORTUNITIES

All U.S. dollar fixed-income sectors (mortgage, investment grade corporates, high yield, Eurobonds, and Brady bonds) are exposed to the risk that spreads over U.S. Treasury rates change. That is, despite a constant Treasury curve, incremental yield (spread) above this curve may increase or decrease for a number of reasons related to perceived risks in the sector. The change in spread impacts total returns just as a change in the underlying Treasury curve does.

Active management opportunities exist because spreads across countries are less than perfectly correlated and because bond structures vary within a country. Exhibit 13.20 shows the correlation of stripped spreads across countries. Each country's perceived creditworthiness does not move in lock-step with the overall market, as noted in the discussion of return attribution. This variation translates into active management opportunities as investors compare the price of sovereign credit risk (spread) versus their own assessment of that sovereign credit risk (value).

EXHIBIT 13.20 EMD Index Stripped Spreads Correlation Matrix (through December 2000)*

	Index Start Date	EMD	Arg	Brz	Bul	Ecu	Mex	Mor	Ngr	Pan	Per	Pol	Rus	Ven
EMD Index	12/90	1.00												
Argentina	4/93	0.94	1.00											
Brazil	12/90	0.86	0.84	1.00										
Bulgaria	11/94	0.83	0.81	0.78	1.00									
Ecuador	6/95	0.73	0.65	0.67	0.66	1.00								
Mexico	12/90	0.84	0.78	0.67	0.65	0.61	1.00							
Morocco	3/96	0.87	0.83	0.75	0.78	0.67	0.71	1.00						
Nigeria	1/92	0.51	0.50	0.42	0.46	0.42	0.36	0.46	1.00					
Panama	7/96	0.77	0.75	0.75	0.61	0.55	0.76	0.65	0.26	1.00				
Peru	3/97	0.78	0.72	0.76	0.76	0.60	0.67	0.72	0.41	0.69	1.00			
Poland	11/94	0.79	0.74	0.72	0.70	0.62	0.63	0.67	0.58	0.63	0.79	1.00		
Russia	7/97	0.85	0.68	0.72	0.69	0.64	0.69	0.71	0.40	0.62	0.64	0.70	1.00	
Venezuela	12/90	0.86	0.81	0.72	0.75	0.62	0.68	0.72	0.44	0.76	0.63	0.65	0.68	1.00

* Correlation of stripped spread changes, logarithmic basis.

EXHIBIT 13.21 Brazil versus Argentina Stripped Spread Difference (through December 2000)

One example of inter-country spread volatility is illustrated in Exhibit 13.21. Even though Argentine and Brazilian spreads are highly correlated, they have provided several opportunities for active management strategies. During the Mexican crisis in 1994, Argentine banks suffered large withdrawals and spreads on Argentine bonds widened accordingly while Brazilian spreads were less affected. During the Brazilian devaluation in 1999, Brazilian spreads increased relative to Argentine spreads.

Opportunities also arise from instrument selection within a country. During times of market volatility, Brady bonds have historically traded at a large discount to Eurobonds. As discussed earlier in this chapter, some market participants argue that, under duress, countries may choose to service Eurobond obligations over Brady obligations just as they discriminated against the old bank loans.

If default risk and volatility distinctions do not warrant higher credit spreads on Brady issues, perhaps the sheer complexity of the Brady formats may explain the relative mispricing. Just as U.S. high-yield bond portfolio managers are often unfamiliar with sovereign credit analysis, others are equally uncomfortable with the unique analytical aspects of the Brady market. Exhibit 13.22 plots the sovereign (stripped) spread of an Argentine Brady bond versus the spread of a Republic of Argentina Eurobond. Despite having identical sovereign credit risk, the Brady bond traded at spreads 400 basis points over the Eurobond during the Russian crisis in 1998 and the Brazilian devaluation in early 1999.

EXHIBIT 13.22   Argentine Bond Spreads, Brady versus Eurobond (Argentine FRB versus Republic of Argentina 2003) (through December 2000)

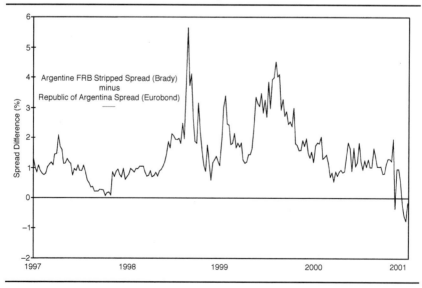

EXHIBIT 13.23   Brazilian Bond Spreads, Brady Bond Comparison (Brazilian FLIRB versus Brazilian C-bond) (through December 2000)

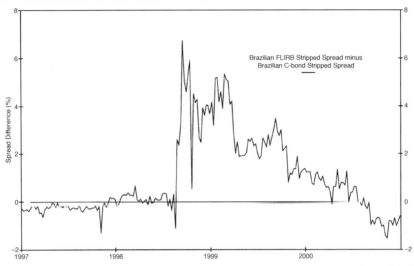

Periods of high volatility cause spread curves to invert and exaggerate spread differences between benchmark securities and less liquid bonds. Exhibit 13.23 looks at the spread differences between two Brazilian Brady bonds: the FLIRB and the C-bond. During the Russian crisis (August 1998) and after Brazil devalued its currency (January 1999), the spread difference between the FLIRB and the C-bond got as high as 600 basis points due to both spread curve inversion and the relatively lower liquidity of the FLIRB.[13]

Emerging markets debt is an asset class with a smaller dedicated investor base than other asset classes. According to market estimates, the dedicated investors such as mutual funds and pension funds make up at most 10% to sovereign debt holders; crossover and local investors make up the remainder. In contrast, dedicated investors account for at least 40% of U.S. high-yield capitalization. Crossover investors make most of their investments in mature markets but will devote a small proportion of their investment funds to EMD.[14]

---

[13] During distressed market conditions, the price of the FLIRB was $15 lower than the price of the C-bond.

[14] Donald J. Mathieson and Garry J. Schinasi, "International Capital Markets Developments, Prospects, and Key Policy Issues," International Monetary Fund (July 2001).

Since crossover investors are a large portion of EMD bond holders, their entry and exit into the market contributes to high emerging market volatility. Crossover preferences for certain types of bonds, particularly corporate bonds, create active management opportunities for the dedicated investor that can purchase corporates opportunistically at distressed levels.

CONCLUSION

Emerging markets debt is an asset class with unique characteristics. Complex security structures, sovereign macroeconomic analysis and unique risk/return characteristics are particular to emerging markets debt.

Emerging markets debt is characterized by periods of high volatility where prices diverge from fundamentals. A lack of a dedicated investor base in EMD contributes to volatility and creates pricing anomalies between instruments. A fundamentally-based, active management style benefits from this volatility and inefficient pricing.

The following factors support the addition of emerging markets debt to a diversified portfolio:

- With the resolution of the Latin debt crisis and the decline of communism, emerging market countries have shifted decisively towards capitalism and democracy.
- Emerging markets debt has grown as an asset class. As of December 2000, it constituted approximately 4.8% of the World Bond Market.
- Emerging markets debt has returned 15.9% annually in premia terms between December 1990 and December 2000.
- Emerging markets debt has low correlation with other segments of the U.S. bond market.

CHAPTER 14

Agency Mortgage-Backed Securities

Frank J. Fabozzi, Ph.D., CFA
Adjunct Professor of Finance
School of Management
Yale University

David Yuen, CFA
Senior Vice President
Portfolio Strategist/Risk Manager
Franklin Templeton Investments

Real estate backed securities are securities backed by a pool (collection) of mortgage loans. Residential or commercial mortgages can be used as collateral for such securities. Real estate securities backed by residential mortgage loans include mortgage passthrough securities, stripped mortgage-backed securities, and collateralized mortgage obligations. Collectively we refer to these securities as *mortgage-backed securities* (MBS). In this chapter we describe those issued by either the Government National Mortgage Association (Ginnie Mae), the Federal National Mortgage Association (Fannie Mae), and the Federal Home Loan Mortgage Corporation (Freddie Mac). For the reasons described later in this chapter, these securities are referred to as agency MBS. In the next chapter, MBS not issued by one of these three entities are described. In Chapter 16 MBS backed by commercial mortgage loans are covered.

WHY IT IS IMPORTANT TO UNDERSTAND
REAL ESTATE-BACKED SECURITIES

The U.S. mortgage market is the largest debt market in the world. A major innovation in the U.S. mortgage market has been the development of a wide range of mortgage designs from which borrowers can select. (We'll discuss the major ones for residential mortgages later in this chapter.) Regardless of the type of mortgage design, as a stand alone investment mortgages typically have unattractive characteristics for both institutional and retail investors. From the perspective of investors, the major innovation in the mortgage market has been the development of securities backed by real estate mortgage loans—mortgage-backed securities or, more generally, real estate-backed securities. In this chapter and the two that follow, these securities are discussed.

An investor who is managing funds where the benchmark or "bogey" is a broad-based bond market index must be familiar with these securities because they represent a major component of the investment-grade bond market (i.e., market for bonds rated at least BBB–). To see this, consider one of the most popular bond indexes followed by institutional investors, the Lehman Brothers' U.S. Aggregate Index. This index includes only investment-grade bonds and is composed of six sectors: Treasury, agency, mortgage passthrough, commercial mortgage-backed, asset-backed, and credit sectors. The mortgage passthrough sector includes securities guaranteed by Ginnie Mae, Fannie Mae, or Freddie Mac. These securities, which we describe later in this chapter, represent the largest sector of the index, constituting about 36%. Add to the mortgage passthrough sector the sector with securities backed by commercial mortgages of about 2% and the real estate-backed securities component increases to about 38% of the Lehman Brothers' Aggregate Index.

The "mortgage sector" is defined by Lehman Brothers to consist of the mortgage passthrough sector and the commercial mortgage-backed sector. However, one more real estate component must be added: asset-backed securities (ABS) where the collateral is residential mortgages. The asset-backed sector is 2% of the index and includes securities backed by both real estate and non-real estate assets. Approximately 25% of the ABS sector is backed by residential real estate mortgages—specifically, home equity loan ABS and manufactured housing ABS, products that are described in the next chapter.

Consequently, a bond portfolio manager who is seeking to build a core portfolio to match the characteristics of the Lehman Brothers' Aggregate Index must understand real estate-backed securities. Moreover, in constructing a portfolio, portfolio managers will depart from the characteristics of an index in order to enhance returns relative to the index. While there are a variety of strategies employed by active managers, one strategy is to look for securities that are not included in the index but are expected to outperform those securities in the index. There are opportunities to do this with real estate-backed securities. This can be done with securities issued by agencies that expose investors to minimal credit risk, called agency collateralized mortgage obligations, which we describe in this chapter. In addition, there are securities issued by private entities that provide return enhancement opportunities for investors willing to accept credit risk that are described in the next chapter.

The bottom line is that a bond portfolio manager seeking to build a core portfolio but who is unfamiliar with real estate-backed securities will be at a competitive disadvantage. Moreover, a portfolio manager who is unfamiliar with real estate-backed securities may miss opportunities to enhance return in products that are not part of the index.

MORTGAGES

We begin our discussion with the raw material for a mortgage-backed security—the mortgage loan. A mortgage loan, or simply mortgage, is a loan secured by the collateral of some specified real estate property, which obliges the borrower to make a predetermined series of payments. The mortgage gives the lender the right if the borrower defaults (i.e., fails to make the contracted payments) to "foreclose" on the loan and seize the property in order to ensure that the debt is paid off. The interest rate on the mortgage loan is called the *mortgage rate* or *contract rate*. Our focus is on residential mortgage loans.

An individual who wants to borrow funds to purchase a home will apply for a loan from a mortgage originator. The individual who seeks funds completes an application form that provides personal financial information, and pays an application fee; then the mortgage originator performs a credit evaluation of the applicant. The two primary factors in determining whether the funds will be lent are the (1) payment-to-income (PTI) ratio, and (2) the loan-to-value (LTV) ratio. The former is the ratio of monthly payments to monthly income and is a measure of the ability of the applicant to make monthly payments (both mortgage and real estate tax payments). The lower this ratio, the greater the likelihood that the applicant will be able to meet the required payments.

LTV is the ratio of the amount of the loan to the market (or appraised) value of the property. The lower this ratio, the greater the protection the lender has if the applicant defaults on the payments and the lender must repossess and sell the property. For example, if an applicant wants to borrow $150,000 on property with an appraised value of $200,000, the LTV is 75%. Suppose the applicant subsequently defaults on the mortgage. The lender can then repossess the property and sell it to recover the amount owed. But the amount that will be received by the lender depends on the market value of the property. In our example, even if conditions in the housing market are weak, the lender will still be able to recover the proceeds lent if the value of the property declines by $50,000. Suppose instead that the applicant wanted to borrow $180,000 for the same property. The LTV would then be 90%. If the lender had to sell the property because the applicant defaults, there is less protection for the lender.

When the lender makes the loan based on the credit of the borrower and on the collateral for the mortgage, the mortgage is said to be a *conventional mortgage*. The lender also may take out mortgage insurance to guarantee the fulfillment of the borrower's obligation. Some borrowers can qualify for mortgage insurance, which is guaranteed by one of three U.S. government agencies: the Federal Housing Administration (FHA), the Veteran's Administration (VA), and the Rural Housing Service (RHS). There are also private mortgage insurers.

There are many types of mortgage designs available in the United States. A mortgage design is a specification of the interest rate, term of the mortgage, and manner in which the borrowed funds are repaid. Here we will discuss the three major ones. With an understanding of the features of these mortgages, securities backed by mortgages can be understood.

Fixed-Rate, Level-Payment, Fully Amortized Mortgage

The basic idea behind the design of the fixed-rate, level-payment, fully amortized mortgage is that the borrower pays interest and repays principal in equal installments over an agreed-upon period of time, called the maturity or term of the mortgage. The frequency of payment is typically monthly. Each monthly mortgage payment for this mortgage design is due on the first of each month and consists of:

1. interest of $\frac{1}{12}$ of the annual interest rate times the amount of the outstanding mortgage balance at the beginning of the previous month, and
2. a repayment of a portion of the outstanding mortgage balance (principal).

The difference between the monthly mortgage payment and the portion of the payment that represents interest equals the amount that is applied to reduce the outstanding mortgage balance. The monthly mortgage payment is designed so that after the last scheduled monthly payment of the loan is made, the amount of the outstanding mortgage balance is zero (i.e., the mortgage is fully repaid or amortized).

To illustrate this mortgage design, consider a 30-year (360-month) $100,000 mortgage with a mortgage rate of 8.125%. The monthly mortgage payment would be $742.50. Exhibit 14.1 shows for selected months how each monthly mortgage payment is divided between interest and repayment of principal. At the beginning of month 1, the mortgage balance is $100,000, the amount of the original loan. The mortgage payment for month 1 includes interest on the $100,000 borrowed for the month. Since the interest rate is 8.125%, the monthly interest rate is 0.0067708 (0.08125 divided by 12). Interest for month 1 is therefore $677.08 ($100,000 times 0.0067708). The $65.42 difference between the monthly mortgage payment of $742.50 and the interest of $677.08 is the portion of the monthly mortgage payment that represents repayment of principal. The $65.42 in month 1 reduces the mortgage balance. Notice that the last mortgage payment in month 360 is sufficient to pay off the remaining mortgage balance.

As Exhibit 14.1 clearly shows, the portion of the monthly mortgage payment applied to interest declines each month, and the portion applied to reducing the mortgage balance increases. The reason for this is that as the mortgage balance is reduced with each monthly mortgage payment, the interest on the mortgage balance declines. Since the monthly mortgage payment is fixed, an increasingly larger portion of the monthly payment is applied to reduce the principal in each subsequent month.

The monthly mortgage payment made by the borrower is not what the investor receives. This is because the mortgage must be serviced. The servicing fee is a portion of the mortgage rate. If the mortgage rate is 8.125% and the servicing fee is 50 basis points, then the investor receives interest of 7.625%. The interest rate that the investor receives is said to be the *net interest* or *net coupon*.

Prepayments and Cash Flow Uncertainty

Our illustration of the cash flows from a fixed-rate, level-payment, fully amortized mortgage assumes that the homeowner does not pay off any portion of the mortgage balance prior to the scheduled due date. But some homeowners do pay off all or part of their mortgage balance prior to the maturity date. Payments made in excess of the scheduled principal repayments are called *prepayments*. Later we will discuss factors that affect prepayments.

EXHIBIT 14.1 Amortization Schedule for a Fixed-Rate, Level-Payment, Fully Amortized Mortgage
   Mortgage loan: $100,000
   Mortgage rate: 8.125%
   Monthly payment: $742.50
   Term of loan: 30 years (360 months)

Month	Beginning Mortgage Balance ($)	Monthly Payment ($)	Monthly Interest ($)	Scheduled Principal Repayment ($)	Ending Mortgage Balance ($)
1	100,000.00	742.50	677.08	65.42	99,934.58
2	99,934.58	742.50	676.64	65.86	99,868.72
3	99,868.72	742.50	676.19	66.31	99,802.41
25	98,301.53	742.50	665.58	76.91	98,224.62
26	98,224.62	742.50	665.06	77.43	98,147.19
27	98,147.19	742.50	664.54	77.96	98,069.23
74	93,849.98	742.50	635.44	107.05	93,742.93
75	93,742.93	742.50	634.72	107.78	93,635.15
76	93,635.15	742.50	633.99	108.51	93,526.64
141	84,811.77	742.50	574.25	168.25	84,643.52
142	84,643.52	742.50	573.11	169.39	84,474.13
143	84,474.13	742.50	571.96	170.54	84,303.59
184	76,446.29	742.50	517.61	224.89	76,221.40
185	76,221.40	742.50	516.08	226.41	75,994.99
186	75,994.99	742.50	514.55	227.95	75,767.04
233	63,430.19	742.50	429.48	313.02	63,117.17
234	63,117.17	742.50	427.36	315.14	62,802.03
235	62,802.03	742.50	425.22	317.28	62,484.75
289	42,200.92	742.50	285.74	456.76	41,744.15
290	41,744.15	742.50	282.64	459.85	41,284.30
291	41,284.30	742.50	279.53	462.97	40,821.33
321	25,941.42	742.50	175.65	566.85	25,374.57
322	25,374.57	742.50	171.81	570.69	24,803.88
323	24,803.88	742.50	167.94	574.55	24,229.32
358	2,197.66	742.50	14.88	727.62	1,470.05
359	1,470.05	742.50	9.95	732.54	737.50
360	737.50	742.50	4.99	737.50	0.00

The effect of prepayments is that the amount and timing of the cash flows from a mortgage are not known with certainty. This risk is referred to as *prepayment risk*. For example, all that the investor in a $100,000, 8.125% 30-year mortgage knows is that as long as the loan is outstanding and the borrower does not default, interest will be received and the principal will be repaid at the scheduled date each month; then at the end of the 30 years, the investor would have received $100,000 in principal payments. What the investor does not know—the uncertainty—is for how long the loan will be outstanding, and therefore what the timing of the principal payments will be. This is true for all mortgage loans, not just fixed-rate, level-payment, fully amortized mortgages.

The majority of mortgages outstanding do not penalize the borrower for prepaying any part or all of the outstanding mortgage balance. In recent years, mortgage *prepayment penalty mortgages* (PPMs) have been originated. In a PPM there is a specified time period, called the "lockout period," where partial prepayments above a specified amount will result in a prepayment penalty. (There is no penalty for prepayment due to the sale of property; only voluntary prepayments are penalized.) After the lockout period there are no penalties for prepayment. The motivation for the PPM is that it reduces prepayment risk for the lender during the lockout period. It does so by effectively making it more costly for the borrower to prepay in order to take advantage of a decline in mortgage rates. In exchange for this reduction in prepayment risk, the lender will offer a mortgage rate that is less than that of an otherwise comparable mortgage loan without a prepayment penalty.

Adjustable-Rate Mortgages

As the name implies, an *adjustable-rate mortgage* (ARM) has an adjustable or floating coupon instead of a fixed one. The coupon adjusts periodically—monthly, semiannually, or annually. Some ARMs even have coupons that adjust every three years or five years. The coupon formula for an ARM is specified in terms of a reference rate plus a quoted margin. The margin is typically 2% to 3%.

At origination, the mortgage usually has an initial rate for an initial period (teaser period) which is slightly below the rate specified by the coupon formula. This is called a "teaser rate" and makes it easier for first time home buyers to qualify for the loan. At the end of the teaser period, the loan rate is reset based on the coupon formula. Once the loan comes out of its teaser period and resets based on the coupon formula, it is said to be fully indexed.

To protect the homeowner from interest rate shock, there are caps or ceilings imposed on the coupon adjustment level. There are periodic caps and lifetime caps. The periodic cap limits the amount of coupon reset upward or downward from one reset period to another. The lifetime cap is the maximum absolute level for the coupon rate that the loan can reset to for the life of the mortgage.

The attributes needed to describe an ARM are the teaser rate, teaser period, index, margin, reset frequency, periodic cap, and lifetime cap. For example, a "6% 1-year CMT + 3% ARM with 2/12 caps" means the loan has a 6% coupon for the first year. It will reset the second year coupon to the then 1-year CMT index rate plus 3% on the anniversary date subject to the 2% periodic cap and 12% lifetime cap constraints. If the prevailing CMT rate is 4.8%, the coupon will simply reset to 7.8% (4.8% + 3%). If the prevailing CMT rate is 5.5%, the coupon can only reset to 8% (not 5.5% + 3%) because the 2% periodic cap only allows a maximum of 2% movement (plus or minus) in the coupon rate from one period to another. The 12% lifetime cap limits the coupon to 12% during the life of the loan.

Two categories of indices have been used in ARMs: (1) market determined rates and (2) calculated cost of funds for thrifts. The index will have an important impact on the performance of an ARM and its value. The most common market determined rates used are the 1-year, 3-year, or 5-year Constant Maturity Treasury (CMT), 3-month or 6-month London Interbank Offered Rate (LIBOR), and the 6-month CD rate.

The cost of funds index for thrifts is calculated based on the monthly weighted average interest cost for liabilities of thrifts. The most popular is the Eleventh Federal Home Loan Bank Board District Cost of Funds Index (COFI). About 25% of ARMs are indexed to this reference rate. The Eleventh District includes the states of California, Arizona, and Nevada. The cost of funds is calculated by first computing the monthly interest expenses for all thrifts included in the Eleventh District. The interest expenses are summed and then divided by the average of the beginning and ending monthly balance. The index value is reported with a one month lag. For example, June's Eleventh District COFI is reported in July. The mortgage rate for a mortgage based on the Eleventh District COFI is usually reset based on the previous month's reported index rate. For example, if the reset date is August, the index rate reported in July will be used to set the mortgage rate. Consequently, there is a two month lag by the time the average cost of funds is reflected in the mortgage rate. This obviously is an advantage to the borrower when interest rates are rising and a disadvantage to the investor. The opposite is true when interest rates are falling.

The second most popular index is the National Cost of Funds Index, which covers all Federal Home Loan Bank districts. A third category is a calculated index based on market rates. An example would be the 12-month moving average of the 1-year Treasury bill rates.

Balloon Mortgages

In a *balloon mortgage*, the borrower is given long-term financing by the lender but at specified future dates the contract rate is renegotiated. Thus, the lender is providing long-term funds for what is effectively a short-term borrowing, how short depending on the frequency of the renegotiation period. Effectively it is a short-term balloon loan in which the lender agrees to provide financing for the remainder of the term of the mortgage. The balloon payment is the original amount borrowed less the amount amortized. Thus, in a balloon mortgage, the actual maturity is shorter than the stated maturity.

MORTGAGE PASSTHROUGH SECURITIES

Investing in mortgages exposes an investor to default risk and prepayment risk. A more efficient way is to invest in a mortgage passthrough security. This is a security created when one or more holders of mortgages form a pool (collection) of mortgages and sell shares or participation certificates in the pool. A pool may consist of several thousand or only a few mortgages. When a mortgage is included in a pool of mortgages that is used as collateral for a mortgage passthrough security, the mortgage is said to be securitized.

The cash flows of a mortgage passthrough security depend on the cash flows of the underlying mortgages. The cash flows consist of monthly mortgage payments representing interest, the scheduled repayment of principal, and any prepayments for all the mortgages in the pool.

Payments are made to security holders each month. Neither the amount nor the timing, however, of the cash flows from the pool of mortgages are identical to that of the cash flows passed through to investors. The monthly cash flows for a passthrough are less than the monthly cash flows of the underlying mortgages by an amount equal to servicing and other fees. The other fees are those charged by the issuer or guarantor of the passthrough for guaranteeing the issue. The coupon rate on a passthrough, called the *passthrough coupon rate*, is less than the mortgage rate on the underlying pool of mortgage loans by an amount equal to the servicing fee and guarantee fee. Consequently, if there are 10,000 certificate issued, then the holder of one certificate is entitled to 1/10,000 of the cash flow from the pool of mortgages after adjusting for all fees.

The timing of the cash flows is also different. The monthly mortgage payment is due from each mortgagor on the first day of each month, but there is a delay in passing through the corresponding monthly cash flow to the security holders. The length of the delay varies by the type of passthrough security.

Not all of the mortgages that are included in a pool of mortgages that are securitized have the same mortgage rate and the same maturity. Consequently, when describing a passthrough security, a weighted average coupon rate and a weighted average maturity are determined. A *weighted average coupon rate*, or WAC, is found by weighting the mortgage rate of each mortgage loan in the pool by the amount of the mortgage balance outstanding. A *weighted average maturity*, or WAM, is found by weighting the remaining number of months to maturity for each mortgage loan in the pool by the amount of the mortgage balance outstanding.

Other features of mortgage passthrough securities vary by issuer. The key features of a passthrough will have an impact on its investment characteristics (particularly its prepayment characteristics). These general features are (1) the type of guarantee, (2) the mortgage design of the loans, and (3) the characteristics of the mortgage loans in a pool.

AGENCY PASSTHROUGHS

Mortgage passthroughs are classified into Government National Mortgage Association (Ginnie Mae), Federal National Mortgage Association (Fannie Mae), Federal Home Loan Mortgage Corporation (Freddie Mac), and private entity mortgage passthroughs. The first three are federal agencies which were described in Chapter 9. Ginnie Mae is a federally related institution while Fannie Mae and Freddie Mac are government sponsored enterprises (GSEs).

There are several practices in the market in referring to the mortgage passthroughs issued by these entities. Some market participants simply refer to them as "agency passthroughs." Other market participants refer to the mortgage passthroughs issued by Ginnie Mae as "agency passthroughs" and those issued by the two GSEs as "conventional passthroughs" and then all three are referred to as "agency/conventional passthroughs." In this chapter, mortgage passthroughs issued by Ginnie Mae, Fannie Mae, and Freddie Mac will be referred to as agency passthroughs.

For a mortgage to be included in the pool of mortgages that is the collateral for an agency passthrough, the loans must meet the criteria established by the agency. These criteria are referred to as "underwriting standards" and they are discussed in the next chapter. A mortgage that meets the underwriting standards is referred to as a "conforming loan" and obviously a loan that fails the underwriting standards is called a "nonconforming loan." The different types of nonconforming loans are discussed in the next chapter.

Private entities are issuers of mortgage passthroughs that are not one of the federal agencies. They include commercial banks, savings and loan associations, investment banking firms, finance companies, and mortgage companies. The mortgage passthrough securities issued by private entities are referred to as "nonagency passthroughs." The mortgages that back nonagency passthrough securities are nonconforming loans.

Default Risk

A Ginnie Mae passthrough—referred to by as a *Ginnie Mae mortgage passthrough security (MBS)*—is guaranteed by the full faith and credit of the U.S. government. That is, the investor will receive timely payment of interest and principal when it is due even if borrowers default on their loans. Thus, a Ginnie Mae MBS is viewed as risk-free in terms of default risk, just like Treasury securities.

Because Fannie Mae and Freddie Mac are GSEs, a mortgage passthrough that they issue is not guaranteed by the full faith and credit of the U.S. government. Market participants, however, view their mortgage passthroughs as having minimal credit risk. A passthrough issued by Fannie Mae—called a *Fannie Mae mortgage-backed security (MBS)*—is guaranteed with respect to the timely payment of interest and principal. A Freddie Mac passthrough—called a *Freddie Mac participation certificate (PC)*—can have one of two guarantees. One type of guarantee is where Freddie Mac guarantees the timely payment of interest and the eventual payment of principal. By "eventual" it is meant that the principal due will be paid when it is collected, but in no circumstance later than one year. The second type of guarantee is one in which Freddie Mac guarantees the timely payment of both interest and principal which the agency refers to as the Gold program. Freddie Mac now only issues Gold PCs.

Because of the guarantee provided by Ginnie Mae, Fannie Mae, and Freddie Mac, principal payment due to defaults are reported as a prepayment. For nonagency passthroughs, there is no explicit or implicit government guarantee. Instead, a private entity that wants to issue a mortgage-backed security must credit enhance the issue. The mechanisms for credit enhancement (internal and external) are explained in the next chapter.

Prepayment Conventions and Cash Flows

The cash flows of a mortgage passthrough are unknown because of prepayments. The only way to project cash flows is to make some assumptions about the prepayment rate over the life of the underlying mortgage pool.

The prepayment rate is sometimes referred to as the *speed*. Two conventions have been used as a benchmark for prepayment rates: conditional prepayment rate and Public Securities Association prepayment benchmark.

Conditional Prepayment Rate

One convention for projecting prepayments and the cash flows of a passthrough assumes that some fraction of the remaining principal in the pool is prepaid each month for the remaining term of the mortgage. The prepayment rate assumed for a pool, called the *conditional prepayment rate* (CPR), is based on the characteristics of the pool (including its historical prepayment experience) and the current and expected future economic environment.

The CPR is an annual prepayment rate. To estimate monthly prepayments, the CPR must be converted into a monthly prepayment rate, commonly referred to as the *single-monthly mortality rate* (SMM). A formula can be used to determine the SMM for a given CPR:

$$SMM = 1 - (1 - CPR)^{1/12}$$

Suppose that the CPR used to estimate prepayments is 6%. The corresponding SMM is:

$$SMM = 1 - (1 - 0.06)^{1/12} = 1 - (0.94)^{0.08333} = 0.005143$$

An SMM of w% means that approximately w% of the remaining mortgage balance at the beginning of the month, less the scheduled principal payment, will prepay that month. That is,

Prepayment for month t = SMM × (Beginning mortgage balance for month t − Scheduled principal payment for month t)

For example, suppose that an investor owns a passthrough in which the remaining mortgage balance at the beginning of some month is $290 million. Assuming that the SMM is 0.5143% and the scheduled principal payment is $3 million, the estimated prepayment for the month is:

$$0.005143 \times (\$290,000,000 - \$3,000,000) = \$1,476,041$$

PSA Prepayment Benchmark

The Public Securities Association (PSA) prepayment benchmark is expressed as a monthly series of CPRs. The PSA benchmark assumes that prepayment rates are low for newly originated mortgages and then will speed up as the mortgages become seasoned.

The PSA benchmark assumes the following prepayment rates for 30-year mortgages:

1. a CPR of 0.2% for the first month, increased by 0.2% per year per month for the next 30 months when it reaches 6% per year, and
2. a 6% CPR for the remaining years.

This benchmark, referred to as "100% PSA" or simply "100 PSA," is mathematically expressed as follows:

if $t \leq 30$ the CPR = 6% $t/30$
if t > 30 then CPR = 6%

where t is the number of months since the mortgage originated.

Slower or faster speeds are then referred to as some percentage of PSA. For example, 50 PSA means one-half the CPR of the PSA benchmark prepayment rate; 150 PSA means 1.5 times the CPR of the PSA benchmark prepayment rate; 300 PSA means three times the CPR of the benchmark prepayment rate. A prepayment rate of 0 PSA means that no prepayments are assumed.

The CPR is converted to an SMM using the formula given above. For example, assuming 165 PSA the SMMs for month 20 after the mortgage is originated is calculated as follows:

$$CPR = 6\% \ (20/30) = 4\% = 0.04$$

$$165 \ PSA = 1.65 \ (0.04) = 0.066$$

$$SMM = 1 - (1 - 0.066)^{1/12} = 0.005674$$

Notice that the SMM assuming 165 PSA is not just 1.65 times the SMM assuming 100 PSA. It is the CPR that is a multiple of the CPR assuming 100 PSA.

For months 31 to 360, the CPR is 6% at 100 PSA and the CPR and SMM for each month for 165 PSA is

$$165 \ PSA = 1.65 \ (0.06) = 0.099$$

$$SMM = 1 - (1 - 0.099)^{1/12} = 0.00865$$

EXHIBIT 14.2 Monthly Cash Flow for a $400 Million Passthrough with a 7.5% Passthrough Rate, a WAC of 8.125%, and a WAM of 357 Months Assuming 165 PSA

(1)	(2)	(3)	(4)	(5)	(6)	(7)	(8)	(9)
Month	Outstanding Balance	SMM	Mortgage Payment	Net Interest	Scheduled Principal	Prepayment	Total Principal	Cash Flow
1	$400,000,000	0.00111	$2,975,868	$2,500,000	$267,535	$442,389	$709,923	$3,209,923
2	399,290,077	0.00139	2,972,575	2,495,563	269,048	552,847	821,896	3,317,459
3	398,468,181	0.00167	2,968,456	2,490,426	270,495	663,065	933,560	3,423,986
4	397,534,621	0.00195	2,963,513	2,484,591	271,873	772,949	1,044,822	3,529,413
5	396,489,799	0.00223	2,957,747	2,478,061	273,181	882,405	1,155,586	3,633,647
26	350,540,672	0.00835	2,656,123	2,190,879	282,671	2,923,885	3,206,556	5,397,435
27	347,334,116	0.00865	2,633,950	2,170,838	282,209	3,001,955	3,284,164	5,455,002
28	344,049,952	0.00865	2,611,167	2,150,312	281,662	2,973,553	3,255,215	5,405,527
29	340,794,737	0.00865	2,588,581	2,129,967	281,116	2,945,400	3,226,516	5,356,483
30	337,568,221	0.00865	2,566,190	2,109,801	280,572	2,917,496	3,198,067	5,307,869
100	170,142,350	0.00865	1,396,958	1,063,390	244,953	1,469,591	1,714,544	2,777,933
101	168,427,806	0.00865	1,384,875	1,052,674	244,478	1,454,765	1,699,243	2,751,916
102	166,728,563	0.00865	1,372,896	1,042,054	244,004	1,440,071	1,684,075	2,726,128
103	165,044,489	0.00865	1,361,020	1,031,528	243,531	1,425,508	1,669,039	2,700,567
200	56,746,664	0.00865	585,990	354,667	201,767	489,106	690,874	1,045,540
201	56,055,790	0.00865	580,921	350,349	201,377	483,134	684,510	1,034,859
202	55,371,280	0.00865	575,896	346,070	200,986	477,216	678,202	1,024,273
203	54,693,077	0.00865	570,915	341,832	200,597	471,353	671,950	1,013,782
353	760,027	0.00865	155,107	4,750	149,961	5,277	155,238	159,988
354	604,789	0.00865	153,765	3,780	149,670	3,937	153,607	157,387
355	451,182	0.00865	152,435	2,820	149,380	2,611	151,991	154,811
356	299,191	0.00865	151,117	1,870	149,091	1,298	150,389	152,259
357	148,802	0.00865	149,809	930	148,802	0	148,802	149,732

Note: Since the WAM is 357 months, the underlying mortgage pool is seasoned an average of 3 months. Therefore, the CPR for month 27 is $1.65 \times 6\%$.

Illustration of Monthly Cash Flow Construction

We now show how to construct a monthly cash flow for a hypothetical passthrough given a PSA assumption. For the purpose of this illustration, the underlying mortgages for this hypothetical passthrough are assumed to be fixed-rate, level-payment, fully amortized mortgages with a weighted average coupon (WAC) rate of 8.125%. It will be assumed that the passthrough rate is 7.5% with a weighted average maturity (WAM) of 357 months.

Exhibit 14.2 shows the cash flow for selected months assuming 165 PSA. The cash flow is broken down into three components: (1) interest (based on the passthrough rate), (2) the regularly scheduled principal repayment, and (3) prepayments based on 165 PSA.

Column (2) gives the outstanding mortgage balance at the beginning of the month. It is equal to the outstanding balance at the beginning of the previous month reduced by the total principal payment in the previous month. Column (3) shows the SMM for 165 PSA. Two things should be noted in this column. First, for month 1, the SMM is for a passthrough that has been seasoned 3 months because the WAM is 357. The total monthly mortgage payment is shown in Column (4). Notice that the total monthly mortgage payment declines over time as prepayments reduce the mortgage balance outstanding. There is a formula to determine what the monthly mortgage balance will be for each month given prepayments but we will not present that formula here. Column (6) gives the regularly scheduled principal repayment. This is the difference between the total monthly mortgage payment [the amount shown in Column (4)] and the gross coupon interest for the month. The gross coupon interest is 8.125% multiplied by the outstanding mortgage balance at the beginning of the month, then divided by 12.

The prepayment for the month is reported in Column (7). The prepayment is found using the formula given above. For example, in month 100, the beginning mortgage balance is \$170,142,350, the scheduled principal payment is \$244,953, and the SMM at 165 PSA is 0.00865. Therefore, the prepayment is:

$$0.00865 \times (\$170{,}142{,}350 - \$244{,}953) = \$1{,}469{,}612$$

The difference between \$1,469,591 shown in Column (7) and the prepayment of \$1,469,612 computed above is simply due to the rounding of the SMM shown in the exhibit to save space.

The total principal payment reported in Column (8) is the sum of Columns (6) and (7). Finally, the projected monthly cash flow for this passthrough is shown in this last column. The monthly cash flow is the sum of the interest paid to the passthrough investor [Column (5)] and the total principal payments for the month [Column (8)].

Factors Affecting Prepayment Behavior

A prepayment model is a statistical model that is used to forecast prepayments. It begins by modeling the statistical relationships among the factors that are expected to affect prepayments. The four main factors that affect prepayment behavior are (1) prevailing mortgage rate, (2) characteristics of the underlying mortgage pool, (3) seasonal factors, and (4) general economic activity.

The single most important factor affecting prepayments because of refinancing is the current level of mortgage rates relative to the borrower's contract rate. The more the contract rate exceeds the prevailing mortgage rate, the greater the incentive to refinance the mortgage loan. For refinancing to make economic sense, the interest savings must be greater than the costs associated with refinancing the mortgage. These costs include legal expenses, origination fees, title insurance, and the value of the time associated with obtaining another mortgage loan. Some of these costs, such as title insurance and origination points, will vary proportionately with the amount to be financed. Other costs, such as the application fee and legal expenses, are typically fixed. It is not only the level of mortgage rates that affects prepayment behavior but also the path that mortgage rates take to get to the current level.

Other secondary factors affecting prepayments include:

- *Loan-to-Value Ratio*—High LTV loans prepay slower, everything else being equal, because there is not sufficient equity to refinance. Low LTV loans with lots of equity also trigger cash-out refinancing.
- *Debt Consolidation*—Sufficient equity also allows for debt consolidation, i.e. refinance into a higher balance mortgage loan to pay off car loans and credit card debts.
- *Loan Size*—Low balance loans prepay slower because the fixed portion of the refinancing cost becomes a bigger hurdle as a percentage of the loan size.
- *Regional economy*—Improving regional economy triggers housing turnover activity.
- *Homeowners' credit*—Improving economy improves homeowners' credit in general. During a recession, homeowners' credit deteriorates (e.g., unemployment) and they cannot refinance even if mortgage rates are low.
- *Proliferation of new mortgage loan types*   —A 30-year mortgagee does not have to refinance into another 30-year mortgage. Given the popularity of ARMs, balloons, and hybrids (fixed for a period then converts to an ARM), which generally offer lower rates in a steep yield curve environment, a 30-year borrower can refinance into these products while a 30-year to 30-year refinancing is not economical.

Average Life

The stated maturity of a mortgage passthrough is an inappropriate measure because of principal repayments over time. Instead, market participants calculate an *average life* which is the average time to receipt of principal payments (scheduled principal payments and projected prepayments), calculating as follows:

1 × (Projected principal received in month 1)
+ 2 × (Projected principal received in month 2)
+ 3 × (Projected principal received in month 3)
  ...
+ T × (Projected principal received in month T)
——
Weighted monthly average of principal received

where T is the last month that principal is expected to be received. Then the average life is found as follows:

$$\text{Average life} = \frac{\text{Weighted monthly average of principal received}}{12 \times (\text{Total principal to be received})}$$

The average life of a passthrough depends on the PSA prepayment assumption. To see this, the average life is shown below for different prepayment speeds for the passthrough we used to illustrate the cash flows in Exhibit 14.2:

PSA speed	50	100	165	200	300	400	500	600	700
Average life	15.11	11.66	8.76	7.68	5.63	4.44	3.68	3.16	2.78

Contraction Risk and Extension Risk

An investor who owns passthrough securities does not know what the cash flows will be because that depends on prepayments. As noted earlier, this risk is called prepayment risk. However, prepayment risk can be divided into two risks, contraction risk and prepayment risk. We will explain these two risk by means of the following example.

Suppose an investor buys a 10% coupon mortgage passthrough at a time when the prevailing mortgage rate is 10%. Suppose further that the expected average life for this mortgage passthrough is 9 years based on a prepayment rate of 110 PSA. Let's consider what will happen to prepayments if mortgage rates decline to, say, 6%. The borrower will have an incentive to prepay all or part of the mortgage resulting in a shortening of the average life of the security from what it was expected to be when the security was purchased. For example, the market might expect that the prepayment speed will increase to 200 PSA resulting in a decrease in the average life to 6 years. The disadvantage to the investor is that the funds received from the prepayments will have to be reinvested at lower interest rates. This risk that the average life of the security will be shortened, forcing the investor to reinvest at lower interest rates, is referred to as *contraction risk*.

Now let's look at what happens if mortgage rates rise to 14%. Prepayments can be expected to slow down because homeowners will not refinance or partially prepay their mortgages resulting in an increase in the expected average life. For example, the market might expect the prepayment rate to decrease to 75 PSA, which would result in an average life of 12 years. Unfortunately, it is in a rising interest rate environment when investors want prepayments to speed up so that they can reinvest the principal received at the higher market interest rate. This adverse consequence of rising mortgage rates is called *extension risk*.

Therefore, prepayment risk encompasses contraction risk and extension risk. Prepayment risk makes passthrough securities unattractive for certain individuals and financial institutions to hold for purposes of accomplishing their investment objectives. Some individuals and institutional investors are concerned with extension risk and others with contraction risk when they purchase a passthrough security. Is it possible to alter the cash flows of a passthrough to reduce the contraction risk or extension risk for institutional investors? This can be done as we will see when we discuss collateralized mortgage obligations.

Trading and Settlement Procedures

Agency passthroughs are identified by a pool prefix and pool number provided by the agency. The prefix indicates the type of passthrough. For example, a pool prefix of 20 for a Freddie Mac PC means that the underlying pool consists of conventional mortgages with an original maturity of 15 years. A pool prefix of AR for a Ginnie Mae MBS means that the underlying pool consists of adjustable-rate mortgages. The pool number indicates the specific mortgages underlying the passthrough and the issuer of the passthrough.

There are specific rules established by the Bond Market Association (previously the Public Securities Association) for the trading and settlement of mortgage-backed securities. Our discussion here is limited to agency passthrough securities.

Many trades occur while a pool is still unspecified and therefore no pool information is known at the time of the trade. This kind of trade is known as a "TBA" (to be announced) trade. In a TBA trade the two parties agree on the agency type, the agency program, the coupon rate, the face value, the price, and the settlement date. The actual pools underlying the agency passthrough are not specified in a TBA trade. However, this information is provided by the seller to the buyer before delivery. There are trades where more specific requirements are established for the securities to be delivered, for example, a Freddie Mac Gold with a coupon rate of 7.0% and a WAC between 7.5% and 7.7%.

There are also *specified pool trades* wherein the actual pool numbers to be delivered are specified.

The price that the buyer pays the seller is the agreed upon sale price plus accrued interest. Given the par value, the dollar price (excluding accrued interest) is affected by the amount of the pool mortgage balance outstanding. The *pool factor* indicates the percentage of the initial mortgage balance still outstanding. So, a pool factor of 90 means that 90% of the original mortgage pool balance is outstanding. The pool factor is reported by the agency each month.

The dollar price paid for just the principal is found as follows given the agreed upon price, par value, and the month's pool factor provided by the agency:

$$\text{Price} \times \text{Par value} \times \text{Pool factor}$$

For example, if the parties agree to a price of 92 for $1 million par value for a passthrough with a pool factor of 85, then the dollar price paid by the buyer in addition to accrued interest is:

$$0.92 \times \$1,000,000 \times 0.85 = \$782,000$$

Trades settle according to a delivery schedule established by the BMA. This schedule is published quarterly with information regarding delivery for the next six months. Each agency and program settles on a different day of the delivery month.

By 3 p.m. eastern standard time two business days before the settlement date, the seller must furnish information to the buyer about pools that will be delivered. This is called the *48-hour rule* . The date that this information must be given is called the *notification date* or *call-out date* . Two parties can agree to depart from BMA guidelines and settle at any time.

When an investor purchases, say, $1 million GNMA 7s on a TBA basis, the investor can receive up to three pools. Three pools can be delivered because the BMA has established guidelines for standards of delivery and settlement of mortgage-backed securities, under which our hypothetical TBA trade permits three possible pools to be delivered. The option of what pools to deliver is left to the seller, as long as selection and delivery satisfy the BMA guidelines.

There are many seasoned issues of the same agency with the same coupon rate outstanding at a given point in time. For example, there are more than 30,000 pools of 30-year Ginnie Mae MBSs outstanding with a coupon rate of 7%. One passthrough may be backed by a pool of mortgage loans in which all the properties are located in California, while another may be backed by a pool of mortgage loans in which all the properties are in Minnesota. Yet another may be backed by a pool of mortgage loans in which the properties are from several regions of the country. So which pool are dealers referring to when they talk about Ginnie Mae 7s? They are not referring to any specific pool but instead to a generic security, despite the fact that the prepayment characteristics of passthroughs with underlying pools from different parts of the country are different. Thus, the projected prepayment rates for passthroughs reported by dealer firms are for generic passthroughs. A particular pool purchased may have a materially different prepayment speed from the generic. Moreover, when an investor purchases a passthrough without specifying a pool number, the seller can deliver the worst-paying pools as long as the pools delivered satisfy good delivery requirements.

In a TBA trade, the BMA delivery standards permit an under- or overdelivery tolerance of $100 per million traded or 0.01%. This means that if $1 million of par value is sold at par, the seller may deliver to the buyer passthroughs with a par value anywhere between $999,900 and $1,000,100. This delivery option used to be a benefit to the seller when the delivery variance was as large as 3%. To understand why, suppose that interest rates decline between the trade date and the settlement date. The value of passthroughs will rise, and therefore it will be beneficial for the seller to deliver less than $1 million. The opposite is true if interest rates rise between the trade date and the settlement date: the seller will deliver the maximum permissible. That delivery option is effectively removed by the current 0.01% variance allowance.

Dollar Rolls

In the MBS market, a special type of collateralized loan has developed because of the characteristics of these securities and the need of dealers to borrow these securities to cover short positions. This arrangement is called a *dollar roll* because the dealer is said to "roll in" securities borrowed and "roll out" securities when returning the securities to the portfolio manager.

As with a repo agreement, it is a collateralized loan that calls for the sale and repurchase of a security. Unlike a repo agreement, the dealer who borrows the securities need not return the identical security. That is, the dealer need only return a "substantially identical security." This means that the security returned by the dealer that borrows the security must match the coupon rate and security type (i.e., issuer and mortgage collateral). This provides flexibility to the dealer. In exchange for this flexibility, the dealer provides 100% financing. That is, there is no over collateralization or margin required. Moreover, the financing cost may be cheaper than in a repo because of this flexibility. Finally, unlike in a repo, the dealer keeps the coupon and any principal paid during the period of the loan.

Determination of the Financing Cost

Determination of the financing cost is not as simple as in a repo. The key elements in determining the financing cost, assuming that the dealer is borrowing securities/lending cash, are:

1. the sale price and the repurchase price
2. the amount of the coupon payment
3. the amount of the principal payments due to scheduled principal payments
4. the projected prepayments of the security sold (i.e., rolled in to the dealer)
5. the attributes of the substantially identical security that is returned (i.e., rolled out by the dealer)
6. the amount of under- or overdelivery permitted

Let's look at these elements. In a repo agreement, the repurchase price is greater than the sale price, the difference representing interest and is called the *drop*. In the case of a dollar roll, the repurchase price need not be greater than the sale price. In fact, in a positively sloped yield curve environment (i.e., long-term rates exceed short-term rates), the repurchase price will be less than the purchase price. The reason for this is the second element, the coupon payment. The dealer keeps the coupon payment.

The third and fourth elements involve principal repayments. The principal payments include scheduled principal and prepayments. As with the coupon payments, the dealer retains the principal payments during the period of the agreement. A gain will be realized by the dealer on any principal repayments if the security is purchased by the dealer at a discount and a loss if purchased at a premium. Because of prepayments, the principal that will be paid is unknown and, as will be seen, represents a risk in the determination of the financing cost.

The fifth element is another risk since the effective financing cost will depend on the attributes of the substantially identical security that the dealer will roll out (i.e., the security it will return to the lender of the securities) at the end of the agreement. Finally, as explained earlier, there are delivery tolerances—that is, permissible under- or overdelivery permitted.

To illustrate how the financing cost for a dollar roll is calculated, suppose that a portfolio manager enters into an agreement with a dealer in which it agrees to sell $10 million par value (i.e., unpaid aggregate balance) of Ginnie Mae 8s at $101\tfrac{7}{32}$ and repurchase substantially identical securities a month later at 101 (the repurchase price). The drop is therefore $\tfrac{7}{32}$. While under- or overdelivery is permitted, we will assume that $10 million par value will be delivered to the dealer by the portfolio manager and the same amount of par value will be returned to the portfolio manager by the dealer. Since the sale price is 101⁷⁄₃₂, the portfolio manager will receive in cash $10,121,875 (101.21875 × $10 million). At the repurchase date, the portfolio manager can repurchase substantially identical securities for 101 or $10,100,000. Therefore, the portfolio manager can sell the securities for $10,121,875 and buy them back for $10,100,000. The difference—which is the drop—is $21,875.

To offset this, the portfolio manager forfeits the coupon interest during the period of the agreement to the dealer. Since the coupon rate is 8%, the coupon interest forfeited is $66,666 (8% × $10 million/12). The dealer is also entitled to any principal repayments, both regularly scheduled and prepayments. Since the dealer purchases the securities from the portfolio manager at $101⁷⁄₃₂, any principal repayments will result in a loss of $1⁷⁄₃₂ per $100 of par value of principal repaid. From the portfolio manager's perspective, this is a benefit and effectively reduces the financing cost. While the regularly scheduled amount can be determined, prepayments must be projected based on some PSA speed. In our illustration, for simplicity let's assume that the regularly scheduled principal payment for the month is $6,500 and the prepayment is projected to be $20,000 based on some PSA speed. Since $1⁷⁄₃₂ is lost per $100 par value repaid, the dealer loses $79 due to the regularly scheduled principal payment (1⁷⁄₃₂ × $6,500/100) and $244 from prepayments (1⁷⁄₃₂ × $20,000/100).

The monthly financing cost is then:

Lost coupon interest			$66,666
Offsets			22,198
Drop (gain from repurchase)		21,875	
Principal repayment premium gained		323	
Due to regularly scheduled principal	79		
Due to prepayments	244		
Total financing cost			$44,468
Monthly financing cost ($44,648/$10,121,875)			0.00439
Annual financing cost (monthly rate × 12)			5.27%

The financing cost as calculated, 5.27%, must be compared with alternative financing opportunities. For example, funds can be borrowed via a repo agreement using the same Ginnie Mae collateral. In comparing financing costs, it is important that the dollar amount of the cost be compared to the amount borrowed. For example, in our illustration we annualized the cost by multiplying the monthly rate by 12. The convention in other financing markets may be different for annualizing. Moreover, it is not proper to compare financing costs of other alternatives without giving recognition to the risks associated with a dollar roll.

Because of the unusual nature of the dollar roll transaction as a collateralized borrowing vehicle, it is only possible to estimate the financing cost. From our illustration, it can be seen that when the transaction prices are above par value, then the speed of prepayments affects the financing cost. The maximum financing cost can be determined by assuming no prepayments. In this case, the total financing cost would be $244 greater or $44,712. This increases the annual financing cost from 5.27% to 5.29%, or 2 basis points. In practice, a portfolio manager can perform sensitivity analysis to determine the effect of prepayments on the financing cost.

STRIPPED MORTGAGE-BACKED SECURITIES

A mortgage passthrough distributes the cash flow from the underlying pool of mortgages on a pro rata basis to the security holders. A *stripped mortgage-backed security* (stripped MBS) is created by altering that distribution of principal and interest from a pro rata distribution to an unequal distribution. In the most common type of stripped mortgage-backed securities, all the interest is allocated to one class—the *interest only class*—and all the principal to the other class—the *principal-only class*.

Principal-Only Securities

A principal-only security, also a called the *PO* or a *principal-only mortgage strip*, is purchased at a substantial discount from par value. The return an investor realizes depends on the speed at which prepayments are made. The faster the prepayments, the higher the investor's return. For example, suppose there is a mortgage pool consisting only of 30-year mortgages with $400 million in principal, and that investors can purchase POs backed by this mortgage pool for $175 million. The dollar return on this investment will be $225 million. How quickly that dollar return is recovered by PO investors determines the actual return that will be realized. In the extreme case, if all homeowners in the underlying mortgage pool decide to prepay their mortgage loans immediately, PO investors will realize the $225 million immediately. At the other extreme, if all homeowners decide to remain in their homes for 30 years and make no prepayments, the $225 million will be spread out over 30 years, which would result in a lower return for PO investors.

Let's look at how the price of the PO would be expected to change as mortgage rates in the market change. When mortgage rates decline below the contract rate, prepayments are expected to speed up, accelerating payments to the PO holder. Thus, the cash flow of a PO improves (in the sense that principal repayments are received earlier). The cash flow will be discounted at a lower interest rate because the mortgage rate in the market has declined. The result is that the PO price will increase when mortgage rates decline. When mortgage rates rise above the contract rate, prepayments are expected to slow down. The cash flow deteriorates (in the sense that it takes longer to recover principal repayments). Couple this with a higher discount rate, and the price of a PO will fall when mortgage rates rise.

Interest-Only Securities

An interest-only security, also called an *IO* or an *interest-only mortgage strip*, has no par value. In contrast to the PO investor, the IO investor wants prepayments to be slow because the IO investor receives interest only on the amount of the principal outstanding. When prepayments are made, less dollar interest will be received as the outstanding principal declines. In fact, if prepayments are too fast, the IO investor may not recover the amount paid for the IO even if the security is held to maturity.

Let's look at the expected price response of an IO to changes in mortgage rates. If mortgage rates decline below the contract rate, prepayments are expected to accelerate. This would result in a deterioration of the expected cash flow for an IO. While the cash flow will be discounted at a lower rate, the net effect typically is a decline in the price of an IO. If mortgage rates rise above the contract rate, the expected cash flow improves, but the cash flow is discounted at a higher interest rate. The net effect may be either a rise or fall for the IO.

Thus, we see an interesting characteristic of an IO: its price tends to move in the same direction as the change in mortgage rates (1) when mortgage rates fall below the contract rate and (2) for some range of mortgage rates above the contract rate. Both POs and IOs exhibit substantial price volatility when mortgage rates change. The greater price volatility of the IO and PO compared to the passthrough from which they were created is because the combined price volatility of the IO and PO must be equal to the price volatility of the passthrough.

An average life for a PO can be calculated based on some prepayment assumption. However, an IO receives no principal payments, so technically an average life cannot be computed. Instead, for an IO a "cash flow average life" is computed, using the projected interest payments in the average life formula instead of principal.

Trading and Settlement Procedures for Stripped Mortgage-Backed Securities

The trading and settlement procedures for stripped mortgage-backed securities are similar to those set by the BMA for agency passthroughs described in the previous section. The specifications are in the types of trades (TBA versus specified pool), calculations of the proceeds, and the settlement dates.

IOs and POs are extreme premium and discount securities and consequently are very sensitive to prepayments, which are driven by the specific characteristics (GWAC, WAM, geographic concentration, average loan size) of the underlying loans. The TBA delivery option on IOs and POs has an economic value and this value is hard to quantify. Therefore, almost all secondary trades in IOs and POs are on a specified pool basis rather than on a TBA basis.

All IOs and POs are given a trust number. For instance, FNMA Trust 1 is a IO/PO trust backed by specific pools of FNMA 9% mortgages. FNMA Trust 2 is backed by FNMA 10% mortgages. FNMA Trust 23 is another IO/PO trust backed by FNMA 10% mortgages. The value of Trust 23 PO may be higher or lower than the value of Trust 2 PO depending on the perceived prepayment behavior of Trust 23 relative to that of Trust 2 based on the GWAC, WAM, and geographical concentration of the two specific trusts. Therefore, an investor must specify which trust he or she is buying.

Since the transactions are on a specified trust basis, they are also done based on the original face amount. For example, suppose an investor agrees to buy $10 million original face of Trust 23 PO for August settlement. At the time of the transaction, the August factor need not be known; however, there is no ambiguity in the amount to be delivered because the seller does not have any delivery option. The seller has to deliver $3 million current face amount if the August factor turns out to be 0.30 and the seller needs to deliver $2.5 million current face amount if the August factor turns out to be 0.25.

The total proceeds of a PO trade are calculated the same way as with a passthrough trade except that there is no accrued interest. For example, suppose a buyer and a seller agree to trade $10 million original face of Trust 23 PO at 75-08 for settlement on August 25. The proceeds for the trade are calculated as follows assuming an August trust factor of 0.25:

$$75.08 \times \$10,000,000 \times 0.25 = \$1,881,250$$

| Price | Original face value | Pool factor | Proceeds |

The market trades IOs based on notional principal. The proceeds include the price on the notional amount and the accrued interest. For example, suppose a buyer and a seller agree to trade $10 million original notional face of Trust 23 IO at 33-20 for settlement on August 25. The proceeds for the trade are calculated as follows assuming an August factor of 0.25:

$$(0.33625 + 0.10 \times 24 \text{ days}/360 \text{ days}) \times \$10,000,000 \times 0.25 = \$857,292$$

| Price coupon | days accrued interest | Orig. notional | Factor | Proceeds |

Agency passthrough trades settle according to a delivery schedule established by the BMA. Stripped mortgage-backed securities trades follow the same delivery schedule.

AGENCY COLLATERALIZED MORTGAGE OBLIGATIONS

Some institutional investors are concerned with extension risk and others with contraction risk when they invest in a mortgage passthrough. This problem can be mitigated by redirecting the cash flows of mortgage passthrough securities to different bond classes, called *tranches*, so as to create securities that have different exposure to prepayment risk and, therefore, different risk/return patterns than the passthrough securities from which the tranches were created. A CMO is an example of a paythrough structure.

When the cash flows of pools of mortgage passthroughs are redistributed to different bond classes, the resulting securities are called *collateralized mortgage obligations*   (CMO). The creation of a CMO cannot eliminate prepayment risk; it can only distribute the various forms of this risk among different classes of bondholders. The CMO's major financial innovation is that the securities created more closely satisfy the asset/liability needs of institutional investors and thus broaden the appeal of mortgage-backed products to bond investors.

Rather than list the different types of tranches that can be created in a CMO structure, we will show how the tranches can be created. This will provide an illustration of financial engineering. Although there are many different types of CMOs that have been created, we will only look at three of the key innovations in the CMO market: sequential-pay tranches, accrual tranches, and planned amortization class bonds. Two other important tranches that are not illustrated here are the floating-rate tranche and inverse floating-rate tranche.

Sequential-Pay CMOs

A sequential-pay CMO is structured so that each class of bond (i.e., tranche) is retired sequentially. To illustrate a sequential-pay CMO, we discuss CMO-1, a hypothetical deal made up to illustrate the basic features of the structure. The collateral for this hypothetical CMO is a mortgage passthrough with a total par value of $400 million and the following characteristics: (1) the security's coupon rate is 7.5%, (2) the weighted average coupon (WAC) is 8.125%, and (3) the weighted average maturity (WAM) is 357 months. This is the same mortgage passthrough that we used earlier in this chapter to describe the cash flow of a passthrough based on some PSA assumption.

EXHIBIT 14.3   CMO-1: A Hypothetical Four-Tranche Sequential-Pay Structure

Tranche	Par Amount	Coupon Rate (%)
A	$194,500,000	7.5
B	36,000,000	7.5
C	96,500,000	7.5
D	73,000,000	7.5
Total	$400,000,000	

Payment rules:
1. *For payment of monthly coupon interest:* Disburse monthly coupon interest to each tranche on the basis of the amount of principal outstanding at the beginning of the month.
2. *For disbursement of principal payments:* Disburse principal payments to tranche A until it is completely paid off. After tranche A is completely paid off, disburse principal payments to tranche B until it is completely paid off. After tranche B is completely paid off, disburse principal payments to tranche C until it is completely paid off. After tranche C is completely paid off, disburse principal payments to tranche D until it is completely paid off.

From this $400 million of collateral, four bond classes or tranches are created. Their characteristics are summarized in Exhibit 14.3. The total par value of the four tranches is equal to the par value of the collateral (i.e., the mortgage passthrough). In this simple structure, the coupon rate is the same for each tranche and also the same as the coupon rate on the collateral. There is no reason why this must be so, and, in fact, typically the coupon rate varies by tranche.

Now remember that a CMO is created by redistributing the cash flow—interest and principal—to the different tranches based on a set of payment rules. The payment rules at the bottom of Exhibit 14.3 describe how the cash flow from the mortgage passthrough (i.e., collateral) is to be distributed to the four tranches. There are separate rules for the payment of the coupon interest and the payment of principal, the principal being the total of the regularly scheduled principal payment and any prepayments.

In CMO-1, each tranche receives monthly coupon interest payments based on the amount of the outstanding balance at the beginning of the month. The disbursement of the principal, however, is made in a special way. A tranche is not entitled to receive principal until the entire principal of the tranche has been paid off. More specifically, tranche A receives all the principal payments until the entire principal amount owed to that tranche, $194,500,000, is paid off; then tranche B begins to receive principal and continues to do so until it is paid the entire $36,000,000. Tranche C then receives principal, and when it is paid off, tranche D starts receiving principal payments.

Although the priority rules for the disbursement of the principal payments are known, the precise amount of the principal in each month is not. This will depend on the cash flow and, therefore, on the principal payments of the collateral, which will depend on the actual prepayment rate of the collateral. An assumed PSA speed allows the cash flow to be projected. Exhibit 14.2 shows the cash flow (interest, regularly scheduled principal repayment, and prepayments) assuming 165 PSA. Assuming that the collateral does prepay at 165 PSA, the cash flow available to all four tranches CMO-1 will be precisely the cash flow shown in Exhibit 14.2.

To demonstrate how the priority rules for CMO-1 work, Exhibit 14.4 shows the cash flow for selected months assuming the collateral prepays at 165 PSA. For each tranche the exhibit shows: (1) the balance at the end of the month, (2) the principal paid down (regularly scheduled principal repayment plus prepayments), and (3) interest. In month 1, the cash flow for the collateral consists of principal payment of $709,923 and interest of $2.5 million (0.075 times $400 million divided by 12). The interest payment is distributed to the four tranches based on the amount of the par value outstanding. So, for example, tranche A receives $1,215,625 (0.075 times $194,500,000 divided by 12) of the $2.5 million. The principal, however, is all distributed to tranche A. Therefore, the cash flow for tranche A in month 1 is $1,925,548. The principal balance at the end of month 1 for tranche A is $193,790,076 (the original principal balance of $194,500,000 less the principal payment of $709,923). No principal payment is distributed to the three other tranches because there is still a principal balance outstanding for tranche A. This will be true for months 2 through 80.

After month 81, the principal balance will be zero for tranche A. For the collateral, the cash flow in month 81 is $3,318,521, consisting of a principal payment of $2,032,196 and interest of $1,286,325. At the beginning of month 81 (end of month 80), the principal balance for tranche A is $311,926. Therefore, $311,926 of the $2,032,196 of the principal payment from the collateral will be disbursed to tranche A. After this payment is made, no additional principal payments are made to this tranche as the principal balance is zero. The remaining principal payment from the collateral $1,720,271, is disbursed to tranche B. According to the assumed prepayment speed of 165 PSA, tranche B then begins receiving principal payments in month 81.

Exhibit 14.4 shows that tranche B is fully paid off by month 100, when tranche C now begins to receive principal payments. Tranche C is not fully paid off until month 178, at which time tranche D begins receiving the remaining principal payments. The maturity (i.e., the time until the principal is fully paid off) for these four tranches assuming 165 PSA would be 81 months for tranche A, 100 months for tranche B, 178 months for tranche C, and 357 months for tranche D.

EXHIBIT 14.4   Monthly Cash Flow for Selected Months for CMO-1 Assuming 165 PSA

	Tranche A			Tranche B		
Month	Balance	Principal	Interest	Balance	Principal	Interest
1	194,500,000	709,923	1,215,625	36,000,000	0	225,000
2	193,790,077	821,896	1,211,188	36,000,000	0	225,000
3	192,968,181	933,560	1,206,051	36,000,000	0	225,000
4	192,034,621	1,044,822	1,200,216	36,000,000	0	225,000
5	190,989,799	1,155,586	1,193,686	36,000,000	0	225,000
6	189,834,213	1,265,759	1,186,464	36,000,000	0	225,000
7	188,568,454	1,375,246	1,178,553	36,000,000	0	225,000
8	187,193,208	1,483,954	1,169,958	36,000,000	0	225,000
9	185,709,254	1,591,789	1,160,683	36,000,000	0	225,000
10	184,117,464	1,698,659	1,150,734	36,000,000	0	225,000
11	182,418,805	1,804,473	1,140,118	36,000,000	0	225,000
12	180,614,332	1,909,139	1,128,840	36,000,000	0	225,000
75	12,893,479	2,143,974	80,584	36,000,000	0	225,000
76	10,749,504	2,124,935	67,184	36,000,000	0	225,000
77	8,624,569	2,106,062	53,904	36,000,000	0	225,000
78	6,518,507	2,087,353	40,741	36,000,000	0	225,000
79	4,431,154	2,068,807	27,695	36,000,000	0	225,000
80	2,362,347	2,050,422	14,765	36,000,000	0	225,000
81	311,926	311,926	1,950	36,000,000	1,720,271	225,000
82	0	0	0	34,279,729	2,014,130	214,248
83	0	0	0	32,265,599	1,996,221	201,660
84	0	0	0	30,269,378	1,978,468	189,184
85	0	0	0	28,290,911	1,960,869	176,818
95	0	0	0	9,449,331	1,793,089	59,058
96	0	0	0	7,656,242	1,777,104	47,852
97	0	0	0	5,879,138	1,761,258	36,745
98	0	0	0	4,117,880	1,745,550	25,737
99	0	0	0	2,372,329	1,729,979	14,827
100	0	0	0	642,350	642,350	4,015
101	0	0	0	0	0	0
102	0	0	0	0	0	0
103	0	0	0	0	0	0
104	0	0	0	0	0	0
105	0	0	0	0	0	0

Let's look at what has been accomplished by creating the CMO. First, the average life for the mortgage passthrough is 8.76 years, assuming a prepayment speed of 165 PSA. On page 361 is the average life of the collateral and the four tranches assuming different prepayment speeds:

EXHIBIT 14.4   (Continued)

	Tranche C			Tranche D		
Month	Balance	Principal	Interest	Balance	Principal	Interest
1	96,500,000	0	603,125	73,000,000	0	456,250
2	96,500,000	0	603,125	73,000,000	0	456,250
3	96,500,000	0	603,125	73,000,000	0	456,250
4	96,500,000	0	603,125	73,000,000	0	456,250
5	96,500,000	0	603,125	73,000,000	0	456,250
6	96,500,000	0	603,125	73,000,000	0	456,250
7	96,500,000	0	603,125	73,000,000	0	456,250
8	96,500,000	0	603,125	73,000,000	0	456,250
9	96,500,000	0	603,125	73,000,000	0	456,250
10	96,500,000	0	603,125	73,000,000	0	456,250
11	96,500,000	0	603,125	73,000,000	0	456,250
12	96,500,000	0	603,125	73,000,000	0	456,250
95	96,500,000	0	603,125	73,000,000	0	456,250
96	96,500,000	0	603,125	73,000,000	0	456,250
97	96,500,000	0	603,125	73,000,000	0	456,250
98	96,500,000	0	603,125	73,000,000	0	456,250
99	96,500,000	0	603,125	73,000,000	0	456,250
100	96,500,000	1,072,194	603,125	73,000,000	0	456,250
101	95,427,806	1,699,243	596,424	73,000,000	0	456,250
102	93,728,563	1,684,075	585,804	73,000,000	0	456,250
103	92,044,489	1,669,039	575,278	73,000,000	0	456,250
104	90,375,450	1,654,134	564,847	73,000,000	0	456,250
105	88,721,315	1,639,359	554,508	73,000,000	0	456,250
175	3,260,287	869,602	20,377	73,000,000	0	456,250
176	2,390,685	861,673	14,942	73,000,000	0	456,250
177	1,529,013	853,813	9,556	73,000,000	0	456,250
178	675,199	675,199	4,220	73,000,000	170,824	456,250
179	0	0	0	72,829,176	838,300	455,182
180	0	0	0	71,990,876	830,646	449,943
181	0	0	0	71,160,230	823,058	444,751
182	0	0	0	70,337,173	815,536	439,607
183	0	0	0	69,521,637	808,081	434,510
184	0	0	0	68,713,556	800,690	429,460
185	0	0	0	67,912,866	793,365	424,455
350	0	0	0	1,235,674	160,220	7,723
351	0	0	0	1,075,454	158,544	6,722
352	0	0	0	916,910	156,883	5,731
353	0	0	0	760,027	155,238	4,750
354	0	0	0	604,789	153,607	3,780
355	0	0	0	451,182	151,991	2,820
356	0	0	0	299,191	150,389	1,870
357	0	0	0	148,802	148,802	930

Prepayment speed (PSA)	Average life for				
	Collateral	Tranche A	Tranche B	Tranche C	Tranche D
50	15.11	7.48	15.98	21.02	27.24
100	11.66	4.90	10.86	15.78	24.58
165	8.76	3.48	7.49	11.19	20.27
200	7.68	3.05	6.42	9.60	18.11
300	5.63	2.32	4.64	6.81	13.36
400	4.44	1.94	3.70	5.31	10.34
500	3.68	1.69	3.12	4.38	8.35
600	3.16	1.51	2.74	3.75	6.96
700	2.78	1.38	2.47	3.30	5.95

Notice that the four tranches have average lives that are both shorter and longer than the collateral, thereby attracting investors who have a preference for an average life different from that of the collateral.

There is still a major problem: There is considerable variability of the average life for the tranches. We'll see how this can be tackled later on. However, there is some protection provided for each tranche against prepayment risk. This is because prioritizing the distribution of principal (i.e., establishing the payment rules for principal) effectively protects the shorter-term tranche A in this structure against extension risk. This protection must come from somewhere, so it comes from the three other tranches. Similarly, tranches C and D provide protection against extension risk for tranches A and B. At the same time, tranches C and D benefit because they are provided protection against contraction risk, the protection coming from tranches A and B.

Accrual Bonds

In CMO-1, the payment rules for interest provide for all tranches to be paid interest each month. In many sequential-pay CMO structures, at least one tranche does not receive current interest. Instead, the interest for that tranche would accrue and be added to the principal balance. Such a bond class is commonly referred to as an *accrual tranche*, or a *Z bond* (because the bond is similar to a zero-coupon bond). The interest that would have been paid to the accrual tranche is then used to speed up paying down the principal balance of earlier tranches.

To see this, consider CMO-2, a hypothetical CMO structure with the same collateral as CMO-1 and with four tranches, each with a coupon rate of 7.5%. The structure is shown in Exhibit 14.5. The difference is in the last tranche, Z, which is an accrual bond.

EXHIBIT 14.5   CMO-02: A Hypothetical Four-Tranche
Sequential-Pay Structure with an Accrual Tranche

Tranche	Par Amount	Coupon rate (%)
A	$194,500,000	7.5
B	36,000,000	7.5
C	96,500,000	7.5
Z (Accrual)	73,000,000	7.5
Total	$400,000,000	

Payment rules:
1. *For payment of monthly coupon interest:* Disburse monthly coupon interest to
tranches A, B, and C on the basis of the amount of principal outstanding at the beginning of the month. For tranche Z, accrue the interest based on the principal plus
accrued interest in the previous month. The interest for tranche Z is to be paid to the
earlier tranches as a principal pay down.
2. *For disbursement of principal payments:* Disburse principal payments to tranche
A until it is completely paid off. After tranche A is completely paid off, disburse principal payments to tranche B until it is completely paid off. After tranche B is completely paid off, disburse principal payments to tranche C until it is completely paid
off. After tranche C is completely paid off, disburse principal payments to tranche Z
until the original principal balance plus accrued interest is completely paid off.

Let's look at month 1 and compare it to month 1 in Exhibit 14.4
based on 165 PSA. The principal payment from the collateral is
$709,923. In CMO-1, this is the principal paydown for tranche A. In
CMO-2, the interest for tranche Z, $456,250, is not paid to that
tranche but instead is used to pay down the principal of tranche A. So,
the principal payment to tranche A is $1,166,173, the collateral's princi-
pal payment of $709,923 plus the interest of $456,250 that was
diverted from tranche Z.

The inclusion of the accrual tranche results in a shortening of the
expected final maturity for tranches A, B, and C. The final payout for
tranche A is 64 months rather than 81 months, for tranche B it is 77
months rather than 100 months, and for tranche C it is 112 rather than
178 months. The average lives for tranches A, B, and C are shorter in
CMO-2 compared to CMO-1 because of the inclusion of the accrual
bond. For example, at 165 PSA, the average lives are as follows:

Structure	Tranche A	Tranche B	Tranche C
CMO-2	2.90	5.86	7.87
CMO-1	3.48	7.49	11.19

The reason for the shortening of the nonaccrual tranches is that the interest that would be paid to the accrual bond is being allocated to the other tranches. Tranche Z in CMO-2 will have a longer average life than tranche D in CMO-1. Thus, shorter-term tranches and a longer-term tranche are created by including an accrual bond. The accrual bond appeals to investors who are concerned with reinvestment risk. Since there are no coupon payments to reinvest, reinvestment risk is eliminated until all the other tranches are paid off.

Planned Amortization Class Tranches

In a planned amortization class (PAC) CMO structure, if prepayments are within a specified range, the cash flow pattern is known for those tranches identified as PAC tranches. The greater predictability of the cash flow for PAC tranches occurs because there is a principal repayment schedule that must be satisfied. PAC tranches have priority over all other tranches in the CMO structure in receiving principal payments from the underlying collateral. The greater certainty of the cash flow for the PAC tranches comes at the expense of the non-PAC tranches, called the *support tranches* or *companion tranches*. It is the support tranches that absorb the prepayment risk.

To illustrate how to create a PAC tranche, we will use as collateral the $400 million mortgage passthrough with a coupon rate of 7.5%, a WAC of 8.125%, and a WAM of 357 months. The second column of Exhibit 14.6 shows the principal payment (regularly scheduled principal repayment plus prepayments) for selected months assuming a prepayment speed of 90 PSA, and the next column shows the principal payments for selected months assuming that the mortgage passthrough prepays at 300 PSA.

The last column of Exhibit 14.6 gives the minimum principal payment if the collateral speed is 90 PSA or 300 PSA for months 1 to 349. (After month 346, the outstanding principal balance will be paid off if the prepayment speed is between 90 PSA and 300 PSA.) For example, in the first month, the principal payment would be $508,169.52 if the collateral prepays at 90 PSA and $1,075,931.20 if the collateral prepays at 300 PSA. Thus, the minimum principal payment is $508,169.52, as reported in the last column of Exhibit 14.6. In month 103, the minimum principal payment is also the amount if the prepayment speed is 90 PSA, $1,446,761, compared to $1,458,618.04 for 300 PSA. In month 104, however, a prepayment speed of 300 PSA would produce a principal payment of $1,433,539.23, which is less than the principal payment of $1,440,825.55 assuming 90 PSA. So, $1,433,539.23 is reported in the last column of Exhibit 14.6. In fact, from month 104 on, the minimum principal payment is the one that would result assuming a prepayment speed of 300 PSA.

EXHIBIT 14.6 Monthly Principal Payment for $400 Million Par 7.5% Coupon Passthrough with an 8.125% WAC and a 357 WAM Assuming Prepayment Rates of 90 PSA and 300 PSA

Month	Principal payment		Minimum principal payment PAC schedule
	At 90% PSA	At 300% PSA	
1	$508,169.52	$1,075,931.20	$508,169.52
2	569,843.43	1,279,412.11	569,843.43
3	631,377.11	1,482,194.45	631,377.11
4	692,741.89	1,683,966.17	692,741.89
5	753,909.12	1,884,414.62	753,909.12
6	814,850.22	2,083,227.31	814,850.22
7	875,536.68	2,280,092.68	875,536.68
8	935,940.10	2,474,700.92	935,940.10
9	996,032.19	2,666,744.77	996,032.19
10	1,055,784.82	2,855,920.32	1,055,784.82
11	1,115,170.01	3,041,927.81	1,115,170.01
12	1,174,160.00	3,224,472.44	1,174,160.00
13	1,232,727.22	3,403,265.17	1,232,727.22
14	1,290,844.32	3,578,023.49	1,290,844.32
15	1,348,484.24	3,748,472.23	1,348,484.24
16	1,405,620.17	3,914,344.26	1,405,620.17
17	1,462,225.60	4,075,381.29	1,462,225.60
18	1,518,274.36	4,231,334.57	1,518,274.36
101	1,458,719.34	1,510,072.17	1,458,719.34
102	1,452,725.55	1,484,126.59	1,452,725.55
103	1,446,761.00	1,458,618.04	1,446,761.00
104	1,440,825.55	1,433,539.23	1,433,539.23
105	1,434,919.07	1,408,883.01	1,408,883.01
211	949,482.58	213,309.00	213,309.00
212	946,033.34	209,409.09	209,409.09
213	942,601.99	205,577.05	205,577.05
346	618,684.59	13,269.17	13,269.17
347	617,071.58	12,944.51	12,944.51
348	615,468.65	12,626.21	12,626.21
349	613,875.77	12,314.16	3,432.32
350	612,292.88	12,008.25	0
351	610,719.96	11,708.38	0
352	609,156.96	11,414.42	0
353	607,603.84	11,126.28	0
354	606,060.57	10,843.85	0
355	604,527.09	10,567.02	0
356	603,003.38	10,295.70	0
357	601,489.39	10,029.78	0

EXHIBIT 14.7 CMO-3: CMO Structure with One PAC Tranche and One Support Tranche

Tranche	Par amount	Coupon rate (%)
P (PAC)	$243,800,000	7.5
S (Support)	156,200,000	7.5
Total	$400,000,000	

Payment rules:
1. *For payment of monthly coupon interest:* Disburse monthly coupon interest to each tranche on the basis of the amount of principal outstanding at the beginning of the month.
2. *For disbursement of principal payments:* Disburse principal payments to tranche P based on its schedule of principal repayments. Tranche P has priority with respect to current and future principal payments to satisfy the schedule. Any excess principal payments in a month over the amount necessary to satisfy the schedule for tranche P are paid to tranche S. When tranche S is completely paid off, all principal payments are to be made to tranche P regardless of the schedule.

If the collateral prepays at any speed between 90 PSA and 300 PSA, the minimum principal payment would be the amount reported in the last column of Exhibit 14.6. For example, if we had included principal payment figures assuming a prepayment speed of 200 PSA, the minimum principal payment would not change: From month 11 through month 103, the minimum principal payment is that generated from 90 PSA, but from month 104 on, the minimum principal payment is that generated from 300 PSA.

This characteristic of the collateral allows for the creation of a PAC tranche, assuming that the collateral prepays over its life at a constant speed between 90 PSA and 300 PSA. A schedule of principal repayments that the PAC bondholders are entitled to receive before any other bond class in the CMO is specified. The monthly schedule of principal repayments is as specified in the last column of Exhibit 14.6, which shows the minimum principal payment. Although there is no assurance that the collateral will prepay between these two speeds, a PAC bond can be structured to assume that it will.

Exhibit 14.7 shows a CMO structure, CMO-3, created from the $400 million, 7.5% coupon mortgage passthrough with a WAC of 8.125% and a WAM of 357 months. There are just two tranches in this structure: a 7.5% coupon PAC tranche created assuming 90 to 300 PSA with a par value of $243.8 million, and a support tranche with a par value of $156.2 million.

The average life for the PAC tranche and the support tranche in CMO-3, assuming various actual prepayment speeds, is shown here:

Prepayment rate (PSA)	PAC tranche (P)	Support tranche (S)
0	15.97	27.26
50	9.44	24.00
90	7.26	18.56
100	7.26	18.56
150	7.26	12.57
165	7.26	11.16
200	7.26	8.38
250	7.26	5.37
300	7.26	3.13
350	6.56	2.51
400	5.92	2.17
450	5.38	1.94
500	4.93	1.77
700	3.70	1.37

Notice that between 90 PSA and 300 PSA, the average life for the PAC tranche is stable at 7.26 years. However, at slower or faster PSA speeds, the schedule is broken, and the average life changes, lengthening when the prepayment speed is less than 90 PSA and shortening when it is greater than 300 PSA. Even so, there is much greater variability for the average life of the support tranche. The average life variability for the support tranche is substantial.

Most CMO structures that have a PAC typically have more than one PAC tranche. The tranches are created by carving up a PAC tranche into a series of sequential-pay PAC tranches.

SUMMARY

In this chapter we have focused on the agency sector of the mortgage-backed securities market. The securities included in this sector are agency passthrough securities, agency stripped mortgage-backed securities, and agency collateralized mortgage obligations. We have explained the raw material for the securities (i.e., the mortgage loans), the structure of the securities, trading and settlement procedures, and the risks associated with these securities.

CHAPTER 15

Nonagency MBS and Real Estate-Backed ABS

Frank J. Fabozzi, Ph.D., CFA
Adjunct Professor of Finance
School of Management
Yale University

John Dunlevy, CFA
Senior Portfolio Manager
Beacon Hill Asset Management

In Chapter 14, mortgage-backed securities issued by Ginnie Mae, Fannie Mae, and Freddie Mac are described. In this chapter, we will look at products backed by residential mortgages that are not issued by one of these entities. These products fall into two groups: nonagency MBS and asset-backed securities backed by residential mortgage loans (i.e., real estate-backed ABS).

The classification of a security as either a nonagency MBS or a real estate-backed ABS is not always clear. This is because there are securities in which the underlying collateral is mixed with various types of mortgage-related loans. That is, the collateral backing a deal may include collateral that is a combination of standard first-lien residential mortgages, second lien mortgages, as well as other products that we will describe in this chapter—home equity loans and manufactured housing loans.[1] The Secu-

---

[1] The purpose of the classification is not to aid in the analysis of these securities, but rather to construct the so-called "league tables" for ranking investment banking firms by deal type.

rities Data Corporation (SDC) has established criteria for classifying a
mortgage product with mixed collateral as either a nonagency MBS or an
ABS. The classification rule is as follows: If at issuance more than 50% of
a deal consists of either manufactured housing loans, home equity loans,
second mortgage loans, or home improvement loans, then the deal is classified as an ABS. For deals in which more than 50% of the loans are first
liens, SDC uses a size test to classify the deal. If more than 50% of the
aggregate principal balance of the loans have a loan balance of more than
$200,000, the deal is classified as a nonagency MBS. A deal in which
50% of the loans are first liens, but more than 50% of the aggregate principal balance of the loans is less than $200,000 is classified as an ABS.

COLLATERAL FOR RESIDENTIAL REAL ESTATE-BACKED SECURITIES

Mortgage loans used as collateral for an agency security are conforming
loans. That is, they must meet the underwriting standards of the agency.
Exhibit 15.1 identifies traditional agency loan guidelines—loan size,
documentation, loan-to-value ratio, property type, and credit score. The
credit score is a measure of the applicant's ability to repay the loan and
is discussed later in this chapter.

The collateral for a nonagency MBS consists of *nonconforming* loans.
A loan may be nonconforming for one or more of the following reasons:

EXHIBIT 15.1   Traditional Agency Loan Guidelines

Conforming Factor	Conforming Guideline
Loan Size	Limit for one unit property is $300,700 as of Jan. 1, 2002
Documentation	Full documentation
	• Verify income (VOI)
	• Verify employment (VOE)
	• Verify deposit (VOA)
	• Appraisal
Ratios	28% Mortgage payment/monthly income
	36% Total debt /monthly income
Loan-to-Value (LTV)	Maximum 80% without private mortgage insurance
Property Type	Single-family
Credit Score	FICO score > 660

1. The mortgage balance exceeds the amount permitted by the agency.
2. The borrower characteristics fail to meet the underwriting standards established by the agency.
3. The loan characteristics fail to meet the underwriting standards established by the agency.
4. The applicant fails to provide full documentation as required by the agency.

There are alternative lending programs for borrowers seeking nonconforming loans for any of the above reasons. A mortgage loan that is nonconforming merely because the mortgage balance exceeds the maximum permitted by the agency guideline is called a *jumbo loan*.

With respect to the characteristics of the borrower, a loan may fail to qualify because the borrower's credit history (as measured by the FICO score) does not meet the underwriting standards or the payment-to-income (PTI) ratio exceeds the maximum permitted. Borrowers who do satisfy the underwriting standards with respect to borrower characteristics are referred to as *A credit borrowers* or *prime borrowers*. An *Alternative A loan* is a loan of an A credit borrower that has a mortgage balance that is below or above the amount necessary to be conforming, but for various reasons fails to qualify to meet the underwriting standards of either the agencies or originators of jumbo loans for one or more of the following reasons:

- Limited/low documentation loans
- Non-conforming ratio loans
- Investor property loans
- Second home/vacation property loans
- Self employed/foreign national loans
- Cash-out refinancing

B and C borrowers or *sub-prime borrowers* are borrowers who fail to satisfy the underwriting standards of the agencies because of borrower characteristics. These characteristics include credit history and maximum PTI. The loans are actually scaled by originators from B to D. Every originator establishes its own profiles for classifying a loan into a rating category.

A characteristic that may result in a loan failing to meet the underwriting standards is that the loan-to-value (LTV) ratio exceeds the maximum established by the agency or the loan is not a first-mortgage lien. There are lenders who specialize in loans that exceed the maximum LTV. These lending programs are sometimes referred to as *125 LTV programs* because the lender may be willing to lend up to 125% of the appraised or market value of the property. Basically, the lender is making a consumer loan based on the credit of the borrower to the extent that the loan amount exceeds the appraised or market value. For this reason, lenders with 125 programs have limited these loans to A credit borrowers. Mortgage-related products in which the underlying loans are 125 LTV loans are considered part of the ABS market and are discussed later in this chapter when ABS are covered.

For borrowers seeking a loan that is not a first lien on the property, a consumer loan in the form of a home equity loan can be obtained. A growing number of home equity loans are now first liens. There are two types of home equity loans, closed-end and open-end loans. With closed-end home equity loans, the lender provides the proceeds at the closing and the borrower must make scheduled monthly payments to amortize the loan as with a standard mortgage loan. In an open-end home equity loan, the lender provides a line of credit and the borrower takes down the line as needed. Mortgage-related products backed by home equity loans are considered part of the ABS market and will be covered later in this chapter.

In assessing whether a loan qualifies for conforming classification, the agencies require documentation (verification) of the information provided in the loan application. These include documents to verify the PTI and the LTV. To verify the PTI, documents to verify income (e.g., pay stubs or tax returns) and employment are needed, as well as a credit report. To verify the LTV, a property appraisal report and documentation of the source of the down payment are required. Failure to provide adequate documentation will result in a loan failing to conform. There are originators who will provide a loan based on no documentation ("no-doc loan") or limited documentation ("low-doc loan") with respect to verification of income. The borrowers are not necessarily subprime borrowers. They may be self-employed individuals or owners of a business where the amount reported in tax returns or paid as income would not meet the PTI standard of the agencies. Originators of no-doc and low-doc loans rely on the collateral (by limiting the LTV to 80% or less) and verification of significant assets that can be used to make the mortgage payments.

FICO Scoring System

Developed by Fair Isaacs & Company, FICO is a credit scoring system that is used by lenders in the credit card, auto, home equity, and home mortgage markets. The system was developed to use past credit data in order to determine the likelihood of an individual borrower default over the next two years. FICO scores are based on the following variables:

■ previous credit history
■ current level of indebtedness

- length of credit history
- number of new credit inquiries
- type of credit available

The range of FICO scores is from a low of 365 (highest risk) to a high of 840 (lowest risk). Freddie Mac uses FICO scores as an important component in its underwriting process. For example, Freddie Mac breaks all mortgage loans into the following three buckets:

Bucket	FICO Range	Underwriting Method
1	less than 620	Cautious review
2	620 to 660	Comprehensive review
3	greater than 660	Basic review

The review that is necessary to approve a mortgage application generally increases as FICO scores decline (that is, credit risk increases). This is the case since historically default experience increases as FICO scores decline. As shown below, according to Fair Issacs & Company, historical default experience increases as FICO scores decline:

	FICO Score				
	<579	580–619	620–659	660–730	740+
% Defaults	9.5%	5.9%	2.7%	1.0%	0.1%

According to Standard & Poor's, 75% of the U.S. population has FICO scores above 660, while only 25% of the population has FICO scores below 660.

PREPAYMENT CONVENTIONS

Dealers involved in the underwriting and market making of real estate-backed securities have developed prepayment models for these loans. Several firms have found that the key difference between the prepayment behavior of borrowers of nonconforming mortgages and conforming mortgages is the important role played by the credit characteristics of the borrower.

Borrower characteristics and the seasoning process must be kept in mind when trying to assess prepayments for a particular deal. In the prospectus of an offering, a base-case prepayment assumption is made—the initial speed and the amount of time until the collateral is seasoned. Thus, the prepayment benchmark is issuer specific. The benchmark speed in the prospectus is called the *prospectus prepayment curve* or PPC. As with the PSA benchmark described in Chapter 14, slower or faster prepayment speeds are a multiple of the PPC. For example, the PPC for a particular nonagency deal might state the following:

> . . . a 100% Prepayment Assumption assumes conditional prepayment rates of 1.5% per annum of the then-outstanding principal balance of the mortgage loans in the first month of the life of the loans and an additional 0.5% per annum in each month thereafter until month 20. Beginning in month 20, 100% Prepayment Assumption assumes a conditional prepayment rate of 11% per annum each month.

For this deal, 100% PPC, 80% PPC, and 150% PPC would then be as follows for the first 20 months:

Month	100% PPC (%)	80% PPC (%)	150% PPC (%)
1	1.5	1.2	2.3
2	2.0	1.6	3.0
3	2.5	2.0	3.8
4	3.0	2.4	4.5
5	3.5	2.8	5.3
6	4.0	3.2	6.0
7	4.5	3.6	6.8
8	5.0	4.0	7.5
9	5.5	4.4	8.3
10	6.0	4.8	9.0
11	6.5	5.2	9.8
12	7.0	5.6	10.5
13	7.5	6.0	11.3
14	8.0	6.4	12.0
15	8.5	6.8	12.8
16	9.0	7.2	13.5
17	9.5	7.6	14.3
18	10.0	8.0	15.0
19	10.5	8.4	15.8
20	11.0	8.8	16.5

Unlike the PSA prepayment benchmark, the PPC is not generic. By this it is meant that the PPC is issuer specific. In contrast, the PSA prepayment benchmark applies to any type of collateral issued by an agency for any type of loan design. This feature of the PPC is important for an investor to keep in mind when comparing the prepayment characteristics and investment characteristics of the collateral between issuers and issues (new and seasoned).

NONAGENCY MBS

As with agency MBS, there are nonagency passthrough securities and nonagency CMOs. Agency CMOs are created from pools of passthrough securities. In the nonagency market, a CMO can be created from either a pool of passthroughs or unsecuritized mortgage loans. It is uncommon for nonconforming mortgage loans to be securitized as passthroughs and then the passthroughs carved up to create a CMO. Instead, in the nonagency market a CMO is carved out of mortgage loans that have not been securitized as passthroughs. Since a mortgage loan is commonly referred to as a whole loan, nonagency CMOs are commonly referred to as whole-loan CMOs. With a nonagency MBS there is no explicit or implicit government guarantee of payment of interest and principal as there is with an agency security. Thus, there is credit risk. The nationally recognized statistical rating organizations rate nonagency securities.

Servicer Advances

The servicer is responsible for the collection of interest and principal, which is passed along to the trustee. The servicer also handles delinquencies and foreclosures. Typically, there will be a master servicer and subservicers. These entities play a critical role and in assessing the credit risk of a nonagency MBS; the rating agencies look carefully at the quality of the servicers.

When there is a delinquency by the homeowner, the investor in a nonagency MBS may or may not be affected. This depends on whether a servicer is required to make advances. Thus, the financial capacity of the servicer to make advances is critical. Typically, a back-up servicer is used just in case the master servicer cannot meet its obligation with respect to advances. The servicer recovers advances when delinquent payments are made or the property is foreclosed and proceeds received.

There are different forms of advancing: (1) mandatory advancing, (2) optional advancing, and (3) limited advancing. The strongest form from the investor's perspective is mandatory advancing wherein failure to advance by a servicer is an event of default. However, a servicer need not advance if it can show that there is not a strong likelihood of recovery of the amount advanced when the property is ultimately disposed of. In an optional or a voluntary advancing, the servicer is not legally obligated to advance so that failure to do so is not an event of default. In a limited advancing the issuer is obligated to advance, but the amount it must advance is limited.

Collateral Risks

For an agency backed product, the investor is not concerned with defaults except to the extent that they increase prepayment. In a nonagency security, defaults may impact the issuer's ability to return principal and pay interest to a tranche. Losses can also result through (1) borrower bankruptcy, (2) borrower fraud, and (3) special hazard risk.

Credit Enhancements

All nonagency securities are credit enhanced. Typically a double A or triple A rating is sought for the most senior tranche in a deal. The amount of credit enhancement necessary depends on rating agency requirements and is referred to as "sizing" the transaction. There are two general types of credit enhancement structures: external and internal. We describe each type in the following sections and also how the rating agencies determine the level of credit enhancement. The same credit enhancements are also included in real estate-backed ABS.

External Credit Enhancements

External credit enhancements come in the form of third-party guarantees that provide for first loss protection against losses up to a specified level, for example, 10%. The most common forms of external credit enhancement are (1) a corporate guarantee, (2) a letter of credit, (3) pool insurance, and (4) bond insurance.

Pool insurance policies cover losses resulting from defaults and foreclosures. Policies are typically written for a dollar amount of coverage that continues in force throughout the life of the pool. However, some policies are written so that the dollar amount of coverage declines as the pool seasons as long as two conditions are met: (1) the credit performance is better than expected and (2) the rating agencies that rated the issue approve. Since only defaults and foreclosures are covered, additional insurance must be obtained to cover losses resulting from bankruptcy (i.e., court mandated modification of mortgage debt—"cramdown"), fraud arising in the origination process, and special hazards (i.e., losses resulting from events not covered by a standard homeowner's insurance policy).

Bond insurance provides the same function as in municipal bond structures. Typically, bond insurance is not used as the primary protection but to supplement other forms of credit enhancement.

A nonagency security with external credit support is subject to the credit risk of the third-party guarantor (called *event risk*). Should the third-party guarantor be downgraded, the issue itself could be subject to downgrade even if the structure is performing as expected.

External credit enhancements do not materially alter the cash flow characteristics of a CMO structure except in the form of prepayment. In case of a default resulting in net losses within the guarantee level, investors will receive the principal amount as if a prepayment has occurred. If the net losses exceed the guarantee level, investors will realize a shortfall in the cash flows.

Internal Credit Enhancements

Internal credit enhancements come in more complicated forms than external credit enhancements and may alter the cash flow characteristics of the loans even in the absence of default. The most common forms of internal credit enhancements are reserve funds, overcollateralization, and senior/subordinated structures.

Reserve Funds   Reserve funds come in two forms, cash reserve funds and excess servicing spread. *Cash reserve funds* are straight deposits of cash generated from issuance proceeds. In this case, part of the underwriting profits from the deal are deposited into a fund which typically invests in money market instruments. Cash reserve funds are typically used in conjunction with some form of external credit enhancement.

Excess servicing spread accounts involve the allocation of excess spread or cash into a separate reserve account after paying out the net coupon, servicing fee, and all other expenses on a monthly basis. For example, suppose that the gross weighted average coupon (gross WAC) is 7.75%, the servicing and other fees are 0.25%, and the net weighted average coupon (net WAC) is 7.25%. This means that there is excess spread of 0.25%. The amount in the reserve account will gradually increase and can be used to pay for possible future losses. This form of credit enhancement relies on the assumption that defaults occur infrequently in the very early life of the loans, but gradually increase in the following two to five years.

Overcollateralization   The total par value of the tranches is the liability of the structure. So, if a structure has two tranches with a par value of $300 million, then that is the amount of the liability. The amount of the collateral backing the structure must be at least equal to the amount of the liability. If the amount of the collateral exceeds the amount of the liability of the structure, the deal is said to be overcollateralized. The amount of overcollateralization represents a form of internal credit enhancement because it can be used to absorb losses. For example, if the liability of the structure is $300 million and the collateral's value is $320 million, then the structure is overcollateralized by $20 million. Thus, the first $20 million of losses will not result in a loss to any of the tranches.

Senior/Subordinated Structure   In a senior/subordinated structure there is a senior tranche and at least one junior or subordinated tranche. For example, suppose a deal has $300 million as collateral. The structure may look as follows:

senior tranche	$270 million
subordinated tranche	$ 30 million

This means that the first $30 million of losses are absorbed by the subordinated tranche.

There is no reason why there must be only one subordinated tranche. The structure can have more than one subordinated tranche. A senior/subordinated structure may look like that shown in Exhibit 15.2. The first tranche to realize any losses is tranche G in the structure shown in Exhibit 15.2. This tranche is referred to as the *first loss tranche*. Notice that the tranche is unrated.

The basic concern in the senior/subordinated structure is that while the subordinated tranches provide a certain level of credit protection for the senior tranche at the closing of the deal, the level of protection changes over time due to prepayments. The objective after the deal closes is to distribute any prepayments such that the credit protection for the senior tranche does not deteriorate over time. There is a well developed mechanism used to address this concern called the shifting interest mechanism. We will discuss the shifting interest mechanism when we discuss structural analysis later.

EXHIBIT 15.2   Example of Senior/Subordinated Structure

	Security	Rating	Class size (%)	Cushion provided by classes below (%)
	Senior class	AAA/AA	94.0	6.0
	B	AA	1.0	4.0
	C	A	1.0	3.0
Junior	D	BBB	1.0	2.0
classes	E	BB	1.0	1.0
	F	B	0.5	0.5
	G	NR	0.5	0.0

Rating Agency Determination of Credit Enhancement Levels

The rating agencies determine the appropriate amount of credit enhancement for a given pool of collateral. For example, Standard & Poor's (S&P) developed its rating standards through analysis of the Great Depression of the 1930s and the regional recessions of the 1980s (such as in Houston, Texas). S&P's analysis begins with a "prime pool" of mortgage loans. The criteria for a prime pool are as follows:

- 300 or more loans
- geographically diverse
- first lien
- single-family detached
- purchase mortgage
- 30-year term
- fully amortizing
- fixed-rate
- full documentation
- owner occupied
- 80% LTV
- balances less than $300,000

For a prime pool, S&P has statistics by rating and loan-to-value ratio for (1) foreclosure frequency and (2) loss severity. The product of the foreclosure frequency and loss severity gives the base case loss coverage required for a prime pool. So, for example, if a AA rating is sought for a prime pool and the corresponding foreclosure and loss severity is 10% and 40%, respectively, then:[2]

base case loss coverage required for a AA prime pool = 10% × 40% = 4%

Adjustments are made to the prime pool loss coverage for each deviation from the prime loan criteria. For example, there will be an adjustment based on the loan-to-value ratio. For a prime pool, the LTV criterion is 80%. Suppose that a target rating of AA is sought but that the loans have an LTV of 90% and the loans have private mortgage insurance. Assuming that the frequency foreclosure and severity loss for a AA rating for a pool which is prime except that the LTV is 90% instead of 80% is 15% and 29%, respectively, then the loss coverage required would be 4.4% (= 15% × 29%). That is, base case loss coverage increases from 4% to 4.4%.

---

[2] The statistics used in this example are for illustration purposes only. However, they are believed to be close to estimates used by S&P at one time. S&P updates its statistics periodically.

After the adjustments for deviations from the prime loss criteria, S&P then scales the base case coverage required for a AA prime loan for any other rating that might be desired. In general, the adjustment is as follows:

base case loss coverage required for a AA prime pool after adjusting for deviations from prime pool × factor based on rating sought

The "factor based on rating sought" will be greater than 1 if a rating higher than AA is sought and less than 1 if a rating lower than AA is sought.

Rating approaches to credit enhancement levels vary by agency. Moody's philosophy is that ratings on mortgage securities are comparable to other types of securities (i.e., corporate and municipal bonds). Therefore, from the analysis of bonds that it has rated, Moody's determines expected credit losses in terms of yield impairment within each rating level. Fitch's approach is similar to S&P's, except Fitch places more emphasis on regional economics.

Structural Analysis

An investor in a nonagency security (as well as a real estate-backed ABS) should understand the deal structure. In addition to understanding the class tranching, this involves understanding the type of senior/subordinated structure, methods of allocating losses, deal triggers, clean-up calls, and compensating interest. We discuss each of these in the sections that follow.

Shifting Interest Structure

In a shifting interest structure, the subordinated classes are designed not to decrease as a percentage of the total outstanding principal. In this structure, amortization and interest are allocated pro-rata among all the deal's classes. Prepayments that would normally be allocated to the subordinated tranches are shifted to the senior tranches for a period of time. For example, for an initial period of five years, 100% of all prepayments on the mortgage pool are allocated to the senior tranches. After the initial prepayment lockout period, a smaller percentage of the pro-rata share of the subordinated tranche's prepayment is paid to the senior classes. A typical shifting interest structure is given in Exhibit 15.3.

In a shifting interest structure, the junior class has a claim not on a particular amount of cash flow, but on a portion of the underlying assets. Realized losses act to reduce the lowest subordinated tranche outstanding balance on a dollar for dollar basis. Hence, the first-loss tranche will be reduced by losses until its principal balance is exhausted, then the next highest rated tranche will absorb losses, and so on.

Methods of Allocating Losses

Losses within a senior/subordinated structure are absorbed by the most junior tranche, although the timing and allocation of cash flow can vary within a deal structure. There are two traditional methods of allocating losses within a senior/subordinated structure: (1) the waterfall method and (2) the direct write-off method. Exhibit 15.4 highlights the differences between these two methods.

Several distinctions should be made between the two methods. First, under the waterfall method, multitranche subordinated structures can be adversely affected with the accrual of interest payments. For example, in the illustration given in Exhibit 15.4, the mezzanine tranche receives only $28,333 of its scheduled $67,667 interest payment. Therefore, a shortfall is created that must be repaid in later periods. If credit problems persist, the unpaid interest can amount to several months without any cash flow. This problem, which arises due to the payment of the senior's share of the loss in cash, can severely impact the liquidity of the tranche in accrual status.[3]

EXHIBIT 15.3   Typical Shifting Interest Mechanism Allocation of Cash Flows

	To Subordinated Tranches			To Senior Tranches				
Year	Pro-rata Interest (%)	Pro-rata Scheduled Principal (%)	Pro-rata Prepayment (%)	Pro-rata Interest (%)	Pro-rata Scheduled Principal (%)	Pro-rata Prepayment (%)		Additional Prepayment
1 through 5	100	100	0	100	100	100	+	100% of Sub.'s Share
6	100	100	30	100	100	100	+	70% of Sub.'s Share
7	100	100	40	100	100	100	+	60% of Sub.'s Share
8	100	100	60	100	100	100	+	40% of Sub's Share
9	100	100	80	100	100	100	+	20% of Sub's Share
10 and up	100	100	100	100	100	100	+	0% of Sub's Share

EXHIBIT 15.4   Comparison of Waterfall and Direct Write-Off Methods

Example		Month 1	
Collateral:	$200,000,000	Interest:	$1,333,333
90% Senior:	180,000,000	Scheduled principal:	200,000
5% Mezzanine:	10,000,000	Prepayments:	800,000
5% Subordinated:	10,000,000	Recovery:	100,000
8% Coupon		Total:	2,433,333
		Realized Losses:	150,000
		Reduction Mortgage Balance:	1,250,000

---

[3] These bonds have additional problems: (1) extension of average life and duration; (2) roll-up of the yield curve; and, (3) no interest-on-interest potential.

EXHIBIT 15. 4 (Continued)

Senior Bonds

	Waterfall Method	Direct Write-Off Method
Interest	$1,200,000	$1,200,000
Scheduled Principal	180,000	180,000
Prepayments	800,000	800,000
Recovery	90,000	100,000
Unrecovered Senior	135,000	0
Total	2,405,000	2,280,000
Beginning Balance	180,000,000	180,000,000
Ending Balance	178,795,000	178,920,000
Change in Balance	−1,205,000	−1,080,000

Mezzanine Bonds

	Waterfall Method	Direct Write-Off Method
Interest	$28,333	$66,667
Scheduled Principal	0	100,000
Prepayments	0	0
Recovery	0	0
Unrecovered Mezzanine	0	0
Payment Unpaid Balance	0	0
Total	28,333	76,667
Write-Down Principal	0	0
Ending Unpaid Account Balance	38,334	0
Beginning Balance	10,000,000	10,000,000
Ending Balance	10,000,000	9,990,000
Change in Balance	0	−10,000

Junior Class

	Waterfall Method	Direct Write-Off Method
Interest	$0	$66,667
Scheduled Principal	0	10,000
Prepayments	0	0
Recovery	0	0
Total	0	76,667
Write-Down Principal	45,000	150,000
Unpaid Interest	66,667	0
Write-Beginning Balance	10,000,000	10,000,000
Ending Balance	9,995,000	9,840,000
Change in Balance	−45,000	−160,000

EXHIBIT 15.5 Average Life at Different Speeds and Step-Down Allowances*

	Prepayment Speed (PSA)		
	250	400	600
All Step-Downs Taken	10.9	9.4	8.2
No Step-Downs Taken	16.0	15.0	13.1

* Assumes 30-year fixed-rate loans, 8.5% gross WAC, 320 WAM, and 4.50% subordinated tranche

Under the direct write-off method, the senior bond is entitled to the proceeds of the liquidated property, and any loss is written off against the most junior tranche. In addition, all interest and scheduled principal are allocated on a pro-rata basis.

Deal Triggers

An important component to be considered when analyzing senior/subordinated tranches is the deal's "triggers." Triggers are step-down tests that allow the subordinated tranches to be reduced as a percentage of the overall deal. For example, as illustrated in Exhibit 15.5, the subordinated bonds in the standard senior/subordinated structure are locked out from unscheduled payments (prepayments) for five years. Following this lockout period, the prepayment protection gradually "steps down" until the subordinated tranches receive their full pro-rata share of prepayments in year 10.

During the initial 5-year lockout period, the subordinated bonds delever, that is, they grow as a percentage of the overall deal. This delevering can occur only if a series of tests (or covenants) are met. These tests address (1) total losses and (2) total delinquencies (60+ days).

These tests are levels of credit performance required before the credit support can be reduced. The tests are applied annually after year 5, and monthly if a test is failed. Of the two tests, the loss test prevents a step-down from occurring if cumulative losses exceed a certain limit (which changes over time). The delinquency test, in its most common form, prevents any step-down from taking place as long as the current over 60-day delinquency rate exceeds 2% of the then-current pool balance.

The above step-down criteria remain in effect on older deals. However, most deals issued after October 1995 are subject to new step-down tests. Following that date new requirements were adopted by the rating agencies, particularly in the area of delinquencies. This was done largely as a result of the fact that many strong deals have performed well and have, in fact, been upgraded by the agencies, despite running delinquencies above 2% of the current pool balance. Under these new tests, the delinquency measures are less stringent and, as a result, present less extension risk for subordinated tranche holders.

Clean-Up Calls

Nonagency deals are usually subject to a 5% to 10% clean-up call; that is, the issuer has the right to collapse a deal if the deal factor is down to 0.05 to 0.10. As shown in Exhibit 15.6, the average life can vary significantly if run to the call date. This option has two major effects on subordinated tranche holders. First, since most subordinated tranches trade at discounts to par, it has a positive impact since par is received. Second, since these calls come into play before maturity, the duration and average life will shorten.

Although most deals use a 10% clean-up call, that does not necessarily mean that these deals will be called. Reasons why many deals may not be called include:

1. Advances in computer technology allow servicers to continue to maintain pool servicing functions economically.
2. Adverse selection (last loans in a pool can be the least creditworthy) may prevent the repurchase of these loans.
3. Issuer of pool often retains economic interest in pool by controlling servicing function and/or by owning the IO-tranche.

Compensating Interest

A feature unique to nonagency MBS is compensating interest. MBS pay principal and interest on a monthly basis. While homeowners may prepay their mortgage on any day throughout the month, the agencies guarantee and pay investors a full month of interest as if all the prepayments occur on the last day of the month. This guarantee does not apply to nonagency MBS. If a homeowner pays off a mortgage on the tenth day of the month, he will not have to pay interest for the rest of the month. Because of the payment delay (for example, 25 days), the investor will receive full principal but only 10 days of interest on the 25th of the following month.

EXHIBIT 15.6   Typical Profile of a Subordinated Bond

	225 PSA +100		300 PSA Base		600 PSA − 100	
	Maturity	Call	Maturity	Call	Maturity	Call
Average Life	11.63	9.56	10.54	8.06	8.06	4.31
Modified Duration	6.86	6.33	6.53	5.62	5.62	3.53
Last Pay	6/23	11/05	6/23	4/03	4/23	9/98

EXHIBIT 15.7 Illustration of the Calculation of Compensating Interest

Assumptions:

Coupon rate = 6.75%

WAM = 357

Servicing = 0.125%

Beginning principal balance:	$300,000,000.00
Accrued bondholder interest:	1,687,500.00
Scheduled amortization:	257,044.75
Prepayments at 25% CPR, 2.3688% SMM:	7,100,438.28

Interest shortfall to bondholder before compensating interest:

$$= \frac{15}{30} \times \frac{1}{12} \times \frac{6.75}{100} \times 7,100,438.28 = 19,969.98$$

Maximum compensating interest available:

$$= \frac{0.125}{100} \times \frac{1}{12} \times (300,000,000 - 7,100,438.28) + \frac{0.125}{100} \times \frac{15}{30} \times \frac{1}{12} \times 7,100,438.28$$

$$= 30,880.19$$

Difference: 30,880.19 − 19,969.98 = 10,910.20

Source: Figure 1 in "Compensating Interest: Rarely an Issue," *PaineWebber Mortgage Strategist* (September 8, 1998), p. 19.

This phenomenon is known as payment *interest shortfall* or *compensating interest* and is handled differently by different issuers. Some issuers will only pay up to a specified amount and some will not pay at all. Actually, it is the servicers who will pay any compensating interest. The servicer obtains the shortfall in interest from the servicing spread. The shortfall that will be made up to the investor may be limited to the entire servicing spread or part of the servicing spread. Thus, while an investor has protection against the loss of a full month's interest, the protection may be limited.

The compensating interest policies of issuers have changed dramatically over the past few years. Whereas at one time some issuers offered no compensating interest, today the compensating interest policies of the major issuers of nonagency securities provide at least 12.5 basis points of compensating interest. There are three aspects regarding the compensating interest policy that the investor should be aware of: (1) the maximum compensating interest, (2) the types of prepayments covered—prepayment in full and curtailments, and (3) the prepayment remittance cycle.

Exhibit 15.7 provides an illustration of the computation of how the maximum compensating interest is computed and how the compensation is determined. The illustration assumes that the issuer will pay compensating interest up to an amount equal to 12.5 basis points per year. Based on the assumptions in the exhibit the maximum compensating interest is $30,880.19. The interest shortfall based on the assumptions is \$19,969.68. Since the maximum compensating interest available is greater than the interest shortfall, the interest shortfall will be covered.

How Do Losses Occur?

Investors in subordinated tranches must understand how losses occur. As shown in the flowchart in Exhibit 15.8, before a pool loss can occur a loan must pass from current status into 30-, 60-, and 90-day delinquency status before finally entering the foreclosure process. During this process, the servicer plays a very important function.

It should be pointed out that the servicer will commonly advance (principal and interest) to bondholders all the way through foreclosure. These advances, which will be reimbursed once the property is liquidated, will be paid before any pool losses are calculated.

The servicer also will work to prevent any losses from occurring to bondholders. The servicer will attempt to minimize losses, once a loan becomes delinquent, by:

1. Contacting the borrower and seeking to bring the balance current.
2. Providing the borrower with a new loan schedule (to bring the balance current).
3. Encouraging owners with equity to sell the property.

If any of these strategies are successful, the servicer has prevented a delinquent loan from resulting in a pool loss.

EXHIBIT 15.8 Flowchart of the Way Losses Occur

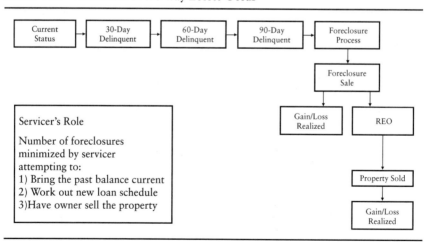

The best defense against pool losses adversely impacting the subordinated tranches is homeowner's equity in the property. That is, the homeowner's down payment or actual perceived equity in a particular property is the first line of defense against default. Defaults rationally occur only when a negative equity condition exists. Otherwise the homeowner would sell the property to prevent default.

Empirical studies of homeowners in negative equity situations show that only a small portion of this universe will default. Statistics show that it requires a period of severe borrower stress (i.e., divorce or unemployment) coupled with a negative equity condition to result in significant levels of default. Mortgage borrowers have resisted default in most negative equity situations due to: (1) the social stigma of losing one's home, (2) fear of tarnishing one's credit rating, and (3) the ongoing need for housing. Furthermore, negative equity/default conditions are not that common to begin with because of annual versus fixed-debt burden.

For a typical 30-year loan with a 75% LTV ratio, the LTV ratio will decline to 71.4% after five years and 66.1% after ten years, assuming no housing inflation. This occurs due to normal amortization of principal over the loan's 30-year life. If any improvement in housing values is assumed (i.e., 2% housing inflation), the LTV ratio will decline to 64.7% after five years and 54.2% after ten years. Thus credit mortgage pools have a normal tendency to improve with time.

In evaluating subordinated tranches, investors attempt to project losses and their timing. A widely used loss curve for this purpose is the Moody's loss curve shown below:

Age	Losses	Cumulative
1	0.5%	0.5%
2	3.5%	4.0%
3	11.0%	15.0%
4	21.5%	36.5%
5	13.5%	57.5%
6	13.5%	71.0%
7	11.5%	82.5%
8	7.5%	90.0%
9	7.0%	97.0%
10+	3.0%	100.0%

This loss curve highlights the expected timing of losses for 30-year collateral fixed-rate single-family pools. The shape of the curve highlights the fact that losses do not typically occur during the first year (since the foreclosure process can often last more than one year), but are typically concentrated in years 3 through 7. During these years the homeowner has not had substantial time to amortize principal or enjoy the benefit of housing inflation. This is in direct conflict with the longer part of the loss curve, where losses become quite rare due to seasoning and the build-up of the homeowner's equity.

NAS and Super-NAS Bonds

In agency CMO deals and nonagency deals, planned amortization class tranches can be included to provide the PAC tranches with prepayment protection, the protection coming from the support tranches in the structure. In the nonagency market, another structure that provides prepayment protection for a some *senior tranches* is the *non-accelerated senior* (NAS) tranches.

Structural Development

There have been three generations of structural development with regard to the NAS market. The phases of development are shown in Exhibit 15.9. The first generation of NAS development was the super-senior bond, which was common in nonagency CMO deals during the early 1990s. The super-senior bond was created in order to ease senior investor fears about the credit risk inherent in nonagency pools which had relatively high California loan concentrations. The thought process was that if the rating agency required 6% subordination on a deal with a high California concentration, then any potential investor credit concerns should be eased if the subordination level were raised to 16%. (See Exhibit 15.10.)

EXHIBIT 15.9   Development of NAS Market

Phase				
1 Super Senior		Mezzanine AAA		
2			NAS	
3				Super-NAS
1990	1992	1994	1996	1998

EXHIBIT 15.10   Creating Super-Senior Bonds

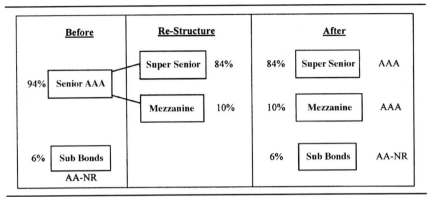

EXHIBIT 15.11   Mezzanine Bond Schedule for Prepayment Allocation

Year	Months	Mezzanine Bond % of Pro Rata Share
1–5	1–60	0
6	61–72	30
7	73–84	40
8	85–96	60
9	97–108	80
10+	+109	100

Super-senior bonds are created by splitting the senior bonds into two parts: the super-senior and the mezzanine bonds. The mezzanine bonds, despite the fact that they enjoy AAA ratings, were subordinated to the other AAA bonds in terms of loss priority.

The AAA mezzanine bonds do, however, enjoy the same hard lock-out features as the subordinated bonds in the structure. That is, during the first five years, 100% of unscheduled principal payments (i.e., the prepayments) from the collateral pool go to pay down the senior bonds. (See Exhibit 15.11.) However, unlike traditional subordinated bonds, not all mezzanine bonds are required to pass the loss and delinquency trigger tests in order to begin to receive their pro rata share of unscheduled principal payments.

The super-senior structure was phased out around 1992–1993 as the California housing market improved, but the AAA mezzanine concept reappeared in 1994 as a method to structure AAA rated bonds with call protection superior to those available in the planned amortization class (PAC) market.

EXHIBIT 15.12   Creating Super-NAS Bonds

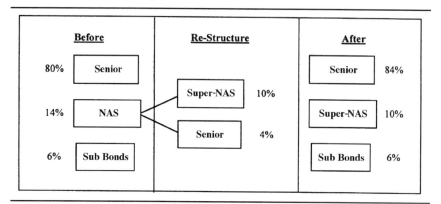

Source: "Super-NAS Bonds: Required Summer Reading," *PaineWebber Mortgage Strategist* (June 9, 1998), p. 16.

Despite the popularity of the AAA mezzanine structure, the second phase of development occurred because AAA mezzanine bonds were not Employee Retirement Income Security Act (ERISA) eligible. ERISA eligibility was an important factor in bringing pension fund investors into this market. ERISA guidelines state that the subordinated status of AAA mezzanine bonds would make them ineligible investments for pension funds. Therefore, Wall Street came up with the non-accelerated senior (NAS) bond.

The NAS bond had all the benefits of the AAA mezzanine plus ERISA eligibility. This was the case since the NAS bond shared losses *pari-pasu* with all other senior bonds in the structure (i.e., it was not subordinated).

The NAS bond is created in a similar way to the PAC bond in that the bond has a schedule which leads to more average life volatility in the other senior bonds. Because of this schedule (i.e., complete 5-year prepay lockout followed by subordinated-like step down schedule), the NAS bond can only receive principal ahead of schedule if all other senior bonds are completely retired. Thus, all senior bonds act to buffer the NAS bond.

The latest or third state of NAS development is the super-NAS. The super-NAS was created in order to further stabilize the average life profile of the NAS bond. Structurally the super-NAS was created as shown in Exhibit 15.12.

The super-NAS is a bond with less average life variability than an ordinary NAS. The super-NAS bond is created by time tranching the NAS cash flows such that the shorter bond becomes the "super-NAS" and the longer bond cash flows are returned to the senior bonds. The result is a shorter and less volatile super-senior with a tighter principal payment window.

EXHIBIT 15.13   NAS Bond Comparison

	10% NAS	20% NAS
NAS Bonds	10%	20%
Sr Bonds	84%	74%
Sub Bonds	6%	6%
	100%	100%
Senior/NAS Ratio	8:4:1	3:7:1

EXHIBIT 15.14   NAS Average Life Comparison

Description	75 PPC*	100 PPC	150 PPC	Avg. Life Range
Deal with 10% NAS				
10-year sequential	13.7	9.4	5.0	8.7
NAS Bond	12.2	11.0	9.4	2.8
Deal with 20% NAS				
10-year sequential	17.5	9.4	4.2	13.3
NAS Bond	12.2	11.0	7.6	4.6

* PPC refers to the prospectus prepayment speed assumption. For example, 100 PPC is the assumed prepayment vector.

NAS Percent of Deal

Another important NAS feature is the size of the NAS relative to the overall deal size. That is, NAS bonds are referred to as 10% NAS bonds, 20% NAS bonds, and so forth. This percentage represents the NAS tranche size as a percentage of the overall deal. For example, assume two NAS bonds are created, one a 10% NAS and the other a 20% NAS. (See Exhibit 15.13.) Additionally, assume both structures have 6% subordination below the NAS bonds. Comparing the structure of the two deals, the larger NAS bond (i.e., 20% NAS) has a lower senior bonds/NAS bond ratio which results in fewer bonds to support or buffer the cash flow variability of the NAS. This means that a smaller NAS, with its lower average life variability, is a better NAS bond.

NAS Bond Profile

Because of its schedule, the NAS bond will have a more stable average life profile than a comparable duration sequential-pay bond from the same deal. Exhibit 15.14 shows the average life profile for two Alternative A deals, one with 10% NAS and one with 20% NAS. As shown previously, the lower the percentage NAS within the deal, the more stable the average life profile of all bonds within the deal. Additionally, NAS bonds have significantly lower cash flow variability than comparable duration sequential-pay bonds. This lower variation in cash flow average lives results in lower option costs on the NAS bonds.

Comparing Super-NAS Bonds with NAS Bonds

As mentioned earlier, super-NAS bonds are a shorter, more stable version of the standard NAS bond. Super NAS bonds also have a tighter principal payment window, since the tail NAS cash flows are placed into the senior bonds. Exhibit 15.15 compares the average life variability and principal windows of a 20% NAS bond with a similar sized super-NAS Alternative A collateralized bond.

The first factor to notice is that the super-NAS has much lower average life dispersion (or range), between 75 PPC and 150 PPC, than does the NAS bond. Additionally, the base case principal window is much narrower (August 2003–September 2012) than the traditional NAS bond (August 2003–June 2028).

At slower prepayment speeds (i.e., 75 PPC), the super-NAS bond extends less than the traditional NAS bond. This is due to the fact that the bond maintains its schedule while the tail cash flow was structured into other senior bonds. This is apparent in the principal window as the final payment date extends only from September 2012 to June 2013 when prepayments slow from 100 PPC to 75 PPC.

Similarly, the super-NAS bond is subject to less contraction risk since it is a shorter average life bond in the base case. It is also apparent from Exhibit 15.14 that the average lives of both bonds at 150 PPC is 7.6 years. Additionally, note that the principal payment window under both bond structures is identical (August 2003–June 2028). The payment window on the super-NAS bond shifts out due to the fact that at these fast prepayment speeds, all of the senior bonds will be paid down prior to the end of the 10-year NAS bond shifting interest schedule. In this scenario, the super-NAS bond becomes the only AAA or senior bond remaining in the deal and must therefore assume the principal window of the underlying collateral.

EXHIBIT 15.15 Super-NAS versus NAS

Description	75 PPC	100 PPC	150 PPC	Avg. Life Range
Deal with 20% NAS				
NAS – Avg. Life	12.2	11.0	7.6	4.6
Window	8/03–6/28	8/03–6/28	8/03–6/28	
Super-NAS – Avg. Life	9.4	8.7	7.7	1.8
Window	8/03–6/13	8/03–9/12	8/03–6/28	

EXHIBIT 15.16 Super-NAS at Faster Prepay Speeds

Description	100 PPC	125 PPC	150 PPC	250 PPC
Deal with 20% NAS				
NAS – Avg. Life	11.0	9.4	7.6	4.1
Window	8/03–6/28	8/03–6/28	8/03–6/28	7/01–11/04
Super-NAS – Avg. Life	8.7	9.1	7.6	4.1
Window	8/03–9/12	8/03–1/20	8/03–6/28	7/01–11/04

As shown in Exhibit 15.16, at fast prepayment speeds, the average lives and principal windows of both the NAS and super-NAS are the same. However, at moderately faster speeds, such as at 125 PPC, the super-NAS actually extends due to the NAS tail (which was combined with the other senior bonds) providing added call protection to the super-NAS. At faster speeds, this tail is paid down and the super-NAS and NAS bonds assume the same profile.

REAL ESTATE-BACKED ASSET-BACKED SECURITIES

In this section we discuss mortgage-related products that are classified in the marketplace as asset-backed securities. The products include bonds backed by home equity loans, 125 loans, and manufactured housing loans.

Closed-End Home Equity Loan-Backed Securities

A *home equity loan* (HEL) is a loan backed by residential property. At one time, the loan was typically a second lien on property that was already pledged to secure a first lien. In some cases, the lien was a third lien. However, the character of a home equity loan has changed. Today, a home equity loan is often a first lien on property where the borrower has either an impaired credit history and/or the payment-to-income ratio is too high for the loan to qualify as a conforming loan for securitization by Ginnie Mae, Fannie Mae, or Freddie Mac. Typically, the borrower used a home equity loan to consolidate consumer debt using the current home as collateral rather than to obtain funds to purchase a new home.

Home equity loans can be either closed-end or open-end. Our focus is on securities backed by closed-end HELs. A closed-end HEL is structured the same way as a fully amortizing residential mortgage loan. That is, it has a fixed maturity and the payments are structured to fully amortize the loan by the maturity date. There are both fixed-rate and variable-rate closed-end HELs. Typically, variable-rate loans have a reference rate of 6-month LIBOR and have periodic caps and lifetime caps. The cash flow of a pool of closed-end HELs is comprised of interest, regularly scheduled principal payments, and prepayments, just as with mortgage-backed securities. We will discuss open-end HELs later.

Payment Structure

As with nonagency mortgage-backed securities discussed earlier, there are passthrough and paythrough home equity loan-backed structures. Typically, home equity loan-backed securities are securitized by both closed-end fixed-rate and adjustable-rate (or variable-rate) HELs. The securities backed by the latter are called *HEL floaters* and most are backed by non-prime HELs. The reference rate of the underlying loans typically is 6-month LIBOR. The cash flow of these loans is affected by periodic and lifetime caps on the loan rate. To increase the attractiveness of home equity loan-backed securities to investors, the securities typically have been created in which the reference rate is 1-month LIBOR. Because of (1) the mismatch between the reference rate on the underlying loans and that of the HEL floater and (2) the periodic and life caps of the underlying loans, there is a cap on the coupon rate for the HEL floater. Unlike a typical floater, which has a cap that is fixed throughout the security's life, the effective periodic and lifetime cap of a HEL floater is variable. The effective cap, referred to as the *available funds cap* or *net funds cap*, will depend on the amount of funds generated by the net coupon on the principal, less any fees.

Let's look at one issue, Advanta Mortgage Loan Trust 1995-2 issued in June 1995. At the offering, this issue had approximately $122 million closed-end HELs. There were 1,192 HELs—727 fixed-rate loans and 465 variable-rate loans. There were five classes (A-1, A-2, A-3, A-4, and A-5) and a residual. The five classes are summarized below:

Class	Par amount ($)	Passthrough coupon rate (%)
A-1	9,229,000	7.30
A-2	30,330,000	6.60
A-3	16,455,000	6.85
A-4	9,081,000	floating rate
A-5	56,917,000	floating rate

The collateral is divided into group I and group II. The 727 fixed-rate loans are included in group I and support Classes A-1, A-2, A-3, and A-4. The 465 variable-rate loans are in group II and support Classes A-5-I and A-5-II certificates. All classes receive monthly principal and interest (based on the passthrough coupon rate).

EXHIBIT 15.17   HEL ABS Structuring

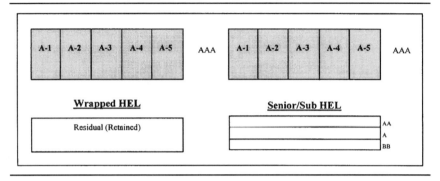

The initial investors in the A-5 floating-rate certificates were given a choice between two sub-classes that offered different floating rates. Sub class A-5-I has a passthrough coupon rate equal to the lesser of (1) 12% or (2) 1-month LIBOR plus 32 basis points with a cap of 12%. Sub-class A-5-II has a passthrough coupon rate equal to the lesser of (1) the interest rate for sub-class A-5-I or (2) the group II available funds cap. The available funds cap is the maximum rate payable on the outstanding Class A-5 certificates principal balance based on the interest due on the variable-rate loans net of fees and minus 50 basis points.

The Class A-4 certificate also has a floating rate. The rate is 7.4% subject to the net funds cap for group I. This is the rate that is paid until the outstanding aggregate loan balances in the trust have declined to 10% or less. At that time, Class A-4 will accrue interest on a payment date that depends on the average net loan rate minus 50 basis points and the net funds cap rate for group I.

Credit Enhancement

All forms of credit enhancement described for nonagency MBS have been used for home equity loan-backed securities. HEL issuers typically have two alternatives when it comes to structuring an ABS transaction. The issuer can pay a premium to an insurer and have the bonds "wrapped" with a AAA guarantee, or try to sell a senior/subordinated deal where the major form of credit protection is internal credit enhancement. Exhibit 15.17 shows a diagram of these alternatives. The senior/subordinate structure was discussed earlier in this chapter. Here we will look at the wrapped deals.

If the issuer tries to have his deal wrapped, the insurer will charge the issuer a premium (which is based on the credit quality of the underlying collateral) in order to obtain the insurer's guarantee of the timely payment of interest and the ultimate payment of principal on all wrapped bonds.

Wrap insurers look at their business like catastrophe insurance; that is, they only expect a minute probability of having to pay a claim. This is the expectation for three reasons. First, HEL ABS transactions are structured so that the internal credit enhancement (i.e., the residual B-pieces, overcollateralization, and reserve accounts) would achieve an investment grade rating on a stand-alone basis. This is called a "shadow rating." Second, the deal's servicer will perform the insurer's role of advancing interest and principal due but not collected. Additionally, the servicer will pay compensating interest on prepayment interest rate shortfalls. Finally, if the deal does start to underperform, "triggers" will protect the insurer by allowing excess spread to be diverted back into the deal.

There are three additional advantages of investing in wrap deals versus senior/subordinated structures—liquidity, credit protection, and expertise. Wrap deals have the benefit of added liquidity since investors look first to the credit of the insurer rather than to the characteristics of the pool. This factor leads to much more liquidity and ability to trade in the underlying bonds. As mentioned previously, the insurer will guarantee the timely payment of interest and the ultimate full payment of principal. Additionally, the obligation is unconditional and irrevocable. This guaranty also covers instances of fraud on the part of the issuer, originator, and/or servicer. These added protections should be of great comfort to the investor and mitigate headline or pool risk. Additionally, since the pool has an investment grade shadow rating, if the AAA insurer is ever downgraded, internal credit enhancement should be adequate to maintain an investment grade rating. Finally, wrap providers bring an added layer of expertise to a transaction. That is, they perform pre-closing due diligence and review individual loan files. Additionally, the insurer monitors collateral performance and oversees the activities of the servicer. This added protection should give the investor comfort in wrapped HEL transactions.

Open-End Home Equity Loan-Backed Securities

With an open-end HEL the homeowner is given a credit line and can write checks or use a credit card for up to the amount of the credit line. The amount of the credit line depends on the amount of equity the borrower has in the property. There is a revolving period over which the homeowner can borrow funds against the line of credit. At the end of the term of the loan, the homeowner either pays off the amount borrowed in one payment or the outstanding balance is amortized. It has been estimated that in the 1990s, HELOCs have been 20% to 25% of all home equity originations. However, only 7% of HELOCs have been securitized.

The revolving period for a HELOC is the period where the borrower can take down all or part of the line of credit. The revolving period can run from 10 to 15 years. At the end of the revolving period, the HELOC can specify either a balloon payment or an amortization schedule (of up to 10 years). Almost all HELOCs are floating-rate loans. The interest rate paid by about 75% of HELOC borrowers is reset monthly to the prime rate (as reported in the *Wall Street Journal*) plus a spread.

The bonds created in HELOC deals are floating-rate tranches. While the underlying loans are priced based on a spread over the prime rate as reported in the *Wall Street Journal*, the securities created are based on a spread over 1-month LIBOR.

Because HELOCs are for revolving lines, the deal structures are quite different for HELOCs and closed-end HELs. As with other ABS involving revolving credit lines such as credit card deals, there is a revolving period, an amortization period, and a rapid amortization period.

Securities Backed by 125 Loans

One of the newer segments of the mortgage market is low/no equity second mortgages. These loans have high loan-to-value (LTV) ratios which generally range between 95% to 125% (hence the name "125 LTV loans"). The origination process involved in these loans focuses on credit rather than property value. That is, 125 LTV lenders target prime borrowers or borrowers who have strong credit histories (i.e., prime or A-borrowers). The well-publicized increase in consumer debt, as well as the attractive economics of the debt consolidation loan, are the basis of the rapid growth of the 125 LTV market. The economics of the debt consolidation loan are very attractive to the high quality borrower.

The "three Cs" of traditional underwriting—credit reputation, capacity, and collateral—are modified in formulating 125 LTV loan guidelines. The primary difference in focus on 125 LTV loans is that the third "C" (collateral) is often missing in the underwriting process. Despite this fact, 125 LTV lenders do file a lien against the borrower's home. The process of securing the loan with a lien creates for most borrowers a sense of obligation. Thus, in the underwriting process, borrower credit is of utmost importance and rates are assigned assuming little or no value can be obtained by foreclosing on the property. 125 LTV lenders seek to attract a borrower with a good credit history with FICO scores in the high 680s.

The most common structure for 125 LTV loan transactions is the senior/subordinated structure. The basic structure of the deal includes a series of AAA-rated sequential-pay bonds. These bonds achieve their AAA rating by virtue of the subordinated tranches M-1 through B-2 (rated AA to BB). In a typical 125 LTV transaction, credit support comes from the following three sources: (1) excess spread, (2) overcollateralization, and (3) subordination.

Typically, prepayment assumptions are considerably slower than other types of mortgage structures, such as home equity loans, nonagency jumbo loans, and agency MBS. The reasons for these slow prepayment assumptions are threefold. First, the typical 125 LTV borrower has a negative equity situation in his or her primary asset (the house). Therefore, the borrower would be ineligible to refinance for most home loan programs. Second, the 125 LTV borrower has recently paid substantial upfront costs (i.e., 5 to 8 points) in order to get into the loan. Therefore, the economics of a rate refinancing would have to be significant given the average balance of the loan (average loan size of $30,000) to justify the refinancing. Third, most new 125 LTV loans contain prepayment penalties which make rate refinancing most uneconomical.

Additionally, prepayments on 125 LTV deals impact the structure differently than on nonagency mortgage deals. That is, like on nonagency deals, subordinated tranches are locked out from prepayments. However unlike nonagency deals, fast prepayments—particularly when they occur early in the deal's life (i.e., while the reserve fund is being built)—can weaken the overall credit structure of the deal. That is, excess spread (which is the primary credit protection on 125 LTV deals) is really like an IO. Therefore, prepayments lessen the scope of the excess spread protection by shrinking the amount of cash available to protect against losses. On the other hand, deleveraging occurs at the subordinated tranche level when prepayments occur. This is the case since the senior bonds must absorb all prepayments for a minimum of 36 months, which causes the subordinated bonds to grow as a percentage of the overall deal.

Manufactured Housing-Backed Securities

Manufactured housing means single-family detached homes constructed off-site and transported to a plot of land or to a manufactured housing community (park). There are two types of manufactured housing (MH) units: (1) single-section (also known as "single-wides") and (2) multisections. Single-wide units, which are transported to their site in one piece, average 1,065 square feet. Multisection units are assembled at the site after being transported in pieces, and average 1,525 square feet.

The typical manufactured housing loan is a 15- to 20-year fully amortizing retail installment loan. Therefore, as with residential mortgage loans and HELs, the cash flow of a pool of MH loans consists of net interest, regularly scheduled principal, and prepayments. Single-section units are usually financed over 15-year terms at rates between 300 to 350 basis points above conventional 30-year rates. Multisection units are usually financed over 20-year terms at rates between 250 to 300 basis points over conventional 30-year rates.

Manufactured housing has proven to be a market which is largely interest rate insensitive. We believe that this is the case for the following reasons. First, MH loans have small balances resulting in minimal saving from refinancings. Even a decline of 200 basis points for a typical $35,000 MH loan would result in only a $44 monthly savings. Second, manufactured housing units, like cars, are subject to depreciation. In the early years of a loan's life, depreciation exceeds amortization leaving the borrower with little equity which is needed to refinance. Third, few refinancing options are currently available for used manufactured housing units. Finally, MH borrowers may not qualify for alternative financings because of their limited financial resources.

OTHER PRODUCTS BACKED BY REAL ESTATE MORTGAGES

We conclude this chapter with two financial products backed by real estate mortgages—both residential and commercial.[4] The two products are real estate investment trusts and collateralized debt obligations.

Real Estate Investment Trusts

The major activity of a real estate investment trust (REIT) is generating income from buying, operating, and selling residential and commercial real estate. As with mutual funds, REITs are passthrough entities under the Internal Revenue Code and therefore free from taxation at the corporate level if certain provisions are satisfied. Specifically, to maintain a tax-free status, a REIT must (1) pay dividends equaling at least 90% of its taxable income and (2) more than 75% of total investment assets must be in real estate assets.

REITs are classified into the following three categories: mortgage REITs, equity REITs, and hybrid REITs. Mortgage REITs lend funds to owners of real estate (residential and commercial), as well as purchasing mortgages in the secondary market and mortgage-backed securities. The primary source of revenue is interest on the loans and MBS. The key to understanding mortgage REITs is understanding the types of mortgage obligations in which they invest and restrictions (covenants) on management activities.

---

[4] Commercial mortgage-backed securities are discussed in Chapter 16.

The primary source of revenue for an equity REIT is rents derived from the ownership and management of real estate property. Of the three categories of REITs, equity REITs are the dominant form, representing more than 90% of all REITs. Hybrid REITs pursue investment strategies of equity REITs and mortgage REITs. That is, they invest in both properties and mortgages.

Collateralized Debt Obligations

A collateralized debt obligation is an asset-backed security with collateral that is a diversified pool of one or more bonds. The first CDOs issued were backed by high-yield corporate bonds. Today, there are CDOs backed by residential and commercial mortgage-backed securities, particularly subordinated tranches. These CDOs are referred to as ABS/MBS CDOs. A CDO issues securities to raise funds to purchase the collateral. The debt tranches are rated by the rating agencies. CDOs are discussed in more detail in Chapter 20.

CHAPTER 16

Commercial Mortgage-Backed Securities

Joseph F. DeMichele
Vice President
Delaware Investments

William J. Adams, CFA
Vice President
Massachusetts Financial Services

Duane C. Hewlett
Vice President
Delaware Investments

Commercial mortgage-backed securities (CMBS) are collateralized by loans on income-producing properties. The CMBS market has grown dramatically from its modest beginnings in the mid-1980s. Issuance, liquidity, and the number of investors participating in the CMBS market have all increased substantially. This chapter gives a brief overview of the history and composition of the CMBS market. It also provides an introduction to the risks involving structure, optionality, and credit quality of CMBS that investors must be aware of when allocating assets to this market sector.

HISTORY

During the 1980s, a strong economy, the deregulation of the financial services industry, and preferential tax treatment led to an explosion in the level of capital flows into the commercial real estate markets. Total commercial debt outstanding grew from over $400 billion in 1982 to approximately $1 trillion by 1990. Inevitably, extreme overbuilding caused the bubble to burst, and the boom of the 1980s was followed by a severe recession in the commercial property markets during the early 1990s. From 1990 to 1993, returns on income-producing properties fell by 28% as reported in the NCREIF Property Index.[1]

During the 1980s, the primary sources of commercial real estate funding were tax shelter syndicates, savings institutions, commercial banks, and life insurance companies. The Tax Reform Act of 1986 withdrew many real estate tax benefits and eliminated the tax shelter syndicates as a major source of funds. The severe devaluation of commercial property values in the early 1990s resulted in sizable losses among thrifts, banks, and insurance companies and led to a major retrenchment of lending activity by these traditional sources of commercial real estate funds. Two significant developments were born of this commercial real estate cycle downturn, one major and one minor, which precipitated the securitization of commercial loans.

The biggest contributing factor leading to the maturation of the CMBS market was the creation of the Resolution Trust Corporation (RTC). The RTC was created by Congress to facilitate the bailout of the ailing thrift industry. The mandate handed down from Congress was for the RTC to liquidate assets it acquired from insolvent thrifts as quickly and efficiently as possible. A large portion of the assets inherited by the RTC from the thrifts it acquired consisted of commercial mortgage loans. The RTC turned to the CMBS market to monetize its "investment." Between 1991 and 1993 it issued nearly $15 billion multifamily and mixed property CMBS. The large number of loans in each deal led to a high level of diversification much like what was found in the widely-accepted residential MBS market. The presence of an over-abundant level of credit protection through subordination, often in the form of cash, made the securities very attractive to investors.

The other occurrence, albeit minor, was the introduction of stricter risk-based capital charges for insurance companies at year-end 1993. These guidelines required insurance companies to hold larger capital reserves for whole-loan commercial mortgages than for securitized commercial mortgages, thus giving insurance companies the incentive to securitize their commercial mortgage holdings.

---

[1] Jonathan Adams, "CMBS Structures and Relative Value Analysis," Chapter 13 in Anand K. Bhattacharya and Frank J. Fabozzi (eds.), *Asset-Backed Securities* (New Hope, PA: Frank J. Fabozzi Associates, 1996).

Issuance has continued to expand since1993, from $17.2 billion to $71.9 billion as of year-end 2001, although the contribution from the RTC has fallen dramatically.[2] As the RTC finished its job of liquidating insolvent thrifts, other issuers opportunistically stepped in to continue the growth of the CMBS market.

Witnessing the success of the RTC's foray into the CMBS market, many insurance companies, pension funds, and commercial banks began to use the CMBS market as a means of restructuring their balance sheets. Institutions began to utilize the CMBS market as a means of liquidity for disposing of unwanted assets, to receive better regulatory treatment for holding securities in lieu of whole loans, or even simply to raise capital for underwriting more loans. As commercial real estate valuations rebounded through the latter half of the 1990s, these traditional lenders stepped up their commercial lending programs and became a consistent source of issuance in the CMBS market.

The emergence of the commercial mortgage conduits further fueled the expansion of CMBS issuance. Almost every major investment bank established a conduit arrangement with a mortgage banker to originate commercial loans for the specific purpose of securitization. The number of commercial mortgage conduits providing real estate funding increased from less than five at the start of 1993 to over 30 at the start of 1995.[3] Conduit issuance has steadily grown as a percentage of total CMBS issuance. Conduit issuance now accounts for roughly 60% of the domestic CMBS market. Today, the market capitalization of the CMBS market exceeds $300 billion. Roughly 20% of all commercial mortgage loans are securitized into CMBS.

TYPES OF CMBS IN TODAY'S MARKET

Agency

All three of the government's housing-related agencies (Ginnie Mae, Fannie Mae, and Freddie Mac) issue forms of CMBS. Because the mission of each of these agencies is to provide funding for residential housing, they have been involved in the issuance of multifamily housing loan securitizations. Ginnie Mae also issues securities backed by loans on nursing home projects and healthcare facilities. All agencies have issued these types of securities since 1985.

---

[2] Morgan Stanley and *Commercial Mortgage Aler* t, Hoboken, N.J.

[3] John Mulligan and Diane Parsley, *Commercial Mortgage-Backed Securities A Market Update* (New York: Donaldson, Lufkin, and Jenrette Securities Corp., February, 1995).

Ginnie Mae issues passthrough securities backed by loans on commercial projects insured by the Federal Housing Authority (FHA). The FHA has established numerous multifamily insurance programs since its inception. Each project pool will vary depending on the underlying FHA insurance program. Specific characteristics such as project type, loan limit, prepayment features, or the presence of rent subsidies, will affect the performance of a particular pool.

Ginnie Mae issues project pools as permanent loan certificates (PLCs) as well as construction loan certificates (CLCs). PLCs are generally backed by 35-year fully amortizing loans with 10 years of call protection. GNMA guarantees full and timely payment of all principal and interest. Project loans also exist with FHA guarantees. These pools carry FHA's implicit government guarantee that only protects 99% of the principal. Data on the underlying loans are much harder to find and the certificates are physical. These attributes cause FHA project pools to be much less liquid than Ginnie Mae project pools.

Like Ginnie Mae, Fannie Mae is active in the multifamily market. Fannie Mae issues CMBS through various programs. The most popular Fannie Mae securities, are issued under the Delegated Underwriting and Servicing (DUS) Program. Specific underwriting guidelines are set by Fannie Mae for designated eligible lenders to originate loans. The loans are fixed rate-mortgages with 5- to 18-year balloon maturities and amortizing terms of 25 to 30 years. These loans are sold to Fannie Mae, which then issues securities. Fannie Mae DUS are differentiated by credit tiering, with each security assigned a rating from one to four. Each DUS is placed in a tier based on its loan-to-value ratio and minimum debt coverage ratio, with tier four being the highest quality. DUSs have stringent call provisions, which have led Fannie Mae to market these securities as substitutes for its bullet-pay agency debentures.

Freddie Mac was the dominant player of the three agencies before 1990. The commercial real estate recession led to a decrease in issuance from Freddie Mac. Since 1993, Freddie Mac has issued securities through its Program Plus which is very similar to the Fannie Mae DUS program.

Private Label

The majority of CMBS issued today are nonagency or private label securities. Some are collateralized by pools of seasoned commercial loans. The RTC deals were examples of CMBS backed by seasoned collateral. Newly-issued deals backed by seasoned collateral are generally the result of balance sheet restructuring by banks or insurance companies. These securitizations provide challenges for investors since many seasoned pools are characterized by a wide range of coupons and loan types and by widely varying prepayment protection.

Today, most private label CMBS are backed by newly originated loans. These CMBS fall into two major categories: those backed by loans made to a single borrower, and those backed by loans made to multiple borrowers. Single borrower deals can involve one property or a group. Usually, they are backed by large properties such as office buildings or regional malls. Although the transactions obviously lack diversity, information is generally more current and comprehensive. Generally, investors demand more stringent underwriting on single property deals to offset the increased risk brought on by the lower level of diversity. Insurance companies are the most common buyer, since many have the necessary real estate lending expertise to evaluate these deals. The attractiveness of the lower reserving requirement for CMBS over commercial whole loans also entices insurance companies.

Single borrower deals are also created with a variety of properties. Properties are run by a single management company. Real Estate Investment Trusts (REITs) sometimes issue this type of CMBS. Typically all the properties backing a particular deal are *cross-collateralized* and *cross-defaulted*. Should one property in the pool experience an impediment to cash flow, the cash generated from the other properties is used to support it. Should one property experience a default, all the remaining properties are defaulted. This is a strong incentive against defaulting, preventing the borrower from walking away from lower quality properties. In essence, this feature allows the cash flow from stronger properties to support weaker ones. Another important characteristic of single borrower pools is the presence of release provisions. A *release provision* requires a borrower to prepay a percentage of the remaining balance of the underlying loans if it wishes to prepay one of the loans and remove the property from the pool. Thus the bondholders are protected from the borrower being able to remove the strongest properties from the pool.

The most common type of private label CMBS is backed by loans underwritten by more than one unrelated borrower on various property types. Conduit deals are the most prevalent example of multiple borrower deals in today's market.

Because the loans are underwritten with the intent of securitization, conduit deals possess certain characteristics that are favorable to investors. Loan types tend to be more homogeneous, and call protection is strong. They also have more uniform underwriting standards, and information on credit statistics is generally readily available.

Another kind of CMBS deal is one backed by leases on a property. These *triple-net lease* or *credit tenant loan deals* are collateralized by lease agreements between the property owner and a tenant. As long as the lease cannot be terminated, the CMBS created have the same credit as any debt obligation of the underlying tenant. Additionally the bonds are secured by the property. The majority of these securities have been collateralized by mortgages on retail stores with lessees, such as Wal-Mart, that are rated by one of the nationally recognized rating organizations. Recently, mortgages on large office buildings with publicly rated tenants such as Merrill Lynch and Chubb have also been securitized.

STRUCTURE OF CMBS

Senior/Subordinate Structure

The majority of private label CMBS created today utilize a *senior/subordinate structure*, whereby the cash flow generated by the pool of underlying commercial mortgages is used to create distinct classes of securities. Monthly cash flow is first used to pay the class with the highest priority, the senior classes. After interest and scheduled principal is paid to the senior classes, the remaining classes are paid in order of stated priority. Should cash flow collected from the pool be insufficient to pay off the bonds designated as senior, the loss will be incurred first by the class with the lowest priority.

In a senior/subordinate structure the lower priority classes provide credit enhancement for the senior securities. The amount of subordination is determined in conjunction with the rating agencies in order to obtain the desired rating on the senior securities. Exhibit 16.1 shows an example of a hypothetical CMBS structure with subordination levels typical in the market today. Note that the majority of securities created are senior classes. Subordination levels are set to attain a AAA credit rating on the senior class. This is the highest rating given by the rating agencies, and signifies bonds deemed to have minimal credit risk. Issuers set subordination levels such that the senior classes will receive this rating, thus being more attractive to investors. Rating agencies determine the appropriate amount of credit enhancement based on an analysis of the credit quality of the pool of commercial loans. This will be discussed in more detail later in the chapter.

In industry jargon, those non-senior securities receiving investment grade ratings are known as *mezzanine bonds*. Those rated non-investment grade are known as subordinate or "B" pieces. The class with the lowest payment priority is called the *first loss piece*. Any shortfall of cash flow on the commercial loan pool would affect this class first, thus putting it at the highest risk of a loss of principal. The risk profile of the other classes changes inversely to the priority of payment schedule.

EXHIBIT 16.1 Hypothetical CMBS Structure

Class	Rating	Size ($MM)	Description	Credit Support (%)	WAL (Years)	Principal Window
A1	AAA	343.00	Senior	32.55	7.00	1/97–7/05
B1	AA	30.60	Mezzanine	26.50	9.70	7/05–8/06
B2	A	30.60	Mezzanine	20.50	9.80	8/06–9/06
B3	BBB	25.50	Mezzanine	15.50	9.90	9/06–10/06
B4	BBB-	12.70	Mezzanine	13.00	9.90	10/06–10/06
B5	BB	30.60	Subordinate	7.00	10.00	10/06–11/06
C	B	17.80	Subordinate	3.50	10.00	11/06–11/06
D	NR	17.77	First Loss	NA	13.70	11/06–11/16
IO	AAA		IO			

A unique feature of the senior/subordinate structure is the fact that credit enhancement can grow over time. Since principal is paid to the senior classes first, if no losses occur these classes will pay down faster than the mezzanine or subordinate pieces. This has the effect of increasing the amount of non-senior classes as a percentage of the entire deal and thus providing more enhancement to the remaining senior classes.

Additional forms of credit enhancement are available. For some deals, such as the RTC originated transactions, a cash account, known as a *reserve fund*, will be maintained to absorb losses and protect investors. *Overcollateralizing* is another form of credit enhancement. It refers to the excess of the aggregate balance of the pool of commercial loans over the aggregate balance of the bond classes created. Like a reserve fund, losses would be absorbed by the amount of excess collateral before affecting any of the bond classes.

Paydown Structures

The most common principal paydown method used in CMBS is the *sequential-pay method*. All principal paydowns, both scheduled and prepaid, are allocated entirely to the most senior class outstanding. Occasionally, a variant of the sequential-pay structure is used. The pool of loans may be segregated into loan groups with each loan group collateralizing a specific set of bond classes. In either paydown structure, principal payments can be designated further to create different bonds within the same class. In Exhibit 16.2, we have altered slightly our hypothetical CMBS to illustrate this technique. The senior class has been further tranched to create two bonds, A1 and A2. Principal is allocated to A1 before A2, thus creating two senior bonds with different average lives.

EXHIBIT 16.2 Hypothetical CMBS Structure with Sequential Pay

Class	Rating	Size	Description ($MM)	Credit Support (%)	WAL (Years)	Principal Window
A1	AAA	130.00	Senior	32.55	5.70	1/97–7/05
A2	AAA	213.00	Senior	32.55	9.40	7/05–7/06
B1	AA	30.60	Mezzanine	26.50	9.70	7/06–8/06
B2	A	30.60	Mezzanine	20.50	9.80	8/06–9/06
B3	BBB	35.50	Mezzanine	15.50	9.90	9/06–10/06
B4	BBB-	12.70	Mezzanine	13.00	9.90	10/06–10/06
B5	BB	30.60	Subordinate	7.00	10.00	10/06–11/06
C	B	17.80	Subordinate	3.50	10.00	11/06–11/06
D	NR	17.77	First Loss	NA	13.70	11/06–11/06
IO	AAA		IO			

Interest Payments

In a CMBS structure, all interest payments generated by the underlying commercial loans can be used to pay either interest or principal payments on the created securities. One alternative is to have all the interest received used to pay interest on the bonds. The principal weighted-average coupon on the bonds can be set to equal the principal weighted-average coupon on the pool of loans. In this case, as different loans with different coupons in the pool pay down, the principal weighted-average coupon on the pool will change. In turn, the amount of cash flow available to pay interest on the bonds will vary. Thus, the coupons on the bonds will be variable. CMBS classes from this structure are said to have *WAC coupons*.

In order to create fixed coupon bonds, the most common method used in CMBS structures is to set the highest coupon on the securities lower than the lowest coupon of the underlying loans. This will ensure that there will be a sufficient amount of interest payments generated by the pool to make all interest payments on the securities. This will lead to a higher level of interest cash flow from the pool of loans than is required to pay interest on the bonds. This extra cash flow is known as *excess interest*.

In some cases excess interest is used to pay down principal on the most senior bonds outstanding. Under this type of structure, the more senior classes will amortize at a rate faster than the junior classes, thus leading to overcollateralization and providing additional credit enhancement for the deal.

More frequently, the excess interest is used to form an *interest-only* or *IO class*. The IO class receives no principal. Its yield is determined solely by the interest cash flow generated by the pool of loans. If the principal balance of a loan is paid prior to its maturity, the yield of the IO will fall. Should a principal payment extend beyond maturity for a loan, the yield will rise. The majority of prepayments in CMBS are generated by defaulted loans and the subsequent recovery on that loan. For this reason the yield on IO securities is very much dependent on the credit quality of the underlying pool of loans.

Underlying Mortgage Type

There are several mortgage loan types that back CMBS deals. The most common are fully amortizing loans, amortizing balloon loans, and interest-only balloons. All else being equal, the faster the amortization of the loan, the faster equity is built up in the property, and the less risk of default. Fully amortizing loans provide the best credit profile. Balloon mortgages also introduce the notion of extension risk, which will be discussed later.

Commercial mortgage loans may have fixed or variable interest rates. If variable rate loans are uncapped and rates rise substantially, the income generated by the property may not be enough to service the debt. Also, if variable rate mortgages are used to structure CMBS with fixed rate classes, basis risk will exist, and interest on the loans may not cover coupon payments on the bonds.

OPTIONALITY

Prepayment Risk

As with most mortgage-backed securities, CMBS have inherent prepayment risk. The underlying commercial mortgages may be prepaid by the borrower. Prepayments on CMBS will affect the yield and average lives of the bonds issued, particularly interest-only securities. Fortunately for investors, most commercial mortgages have explicit provisions that preclude borrowers from prepaying.

The most onerous to a borrower is the *prepayment lock-out*. Written into the loan agreement, a lock-out is a provision preventing any prepayments for a set time period. The time may vary, but generally will range from three to five years.

Another form of prepayment protection in CMBS structures is called *yield maintenance*. The yield maintenance provision is designed to create an incentive for the borrower *not* to prepay. If the borrower chooses to prepay, the lender must be compensated for any lost yield. If market interest rates are lower than when the loan was originated, the borrower must reimburse the lender for any lost interest income. The yield maintenance penalty would be equal to the income that would have been earned by the lender less what would now be earned by reinvesting the prepaid proceeds at the risk-free Treasury rate.

A third form of prepayment protection is the prepayment penalty in the case of a prepaid loan. This will typically take the form of a fixed percentage of the remaining principal balance of the loan. The most common penalty in today's market is the "5-4-3-2-1" penalty. During the first year of the penalty period, the prepayment penalty would be equal to 5% of the unpaid principal balance of the loan. In year two, the penalty would decline to 4%, and so on.

Today, most commercial mortgages backing CMBS possess some combination of these three prepayment provisions. However, many loan agreements allow for prepayment penalties to decrease over time with the loans becoming freely prepayable during the last six to nine months of the life of each loan.

During the time that these prepayment provisions are in place, the predominant cause of prepayments will be defaults. After these provisions have expired, the prevailing interest rate environment will become a determinant of prepayments as in the residential mortgage market. Other factors, such as retained equity, will affect the level of prepayments. If capital improvements are needed and cheaper financing cannot be found, the owner will most likely prepay the loan in order to refinance. If the property has appreciated sufficiently in value or net operating income has grown enough to cover additional leverage, the owner will most likely do an equity take-out refinancing.

Unfortunately, the amount of data available on prepayments in the CMBS market pales in comparison to the residential mortgage market. Data available are mostly from the RTC deals. Underwriting standards as well as the current real estate market environment are much different today and bring the validity of comparisons on prepayments into question. Additionally, the lack of a dominant, measurable variable, such as interest rates, makes option analysis much more difficult than with residential mortgage-backed securities. Fortunately, the call protection provided by the various prepayment provisions in CMBS helps to significantly offset these factors.

Extension Risk

The majority of CMBS issued today are collateralized by balloon mortgages. In order to meet the balloon principal payment the borrower will have to either sell the property or refinance the loan. Should neither be possible, the servicer usually has the option to extend the loan beyond the balloon date. The extension option varies but typically cannot exceed three years. Rating agencies generally require the stated final maturity of the bond to be four or five years beyond the maturity of the underlying loans. This would allow time for foreclosure and workout should refinancing be unavailable.

Factors that affect extension risk are loan-to-value (LTV) and the interest rate environment at the balloon date. Should property values fall, LTV will rise, and refinancing will be more difficult, thus increasing extension risk. Likewise, if interest rates are high enough such that the income produced by the property does not generate an acceptable debt service ratio, refinancing may not be obtainable.

EVALUATING CREDIT QUALITY IN COMMERCIAL MORTGAGE-BACKED SECURITIES

As the commercial mortgage-backed securities market continues to grow in both dollar amount and investor acceptance, a move toward an acceptance of standardization appears evident. This may prove to be an alarming trend if investors in these securities are lowering credit standards or reducing their level of analysis in exchange for yield and favorable regulatory treatment. Prudent investors must remember that these securities require a consistent level of credit and cash flow analyses, well beyond that of standardized structured collateral. The best analysis for the securities must combine elements of both structured finance and fundamental collateral and credit analyses. Therefore, in this section, we attempt to build a basic, analytical framework for CMBS transactions, which starts with the previously discussed development and appreciation of the forces which created this market. Next, the inherent volatility and cash flow variability of the underlying commercial mortgages are described. Finally, a means of dealing with the unique characteristics of the collateral, including underwriting standards and structural features, is presented. The point of this section is to focus investor attention on relative value and issues affecting the quality of various CMBS transactions in the market.

Earlier, we discussed the development of liquidity in the CMBS market from direct real estate lending to securitization. Readily available capital for the asset class led to excessive development which culminated in the early 1990s real estate recession. The RTC was created to monetize problem commercial real estate. It did so through structured securities, thereby broadening the investor base and creating many of the structural and legal features of the market today. During this time, a black cloud formed over commercial real estate as an investment. Traditional real estate investors left the market, creating both a liquidity crisis for any new and/or existing financing and an oversupply of additional product due to a reduction in exposure to the asset class. In this void, Wall Street's expertise and capital was required, thereby fueling the CMBS market as we know it today.

The current commercial real estate market combines the two elements described above: the RTC's structure and Wall Street's capital. Despite weak economic environment at the time of this writing, commercial real estate has recovered from the problems of the early 1990s. Fewer banks and insurers are selling the asset class (in fact, many traditional long-term real estate investors have returned to the market), and, most important, Wall Street's capital remains in the market in the form of conduits. Conduits are now the (re)financing vehicle of choice for real estate owners and developers starved for regular sources of capital. Conduits originate and then securitize real estate loans, rather than maintain the credit risk on their own balance sheet. Typically, conduits take the form of mortgage brokers/bankers backed by an investment bank or commercial banks. Mortgage brokers originate and underwrite commercial mortgages using the capital, warehousing, and distribution channels of the investment bank. A commercial bank provides all such functions, thereby offering it a viable commercial real estate operation, while maintaining significantly lower levels of direct real estate exposure on its balance sheet.

As the CMBS market has evolved, the commercial mortgage market has taken an interesting turn (or return, in this case). With traditional real estate lenders returning to the market along with the capital provided by real estate investment trusts, the highest quality properties (Class A) are rarely available for conduit programs. As such, most commercial real estate underwritten by conduits is average, at best, typically Class B and C quality. Historically, this asset class was the domain of the S&Ls. Wall Street's capital, therefore, is filling a financing void left by the S&Ls, while securitization is transferring risks. These two points are key. It is important to understand the issues and reasons why S&L collateral became RTC collateral and avoid those mistakes again. By structuring commercial real estate mortgages, investors best suited to manage real estate risks are those investors getting paid for it, while investors without the necessary real estate analysis capabilities receive the benefits of the asset class without having to staff a complete real estate operation.

While this brief description of the evolution of commercial real estate lending is obviously simplified, we discuss the nature and role of conduits to raise specific points about evaluating CMBS. This is a highly competitive business involving many constituencies with conflicting interests. The competition is likely causing both spread compression (cheaper capital) and lower quality underwriting standards and/or property quality; these are two inconsistent forces. However, demand for the securities from the investment community remains strong, and, as such, issuance is likely to continue its current rapid pace. Therefore, within this environment, it is even more important to provide a proper framework for credit analysis for CMBS.

THE UNDERLYING COMMERCIAL REAL ESTATE MORTGAGES

If Wall Street's conduit programs have truly replaced S&L's historical financing role, obviously the historical performance of this class of commercial mortgage assets should be assessed when analyzing today's conduit product. However, the lack of historical information on the CMBS market is problematic. The traditional real estate asset is far from standardized, varying significantly by property type, market, transaction, and ownership structure. As such, consistent and standardized historical performance information is not available to the market, and, therefore, credit ratings and valuation decisions are often driven largely by generalizations about the collateral, near-term performance of the assets, and analysis of small, non-uniform portfolio characteristics. While this market is often standardized under the CMBS heading, it is crucial to consider the significant differences among the variety of assets found in a pool, as well as the resulting differences in underwriting criteria demanded. Thus, investors will have a better sense of the differences found in today's CMBS pools and the stability of the individual cash flows and valuations.

Multifamily

Multifamily housing generally is considered to be a more stable real estate investment. Cash flows typically are quite consistent, and valuations are much less volatile than other types of income producing properties, due to the stable demand for rental housing. However, the asset also tends to be the most commodity-like income-producing property type, making it more susceptible to competitive pressures and rapid changes in supply and demand. Multifamily properties are unique in that they combine elements of both commercial, income-producing real estate, and residential housing. As such, the traditional analysis of commercial real estate (location, property quality, market dynamics, etc.) is an important consideration for the properties, while the impact of its residential characteristics also needs to be recognized.

The primary difference between multifamily properties and other types of income-producing properties involves the lease term of the typical tenant, and the diversification provided by the large number of available units for rent relative to office or retail space. Residents in multifamily properties are obligated on short-term leases, ranging from six months to two years. This is a positive characteristic of the projects in that it permits the property to adjust quickly to improving market conditions, and also provides owners with regular opportunities to pass through increased operating costs. However, the inverse is also true, as multifamily properties are susceptible to increased supply or competitive pressures and weakening economic or demographic trends within the market. This is especially true in strong multifamily markets, as the barriers to entry are low enough for multifamily developers to quickly bring supply into any given market.

These characteristics demand an understanding of key housing trends in the local geographic areas, and the age and condition of the individual property, as well as its ability to remain competitive within its market. Property owners and underwriters must allocate money for maintenance spending. Absent such upkeep, apartments can quickly deteriorate and show significant underperformance of cash flows. Also, consider historical performance of the market (boom/bust versus conservative capital allocation) as well as the outlook for markets in which the pool is heavily weighted. One year's operating performance is the typical underwriting period for multifamily properties, often completed with little sense of the past or expected market conditions going forward.

Retail/Shopping Center

Retail real estate ranges from large super-regional malls to smaller neighborhood shopping centers. As implied by the names, this space is differentiated by its size. Regional and super-regional malls are typically enclosed structures, ranging from 500,000 square feet to upwards of 3 million square feet. These properties generally are well-known, high quality shopping centers within the property's given market and surrounding area. The malls are anchored by nationally-recognized department stores and retail tenants, and maintain significant fill-in, small shop space. The assets are primarily the domain of long-term, direct real estate investors (such as insurers or pension funds) or equity REITs, and are rarely found in pooled CMBS transactions; those assets in the CMBS market primarily are in the form of single asset transactions. Given the unique positioning and retail exposure of most large malls, as well as high barriers to entry, cash flows are often quite stable for this asset class.

Community and neighborhood shopping centers are more likely to be found in today's conduit transactions, and these properties' cash flows can prove to be more volatile. The properties are usually an open-air format, ranging in size from under 100,000 square feet to 500,000 square feet, serving a smaller market area than the larger malls. The properties often are anchored by necessity-based retailers, such as national and regional discount chains, grocery markets, and drug stores. Smaller centers are sometimes unanchored. The anchors serve as a drawing point for customer traffic to the smaller, in-line stores, which also are often characterized by necessity shopping and convenience (banks, dry cleaners, video rental, small restaurants, for instance). The properties are standardized, non-descript neighborhood convenience centers, which implies that an accessible location is a key valuation feature. Also, the properties are susceptible to competition and new development, so regular maintenance spending is important in keeping the centers competitive.

When evaluating retail real estate, an investor should consider the following: the age and quality of the property, the presence and quality of anchors tenants in the center, location and accessibility, sales volume on a square foot basis, competitive development, sales trends, and occupancy costs in relation to sales volumes. Recognize the excessive growth in retail real estate space over the past ten years. According to some national surveys, the growth of retail space in the United States over the past decade increased almost 40%, exceeding annualized population growth by more than a full percentage point. Certainly, some space has been removed from service over this time as well. However, the growth trends remain striking. Of particular interest for conduit investors is the above-average growth of neighborhood and community centers. As stated earlier, retail exposure in today's conduit transactions is typically neighborhood and community centers in the Class B and Class C quality range.

Office

Office space is a unique component of the commercial real estate market. Office buildings comprise over 25% of real estate space in the United States, but the exposure is highly fragmented and diverse. Significant differences between various classes of space exist, ranging from renowned Class A landmarks to poorly located, aging Class C space in need of both deferred maintenance spending and capital improvements. Properties are also classified by location, ranging from the central business district (CBD) to suburban space. CBD settings are tightly grouped on small parcels of land, typically representing the "downtown" business districts of the representative market. Suburban space, on the other hand, is more widely dispersed on larger areas of land often grouped in the business park setting. During the past decade nearly 70% of office space constructed in the United States was built in a suburban setting, due in part to cheaper construction and lower priced land costs, as well as the continued "suburbanization" of corporate America. These facts along with excellent, decentralized distribution locations will likely keep suburban office space competitive over the long term.

The office sector also presents unique credit issues to analyze. The sector experienced significant overbuilding in the 1980s and also proved susceptible to corporate downsizing. Rental rates are extremely volatile and occupancy levels can swing dramatically. The properties typically are subject to longer-term leases and require significant spending for maintenance and improvements, tenant buildouts, and leasing commissions. Information regarding lease rollover schedules, tenant quality and retention rates, down time between leases, and rental stream forecasting (effective rent versus straight line rents in periods of free rent and over/under market rent conditions) are necessary to understand the performance of office properties. Future market conditions are also important to consider, since markets can change dramatically with the addition of new, large projects. Given this cash flow volatility, both investors and rating agencies continue to demand strong debt service coverage ratios and adequate credit enhancement for office properties within conduit pools.

Hotel

Hotels are considered nontraditional real estate collateral because the performance of a hotel mortgage and the underlying collateral are largely dependent on the success of the hotel business operation at the property. The success of the hotel business operation will be influenced by a number of factors including: the popularity of the hotel franchise or brand, the quality of the hotel management, the amenities and condition of the hotel improvements, and the balance between supply and demand of rooms within the subject's submarket. Because of the many "non-real estate" factors that determine the success of a hotel property, loans secured by hotel properties are subject to more stringent underwriting standards relative to other property types.

Hotel properties serve as collateral for approximately 10% of the outstanding balance of CMBS loans. The types of hotels serving as collateral can be characterized by the level of guest services the hotel provides. The most common hotel types include: limited-service, full-service, extended-stay, and resort. Each of these hotel types has advantages and disadvantages from a lender's perspective. Limited-service hotels are the least management and capital intensive of the hotel types and are therefore considered to possess less barriers to entry than hotels providing more guest services. While this means limited-service hotels are more at-risk to new construction and periods of oversupply, from a loan workout perspective, limited-service hotels can typically be liquidated more quickly and with less required capital expense. On the other end of the spectrum are resort hotels which are very management and capital intensive because of the high level of guest service and extensive physical improvements and amenities. As a result, barriers to entry are high and this type of hotel is less likely to experience a rapidly oversupplied market. However, because of the management and capital requirements, an underperforming resort hotel takes much longer to turn around and is less liquid in a workout scenario.

Regardless of the hotel type, factors that determine the success of a hotel property and related mortgage include the franchise or branding of the hotel, the quality of management, and condition of the hotel. Hotels having the most popular branding in their respective service segment have a competitive advantage over other hotels in the market. The most popular hotel franchises can enforce the highest and most consistent quality standards. As a result, knowing a hotel's franchise typically reflects the quality of management at the hotel and condition and quality of the hotel improvements. However, a CMBS investor must keep in mind that unless the quality of a hotel's services and physical condition remain consistent over time with those of the franchisor, the franchise license can be terminated by the franchisor. For this reason, reviewing the most recent hotel property inspection reports as well as hotel operating results is a necessary part of investor due diligence and ongoing surveillance.

A final factor that will influence the success of a hotel property and related mortgage is the condition of the local hotel submarket. The relationship between room supply and room demand determine a hotel submarket's overall occupancy levels and average daily rates. Depending on the level of hotel exposure in a CMBS pool, the investor should assess the condition of a local hotel submarket room supply and demand by referring to third-party venders such as Smith Travel Research as well as local sources such as a region's convention and visitors bureau and local/regional hotel brokers.

Healthcare

Like hotels, healthcare properties are considered nontraditional real estate because their success is dependent upon a single business operation rather than the forces of supply and demand for space within a property type. Healthcare facilities are special-purpose facilities designed for providing one or more of the healthcare services along the healthcare continuum. The facilities are typically operated by a single healthcare provider who either owns the facility or leases the facility. In either case, the primary source of repayment for the mortgage loan is the cash flow of the healthcare business. While the secondary source of repayment is liquidation of the real estate collateral, the value of the real estate collateral is greatly diminished absent a viable healthcare business at the facility. For this reason, when evaluating healthcare exposure within a CMBS transaction, the investor needs to assess the quality and financial strength of the healthcare operating company at the facilities and the recent trend in occupancy and profitability of the collateral properties. Because of the business aspect of healthcare facilities, underwritten loan-to-value measures typically assume a successful business operation and, in a distressed situation, can prove unreliable.

Healthcare properties serve as collateral for about 5% of the overall outstanding balance of CMBS loans. The most common types of healthcare facilities found in CMBS transactions include skilled nursing facilities, assisted living facilities, and independent living facilities. These facility types are distinguished by the level of medical care provided at the facility.

Skilled nursing facilities (SNFs) provide care for residents requiring the highest acuity of care. SNF residents typically need full-time medical attention and skilled nursing care. Because of the level of medical care provided at SNF's, these facilities are most heavily regulated by federal and state agencies and the majority of resident care is paid for by the federally funded Medicare and state funded Medicaid programs. The supply of SNFs is regulated to the extent that many states require operators to obtain a Certificate of Need (CON) license before they can open or expand a SNF facility. The demand for SNFs is largely influenced by the aging U.S. population and increase in elderly population, the population segment which represents the greatest demand for SNF beds. An offset to this increased demand is the proliferation of assisted living facilities (ALFs), a suitable and often preferable alternative to the SNF for certain residents. ALFs are designed for residents who do not require full-time medical attention and skilled nursing care but do need assistance with certain daily activities such as bathing, dressing, and/or eating. Because of the lower level of care acuity, the majority of resident occupancy and care cost is paid for from private sources rather than government funded Medicare and Medicaid. Also because of the lower level of care acuity, there is less regulation of facility development. As a result, during the second half of the 1990s, the number of new ALFs grew dramatically and as of this writing the sector is overbuilt.

Independent living facilities (ILFs) are designed for residents that are typically 65 and older and who require little or no medical attention. Residents typically choose to live in a ILF to benefit from increased social activities among a similar age group. Most ILF residents are private-pay residents.

UNDERWRITING CRITERIA

One method analysts use to evaluate cash flow volatility among different property types and property qualities is the analysis of mortgage underwriting standards. Clearly, the credit quality of any commercial mortgage pool is determined by the underlying collateral's ability to function as an income producing, debt servicing property over a defined time period. Several financial ratios are available for determining the credit quality of the property, including a ratio of cash flow to the required debt service (DSC) and a ratio of the mortgage loan amount to the value of the property (loan to value or LTV).

In many ways, debt service coverage is a more important credit analysis tool available for real estate securities than is valuation. This cash flow ratio compares a property's net operating income (NOI) to its required debt service payments, with NOI defined as income less property operating expenses and an allowance for maintenance capital spending or replacement reserves. Typically, NOI also will include other recurring expense items demanded by an individual property, such as leasing commissions for retail properties or tenant buildout costs for office properties. The data are often calculated on a trailing 12-month basis. However, shorter reporting periods are annualized or longer reporting periods averaged. Whatever the case, a true picture of normalized operating performance is required to understand the property's ability to service its debt load.

More often than not, a reporting period may overstate NOI due to above-market leases, stronger than expected occupancy levels, or leasing commissions/tenant buildout costs not commensurate with the existing lease rollover schedule. In such a case, it is imperative to normalize operating cash flow, and consider its impact on the credit profile of the individual property or collateral pool. The credit rating agencies attempt to quantify the process of normalizing cash flow by reporting the agency's variance figure. Expressed on a percentage basis, the variance figure calculates the rating agency's re-underwritten (or normalized) cash flow figure relative to the cash flow reported by the mortgage originators.

Recently, the rating agencies have "haircut" reported NOI for a variety of reasons, including above-market rents and occupancy levels, below-market mortgage interest rates, normalized amortization, management fees, tenant buildout costs, leasing commissions, replacement reserves, and deferred maintenance.

Potentially volatile cash flows derived from a property or the pool must be accounted for in the initial valuation of the CMBS transaction. Additionally, when armed with both underwritten and normalized NOI, investors can determine the appropriate level of DSC for a given property or pool to account for volatility in the cash flows and its ability to service debt. This figure can be as low as 1.1 to 1.15 for stable properties with a positive outlook to greater than two times (2×) for properties subject to highly volatile cash flows.

Loan to value is another analytical tool used to compare the property's debt level to its current valuation, as well as its loan balance at maturity. While third-party appraisals are used in this process, which are subject to significant interpretation, a general sense of a property's or pool's loan to value ratio allows one to address refinancing risks. Clearly, lenders and investors should require equity, in line with the property's quality and cash flow volatility. Equally important is an acceptable level of debt amortization over the life of the loan. In doing so, investors protect themselves from shifts in valuation, whether driven by true changes in cash flows or the required rate of return demanded for the asset class.

The equity portion of a property's capitalization also tends to give property owners the incentive to properly maintain the asset. Finally, investors protect themselves at maturity by reducing the LTV ratio over the life of the loan through amortization, thereby increasing the likelihood of refinancing the property when the loan is due.

If refinancing at maturity is unlikely, then investors must factor in principal shortfalls or extension risks. To repeat, standards for LTV ratios vary by property type with stable multifamily units pressing the 75% level and riskier hotels or offices sometimes as low as 50% to 55%.

Portfolio Issues

CMBS investors also must focus on a number of portfolio issues, especially those involving the composition of the total collateral pool. The benefits of the CMBS structure are derived from an ability to make real estate investments without the risks associated with direct mortgage or equity placements (i.e., diversification by property type, loan size and type, geography, borrower, and tenant). As discussed, diversification by property type should be evident, as a well-mixed pool clearly will overcome the cash flow volatility of any one property type. Geographic diversification is also important, because commercial real estate performance is a function of local and regional economics, demographics, and employment conditions.

Higher state concentrations increase the correlation amongst properties, thus offsetting the benefits of diversification. Loan size and borrower/tenant concentration are also important features of a well-diversified mortgage pool, as greater loan diversity by size or borrower diminishes investor reliance upon and exposure to any one property, set of properties, or individual borrower or tenant performance.

STRUCTURING—TRANSFERRING RISKS AND RETURNS

We have attempted to provide a continuum of stability amongst the various property types typically found in today's CMBS transactions, as well as the resulting underwriting issues created by cash flow variability. As discussed, the standard structure in today's conduit deals is a senior/subordinate structure which transfers significant risk to the underlying equity and support bonds. This risk is typically borne by the master or special servicers or some other real estate professionals, which will be discussed in more detail later. On a portfolio level, these issues are manifested by the level of credit enhancement demanded by the rating agencies for any given rating category. Therefore, one must recognize that varying levels of credit enhancement and the subsequent differences in valuation from one security to the next represent the ratings agencies' and investment community's attempt to cope with the cash flow and valuation variability of the underlying collateral. As such, excessive credit enhancement for a pool is not necessarily a good investment characteristic, but could indicate high expected cash flow volatility and/or poor property quality.

Compare standardized residential mortgage pools requiring 2.5% to 3% credit support at the AAA level, versus 15% to 22% credit support often found in commercial mortgage pools. The CMBS level of credit support is designed specifically to recognize the lack of standardization of the underlying collateral, cash flow volatility, and the higher default frequency and loss severity on commercial mortgage securities. As stated, some commercial properties require DSC ratios as high as 2×, indicating cash flow variability in excess of 40%. The property's ability to service its debt load is driven by any number of controllable and noncontrollable factors. Residential housing, on the other hand, is owned by its occupants and holds a much more meaningful position to its occupants, other than holding a put option on the property. As such, volatility is significantly higher for commercial mortgages, and the level of credit support required to protect senior investors is more substantial.

Default frequency and loss severity are also important issues to consider when investing in commercial mortgage securities. Typically, individual assets are structured in bankruptcy-remote entities or some other type of isolation from third-party bankruptcy risks. Therefore, there is no recourse to the borrower's assets beyond the equity in the property. While low LTV ratios alleviate some risks in this scenario, maintaining equity value when a commercial mortgage has reached the point of default is often futile. Often, property level cash flows have fallen, and, for properties underwritten with a low DSC ratio, debt service requirements may exceed cash flow. Additionally, property cash flow problems which are driven by macroeconomic issues (overbuilding or weakening economic conditions, for instance) will have a substantial impact on valuations. In this environment, equity withers and properties that do not cover debt service become uneconomical. Borrowers without a contractual obligation, incentive, and/or an ability to fund losses are forced to default, and the decision to do so is certainly easier than that of a residential mortgage.

Loss severity on the typical commercial real estate default is also impacted in this scenario and is often higher than residential mortgage losses. Valuation drops as the property's performance weakens. However, this loss is exacerbated by market forces which demand either higher rates of return on the asset class and/or stronger equity coverage (i.e., more mortgage losses on the original loan balance). Finally, the costs of liquidating commercial mortgages exceeds those of residential mortgages. The assets are large and unique, and often in need of capital improvements or deferred maintenance. The investor population is smaller, more sophisticated, and specialized, while there are costs associated with the property (taxes, insurance, etc.) that must be carried often for extended marketing periods. As such, loss severities approaching 30% or 40% are not unreasonable.

Clearly, for this asset class, the original cash flows, debt service coverage, and loan to value ratios are mitigated by these risks, and, therefore, must be thoroughly analyzed and understood when the transactions are originated.

Master and Special Servicers

A final important structural feature of CMBS transactions is the presence of both master and special servicers. Master servicers manage the routine, day-to-day administration functions required by all structured securities or collateralized transactions, while special servicers are used to handle delinquent loans and workout situations. Assigned the task of maximizing the recovery on a defaulted loan, special servicers play an important role in CMBS transactions as both defaults and work-outs are frequent and specialized. Most often, the servicer's interests are aligned with investors, as most servicers invest in non-rated and subordinate bonds within the deals they service. Thus, it is important to assess the quality and competency of the servicer. Investors should consider the level of latitude and advancing capabilities provided the servicer in a work-out situation, its financial condition, historical performance and experience within the commercial real estate asset class (and in work-out situations, if applicable), and the monitoring, reporting, and servicing capabilities (including cash management and collections operations). Investors must be comfortable with the servicer's ability to function effectively in that role, as well as the outlook for the servicer's continued viability.

Regulatory Issues

Increasingly, CMBS have been afforded favorable regulatory treatment. The National Association of Insurance Commissioners (NAIC) recognizes CMBS as securities rather than real estate. This allows for a capital reserve requirement ranging from 0.03% to 1.0% for investment grade fixed-income securities compared with 3.0% for commercial mortgages. In August 2000, the Department of Labor granted an ERISA exemption to CMBS allowing investment-grade CMBS to become eligible investments for ERISA-guided plans. Additionally, the Basel Committee of the Bank of International Settlements (BIS) has finally issued its long-awaited proposal on risk weightings for structured securities, including CMBS. Currently, the risk weighting for commercial real estate is 100%. Under the BIS proposal, highly rated CMBS will receive the same risk weighting as government sponsored enterprises (GSEs). GSEs carry a 20% weighting. Clearly, the growing CMBS market would benefit from these changes. Participation by investors should increase, allowing for new capital to support demand for the securities and improving liquidity.

CONCLUSION

In this chapter, we presented an overview of the development of the CMBS market and a discussion of the current issues facing investors today. Commercial real estate lending is evolving into sophisticated, structured securities that represent a growing portion of the fixed income market. Despite trading under the general CMBS heading, the securities and the underlying collateral are specialized and unique, thereby presenting investors with new challenges, as well as potentially higher returns. As pointed out, the securities must be recognized for the individual characteristics which differentiate them, thereby demanding prudent analysis. If recent issuance is any indication, this market should continue to expand, and new investors will continue to enter the market. With the continued expansion of available securities and investors, as well as new performance data, the market likely will differentiate the securities by quality. This chapter presents an introduction to those issues and security types that affect the quality of CMBS transactions and the market's investment potential to go forward.

CHAPTER 17

Non-Real Estate
Asset-Backed Securities

Frank J. Fabozzi, Ph.D., CFA
Adjunct Professor of Finance
School of Management
Yale University

Thomas A. Zimmerman
Executive Director
Head, ABS Research
UBS Warburg

Asset-backed securities are securities backed by loans or receivables. The securitization of residential mortgage loans is by far the largest type of asset that has been securitized and these securities are covered in Chapters 14 and 15. The collateral includes standard residential mortgage loans, home equity loans, and manufactured housing loans. Securities backed by commercial mortgage loans, commercial mortgage-backed securities (CMBS), are covered in Chapter 16. For asset-backed securities not backed by real estate, the largest sector is securities backed by credit card receivables, covered in Chapter 18.

In this chapter, we discuss the basic features of asset-backed securities and the credit risks associated with investing in them. We then look at several types of asset-backed securities not backed by real estate or credit card receivables.

FEATURES OF AN ABS

Before we discuss the major types of asset-backed securities, let's first look at the general features of the underlying collateral and the structure.

Credit Enhancement

All asset-backed securities are credit enhanced. This means that support is provided for one or more of the bondholders in the structure. Credit enhancement levels are determined relative to a target rating desired by the issuer for a security by each rating agency. There are two general types of credit enhancement structures: external and internal. We describe each type in Chapter 15.

Amortizing versus Nonamortizing Assets

The collateral for an ABS can be classified as either amortizing or non-amortizing assets. *Amortizing assets* are loans in which the borrower's periodic payment consists of scheduled principal and interest payments over the life of the loan. The schedule for the repayment of the principal is called an *amortization schedule*. The standard residential mortgage loan falls into this category. Auto loans and closed-end home equity loans are amortizing assets. Any excess payment over the scheduled principal payment is called a *prepayment*.

In contrast to amortizing assets, nonamortizing assets do not have a schedule for the periodic payments that the individual borrower must make. Instead, a *nonamortizing asset* is one in which the borrower must make a minimum periodic payment. If that payment is less than the interest on the outstanding loan balance, the shortfall is added to the outstanding loan balance. If the periodic payment is greater than the interest on the outstanding loan balance, then the difference is applied to the reduction of the outstanding loan balance. There is no schedule of principal payments (i.e., no amortization schedule) for a nonamortizing asset. Consequently, the concept of a prepayment does not apply. Credit card receivables and open-end home equity loans are examples of nonamortizing assets.

For an amortizing asset, projection of the cash flows requires projecting prepayments. One factor that may affect prepayments is the prevailing level of interest rates relative to the interest rate on the loan. In projecting prepayments it is critical to determine the extent to which borrowers take advantage of a decline in interest rates below the loan rate in order to refinance the loan.

As with nonagency mortgage-backed securities (MBS) which are described in Chapter 15, modeling defaults for the collateral is critical in estimating the cash flows of an asset-backed security. Proceeds that are recovered in the event of a default of a loan prior to the scheduled principal repayment date of an amortizing asset represents a prepayment and are referred to as an *involuntary prepayment*. Projecting prepayments for amortizing assets requires an assumption of the default rate and the recovery rate. For a nonamortizing asset, while the concept of a prepayment does not exist, a projection of defaults is still necessary to project how much will be recovered and when.

The analysis of prepayments can be performed on a pool level or a loan level. In pool-level analysis it is assumed that all loans comprising the collateral are identical. For an amortizing asset, the amortization schedule is based on the gross weighted average coupon (GWAC) and weighted average maturity (WAM) for that single loan. Pool-level analysis is appropriate where the underlying loans are homogeneous. Loan-level analysis involves amortizing each loan (or group of homogeneous loans).

The maturity of an asset-backed security is not a meaningful parameter. Instead, the average life of the security is calculated. This measure is introduced in Chapter 14.

Fixed-Rate versus Floating-Rate

There are fixed-rate and floating-rate asset-backed securities. Floating-rate asset-backed securities are typically created where the underlying pool of loans or receivables pay a floating rate. The most common are securities backed by credit card receivables, home equity line of credit receivables, closed-end home equity loans with an adjustable rate, student loans, Small Business Administration loans, and trade receivables. With the use of derivative instruments, fixed-rate collateral also can be used to create a structure that has one or more floating-rate tranches. For example, there are automobile loan-backed securities with a fixed rate that can be pooled to create a structure with floating-rate tranches.

Passthrough versus Paythrough Structures

How a mortgage passthrough security is created is explained in Chapter 14. A pool of mortgage loans is used as collateral and certificates (securities) are issued with each certificate entitled to a pro rata share of the cash flow from the pool of mortgage loans. So, if a $100 million mortgage pool is the collateral for a passthrough security and 10,000 certificates are issued, then the holder of one certificate is entitled to 1/10,000 of the cash flow from the collateral.

The same type of structure, a passthrough structure, can be used for an asset-backed security deal. That is, each certificate holder is entitled to a pro rata share of the cash flow from the underlying pool of loans or receivables. For example, consider the following asset-backed security structure:

senior tranche	$280 million	10,000 certificates issued
subordinated tranche	$20 million	1,000 certificates issued

Each certificate holder of the senior tranche is entitled to receive 1/10,000 of the cash flow to be paid to the senior tranche from the collateral. Each certificate holder of the subordinated tranche is entitled to receive 1/1,000 of the cash flow to be paid to the subordinated tranche from the collateral.

How a passthrough security can be used to create a collateralized mortgage obligation (CMO) is also explained in Chapter 14. That is, passthrough securities are pooled and used as collateral for a CMO. Another name for a CMO structure is a *paythrough structure*. In the case of an ABS, the loans are either pooled and issued as a passthrough security or as a paythrough security. That is, unlike in the agency mortgage-backed securities market, a passthrough is not created first and then the passthrough is used to create a paythrough security. This is the same process as with a nonagency mortgage-backed security.

In a paythrough structure, the senior tranches can be simple sequential-pays, as described for CMOs in Chapter 14. Or, there could be a planned amortization class (PAC) structure with, say, senior tranche 1 being a short average life PAC, senior tranche 2 being a long average life tranche, and the other two senior tranches being support tranches.

It is important to emphasize that the senior-subordinated structure is a mechanism for redistributing credit risk from the senior tranche to the subordinated tranches and is referred to as *credit tranching*. When the senior tranche is carved up into tranches with different exposures to prepayment risk in a paythrough structure, prepayment risk can be transferred among the senior tranches as in a nonagency CMO. This is referred to as *prepayment tranching* or *time tranching*.

Optional Clean-Up Call Provisions

For asset-backed securities there is an optional clean-up call provision granted to the issuer. There are several types of clean-up call provisions.

In a *percent of collateral call,* the outstanding bonds can be called at par value if the outstanding collateral's balance falls below a predetermined percent of the original collateral's balance. This is the most common type of clean-up call provision for amortizing assets, and the predetermined level is typically 10%.

A *percent of bonds* clean-up call provision is similar to a percent of collateral call except that the percent that triggers the call is the percent of the amount of the bonds outstanding relative to the original amount of bonds issued. In structures where there is more than one type of collateral, such as in home equity loan-backed securities, a percent of tranche clean-up call provision is used.

A *call on or after specified date* operates just like a standard call provision for corporate, agency, and municipal securities. In a *latter of percent or date call* the outstanding bonds can be called if either (1) the collateral outstanding reaches a predetermined level before the specified call date or (2) the call date has been reached even if the collateral outstanding is above the predetermined level.

In an *auction call*, common in certain types of home equity loan-backed securities, at a certain date a call will be exercised if an auction results in the outstanding collateral being sold at a price greater than its par value. The premium over par value received from the auctioned collateral is retained by the trustee and eventually paid to the issuer through the residual.

In addition to the above clean-up call provisions, which permit the trustee to call the bonds, there may be an insurer call. Such a call permits the insurer to call the bonds if the collateral's cumulative loss history reaches a predetermined level.

CREDIT RISKS ASSOCIATED WITH INVESTING IN ABS

In evaluating credit risk, the rating agencies focus on four areas:

- asset risks
- structural risks
- legal and regulatory considerations
- third parties to the structure

We discuss each area below.

Asset Risks

Evaluating asset risks involves the analysis of the credit quality of the collateral. The rating agencies will look at the underlying borrower's ability to pay and the borrower's equity in the asset. The latter will be a key determinant as to whether the underlying borrower will default or sell the asset and pay off a loan. The rating agencies will look at the experience of the originators of the underlying loans and will assess whether the loans underlying a specific transaction have the same characteristics as the experience reported by the issuer.

The concentration of loans is examined. The underlying principle of asset securitization is that a large number of borrowers in a pool will reduce the credit risk via diversification. If there are a few borrowers in the pool that are significant in size relative to the entire pool balance, this diversification benefit can be lost, resulting in a higher level of default risk. This risk is called *concentration risk*. In such instances, rating agencies will set concentration limits on the amount or percentage of receivables from any one borrower. If the concentration limit at issuance is exceeded, the issue will receive a lower credit rating than if the concentration limit was not exceeded. If after issuance the concentration limit is exceeded, the issue may be downgraded.

The rating agencies will use statistical analysis to assess the most likely loss to an investor in an ABS tranche due to the performance of the collateral. The rating agencies will analyze various scenarios, and from the results of these scenarios they can determine an expected (or weight average) loss for the investor in a tranche and the variability of the loss.

Structural Risks

As explained earlier in this chapter, the payment structure of an asset-backed deal can be either a passthrough or paythrough structure. The former simply has one senior tranche and the cash flow is distributed on a pro rata basis to the bondholders. In a paythrough structure, the senior tranche is divided into more than one tranche and there are payment rules as to how the cash flows from the collateral are to be distributed amongst the senior tranches.

The decision as to whether a passthrough or paythrough structure is used is made by the issuer. Once selected, the rating agencies examine the extent to which the cash flow from the collateral can satisfy all of the obligations of the ABS deal. The cash flow of the underlying collateral is interest and principal repayment. The cash flow payments that must be made are interest and principal to investors, servicing fees, and any other expenses for which the issuer is liable. The rating companies analyze the structure to test whether the collateral's cash flows match the payments that must be made to satisfy the issuer's obligations. This requires that the rating agency make assumptions about losses and delinquencies and consider various interest rate scenarios after taking into consideration credit enhancements.

In considering the structure, the rating agencies will consider (1) the loss allocation (how losses will be allocated to the tranches in the structure), (2) the cash flow allocation (i.e., in a paythrough structure the priority rules for the distribution of principal and interest), (3) the interest rate spread between the interest earned on the collateral and the interest paid to the tranches plus the servicing fee, (4) the potential for a trigger event to occur that will cause the rapid amortization of a deal, and (5) how credit enhancement may change over time.

Legal Structure

A corporation issuing an ABS seeks a rating on the securities it issues that is higher than its own corporate rating. This is done by using the underlying loans as collateral for a debt instrument rather than the general credit of the issuer. Typically, however, the corporate entity (i.e., seller of the collateral) retains some interest in the collateral. For example, the corporate entity can retain a subordinated tranche. Because the corporate entity retains an interest, rating companies want to be assured that a bankruptcy of that corporate entity will not allow the issuer's creditors access to the collateral. That is, there is concern that a bankruptcy court could redirect the collateral's cash flows or the collateral itself from the security holders in an ABS transaction to the creditors of the corporate entity if it became bankrupt.

To solve this problem, a bankruptcy-remote special-purpose vehicle (SPV) is formed. The issuer of the asset-backed security is then the SPV. Legal opinion is needed stating that in the event of bankruptcy of the seller of the collateral, counsel does not believe that a bankruptcy court will consolidate the collateral sold with the assets of the seller.

The SPV is set up as a wholly owned subsidiary of the seller of the collateral. Although it is a wholly owned subsidiary, it is established in such a way that it is treated as a third-party entity relative to the seller of the collateral. The collateral is sold to the SPV, which, in turn, resells the collateral to the trust. The trust holds the collateral on behalf of the investors. The SPV holds the interest retained by the seller of the collateral.

Third-Party Providers

In an ABS deal there are several third parties involved. These include third-party credit enhancers, the servicer, a trustee, issuer's counsel, a guaranteed investment contract provider (this entity insures the reinvestment rate on investable funds), and accountants. The rating agency will investigate all third-party providers. For the thirty-party enhancers, the rating agencies will perform a credit analysis of their ability to pay.

All loans must be serviced. Servicing involves collecting payments from borrowers, notifying borrowers who may be delinquent, and, when necessary, recovering and disposing of the collateral if the borrower does not make loan repayments by a specified time. These responsibilities are fulfilled by a third party to an ABS transaction, the servicer. Moreover, while still viewed as a "third party" in many asset-backed securities transactions, the servicer is likely to be the originator of the loans used as the collateral.

In addition to the administration of the loan portfolio as just described, the servicer is responsible for distributing the proceeds collected from the borrowers to the different bondholders in an ABS transaction according to the payment priorities. Where there are floating-rate securities in the transaction, the servicer will determine the interest rate for the period. The servicer may also be responsible for advancing payments when there are delinquencies in payments (that are likely to be collected in the future), resulting in a temporary shortfall in the payments that must be made to the bondholders.

The role of the servicer is critical in an ABS transaction. Therefore, rating agencies look at the ability of a servicer to perform all the activities that a servicer will be responsible for before they assign a rating to the bonds in a transaction. For example, the following factors are reviewed when evaluating servicers: servicing history, experience, underwriting standard for loan originations, servicing capabilities, human resources, financial condition, and growth/competition/business environment. Based on its analysis, a rating agency determines whether the servicer is acceptable or unacceptable. Transactions including the latter are not rated, or the rating agency may require a backup servicer if there is a concern about the ability of a servicer to perform.

Remember that the issuer is not a corporation with employees. It simply has loans and receivables. The servicer therefore plays an important role in ensuring that the payments are made to the bondholders.

REVIEW OF SEVERAL NON-REAL ESTATE ABS

The list of non-real estate assets that have been securitized continues to grow. Below we restrict our discussion to a few asset types that have been securitized—auto loan-backed securities, student-loan backed securities, SBA-loan backed securities, aircraft ABS, franchise-loan backed securities, and rate reduction bonds.

Auto Loan-Backed Securities

Auto loan-backed securities represent one of the oldest and most familiar sectors of the ABS market. A key factor in the appeal of auto ABS securities is the historically strong credit quality of the underlying collateral. Of the most active sectors in the ABS arena—autos, credit cards, home equity loans (HELs)—autos are generally considered to have the strongest credit quality (that is, before credit enhancement brings virtually all senior securities across sectors to a triple-A rating).

Auto ABS are issued by:

1. the financial subsidiaries of auto manufacturers (domestic and foreign)
2. commercial banks

3. independent finance companies and small financial institutions specializing in auto loans

The auto loan market has traditionally played a major role in the ABS universe, representing about 16% of the outstanding ABS market. Since 1999 there has been explosive growth in this sector attributed largely to the "prime market"—specifically, to loans originated by the Big Three auto company part of that market. Other parts of the prime auto loan sector also had strong increases, with Japanese captive finance companies leading the way.

Prime auto loans are of fundamentally high credit quality for the following reasons. First, they are a secured form of lending (credit cards are unsecured lending). Second, they begin to repay principal immediately through amortization (credit cards require only a minimum payment). Third, they are short-term in nature (HELs have 15–30 year maturities). Finally, for the most part, major issuers of auto loans have tended to follow reasonably prudent underwriting standards.

Unlike the sub-prime mortgage industry, there is less consistency on what actually constitutes various categories of prime and sub-prime auto loans. According to Moody's, the *prime* market is composed of issuers typically having cumulative losses (on a static pool basis) of less than 3%; *near-prime* issuers that have cumulative losses of 3–7%; and *sub-prime* issuers with losses exceeding 7%.

Cash Flows and Prepayments

The cash flow for auto loan-backed securities consists of regularly scheduled monthly loan payments (interest and scheduled principal repayments) and any prepayments. For securities backed by auto loans, prepayments result from

- sales and trade-ins requiring full payoff of the loan
- repossession and subsequent resale of the automobile
- loss or destruction of the vehicle
- payoff of the loan with cash to save on the interest cost
- refinancing of the loan at a lower interest cost

While refinancings may be a major reason for prepayments of mortgage loans, they are of minor importance for automobile loans. Moreover, the interest rates for automobile loans underlying some deals are substantially below market rates since they are offered by manufacturers as part of a sales promotion.

Prepayments for auto loan-backed securities are measured in terms of the *absolute prepayment speed* (ABS). The ABS measure is the monthly prepayment expressed as a percentage of the original collateral amount. As explained in Chapter 14, the single monthly mortality rate (SMM) is a monthly conditional prepayment rate (CPR) that expresses prepayments based on the prior month's balance.

Structures

There are auto loan-backed deals that are passthrough structures and pay-through structures. In the typical passthrough structure there is a senior tranche and a subordinate tranche. There is also an interest-only class. While more deals are structured as passthroughs, this structure is typically used for smaller deals. Larger deals usually have a paythrough structure.

Since inception of the grantor trust passthrough in the mid-1980s through late-1999, only a few innovations have been introduced into this sector. These included an owner's trust structure (which permitted tranching), the securitization of non-prime loans, and the use of auto leases as collateral. Other than those few developments, the sector was, for the most part, relatively boring and predictable. Investors came to appreciate that this area was dominated by the "Big Three" auto makers, offered low credit losses, and represented a safe, liquid part of the short end of the ABS maturity spectrum.

However, several interesting developments in 2000 and 2001 made the auto sector somewhat less steady. First was the introduction of a soft bullet in late-1999, a structure that had been the norm in credit cards for many years. Second was the shift towards greater floating-rate issuance, a sharp contrast to the long-term convention of fixed-rate auto ABS. The final change was use of an initial revolving period, which extends the average life of the securities.

Although none of these structural changes are revolutionary, on balance they represent a major change in the auto sector. This is important, because the greater diversity of security types has attracted a wider range of investors. Below we examine these relatively new features.

Soft Bullets   Perhaps the most interesting innovation was the introduction of the soft bullet structure. Since the inception of auto ABS in the mid-1980s, auto ABS have been structured with amortizing principal payments. This cash flow structure of the security mirrors the underlying payments on the collateral, which typically are 4- to 5-year amortizing loans. Although the owner trust structure allowed for prioritization of cash flows across different classes, the amortization of principal had not been dealt with until 2001.

EXHIBIT 17.1   CARAT 1999-2

Class	Amount ($MM)	Coupon	Maturity	Avg. Life
A-1	427.00	5.99%	7/16/01	0.5
A-2	370.00	6.06%	6/17/02	1.0
A-3	306.50	6.25%	3/17/03	1.5
A-4	400.00	6.30%	5/17/04	2.0
A-5	76.78	6.45%	1/18/05	3.0
VPTN-1	481.00	1ML + 0.12%	1/18/05	—
Certificates	63.75	6.70%	1/18/05	1.6

Source: Moody's Investor Service.

The Capital Auto Receivables Asset Trust (CARAT) 1999-2 issue by GMAC in August 1999 marked the first time that investors were able to buy auto loan ABS with a soft bullet maturity. Exhibit 17.1 presents the details of the different classes from that deal. This structure was able to offer soft bullet classes instead of amortizing classes, because it included a new type of security that could (1) absorb the amortizing principal cash flows prior to the bullet date and (2) provide the cash flow to meet the bullet principal payment at maturity.

In the CARAT structure, this security was christened a "variable pay term note" (VPTN). At origination, the deal contained a VPTN-1 class that received all principal payments until class A-1 targeted final maturity date, at which point the VPTN-1 class would be paid down. At that point the trust would issue a new VPTN-2 class, the proceeds from which would be used to pay down the A1 class. During the next period, principal payments would go to pay down the VPTN-2 class. On the maturity date of the A2 class, a new class, VPTN-3, would be issued; the proceeds would pay off the A2 bullet class. This process of creating new variable notes and paying them down continues until all the bullet securities are paid off.

Beginning with the CARAT 2000-2 deal, GMAC modified its soft bullet structure by using a single variable pay note rather than a series of notes. At the maturity date of each bullet class, the VTPN in this revised structure is increased by the amount needed to pay off the bullet class. Then the enlarged variable pay note is paid down until the next bullet maturity date.

Ford's soft bullet deals utilized a structure similar to that in the early CARAT deals. The first such Ford deal, Ford 2000-B, was issued in April 2000.

EXHIBIT 17.2   Toyota Auto Receivables 2001-B Owner Trust

Class	Amount ($MM)	Coupon	Final Payment	Avg. Life
A-1	417.84	4.30%	5/15/02	—
A-2	500.00	1ML + 0.06%	12/15/03	1.00
A-3	360.00	1ML + 0.08%	3/15/05	2.01
A-4	175.00	1ML + 0.10%	10/15/07	2.13

Source: Moody's Investor Service.

Since the initial CARAT soft bullet deal, the use of the soft bullet structure has been irregular. So far, only GMAC (via CARAT deals) and Ford have used the structure. Ford used it on three deals in 2000: Ford Credit Auto Owner Trusts 2000-B, 2000-D, and 2000-F. Ford has not revisited the soft bullet structure as of this writing. On the other hand, GMAC has used it exclusively since the initial CARAT 1999-2.

Floating-Rate Autos   The second major change in the auto sector was the increased issuance of floaters. In response to the volatile environment for corporates in 2001 and early 2002, the auto ABS market experienced a dramatic increase in floater issuance. Until that time, auto loans were almost exclusively a fixed-rate product. Floating-rate issuance in 2000 accounted for only 4.3% of total auto ABS issuance. In the first half of 2001, however, that percentage shot up to 25.5%.

An example of a floating-rate auto loan ABS is the Toyota Motor Credit of May 2001 (Toyota Auto Receivables 2001-B Owner Trust), the first auto deal entirely comprised of floating-rate tranches.[1] This $1.5 billion issue was divided into four tranches, three of which were sold publicly. The fourth tranche, a $418 million money-market class, was placed privately. Details of this issue are presented in Exhibit 17.2.

Revolving Period   Another recent innovation, introduced in the Ford 2000-F deal, is an initial revolving period during which the securities receive no principal payments. Instead, during this time, collateral payments are used to purchase additional receivables. After the revolving period ends, the securities pay down in sequential order. The revolving period in this

---

[1] In order to provide floating-rate tranches, the Trust entered into a swap agreement with Toyota Motor Credit Corporation (TMCC) in which TMCC receives the fixed-rate payments from the collateral and pays a floating-rate to the Trust (net of fees). The Trust is then able to pay the floating-rate coupon to investors. However, because the deal contains a fixed-to-floating swap, the ratings of the deal are subject to the counterparty risk of TMCC. Unlike the bullet structure, it is easy for most issuers to incorporate a swap into their deals and to issue floaters.

deal added 1.5 years to the average life of each class. We can see this in Exhibit 17.3, which compares average lives of Ford 2000-F tranches with those from Ford 2000-D, a deal typical of other Ford soft bullet deals. The advantage to investors is that they can purchase an auto ABS with a longer average life than found in other auto deals. However to our knowledge, this is the only public auto deal using this technique, which suggests that demand for this structure was not great enough to encourage a follow-up deal.[2]

Student Loan-Backed Securities

Student loans are made to cover college cost (undergraduate, graduate, and professional programs such as medical school and law school) and tuition for a wide range of vocational and trade schools. Securities backed by student loans are popularly referred to as SLABS (student loan asset-backed securities).

The student loans that have been most commonly securitized are those that are made under the Federal Family Education Loan Program (FFELP). Under this program, the government makes loans to students via private lenders. The decision by private lenders to extend a loan to a student is not based on the applicant's ability to repay the loan. If a default of a loan occurs and the loan has been properly serviced, then the government will guarantee up to 98% of the principal plus accrued interest.

Loans that are not part of a government guarantee program are called *alternative loans*. These loans are basically consumer loans, and the lender's decision to extend an alternative loan will be based on the ability of the applicant to repay the loan. Alternative loans have been securitized.

EXHIBIT 17.3 Average Life: Revolving versus Non-Revolving

	No Revolving Period	Revolving Period
	Ford 2000-D	Ford 2000-F
A1	0.47	2.00
A2	0.97	2.50
A3	1.47	3.00
A4	1.97	3.50
A5	2.47	4.00

[2] However, the revolving structure has been used in several 144a deals.

Congress created Fannie Mae and Freddie Mac to provide liquidity in the mortgage market by allowing these government-sponsored enterprises to buy mortgage loans in the secondary market. Congress created the Student Loan Marketing Association (Sallie Mae) as a government-sponsored enterprise to purchase student loans in the secondary market and to securitize pools of student loans. Sallie Mae is the major issuer of SLABS, and its issues are viewed as the benchmark issues. Other entities that issue SLABS are either traditional corporate entities (e.g., the Money Store and PNC Bank) or nonprofit organizations (Michigan Higher Education Loan Authority and the California Educational Facilities Authority). The SLABS of the latter typically are issued as tax-exempt securities and therefore trade in the municipal market.

Collateral

There are different types of student loans under the FFELP, including subsidized and unsubsidized Stafford loans, Parental Loans for Undergraduate Students (PLUS), and Supplemental Loans to Students (SLS). These loans involve three periods with respect to the borrower's payments—deferment period, grace period, and loan repayment period. Typically, student loans work as follows. While a student is in school, no payments are made by the student on the loan. This is the *deferment period*. Upon leaving school, the student is extended a *grace period* of usually 6 months when no payments on the loan must be made. After this period, payments are made on the loan by the borrower.

Prepayments typically occur due to defaults or loan consolidation. Even if there is no loss of principal faced by the investor when defaults occur, the investor is still exposed to contraction risk. This is the risk that the investor must reinvest the proceeds at a lower spread and, in the case of a bond purchased at a premium, the premium will be lost. Studies have shown student loan prepayments are insensitive to the level of interest rates. Consolidation of a loan occurs when the student who has loans over several years combines them into a single loan. The proceeds from the consolidation are distributed to the original lender and, in turn, distributed to the bondholders.

Structures

Structures on student loan floaters have experienced more than the usual amount of change since 2000. The reason for this is quite simple. The underlying collateral—student loans—is exclusively indexed to 3-month Treasury bills, while a large percentage of securities are issued as LIBOR floaters. This creates an inherent mismatch between the collateral and the securities.

EXHIBIT 17.4   Alternative Structures for Student Loan ABS

Collateral Index	Internal to the Deal From 3rd Party		Security Issued
	Swap	Cap	
3-mo. T-Bill	no	no	T-Bill/student loan rate cap
	no	no	3-mo. LIBOR/student loan rate cap
	no	yes	3-mo. LIBOR/capless
	3-mo. T-Bill/3-mo. LIBOR	no	3-mo. LIBOR/capless

Issuers have dealt with the mismatch in a variety of ways. Some issued Treasury bill floaters which eliminate the mismatch, others issued hedged or unhedged LIBOR floaters, while others switched back and forth between the two. Recently, some have issued both Treasury and LIBOR floaters in the same transaction.[3]

Exhibit 17.4 lists the main structural permutations from which issuers can chose. They can issue securities linked to Treasury bills. If they chose this route, there is minimal mismatch risk because the coupon on the bonds will rise and fall in line with the index on the collateral. Such floaters are essentially capless, although typically they do contain a "student loan rate" cap for liquidity management purposes.

Investors who prefer LIBOR-indexed assets, and who want to invest in student loan floaters from such an issuer, are forced to enter into an interest rate swap outside the deal. The other issuance selection is to issue LIBOR floaters. When no cap protection is provided, the bonds have an available funds cap (i.e., a student loan rate cap). This cap is generally defined as the monthly or quarterly cash flow from the student loan rate, less servicing and administration fees. The student loan rate is a weighted average of the various types of loans in a particular deal plus the rates on the special allowance supplement (SAP) payments.

If LIBOR spiked relative to the 3-month Treasury bill rate, or if bills dropped in a flight to quality, it is possible there would be insufficient funds available to meet bond interest payments. In such structures, it is typical to have a make-up or carryover provision. Once the index on the collateral rises (or the coupon on the bonds falls) sufficiently, the increased cash flow is used to make up the interest carryover amount. While it is conceivable that the spread between Treasuries and LIBOR

---

[3] Also in conjunction with the choice of index, issuers have incorporated a variety of basis swaps and/or have bought cap protection from third parties, while some have used internal structures to deal with the risk.

could widen and stay permanently at a level that the shortfall might never be recouped, this is a highly unlikely event based on historical experience.

It is important to bear in mind that when an ABS structure contains a basis mismatch, it is not only the investor, but the issuer that bears a risk. Student loan deals (like deals in many other ABS classes) have excess spread, i.e., roughly the difference between the net coupon on the collateral and the coupon on the bonds.

In mortgage-related ABS, the excess spread is much larger than in the student loan sector, and is used to absorb monthly losses. Since losses in federally guaranteed student loans are relatively small, the vast majority of the excess spread flows back to the issuer. Hence, the Treasury bill/LIBOR basis risk is of major concern to issuers. When an issuer incorporates a swap in the deal, it not only reduces the risk to the investor (by eliminating the effect of an available funds cap) but reduces risk to the issuer, as well, by protecting a level of excess spread. When a cap is purchased, it is primarily for the benefit of the investor, because the cap only comes into play once the excess spread in the deal has been effectively reduced to zero.

The indices used on private and public student loan ABS transactions since the earliest deals in 1993 have shifted over time (even though throughout this period, the index on the underlying loans was always 3-month Treasury bills). During 1993–1995, most issuers, with the notable exception of Sallie Mae, used 1-month LIBOR, which indicated strong investor preference for LIBOR floaters. By contrast, from Sallie Mae's first deal in late 1995-on, that issuer chose to issue Treasury bill floaters to minimize interest rate risk.

In 1999, Congress changed the formula for the special allowance supplement (SAP) paid to banks that originate student loans. Student loan rates are capped. If interest rates increase to a point where the student loan rate is capped out, the Education Department supplements the students' payments to the lending bank. Traditionally, these SAP payments, like the student loan rate, were indexed to the 3-month Treasury-bill rate. Under the new formula, SAP payments on newly originated loans are indexed to 3-month commercial paper. Since SAP payments can represent a sizeable amount of the cash flow in a student loan deal, and commercial paper is highly correlated to LIBOR, this change reduces the "natural" mismatch between student loan collateral and student loan ABS.

SBA Loan-Backed Securities

The Small Business Administration (SBA) is an agency of the U.S. government empowered to guarantee loans made by approved SBA lenders to qualified borrowers. The loans are backed by the full faith and credit of the

U.S. government. Most SBA loans are variable-rate loans where the reference rate is the prime rate. The rate on the loan is reset monthly on the first of the month or quarterly on the first of January, April, July, and October. SBA regulations specify the maximum coupon allowable in the secondary market. Newly originated loans have maturities between 5 and 25 years.

The Small Business Secondary Market Improvement Act passed in 1984 permitted the pooling of SBA loans. When pooled, the underlying loans must have similar terms and features. The maturities typically used for pooling loans are 7, 10, 15, 20, and 25 years. Loans without caps are not pooled with loans that have caps.

Most variable-rate SBA loans make monthly payments consisting of interest and principal repayment. The amount of the monthly payment for an individual loan is determined as follows. Given the coupon formula of the prime rate plus the loan's quoted margin, the interest rate is determined for each loan. Given the interest rate, a level payment amortization schedule is determined. This level payment is paid until the coupon rate is reset.

The monthly cash flow that the investor in an SBA-backed security receives consists of:

- the coupon interest based on the coupon rate set for the period
- the scheduled principal repayment (i.e., scheduled amortization)
- prepayments

Prepayments for SBA-backed securities are measured in terms of CPR. Voluntary prepayments can be made by the borrower without any penalty. There are several factors contributing to the prepayment speed of a pool of SBA loans. A factor affecting prepayments is the maturity date of the loan. It has been found that the fastest speeds on SBA loans and pools occur for shorter maturities. The purpose of the loan also affects prepayments. There are loans for working capital purposes and loans to finance real estate construction or acquisition. It has been observed that SBA pools with maturities of 10 years or less made for working capital purposes tend to prepay at the fastest speed. In contrast, loans backed by real estate that are long maturities tend to prepay at a slow speed. All other factors constant, pools that have capped loans tend to prepay more slowly than pools of uncapped loans.

Aircraft ABS

Aircraft financing has gone through an evolution over the past several years. It started with mainly bank financing, then moved to equipment trust certificates (ETCs), then to enhanced ETCs (EETCs), and finally to aircraft ABS. Today, both EETCs and aircraft ABS are widely used.

EETCs are corporate bonds that share some of the features of structured products, such as credit tranching and liquidity facilities. Aircraft ABS differ from EETCs in that they are not corporate bonds, and they are backed by leases to a number of airlines instead being tied to a single airline. The rating of aircraft ABS is based on the cash flow from the pool of aircraft leases or loans and the collateral value of that aircraft, not on the rating of lessee airlines.

One of the major characteristics that set aircraft ABS apart from other forms of aircraft financing is their diversification. ETCs and EETCs finance aircraft from a single airline. An aircraft ABS is usually backed by leases from a number of different airlines, located in a number of different countries and flying a variety of aircraft types. This diversification is a major attraction for investors. In essence, they are investing in a portfolio of airlines and aircraft types rather than a single airline—as in the case of an airline corporate bond. Diversification also is one of the main criteria that rating agencies look for in an aircraft securitization. The greater the diversification, the higher the credit rating, all else being equal.

Aircraft Leasing

Although there are various forms of financing that might appear in an aircraft ABS deal—including operating leases, financing leases, loans, or mortgages—to date, the vast majority of the collateral in aircraft deals has been operating leases. In fact, all of the largest deals have been issued by aircraft leasing companies. This does not mean that a diversified finance company or an airline itself might not at some point bring a lease-backed or other aircraft ABS deal. It just means that so far, aircraft ABS have been mainly the province of leasing companies. Airlines, on the other hand, are active issuers of EETCs.

Aircraft leasing differs from general equipment leasing in that the useful life of an aircraft is much longer than most pieces of industrial or commercial equipment. In a typical equipment lease deal, cash flow from a particular lease on a particular piece of equipment only contributes to the ABS deal for the life of the lease. There is no assumption that the lease will be renewed. In aircraft leasing, the equipment usually has an original useful life of 20+ years, but leases run for only around 4–5 years. This means that the aircraft will have to be re-leased on expiration of the original leases. Hence, in the rating agencies' review, there's a great deal of focus on the risks associated with re-leasing the aircraft.

The risk of being able to put the plane back out on an attractive lease can be broken down into three components: (1) the time it takes to re-lease the craft, (2) the lease rate, and (3) the lease term. Factors that can affect re-leasing include:

- *General health of the economy* —Although there is a long-term, secular rise in both passenger and freight miles flown, the airline industry is well known for its sharp cyclical swings, and it typically experiences sharp declines during recessions.
- *Health of the airline industry* —Periods of overbuilding (which there have been) can create sharp declines in aircraft values and lease rates.
- *Obsolescence* —Older aircraft run the risk of becoming technically (or legislatively) obsolete. The older the aircraft, in general, the more difficult it is to obtain high lease rates on renewal.
- *Type of aircraft*— Today, wide-body aircraft are less in demand than are narrow-bodied craft. This is partly from the recession in Asia as of this writing. Most of the Pacific fleet are wide-bodies; and with the decline of demand, a surplus developed. Some aircraft are more desirable for freighters than others. For example, in the air freight business, some McDonnell Douglas aircraft are viewed as virtually indestructible and valuable because they can fly (almost) indefinitely.

Servicing

Servicing is important in many ABS sectors, but it is crucial in a lease-backed aircraft deal, especially when the craft must be re-marketed when their lease terms expire before the term of the aircraft ABS. It is the servicer's responsibility to re-lease the aircraft. To fulfill that function in a timely and efficient manner, the servicer must be both well-established and well-regarded by the industry.

As Moody's states, the servicer "should have a large and diverse presence in the global aircraft marketplace in terms of the number of aircraft controlled. Market share drives the ability of a servicer to meet aircraft market demand and deal with distressed airlines."[4]

The servicer is also the key to maintaining value of the aircraft, through monitoring usage of the craft by lessees. If a lessee is not maintaining an aircraft properly, it is the servicer's responsibility to correct that situation. Because of servicers' vital role to the securitization, the rating agencies spend a great deal of effort ascertaining how well a servicer is likely to perform.

Defaults

In addition to the risk from needing to re-lease craft, rating agencies are also concerned about possible defaults. Because of protections under Section 1110 of the U.S. bankruptcy code, and international statutes that favor aircraft creditors, there is relatively little risk of losing an aircraft. There

---

[4] Moody's *Approach to Pooled Aircraft-Backed Securitization*, Moody's Investors Service, March 12, 1999, p. 9.

are, however, repossession costs, plus the loss of revenues during the time it takes to repossess and restore the aircraft to generating lease income.

The rating agencies will "stress" an aircraft financing by assuming a default rate, a period of time, and cost for repossessing the aircraft. A major input into base default assumptions is the credit rating of airline lessees. For this part of the review, the ABS rating analyst relies on the corporate rating of the airline.

While there is little risk of not recovering the aircraft in event of a default, the rating agencies do carefully review the legal and political risks that the aircraft may be exposed to, and evaluate the ease with which the aircraft can be repossessed in the event of a default, especially if any of the lessees are in developing countries.

Enhancement Levels

In aircraft ABS, as in every other ABS sector, the rating agencies attempt to set enhancement levels that are consistent across asset types. That is, the risk of not receiving interest or principal in an aircraft deal rated a particular credit level should be the same as in a credit card or home equity deal (or, for that matter, even for a corporate bond) of the same rating. The total enhancement ranges from 34% to 47%.

Since the early deals, there has been a change in enhancement levels. Early deals depended largely on the sale of aircraft to meet principal payments on the bonds. Since then, the aircraft ABS relied more on lease revenue. Since lease revenue is more robust than sales revenue, the enhancement levels have declined. To understand why a "sales" deal requires more enhancement than a "lease" deal, consider the following. If an aircraft is sold during a recession, the deal suffers that entire decline in market value. On the other hand, if a lease rate declines during a recession, the deal sustains only the loss on the re-lease rate.

Franchise-Loan Backed Securities

Franchise loan securities are a hybrid between the commercial mortgage-backed securities (CMBS) and ABS markets. They are often backed by real estate, as in CMBS, but the deal structures are more akin to ABS. Also, franchise loans resemble Small Business Administration (SBA) loans and collateralized debt obligations (CDOs) more than they do consumer loan-backed ABS securities. Greater reliance is placed on examining each franchise loan within the pool than on using aggregate statistics. In a pool of 100 to 200 loans (typical franchise loan group sizing) each loan is significant. By contrast within the consumer sector, any individual loan from a pool of 10,000 loans (as in home equity deals) does not represent as large a percentage, thus is not considered quite as important.

Franchise loans are similar to SBA loans in average size, maturity, and end use. But whereas most SBA loans are floating-rate loans indexed to the prime rate, most securitized franchise loans are fixed-rate; if they are floating, they are likely to be LIBOR-linked.

Franchise loans are used to fund working capital, expansion, acquisitions, and renovation of existing franchise facilities.

The typical securitized deal borrower owns a large number of units, as opposed to being a small individual owner of a single franchise unit. However, individual loans are usually made on a single unit, secured either by the real estate, the building, or the equipment in the franchise.

The consolidation within the industry and the emergence of large operators of numerous franchise units have improved industry credit performance. A company owning 10 to 100 units is in a better position to weather a financial setback than is the owner of a single franchise location.

Loans can be either fixed or floating rate, and are typically closed-end, fully amortizing with maturities of 7 to 20 years. If secured by equipment, maturities range from 7 to 10 years. If they are secured by real estate, maturities usually extend 15 to 20 years.

Security Characteristics

Because franchise loan collateral is relatively new to the ABS market, and deal size is small, most of these securitized packages have been issued as a 144A. Issuers also prefer the 144A execution for competitive reasons, because they are reluctant to publicly disclose details of their transactions.

Deals typically range from $100–$300 million, and are customarily backed by 150 to 200 loans. Average loan size is around $500,000, while individual loans may range from $15,000–$2,000,000.

Most deals are structured as sequential-pay bonds with a senior/subordinate credit enhancement. Prepayments can occur if a franchise unit closes or is acquired by another franchisor. However, few prepayments have been experienced within securitized deals as of this writing, and most loans carry steep prepayment penalties that effectively discourage rate refinancing. Those penalties often equal 1% of the original balance of the loan.

Major Sectors

The vast majority of franchise operations consist of three types of retail establishments: restaurants, specialty retail stores, and retail energy outlets. The restaurant category has three major subsectors: quick service restaurants (QSRs), casual restaurants, and family restaurants. Exhibit 17.5 shows some of the franchise "concepts" that fall within these categories.

EXHIBIT 17.5 Types of Retail Establishments

Restaurants

Quick Service Restaurants (QSRs):
McDonald's, Burger King, Wendy's, Pizza Hut
Casual
T.G.I. Fridays, Red Lobster, Don Pablo's
Family
Denny's, Perkins, Friendly's

Specialty Retail
Convenience stores, Blockbuster, 7-11, Jiffy Lube,
Meineke Muffler

Energy Retail
Texaco

A "concept" is simply another name for a particular franchise idea, since each franchise seeks to differentiate itself from its competitors. Hence, even though Burger King and Wendy's are both QSRs specializing in sandwiches, their menu and style of service are sufficiently different that each has its own business/marketing plan—or "concept." For example, Wendy's has long promoted the "fresh" market, as the firm mandated fresh (not frozen) beef patties in their hamburgers, and helped pioneer the industry's salad bars. Burger King is noted for its "flame broiled" burgers, as well as having it "your way."

In addition to segmenting the industry by functional types, it is also segmented by credit grades. For example, Fitch developed a credit tiering system based on expected recoveries of defaulted loans. Tier I concepts have a much lower expected default level than Tier II concepts, etc. Many financial and operational variables go into these tiered ratings, including the number of outlets nationwide (larger, successful concepts benefit from better exposure, national advertising, etc.); concept "seasoning" (especially if it has weathered a recession); and viability in today's competitive environment (yesterday's darlings may have become oversaturated, or unable to respond to changing tastes or trends by revamping and updating).

Risk Considerations

There are several risk factors to be aware of when comparing franchise loan pools, and the following are some of the most important.

Number of Loans/Average Size High concentrations of larger loans represent increased risk, just as in any other pool of securitized loans.

Loan-to-Value Ratio LTVs can be based on either real estate or business values. It is important to determine which is being used in a particular deal in order to make a valid comparison with other franchise issues. Note that when business value is used to compute LTV, it is common for a nationally recognized accounting firm to provide the valuation estimate.

Fixed Charge Coverage Ratio The fixed charge coverage ratio (FCCR) is calculated as follows:

$$\text{FCCR} = \frac{\text{adjusted free cash flow less occupancy costs}}{\text{occupancy costs plus debt service}}$$

Typical FCCRs range from 1.00–3.00, and average around 1.5. A deal with most unit FCCRs below 1.5 would be viewed as having greater risk than average, while one with most FCCRs above 1.5 would be perceived as having less risk than average.

Diversification As in all ABS sectors, a primary risk factor is the degree of diversification. In a franchise loan deal, important areas for diversification include franchise owner, concept, and location.

A typical franchise pool includes loans to 10–15 franchisees, each having taken out loans on 5–20 individual units. A large concentration of loans to any single franchise operator might increase deal risk. However, such concentration is sometimes allowed, and rating agencies will not penalize extensively, if that particular franchisee has a very strong record and the individual franchise units have strong financials. It might even be better to have a high concentration of high quality loans than a more diverse pool of weaker credits.

Concept diversification is also important. Franchise loans extend for 10 to 20 years, and a profitable concept today may become unprofitable as the loans mature.

It is not as important that pooled loans include representation across several major sectors (such as more than one restaurant subsector, or loans from all three major groups). Many finance companies specialize in one or two segments of the industry, and know their area well. Thus a deal from only one of the major sectors does not add any measurable risk as long as there is diversification by franchisee and concept.

Geographical diversification is also important, as it reduces risk associated with regional economic recessions.

Control of Collateral   A key factor in the event of borrower (franchisee) default is control of the collateral. If a franchise loan is secured by a fee simple mortgage, the lender controls disposition of collateral in a bankruptcy. However, if that collateral is a leasehold interest (especially if the lessor is a third party and not the franchisor), the lender may not be able to control disposition in the event of default.

Rate Reduction Bonds

The concept of *rate reduction bonds* (RRBs)—also known as *stranded costs* or *stranded assets*—grew out of the movement to deregulate the electric utility industry and bring about a competitive market environment for electric power. Deregulating the electric utility market was complicated by large amounts of "stranded assets" already on the books of many electric utilities. These stranded assets were commitments that had been undertaken by utilities at an earlier time with the understanding that they would be recoverable in utility rates to be approved by the states' utility commissions. However, in a competitive environment for electricity, these assets would likely become uneconomical, and utilities would no longer be assured that they could charge a high enough rate to recover the costs. To compensate investors of these utilities, a special tariff was proposed. This tariff, which would be collected over a specified period of time, would allow the utility to recover its stranded costs.

This tariff, which is commonly known as the *competitive transition charge* (or CTC), is created through legislation. State legislatures allow utilities to levy a fee, which is collected from their customers. Although there is an incremental fee to the consumer, the presumed benefit is that the utility can charge a lower rate as a result of deregulation. This reduction in rates would more than offset the competitive transition charge. In order to facilitate the securitization of these fees, legislation typically designates the revenue stream from these fees as a statutory property right. These rights may be sold to an SPV, which may then issue securities backed by future cash flows from the tariff.

The result is a structured security similar in many ways to other ABS products, but different in one critical aspect—the underlying asset in a RRB deal is created by legislation, which is not the case for other ABS products.

In the first quarter of 2001 there was a good deal of concern regarding RRBs. The sector came under intense scrutiny as a result of the financial problems experienced by California's major utilities. Yet despite the bankruptcy motion filed by Pacific Gas and Electric (PG&E) in 2001—a bellwether issuer of RRBs—rating agencies maintained their triple-A ratings on California's existing RRB issues. This is not the first time the RRB sector had found itself in turmoil. Over much of 1998, the sector was roiled by a movement in California to overturn the existing legislation which had been created specifically for RRB securitization. This put existing RRB issues in jeopardy; however, the ultimate result (voter initiative was defeated) proved to be positive for this product. The ability of this asset class to retain its rating despite a significant credit crisis at an underlying utility, as well as a serious challenge to the legislation that allows for the creation of these securities, speaks volumes for the soundness of the structures of RRB deals.

Structure

As noted previously, state regulatory authorities and/or state legislatures must take the first step in creating RRB issues. State regulatory commissions decide how much, if any, of a specific utility's stranded assets will be recaptured via securitization. They will also decide upon an acceptable time frame and collection formula to be used to calculate the tariff (the CTC). When this legislation is finalized, the utility is free to proceed with the securitization process.

The basic structure of an RRB issue is straightforward. The utility sells its rights to future CTC cash flows to an SPV created for the sole purpose of purchasing these assets and issuing debt to finance this purchase. In most cases, the utility itself will act as the servicer since it collects the CTC payment from its customer base along with the typical electric utility bill. Upon issuance, the utility receives the proceeds of the securitization (less the fees associated with issuing a deal), effectively reimbursing the utility for its stranded costs immediately.

RRBs usually have a "true-up" mechanism. This mechanism allows the utility to recalculate the CTC on a periodic basis over the term of the deal. Because the CTC is initially calculated based on projections of utility usage and the ability of the servicer to collect revenues, actual collection experience may differ from initial projections. In most cases, the utility can re-examine actual collections, and if the variance is large enough (generally a 2% difference), the utility will be allowed to revise the CTC charge. This true-up mechanism provides cash flow stability as well as credit enhancement to the bondholder.

Enhancement Levels

Credit enhancement levels required by the rating agencies for RRB deals are very low relative to other ABS asset classes. Although exact amounts and forms of credit enhancement may vary by deal, most transactions require little credit enhancement because the underlying asset (the CTC) is a statutory asset and is not directly affected by economic factors or other exogenous variables. Furthermore, the true-up mechanism virtually assures cash-flow stability to the bondholder.

As an example, the Detroit Edison Securitization Funding 1 issued in March 2001 was structured with 0.50% initial cash enhancement (funded at closing) and 0.50% overcollateralization (to be funded in equal semi-annual increments over the term of the transactions). This total of 1% credit enhancement is minuscule in comparison to credit cards (for example), which typically require credit enhancement in the 12%–15% range for large bank issuers.

Unique Risks

RRBs are subject to risks that are very different from those associated with more traditional structured products (e.g., credit cards, HELs, etc.). For example, risks involving underwriting standards do not exist in the RRB sector, since the underlying asset is an artificial construct. Underwriting standards are a critical factor in evaluating the credit of most other ABS. Also, factors that tend to affect the creditworthiness of many other ABS products—such as levels of consumer credit or the economic environment—generally do not have a direct effect RRBs. Instead, other unique factors must be considered when evaluating this sector. The most critical risks revolve around the legislative process and environment plus the long-term ability of the trust to collect future revenues to support the security's cash flows.

In examining a specific RRB deal, several points must be considered.

■ Is the CTC determined by legislation to be a property right? If the legislation defines the fee as a property right, then the utility may sell these rights to an SPV for securitization.
■ Is the transfer considered a true sale? This determines actual ownership of the asset. A true sale safeguards the trust from future claims that may be made against the utility itself, and fully separates the assets from the utility (this true sale now allows for current California RRBs to maintain their triple-A ratings).
■ Is the CTC irrevocable? Since the CTC is created by legislation, it is important to consider whether future legislation could challenge or modify the existing legislation. It is also wise to consider the overall legislative environment, to attempt quantifying the likelihood of any future challenge to existing legislation.
■ Is the utility a good generator and servicer? Since the asset that securitizes an RRB deal is based on a future cash flow stream, the ability of a utility to generate and collect fees must be considered. Electric power is an essential service, so even utilities that find themselves in financial distress usually continue to generate power and collect fees (as is the case in California as of this writing).

CHAPTER 18

Credit Card ABS

John N. McElravey, CFA
Director, Structured Debt Research Group
Banc One Capital Markets, Inc.

redit card asset backed securities (ABS) have been issued in the public
debt market since 1987. Over the years, they have become the largest
and most liquid sector in the ABS market. Average annual new issuance
of credit card ABS since 1995 has been about $46 billion, with a peak
amount of $58.2 billion in 2001. Because of its liquidity, transparency,
and relatively high credit quality issuers, credit card ABS has become
something of a safe haven in times of trouble for ABS investors. Indeed,
investors making their first foray into ABS generally dip their toes into
credit cards before diving in to the many other asset types available.

The size of the credit card ABS sector corresponds with the growth
in the credit card market overall as consumers have come to rely on
credit cards as a convenient method of payment for an expanding universe of goods and services, and as a means of accessing credit. In this
chapter, we summarize the key structural features of credit card securitizations and provide an overview of the credit card ABS market.

SECURITIZATION OF CREDIT CARD RECEIVABLES

The earliest credit card securitizations in the late 1980s were executed
as a means of diversifying the funding sources for banks active in the
credit card market. In the early 1990s, the banking industry faced the
imposition of stricter capital standards by regulators. Securitization
provided a vehicle to help meet these new standards by reducing balance

sheet assets and thereby improving regulatory capital ratios. Securitization also allowed for specialized credit card banks to enter the market and grow rapidly without having to rely heavily on customer deposit accounts as a funding source. These specialty banks, such as MBNA, First USA, and Capital One, were able to access the credit markets directly and achieve funding costs that were more comparable with established bankcard issuers. Much of the increased competition and innovation in the credit card market seen during the 1990s can be traced to these banks, which could not have grown as rapidly as they did without the benefits afforded by securitization.

Basic Master Trust Structure

The structure used for credit card securitization until 1991 was a stand-alone trust formed with a dedicated pool of credit card accounts and the receivables generated by those accounts. Each securitization required a new trust and a new pool of collateral. Since 1991, the *master trust* has become the predominant structure used in the credit card market (see Exhibit 18.1). As the name implies, the credit card issuer establishes a single trust that can accept numerous additions of accounts and receivables and issue additional securities. All of the securities issued by the master trust are supported by the cash flows from all of the receivables contributed to it. The collateral pool is not segregated to support any individual securities.

EXHIBIT 18.1   Basic Master Trust Structure

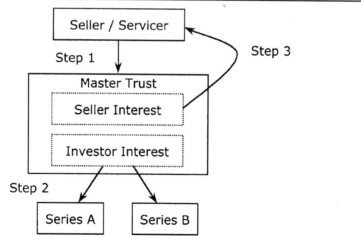

Step 1: Receivables from designated accounts are transferred to the master trust.
Step 2: Pro rata share of charge-offs and cash flows are allocated to investors.
Step 3: Pro rata share of charge-offs and cash flows are allocated to the seller.

For the credit card issuer, this structure lowers costs and provides greater flexibility because a new trust need not be established using a unique set of accounts each time additional securities are issued. From the investors' point of view, assessing the credit quality of a new issue requires less effort because there is only one pool of collateral to review. As the collateral pool grows, it becomes more diversified. While the characteristics of the collateral pool can change over time due to changes in interest rates, underwriting criteria, industry competition, and so on, any change in a master trust would be more gradual than would the differences in stand alone pools.

Master Owner Trust Structures

The state of the art in credit card structures has evolved since 2000 to the *master note trust* or *master owner trust* (MOT) structure. The most prolific credit card ABS issuers have already adopted, or are in the process of readying, issuance vehicles that make use of the latest technology. The securities issued by the MOT are still backed by a revolving pool of credit card receivables, and the credit analysis required of the underlying collateral pool is not affected. However, there are important structural differences from previously issued credit card ABS using earlier master trust technology.

Most issuers adopting the MOT structure already have existing credit card master trusts, and some banks service more than one outstanding master trust because of the consolidation that has taken place in the credit card industry. Exhibit 18.2 presents an example of a MOT structured for an issuer currently active in the ABS market. The issuer's existing credit card master trust issues a "collateral certificate," which is treated like any other series issued by the master trust. The collateral certificate represents an undivided interest in the assets of the master trust, and is allocated its proportionate share of principal collections, finance charges, losses, and servicing fees. For credit card banks with more than one existing credit card master trust, it is conceivable that each one could issue a collateral certificate that could be used to back ABS. The cash flows allocated to the collateral certificate are passed through to the MOT. Securities are issued by the MOT to ABS investors.

Credit card ABS issuers may prefer the MOT structure for several different reasons. First, MOT structures can incorporate flexibility similar to that of a corporate medium-term-note program. For example, different classes of a series can be issued at different times, in varying sizes, and with different maturity profiles. Flexibility of this sort allows the issuer to be opportunistic with regard to the market timing of a new issue, and to tailor securities to a target investor base. This characteristic of the MOT is sometimes referred to as a "de-linked" issuance structure because the AAA securities can be issued separately from the A-rated or BBB-rated securities that provide credit enhancement for the senior notes. Most credit card ABS currently outstanding have been issued as a single series with senior and subordinate classes issued concurrently and having the same maturity. The subordinate classes support only the senior class with which they were issued.

In the MOT structure, all of the subordinate classes outstanding support all of the senior classes outstanding. These are known as "shared enhancement series" (see Exhibit 18.2). Senior securities can only be issued to the extent that there is a sufficient amount of subordinate notes already outstanding. For example, in order to issue Class B securities, there must be a sufficient amount of Class C notes outstanding to support them. A "sufficient amount" is that amount determined by the rating agencies to provide credit enhancement to maintain the desired ratings on the notes.

EXHIBIT 18.2   Master Owner Trust Structure

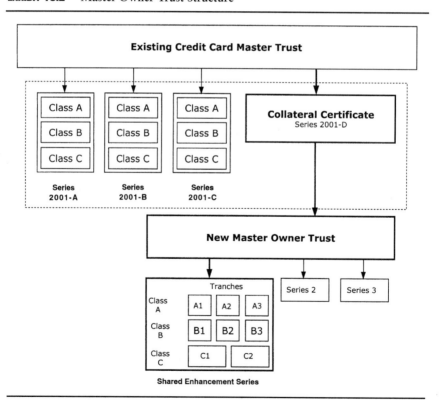

In turn, to issue Class A securities there must be the appropriate amount of Class B and Class C notes outstanding. The subordinate notes are allowed to have a different maturity date than the Class A notes. If a class of subordinate notes matures prior to the senior class, then a replacement subordinate note must be issued prior to the existing subordinate note's maturity. To the extent that a replacement note is not issued before paying the maturing note, then principal collections will be deposited into an account that will be used to support the senior notes. Thus, the senior notes will always have the required amount of credit enhancement outstanding. Senior notes benefit from subordination up to and including the required amount. They do not have the benefit of subordinate notes issued in excess of the required amount. Even if de-linked series are issued, other securities issued by MOTs still can be structured to allow for the issuance of credit card ABS in a single series with "linked" subordinate classes that do not provide shared enhancement (classic credit card ABS). Series 2 and Series 3 in Exhibit 18.2 depict such a scenario.

Another reason for the MOT structure is that issuers can expand their potential investor base by structuring securities to be issued as notes rather than as passthrough certificates. By doing this, all classes of a series issued, including the subordinate classes, can achieve ERISA eligibility. This feature is important because pension funds, a significant source of fixed income investor funds, can only buy securities that meet ERISA guidelines. In this way, the total investor base for credit card ABS expands, especially for the subordinate bonds where liquidity has lagged the senior classes. In addition to expanding the investor base, the flexibility in the MOT structure allows for better and more timely execution of reverse-inquiry issuance.

Investor Interest/Seller Interest

Credit card master trusts allocate cash flow between the ABS investors and the credit card issuer. The "investor interest" is simply the principal amount owed to investors in the ABS. The "seller interest" is a residual ownership interest that the credit card issuer is required to maintain. This seller interest aligns the incentives of the seller with that of the investors because it has a *pari passu* claim on the cash flows. The minimum required seller interest for most master trusts tends to be in the 4% to 7% range of outstanding receivables. The seller interest in a master trust is likely to be higher in practice, in some cases much higher, than the minimum. For example, the average seller interest for trusts included in the Banc One Capital Markets Credit Card Performance Index tend to be in the 20% to 25% range. The actual level of seller interest will be driven by the issuer's strategy with regard to its use of securitization for its funding needs.

The seller interest absorbs seasonal fluctuations in the amount of outstanding receivables, and is allocated dilutions from returned merchandise and ineligible receivables. The seller interest does *not* provide credit enhancement for the ABS. Credit enhancement for the ABS, discussed more fully later, is provided by subordinated securities, which are part of the investor interest, or by other means provided for in the structure of the series.

As an issuer's credit card business grows, accounts that meet the eligibility criteria can be added to a master trust. An account addition normally requires rating agency approval unless it is a relatively small percentage of the current balance (usually 10% to 15%). Sellers are obligated to add accounts if the seller interest falls below its required minimum level. If the seller is unable to add accounts to the trust, then an early amortization event is triggered and investors begin receiving principal payments immediately. The risk of an early amortization gives the seller a powerful incentive to keep the seller interest above the minimum level.

The Credit Card ABS Life Cycle

Under normal circumstances, the life cycle of credit card ABS is divided into two periods: the revolving period and the amortization period. We discuss each period below.

Revolving Period

During the revolving period, investors receive interest payments only. Principal collections on the receivables are used to purchase new receivables or to purchase a portion of the seller interest if there are not enough new receivables generated by the designated accounts. The revolving period is used by an issuer to finance short-term credit card loans over a longer time period. The revolving period is used to maintain a stable average life and to create more certainty for the expected maturity date.

Amortization Period

After the end of the revolving period, the amortization period begins and principal collections are used to repay ABS investors. The amortization period may be longer or shorter depending on the monthly payment rate of the accounts in the master trust. The payment rate is the percentage of the outstanding receivables balance paid each month. Trusts with lower monthly payment rates will require longer amortization periods. For example, credit card ABS with a 5-year expected maturity might revolve for 48 months, and then enter amortization for the final 12 months of its life. This part of the credit card ABS life cycle is usually accomplished through one of two mechanisms: *controlled amortization* or *controlled accumulation*.

EXHIBIT 18.3   Controlled Amortization

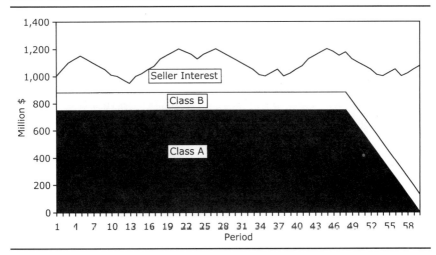

In a controlled amortization, principal is paid to the ABS investors in equal payments (see Exhibit 18.3). The example assumes one series issued out of the master trust with two classes, a Class A senior certificate and a Class B subordinated certificate. During the 4-year revolving period, investors receive only interest payments. Principal collections are used to purchase new receivables. The total amount of receivables varies over time, and these fluctuations are absorbed by the seller interest. At the beginning of year five, the revolving period ends and a controlled amortization begins. Investors receive principal payments in 12 equal installments. Principal collections not needed to repay ABS investors are used to purchase new receivables. Interest payments continue based on the declining principal balance of the ABS. The Class B amount remains fixed during Class A amortization, and the seller interest grows proportionately until the ABS investors are repaid.

In a controlled accumulation, principal collections needed to repay ABS investors are deposited into a trust account each month and held until maturity after the end of the revolving period (see Exhibit 18.4). This example again assumes a simple senior/subordinated structure and a 4-year revolving period. After the end of the revolving period, principal collections are trapped in an account in 12 equal installments to be used to repay the Class A investors. Excess principal collections are used to purchase new receivables. Interest payments to investors during the accumulation period are made based on the original outstanding invested amount. A single "bullet" payment of principal is made at maturity to the ABS investors. This structural device developed as a way to emulate the cash flow characteristics of a corporate bond.

EXHIBIT 18.4   Controlled Accumulation

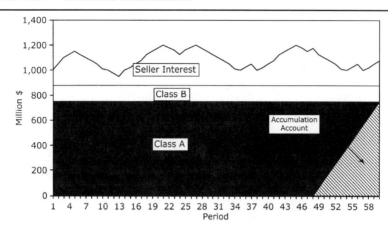

EXHIBIT 18.5   Early Amortization Triggers

Seller/Servicer Issues

1. Failure to make required deposits or payments.
2. Failure to transfer receivables to the trust when necessary.
3. Breach of representations or warranties.
4. Events of default, bankruptcy, or insolvency of the seller or servicer.

Collateral Performance Issues

5. Three-month average excess spread falls below zero.
6. Seller interest falls below the minimum level.
7. Collateral portfolio balance falls below the invested amount.

Legal Issues

8. Trust is reclassified as an "investment company" under the Investment Company Act of 1940.

Early Amortization

Under certain circumstances, such as poor credit performance or a financially troubled servicer, an early amortization of the ABS could occur. Trigger events are put in place to reduce the length of time that investors would be exposed to a troubled transaction. Exhibit 18.5 lists common early amortization trigger events found in credit card master trusts. If an early amortization trigger is hit, then a transaction that is in its revolving period stops revolving and immediately begins to pass principal collections through to the ABS investors. One structural enhancement available to protect investors allows for principal to be passed through on an uncontrolled, or rapid amortization, basis. This mechanism diverts principal due to the seller toward payment of the ABS in order to get investors repaid more quickly.

Cash Flow Allocations

Credit card master trusts may have a large number of series outstanding at any one time. As a result, the allocation of cash flows can become complex. This section discusses the key elements of master trust cash flows.

Groups

A credit card master trust may utilize the concept of a "group," which is a structural device used to help allocate cash flow. Within the hierarchy of the master trust, one or more groups may be established, and each series of securities issued to investors will be assigned to a group. At its highest level, the master trust allocates cash on a pro rata basis between the investor interest and seller interest. The investor interest is subdivided further on a pro rata basis at the group level. While many trusts have only one group that encompasses all of the series issued, other trusts may have two or more. In trusts with more than one group, series with similar characteristics could be grouped together. For example, a master trust with two groups could place all of the fixed-rate coupon series in one group and all of the floating-rate coupon series in a second group. The sharing of excess principal or finance charge collections, if called for in the master trust structure, will be determined at the group level.

Finance Charge Allocations

The components of the finance charge collected by a master trust include the monthly interest on the account balance, annual or late fees, recoveries on charged-off receivables, interchange,[1] and discounted receivables.[2] When expressed as a percentage of the trust's receivables balance, finance charges are called the *portfolio yield*.

---

[1] Interchange is a fee paid to the bank that issues the credit card. It compensates the bank for taking on credit risk and allowing a grace period. Interchange is created when a bank discounts the amount paid to a merchant for a credit card transaction. Interchange is shared by the merchant's bank, the bank issuing the credit card, and Visa or MasterCard for clearing the transaction.

[2] Some master trusts allow receivables to be added at a discount. The discount typically ranges between 1% and 5%. When the face amount of the receivable is collected, the discounted portion is included as a finance charge collection. This practice can temporarily increase the portfolio yield on the collateral pool.

Finance charge collections are allocated by most master trusts pro rata based on the outstanding invested amount of each series. This "floating" allocation adjusts as a series amortizes or accumulates principal collections in a principal funding account. Excess finance charge collections may or may not be shared by series in the same group depending on the structure of the master trust. Some master trusts, such as Discover Card Master Trust, utilize a "fixed" allocation of finance charges. In this structure, the proportion to be allocated to a particular series is fixed at the end of the revolving period and is based on the original principal balance of the series. This structure allows for a greater relative proportion of finance charge collections to go to amortizing series. In an early amortization, a portion of the seller's finance charges can be reallocated to investors to cover any potential shortfall when the portfolio is under stress.

Master trusts that allocate finance charges *pro rata* based on the size of the series invested amount are known as "nonsocialized" master trusts. Finance charges are available to each series to cover its allocated charge-offs, servicing fees, and to pay the coupon to the ABS investors each month. Some nonsocialized master trusts do not share excess finance charges. In other nonsocialized trusts, once all of the expenses are covered, the series included in the same group may share excess finance charges. If excess finance charges are shared by the series in a group, then they are distributed to the other series based on need. Any excess finance charges left over are considered excess spread.

The advantage of a nonsocialized master trust is that the risk of early amortization can be isolated at the series level. The disadvantage is that high coupon series are at a relatively greater risk of early amortization if there is a shortfall in finance charge collections. The sharing of excess finance charges helps mitigate, but does not eliminate, this risk. Most master trusts, such as the Sears Credit Card Master Trust II, are structured as nonsocialized trusts that allow for sharing excess finance charges.

An alternative structure, used by a small number of credit card ABS issuers, is a "socialized" master trust. In such a structure, finance charges are allocated to series within a group based on need. Need is determined by the costs of each series—the coupon, servicing fees, and allocated charge-offs. Charge-offs are allocated to a series *pro rata* based on its size within the group. The expenses for the group are the weighted average of the expenses for each series. Series with higher coupon costs will receive a larger allocation of finance charge collections. The advantage of socialization is that finance charge collections are combined to help support higher cost series, and thus help avoid an early amortization. However, the fates of all series are linked. All series in a group will make payments as expected, or they will all enter early amortization together. Citibank Credit Card Master Trust I and Household Affinity Master Trust I are two examples of socialized master trusts.

Principal Collections

Principal collections are allocated on a *pro rata* basis to each series in the same group based on the size of its invested amount. The allocation of principal to each series is determined by where it is in the ABS life cycle. Series that are in their revolving period receive no principal collections. Their principal collections can be reallocated, and may be shared with other series that are amortizing. Sharing principal collections is a structural enhancement that helps to ensure the timely payment of principal to ABS investors. Principal that is not needed to repay investors is reinvested in new receivables.

For a series in its amortization or accumulation period, principal collections allocated to it will be used to repay investors. The allocation of principal is determined by the size of the invested amount of the series at the end of its revolving period. Even though the certificates are amortizing, the allocation percentage to the series will be fixed based on its original invested amount. If the credit card ABS accumulate principal or amortize over 12 months, then $\frac{1}{12}$ of the principal amount of that series will be paid to it. Principal collections in excess of what is necessary for amortization, depending on the structure of the trust, may be shared with other series in the same group as needed to meet their amortization schedules. Otherwise, excess principal is used to purchase additional receivables.

Credit Enhancement

In order to establish an investment grade rating on credit card ABS, credit enhancement is necessary to absorb losses. The amount of credit enhancement needed will vary from one master trust to another based on the desired rating level and the credit performance of an issuer's credit card portfolio. Early credit card transactions carried letters-of-credit from commercial banks as credit enhancement. However, downgrades of a number of credit enhancers exposed ABS investors to downgrades on their investments. While some issuers still rely on surety bonds, internal forms of credit enhancement have become the norm.

Excess Spread

Excess spread is perhaps the most important measure of the health of a credit card master trust, is a key early amortization trigger, and is the first line of defense against losses. Excess spread is simply the cash flow left over each month after the investor coupon, servicing fees, and charge-offs have been allocated to each series. The calculation of excess spread is fairly straightforward, as shown in Exhibit 18.6, with the values expressed as an annualized percentage of the outstanding receivables balance. If the 3-month moving average of excess spread for a particular series in a non-socialized master trust falls below zero, then an early amortization event with regard to that series has occurred. In socialized master trusts, the excess spread for all series in the same group will be equal because they share finance charge collections based on the weighted-average cost of the group. An early amortization trigger based on a decline in excess spread will, therefore, affect all series in the group.

Cash Collateral Account

A *cash collateral account* (CCA) is a cash reserve account funded at closing and held by the trust. The cash to fund the CCA is usually lent by a third party and invested in high-grade, short-term securities. The CCA is used to protect against shortfalls in cash flow due to rising charge-offs, and any draws on it are reimbursed from future excess spread.

Collateral Invested Amount

An alternative to a cash reserve is a *collateral invested amount* (CIA), which is a privately placed subordinated tranche of a series. The CIA is placed with a third-party investor, and the investor may or may not require a rating on the CIA. The CIA is an improvement for the issuer over the CCA because this tranche is backed by collateral from the master trust rather than cash. Like the CCA, the CIA is available to protect against shortfalls in cash flow due to declining excess spread. The CIA tranche has the benefit of a spread account, which is not available as credit enhancement to other investors. Draws on the CIA also are reimbursed through excess spread.

EXHIBIT 18.6   Excess Spread Calculation

Gross Portfolio Yield	19%
Less:	
Charge-Offs	6%
Net Portfolio Yield	13%
Less:	
Investor Coupon	6%
Servicing Fee	2%
Excess Spread	5%

EXHIBIT 18.7   Credit Card Series Structure

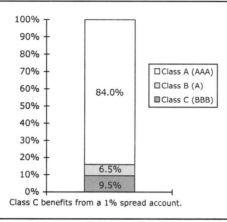

Class C benefits from a 1% spread account.

Subordination

As credit card ABS have evolved, structures have become more complex. Letters-of-credit have given way to CCAs or CIAs, which in turn have been replaced with rated subordinated securities. The subordinated classes also are placed with public ABS investors and tend to be rated in the single-A or triple-B categories. A typical structure might include AAA-rated Class A senior certificates, a single-A rated Class B subordinated tranche, and a Class C tranche issued to investors rated at triple-B level (see Exhibit 18.7). The Class C tranche is credit enhanced by a spread account that can trap additional cash out of excess spread if certain credit performance triggers are tripped. Using subordinated tranches allows the issuer to monetize a larger portion of its collateral portfolio, and allows it to reach a wider investor audience. As noted above, the development of the master owner trust is the latest step toward a liquid, ERISA-eligible, subordinated credit card ABS market sector.

Rating Agency Considerations

Rating agency criteria have evolved over time as new structures, such as rated C-pieces or the master owner trust, have been introduced. In general, the rating criteria from the agencies are not substantially different for the MOT structure than it was for the classic credit card master trusts. Stressing the historical performance of critical variables related to the cash flows tests the structural integrity of credit card ABS. The rating agencies generally require three to five years of historical data, and will examine vintage data in order to estimate loss curves and the ultimate level of charge-offs. Once baseline performance is determined, then different cash flow stresses are used depending on the desired rating. The key quantitative variables for analyzing credit card securitizations include portfolio yield, charge-offs, monthly payment rate, monthly purchase rate, and the investor coupon.[3] Each is discussed below.

- *Portfolio yield* , as noted above, is a measure of the income generated by the credit card receivables. While portfolio yield is driven largely by the APR on accounts and fees, usage by account holders also plays an important role. All else being equal, a portfolio with proportionately more revolving accounts relative to convenience users will translate into a higher portfolio yield.
- *Charge-offs* are the credit losses experienced by the portfolio, and are taken by most issuers at 180 days past due. Peak losses on a static pool basis for credit card accounts have been observed at about 24 months of seasoning.
- The *monthly payment rate* is an important variable in the analysis because high payment rates can be a source of strength and implied credit enhancement. A large proportion of convenience users, while depressing portfolio yield, can sharply increase payment rates. A higher payment rate means that investors can be repaid more quickly during an early amortization.
- Related to the payment rate is the *purchase rate* , which is the generation of new receivables by the designated accounts. Higher purchase rates mean more receivables are being generated to support outstanding ABS. Bankruptcy of the seller of the receivables, such as a department store chain, is the main risk with regard to the purchase rate because cardholders may stop using the card. As the amount of receivables declines, the credit quality of the portfolio may deteriorate.
- *Floating-rate ABS* generally require more credit enhancement than fixed-rate transactions because the rating agencies assume in their stress scenarios that market interest rates increase dramatically. Higher funding costs for the ABS reduce the available excess spread.

The stress tests run by the rating agencies force portfolio yields, payment rates, and purchase rates down sharply at the same time that charge-offs rise. This combination compresses excess spread and causes an early amortization of the transaction. Exhibit 18.8 shows generic stress scenarios for credit card ABS transactions for Standard & Poor's. The rating agencies may deviate from these benchmark levels depending

---

[3] The methodology and variables used are based on Standard & Poor's rating criteria. The other rating agencies perform a similar analysis when rating credit card ABS.

on the qualitative factors of a seller's business. Some of the key qualitative elements that go into the rating analysis are new account underwriting, servicing and collections, marketing, card type (private label versus general purpose), geographic diversification, strategic objectives of the firm, account seasoning, and the competitive position of issuer. These qualitative factors, among others, determine how the generic stress factors will be modified and applied to an individual issuer's credit card portfolio.

THE CREDIT CARD ABS MARKET

Credit card ABS is the largest and most liquid part of the ABS market. In 2001, total new public issuance of credit card ABS reached $58.2 billion, and we expect issuance to remain at high levels in the near future. In addition, there are about $270 billion of credit card ABS outstanding. The large number of issuers and dollar amount outstanding makes this sector particularly active for secondary trading. Consequently, pricing spreads for credit card ABS tend to be used as a benchmark for comparison to other ABS sectors.

During the past decade, the credit card industry has experienced rapid growth and increasing competition. That dynamic culminated in sharp increases in outstanding receivables in 1995 and 1996, and was reflected in the amount of new credit card ABS issued during that period. However, rapid growth and intense competition also led to problems with asset quality (see Exhibit 18.9). Charge-offs rose steadily and excess spreads dropped from the middle of 1995 through the middle of 1997 as consumer bankruptcy rates reached record levels. It has been generally acknowledged that competition for new accounts, the use of introductory "teaser rates," and weaker underwriting led to many of the credit problems seen in the credit card sector.

EXHIBIT 18.8   Standard & Poor's Benchmark Credit Card Stress Scenarios

	AAA-Rating	A-Rating
Charge-Offs	3–5× steady-state levels	2–3× steady-state levels
Portfolio Yield[1]	11%–12% annual rate	12% annual rate
Payment Rate	45%–55% of steady state level	50%–60% of steady state level
Purchase Rate	0%–5% annual rate	0%–5% annual rate
Investor Coupon[2]	15%	14%

[1] Based on proposed legislative caps.
[2] Coupon for uncapped floaters.

EXHIBIT 18.9   Banc One Capital Markets Credit Card Performance Indices

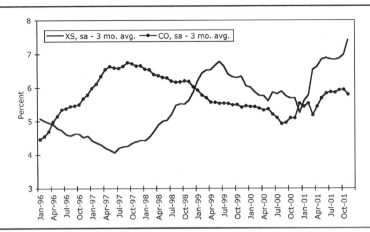

Credit performance stabilized in the late 1990s as credit card companies re-examined their marketing strategies and underwriting procedures. Charge-off rates slowly fell back to about 5% by the summer of 2000, but excess spreads remained relatively high as banks instituted more thorough risk-based pricing of customer accounts (see Exhibit 18.9). As the economy slowed and the recession took hold, charge-off rates began to climb again, and peaked at about 6% by year-end 2001. Nevertheless, excess spreads have increased sharply due to dramatically lower interest rates. The majority of ABS are issued as floating-rate notes. As LIBOR rates fell, funding costs dropped, and margins on credit card master trusts soared to record levels.

Industry Consolidation

To better meet their credit underwriting and customer service needs, stronger credit card companies invested heavily in technology, and increased their scale of operations to spread the costs of that investment over more accounts. Many smaller or weaker firms have been unable or unwilling to meet the challenge of the new competitive environment, and have decided to exit the business. As a result, consolidation has been one of the key themes in the credit card business for the past few years. To illustrate, at the start of 1987 there were slightly more than $80 billion of credit card receivables outstanding in the United States, and the top ten credit card companies had a combined market share of about 40%. By the end of 2000, there were about $700 billion of outstanding credit card receivables, and the top ten credit card companies had a combined market share of 68% (see Exhibit 18.10).

EXHIBIT 18.10 Top Ten U.S. General Purpose Credit Card Issuers

Rank 2001	Rank 2000	Sponsor Name	Corporate Ratings (M/S)	Managed Receivables ($B)	Market Share[4] (%)	Receivables Growth[5] (%)	Securitized Receivables[6] (%)	Trust Size[7] ($B)	Outstanding Securities[8] ($B)	Series Issued in 2000	Series Issued in 2001
1	1	Citigroup	Aa2/AA−	$97.90	14.0%	23.8%	43.5%	$73.39	$32.55	7	8
2	3	First USA/Bank One*	Aa3/A	70.54	10.1	6.4	57.1	59.36	30.79	0	4
3	2	MBNA	Baa2/BBB	70.50	10.1	15.4	72.5	59.18	39.13	11	6
4	5	Discover[1]	Aa3/AA−	50.20	7.2	14.9	57.9	36.71	25.00	10	5
5	4	American Express[2]	A1/A+	50.16	7.2	16.1	33.3	21.93	15.37	5	6
6	6	JP Morgan Chase	Aa3/AA−	37.40	5.3	17.2	47.4	21.46	14.86	3	3
7	7	Providian Financial	Ba1/BB+	30.50	4.4	41.9	21.9	8.29	5.20	3	0
8	8	Capital One	Baa3/BB+	29.90	4.3	87.5	54.6	19.23	11.90	5	4
9	9	Bank of America	Aa2/A+	25.46	3.6	22.3	34.4	11.11	7.62	0	1
10	10	Household Bank	A3/A	14.89	2.1	9.5	30.4	10.21	3.56	2	2
		Top Ten Total		$477.45	68.2%	20.2%	49.0%	$320.87	$185.97	46	39
		Market Total		$700.3[3]		15.0%			$259.60	61	44

[1] Managed Receivables and Receivables Growth Reported as of 5/31/01
[2] Managed Receivables and Receivables Growth Reported as of 12/31/00
[3] Total Consumer Revolving Credit—Federal Reserve Release G.19 (excludes mortgage products)
[4] Managed Receivables over Total Consumer Revolving Credit
[5] Year-over-year growth since June 30, 2000, except where otherwise noted
[6] (1-Weighted Average Master Trust Investor Interest)/Managed Receivables
[7] Receivables transferred to all of the Sponsor's Master Trusts
[8] Term, public, U.S. dollar denominated transactions
* Includes $7.5 billion purchase of Wachovia's portfolio, of which $1.3 billion was subsequently sold back to Wachovia
Data Sources: The Nilson Report, Moody's, Bloomberg, Intex, Federal Reserve Bank, and Sponsor Financial Statements
All data through June 2001 unless otherwise noted.

As the credit card industry has consolidated, so has the market for credit card ABS. The three largest credit card issuers accounted for about 45% of credit card ABS outstanding as of year-end 2001, and the top five were responsible for approximately 63%. While consolidation has reduced the number of issuers in the market, the overall credit quality of those that remain has improved. Seven of the top ten sponsors have corporate debt ratings of A2/A or better. From the standpoint of liquidity and issuer quality, this sector is the strongest in the ABS market.

Credit Card Market Segments

The major issuers of credit card ABS fall into four major categories: commercial banks, consumer finance companies, independent networks, and retailers. Some examples of the issuers in each of these categories follow:

- Commercial Banks: Bank One, Citibank, Chase, BankAmerica
- Consumer Finance: MBNA, Household, Capital One, Providian
- Independent Networks: Discover, American Express
- Retailers: Sears, Target, World Financial Network, Federated

General Purpose Cards

The credit card ABS market is divided into two major segments: general-purpose cards and private label cards. The larger of these two segments includes transactions sponsored by issuers of general-purpose credit cards. General-purpose credit cards include both Visa and MasterCard cards issued by commercial banks and consumer finance companies, as well as the independent networks of merchants built by Discover Card and American Express. This group of issuers represents the vast majority of the credit card ABS market. Issuers of general-purpose cards tend to price new ABS at tighter spreads relative to private label issuers. Tiering in that market favors the largest, most frequent issuers with stable credit performance. Nevertheless, most issuers price new credit card ABS transactions within a very tight range of only a few basis points. At this point in time, Citibank and MBNA are generally considered to be the benchmark issuers in this market segment.

Teaser Rate Cards

In an attempt to gain market share in the face of fierce competition, credit card issuers devised a number of innovations to establish brand loyalty with new customers. Low-price cards, with no annual fee and up-front "teaser" rates, have been used to lure customers away from competitors. These accounts often allow the new customer to transfer existing balances from other, higher interest rate cards. The teaser rate usually is in effect for 6 to 12 months, and then steps up to a higher rate based on the borrower's credit risk. Balance transfers have been used to great effect by card issuers, though many borrowers have become adept at rolling balances from one card to another at the end of the teaser rate period. One of the problems with this approach is the potential for adverse selection in the account base. Borrowers with poor credit are more likely to respond to a teaser rate, and may be less likely to roll balances to a new card in the future because they have less credit options. Most credit card banks have moved away from the blanket marketing of teaser rate accounts to concentrate on other ways to establish brand loyalty among cardholders.

Affinity and Co-Branded Programs

One of the uses of the technological investment made by credit card issuers has been in the customer retention effort. A package of interest rates, credit limits, and other services can be offered to entice customers to stay once the teaser period ends. These packages may come in thousands of possible combinations, and are offered based on the credit profile and card usage patterns of the cardholder. The method of "mass customization" is made possible by the sophisticated computer systems that search for new customers in huge databases, and track the credit performance and profitability of existing customers. One of the most successful issuers practicing a mass customization strategy is Capital One.

Two popular products created by issuers to differentiate themselves in the minds of cardholders and retain them as customers are *affinity* and *co-branded* programs. Affinity cards are issued by a bank in association with a special interest group, such as a college alumni association, professional group, or sports team. The group receives a fee from the bank, and the bank uses its affinity program to attract a certain demographic group to use its card. Co-branded cards are programs that associate a bank's credit card with a particular commercial firm. Customers can earn certain rewards from the commercial firm for making purchases with the card, such as mileage awards toward free tickets on airlines, which is probably the most popular of the bank co-brand programs.

Private Label Credit Cards

The other, much smaller segment of the credit card market includes private label credit cards, which are sponsored by retailers for use in their own stores. This segment has been dominated by issuance from Sears, which represents about one-third of the private label market. Retail credit card accounts are most often viewed by the sponsor as a means to increase sales, and credit underwriting may not be as stringent as it is for general-purpose credit cards. As a result, charge-offs tend to be higher on private label credit card master trusts than they are for general-purpose card master trusts. On the other hand, APRs and portfolio yields do tend to be higher to compensate for the greater risk in the private label portfolio. Private label credit card ABS transactions tend to be less frequent and somewhat smaller, and as result they tend to price at a concession to ABS transactions sponsored by general-purpose card issuers. Nevertheless, good value can be found among private label issuers by investors willing to investigate them.

CONCLUSION

The credit card ABS market currently is the largest and most liquid asset-backed sector. For this reason, it is viewed by many as a safe haven for ABS investors in stressful market times. Indeed, spreads on credit card ABS are usually the first to recover from market dislocations. Over the past several years, a growing economy, healthy consumer balance sheets, and greater acceptance of credit cards for non-traditional uses led to a sharp increase in outstanding receivables. Meanwhile, the market weathered a deteriorating credit situation from 1995 through 1997. Nevertheless, a growing need for technology and intense competition led to consolidation in the industry, though competition still appears to be quite strong. Increasing issuance in the European market should produce a more global credit card ABS market in coming years, and additional innovations are sure to follow. Given the commitment most credit card issuers have made to the ABS market, it seems likely that the credit card ABS market should continue to be a benchmark sector for the foreseeable future.

CHAPTER 19

Leveraged Loans

Steven Miller
Managing Director
PMD Group
Standard & Poor's

The leveraged loan market has evolved since the mid-1980s to an institutional investor-driven segment of the capital markets from the sole province of banks. Though the market retains some of the vestiges of a private market—including cumbersome documentation and transfer provisions and some measure of non-public information—institutional accounts now represent more than 50% of the funding for leveraged loans. As of September 30, 2001, roughly 80 institutional investors were active in the leveraged loan market.

These accounts are divided into three main segments: (1) retail mutual funds, (2) securitization vehicles, primarily collateralized loan obligations (CLOs), and (3) proprietary accounts of insurance companies, hedge funds, and a small number of pension funds; hedge funds and pensions tend to invest through total rate of return swaps.

As the institutional investor base has grown, banks' appetite for leveraged loans has receded. In fact, most banks now are afflicted with anorexia when it comes to buying new loan assets. Since 1999, the number of banks that have actively bought leveraged loans on a retail basis[1] has withered to 31 as of September 30, 2001 from 110. The reasons are straightforward:

---

[1] We define this as banks that participated in 10 or more primary loans in a non-underwriting capacity.

- Most banks are husbanding their capital for fee-generating businesses rather than investing in credit products; in fact, the chance of capturing fees as a memeber of the bond syndicate is one of the most powerful draws to bring banks into leveraged loan syndicates.
- With default up over this period (discussed later) and credit quality deteriorating, even those banks that remain active have pulled in their horns.
- The banking industry has endured wave upon wave of consolidation with underwriting banks buying up many of their best bank investors. Examples: in recent years Fleet Bank has bought Bank of Boston and Summit bank and First Union has bought Corestates and Wachovia.
- The Japanese banks have become very reticent players in recent years. During the first three quarters of 2001, these banks bought just 2% of primary leveraged loans. As recently as 1994, Japanese banks represented 17% of the primary market.

WHAT IS A SYNDICATED LOAN?

Syndicated loans are loans that are sufficiently large that they are provided by a group of banks under one master credit agreement, just like bonds. And, just like bonds, the loan is led by an arranger or a group of co-arrangers and syndicated to a group of banks and institutional investors.

Syndicating loans has been a practice of banks long before J. Pierpont Morgan came on the scene in the late 1800s and helped to popularize this form of fund raising by tapping European capital providers for American corporations. But the syndicated loan market is a relatively recent innovation. It was more or less invented in the mid-1980s as a way to finance large leveraged buyout loans like RJR Nabisco. The syndicated loan market has evolved over the past decade from something of a backwater lending segment to a capital markets-like model, particularly in the leveraged loan segment where institutional investors now predominate. Today, the leveraged loan market sports many of the trappings of the bond market—though loans continue to be private instruments and loan investors often receive information from the issuer that is not filed with the SEC—including third-party ratings and a trade association focused on increasing the efficacy of settlement and trading, mark-to-market pricing, news and data, and market statistics.

And since the early 1990s, as discussed previously, institutional investors have steadily increased their participation as banks have withdrawn. Institutional investors buy only non-investment grade loans—specifically, only term loans. As a result, in this chapter we'll focus on these tranches, or "institutional loans" in market parlance. These are floating-rate, funded loans with back-end loaded amortization that are, virtually without exception, secured. Most loans are secured by all assets, though there are cases where capital stock in operating units are the primary form of collateral and still others where it is inventories and receivables. Leveraged loans are almost always for non-investment grade or non-rated companies, though there is the occasional BBB or BBB– issuer that is forced to tap the institutional loan market for secured, funded debt. These issuers are usually in the throes of financial distress or a large transaction that requires them to leverage up their balance sheets.

Leveraged loans bought by institutional investors have traditionally paid a rate of interest in the range of 2.0% to 5.0% over LIBOR. The issuer is given the option to fix the rate of the loan in 1- to 12-month intervals at the prevailing LIBOR rate plus the spread. In most cases, the issuer is given a great deal of flexibility and can have numerous LIBOR contracts under a single facility. That is, in a $100 million loan, the issuer may have three equal sized LIBOR contracts one of which is set for three months, one for six months, and one for nine months.

STRUCTURING AND SYNDICATING LOANS

In structuring and syndicating a loan, agent banks must deal with two primary constituencies: (1) the borrower and (2) potential lenders.

The borrower is the client, paying the agent a fee to structure and syndicate the loan. The fee increases with the complexity of the loan. If the loan is a plain vanilla (or standard) loan to an large, high-quality company, there will be little or no fee. And, often, these borrowers will syndicate a loan themselves, using the agent simply to set documentation and administer the process. As the risk of the borrower or the transaction increases, so does the fee. As a result, the most profitable loans are those to leveraged borrowers.

Lenders are the "retail" market for a syndicated loan. An agent must gauge market appetite for a particular credit before pricing it. An agent will price a loan where it believes it will clear the market. The loan market, however, remains unique among the major capital markets because loans are priced and then syndicated over several weeks or months period. In the bond market, by contrast, a bond is priced to market on the day of the offering, ensuring that pricing will clear the market.

Once pricing and structure are set, the agent(s)—often with borrower approval or at least knowledge—will set several commitment tiers for the retail market. Lenders are usually paid an upfront fee based on their commitment tier, with larger commitments bringing larger fees. After the syndication is complete, the agent(s) will make allocations to the syndicate group based on how well the loan was subscribed (how much money was raised). If, for instance, a $100 million is raised for a $100 million syndicated loan, lenders will be allocated exactly what they committed. If, however, $200 million was raised, lenders may be allocated only half of the amount they committed.

There are three types of syndications:

■ *Underwritten Deal*— In an underwritten deal, the agent or agents guarantee the entire commitment and then syndicate the loan. Even if the agent syndicate less than the committed amount, it must provide the funds. Fully underwritten deals can be used as a competitive tool by agents to win mandates. They also tend to be more richly priced because the agent is on the hook if potential lenders balk.

■ *Best Efforts*—In a best-efforts syndicate, the agent or agents commit to underwrite less than the entire amount of the loan; leaving it at the mercy of the market. If other lenders elect not to join the deal, then the credit will not close. Best-efforts syndications tend to be used for risky borrowers or complex transactions, when the chances that the other lenders will pass on the deal are higher. Pricing and fees tend to be lower than those paid to a fully underwritten syndication.

■ *Club Deal* —Smaller deals (usually $200 million or less) that are premarketed to a group of relationship banks. The agent is generally a first among equals.

Buying Syndicated Loans

Investors generally buy loans in the primary or secondary market in initial investments of at least $2 to $5 million and incremental investments of $1 million. As we discuss later, the assignment provisions of loans are cumbersome and transfer fees are often costly.

Most participants say that committing $500 million to the leveraged loan is the minimum required to be a "player" and be consistently invited into the primary by large underwriters. Those who want to commit less generally invest through a fund manager. There are, however, a number of hedge funds that buy opportunistically through total rate of return swaps as part of their overall high-yield investment strategy.

There are four primary ways that institutional investors buy leveraged loans.

Retail Mutual Funds

At the close of 2001, there were roughly 30 of these funds with net assets of about $23 billion according to one source, Lipper. Most retail loan funds are closed-end, continuously offered vehicles that are redeemable through tenders conducted quarterly. Some of the newer funds, however, have monthly or even daily redemptions. These are the exception, though, not the rule.

Securitization Vehicles

Since the mid-1990s, loan vehicles—or collateralized loan obligations (CLOs) as they are popularly known—have become the largest form of institutional investment in the loan market. At the end of 2001, these vehicles held roughly $70 billion of leveraged loans. Like all asset-backed securities, CLOs carve up the risk into various layers of liabilities, typically a AAA-rated senior tranche, a AA rated senior tranche, a BBB or BB mezzanine tranche and, of course, an equity tranche. The typically run 5 to 7 years and are highly structured with all sorts of covenant tests including industry diversification and minimum collateral rating. The size of these vehicles ranges from $300 million to a billion; though the rule in 2001 was for deals of $300–600 million.

Proprietary Investing

Proprietary investing is done mainly by insurance companies who have internal managers. Again, a $500 million commitment of capital is required for a seat at the table.

Managed Accounts

While managed accounts are used by endowments, insurance companies also use them to dip their toes in the loan market. These accounts can run between $50 million and several hundred million dollars. The investor pays a fee to access a manager's relationship with underwriters and his or her position in the market.

Total Rate of Return Swaps

Total rate of return swaps are primarily used by hedge funds to invest in loans. These swaps allow the funds to take a leveraged position in the performance of one loan or a basket of loans in exchange for a fee.

WINNING A MANDATE

Normally, a borrower will solicit several bids from potential agents before awarding a mandate to one or more agents. Potential agents will normally include the borrower's traditional agent, large relationship lenders and, perhaps, other lenders that have expertise in the borrower's industry or segment. Potential agents will propose pricing and structure based on comparables (the most recent credits of similar, or comparable, borrowers), taking into account several driving factors discussed below.

Borrower Risk

The likelihood that a borrower will be unable to repay the loan on time. It is based on the borrower's financial condition, industry segment and conditions within that industry, economic variables, and intangibles like company management. Borrower Risk will often be determined by a rating from Standard & Poor's Corp. (S&P) or Moody's Investors Service. These ratings range (at close) from AAA for the most creditworthy borrowers to B– for the least. The market is divided, roughly, into two segments: Investment Grade (borrowers rated BBB– or higher by S&P or Baa3 or higher by Moody's) and Leveraged (borrowers rated lower by either agency). Borrower risk varies widely within each of these broad segments. If a borrower rating is not available (either because the company is too small or has no public debt to rate) then financial measures, like revenue size, leverage, and coverage (see the next section for an explanation) are used to determine risk.

Facility Risk

Facility risk is the potential loss to the bank if the borrower does indeed default. This is based on the collateral (if any) backing the loan and the amount of other debt and equity that are subordinated to the loan.

Sponsor

If a transaction has a strong sponsor group, agents may be able to offer the borrower more attractive pricing. Many leveraged companies are owned by a group of equity sponsors. These are entities, like Kohlberg Kravis & Roberts (KKR), which invest in many companies that have leveraged capital structures. To the extent the sponsor or sponsor group has a strong following in the syndicated loan market, a loan is easier to syndicate and, therefore, can be priced lower. If the sponsor group does not have a loyal set of relationship lenders, by contrast, the deal may need to be priced higher to attract potential investors.

Supply/Demand

With respect to supply and demand, two factors are important—deal size and market activity. The size of the deal must be weighed against potential market demand. Clearly, the larger the deal in comparison to market demand, the higher the pricing must be to attract lenders. By contrast, if demand far outstrips the deal size, the pricing can be set tighter. Market activity is similar to the last point. If there are many deals competing for market attention, an agent must make sure that its deal will be compelling by setting pricing higher. If, by contrast, the market is dry, pricing can be set more aggressively.

TYPES OF SYNDICATED LOAN FACILITY

Revolving Credit

In a revolving credit (RC), borrowers can draw down, repay, and re-borrow. The facility acts much like a credit card, except that borrowers are charged a fee on unused amounts. Many revolvers to leveraged grade borrowers are tied to the Borrowing Base lending formula. This limits borrowing to a certain percentage of collateral, most often receivables and inventory. There a number of options that can be offered within a RC:

- *Swingline* —A small overnight borrowing line typically provided by the agent.
- *Multi-Currency*—The borrower may have the right to borrow in several currencies.
- *Competitive Bid Option (CBO)*—Allows borrowers to solicit the best bids from its syndicate group. The agent will conduct what amounts to an auction to raise funds for the borrower. The best bids are accepted and used. Typically available to large, investment-grade borrowers.
- *Term-Out*—Many RCs allow the borrower to term-out borrowings at a given conversion date. Under the option, borrowers may take what is outstanding under the facility and pay it off on a predetermined repayment schedule.
- *Evergreen* —The option for the borrower—with consent of the syndicate group—to extend the facility each year for an additional year.

364-Day Facility

A 364-day facility is precisely that—a revolving credit that runs 364 days. The reason is that regulatory capital guidelines set a one-year cutoff on whether banks must reserve capital against unused amounts under revolving credits. Therefore, banks offer more attractive undrawn fees (commitment and/or annual fees) on 364-day facilities than on multiyear RCs.

Term Loan

With a term loan, or installment loan, the borrower may draw down the loan during a set initial commitment period. Then the borrower repays the loan based on a scheduled series of repayments or a one-time payment at maturity (bullet payment). A common example is an auto loan.

Amortizing Term Loan

An amortizing term loan is a term loan with a progressive repayment schedule that typically run six years or less in term. These loans are normally syndicated to banks along with revolving credits as part of a syndication.

Institutional Term Loan

Institutional term loans (B/C/D Term Loans) are term loan facilities carved out for nonbank, institutional investors. These loans are priced higher than amortizing term loans because they have longer maturities and back-end loaded repayment schedules. The loans are named in alphabetical order: TLb/c/d.

Letter of Credit

There are a number of different letters of credit (LC) which, simply put, are guarantees provided by the bank to pay off debt or obligations if the borrower cannot.

Equipment Lines

Equipment lines provide credit that may be drawn down for a given period to purchase specified assets or equipment. The lines are then repaid over a specified period. Repaid amounts may not be borrowed.

SYNDICATING A LOAN BY FACILITY

Most loans in the leveraged market comprise a revolving credit, an amortizing term loan (TLa) and several institutional term loan tranches. Most loans are structured and syndicated to accommodate the two primary syndicated lender constituencies: Banks (domestic and foreign) and institutional investors (primarily mutual funds and insurance companies).

Most times, loan facilities are divided into two pieces to appeal to these groups:

- *Pro Rata*—This comprises the RC and TLa, which are packaged together and normally syndicated to banks. In some deals, however, institutional investors take pieces of the TLa and, less often, RC.
- *Institutional*—This comprises institutional term loans. In most deals these facilities are packaged together and sold to institutional investors, though some banks are buyers of institutional term loans.

SECONDARY SALES

After the loan is syndicated and closed, the lender may sell pieces of their commitment to other lenders. New lenders may buy basically in two ways: assignments and participations.

Assignments

The assignee becomes a direct signatory to the loan and receives interest and principal payments directly from the administrative agent. Assignments typically require the consent of the borrower and agent. Consent may be withheld only if a reasonable objection is made. The amount of the assignment usually must exceed a certain amount (typically $5–$10 million) and the assigning bank must pay a fee to the administrative agent (the fee can range broadly but usually is $2,000–$3,500). This fee also may be less if the assignee is an existing lender that is just increasing its position in the loan.

Traditionally arrangers have waived assignments for their best institutional accounts on secondary trades that they've executed. And since 2001, several league table banks have instituted policies where they would waive fees on trades made away from them—on loans for which they are the administrative agent—if, of course, the dealer that made that particular trade adopted a similar policy. At this writing, in December 2001, five or six of the 25 active dealers had adopted such a policy, so it was not yet a market convention. But, institutional accounts, discussed previously, are gaining increasing power in the market and are exerting a great deal of pressure on the sell side to do away with fees altogether.

Participations

A participation is an agreement between a lender and a participant. The participant is essentially participating in the lender's loan. The lender remains the official holder of the loan with the participant owning the rights to the amount purchased. Consents, fees, or minimums are almost never required. The participant only has the right to vote on material changes in the loan document (rate, term, and collateral). Non-material changes do not require approval of participants. A participation can be a more risky way of purchasing a loan because if the lender becomes insolvent or defaults, the participant does not have a direct claim on the loan. In this case, the participant become a creditor of the lender and often must wait for claims to be sorted out in order to collect on its participation.

PRICING

Rates

Bank loans usually offer borrowers different interest rate options. Several of these options allow borrowers to lock in a given rate for a one-month to one-year period. Pricing on many loans is tied to performance grids, which adjust pricing by one or more financial criteria. Pricing is typically tied to rating in investment-grade loans and financial ratios in leveraged loans. Communications loans are invariably tied to the borrower's debt to cash flow ratio. Pricing options include those described below.

Prime

This is a floating-rate option. Borrowed funds are priced at a spread over the reference bank's prime lending rate. The rate is reset daily and borrowers may be repaid at any time without penalty. This is typically an overnight option, because the prime option is more costly to the borrower than LIBOR or CDs.

LIBOR (or Eurodollars)

Interest on borrowings is set at a spread over LIBOR (London Interbank Offered Rate) for a period of one month to one year. The corresponding LIBOR rate is used to set pricing. Borrowings cannot be prepaid before the end of the period unless the borrower receives the consent of banks or reimburses the banks for any potential loss resulting from the prepayment.

CD

This option works precisely like the LIBOR option except the base rate is certificates of deposit (CDs) sold by a bank to institutional investors.

Other Fixed-Rate Options

There are a number of other options that are less common but work like the LIBOR and CD options. These include federal funds (the overnight rate charged by the Federal Reserve to member banks) and cost of funds (the bank's own funding rate).

Fees

There are a number of fees associated with syndicated loans. They are described as follows.

Upfront Fee

More recently as the market has matured, participants have taken to adopting bond market parlance and referring to this fee as an original issue discount. In any case, it is the fee paid by the borrower to the banks for making the loan. The fee is often tiered, with the agent (or agents) receiving a larger amount in consideration of structuring and/or underwriting the loan, thereby assuming greater risk. Once pricing and structure are set, the agent(s)—often with borrower approval or at least knowledge—will set several fee tiers for the retail market, with lenders making larger commitments and receiving higher fees. Most often, fees are paid on a lender's final allocation. For example, a loan has two fee tiers: 100 basis points (or 1.0%) for $25 million commitments and 50 basis points for $15 million commitments. A lender committing to the $25 million tier will be paid on its final allocation rather than on its initial commitment. In this example, the loan is oversubscribed and lenders committing $25 million are allocated $20 million; these lenders will receive a fee of $200,000 (or 1.0% of $20 million). Sometimes upfront fees will be structured as a percent of final allocation plus a flat fee. This happens most often for larger fee tiers to encourage potential lenders to step up for larger commitments. The flat fee is paid regardless of the lender's final allocation.

Commitment Fee

A commitment fee, of up to 0.50% annually, is paid to lenders on undrawn amounts under a revolving credit or a term loan prior to draw down. On term loans, this fee is usually referred to as a "ticking" fee.

Facility Fee

Facility fees are paid on a facility's entire committed amount, regardless of usage. This fee is often charged on revolving credits to investment-grade borrowers, instead of a commitment fee. The reason: These facilities typically have competitive bid options (CBOs) that allow a borrower to solicit the best bid from its syndicate group for a given borrowing. The lenders that do not lend under the CBO are still paid for their commitment.

Administrative Agent Fees

The agent is typically paid an annual fee to administer the loan (including distributing interest payments to the syndicated group, updating lender lists and managing borrowings). For secured loans (particularly those backed by receivables and inventory) the agent often collects a collateral monitoring fee, to ensure that the promised collateral is in place.

Letter of Credit Fees

There are several types of letter of credit fees. The most common—a fee for standby or financial letters of credit—guarantees that lenders will support various corporate activities. Because these LCs are considered borrowed funds under capital guidelines, the fee is typically the same as the LIBOR margin. Fees for commercial LCs (those supporting inventory or trade) are typically lower because actual collateral is submitted). The LC is usually issued by a fronting bank (usually the agent) and syndicated to the lender group on a pro rata basis. The group receives the LC fee on their respective shares, while the fronting bank receives an issuing (or fronting, or facing) fee for issuing and administering the LC. This fee is almost always 12.5–25.0 bps (0.125–0.250%) of the LC commitment.

Cancellation/Prepayment Fees

Cancellation/prepayment fees are found only in loans to the most risky borrowers. They are fees paid to banks if the borrower repays early. Most have a sliding scale, so that borrowings prepaid in year one are charged a higher fee, which declines over time. Prepayment fees are often featured on Amortization Extended Loans (Axels), a version of institutional term loans from Goldman Sachs.

VOTING RIGHTS

Amendments (changes) to a loan agreement must be approved by a certain percentage of lenders. Most loan agreements have three levels of approval:

- *Required Lenders*—Typically the percentage of lenders required to approve non-material amendments and waivers. This number is usually a simple majority. In addition, changes affecting one facility within a deal almost always require the approval of a majority of that facility's lenders.
- *Full Vote*—Approval of all lenders (including participants) is required to approve material changes. These are typically RATS

rights (Rate, amortization, term, and security/collateral), though, as described below, sometimes changes in amortization and collateral may be approved by a lower percentage of lenders (a supermajority).

■ *Supermajority* —Many loans also have a supermajority voting tier (typically 67–80%) under which certain material changes can be made. These include changes in amortization (in-term repayments) and release of collateral.

COVENANTS

Loan agreements have a series of restrictions which dictate, to varying degrees, how borrowers can operate and how they can carry themselves financially. For instance, one covenant may require the borrower to maintain its fiscal-year end. Another may prohibit the borrower from taking on new debt. Most agreements also have financial compliance covenants. For instance, a borrower must keep a certain level of equity; if not, banks have the right to terminate the agreement or push the borrower into default. The size of the covenant package increases in proportion to a borrower's financial risk. Agreements to investment-grade companies are usually thin and easy. Agreements to leveraged borrowers often are much more onerous. There are three primary covenant types that are described next.

Affirmative Covenants

Affirmative covenants state what the borrower must do to be in compliance with the loan. An example would be that the borrower must maintain insurance. These covenants are usually boiler-plate and require a borrower to pay the bank interest and fees, maintain insurance, pay taxes, and so forth.

Negative Covenants

Negative covenants limit the borrower's activities. An example would be a limit on new investments. Negative covenants are highly structured and customized to a borrower's specific condition. They can limit the type and amount of investments, new debt, liens, asset sales, acquisitions and guarantees.

Financial Covenants

Financial covenants enforce minimum financial performance measures on the borrower. For example, the borrower must maintain a higher level of current assets than current liabilities. These covenants become more tightly wound and extensive as a borrower's risk increases. In general, there are five types of financial covenants:

- *Coverage*—The borrower must maintain a minimum level of cash flow or earnings, relative to specified expenses, most often interest, debt service (interest and repayments), fixed charges (debt service, capital expenditures and/or rent).
- *Leverage*—A maximum level of debt relative to either equity or cash flow. The debt to cash flow level is far more common.
- *Current Ratio*—The borrower must maintain a minimum ratio of current assets (cash, marketable securities, accounts receivable, and inventories) to current liabilities (accounts payable, short-term debt of less than one year). Sometimes, a Quick Ratio is substituted. The only difference: Inventories are not excluded from the numerate.
- *Tangible Net Worth* (TNW)—Most borrowers are required to have a minimum level of TNW (net worth less intangible assets such as goodwill, intellectual assets, excess value paid for acquired companies). There often is a build-up provision increasing the minimum by a percentage of net income or equity issuance.
- *Maximum Capital Expenditures*—Borrower must limit capital expenditures (purchases of property, plant, and equipment) to a certain amount. The amount may be increased by some percentage of cash flow or equity issuance. Also, the borrower often can carry forward amounts not used in the current year to the next year.

Mandatory Prepayments

Usually, leveraged loans require a borrower to prepay with proceeds of excess cash flow, asset sales, and debt or equity issuance.

- *Excess Cash Flow*—Typically defined as Cash Flow after all cash expenses, required Dividends, Debt Repayments, Capital Expenditures and changes in Working Capital. Typical percent: 50–75%.
- *Asset Sales*—Net proceeds of asset sales, normally excluding receivables or inventories. Typical percent: 100%.
- *Debt Issuance*—Net proceeds from debt issuance. Typical percent: 100%.
- *Equity Issuance*—Net proceeds of equity issuance. Typical percent: 25–50%.

CHAPTER 20

Collateralized Debt Obligations

Laurie S. Goodman, Ph.D.
Managing Director
UBS Warburg

Frank J. Fabozzi, Ph.D., CFA
Adjunct Professor of Finance
School of Management
Yale University

A collateralized debt obligation (CDO) is an asset-backed security backed by a diversified pool of one or more of the following types of debt obligations:

- U.S. domestic investment-grade and high-yield corporate bonds
- U.S. domestic bank loans
- emerging market bonds
- special situation loans and distressed debt
- foreign bank loans
- asset-backed securities
- residential and commercial mortgage-backed securities

When the underlying pool of debt obligations consists of bond-type instruments (corporate and emerging market bonds), a CDO is referred to as a *collateralized bond obligation* (CBO). When the underlying pool of debt obligations are bank loans, a CDO is referred to as a *collateralized loan obligation* (CLO).

In this chapter we explain the basic CDO structure, the types of CDOs, the risks associated with investing in CDOs, and the general principles for creating a portfolio of CDOs.

STRUCTURE OF A CDO

In a CDO structure, there is an asset manager responsible for managing the portfolio. There are restrictions imposed (i.e., restrictive covenants) as to what the asset manager may do and certain tests that must be satisfied for the CDO securities to maintain the credit rating assigned at the time of issuance. We'll discuss some of these requirements later.

The funds to purchase the underlying assets (i.e., the bonds and loans) are obtained from the issuance of debt obligations. These debt obligations are referred to as *tranches*. The tranches are:

■ senior tranches
■ mezzanine tranches
■ subordinate/equity tranche

There will be a rating sought for all but the subordinate/equity tranche. For the senior tranches, at least an A rating is typically sought. For the mezzanine tranches, a rating of BBB but no less than B is sought. Since the subordinate/equity tranche receives the residual cash flow, no rating is sought for this tranche.

The ability of the asset manager to make the interest payments to the tranches and pay off the tranches as they mature depends on the performance of the underlying assets. The proceeds to meet the obligations to the CDO tranches (interest and principal repayment) can come from

■ coupon interest payments from the underlying assets
■ maturing assets in the underlying pool
■ sale of assets in the underlying pool

In a typical structure, one or more of the tranches is a floating-rate security. With the exception of deals backed by bank loans that pay a floating rate, the asset manager invests in fixed-rate bonds. Now that presents a problem—paying tranche investors a floating rate and investing in assets with a fixed rate. To deal with this problem, the asset manager uses derivative instruments to be able to convert a portion of the fixed-rate payments from the assets into floating-rate cash flow to pay floating-rate tranches. In particular, interest rate swaps are used. This instrument allows a market participant to swap fixed-rate payments for floating-rate payments or vice versa. Because of the mismatch between the nature of the cash flows of the assets in which the manager invests and the floating-rate liability of any of the tranches, the asset manager must use an interest rate swap. A rating agency will require the use of swaps to eliminate this mismatch.

Arbitrage versus Balance Sheet Transactions

CDOs are categorized based on the motivation of the sponsor of the transaction. If the motivation of the sponsor is to earn the spread between the yield offered on the assets in the underlying pool and the payments made to the various tranches in the structure, then the transaction is referred to as an *arbitrage transaction*. If the motivation of the sponsor is to remove debt instruments (primarily loans) from its balance sheet, then the transaction is referred to as a *balance sheet transaction*. Sponsors of balance sheet transactions are typically financial institutions such as banks seeking to reduce their capital requirements by removing loans due to their higher risk-based capital requirements. Our focus in this chapter is on arbitrage transactions.

ARBITRAGE TRANSACTIONS

The key as to whether it is economically feasible to create an arbitrage CDO is whether a structure can offer a competitive return for the subordinate/equity tranche.

To understand how the subordinate/equity tranche generates cash flows, consider the following basic $100 million CDO structure with the coupon rate to be offered at the time of issuance as follows:

Tranche	Par value	Coupon type	Coupon rate
Senior	$80,000,000	Floating	LIBOR + 70 basis points
Mezzanine	10,000,000	Fixed	Treasury rate + 200 basis points
Subordinate/Equity	10,000,000	—	—

Suppose that the collateral consists of bonds that all mature in 10 years and the coupon rate for every bond is the 10-year Treasury rate plus 400 basis points. The asset manager enters into an interest rate swap agreement with another party with a notional principal of $80 million in which it agrees to do the following:

■ Pay a fixed rate each year equal to the 10-year Treasury rate plus 100 basis points
■ Receive LIBOR

The interest rate agreement is simply an agreement to periodically exchange interest payments. The payments are benchmarked off a notional principal. This amount is not exchanged between the two parties. Rather it is used simply to determine the dollar interest payment of each party. This is all we need to know about an interest rate swap in order to understand the economics of an arbitrage CDO transaction.[1] Keep in mind, the goal is to show how the subordinate/equity tranche can be expected to generate a return.

Let's assume that the 10-year Treasury rate at the time the CDO is issued is 7%. Now we can walk through the cash flows for each year. Look first at the collateral. The collateral will pay interest each year (assuming no defaults) equal to the 10-year Treasury rate of 7% plus 400 basis points. So the interest will be:

Interest from collateral: $11\% \times \$100,000,000 = \$11,000,000$

Now let's determine the interest that must be paid to the senior and mezzanine tranches. For the senior tranche, the interest payment will be:

Interest to senior tranche: $\$80,000,000 \times (\text{LIBOR} + 70 \text{ bp})$

The coupon rate for the mezzanine tranche is 7% plus 200 basis points. So, the coupon rate is 9% and the interest is:

Interest to mezzanine tranche: $9\% \times \$10,000,000 = \$900,000$

Finally, let's look at the interest rate swap. In this agreement, the asset manager is agreeing to pay some third party (we'll call this party the "swap counterparty") 7% each year (the 10-year Treasury rate) plus 100 basis points, or 8%. But 8% of what? As explained above, in an interest rate swap payments are based on a notional principal. In our illustration, the notional principal is $80 million. The asset manager selected the $80 million because this is the amount of principal for the senior tranche. So, the asset manager pays to the swap counterparty:

Interest to swap counterparty: $8\% \times \$80,000,000 = \$6,400,000$

---

[1] Interest rate swaps are covered in Chapter 29.

The interest payment received from the swap counterparty is LIBOR based on a notional amount of $80 million. That is,

Interest from swap counterparty: $80,000,000 \times LIBOR$

Now we can put this all together. Let's look at the interest coming into the CDO:

Interest from collateral	=	$11,000,000
Interest from swap counterparty	=	$80,000,000 \times LIBOR$
Total interest received	=	$11,000,000 + $80,000,000 \times LIBOR$

The interest to be paid out to the senior and mezzanine tranches and to the swap counterparty include:

Interest to senior tranche	=	$80,000,000 \times (LIBOR + 70 \text{ bp})$
Interest to mezzanine tranche	=	$900,000
Interest to swap counterparty	=	$6,400,000
Total interest paid	=	$7,300,000 + $80,000,000 \times (LIBOR + 70 \text{bp})$

Netting the interest payments coming in and going out we have:

Total interest received	=	$11,000,000 + $80,000,000 \times LIBOR$
−Total interest paid	=	$7,300,000 + $80,000,000 \times (LIBOR + 70 \text{ bp})$
Net interest	=	$3,700,000 − $80,000,000 \times (70 \text{ bp})$

Since 70 bp times $80 million is $560,000, the net interest remaining is $3,140,000 (= $3,700,000 − $560,000). From this amount any fees (including the asset management fee) must be paid. The balance is then the amount available to pay the subordinate/equity tranche. Suppose that these fees are $614,000. Then the cash flow available to the subordinate/equity tranche is $2.5 million. Since the tranche has a par value of $10 million and is assumed to be sold at par, this means that the potential return is 25%.

Obviously, some simplifying assumptions have been made. For example, it is assumed that there are no defaults. It is assumed that all of the issues purchased by the asset manager are noncallable (or not prepayable) and therefore the coupon rate would not decline because issues are called. Moreover, as explained later, after some period the asset manager must begin repaying principal to the senior and mezzanine tranches. Consequently, the interest swap must be structured to take this into account since the entire amount of the senior tranche is not outstanding for the life of the collateral. Despite these simplifying assumptions, the illustration does demonstrate the basic economics of the CDO, the need for the use of an interest rate swap, and how the subordinate/equity tranche will realize a return.

Early Termination

A deal can be terminated early if certain events of default occur. These events basically relate to conditions that are established that would materially adversely impact the performance of the underlying assets. Such events include (1) the failure to comply with certain covenants, (2) failure to meet payments (interest and/or principal) to the senior tranches, (3) bankruptcy of the issuing entity of the CDO, and (4) departure of the portfolio management team if an acceptable replacement is not found.

Types of Arbitrage Transactions

Arbitrage transactions can be divided into two types depending on what the primary source of the proceeds from the underlying assets are to satisfy the obligation to the tranches. If the primary source is the interest and maturing principal from the underlying assets, then the transaction is referred to as a *cash flow transaction*. If instead the proceeds to meet the obligations depend heavily on the total return generated from the portfolio (i.e., interest income, capital gain, and maturing principal), then the transaction is referred to as a *market value transaction*.

CASH FLOW TRANSACTIONS

In a cash flow transaction, the objective of the asset manager is to generate cash flow for the senior and mezzanine tranches without the need to actively trade bonds. Because the cash flows from the structure are designed to accomplish the objective for each tranche, restrictions are imposed on the asset manager. The asset manager is not free to buy and sell bonds. The conditions for disposing of issues held are specified and are usually driven by credit risk considerations. Also, in assembling the portfolio, the asset manager must meet certain requirements set forth by the rating agency or agencies that rate the transaction.

There are three relevant periods. The first is the *ramp-up period*. This is the period that follows the closing date of the transaction where the asset manager begins investing the proceeds from the sale of the debt obligations issued. This period usually lasts from 1 to 2 years. The *reinvestment period* or *revolving period* is where principal proceeds are reinvested and is usually for 5 or more years. In the final period, the portfolio assets are sold and the debtholders are paid off as described as follows.

Distribution of Income

Income is derived from interest income from the underlying assets and capital appreciation. The income is then used as follows. Payments are first made to the trustee and administrators and then to the senior asset manager. Once these fees are paid, then the senior tranches are paid their interest. At this point, before any other payments are made, certain tests must be passed. These tests are called *coverage tests* and are discussed later. If the coverage tests are passed, then interest is paid to the mezzanine tranches. Once the mezzanine tranches are paid, interest is paid to the subordinate/equity tranche.

In contrast, if the coverage tests are not passed, then payments are made to protect the senior tranches. The remaining income after paying the fees and senior tranche interest is used to redeem the senior tranches (i.e., pay off principal) until the coverage tests are brought into compliance. If the senior tranches are paid off fully because the coverage tests are not brought into compliance, then any remaining income is used to redeem the mezzanine tranches. Any remaining income is then used to redeem the subordinate/equity tranche.

Distribution of Principal Cash Flow

The principal cash flow is distributed as follows after the payment of the fees to the trustees, administrators, and senior managers. If there is a shortfall in interest paid to the senior tranches, principal proceeds are used to make up the shortfall. Assuming that the coverage tests are satisfied, during the reinvestment period the principal is reinvested. After the reinvestment period or if the coverage tests are failed, the principal cash flow is used to pay down the senior tranches until the coverage tests are satisfied. If all the senior tranches are paid down, then the mezzanine tranches are paid off and then the subordinate/equity tranche is paid off.

After all the debt obligations are satisfied in full and if permissible, the subordinate/equity investors are paid. Typically, there are also incentive fees paid to management based on performance. Usually, a target return for the subordinate/equity investors is established at the inception of the transaction. Management is then permitted to share on some pro rata basis once the target return is achieved. Later when we explain how to assess a CDO, we will see that the incentive fee structure is an important factor.

Restrictions on Management

The asset manager must monitor the collateral to ensure that certain tests are being met. There are two types of tests imposed by rating agencies: quality tests and coverage tests.

Quality Tests

In rating a transaction, the rating agencies are concerned with the diversity of the assets. Consequently, there are tests that relate to the diversity of the assets. These tests are called *quality tests*. An asset manager may not undertake a trade that will result in the violation of any of the quality tests. Quality tests include

- a minimum asset diversity score
- a minimum weighted average rating
- maturity restrictions
- restrictions imposed on the concentration of bonds in certain countries or geographical regions for collateral consisting of emerging market bonds

Diversity Score An asset diversity score is a measure that is constructed to gauge the diversity of the collateral's assets. Moody's has developed a measure. It is beyond the scope of this chapter to discuss this measure and the theory underlying its construction. Rather, what is important to understand is that every time the composition of the portfolio changes, a diversity score is computed. There is a minimum diversity score needed to achieve a particular rating.

Weighted Average Rating A measure is also needed to gauge the credit quality of the collateral's assets. Certainly one can describe the distribution of the credit ratings of a portfolio in terms of the percentage of the collateral's assets in each credit rating. However, such a measure would be of limited use in establishing tests for a minimum credit rating for the portfolio. There is a need to have one figure that summarizes the rating distribution.

Moody's and Fitch have developed a measure to summarize the rating distribution. This measure is commonly referred to as the *weighted average rating factor* (WARF) for the collateral's assets. This involves assigning a numerical value to each rating. These numerical values are referred to as "rating factors." For example, Moody's assigns a rating factor of 1 for Aaa rated issues scaling up to 10,000 for Ca rated issues. For each issue in the collateral portfolio, the current *face value* of the issue is multiplied by its corresponding rating factor. The values are then summed to give the WARF and a WARF value would then correspond to a rating for the collateral portfolio. The asset manager must maintain a minimum average rating score.

Unlike Moody's and Fitch, S&P uses a different system. S&P specifies *required rating* percentages that the collateral portfolio must maintain. Specifically, S&P requires strict percentage limits for lower rated assets in the portfolio.

Coverage Tests

There are tests to ensure that the performance of the collateral is sufficient to make payments to the various tranches. These tests are called *coverage tests*. There are two types of coverage tests: par value tests and interest coverage tests. Recall that if the coverage tests are violated, then income from the collateral is diverted to pay down the senior tranches.

Par value test   A separate par value test is used for each rated bond issued in the transaction. A *par value test* specifies that the par value of the collateral's portfolio be at least a specified percentage above the liability to the bondholders. For example, suppose that the par value of the senior notes in a CDO deal is $50 million. The par value test might specify that the collateral's par value must be 120% of the par value of the senior notes. That is, the par value of the collateral must be at least $60 million ($50 million times 120%). Basically, this is an *overcollateralization test* for a rated bond issued since it is a measure of the cushion provided by the collateral's assets over the obligation to the bondholders *in terms of par value*.

The percentage in the par value test is called the *trigger*, and as indicated, the trigger is different for each rated bond. Specifically, the trigger declines as the rating declines. For example, if the trigger for the senior tranches is 120%, then the trigger will be less than 120% for the mezzanine tranches. This simply means that the overcollateralization in terms of par value declines as the rating of a bond issued in the transaction declines.

Interest coverage test   While par value tests focus on the market value of the collateral relative to the par value of the bonds issued, *interest coverage tests* look at the ability to meet interest payments when due.

MARKET VALUE TRANSACTIONS

Cash flow transactions are dependent on the ability of the collateral to generate sufficient current cash flow to pay interest and principal on the rated tranches issued by the CDO. The ratings are based on the effect of collateral defaults and recoveries on the receipt of timely interest and principal payments from the collateral. The asset manager focuses on controlling defaults and recoveries. *Overcollateralization*, in terms of par value of the collateral's assets, provides important structural protection for bondholders. If par value (overcollateralization) tests are not met, then cash flow is diverted from the mezzanine and subordinated tranches to pay down senior notes, or cash flow is trapped in a reserve account. There are no forced collateral liquidations.

In contrast, market value transactions depend upon the ability of the asset manager to maintain and improve the market value of the collateral. Funds to be used for liability principal payments are obtained from liquidating the collateral. Liability interest payments can be made from collateral interest receipts, as well as collateral liquidation proceeds. Ratings are based on collateral price volatility, liquidity, and market value. The asset manager focuses on maximizing total return while minimizing volatility.

Overcollateralization tests are conducted regularly. However, in market value transactions, the overcollateralization tests are based on the *market value* of the collateral portfolio, not the par value. Market value overcollateralization tests require that the market value of assets multiplied by the "advance rates" (discussed later) be greater than or equal to debt outstanding. If that is not the case, collateral sales and liability redemptions may be required to bring overcollateralization ratios back into compliance.[2] As with cash value transactions, market value transactions do have diversity, concentration, and other portfolio constraints, albeit less than cash flow transactions. Exhibit 20.1 summarizes the salient features of cash flow versus market value transactions.

Why are market value structures used? While market value deals are a distinct minority of CBOs, they are the structure of choice for certain types of collateral (such as distressed debt), where the cash flows are not predictable with a reasonable degree of certainty. It is very difficult to use unpredictable cash flows within the confines of a cash flow structure. Moreover, market value structures may also appeal to asset managers and equity buyers who like the greater trading flexibility inherent in these deals. Finally, market value transactions also facilitate the purchase of assets that mature beyond the life of the transaction, because the price volatility associated with the forced sale of these assets is explicitly considered.

Let's illustrate the structure with the hypothetical transaction shown in Exhibit 20.2. The first column of the exhibit shows the capital structure of the transaction. The capital structure includes a senior facility, senior notes, senior-mezzanine notes, subordinate notes, and equity. The senior facility is a floating-rate revolving loan. This structure has a subordinated tranche as well as an equity tranche. The second column shows the capital structure at the closing date.

During the ramp-up period, the asset manager obtains additional funding based on the target leverage. The additional leverage is provided from the senior borrowing facility and additional amount provided by senior notes. Additional equity is also injected. The last column shows the capital structure when the transaction is fully ramped up.

---

[2] There other alternatives to bring the portfolio into compliance: higher quality securities with higher advance rates can be substituted for lower quality securities with lower advance rates. The point is that action must be taken to safeguard the interest of the bondholders.

EXHIBIT 20.1   Overview of Cash Flow versus Market Value Transactions

	Cash Flow Deal	Market Value Deal
Objective	Cash Flow deals depend on the ability of the collateral to generate sufficient current cash to pay interest and principal on rated notes issued by the CBO/CLO.	Market Value transactions depend on the ability of the fund manager to maintain and improve the market value of the collateral.
Rating Focus	The ratings are based on the effect of collateral defaults and recoveries on the timely payment of interest and principal from the collateral.	Ratings are based on collateral price volatility, liquidity and market value.
Manager Focus	Manager focuses on controlling defaults and recoveries.	Manager focuses on maximizing total return while minimizing volatility.
Structural Protection	Overcollateralization is measured on the basis of the portfolio' s par value. If overcollateralization tests are failed, then cash flow is diverted from the mezzanine and subordinated classes to pay down senior notes, or cash flow is trapped in a reserve account. There are no forced collateral liquidations.	Market Value overcollateralization tests are conducted regularly. The market value of assets multiplied by the advance rates* must be greater than or equal to the debt outstanding; otherwise collateral sales and liability redemptions may be required to bring overcollateralization ratios back into compliance.
Diversity and Concentration Limits	Very strict.	Substantial diversification is required. More is "encouraged" by the structure of advance rates.
Trading Limitations	There are limitations on portfolio trading.	There is greater portfolio trading flexibility.
Collateral	Typical Cash Flow assets include bank loans, high yield bonds, emerging market bonds/loans, and project finance.	Typical Market Value assets include assets eligible for inclusion in Cash Flow CBOs/CLOs as well as distressed debt, equities, and convertibles.

* Advance rate: percentage of the market value of a particular asset that may be issued as rated debt. Advance rates depend upon the price volatility and quality of price/return data and the liquidity of the assets. Assets with lower price volatility and greater liquidity are typically assigned higher advance rates.

EXHIBIT 20.2   Illustration of a Hypothetical Market Value Transaction
(in millions of dollars)

Capital Structure	At Closing Date	Fully Ramped Up
Senior facility	$0	$364
Senior note	40	160
Senior-subordinated notes	80	80
Subordinated notes	40	40
Equity	8	160

The order of priority of the principal payments in the capital structure is as follows. Fees are paid first for trustees, administrators, and managers. After these fees are paid, the senior facility and the senior notes are paid. The two classes in the capital structure are treated *pari passu* (i.e., equal in their rights to their claim on cash proceeds from the underlying assets). That is, their payments are pro rated if there is a shortfall. If the senior facility or senior notes are amortizing, they would have the next priority on the cash proceeds from the underlying assets with respect to the payment of the principal due. The senior-subordinated notes would be paid, followed by the subordinated notes. All of this assumes that the overcollateralization tests are satisfied. If not, the senior notes are then paid down until the overcollateralization tests are brought into compliance.

The Rating Process

The credit enhancement for a market value deal is the cushion between the current market value of the collateral and the face value of the structure's obligations. Within this framework, the collateral must normally be liquidated (either in whole or in part) if the ratio of the market value of the collateral to the debt obligations falls below a predetermined threshold. The liquidated collateral is used to pay down debt obligations, which brings the structure back into compliance.

The biggest risk in a market value transaction is a sudden decline in the value of the collateral pool. Thus, the rating agencies focus on the price volatility and liquidity of the assets that may be incorporated into these structures. Volatility and liquidity are assumed to be reflected in a set of advance rates that are designed to provide a cushion against market risk, and represent adjustments to the value of each asset.

A market value deal simply requires that the market value of the collateral times the advance rate (the adjustment to the value of the assets to provide a cushion against market risk) be greater than the book value of the liabilities. Moody's and Fitch, the rating agencies that have rated the majority of market value deals thus far, both use a set of advance rates to determine how much rated debt can be issued against the market value of an asset.

To get a handle on what this all means, Exhibit 20.3 shows Moody's advance rates in the simplest case of a one-tranche structure—one with subordination provided only by the advance rate. In producing the advance rates shown in Exhibit 20.3, Moody's assumed the following regarding portfolio diversification:

1. Maximum allowable investment in one issuer = 5%
2. Maximum allowable investment in any one industry = 20%
3. Maximum allowable investment in any one asset type = 100%

Thus, the least diversified portfolio consists of 20 issuers, 5 industries, and one asset type.

If an asset class consists of performing high-yield bonds rated B, and the deal is carved only into a bond rated A2 and equity, then (from Exhibit 20.3) Moody's advance rate would be 0.79. Thus, the market value of the deal times the advance rate (0.79 in this case) must be greater than the market value of the bonds. If a deal has several tranches, then the par value of the debt within each rating is weighted to find the weighted average advance rate. Thus, if the liabilities consisted of equal parts of bonds rated A2 (with an advance rate of 0.79) and those rated Baa2 (with an advance rate of 0.83), then the weighted average advance rate would be 0.81. Note that if there were greater diversification within this deal, then the advance rates would be somewhat higher.

In addition to the protection provided by advance rates, Fitch also has a required quarterly minimum net worth test to protect the rated debt. This requires that 60% of the original equity remains to protect the senior tranche, and 30% to protect the subordinated tranche. If the equity falls below that, noteholders of the senior tranche may vote to accelerate payment of the debt, at which point the asset manager must liquidate assets and fully pay down the debt related to the test that has failed.

Advance rates are the crucial variable in market value deals. Advance rates determined by the rating agencies are actually a combination of three factors—price volatility of the securities, correlation among securities, and liquidity.

Many CBO investors have tended to steer away from the debt in market value deals, believing that purchasing the debt is like making an investment in a hedge fund. As a result, market value deals trade at similar or slightly wider spreads than cash flow deals launched at the same time. However, the protections built into market value deals are quite powerful from the bondholder's point of view, and that this paper will eventually trade tighter than paper from cash flow deals with the same rating issued at the same time. Investors should regard the rated bonds in market value deals (offered at similar or slightly wider spreads than equivalently rated bonds in cash flow deals) as a buying opportunity.

EXHIBIT 20.3 Advance Rates for Different Asset Types and Rating Levels (20 issuers, 5 industries, 100% investment in one asset type, 5-year maturity)

Asset Type	Aaa	Aa1	Aa2	Aa3	A1	A2	A3	Baa1	Baa2	Baa3
Performing Bank Loans Valued $0.90 and above	0.870	0.890	0.895	0.900	0.905	0.910	0.915	0.930	0.935	9.400
Distressed Bank Loans Valued $0.85 and above	0.760	0.780	0.790	0.795	0.810	0.815	0.820	0.830	0.840	0.870
Performing High-Yield Bonds Rated Baa	0.76	0.79	0.80	0.81	0.83	0.84	0.85	0.87	0.88	0.90
Performing High-Yield Bonds Rated B	0.72	0.75	0.76	0.77	0.78	0.79	0.80	0.82	0.83	0.85
Distressed Bank Loans Valued Below $0.85	0.58	0.62	0.63	0.64	0.67	0.68	0.69	0.71	0.72	0.74
Performing High-Yield Valued Below Caa	0.45	0.49	0.50	0.51	0.56	0.58	0.60	0.62	0.64	0.67
Distressed Bonds	0.35	0.39	0.40	0.41	0.47	0.48	0.50	0.54	0.56	0.57
Reorganized Equities	0.31	0.37	0.38	0.39	0.44	0.46	0.47	0.51	0.52	0.54

Source: Moody's Investors Service, "Moody's Approach to Rating Market-Valued CDOs" (April 13, 1998).

SYNTHETIC CDOS

A *synthetic CDO* is so named because the CDO does not actually own the pool of assets on which it has the risk. Stated differently, a synthetic CDO absorbs the economic risks, but not the legal ownership, of its reference credit exposures. Synthetic CDO structures are now widely used in both arbitrage and balance sheet transactions.

The building block for synthetic securitizations is a credit derivative.[3] More specifically, it a credit default swap, which allows institutions to transfer the economic risk, but not the legal ownership, of underlying assets. A credit default swap is conceptually similar to an insurance policy. A protection buyer (generally the CDO's asset manager) purchases protection against default risk on a reference pool of assets. Those assets can consist of any combination of loans, bonds, derivatives, or receivables. The protection buyer pays a periodic fee (like an insurance premium) and receives, in return, payment from the protection seller (the CDO investors) in the event of a "credit event" affecting any item in the reference pool.

Credit events on a debt instrument generally include: bankruptcy or failure to pay when due, cross default/cross acceleration, repudiation, and restructuring. The bottom line is that the CDO and its investors receive a periodic fee (for accepting the economic risks on the reference pool), and the CDO pays out to the asset manager in the event a defined "credit event" occurs on those reference assets. In the event a credit event occurs, there is an intent that the protection buyer be made whole: The protection buyer should be paid the difference between par and the "fair value" of the securities.[4]

What is the motivation for the creation of synthetic CDOs? By embedding a credit default swap within a CDO structure, financial institutions can shed the economic risk of assets without having to notify any borrowers, or worse, seek borrowers' consent to put their loans into "other hands." In traditional balance sheet collateralized loan obligations (CLOs), transfer of a loan to any special purpose vehicle (SPV) requires at least customer notification, and often customer consent. Thus synthetic

---

[3] Credit derivatives are discussed in Chapter 31.

[4] The settlement on the credit default swap can take the form of either physical settlement or cash settlement. In a physical settlement, the buyer of the protection delivers to the seller an obligation of the reference entity that has experienced a credit event. The obligation must have the same status in the reference entity's capital structure. The protection seller pays par for the asset that has experienced a credit event, even though its current value may be less, thus making the protection buyer whole. In a cash settled swap, the defaulted credit is marked to market, and the protection buyer is paid the difference between par and post-default market value. Most synthetic CDOs have an embedded cash settled swap.

CDOs were initially set up to accommodate European bank balance sheet deals, as it is considered particularly bad form and poor customer relationship management on that continent to sell customer loans.

From an investor's perspective, the concern with synthetic CDOs has been the downgrading of some of the earlier deals. The downgrading reflected the concerns of the rating agencies with respect to the composition of reference pools. Current deals build in substantially better investor protection than was the case in early synthetic CDOs. This improved protection centers on two basic areas: narrowing the definition of credit events in the credit default swap and improving pool disclosure.

MANAGING A CDO PORTFOLIO

Portfolio managers have accumulated positions in a number of CDOs. Some even have quite an extensive collection, with positions in more than 100 different CDO deals. Yet most portfolio managers tend to look at buying each additional CDO as if they were buying their first. In doing that, they spend a disproportionate amount of time trying to evaluate the manager, and often end up trying to differentiate on the basis of track records.

Although one should look at individual deals, it is crucial to look at the incentive structure in a CDO. Performance of existing CDOs provides much more information than do track records of CDO managers. Moreover, it is of utmost import to manage a portfolio of CDOs within general portfolio framework and parameters.

The key to diversification in CDOs comes from holding different types of collateral. A CDO with a low diversity score may actually increase the diversity of a portfolio, depending on its contents. Style (or asset class) is the most important factor in explaining investment returns.

General Rules For CDO Portfolio Management

Here are four general rules for CDO portfolio management:

Rule 1. In picking managers, track records cannot be taken at face value. Common sense goes a long way.

Rule 2. Look at the incentive structure for a manager. If possible, see how strong an impact that has had in outstanding deals.

Rule 3. Collect CDOs backed by different types of collateral. Asset class is a far more important determinant of returns than is choice of specific managers. Buy a certain type of CDO when you believe the underlying collateral is cheap.

Rule 4. Look at diversity on a portfolio basis. Buying a number of CDOs, backed by different types of collateral, creates your own diversification. So don't necessarily avoid CDOs with low diversity scores.

We discuss the reasoning behind each of these rules below.

Track Records

When marketing a CDO deal, the first words spoken to the investor are often "The most important aspect of picking a CDO is selecting a manager; so look at the track record of this manager." But we believe it is very difficult for investors to assess a manager on track records alone, as they do not necessarily allow easy comparison. The best one can hope to establish is that a manager has been managing that particular asset class for a long period of time, their investment approach can be articulated clearly, and risk management parameters are strictly adhered to.

There is good reason to be very skeptical about track records. They contain three biases—"creation bias," "survivorship bias," and "size bias." A discussion of these biases are beyond the scope of this chapter. It should be noted, however, that there is a good deal of academic literature on these biases as they pertain to the equity mutual fund arena. The same biases apply to fixed income funds, as well.

Common Sense

Rule 1 states that the key to evaluating manager performance is to use common sense. Don't be duped by performance numbers. Here is what to look for:

- Make sure the firm has a track record with every asset class it is including, and that the asset manager is not stretching into asset classes in which they have not historically been active.

- Make sure the firm has a disciplined, consistent approach to investing, which is followed in good times and bad.

- Look at the stability of both the firm and the manager. A management team that has been at a firm for a long period of time, with significant equity, is less likely to leave. (Ideally, CDO investors would like to handcuff managers to the firm for the life of their deal. One obviously can't do that, but bigger manager stakes mean there's less likelihood of leaving.) Moreover, the longer a group of people has been working together, the less chance of a sudden shift in strategy.

There is an assumption on the part of investors that Wall Street dealers who underwrite CDOs act as gatekeepers, allowing only the top-notch performing managers to pass through their pearly gates. That blind trust is to some extent misplaced. More money management firms wish to manage CDOs than there is dealer pipeline capacity. Thus, a dealer wants to underwrite CDOs (from managers) they believe will sell quickly.

However there are often other considerations, including overall quality of the relationship between the dealer and an asset manager, as well as help the asset manager can provide in marketing the deal and taking some of the equity. Consider two asset managers; one has a very good track record, the other only an average one. The manager with the average track record will take all the equity in the CDOs, plus some of the subordinate securities. The manager with the better track record wants the underwriters to market all the equity. Who will the underwriters pick? It's a no brainer—the manager with the average track record who is willing to provide more help in underwriting the deal.

Realize that the Wall Street dealer community does require at least a minimum performance threshold. The manager's investment philosophy and track record do have to be good enough to market the deal. Moreover, since dealers are looking at the overall quality of the relationship between the dealer and asset manager, as well as an asset manager's willingness to take down some of the equity, it's natural that larger, better established money management firms are likely to have an edge. This is a good thing for investors, per our common sense tests above.

Checking Out the Incentive Structures in Existing CDO Deals

One of the most important pieces of analysis in evaluating a new CDO deal is to look at how managers have responded to incentive structures on their outstanding deals. In most deals, the deal manager owns between 25% and 49.5% of the equity. (If they owned 50% or more, the entire deal would get consolidated onto their balance sheet.) We believe that in a CDO structure, a deal manager usually has a powerful incentive to keep cash flow going to the equity tranche, even if that works to the detriment of bondholders and net asset value of the deal.

Recall that cutting off cash flows to the equity tranche due to violation of coverage tests generally cuts seriously into equity holders' return. Once equity holders lose the cash flows, it is difficult to get them back later on, since the deal begins to de-lever. Thus, when the manager is also the equity holder, he has every incentive to avoid tripping the overcollateralization and interest coverage tests. Let's look at how this can be done.

Asset managers are often able to forestall violation of coverage tests by judicious portfolio trading. If the overcollateralization test is close to being tripped, selling a bond trading at par, and buying two bonds priced at 50, can temporarily boost the overcollateralization test. Additionally, sometimes if a bond is priced at 75 on the way to 40, it might also be kept in the pool. Moody's acknowledged this problem in a *Special Report* where it stated:

> We have noted some managers that are lax in righting a deteriorating portfolio, while concurrently distributing excess interest out of the structure. These collateral managers do not actively utilize the O/C test at a possible corrective lever that can efficiently be used to remedy a deteriorating deal. Some common examples include cases where a collateral manager is tardy at treating a security as a defaulted securities, buying deep discounted securities, or holding on to severely impaired securities.[5]

It is very difficult for an equity holder to manage a deal and totally ignore their own incentive interests. However, some managers can be egregiously self-serving. This can usually be spotted by looking for a huge deterioration in WARF scores or a big growth in the allocation to assets that fall into the CCC rated bucket.

Realize that poor performance on previous deals is not necessarily indicative of abusive management. Often, market conditions have deteriorated, and most CDOs of that asset type have been impacted. Thus, if a deal is performing poorly, it is very important to look at the reasons why.

Diversification

Thus far, we have examined what to focus on when looking at an individual deal—making the case that rather than focusing on the manager's track record, focus on the performance of outstanding CDO deals, and how the manager has balanced his or her interests with those of the noteholders. We now shift gears, and argue that not only should CDO buyers look at individual deals, but they should look at their CDO holding in a portfolio framework.

The key to managing a CDO portfolio is diversification. One of the few indisputable facts is that the types of securities purchased (the style) is key—far more important than skills of a particular manager. Roger Ibbotson, one of the key researchers in the performance area, writes:

> relying on past performance is not as simple as it appears. The investment styles of mutual funds typically explain more than 90 percent of the variation in returns. Just knowing that a fund is a large or small capitalization fund, a growth or value fund, an inter-

---

[5] Gus Harris, "Commonly Asked CDO Questions: Moody's Responds," Moody's Investor Service, *Structured Finance, Special Report* , February 23, 2001.

national stock fund, or a combination of these categories largely explains its performance. The skill of the manager is demonstrated relative to the fund's investment style. . .[6]

While it is indisputable that style matters, there is a question as to whether good or poor performance in one period is indicative of the performance going forward. That is, are some managers just far superior to others? While there have been studies of mutual funds that have examined this issue, in short, the debate seems to be whether style (asset class) accounts for 90% or 99% of return variation. There is no disputing the fact that it is the key factor. Bottom line—diversify across asset classes.

Many investors buying a large number of positions still tend to look at each purchase individually. Yes, it is important to look at each deal, but some parameters may be unacceptable if a particular deal was the only one purchased, and less important when the security will become part of a portfolio. Diversity is one such parameter.

In fact, it is important to look at holdings on a consolidated basis. Adding deals with low diversification may, in some circumstances, help a CDO portfolio. For example, a REIT-only deal may have a low diversity score, but if it is part of a larger CDO portfolio, and REIT holdings elsewhere are limited, then the purchase may actually increase diversification. By contrast, if one purchased three high-yield deals within a short period of time, each with very high diversity scores, the additional diversification provided by buying all three deals may actually be limited, as they may own substantially the same securities. The rating agencies generally tend to require less subordination on a deal with a higher diversity score. However, when an investor purchases a large number of CDOs, they are creating their own diversification.

In point of fact, favoring deals with low diversity scores actually conflicts with the Rule 3—trying to collect CDOs backed by different types of collateral. High-yield and investment-grade corporate deals tend to have much higher diversity scores than do ABS or CBO deals backed by CDO collateral deals. Thus, if one was trying to accumulate deals with low diversity scores, you would be accumulating predominately ABS deals and not achieving that desired diversification.

Thus, the practical advice is

1. an investor should not shun low diversity score deals since the investor also creates his or her own diversification; and
2. an investor should look at holdings in his or her CDO portfolio on a consolidated basis.

---

[6] Roger Ibbotson, "Style Conscious," *Bloomberg Personal*, March/April 2001.

CHAPTER 21

Investment Companies

Frank J. Jones, Ph.D.
Chief Investment Officer
The Guardian Life Insurance Company of America

Frank J. Fabozzi, Ph.D., CFA
Adjunct Professor of Finance
School of Management
Yale University

Investment companies are entities that sell shares to the public and invest the proceeds in a diversified portfolio of securities. Each share sold represents a proportional interest in the portfolio of securities managed by the investment company on behalf of its shareholders. The type of securities purchased depends on the company's investment objective.

TYPES OF INVESTMENT COMPANIES

There are three types of investment companies: open-end funds, closed-end funds, and unit trusts.

Open-End Funds (Mutual Funds)

Open-end funds, commonly referred to simply as *mutual funds*, are portfolios of securities, mainly stocks, bonds, and money market instruments. There are several important aspects of mutual funds. First, investors in mutual funds own a pro rata share of the overall portfolio. Second, the investment manager of the mutual fund actively manages the portfolio, that is, buys some securities and sells others (this characteristic is unlike unit investment trusts, discussed later).

Third, the value or price of each share of the portfolio, called the *net asset value* (NAV), equals the market value of the portfolio minus the liabilities of the mutual fund divided by the number of shares owned by the mutual fund investors. That is,

$$NAV = \frac{\text{Market value of portfolio} - \text{Liabilities}}{\text{Number of shares outstanding}}$$

For example, suppose that a mutual fund with 10 million shares outstanding has a portfolio with a market value of $215 million and liabilities of $15 million. The NAV is

$$NAV = \frac{\$215,000,000 - \$15,000,000}{\$10,000,000} = \$20$$

Fourth, the NAV or price of the fund is determined only once each day, at the close of the day. For example, the NAV for a stock mutual fund is determined from the closing stock prices for the day. Business publications provide the NAV each day in their mutual fund tables. The published NAV's are the closing NAV's.

Fifth, and very importantly, all new investments into the fund or withdrawals from the fund during a day are priced at the closing NAV (investments after the end of the day or on a non-business day are priced at the next day's closing NAV).

The total number of shares in the fund increases if there are more investments than withdrawals during the day, and vice versa. For example, assume that at the beginning of a day a mutual fund portfolio has a value of $1 million, there are no liabilities, and there are 10,000 shares outstanding. Thus, the NAV of the fund is $100. Assume that during the day $5,000 is deposited into the fund, $1,000 is withdrawn, and the prices of all the securities in the portfolio remain constant. This means that 50 shares were issued for the $5,000 deposited (since each share is $100) and 10 shares redeemed for $1,000 (again, since each share is $100). The net number of new shares issued is then 40. Therefore, at the end of the day there will be 10,040 shares and the total value of the fund will be $1,004,000. The NAV will remain at $100.

If, instead, the prices of the securities in the portfolio change, both the total size of the portfolio and, therefore, the NAV will change. In the previous example, assume that during the day the value of the portfolio doubles to $2 million. Since deposits and withdrawals are priced at the end-of-day NAV, which is now $200 after the doubling of the portfolio's value, the $5,000 deposit will be credited with 25 shares ($5,000/$200) and the $1,000 withdrawn will reduce the number of shares by 5 shares ($1,000/$200). Thus, at the end of the day there will be 10,020 shares (25 − 5) in the fund with an NAV of $200, and the value of the fund will be $2,004,000. (Note that 10,020 shares × $200 NAV equals $2,004,000, the portfolio value).

Overall, the NAV of a mutual fund will increase or decrease due to an increase or decrease in the prices of the securities in the portfolio. The number of shares in the fund will increase or decrease due to the net deposits into or withdrawals from the fund. And the total value of the fund will increase or decrease for both reasons.

Closed-End Funds

The shares of a *closed-end fund* are very similar to the shares of common stock of a corporation. The new shares of a closed-end fund are initially issued by an underwriter for the fund. And after the new issue, the number of shares remains constant. After the initial issue, there are no sales or purchases of fund shares by the fund company as there are for open-end funds. The shares are traded on a secondary market, either on an exchange or in the over-the-counter market.

Investors can buy shares either at the time of the initial issue (as discussed below), or in the secondary market. Shares are sold only on the secondary market. The price of the shares of a closed-end fund are determined by the supply and demand in the market in which these funds are traded. Thus, investors who transact closed-end fund shares must pay a brokerage commission at the time of purchase and at the time of sale.

The NAV of closed-end funds is calculated in the same way as for open-end funds. However, the price of a share in a closed-end fund is determined by supply and demand, so the price can fall below or rise above the net asset value per share. Shares selling below NAV are said to be "trading at a discount," while shares trading above NAV are "trading at a premium." Newspapers list quotations of the prices of these shares under the heading "Closed-End Funds."

Consequently, there are two important differences between open-end funds and closed-end funds. First, the number of shares of an open-end fund varies because the fund sponsor will sell new shares to investors and buy existing shares from shareholders. Second, by doing so, the share price is always the NAV of the fund. In contrast, closed-end funds have a constant number of shares outstanding because the fund sponsor does not redeem shares and sell new shares to investors (except at the time of a new underwriting). Thus, the price of the fund shares will be determined by supply and demand in the market and may be above or below NAV, as discussed above.

Although the divergence of the price from NAV is often puzzling, in some cases the reasons for the premium or discount are easily understood. For example, a share's price may be below the NAV because the fund has a large built-in tax liability and investors are discounting the share's price for that future tax liability.[1] (We'll discuss this tax liability issue later in this chapter.) A fund's leverage and resulting risk may be another reason for the share's price trading below NAV. A fund's shares may trade at a premium to the NAV because the fund offers relatively cheap access to, and professional management of, stocks in another country about which information is not readily available to small investors.

Under the Investment Company Act of 1940, closed-end funds are capitalized only once. They make an initial IPO (initial public offering) and then their shares are traded on the secondary market, just like any corporate stock, as discussed earlier. The number of shares is fixed at the IPO; closed-end funds cannot issue more shares. In fact, many closed-end funds become leveraged to raise more funds without issuing more shares.

An important feature of closed-end funds is that the initial investors bear the substantial cost of underwriting the issuance of the funds' shares. The proceeds that the managers of the fund have to invest equals the total paid by initial buyers of the shares minus all costs of issuance. These costs, which average around 7.5% of the total amount paid for the issue, normally include selling fees or commissions paid to the retail brokerage firms that distribute them to the public. The high commissions are strong incentives for retail brokers to recommend these shares to their retail customers, and also for investors to avoid buying these shares on their initial offering.

The relatively new exchange traded funds (EFTs) which are discussed Chapter 22, pose a threat to both mutual funds and closed-end funds. ETFs are essentially hybrid closed-end vehicles, which trade on exchanges but which typically trade very close to NAV.

Since closed-end funds are traded like stocks, the cost to any investor of buying or selling a closed-end fund is the same as that of a stock. The obvious charge is the stock broker's commission. The bid/offer spread of the market on which the stock is traded is also a cost.

Unit Trusts

A *unit trust* is similar to a closed-end fund in that the number of unit certificates is fixed. Unit trusts typically invest in bonds. They differ in several ways from both mutual funds and closed-end funds that specialize in

---

[1] Harold Bierman, Jr. and Bhaskaran Swaminathan, "Managing a Closed-End Investment Fund," *Journal of Portfolio Management* (Summer 2000), p. 49.

bonds. First, there is no active trading of the bonds in the portfolio of the unit trust. Once the unit trust is assembled by the sponsor (usually a brokerage firm or bond underwriter) and turned over to a trustee, the trustee holds all the bonds until they are redeemed by the issuer. Typically, the only time the trustee can sell an issue in the portfolio is if there is a dramatic decline in the issuer's credit quality. As a result, the cost of operating the trust will be considerably less than costs incurred by either a mutual fund or a closed-end fund. Second, unit trusts have a fixed termination date, while mutual funds and closed-end funds do not.[2] Third, unlike the mutual fund and closed-end fund investor, the unit trust investor knows that the portfolio consists of a specific portfolio of bonds and has no concern that the trustee will alter the portfolio. While unit trusts are common in Europe, they are not common in the United States.

All unit trusts charge a sales commission. The initial sales charge for a unit trust ranges from 3.5% to 5.5%. In addition to these costs, there is the cost incurred by the sponsor to purchase the bonds for the trust that an investor indirectly pays. That is, when the brokerage firm or bond-underwriting firm assembles the unit trust, the price of each bond to the trust also includes the dealer's spread. There is also often a commission if the units are sold.

In the remainder this chapter of our primary focus chapter is on open-end (mutual) funds.

FUND SALES CHARGES AND ANNUAL OPERATING EXPENSES

There are two types of costs borne by investors in mutual funds. The first is the *shareholder fee*, usually called the *sales charge*. This cost is a "one-time" charge debited to the investor for a specific transaction, such as a purchase, redemption or exchange. The type of charge is related to the way the fund is sold or distributed. The second cost is the annual fund operating expense, usually called the *expense ratio*, which covers the funds' expenses, the largest of which is for investment management. This charge is imposed annually. This cost occurs on all funds and for all types of distribution. We discuss each cost next.

Sales Charge

Sales charges on mutual funds are related to their method of distribution. The current menu of sales charges and distribution mechanisms

---

[2] The are, however, exceptions. Target term closed-end funds have a fixed termination date.

has evolved significantly and is now much more diverse than it was a decade ago. To understand the current diversity and the evolution of distribution mechanisms, consider initially the circumstances of a decade ago. At that time, there were two basic methods of distribution, two types of sales charges, and the type of the distribution was directly related to the type of sales charge.

The two types of distribution were sales-force (or wholesale) and direct. *Sales-force (wholesale) distribution* occurred via an intermediary, that is via an agent, a stockbroker, insurance agent, or other entity who provided investment advice and incentive to the client, actively "made the sale," and provided subsequent service. This distribution approach is active, that is the fund is typically sold, not bought.

The other approach is *direct* (from the fund company to the investor), whereby there is no intermediary or salesperson to actively approach the client, provide investment advice and service, or make the sale. Rather, the client approaches the mutual fund company, most likely by a "1-800" telephone contact, in response to media advertisements or general information, and opens the account. Little or no investment counsel or service is provided either initially or subsequently. With respect to the mutual fund sale, this is a *passive* approach, although these mutual funds may be quite active in their advertising and other marketing activities. Funds provided by the direct approach are bought, not sold.

There is a *quid pro quo*, however, for the service provided in the sales-force distribution method. The *quid pro quo* is a sales charge borne by the customer and paid to the agent. The sales charge for the agent-distributed fund is called a *load*. The traditional type of load is called a *front-end load*, since the load is deducted initially or "up-front". That is, the load is deducted from the amount invested by the client and paid to the agent/distributor. The remainder is the net amount invested in the fund in the client's name. For example, if the load on the mutual fund is 5% and the investor invests $100, the $5 load is paid to the agent and the remaining $95 is the net amount invested in the mutual fund at NAV. Importantly, only $95, not $100, is invested in the fund. The fund is, thus, said to be "purchased above NAV" (i.e., the investor pays $100 for $95 of the fund). The $5 load compensates the sales agent for the investment advice and service provided to the client by the agent. The load to the client, of course, represents income to the agent.

Let's contrast this with directly placed mutual funds. There is no sales agent and, therefore, there is no need for a sales charge. Funds with no sales charges are called *no-load mutual funds* . In this case, if the client provides $100 to the mutual fund, $100 is invested in the fund in the client's name. This approach to buying the fund is called buying the fund "at NAV," that is, the whole amount provided by the investor is invested in the fund.

A decade ago, many observers speculated that load funds would become obsolete and no-load funds would dominate because of the sales charge. Increasingly financially sophisticated individuals, the reasoning went, would make their own investment decisions and not need to compensate agents for their advice and service. But, as will be shown, the actual trend has been quite different.

Why has there not been a trend away from the more costly agent distributed funds as many expected? There are two reasons. First, many investors have remained dependent on the investment counsel and service, and perhaps more importantly, the initiative of the sales agent. Second, sales-force distributed funds have shown considerable ingenuity and flexibility in imposing sales charges, which both compensate the distributors and appear attractive to the clients. Among the recent adaptations of the sales load are *back-end loads* and *level loads*. While the front-end load is imposed at the time of the purchase of the fund, the back-end load is imposed at the time fund shares are sold or redeemed. Level loads are imposed uniformly each year. These two alternative methods both provide ways to compensate the agent. However, unlike with the front-end load, both of these distribution mechanisms permit the client to buy a fund at NAV—that is, not have any of their initial investment debited as a sales charge before it is invested in their account.

The most common type of back-end load currently is the *contingent deferred sales charge* (CDSC). This approach imposes a gradually declining load on withdrawal. For example, a common "3,3,2,2,1,1,0" CDSC approach imposes a 3% load on the amount withdrawn after one year, 3% after the second year, 2% after the third year, and so on. There is no sales charge for withdrawals after the seventh year.

The third type of load is neither a front-end load at the time of investment nor a (gradually declining) back-end load at the time of withdrawal, but a constant load each year (e.g., a 1% load every year). This approach is called a *level load*. This type of load appeals to the types of financial planners who charge annual fees (called *fee-based* financial planners) rather than commissions, such as sales charges (called *commission-based* financial planners).

Many mutual fund families often offer their funds with all three types of loads—that is, front-end loads (usually called "A shares"); back-end loads (often called "B shares"); and level loads (often called "C shares") and permit the distributor and its client to select the type of load they prefer.[3]

According to the National Association of Securities Dealers (NASD), the maximum allowable sales charge is 8.5%, although most funds impose lower charges.

---

[3] Edward S. O'Neal, "Mutual Fund Share Classes and Broker Incentives," *Financial Analysts Journal* (September/October 1999), pp. 76–87.

The sales charge for a fund applies to most, even very small, investments (although there is typically a minimum initial investment).For large investments, however, the sales charge may be reduced. For example, a fund with a 4.5% front-end load may reduce this load to 3.0% for investments over $1 million. There may be in addition further reductions in the sales charge at greater investments. The amount of investment needed to obtain a reduction in the sales charge is called a *breakpoint*— the breakpoint is $1 million in this example. There are also mechanisms whereby the total amount of the investment necessary to qualify for the breakpoint does not need to be invested up front, but only over time (according to a "letter of intent" signed by the investor).[4]

The sales charge is, in effect, paid by the client to the distributor. How does the fund family, typically called the *sponsor* or manufacturer of the fund, cover its costs and make a profit? That is the topic of the second type of "cost" to the investor, the fund annual operating expense.

Annual Operating Expenses (Expense Ratio)

The *operating expense*, also called the *expense ratio*, is debited annually from the investor's fund balance by the fund sponsor. The three main categories of annual operating expenses are the management fee, distribution fee, and other expenses.

The *management fee*, also called the *investment advisory fee* is the fee charged by the investment advisor for managing a fund's portfolio. If the investment advisor is part of a company separate from the fund sponsor, some or all of this investment advisory fee is passed on to the investment advisor by the fund sponsor. In this case, the fund manager is called a *subadvisor*. The management fee varies by the type of fund, specifically by the difficulty of managing the fund. For example, the management fee may increase from money market funds to bond funds, to U.S. growth stock funds, to emerging market stock funds, as illustrated by examples to come.

In 1980, the SEC approved the imposition of a fixed annual fee, called *the l2b-1 fee*, which is, in general, intended to cover *distribution costs*, including continuing agent compensation and manufacturer marketing and advertising expenses. Such l2b-1 fees are now imposed by many mutual funds. By law, 12b-1 fees cannot exceed 1% of the fund's assets per year. The 12b-1 fee may include a service fee of up to 0.25% of assets per year to compensate sales professionals for providing services or maintaining shareholder accounts. The major rationale for the

---

[4] Daniel C. Inro, Christine X. Jaing, Michael Y. Ho, Wayne Y. Lee, "Mutual Fund Performance: Does Fund Size Matter?" *Financial Analysts Journal* (May/June 1999), pp. 74–87.

component of the l2b-1 fee which accrues to the selling agent is to provide an incentive to selling agents to continue to service their accounts after having received a transaction-based fee such as a front-end load. As a result, a 12b-1 fee of this type is consistent with sales-force sold, load funds, not with directly sold, no-load funds. The rationale for the component of the 12b-1 fee which accrues to the manufacturer of the fund is to provide incentive and compensate for continuing advertising and marketing costs.

Other expenses include primarily the costs of (1) custody (holding the cash and securities of the fund), (2) the transfer agent (transferring cash and securities among buyers and sellers of securities and the fund distributions, etc.), (3) independent public accountant fees, and (4) directors' fees.

The sum of the annual management fee, the annual distribution fee, and other annual expenses is called the *expense ratio*. All the cost information on a fund, including selling charges and annual expenses, are included in the fund prospectus.

Exhibit 21.1 shows the expense ratios from the current prospectuses of the three largest mutual funds—the Fidelity Magellan Fund, the Vanguard S&P 500 Index Fund, and the American Income Fund of America Fund. The first two are direct funds and the third is a sales-force fund. The Fidelity Magellan and Vanguard S&P 500 Index funds are directly sold and, thus, have no 12b-1 distribution expenses. The American Income Fund of America, on the-other hand, is sales-force sold and has a distribution or 12b-1 fee. With respect to the management fee, index funds are easier to manage and, thus, the Vanguard S&P 500 Index fund has the lowest management fee. The Fidelity Magellan is a very actively managed pure stock fund, which is difficult to manage, and has the highest management fee.

EXHIBIT 21.1 Annual Operating Expenses for Three Mutual Funds

Type of Expense	Fidelity: Magellan	Vanguard: S&P 500 Index	American: Income Fund of America-A
Management Fee	0.57%	0.16%	0.28%
Distribution and/or Service (12b-1) Fees	0.00%	0.00%	0.24%
Other Expenses	0.18%	0.02%	0.07%
Total	0.75%	0.18%	0.59%

EXHIBIT 21.2 Shareholders Fees for the Three Largest Funds

Type of Fee	Fidelity: Magellan	Vanguard: S&P 500 Index	American: Income Fund of America-A
Sales Charge on Purchases	3%	0%	5.75%
Sales Charge on Reinvested Dividend	0%	0%	0%
Redemption Fee	0%	0%	0%
Exchange Fee	0%	0%	0%

EXHIBIT 21.3 Hypothetical Sales Charges and Annual Expenses of Funds of Different Classes for an Agent Distributed Stock Mutual Fund

	Sales Charge			Annual Operating Expenses			
	Front	Back	Level	Management Fee	Distribution (12b-1 Fee)	Other Expenses	Expense Ratio
A	4.5%	0	0%	0.90%	0.00%	0.15%	1.05%
B	0	a	0%	0.90%	0.75%	0.15%	1.80%
C	0	0	1%	0.90%	0.75%	0.15%	1.80%

[a] 3%, 3%, 2%, 2%, 1%, 0%

In addition to the annual operating expenses, the fund prospectus provides the fees which are imposed only at the time of a transaction. These fees are provided in Exhibit 21.2 for the three largest funds. The Vanguard fund is directly distributed and is a pure no-load fund. The American fund is sales-force distributed and is a front-end load (A share) fund. The Fidelity fund is directly distributed but has a moderate front-end load.

As we explained earlier, many agent-distributed funds are provided in different forms, typically the following: (1) A shares: front-end load; (2) B shares: back-end load (contingent deferred sales charge); and, (3) C shares: level load. These different forms of the same fund are called share *classes*. Exhibit 21.3 provides an example of hypothetical sales charges and annual expenses of funds of different classes for an agent distributed stock mutual fund. The sales charge accrues to the distributor. The management fee accrues to the mutual fund manager. Other expenses, including custody and transfer fees and the fees of managing the fund company, accrue to the fund sponsor to cover expenses.

Multiple Share Classes

Share classes were first offered in 1989 following the SEC's approval of multiple share class. Initially share classes were used primarily by sales-force funds to offer alternatives to the front-end load as a means of compensating brokers. Later, some of these funds used additional share classes as a means of offering the same fund or portfolio through alternative distribution channels in which some fund expenses varied by channel. Offering new share classes was more efficient and less costly than setting up two separate funds.[5] By the end of the 1990s, the average long-term sales-force fund offered nearly three share classes. Direct market funds tended to continue to offer only one share class.

ADVANTAGES OF INVESTING IN MUTUAL FUNDS

There are several advantages of the indirect ownership of securities by investing in mutual funds. The first is risk reduction through diversification. By investing in a fund, an investor can obtain broad-based ownership of a sufficient number of securities to reduce portfolio risk. While an individual investor may be able to acquire a broad-based portfolio of securities, the degree of diversification will be limited by the amount available to invest. By investing in an investment company, however, the investor can effectively achieve the benefits of diversification at a lower cost even if the amount of money available to invest is not large.

The second advantage is the reduced cost of contracting and processing information because an investor purchases the services of a presumably skilled financial advisor at less cost than if the investor directly and individually negotiated with such an advisor. The advisory fee is lower because of the larger size of assets managed, as well as the reduced costs of searching for an investment manager and obtaining information about the securities. Also, the costs of transacting in the securities are reduced because a fund is better able to negotiate transactions costs; and custodial fees and recordkeeping costs are less for a fund than for an individual investor. For these reasons, there are said to be economies of scale in investment management.

Third, and related to the first two advantages, is the advantage of the professional management of the mutual fund. Fourth is the advantage of liquidity. Mutual funds can be bought or liquidated any day at the closing NAV. Fifth is the advantage of the variety of funds available, in general, and even in one particular funds family, as discussed later.

---

[5] Brian Reid, *The 1990's: A Decade of Expansion and Changes in the U.S. Mutual Fund Industry*, Investment Company Institute, p. 15.

Finally, money market funds and some other types of funds provide payment services by allowing investors to write checks drawn on the fund, although this facility may be limited in various ways.

TYPES OF FUNDS BY INVESTMENT OBJECTIVE

Mutual funds have been provided to satisfy the various investment objectives of investors. In general, there are stock funds, bond funds, money market funds, and others. Within each of these categories, there are several sub-categories of funds. There are also U.S.-only funds, international funds (no U.S. securities), and global funds (both U.S. and international securities). There are also passive and active funds. Passive (or indexed) funds are designed to replicate an index, such as: the S&P 500 Stock Index; the Lehman Aggregate Bond Index; or the Morgan Stanley Capital International EAFE Index (Europe, Australasia, and the Far East). Active funds, on the other hand, attempt to outperform an index and other funds by actively trading the fund portfolio. There are also many other categories of funds, as discussed below. Each fund's objective is stated in its prospectus, as required by the SEC and the "1940 Act," as discussed below.

Stock funds differ by:

- the average market capitalization ("market cap;" large, mid, and small) of the stocks in the portfolio;
- style (growth, value, and blend); and
- sector—"sector funds" specialize in one particular sector or industry, such as technology, healthcare or utilities.

The categories for market cap, while not fixed over time, were as of late 2000 approximately:

- small—$0 to $2 billion;
- mid—$2 billion to $12 billion; and
- large—over $12 billion.

With respect to style, stocks with high price-to-book and price-to-earnings ratios are considered "growth stocks," and stocks with low price-to-book and price-to-earnings ratios are considered value stocks, although other variables are also considered. There are also blend stocks with respect to style.

Bond funds differ by the creditworthiness of the issuers of the bonds in the portfolio (for example, U.S. government, investment grade corporate, and high yield corporate) and by the maturity (or duration) of the bonds (long, intermediate, and short.) There is also a category of bond funds called municipal bond funds whose coupon interest is tax exempt. Municipal funds may also be single state (that is, all the bonds in the portfolio were issued by issuers in the same state) or multi-state.

There are also other categories of funds such as asset allocation, hybrid, or balanced funds (all of which hold both stocks and bonds), and convertible bond funds.

There is also a category of money market funds (maturities of one year or less) which provide protection against interest rate fluctuations. These funds may have some degree of credit risk (except for the U.S. government money market category). Many of these funds offer check-writing privileges. In addition to taxable money market funds, there are also tax exempt municipal money market funds.

Among the other fund offerings are *index funds* and *funds of funds*. Index funds, as discussed above, attempt to passively replicate an index. With respect to index funds, the number of index funds rose from 15 in 1990 to 193 in 1999 with $383 billion in total assets. The variety of index funds also expanded, domestically and internationally. Equity funds are the most common type of index funds, accounting for about 88% of these funds and $357 billion in assets.

Funds of funds invest in other funds not in individual securities. A fund of funds is a fund that invests in other mutual funds. In 1990, there were only 16 fund of funds with $1.4 billion in assets. By 1999, there were 213 fund of funds with $48 billion in assets.[6]

Several organizations provide data on mutual funds. The most popular ones are Morningstar and Lipper. These firms provide data on fund expenses, portfolio managers, fund sizes, and fund holdings. But perhaps most importantly, they provide performance (that is, rate of return) data and rankings among funds based on performances and other factors. To compare fund performance on an "apples to apples" basis, these firms divide mutual funds into several categories which are intended to be fairly homogeneous by investment objective. The categories provided by Morningstar and Lipper are similar but not identical and are shown and compared in Exhibit 21.4. Thus, the performance of one Morningstar "large cap blend" fund can be meaningfully compared with another fund in the same category, but not with a "small cap value" fund. Morningstar's ranking system whereby each fund is rated from one-star (the worst) to five-stars (the best) relative to the other funds in its category is well known.

[6] Reid, *The 1990's: A Decade of Expansion and Changes in the U.S. Mutual Fund Industry*, pp. 14–15.

EXHIBIT 21.4   Fund Categories: Morningstar versus Lipper

Morningstar		Lipper	
LG	Large Growth	LG	Large Cap Growth
LV	Large Value	LV	Large Cap Value
LB	Large Blend	LC	Large Cap Core
MG	Mid Cap Growth	MG	Mid Cap Growth
MV	Mid Cap Value	MV	Mid Cap Value
MB	Mid Cap Blend	MC	Mid Cap Core
		XG	Multi Cap Growth
		XC	Multi Cap Core
		XV	Multi Cap Value
SG	Small Growth	SG	Small Cap Growth
SV	Small Value	SV	Small Cap Value
SB	Small Blend	SC	Small Cap Core
DH	Domestic Hybrid	EI	Equity Income
		BL	Balanced
FS	Foreign Stock	IL	International Stock (non U.S.)
WS	World Stock	GL	Global Stock (incl. U.S.)
ES	Europe Stock	EU	European Region
EM	Diversified Emerging Mkt.	EM	Emerging Markets
DP	Diversified Pacific Asia	PR	Pacific Region
PJ	Pacific Asia ex-Japan		
JS	Japan Stock		
LS	Latin America Stock	LT	Latin American
IH	International Hybrid	SE	Sector
		SQ	Specialty Equity
ST	Technology	TK	Science & Technology
SU	Utilities	UT	Utility
SH	Health	HB	Health & Biotech
SC	Communication		
SF	Financial		
SN	Natural Resources	NR	Natural Resources
SP	Precious Metals		
SR	Real Estate		

EXHIBIT 21.4 (Continued)

Morningstar		Lipper	
CS	Short-Term Bond	SB	Short-Term Bond
GS	Short Government	SU	Short-Term U.S.
GI	Interm. Government	IG	Intmdt U.S. Govt.
CI	Inter-Term Bond	IB	Intermediate Bond
MT	Mortgage		
CL	Long-Term Bond	AB	Long-Term Bond
GL	Long Government	LU	Long-Term U.S. Funds
		GT	General U.S. Taxable
CV	Convertibles		
UB	Ultrashort Bond		
HY	High-Yield Bond	HC	High-Yield Taxable
MO	Multisector Bond		
IB	International Bond	WB	World Bond
EB	Emerging Bond		
		GM	General Muni Debt
ML	Muni National Long		
MI	Muni National Interm	IM	Intmdt. Muni Debt
		SM	Short-Term Muni
		HM	High-Yield Muni
		NM	Insured Muni
SL	Muni Single St. Long	SS	Single State Muni Debt
SI	Muni Single St. Interm.		
MS	Muni Single St. Short		
MY	Muni New York Long		
MC	Muni California Long		
MN	Muni New York Interm		
MF	Muni California Interm		

Mutual fund data are also provided by the Investment Company Institute, the national association for mutual funds.

THE CONCEPT OF A FAMILY OF FUNDS

A concept that revolutionized the fund industry and benefitted many investors is what the mutual fund industry calls *a family of funds*, a group of funds or a complex of funds. That is, many fund management companies offer investors a choice of numerous funds with different investment objectives in the same fund family. In many cases, investors may move their assets from one fund to another within the family at little or no cost, and with only a phone call. Of course, if these funds are in a taxable account, there may be tax consequences to the sale. While the same policies regarding loads and other costs may apply to all the members of the family, a management company may have different fee structures for transfers among different funds under its control.

Large fund families usually include money market funds, U.S. bond funds of several types, global stock and bond funds, broadly diversified U.S. stock funds, U.S. stock funds which specialize by market capitalization and style, and stock funds devoted to particular sectors such as healthcare, technology or gold companies. Well-known management companies, such as Fidelity, Vanguard, and American Funds, the three largest fund families, sponsor and manage varied types of funds in a family. Fund families may also use external investment advisors along with their internal advisors in their fund families. The number of family funds has grown from 123 in 1980 to 433 in 1999.

Fund data provided in newspapers group the various funds according to their families. For example, all the Fidelity funds are listed under the Fidelity heading, all the Vanguard funds are listed under their name, and so on.

TAXATION OF MUTUAL FUNDS

Mutual funds must distribute at least 90% of their net investment income earned (bond coupons and stock dividends) exclusive of realized capital gains or losses to shareholders (along with meeting other criteria) to be considered a *regulated investment company* (RIC) and, thus, not be required to pay taxes at the fund level prior to distributions to shareholders. Consequently, funds make these distributions. Taxes, if this criterion is met, are then paid on distributions, only at the investor level, not the fund level. Even though many mutual fund investors choose to reinvest these distributions, the distributions are taxable to the investor, either as ordinary income or capital gains (long term or short term), whichever is relevant.

Capital gains distributions must occur annually, and typically occur late during the calendar year. The capital gains distributions may be either long-term or short-term capital gains, depending on whether the fund held the security for a year or more. Mutual fund investors have no control over the size of these distributions and, as a result, the timing and amount of the taxes paid on their fund holdings is largely out of their control. In particular, withdrawals by some investors may necessitate sales in the fund, which in turn cause realized capital gains and a tax liability to accrue to investors who maintain their holding.

New investors in the fund may assume a tax liability even though they have no gains. That is, all shareholders as of the date of record receive a full year's worth of dividends and capital gains distributions, even if they have owned shares for only one day. This lack of control over capital gains taxes is regarded as a major limitation of mutual funds. In fact, this adverse tax consequence is one of the reasons suggested for a closed-end company's price selling below par value. Also, this adverse tax consequence is one of the reasons for the popularity of exchange traded funds to be discussed later.

Of course, the investor must also pay ordinary income taxes on distributions of income. Finally, when the fund investors sell the fund, they will have long-term or short-term capital gains, taxes on the gains, or losses, depending on whether they held the fund for a year or not.

REGULATION OF FUNDS

There are four major laws or Acts which relate either indirectly or directly to mutual funds. The first is the Securities Act of 1933 ("the '33 Act") which provides purchasers of new issues of securities with information regarding the issuer and, thus, helps prevent fraud. Because open-end investment companies issue new shares on a continuous basis, mutual funds must comply with the '33 Act. The Securities Act of 1934 ("the '34 Act") is concerned with the trading of securities once they have been issued, with the regulation of exchanges, and with the regulation of broker-dealers. Mutual fund portfolio managers must comply with the '34 Act in their transactions.

All investment companies with 100 or more shareholders must register with the SEC according to the Investment Company Act of 1940 ("the '40 Act"). The primary purposes of the '40 Act are to reduce investment company selling abuses and to ensure that investors receive sufficient and accurate information. Investment companies must provide periodic financial reports and disclose their investment policies to investors. The '40 Act prohibits changes in the nature of an investment company's fundamental investment policies without the approval of shareholders. This Act also provides some tax advantages for eligible Regulated Investment Companies (RIC), as indicated below. The purchase and sale of mutual fund shares must meet the requirements of fair dealing that the SEC '40 Act and the NASD (National Association of Securities Dealers), a self-regulatory organization, have established for all securities transactions in the United States.

Finally, the Investment Advisors Act of 1940 specifies the registration requirements and practices of companies and individuals who provide investment advisory services. This Act deals with Registered Investment Advisors (RIAs).

Overall, while an investment company must comply with all aspects of the '40 Act, it is also subject to the '33 Act, the '34 Act, and the Investment Advisors Act of 1940.

The SEC also extended the '34 Act in 1988 to provide protections such that advertisements and claims by mutual funds would not be inaccurate or misleading to investors. New regulations aimed at potential self-dealing were established in the Insider Trading and Securities Fraud Enforcement Act of 1988, which requires mutual fund investment advisors to institute and enforce procedures that reduce the chances of insider trading.

An important feature of the '40 Act exempts any company that qualifies as a "regulated investment company" from taxation on its gains, either from income or capital appreciation, as indicated above. To qualify as an RIC, the fund must distribute to its shareholders 90% of its net income excluding realized capital gains each year. Furthermore, the fund must follow certain rules about the diversification and liquidity of its investments, and the degree of short-term trading and short-term capital gains.

Fees charged by mutual funds are also, as noted previously, subject to regulation. The foundation of this regulatory power is the government's de facto role as arbiter of costs of transactions regarding securities in general. For example, the SEC and the NASD have established rules as part of the overall guide to fair dealing with customers about the markups dealers can charge financial institutions on the sale of financial assets. The SEC set a limit of 8.5% on a fund's load but allows the fund to pass through certain expenses under the 12b-1 rule, as indicated below. Effective July 1, 1993, the SEC has amended the rule to set a maximum of 8.5% on the total of all fees, inclusive of front-end and back-end loads as well as expenses such as advertising.

Some funds charge a *12b-1 fee*, as authorized in the '40 Act. The 12b-1 fee may be divided into two parts. The first component is a *distri-*

bution fee, which can be used for fund marketing and distribution costs. The maximum distribution fee is 0.75% (of net assets per year). The second is a *service fee* (or *trail commission*), which is used to compensate the sales professionals for their ongoing services. The maximum service fee is 0.25%. Thus, the maximum 12b-1 fee is 1%. While no-load funds can have 12b-1 fees, the practice has been that in order to call itself a no-load funds, its 12b-1 fee must be at most 0.25% (all of which would be a distribution fee.) In general, the distribution fee component of the 12b-1 fee is used to develop new customers while the service fee is used for servicing existing customers.

A rule called "prospectus simplification" or "Plain English Disclosure" was enacted on October 1, 1998 to improve the readability of the fund prospectus and other fund documents. According to the SEC, prospectuses and other documents were written by lawyers for other lawyers and not for the typical mutual fund investor. This initiative mandated that prospectuses and other document be written in "plain English" for individual investors.

Among the recent SEC priorities which directly affect mutual funds are:

1. Reporting after-tax fund returns. This requires funds to display the pre-liquidation and post-liquidation impact of taxes on one, five, and ten year returns both in the fund's prospectus and in annual reports. Such reporting could increase the popularity of tax–managed funds (funds with a high tax efficiency).
2. More complete reporting of fees, including fees in dollars and cents terms as well as in percentage terms.
3. More accurate and consistent reporting of investment performance.
4. Requiring fund investment practices to be more consistent with the name of a fund to more accurately reflect their investment objectives. The SEC is considering requiring that 80% of a fund's assets be invested in the type of security that its name implies (e.g. healthcare stocks). The requirement is currently 65%.
5. Disclosing portfolio practices such as "window dressing" (buying or selling stocks at the end of a reporting period to include desired stocks or eliminate undesired stocks from the reports at the end of the period in order to improve the appeared composition of the portfolio), or "portfolio pumping" (buying shares of stocks already held at the end of a reporting period to improve performance during the period).
6. Requiring fund managers to list their security holdings more frequently than the current twice a year.
7. Various rules to increase the effectiveness of independent fund boards.

STRUCTURE OF A FUND

A mutual fund organization is structured as follows:

1. A *board of directors* (also called the *fund trustees*), which represents the *shareholders* who are the owners of the mutual fund.
2. The mutual fund, which is an entity based on the Investment Company Act of 1940.
3. An *investment advisor* , which manages the fund's portfolios and is a registered investment advisor (RIA) according to the Investment Advisor's Act of 1940.
4. A *distributor* or broker/dealer, which is registered under the Securities Act of 1934.
5. Other service providers, both external to the fund (the independent public accountant, custodian, and transfer agent) and internal to the fund (marketing, legal, reporting, etc.).

The role of the board of directors is to represent the fund shareholders. The board is composed of both "interested" (or "inside") directors who are affiliated with the investment company (current or previous management) and "independent" (or "outside") directors who have no affiliation with the investment company. The practice is changing such that a majority of the board must be outside directors.

The mutual fund enters into a contract with an investment advisor to manage the fund's portfolios. The investment advisor can be an affiliate of a brokerage firm, an insurance company, a bank, an investment management firm, or an unrelated company.

The distributor, which may or may not be affiliated with the mutual fund or investment advisor, is a broker-dealer.

The role of the custodian is to hold the fund assets, segregating them from other accounts to protect the shareholders' interests. The transfer agent processes orders to buy and redeem fund shares, transfers the securities and cash, collects dividends and coupons, and makes distributions. The independent public accountant audits the fund's financial statements.

RECENT CHANGES IN THE MUTUAL FUND INDUSTRY

There have been several significant recent changes in the mutual fund industry in addition to those discussed earlier in this chapter. Next we discuss these changes.

Distribution Channels

As explained earlier in this chapter, at the beginning of the 1990s there were two primary distribution channels, direct sales to investors and sales through brokers. Since then, fund companies and fund distributors developed and expanded sales channels beyond the two traditional channels. By the end of the 1990s, fund companies' use of multiple distribution channels resulted in a blurring of the distinction between direct and sales-force funds that had characterized funds at the beginning of the decade.

Fund companies and distribution companies developed new outlets for selling mutual funds and expanded their traditional sales channels. The changes that occurred are evident in the rising share of sales through third parties and intermediaries. In particular, the estimated share of new direct sales of long-term funds was 18% in 1999, down from 23% in 1990. Over the same period, new sales of long-term funds made through a third party or an intermediary rose from 77% to 82%. However, of this total third party sales market, the sales force market also declined, from 63% to 58%. Only the sales through third parties-direct market increased, from 14% to 24%.[7]

Significant market trends account for these changes. In particular, many funds that had previously marketed only directly turned increasingly toward third parties and intermediaries for distribution. For example, in 1990 an estimated 62% of new sales of direct-market funds came through traditional direct sales whereas by 1999 this share had fallen to 43%. The nontraditional, third-party distribution channels used by direct-market funds were mutual fund supermarkets; mutual fund wrap-account programs; fee-based advisors; variable annuities; employer-sponsored pension plans and bank trust departments.

Like direct-market funds, funds that were traditionally sold through a sales force moved increasingly to nontraditional sources of sales such as employer-sponsored pension plans, banks and life insurance companies in the 1990s. Only 41% of new sales of sales-force funds came through nontraditional sources in 1990, whereas 65% came through nontraditional sources in 1999.

Below we describe the various nontraditional distribution channels.

Supermarkets

The introduction of the first mutual fund supermarket in 1992 marked the beginning of a significant change in the distribution of direct market funds. Specifically, during 1992, Charles Schwab & Co. introduced its *OneSource* service. With this and other supermarket programs, the

---

[7] Reid, *The 1990's: A Decade of Expansion and Changes in the U.S. Mutual Fund Industry*, pp. 11–12.

organizer of the supermarket offers no-load funds from a number of different mutual fund companies. These supermarkets allow investors to purchase funds from participating companies without investors having to contact each fund company. The organizer of the supermarket also provides the investor with consolidated recordkeeping and a simple account statement.

These services provide a non-transaction-fee program to provide access to multiple fund families under one roof and to help service the back-office needs of financial advisors. Through this service, investors can access many mutual fund families through one source and buy all the funds with no transaction fee (i.e., no load).

On the one hand, these services make a mutual fund family more accessible to many more investors. On the other hand, they break the direct link between the mutual fund and the investor. According to these services, the mutual fund company does not know the identity of its investors through the supermarkets; only the supermarket, which distributes the funds directly to the investor knows their identity. These supermarkets fit the needs of fee-based financial planners very well. For individual investors and planners as well, supermarkets may offer one-stop shopping including the current "best of the breed."

Currently, in addition to Schwab, Fidelity and Waterhouse are other major mutual fund supermarkets. Assets in mutual fund supermarkets reached an estimated $500 billion in 1999.

Wrap Programs

Wrap accounts are managed accounts, typically mutual funds "wrapped" in a service package. The service provided is often asset allocation counsel; that is, advice on the mix of managed funds. Thus, mutual fund wrap programs provide investors with advice and assistance for an asset-based fee rather than the traditional front-end load. Wrap products are currently offered by many fund and non-fund companies. Wrap accounts are not necessarily alternatives to mutual funds, but may be different ways to package the funds.

Traditional direct market funds as well as sales force funds are marketed through this channel. Mutual funds in wrap programs were an estimated $94 billion in late 1999.

Fee-Based Financial Advisors

Fee-based financial advisors are independent financial planners who charge investors an annual fee, typically as a percentage of assets under management. In return, they provide investment advice to their clients by selecting portfolios of mutual funds and securities. While many planners recommend mutual funds to their clients, others recommend portfolios of planner-selected securities. Mutual fund assets in these accounts reached $150 billion at end of 1999.

Variable Annuities

Variable annuities represent another distribution channel. Variable annuities are "mutual funds in an insurance wrapper." Among their insurance features are the tax deferral of investment earnings until they are withdrawn, and higher charges (there is a mortality charge for an insurance feature provided). Variable annuities are sold through insurance agents and other distributors as well as directly through some fund companies. Assets in variable annuities exceeded $800 billion in 1999.

Changes in the Costs of Purchasing Mutual Funds

The purchase cost (or price) of mutual funds declined significantly during the rapid growth of the 1990s. Purchase cost is measured by total shareholder costs: which includes both costs from annual fund expenses and from transaction-based sales loads. The decline in total shareholder costs occurred across all major types of funds. For equity funds, total shareholder costs were 181 basis points per year in 1990 and declined to 135 basis per year in 1998, a decrease of 25%. The corresponding decline for bond funds was from 171 basis points per year in 1990 to 109 basis points. There were also smaller decreases in money market funds.[8]

In general, load funds responded to the competition of no-load funds by lowering distribution costs. Distribution cost is defined as the sum of the annualized sales load and 12b-1 fees. The distribution cost is the component of total shareholder cost that reflects the cost of advice and assistance provided by brokers and sales professionals to buyers of mutual funds.

Load funds lowered distribution costs, in part, by reducing front-end sales loads. In addition, load funds introduced alternatives to front-end loads that, depending on the investor's circumstances, could be less costly than front-end loads as a means of compensating sales professionals. One common distribution cost structure combined a 12b-1 fee with a contingent deferred sales load that would be paid by the investor when the shares were redeemed, and, depending on the time the fund was held, could be zero.

The reduction in and reallocation of distribution costs during the 1990s was significant. For both equity and bond funds, the lowering of

---

[8] For a further discussion of this topic, see Reid, *The 1990's: A Decade of Expansion and Changes in the U.S. Mutual Fund Industry* .

front-end loads along with the growth of alternatives to front-end loads together with more funds adopting 12b-1 fees resulted in 12b-1 fees being a much larger portion of distribution costs.

A final element in the decline of total shareholder cost was the achievement of economies of scale by many individual costs. Some of the annual fund expenses, mainly those included in "other expenses" and those affected by breakpoints, have declined with the increase in size of some of the larger funds.

"Mix and Match"

Until recently, fund manufacturers distributed only their own funds; fund distributors distributed only one manufacturer's funds; and typically employee defined contribution plans, such as 401(k)s, offered funds from only one distributor. However, the investors' demands for choice and convenience, and also the distributors' need to appear independent and objective, have incented essentially all institutional users of funds and distribution organizations to offer funds from other fund families in addition to their own (that is, if they also manufacture their own funds). In addition, mutual fund supermarkets distribute funds of many fund families with considerable facility and low costs. Even the biggest fund families, including Fidelity and Vanguard, offer funds from other families.

The balance of power between fund manufacturers and distributors currently significantly favors distribution. That is, in general there are more funds available than distributors to sell them. In the mutual fund business, "distribution is king."

ALTERNATIVES TO MUTUAL FUNDS

Due to the success of mutual funds, investment management companies have developed several alternatives to mutual funds. The major alternatives are exchange-traded funds, segregated accounts, and "folios." We discuss each in the sections that follow.

Exchange-Traded Funds

While mutual funds have become very popular with individual investors during the 1980s and 1990s, they are often criticized for two reasons. First, mutual funds shares are priced at, and can be transacted only at, the end-of-the-day (closing) price. Specifically, transactions (i.e., purchases and sales) cannot be made at intra-day prices, but only at the end of the day closing prices. The second issue relates to taxes and the investors' control over taxes. As noted earlier in this chapter, withdrawals by some fund shareholders may cause taxable realized capital gains for shareholders who maintain their positions.

During 1993, a new investment vehicle which has many of the same features of mutual funds but responds to these two limitations was introduced. This investment vehicle, called *exchange-traded funds* (ETFs), consists of investment companies that are similar to mutual funds but trade like stocks on an exchange. EFTs are described in more detail in Chapter 22. While they are open-ended, ETFs are, in a sense, similar to closed-end funds which have very small premiums or discounts from their NAV.

Since their introduction in 1993, they have only been traded on the American Stock Exchange. Through 2000, these ETFs have been based only on U.S. (e.g., the S&P500) and international (e.g., MSCI EAFE) stock indexes and subindexes, not actively managed portfolios or funds. In addition to broad stock indexes, ETFs are also based on style, sector, and industry oriented indexes.

In an ETF, it is the investment advisor's responsibility to maintain the portfolio such that it replicates the index and the index's return accurately.[9] Because supply and demand determine the secondary market price of these shares, the exchange price may deviate slightly from the value of the portfolio and, as a result, may provide some imprecision in pricing. The deviation will be small, however, because arbitrageurs can create or redeem large blocks of shares on any day at NAV, significantly limiting the deviations.

Along with being able to transact in ETFs at current prices throughout the day comes the flexibility to place limit orders, stop orders, orders to short sell and buy on margin, none of which can be done with open-end mutual funds. These types of orders are discussed in Chapter 4.

The other major distinction between open-ended mutual funds and ETFs relates to taxation. For both open-ended funds and ETFs, dividend income and capital gains realized when the funds or ETFs are transacted are taxable to the investor. However, in addition, when there are redemptions, open-end mutual funds may have to sell securities (if the cash position is not sufficient to fund the redemptions), thus causing a capital gain or loss for those who held their shares, while ETFs do not have to sell portfolio securities since redemptions are effected by an in-kind exchange of the ETF shares for a basket of the underlying portfolio securities—not a taxable event to the investors according to the IRS. Therefore, investors in ETFs are subject to significant capital gains taxes only when they sell their ETF shares (at a price above the original purchase

---

[9] Among the early investment advisors have been State Street Global Advisors and Barclays Global Investors.

price). However, ETFs do distribute cash dividends and may distribute a limited amount of realized capital gains and these distributions are taxable. Overall, with respect to taxes, ETFs, like index mutual funds, avoid realized capital gains and the taxation thereof due to their low portfolio turnover. But unlike index mutual funds (or other funds for that matter), they do not cause potentially large capital gains tax liabilities which accrue to those who held their positions in order to meet shareholder redemptions due to the unique way in which they are redeemed.

The pros and cons of mutual funds and ETF's are summarized in Exhibit 21.5. Exhibit 21.6 considers the tax differences in more detail. Overall, the ETFs have the advantages of intra–day pricing and tax management, and many, but not all, have lower expenses than their corresponding index mutual funds. However, since open-ended funds are "transacted" through the fund sponsor and ETFs are traded on an exchange, the commissions on each ETF trade may make them unattractive for a strategy that involves several small purchases, as for instance, would result from strategies such as dollar cost averaging or monthly payroll deductions. However, ETFs may provide a viable alternative to mutual funds for many other purposes.

Among the earliest and currently the most popular ETFs are:

- *SPDRS* (pronounced "Spiders"—Standard and Poor's Depository Receipts) (ticker symbol: SPY)—tracks the S&P500.
- *DIAMONDS* (ticker symbol: DIA)—tracks the Dow Jones Industrial Average.
- *WEBS* (World Equity Benchmarks)—tracks the Morgan Stanley Capital International indexes of various countries. These have been recently renamed *iShares MSCI*.
- *QQQs* (often called Qubes) (ticker symbol:QQQ)—tracks the Nasdaq 100 index.
- *i Shares*—provided by Barclays Global Investors and tracks 42 different stock indexes.

With respect to continued growth, all the current ETFs are indexed. ETFs based on actively traded portfolios are being planned in the United States and have begun trading in Germany.

Segregated (Separately Managed) Accounts

Many high net worth individuals object to mutual funds because of their lack of control over taxes, their lack of any input into investment decisions, and the absence of "high touch" service. Separate accounts respond to all these limitations of mutual funds, although they are more expensive.

EXHIBIT 21.5   Mutual Funds versus Exchange Traded Funds

	Mutual Funds	ETFs
Variety	Wide choice	Choices currently limited to stock indexes, but on many stock indexes.
Taxation	Subject to taxation on dividend and realized capital gains. May have gains/losses when other investors redeem funds. May have gains/losses when stocks in index are changed.	Subject to taxation on dividend and realized capital gains. No gains/losses when other investors redeem funds. May have gains/losses when stocks in index are changed.
Valuation	NAV based on actual stock market prices.	Creations and redemptions at NAV. Secondary market prices may be valued somewhat above or below NAV, but deviation typically small due to arbitrage.
Pricing	End-of-Day	Continuous
Expenses	Low for Index Funds	Low, and in some cases, even lower than for index mutual funds
Transaction Cost	None (for no-load funds); sales charge for load funds.	Commission or brokerage
Management Fee	Depends on fund; even index funds have a range of management fees.	Depends on fund; tends to be very low on many stock index funds

EXHIBIT 21.6   Taxes: Mutual Funds versus ETFs

	Mutual Funds	ETFs
Holding/Maintaining		
1. Taxes on Dividend, Income and Realized Capital Gains	Fully Taxable	Fully Taxable
2. Turnover of Portfolio	Withdrawal by other investors may necessitate portfolio sales and realized capital gains for holder.	Withdrawal by others does not cause portfolio sales and, thus, no realized capital gains for holder.
Disposition		
3. Withdrawal of Investment	Capital gains tax on difference between sales and purchase price.	Capital gains tax on difference between sales and purchase price.
4. Overall	Due to some portfolio turnover, will realize capital gains.	Due to very low portfolio turnover, will not realize significant capital gains.

Previously, money managers managed separate accounts for only very large portfolios, typically $1 million and more. Currently, however, many money managers are significantly decreasing the minimum size of their separately managed accounts. As a result, many investors with mid-sized portfolios are utilizing segregated, individually-managed accounts provided by many companies and other investment managers. Typically, asset managers earn higher fees on separately managed accounts but also have higher service costs relative to mutual funds.

"Folios"

A very recent internet-based product offers a variety of pre-selected portfolios consistent with any particular investment strategy that investors may desire. For instance, it offers a pre-selected large cap equity growth portfolio, a small cap equity value portfolio, and so on. These preselected portfolios are called "folios." Investors can also alter the portfolio selections if they choose. After an investor selects and alters one of these portfolios, the portfolio can be transacted through an internet service at a discount price. Folios are being marketed as an alternative to mutual funds. Among the early products in this field are: Folio[fn]; NetFolio; Personal Fund; $$$ Smartleaf; and UNX.com.

CHAPTER 22

Exchange-Traded Funds and Their Competitors

Gary L. Gastineau
Managing Director
ETF Advisors, LLC

Exchange-traded funds (ETFs) are the most important—and potentially the most versatile—financial instruments introduced since the debut of financial futures 30 years ago. We begin this chapter by explaining the origins of ETFs and some of their important features like intra-day trading on a stock exchange, creation and redemption of fund shares "in-kind," and tax efficiency. We also compare the recently popular open-end ETFs to competitive products like closed-end funds, conventional mutual funds, HOLDRs, and Folios in terms of costs, applications, and tax efficiency.

THE HISTORY AND STRUCTURE OF ETFS AND SOME COMPETITORS[1]

Exchange-traded funds, referred to by friends and foes alike as "ETFs," are outstanding examples of step-by-step evolution of new financial instruments starting with a series of proto-products that led in a natural progres-

---

[1] The history discussion appeared in an extended form in Gary L. Gastineau, "Exchange-Traded Funds—An Introduction," *The Journal of Portfolio Management* (Spring 2001), pp. 88–96. Most of the remainder first appeared in Gary L. Gastineau, *The Exchange-Traded Funds Manual* (New York: John Wiley & Sons, 2002).

sion to the current generation of exchange-traded funds and set the stage for products yet to come.

Portfolio Trading

The basic idea of trading an entire portfolio in a single transaction did not originate with the TIPS or SPDRS, which are the earliest successful examples of the modern portfolio-traded-as-a-share structure. The idea originated with what has come to be known as "portfolio trading" or "program trading." In the late 1970s and early 1980s, program trading was the then revolutionary ability to trade an entire portfolio, often a portfolio consisting of all the S&P 500 stocks, with a single order placed at a major brokerage firm. Some modest advances in electronic order entry technology at the NYSE and the Amex and the availability of large order desks at some major investment banking firms made these early portfolio or program trades possible. At about the same time, the introduction of S&P 500 index futures contracts at the Chicago Mercantile Exchange provided an arbitrage link between the futures contracts and the traded portfolios of stocks. It even became possible, in a trade called an *exchange of futures for physicals* (EFP) to exchange a stock portfolio position, long or short, for a stock index futures position, long or short. The effect of these developments was to make portfolio trading either in cash or futures markets an attractive activity for many trading desks and for many institutional investors.

As a logical consequence of these developments affecting large investors, there arose interest—one might even say insistent demand—for a readily tradable portfolio or basket product for smaller institutions and the individual investor. Before the introduction of "mini" contracts, futures contracts were relatively large in notional size. Even with "mini" contracts, the variation margin requirements for carrying a futures contract are cumbersome and relatively expensive for a small investor. Perhaps even more important, there are approximately ten times as many securities salespeople as futures salespeople. The need for a security—that is, an SEC-regulated portfolio product—that could be used by individual investors was apparent. One of the first such products introduced were the Index Participation Shares.

Index Participation Shares (IPS)

The Index Participation Shares, known as "IPS," were a relatively simple, totally synthetic, proxy for the S&P 500 Index. While IPS on other indexes were also available, S&P 500 IPS were the most active. They began trading on the American Stock Exchange and the Philadelphia Stock Exchange in 1989. IPS traded with a level of activity that showed significant public interest, in spite of a lawsuit by the Chicago Mercantile Exchange (CME) and the Commodity Futures Trading Commission (CFTC) which charged that IPS were futures contracts. As futures contracts, they would be required by law to trade on a futures exchange regulated by the CFTC, not on a securities exchange. In spite of the cloud cast by this litigation, IPS volume and open interest began to grow.

The IPS were, candidly, much like a futures contract; but they were margined and collateralized like stocks. Like futures, there was a short for every long and a long for every short. IPS were carried and cleared by the Options Clearing Corporation and they provided a return essentially identical to the long or short return on the underlying shares in the index with an appropriate quarterly credit for dividends on the long side and a debit for dividends on the short side.

Alas, success eluded the IPS. A federal court in Chicago found that the IPS were indeed illegal futures contracts and had to be traded on a futures exchange if they were traded at all. The stock exchanges began to close down IPS trading and investors were required to liquidate their IPS positions in an orderly manner.

While a number of efforts to find a replacement product for IPS that would pass muster as a security were underway in the United States, another effort achieved success first in Toronto. There, the TIPs (*Toronto Stock Exchange Index Participations*) were introduced.

Toronto Stock Exchange Index Participations (TIPs)

TIPs were a warehouse receipt-based instrument designed to track the TSE-35 index and a later product tracked the TSE-100 index as well. The TSE-100 product was initially called HIPs. These products traded actively and attracted substantial investment from Canadians and from international indexing investors. TIPs were unique in their expense ratio. The ability of the trustee (State Street Bank) to loan out the stock in the TIPs portfolio and frequent demand for stock loans on shares of large companies in Canada led to what was, in effect, a negative expense ratio at times.

The TIPs were a victim of their own success. They proved costly for the Exchange and for some of its members who were unable to recover their costs from investors. Early in 2000, the Toronto Stock Exchange decided to get out of the portfolio share business and TIPs positions were liquidated or rolled into a Barclays Global Investors (BGI) 60 stock index share at the option of the TIPs holder. The BGI fund was relatively low cost, but not as low cost as the TIPs, so a large fraction of the TIPs shares were liquidated.

While the TIPs were flourishing in Toronto, two other portfolio share products were under development in the United States: Supershares and SPDRs.

Supershares

Supershares, developed by Leland, O'Brien, Rubinstein Associates (LOR), were a complex product using both a trust and a mutual fund structure—one inside the other. Supershares were a high cost product, particularly after a fee was extracted to compensate the creators and sponsors. The complexity of the product, which permitted division of the Supershares into a variety of components, some with option characteristics, made sales presentations long and confusing for many customers. The Supershares never traded actively, and the trust was eventually liquidated.

Standard & Poor's Depository Receipts (SPDRS)

SPDRS (pronounced "spiders") were developed by the American Stock Exchange (Amex) approximately in parallel with Supershares, although their introduction was deferred until after the Supershares were offered.[2] SPDRs are the shares of a unit trust which holds an S&P 500 portfolio that, unlike the portfolios of most U.S. unit trusts, can be changed as the index changes. The reason for the selection of the unit trust structure was the Amex's concern for simplicity and costs. A mutual fund must pay the costs of a board of directors, even if the fund is very small. The Amex was uncertain of the demand for SPDRs and did not want to build a more costly infrastructure than was necessary. While SPDRs are the essence of simplicity relative to Supershares, they are more complex than TIPs and IPS, and the education process has been a long one. SPDRs traded reasonably well on the Amex in their earlier years, but only in the late 1990s did SPDRs asset growth become truly exponential. Investors began to look past the somewhat esoteric in-kind share creation and redemption process (used by market makers and large investors to acquire and redeem SPDRs in large blocks) and focused on the investment characteristics and tax efficiency of the SPDRs shares.

Today, the S&P 500 SPDRs have more assets than any other index fund except the Vanguard 500 mutual fund. The SPDRs account for more than one-third of ETF assets in the United States. Interestingly, however, from 70% to 90% of traditional U.S. index fund money goes into S&P 500 portfolios. Clearly, the interest in ETFs based on indexes other than the S&P 500 suggests that there is more to ETFs than an alternative to conventional index funds.[3]

---

[2] The elaborate structure of the Supershares helped clear the way for the SPDRs and later ETFs.

[3] For specific analysis of the 500 SPDRs see Edwin J. Elton, Martin J. Gruber, George Comer, and Kai Li, "Where Are the Bugs?" Forthcoming in *The Journal of Business*.

World Equity Benchmark Shares (WEBS)— Renamed iShares MSCI Series

The WEBS, originally developed by Morgan Stanley, are important for two reasons. First, they are foreign index funds. More precisely, they are U.S.-based funds holding stocks issued by non-U.S.-based firms. Second, they are one of the earliest exchange-traded index products to use a mutual fund as opposed to a unit trust structure. The mutual fund structure has more investment flexibility and there are some other differences in dividend reinvestment and stock lending, but most of these differences are in the process of being eliminated. We would expect most new funds to use the mutual fund structure, but competitors' whispers that the SPDRs and other ETFs structured as unit trusts suffer from an evil affliction called "dividend drag" are gross exaggerations.

A product similar to WEBS was introduced on the NYSE at about the same time WEBS appeared on the Amex. For a variety of reasons (the most important of which were structural flaws in the product) these "Country Baskets" failed and the trust was liquidated.

In addition to WEBS, a variety of additional ETF products are now available. The Mid-Cap SPDRs (a unit trust run by the Bank of New York) actually came before WEBS, and the DIAMONDS (a unit trust based on the Dow Jones Index Industrial Average and run by State Street Bank) and the Nasdaq 100 (a unit trust run by the Bank of New York) were introduced later. The Select Sector SPDRs used a mutual fund structure similar to the WEBS and were introduced in late 1998. Of these products, the Nasdaq 100 and the Sector SPDRs deserve a closer look.

NASDAQ 100 Index Tracking Stock (Trading Symbol QQQ)

In spite of the name, the Nasdaq 100 Trust, sponsored by Nasdaq, is not a tracking stock as the term is generally used in the United States—and, from a strictly technical point of view, it's not even a stock. The basic unit of trading, however, is a "share" and the Nasdaq 100 Trust, as a unit trust, is more like the original SPDR than most of the other currently traded ETFs. The reason for focusing on the Nasdaq 100 Trust is its spectacular success, partly as a result of a sound marketing effort by Nasdaq, but primarily because of the spectacular performance—until March, 2000—of stocks listed on the Nasdaq market. The Nasdaq 100, perhaps more than any of the other ETF products, illustrates the variety of applications for and reasons for investment in exchange-traded funds. The Nasdaq 100 Shares serve as a volatile trading vehicle on both the long and short side of the market and as a proxy for the technology sector. Heavy trading volume and narrow bid-asked spreads for small orders attracted both large and small traders and the growth in volume attracted more traders, leading to even more volume.

Sector SPDRs

The Sector SPDRs, developed by Merrill Lynch, provide another interesting perspective on the ETF world. Although each stock in the S&P 500 is assigned to a Sector SPDR, the balance of investor interest has been very different from sector capitalization weights. Investor interest has been greatest in the Technology Sector SPDR, followed at a considerable distance by the Financial Sector SPDR and at a great distance by all the other sectors. These sector funds have served, at least initially, primarily as a mechanism for expressing a strongly held view about a particular segment of the market. In part because their relatively low share prices increase transaction costs for many investors, sector funds have not yet caught on in a major way as the basis for weighting a portfolio more heavily in favored sectors, or less heavily if the sector is relatively unattractive. The very slow start of the high cost iShares Dow Jones sector funds suggests a need for more information, education, and appropriate allocation tools to help individual investors and their advisors use sector funds effectively.

BGI iShares Funds

Barclays Global Investors, a major institutional index portfolio manager, launched iShares in a bid to develop a retail branded family of financial products. Whether or not the extremely low expense ratio on the S&P 500 fund, which is part of the iShares offering and the former WEBS (for which BGI has served as investment advisor since inception) get special attention, many observers feel that BGI has yet to demonstrate that it can succeed in the ETF market. By early October 2001, BGI accounted for more than 73% of U.S.-based exchange-traded funds and about 18% of U.S. ETF assets. Most of these assets are in funds with expense ratios of 20 basis points or less.

State Street Global Advisors streetTRACKS Funds

The original 500 SPDRs and the DIAMONDS were developed cooperatively by the Amex, outside counsel, and State Street; and the Sector SPDRs were developed with important participation by Merrill Lynch. The streetTRACKS Funds represent State Street's first solo ETF effort in the United States. BGI's strategy of cornering many branded benchmark index licenses left State Street with an unusual collection of indexes as the basis for its funds. All in all, State Street's recent U.S. effort has been mildly disappointing, but they have done much better in the launch of the Hong Kong TraHKers Fund and other funds for investors outside the United States.

Nuveen Investments Fixed Income Funds and Selected Equity Index Funds

The focus of Nuveen's initial effort in index ETFs has been on the development and licensing of fund-friendly indexes as templates for its proposed index fund products. Nuveen attempts to develop funds which meet specific investor needs rather than launch a fund simply because an index happens to be available. Nuveen was the first advisor to file an exemptive request with the SEC to launch fixed-income index funds.[4]

ETFS AND OTHER TRADABLE BASKET PRODUCTS

While most readers think of the fund products described above as ETFs, various financial instruments, each referred to by some of its advocates as an exchange-traded fund, are designed to meet specific portfolio investment needs. In many cases, the needs met are practically identical; in other cases, they are quite different. In spite of some confusion about what the term ETF includes, most observers agree that a range of exchange-traded portfolio basket products compete for investors' dollars.

Our purpose in this section is to introduce the major categories of financial instruments which sometimes have been called "ETFs" or which compete with ETFs. We will appraise the features of each. Our objective is to provide a relatively straightforward comparison of features. The purpose of the comparison is not to suggest that one structure is always superior or that the emphasis should always be on competition between the products. In fact, folio customers have been important users of the fund-type ETFs described in the previous section and of HOLDRs which are described next.

Closed-End Funds

Nuveen Investments began using the term "exchange-traded funds" for its closed-end municipal bond funds traded on the New York and American Stock Exchanges in the very early 1990s, several years before the first SPDRs began trading on the American Stock Exchange. The use of the name "exchange-traded funds" was selected to emphasize the fact that someone buying and selling these municipal bond fund shares enjoyed the investor protections afforded by investment company (fund) regulation and by the auction market on a major securities exchange. Interestingly, the

---

[4] For a slightly different perspective of the ETF landscape with more data on individual funds, see Albert J. Fredman, "An Investor's Guide to Analyzing Exchange-Traded Funds," *AAII Journal* (May 2001), pp. 8–13.

intra-day trading convenience and trading cost reduction of the pooled portfolio structure and exchange trading for these closed-end funds was similar in many respects to the contribution of the pooled portfolio structure and exchange trading to the newer "open" exchange-traded funds, originating with the TIPs in Canada and the SPDRs in the United States.

Both these types of exchange-traded funds provide an efficient means to assemble and trade a portfolio of securities—in the case of the closed-end funds, recent offerings have been primarily municipal bond portfolios; in the case of the "open" ETFs, they have been primarily stock portfolios. Typically, both these vehicles are able to trade the components of their portfolios at narrower spreads and manage these portfolios at lower cost than an individual, an institutional manager of separate accounts, or the manager of a conventional "open-end" mutual fund. Limited liquidity in the municipal bond markets makes it especially difficult to manage a municipal bond portfolio with as high a degree of efficiency in an "open-end" portfolio structure as in a closed-end fund. Creation and redemption in-kind—in some respects the defining characteristic of "open" ETFs—is not yet practical in U.S. municipal bond markets.

Given the diversity and relative illiquidity of most individual municipal bond positions, the closed-end fund structure seems to be the most efficient choice for that market today. The relative increase in liquidity for the fund shares and the reduction in portfolio transaction costs available in a well-managed, closed-end municipal bond fund usually more than compensate for the occasional discount from net asset value associated with the fixed capitalization of a closed-end fund. Depending on an investor's objectives, the liquidity and cost advantages of the closed-end municipal bond fund may be as important as the cost and liquidity advantages of the newer "open" ETFs.

"Open" Exchange-Traded Funds

The SEC requires that references to what we have been calling exchange-traded funds as open-end funds be made only in the context of a comparison with conventional open-end investment companies (mutual funds). We are about to make such a comparison so we will now drop the quotes around open, and fully qualify the limits of openness in such funds. Shares in open ETFs are issued and redeemed directly by the fund at their net asset value (NAV) only in creation unit aggregations, typically 50,000 fund shares or multiples of 50,000 shares. The shareholder who wants to buy or sell fewer than 50,000 shares may only buy and sell smaller lots on the secondary market at their current market price. The secondary market participant is dependent on competition among the exchange specialist, other market makers and arbitrageurs to keep the market price of the shares very near the intra-day value of the fund portfolio. The effectiveness of market forces in promoting tight bid asked spreads and fair pricing has been impressive. ETF shares have consistently traded very, very close to the value of the underlying portfolio in a contemporaneously priced market.

Before we move beyond the issue of share creation and redeemability to compare these new funds with conventional mutual funds in more detail, it is worth noting that the first open exchange-traded funds were not mutual funds. They were, as noted earlier, unit investment trusts (UITs) selected by the AMEX for simplicity and cost-saving reasons. The AMEX was concerned that the new "funds" might turn out to be very small, leaving the Exchange with the expenses of compensating a board of directors in perpetuity. In fact, the portfolios of the unit trust-based products have grown quite large. At the end of December 2000, the 500 SPDR would have been ranked twenty-first in size among mutual funds, just behind Janus Twenty and ahead of AimValue. The Nasdaq 100 Trust would have ranked twenty-third, ahead of Vanguard Windsor.

The differences between the SPDRs and Nasdaq 100 UIT structure and the open-end investment company structure used for most of the newer ETFs are not important to most investors in an equity index fund. Some providers of open ETFs structured as management investment companies have criticized the older UIT structures because dividends from their portfolio stocks cannot be equitized (i.e., reinvested in portfolio shares). The dividends must be retained as cash and invested, in effect, in money market instruments until the dividend payment is made.[5] Furthermore, securities in the UIT portfolios cannot be lent out to obtain securities lending income to help offset portfolio expenses. The impact of these differences is not material under most circumstances, but State Street Bank, trustee of the 500 SPDR and the DIAMONDS, has asked the Securities and Exchange Commission to permit a change in the rules of the trust to facilitate equitization of dividends and securities lending. There is every reason to believe that this application will be approved in time, making the equity index UIT ETFs and the investment company ETFs functionally equivalent for all practical purposes.[6] The UIT structure and the investment company structure share a broad range of similar characteristics, most of which are advantages relative to the traditional open-end mutual fund structure.

For the typical retail or even institutional investor, purchasing and selling ETF shares is the essence of simplicity. The trading rules and prac-

---

[5] Actually, the trustee uses the cash and credits the Trust's expense account with the equivalent of interest.
[6] The Bank of New York will undoubtedly file a similar application for the Mid-Cap SPDRs and Nasdaq 100 Trust when approval of the State Street filing nears.

tices are those of the stock market. ETF shares are purchased and sold in the secondary market, much like stocks or shares of closed-end funds, rather than being purchased *from* the fund and resold *to* the fund, like conventional mutual fund shares.

Because they are traded like stocks, shares of ETFs can be purchased or sold any time during the trading day, unlike shares of most conventional mutual funds which are sold only at the 4:00 p.m. net asset value (NAV) as determined by the fund and applied to all orders received since the prior day's share trading deadline. While the opportunities for intra-day trading may not be important to every investor, they certainly have appeal to many investors during a period when there is concern about being able to get out of a position before the market close when prices are volatile.

Primary market transactions in ETF shares, that is, trades when shares are bought and redeemed with the fund itself as a party to the trade, consist of in-kind creations and redemptions in large size. For example, the SPDR and Nasdaq 100 creation aggregations are 50,000 fund shares, and creation/redemption occurs only in multiples of 50,000 shares. There have been several occasions when creation and redemption of fund shares has resulted in asset flows of $1 billion dollars or more in or out of the SPDR or the Nasdaq 100 Trust in a single day. Exchange specialists, market makers, and arbitrageurs buy ETF shares from the fund by depositing a stock portfolio and a cash balancing component that essentially match the fund in content and are equal in value to 50,000 ETF shares on the day the fund issues the shares. The same large market participants redeem fund shares by tendering them to the fund in 50,000 share multiples and receiving a stock portfolio plus or minus balancing cash equivalent in value to the 50,000 ETF shares redeemed. The discipline of possible creation and redemption at each day's market closing NAV is a critical factor in the maintenance of fund shares at a price very, very close to the value of the fund's underlying portfolio, not just at the close of trading, but intra-day. A proxy for intra-day net asset value per share is disseminated for each ETF throughout the trading day to help investors check the reasonableness of bids and offers on the market.[7]

An extremely important feature of the creation and, more particularly, the redemption process is that redemption-in-kind does more than provide an arbitrage mechanism to assure a market price quite close to net asset value. Redemption in kind also reduces the fund's transaction costs slightly and enhances the tax efficiency of the fund. While a conventional mutual fund can require shareholders to take a redemption payment in-kind rather than in cash for large redemptions, most funds are reluctant to do this, and most shareholders have fund positions consider-

---

[7] This proxy value does not have the status of a formal NAV calculation.

ably smaller than the $250,000 minimum usually required for redemption in-kind. As a consequence, most redemptions of conventional mutual fund shares are for cash, meaning that an equity fund faced with significant shareholder redemptions is required to sell shares of portfolio stocks, frequently shares that have appreciated from their original cost. When gains taken to obtain cash for redemptions are added to gains realized on merger stocks that are removed from the index for a premium over the fund's purchase price, many conventional index funds distribute substantial capital gains to their shareholders, even though the continuing shareholders who pay taxes on these distributions have made no transactions, and the fund, looked at from a longer perspective, has been a net buyer of most or all of its index's component securities.

The in-kind redemption process for exchange-traded funds enhances tax efficiency in a simple way. The lowest cost shares of each stock in the portfolio are delivered against redemption requests. In contrast to a conventional fund which would tend to sell its highest cost stocks first, leaving it vulnerable to substantial capital gains realizations when a portfolio company is acquired at a premium and exits the index and the fund, the lowest cost lot of stock in each company in the portfolio is tendered to ETF shareholders redeeming in multiples of 50,000 fund shares. The shares of stock in each company remaining in the portfolio have a relatively higher cost basis, which means that acquired companies generate smaller or no gains when they leave the index and are sold for cash by the fund.

One further feature of the existing exchange-traded funds which causes a degree of misunderstanding and which seems to create an expectation that all ETFs will be extremely low cost funds requires an explanation. First, the existing ETFs are all index funds. Index funds generally have lower management fees than actively-managed funds, whatever their share structure. Second, ETFs enjoy somewhat lower operating costs than their conventional fund counterparts. The principal reasons for lower costs are (1) the opportunity to have a somewhat larger fund because of the popularity of the exchange-traded fund structure, (2) slightly lower transaction costs due to in-kind deposits from and payments to buyers and redeemers in the primary market and, most importantly, (3) the elimination of the transfer agency function—that is, the elimination of shareholder accounting—at the fund level.

As all U.S. ETFs are "book entry only" securities, an exchange-traded fund in the United States has one registered shareholder: the Depository Trust Company (DTC). If you want a share certificate for a SPDR or QQQ position, you are out of luck. Certificates are not available. The only certificate is held by the Depository Trust Company, and the number of shares represented by that certificate is "marked to market" for increases and decreases in shares as creations and redemptions occur.

Shareholder accounting for ETFs is maintained at the investor's bro-kerage firm, rather than at the fund. This creates no problems for the shareholder, although it does have some significance for the distribution of exchange-traded funds. One of the traditional functions of the mutual fund transfer agent is to keep track of the salesperson responsible for the placement of a particular fund position, so that any ongoing payments based on 12b-1 fees or other marketing charges can be made to the credit of the appropriate salesperson. There is no way for the issuer of an ETF to keep track of salespeople because these fund positions do not carry the record keeping information needed to use the DTC Fund/SERV pro-cess. They are, in a word, just like shares of a stock—and a stock with no certificates at that. The elimination of the individual shareholder transfer agency function reduces operating costs by a minimum of five basis points and probably by much more in many cases. ETF expenses tend to reflect the cost savings on this function.

The trading price of an exchange-traded fund share will be subject to a bid-asked spread in the secondary market (although these are very narrow on most products) and a brokerage commission. A simple breakeven anal-ysis divides the round-trip trading costs by the daily difference in operat-ing expenses. Anyone planning to retain a reasonably large fund position for more than a short period of time and/or anyone who values the intra-day purchase and sale features of the exchange-traded funds will find the combination of the lower expense ratio and greater flexibility make the ETF share more attractive than a conventional mutual fund share.

Powerful advantages notwithstanding, there are a few disadvantages in the exchange-traded fund format for some investors. An investor can-not be certain of his or her ability to buy or sell shares at a price no worse than net asset value without incurring some part or all of a trading spread and a commission. It is the trading spread in the secondary market which covers the costs of insulating the ongoing shareholder from the cost of in-and-out transactions by active traders. These transaction costs in open market ETF trades means that, even with lower fund expenses, certain small investors will not find ETFs as economical as traditional funds if they are in the habit of making periodic small investments. Since most conventional mutual funds take steps to refuse investments from in-and-out traders if they trade in and out too frequently, the transaction costs associated with ETFs are simply a more equitable allocation of these costs among various fund shareholders. A long-term investor, particularly a taxable long-term investor, will benefit greatly from the exchange-traded fund structure because in the long run that investor should enjoy lower fund expenses and a higher after-tax return than he would find in an oth-erwise comparable conventional fund. This allocation of costs and bene-fits is ironic given the only significant criticism which has been leveled at exchange-traded funds, i.e., that they encourage active trading. In fact, the long-term taxable investor enjoys the greatest benefits from the ETF structure. Even so, the ETF structure has probably reduced the active trader's costs as well, given the obstacles and special redemption fees these traders often incur when they use conventional funds.

As noted, all current open exchange-traded funds are equity index funds. As time goes by, there will be a wider variety of funds available. The introduction of fixed-income index funds, enhanced index funds, and ultimately, actively-managed funds, seems inevitable. It is in the advance from simple indexation with full replication of the index in the portfolio that the investment management company structure shows its greatest advantages over the open UIT structure because the latter structure does not provide a mechanism for anything beyond full replication of an index. The open-end management investment company structure permits a portfolio to differ from the structure of an index fairly easily if the index structure is not consistent with the diversification requirements that allow the fund to qualify as a regulated investment company (RIC) for tax purposes. The UIT structure provides for replication of an index with limited variations based on rounding share positions and limited timing adjustments of index replicating transactions by advancing or deferring them for a few days. As in most evolutionary developments, whether in biology or finance, there is more than one way to accomplish an objective.

Alternative portfolio or basket structures differ both from the UIT and the exchange-traded investment management company. These other structures have their own unique features. Foremost among these are HOLding company Depository Receipts, (HOLDRs), a structure pioneered by Merrill-Lynch, and Folios, which have been introduced by a number of firms that would otherwise be characterized primarily as deep discount brokers. Both HOLDRs and Folios are unmanaged baskets of securities which may have an initial structure based on an index, a theme, or just a diversification policy.

HOLding Company Depository Receipts (HOLDRs)

HOLDRs use a grantor trust structure which makes them similar to the open ETFs discussed above in that additional HOLDRs shares can be created and existing HOLDRs can be redeemed. The creation unit aggregation for the open ETF management company structures is typically 50,000 fund shares and the minimum trading unit on the secondary market is a single fund share. In contrast, the creation unit *and* the minimum trading unit in HOLDRs is generally 100 shares. Most brokerage firms will not deal in fractional shares or odd lots of HOLDRs.[8] An investor can buy and sell HOLDRs in the secondary market or an existing HOLDRs position can be redeemed (exchanged for its specific underlying stocks). A new HOLDRs position can be created by simply depositing the stocks behind the 100-share HOLDRs unit with the Bank of New York.[9]

The creation/redemption fee for HOLDRs will generally be roughly similar in *relative* magnitude to the comparable fee on investment company ETFs and the pricing principles and arbitrage pricing constraints operate in a similar way. To the extent that one of the stocks in a HOLDRs basket performs poorly and the investor wants to use the loss on that stock to offset gains elsewhere, the HOLDRs can be taken apart and reassembled without affecting the tax status of any shares not sold. The ability to realize a loss on an individual position may give the HOLDRs structure a slight tax advantage over the investment company-based ETFs. On the other hand, unlike the redemption in-kind of the shares of an open ETF, the HOLDRs structure does not permit elimination of a low-cost position in the HOLDRs portfolio without realization of the gain by the investor.

An investor who maintains an account at Merrill Lynch will probably be able to obtain good tax reporting for HOLDRs positions. An investor transferring an account or carrying a HOLDRs position elsewhere may find tax preparation cumbersome and time consuming.

The first HOLDRs were based on the split-up of Telebras into 12 separate companies in mid-1998. They were designed to provide a single vehicle to absorb the split-off companies much as earlier unit trusts were designed to absorb the component pieces of AT&T at the time of the court-mandated divestiture of the regional operating companies. The Telebras HOLDRs traded an average of over 700,000 shares per day in the first half of 2001. Subsequent HOLDRs baskets were created initially out of 20 securities in each of a number of relatively narrowly defined industries and, more recently, out of a larger number of companies with various investment characteristics.

The principal disadvantages of HOLDRs are that they lack the indefinite life of an investment company and there is no provision for adding positions to offset attrition through acquisitions of basket com-

---

[8] DTC does not transfer fractional shares or fractions of the basic trading unit of a security, which is 100 shares in the case of the HOLDRs. However, some firms use trading and accounting systems that accommodate the New York Stock Exchange's Monthly Investment Plan (MIP). MIP was designed to let investors buy odd lots and fractional shares as a start in owning their share of America. Firms that can accommodate fractional share positions (including Foliofn) see the ability to handle fractional shares as a competitive advantage.

[9] The stock basket underlying a 100-share HOLDRs unit will initially consist of whole shares of the component stocks. In the event of a merger affecting one of the companies, any cash proceeds will be distributed. The surviving company's whole shares will usually be retained in the HOLDRs basket.

ponents by other companies. No HOLDRs component that disappears in a cash merger or bankruptcy can be replaced in the HOLDRs basket. If some stocks do well and others do poorly, there is no mechanism for rebalancing positions. There is a provision in some of the HOLDRs trusts that once the number of stocks represented in the HOLDRs portfolio drops below a certain level, the trust will be dissolved and the remaining shares will be delivered to the holders of HOLDRs in proportion to their ownership. The thematic nature of many of the HOLDRs baskets reflects this relatively temporary structure, though the Telebras HOLDRs and many of the recent broadly diversified portfolios have a longer term orientation.

The HOLDRs share one very important characteristic with the index ETFs: It is frequently less costly to trade the basket in the form of HOLDRs than it is to trade the individual shares, particularly for a small- to mid-sized investor who might be trading odd lots in many of the basket components if HOLDRs or ETFs were unavailable.

HOLDRs also feature a variation on a front-end load in their initial public offering (IPO). Once the HOLDRs are trading in the secondary market, additional HOLDRs can be created and redeemed at relatively low cost. The IPO structure may turn out to be an important feature of HOLDRs. If HOLDRs can continue to be launched in environments less favorable to the IPO structure, they may have a lasting role in the financial engineer's repertoire of financial instruments.

Folios

In contrast to the other ETF variations and competitors described here, Folios are not standardized products nor are they investment companies or some kind of trust. They are baskets of stocks that can be modified one position at a time or traded with a single order through a brokerage firm. The firms which advocate and provide Folio baskets for trading do provide semi-standardized baskets—in some cases based on indexes, and in other cases based on a simple diversification rule. In practice, however, each investor's implementation of the Folio basket may be slightly different.

An investor may have $20,000 to invest. Upon examination of the group of "prefabricated" Folios suggested by the firm she trades with, she may decide she likes a specific basket of 40 stocks. The investor can choose how many shares of each stock she would like to buy or she can request a customized basket prepared by the firm and giving her an "appropriate" number of whole and sometimes fractional shares of each stock in the selected basket. She can modify the basket immediately—or later—until she finds a mix that matches her needs and inclinations.

Because Folio baskets will not be standardized, Folios cannot be traded like fund shares or like HOLDRs. Each of the stocks in a Folio will trade separately. While the brokerage firm can provide low-cost commissions and even the opportunity to execute trades against its other customer trades at selected times during the day, if the basket does not trade as a standardized basket, the investor will miss some of the transaction cost advantages which traders in standardized basket shares often enjoy.

A tax advantage of Folios over investment companies in certain circumstances is similar to a tax feature of HOLDRs. An investor can sell one position out of a Folio to take a loss and use that loss to offset gains obtained elsewhere—outside the Folio basket. In contrast, a fund taxed as a regulated investment company cannot pass losses through to shareholders. If the fund experiences large losses, an investor can take a loss on the fund shares by selling the share position; but losses on an individual portfolio component are not available to the investor who continues to hold the shares as a passthrough. In a reasonably bullish market environment, the ability of the UIT or management company ETF to modify its portfolio with creations and redemptions without taxable gain realizations will probably be more important to an individual investor than the ability to take specific losses in either HOLDRs or Folios. Other market environments may make the selected loss realization opportunity of the HOLDRs or Folios more valuable.

Folios, like HOLDRs, can be difficult from a tax accounting perspective, although all the Folio providers offer a service whereby careful entry of the cost of each position delivered into the account and automatic entry of positions purchased and sold in the account can be translated into a relatively simple schedule of gains and losses, suitable for attachment to the investor's tax return. An important competitive advantage of FolioFN compared to some other purveyors of basket products is the combination of its ability to provide and carry fractional share positions and a portfolio management and reporting system designed for use by independent advisors working with investors.

Folios have been criticized for the tendency of their promoters to minimize the true costs of acquiring and holding a Folio basket. While the promoters of Folios provide tools for measuring diversification effects of changes in the portfolio to realize losses or to make a change in the composition of the basket, the Folio baskets lack the inherent discipline of a product which is modified in response to a change in an index or in response to a decision by a portfolio manager. Investment managers and index publishers make mistakes and bad decisions, but they are unlikely to let a portfolio drift from neglect, as could easily happen with an unsupervised Folio basket. We expect Folios to become primarily a vehicle for advisors working with clients rather than a service for the online trader who trades his own account. Folios will use ETFs like stocks in the construction of Folio accounts.

In contrast to the ETFs' fund structure, there is no "tax-realization-free" mechanism for reducing the impact of a very successful position in either HOLDRs or Folios. In the regulated investment company structures (exchange-traded unit trusts or funds), tax rules would limit the size of any single stock to 25% of the assets of the fund under most circumstances. Reductions in the commitment to a particular position in a regulated investment company with redemptions in-kind might be obtainable without realization of taxable gains. This would not be possible for very successful positions underlying HOLDRs or for components of a Folio. Basket mechanisms that do not offer a way to reduce a large, successful position without capital gains realization force the investor to choose between tax deferral and diversification.

In the long run, Folios are more likely to be co-opted by specialized investment managers than they are to succeed in the format in which they were first introduced. Without an increase in fees charged to the individual customer or substantial income from sale of their investors' order flow, it seems unlikely that the retail, discount brokerage Folio service is an economically viable business model. Nonetheless, the Folio structure and flexibility is intriguing. While the initial product probably tried to take some aspects of do-it-yourself portfolio management too far, Folios can be an excellent vehicle for an advisor serving individual investors.

A Side-by-Side Comparison of Tradable Basket Products [10]

Exhibit 22.1 provides an eclectic comparison of the mutual fund-style and UIT-style versions of open exchange-traded funds and conventional mutual funds to the other basket products we have discussed. Most of the items on this comparison table are relatively straightforward and readily understandable from the previous text, but several items do require some discussion. First, these comparisons are based on the current product offerings in each category. At present, all open ETFs and open UITs are based on equity indexes. The lack of active management is virtually inherent in the open UIT, but there is reason to believe that open mutual fund-type ETFs will be able to serve as the vehicle for enhanced index funds and actively-managed funds in the future. Active management is also compatible with the closed-end funds, but not with the HOLDRs. Actively-managed Folios become the equivalent of separate accounts, something very different from all the other basket products.

---

[10] For a slightly different but useful perspective, see Albert J. Fredman, "Sizing Up Mutual Fund Relatives: Low-Cost Alternative Investing," *AAII Journal* (July 2001), pp. 9–14.

EXHIBIT 22.1 Basket Product Comparisons

Feature/Product Structure	Open ETFs	Open UITs	Conventional Mutual Funds	Closed ETFs	HOLDRs	Folios
Creation of Shares—primary market	In-kind deposit	In-kind deposit	Cash deposit with fund	IPO	IPO/in-kind deposit	NA
Purchase of Shares—secondary market	Open market purchase	Open market purchase	NA	Open market purchase	Open market purchase	Open market purchase
Sale of Shares—secondary market	Open market sale	Open market sale	NA	Open market sale	Open market sale	Open market sale
Redemption of Shares—primary market	In-kind redemption	In-kind redemption	Cash redemption	NA	In-kind redemption	NA
Underlying portfolio structure (available today)	Index	Index	Index or managed	Managed	Preset basket	Investor's choice
Tax structure	RIC	RIC	RIC	RIC	Structure is tax transparent	No structure
Tax-efficiency factors	Redemption in-kind	Redemption in-kind	Cash redemption	Cash redemption	Separable losses	Separable losses
Investor tax-efficiency rating	1	1	5	4	3	2
Effect of structure on shareholder's trading cost	Usually reduces	Usually reduces	Usually reduces	Usually reduces	Usually reduces	No effect except discount brokerage
Investor's Trading cost rating	1	1	2	1	1	3
Shareholder attention required	Minimal dividend reinvestment	Minimal dividend reinvestment	Minimal dividend reinvestment	Minimal dividend reinvestment	Dividend reinvestment principal reinvestment tax loss sales and replacements significant	Dividend reinvestment principal reinvestment tax loss sales and replacements significant

Ratings 1 = best, 5 = worst. See text for discussion.

In assigning tax-efficiency ratings, we have placed significantly greater value on the redemption in-kind feature of the open ETFs and open UITs than on the separable loss feature available in Folios with no particular change and in HOLDRs through the exchange of the HOLDR for the basket of underlying securities followed by realization of the loss, re-establishment of the position that incurred the loss after the wash sale period is past and reconstitution of the HOLDR—a relatively complex and non-user-friendly process.

Closed-end funds are rated higher than conventional mutual funds on tax-efficiency because they are characterized by a closed portfolio and do not face the forced realization of gains which can come about through cash redemptions in an open-end mutual fund.

The investor's trading cost ratings are based on the advantages associated with trading a basket at the share level versus transacting separately in all the securities making up the basket. All of the standardized ETFs are ranked highly because trading in the composite share should be more efficient than trading in the underlying positions separately. It is certainly possible to differentiate among individual products in terms of the cost of trading the product or trading the underlying securities separately, but the difference is more related to the nature of the underlying market and the quality of the market in the basket product than it is on anything systematically related to the product structure. The conventional mutual funds are rated slightly below the exchange-traded products other than the unstructured Folios on the assumption that, on average, a redemption charge or other obstacles to short-term trading will increase an investor's costs of trading.[11] Folios are rated least favorably on trading cost simply because they do not provide any of the advantages associated with trading the other products as portfolios or baskets. Even when the transactions in a Folio are aggregated, each stock is traded separately. None of the Folio providers have reached a size that permits them to match and offset many customer orders to eliminate the bid-asked spread.

The topic that probably requires the most consideration for long-term investors is the shareholder attention required to use each product effectively. Any basket or portfolio product will typically be less risky than a random collection of a few of its component securities, and any basket product will provide at least a degree of diversification, though some of the more specialized HOLDRs baskets or, for that matter, sector funds provide only minimal internal diversification. Nonetheless, these basket products are generally designed to require minimal share-

---

[11] An investor can do an in-and-out trade in some conventional mutual funds with almost no transaction cost, but many funds will probably not accept a repeat order from that investor.

holder attention from day to day and even from year to year. Most, for example, provide either automatic dividend reinvestment or let an investor make a variety of arrangements for automatic reinvestment of the dividends with the brokerage firm holding the account.

HOLDRs and Folios require somewhat greater investor (or manager) attention than the conventional fund or exchange-traded fund products for at least two reasons: First, to the extent that any of the companies in the HOLDRs or Folios are taken over in a cash acquisition, the shares will automatically be turned into cash and the shareholder will have to deal with reinvestment of the principal. Also, both these less structured products provide for their variety of tax-efficiency by permitting tax loss sales of individual securities. Folios, which are marketed principally as a way to take advantage of the automatic diversification a portfolio of stocks provides, require some kind of replacement or re-balancing activity to maintain a useful degree of diversification. With the other products, either a portfolio manager or the process for weighting or re-weighting the index and insuring regulated investment company diversification compliance in the fund will retain a minimal level of diversification without action by the investor or an advisor employed to manage the investor's position.

TAXES AND TAX EFFICIENCY IN ETFS AND THEIR COMPETITORS

Advocates of conventional mutual funds, exchange-traded funds, and separate stock portfolios (including HOLDRs and Folios) have engaged in extensive discussions about the relative tax-efficiency of their respective approaches to equity portfolio management. The purpose of this section is to codify appropriate information for investors who may be justifiably confused by what they have been hearing or reading from diverse sources. While we have attempted to summarize our conclusions on the relative tax-efficiency of the three portfolio structures in Exhibit 22.2, the answer to the question, "Which way of holding a portfolio of common stocks offers the greatest tax-efficiency?" is still, of course, "It depends on investment results."

Discussing the principal tax issues as we work down Exhibit 22.2, our objective is to help investors understand which tax features are most important as the first step in making an informed choice, given their personal circumstances. In many instances, the appropriate choice will depend on holdings (or gains and losses) outside the fund or basket under consideration. As with any tax issue, investors should consult their personal tax advisors. We offer this material only to help investors approach the tax issues of interest to them, not as tax advice.

EXHIBIT 22.2 Factors Affecting Tax Efficiency of Mutual Funds, ETFs, and Separate Accounts (inc. HOLDRs, Folios, etc.)

	Mutual Funds	Exchange-Traded Funds	Separate Accounts (inc. HOLDRs, Folios)
Deductibility of investment management expenses	+	+	−
Passthrough of losses	−	−	+
Passthrough of STG (in character)	−	−	+
Deferral of STG	−	+	−
Deferral of LTG (with changing portfolio)	o	+	o
Step-up of basis at death	o	+	+
Appreciated shares for charitable gifts	−	o	+
Tax impact of stocks acquired for cash in mergers	−	+	−
Successful portfolio—little turnover	o	+	o
Successful portfolio—high turnover	−	+	−
Mediocre portfolio	o	o	+
Capital gain/loss accounting	+	+	check with advisor

Key: + Best
       o Okay
       − Worst
      STG Short-Term Capital Gains
      LTG Long-Term Capital Gains

Deductibility of Investment Management Expenses

As suggested by the +'s in the fund columns of Exhibit 22.2, any investment management expenses incurred by the fund are deductible from the fund's income before anything is distributed to shareholders. This expense deductibility holds for both conventional mutual funds and exchange-traded funds. An investor who pays any investment advisory expenses, such as a wrap fee which covers advice as well as replaces stock trading commissions in connection with HOLDRs or Folios, will not be able to deduct those expenses for tax purposes unless they and other miscellaneous itemized deductions exceed 2% of the investor's adjusted gross income. The magnitude of the amounts involved is relatively easy to estimate, but it is probably not large enough to be a material consideration for most investors if the only funds used are low-cost index ETFs. On the other hand, higher fees embedded in actively-managed ETFs or conventional funds may be tax-advantaged relative to a separate, non-deductible, or less deductible advisory fee.

Passthrough of Losses

Here, the separate portfolio investor is at an advantage over the investor who purchases shares in a fund. If some of the stocks in the underlying portfolio go up and some go down, the mutual fund and exchange-traded fund cannot pass net losses through to the shareholder. In contrast, the separate account, HOLDRs and Folio/basket product shareholder owns each of the securities in the basket product, and can (perhaps with effort and some modest expense in the case of the HOLDRs) decompose the portfolio, take losses on positions that have experienced losses, and let gains run. Of course, the funds' losses cannot be passed through to the shareholder for offset against gains on positions outside the portfolio. The only way to take a capital loss on a fund is to sell the fund shares.

Passthrough of Short-Term Gains with Character Retained

In the taxation of regulated investment companies, any net short-term gains are reported and taxed as ordinary income as opposed to short-term gains in the fund investor's tax returns. An investor with realized or unrealized long-term or short-term capital losses in other investments would be unable to offset short-term capital gains from distributions made by a fund against capital losses outside the fund. The investor in HOLDRs, Folios or other separate stock basket products could reflect realized short-term stock gains on his tax return and offset them with capital losses realized from another source. Short-term capital gains are unlikely to be a material issue for most equity funds. Unless a fund manager is making extensive use of initial public offerings (new issues) to spike performance or assumes most fund shareholders do not benefit from the lower tax rate on long-term capital gains, realized net short-term gains in an equity fund that is more than a year old are improbable, unless the fund is an index fund based on an index that is very fund-unfriendly.[12]

Deferral of Short-Term Gains

Whenever deferral of a portfolio capital gain (short term or long term) is desired, the ETFs stand out relative to both conventional mutual funds and the separate portfolio products for the simple reason that an astute ETF portfolio manager should be able to redeem out enough of the portfolio's net capital gains so that the *value* of gains can be retained, untaxed, in the fund even if the portfolio is changed. Barring the presence of offsetting

---

[12] For a discussion of fund-friendly indexes, see Chapter 6 in Gary L. Gastineau, *The Exchange-Traded Funds Manual* (NY: John Wiley & Sons, 2002).

losses, holders of a conventional mutual fund or a separate portfolio product will be taxed at their full marginal ordinary income tax rate on any short-term capital gains. Holders of mutual fund shares will not be able to offset the short-term gain with capital losses outside the fund because the short-term gain will be taxed as an ordinary income dividend. Again, net realized short-term gains should be rare in most equity fund portfolios.

Deferral of Long-Term Capital Gains

Each of these vehicles should be able to defer long-term gains—as long as there are no changes made in the portfolio. If changes are made and resulting realized long-term gains are likely to be material, the ETF once again stands out as the vehicle of choice. The investor who owns any other non-fund portfolio products may be able to offset long-term gains with losses on other components of the portfolio or other positions outside the portfolio, but this process offers less flexibility than the ETF that defers the gains, but permits a very wide range of changes in the portfolio—including complete portfolio turnover without realization of taxable gains at the extreme.

Step-Up of Cost Basis of Stocks at Death as a Meaningful Feature of the Portfolio Structure[13]

Here both the ETFs and the separate stock portfolio products can shine. Other things equal, the very long-term holder of an ETF should have most of a lifetime's return in the form of unrealized capital gains. With astute management, the holder of a separate stock portfolio might approach this ideal, but rating the separate portfolio as equal to the ETF is probably generous. Under the assumption that the investor has held a number of stocks for most of the period from initiation of the position until death, the heirs of the holder of the conventional mutual fund are unlikely to avoid as much capital gains tax as ETF or separate portfolio investors because more capital gains will have been realized, distributed, and taxed over time in the conventional fund.

Appreciated Shares Usable for Charitable Gifts

Here the separate portfolio products triumph. With individual stock positions that can be separated, the one with the greatest appreciation—i.e., the one with the lowest relative cost basis—can be donated to charity to maximize the deductible donation without paying capital gains tax on the gain. In the case of the ETF, the stock positions are combined or averaged so the

---

[13] Step-up of cost basis at death is scheduled to disappear in 2010 and, like most changes made by the 2001 tax law, it is scheduled to be reinstated in 2011.

appreciation of the fund shares will be approximately the average capital gain return on the portfolio as opposed to the separate account portfolio where the most appreciated security would be the one chosen for a charitable deduction. With a conventional mutual fund, more capital gains likely will have been realized so that some of the appreciation of the shares will have been taxed previously. Over time, the tax basis on conventional fund shares may be increased by reinvestment of realized gains, making the conventional fund shares poor candidates for in-kind charitable contributions.

Tax Impact of Low-Basis Stock Acquired by Another Company for Cash

Here the dominant portfolio format is the exchange-traded fund under the assumption that the portfolio manager will be able to redeem out the appreciated stock in-kind. If the stock is redeemed out in-kind rather than sold, no gain is realized at the fund level and, thus, nothing is distributed to shareholders and taxed. In contrast, of course, the conventional mutual fund and the separate portfolio product would have experienced taxable capital gains with fewer opportunities to shelter or defer them.

CHAPTER 23

Stable-Value
Pension Investments

John R. Caswell, CFA
Managing Partner
Galliard Capital Management

Karl P. Tourville
Managing Partner
Galliard Capital Management

The rapid formation and widespread use of defined-contribution pension plans in the United States over the last 15 to 25 years has significantly impacted the U.S. financial markets. The key feature of all of these plans that has profoundly impacted investment management trends has been the shift in responsibility for investment decision-making from plan sponsors to individual plan participants. For conservative participants whose primary investment objective is preservation of capital, stable-value investments have been widely used in both the corporate and public plan sectors due their attractive yields, stability, and safety.

A stable-value investment is an instrument in which contractual terms provide for a guaranteed return of principal at specified rate of interest. Examples of stable-value assets include fixed annuities and traditional guaranteed investment contracts (GICS), bank investment contracts (BICs), and GIC alternatives such as separate-account GICs and synthetic GICs. Stable-value pooled funds, which are professionally managed collective trusts investing in these assets, are also utilized. Growth in stable-value assets has paralleled that of the overall defined-contribution market, rising to over $225 billion by December 2001.

A key feature of a stable-value asset is its treatment from an accounting standpoint. According to Generally Accepted Accounting Principles (GAAP), stable-value instruments can be held at contract value, provided that established criteria are met. Contract value is the acquisition cost of the contract plus accrued interest, adjusted to reflect any additional deposits or withdrawals. This is also referred to as book value. Book-value accounting eliminates the market-value fluctuations experienced by other asset classes and contributes to the high, risk-adjusted returns of stable-value instruments.

Initially, traditional GICs were the dominant stable-value instrument. This was true of the corporate market initially and remains the case for a majority of the public fund plans. The perceived risk in these products was minimal and they faced little, if any, competition until the insolvency of several major GIC issuers. While these defaults proved to be a great challenge to an industry unaccustomed to such difficulties, they also proved to be the catalyst for tremendous change resulting in the development of a new generation of products, popularly known as synthetic GICs. Investors, and ultimately plan participants, now benefit from a broader variety of products, providers, and strategies.

This chapter will review the various instruments utilized in today's stable-value portfolios with an emphasis on GIC alternatives, the most rapidly growing segment of the market. Also discussed are contract terms and portfolio management considerations along with some thoughts on the future direction of the stable-value asset class.

STABLE-VALUE PRODUCTS

Stable-value products include investment contracts (GICs and BICs), GIC alternatives, separaet account GICs, synthetic GICs, buy-and-hold synthetics, actively-managed synthetics, alpha synthetics, and stable-value pooled funds.

Investment Contracts

Traditional guaranteed investment contracts (also called guaranteed insurance, interest, or income contracts) were the foundation of today's stable-value industry. A GIC is issued by an insurance company, utilizing a group annuity contract format. As insurance contracts, the obligation is backed by the general account of the issuer. In an effort to diversify its depositor base and obtain funding at attractive rates, the banking industry began issuing competing bank investment contracts (BICs) in 1987. While providing stable-value portfolios with industry diversification, BICs achieved only modest market share as a limited number of issuers constrained supply.

While different in legal structure and regulatory purview, GICs and BICs are functionally similar in that the issuer of the contract receives a deposit of funds from a qualified investor and, in return, guarantees a specified rate of interest for a predetermined period of time. Interest is accrued on either a simple interest or a fully compounded basis and paid either annually or at the end of the contract term. The contracts include a variety of terms (discussed later), the most important of which is a guarantee that payments will be made at the contract's book value for qualified participant withdrawals. This feature allows these contracts to be valued at their book value rather than at some calculated market value equivalent.

While traditional GICs still play an important role in most stable-value portfolios, diversification considerations relative to life insurance industry exposure have led to their diminishing use vis-à-vis GIC alternatives. Although some portfolios have significant investments in traditional GICs, more often these products are evaluated versus other investment alternatives and purchased on the basis of their relative value—similar to corporate bonds in a marketable bond portfolio.

GIC Alternatives

Designed to preserve the benefits of traditional GICs while providing added portfolio diversification and investor control, GIC alternatives now account for a significant and increasing amount of the stable-value marketplace. The two primary forms of alternatives are separate-account GICs offered through life insurance companies and synthetic contracts issued by insurance companies, banks, and other financial institutions.

Separate-Account GICs

Separate-account GICs are the closest cousins to traditional GICs in that they are contractually issued as a group annuity policy with terms negotiated between the parties. However, unlike a GIC—which is backed by the general assets of the issuer—in a separate account, the insurance company segregates the assets on its balance sheet for the exclusive benefit of the contract holder. Legal ownership remains with the insurance company, but the contract holder's beneficial interest in the securities has been clearly established in most states. Therefore, in the event of an insolvency, the assets are not subject to claims of general policy holders.

The separate-account assets may be managed by the insurance company or, in some cases, by an outside money manager selected by the contract holder with the approval of the insurance company. An initial crediting rate of interest is established which reflects the yield of the underlying securities as well as the insurance company's underwriting, administration, and investment management fees.

The contract may have a specific maturity date or the assets may be managed to a constant duration, in which case the contract has no specified maturity date (referred to as "evergreen"). Additional flexibility is provided to the contract holder within this structure to establish individual investment guidelines for maturity, credit quality, and diversification. A variety of terms and conditions may be included in the contract, but the key feature is the provision for payments to plan participants at book value for qualified withdrawals.

Synthetic GICs

Synthetic GICs provide the features of a separate-account GIC with the additional advantage that the contract holder retains actual ownership and custody of the assets underlying the contract. In a typical synthetic structure, the investor purchases a fixed-income security (or portfolio of securities) and enters into a contract with a third-party guarantor. This third party is typically a bank or an insurance company, which agrees to accommodate benefit payments and other qualified participant withdrawals at the contract's book value. The contract is typically referred to as a wrapper agreement, and the issuer is called a wrap provider.

The investor retains ownership of the underlying pool of securities and receives an interest crediting rate equal to the annualized effective yield of the securities with an adjustment for fees and other factors. Additionally, the contract guarantees the investor a minimum rate of interest, usually 0%, to protect against a loss of principal. In exchange for these considerations, the wrap provider receives a fee that varies according to the risk assumed.

A synthetic GIC arrangement may involve as many as four parties, including an investor, a wrap provider, an outside money manager, and a trustee/custodian. One financial institution may provide all services for an investor (bundled product) or the service providers may be different entities (unbundled product). Regardless of the parties involved, the structural mechanics are similar. The terms of the wrap agreement transform a portfolio of marketable securities, whose values fluctuate, into a synthetic GIC.

Buy-and-Hold Synthetics

In a buy-and-hold synthetic structure, the investor purchases a single security which is usually held to its final maturity. The contract's crediting rate generally remains fixed, although rate resets may occur if expected or actual cash flows change. In these respects, buy-and-hold synthetics closely resemble traditional GICs. To date, asset-backed and mortgage-backed securities have been used heavily in buy-and-hold structures due to their high credit quality and relatively attractive yields. The buy-and-hold synthetic can also be structured with an interest rate swap embedded within a wrap agreement. With this version of the product, a floating-rate security is purchased and the floating interest rate is exchanged for a fixed rate. A wide array of features have been used in these arrangements, although use of callable, extendible, or amortizable (based on the performance of an index) structures have been most common.

Actively Managed Synthetics

The rationale behind the utilization of managed synthetics is the belief that active investment management enhances investment returns and leads to higher contract crediting rates. Added benefits include broader diversification and the ability to buy and sell securities or adjust the portfolio's duration, which enhances flexibility. Portfolios are constructed using the full range of fixed-income securities including U.S. Treasuries and agencies, mortgage-backed and asset-backed securities, and corporate bonds.

More complex instruments, such as interest rate swaps, futures, and options are also utilized, although to a lesser degree. The interest earned by investors over time equals the total return on the underlying portfolio of securities, less wrap and investment management fees. With managed synthetics, the volatility of annual returns is greatly reduced because of book value accounting. Exhibit 23.1 illustrates the smoothing effects of a wrap contract on a portfolio of marketable securities. Quarterly returns from the Lehman Brothers Intermediate Government/Corporate Bond Index are charted over a recent 10-year period. Overlaid on this exhibit are the returns that would have resulted in each period had the index had been wrapped, net of annual wrap fees of 10 basis points. As can be seen, the wrapped portfolio's quarterly returns are considerably more stable.

Managed synthetics are available in two forms, immunized and constant duration (evergreen). An immunized contract has a fixed maturity and, hence, the duration of the underlying portfolio is lowered over time to meet the maturity date. Evergreen contracts are managed within established duration bands and a specific maturity date is not usually established. To date, evergreen contracts have been the most commonly used managed synthetic.

EXHIBIT 23.1   Quarterly Return Comparisons (January 1987–June 2001)

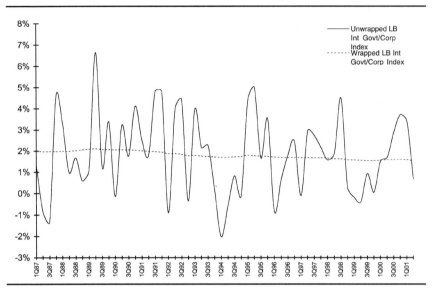

Alpha Synthetics

A newer hybrid referred to as the alpha synthetic combines the character-istics of the buy-and-hold and managed structures. In the alpha structure, an interest rate swap is embedded in a wrap contract. The investor agrees to pay the total return of an established benchmark for a specified period of time in exchange for a fixed rate of return known as the base rate. The base rate paid is a function of current Treasury yields and interest rate swap spreads relative to the index selected. The portfolio is then actively managed to outperform the selected index and any positive performance margin, referred to as portfolio alpha, is earned by the investor.

The initial crediting rate usually equals the base rate less wrap and investment management fees. Sometimes an estimate of the expected outperformance of the manager is added to the base rate to establish the initial crediting rate. The crediting rate is then reset periodically, often annually, to reflect the actual performance of the portfolio.

Stable-Value Pooled Funds

Individual stable-value portfolios may typically invest in most, if not all, of the products described in this chapter. However, many employee ben-efit plans have opted to utilize a professionally managed stable-value collective fund rather than attempt to manage their own portfolio. This is especially true in small to midsize plans, where it is increasingly difficult to attain appropriate portfolio diversification without incurring significant transaction costs. In addition, many larger plans utilize a pooled fund vehicle as a buffer within their portfolio to provide immediate liquidity for qualified withdrawals. Such a liquidity fund or buffer is often a contractual requirement stipulated by the issuer to minimize the likelihood of tapping its contracts for book-value payments. For that reason, investing in a stable-value collective fund can serve to enhance a portfolio's overall yield given that, over time, it outperforms shorter-term investments such as money market funds.

Stable-value pooled funds operate similar to mutual funds except that they are exempt from registration as securities with the Securities and Exchange Commission. The funds are collective trusts offered through banks and trust companies to fiduciary clients and can accept only qualified employee benefit plans as investors—including any plan qualified under section 401(a) of the Internal Revenue Service Code and deferred-compensation plans described in section 457 of the Code. The funds are typically valued daily in the same way as mutual funds and, therefore, offer substantial flexibility to a plan sponsor for investing participant contributions and paying out plan benefits. Pooled funds invest in the full range of stable-value products, offering to a plan ongoing professional management, broad diversification, high credit quality, and competitive returns.

THE EVOLUTION OF STABLE VALUE

Having defined the various stable-value products available today, a review of the market from an historical perspective may provide some insight into both the current use of these products within the context of portfolio management and where stable value may evolve in the future.

The Beginnings

Following enactment of the Employee Retirement Income and Security Act of 1974 (ERISA), the concept began to emerge of plan participants directing their own investments in defined-contribution plans. A significant result of this legislation was the increased utilization of guaranteed annuity contracts (GACs), which would hold a dominant position within these plans for years to come. Offered by the life insurance industry, which has been in the forefront of pension development and management in the United States, the GAC (also referred to as an immediate participation guarantee contract) was a nonmaturing contract featuring a fixed rate of interest that was convertible to an individual annuity upon retirement. This option was popular until the substantial rise in interest rates in the late 1970s and early 1980s, when the comparatively low rates of interest of the GAC created dissatisfaction among participants versus the double-digit, short-term market rates available at the time. These events prompted the creation of the guaranteed investment contract (GIC) of today, which retained the fixed-rate feature while offering relatively short, set maturity dates to allow for more rapid reinvestment and competitive returns.

Concurrent with these events, there were significant overhauls in the U.S. tax code, ultimately providing for tax-deferred contributions by participants to qualified employee benefit plans—including the 401(k) plan. These modifications prompted explosive growth in defined contribution plan formation, rising employee participation, and placed the investment decision-making responsibility in the hands of the individual plan participant. GICs were easy to understand. The fixed-rate, fixed-maturity structure was quite similar to bank certificates of deposit (CDs), so they were a likely beneficiary of the changes and grew rapidly. This growth attracted competition and, in 1987, a limited number of banks began issuing BICs to compete with GICs.

During this period, many plan sponsors managed their GIC options internally and purchased GIC and BIC contracts directly from the issuers or through consultants or GIC brokers. Some plans utilized a single insurance company's GIC, offering either a class year structure (participants received a new rate each year on their contributions) or a blended rate, which changed each year. In an effort to provide a diversified GIC option to smaller plans or to larger plans in their startup phase, many banks began offering GIC pooled funds in the mid-1980s. These funds featured independent professional management, credit oversight, diversification, and a mutual-fund-type structure and liquidity (subject to certain restrictions).

The Rise of Alternatives (Synthetics)

Traditional GICs were thought to be relatively safe, offering a guarantee of principal and interest to the participant. This perception began to change in the wake of the savings & loan crisis of the late 1980s, which was accompanied by credit concerns about banks and insurance companies, as well. It culminated with the default and seizure of Executive Life by the California state insurance commissioner in 1991.

In response to the growing credit and diversification concerns of GIC investors, Bankers Trust began offering the first synthetic GIC alternative in 1990, called BASIC—benefits accessible securities investment contract—which provided a book-value guarantee (wrapper) on an individual marketable fixed-income security. Bankers Trust followed in 1991 with the managed BASIC, which wrapped a portfolio of securities.

As synthetics gradually filtered into the marketplace, Bankers Trust was one of a limited number of active issuers. Purchasers of these early products tended to be more sophisticated investors, such as plan sponsors that managed their pension plans internally or professional stable-value managers. Following the highly publicized defaults of Mutual Benefit Life (1992) and Confederation Life (1994), however, synthetic GICs became widely used to enhance portfolio diversification and to reduce credit risk.

A time line of key market developments appears in Exhibit 23.2. The insurance industry quickly followed Bankers Trust's lead. It responded with a wrap contract of its own as well as increased efforts to market separate account GICs that offer features similar to wrapper agreements, although asset ownership and custody remained with the insurance company. Pooled funds also grew in popularity as plan sponsors sought to hire outside fiduciaries to manage their portfolios following issuer defaults. The larger, well diversified pooled funds were found to be an attractive alternative to in-house management.

The Stable-Value Market Today

Because of its unique position in the defined contribution market, the stable-value market has evolved from the old GIC mantle to an entire industry with its own association. Many stable-value professionals are now advancing the argument that stable value is an asset class separate to itself, given its unique risk/return characteristics. Indeed, many plan sponsors and plan participants must agree, as stable-value assets, by some estimates, now exceed $225 billion.

EXHIBIT 23.2 Evolution of Stable Value

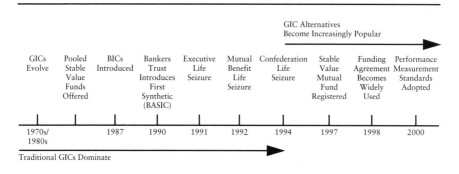

EXHIBIT 23.3   Product Market Share as of December 31, 2000

	Total Assets ($ Billion)
Guaranteed investment contracts	91
Separate account contracts	8
Synthetic GICs	115
Other	11
Total	225

Source: John Hancock, Life Insurance Marketing and Research Association (LIM-RA) and the Stable Value Investment Association, by permission.

While traditional GICs historically captured the largest share of invested assets within the stable-value market, they have recently been eclipsed by synthetic GICs as the dominant asset as investors have been attracted to the diversification and improved flexibility synthetics provide. According to data released by the Life Insurance Marketing and Research Association (LIMRA) and the Stable Value Investment Association, synthetic GICs now have a 51% market share ($115 billion) as compared with traditional GICs which now have a 40% market share ($91 billion). The migration toward synthetics has been especially prevalent among professional stable-value managers. According to Hueler Analytics, synthetic GICs accounted for 67% of stable-value pooled fund assets as of September 30, 2001. A breakdown of stable-value assets by product market share is provided in Exhibit 23.3.

Enticed by rising demand and relatively attractive fees, numerous wrap providers have now entered the market. Banks, including the domestic branches of foreign institutions, now dominate with an estimated 67% share of total wrapped assets. Insurance companies, despite some restrictions that have limited their ability to provide synthetics, have captured 33% of the market. A list of active wrap providers appears in Exhibit 23.4.

STABLE-VALUE PORTFOLIO MANAGEMENT

Stable-value portfolio management has changed dramatically in recent years as the combination of innovative products and new providers has virtually redefined how portfolios are structured and managed. The increased use of GIC alternatives such as synthetics has advanced portfolio management to the point where most traditional bond management strategies can be emulated within stable-value portfolios, while maintaining the low return volatility characteristics of stable value through book-value wrappers. In fact, major bond market participants such as multinational banks, securities dealers, and fixed-income managers have been at the forefront of product development and industry change as they have sought ways to apply their expertise to a market which, until recently, had been dominated by insurance companies.

This section highlights some general considerations in managing the traditional stable-value portfolio, with an emphasis on the use of synthetics. It also discusses some of the relevant contract terms and considerations impacting the portfolio structuring process.

EXHIBIT 23.4   Synthetic GIC Issuers and Wrapped Assets Outstanding as of December 31, 2000

Insurance Companies	$ Amount Outstanding
Aegon	$22,000,000,000
AIG Financial	10,000,000,000
Allstate	3,470,254,282
Pacific Life	2,100,000,000
C.N.A.	1,779,327,411
Prudential	755,000,000
Security Life of Denver	406,895,941
Jackson National	46,000,000
Met Life	3,000,000,000
Subtotal	$40,557,477,634

Banks	$ Amount Outstanfing
JP Morgan	$20,000,000,000
Union Bank Switzerland	12,000,000,000
State Street	11,700,000,000
Deutsche Bank	10,300,000,000
CDC Investment	8,000,000,000
Rabobank	7,600,000,000
Bank of America	7,286,000,000
Westdeutsche Landesbank	5,800,000,000
Subtotal	$82,686,000,000
Total	$123,243,477,634

Source: Galliard Capital Management

Stable-Value Portfolio Objectives

Consistent with the role of stable value as the safe option in most defined contribution plans today, the overriding objective in managing these portfolios is preservation of principal. Liquidity to meet participant withdrawals is an additional factor, as is earning a fairly stable return which exceeds that of shorter-maturity alternatives. Portfolio management strategies should address these objectives and should guide the selection of individual issues.

Credit Quality

All holdings in a stable-value portfolio—whether traditional GICs/BICs, wrap contracts, or assets underlying wrap contracts—must be high-quality instruments. A stringent credit review process is used initially to review issuers and to monitor them on an ongoing basis. Most managers establish minimum credit quality rating standards of single-A or double-A and require that the overall quality rating of the portfolio exceed Aa3 as measured by Moody's Investors Service or AA– by Standard & Poor's. Synthetic GICs can improve portfolio credit quality, since their underlying securities are often obligations of the U.S. government or its agencies, well structured mortgage/asset-backed securities, or highly rated corporate bonds. Investors must look deeper than the financial statements and the opinions of the rating agencies, however. Factors including the issuer's mix of business, amount of leverage, investment portfolio structure and liquidity, and the breadth and depth of management must also be explored.

Diversification

Diversification is a critical element in any portfolio management process and was a particularly thorny issue in stable-value portfolios prior to the advent of synthetics. Fiduciaries of employee benefit plans are charged with adequately diversifying portfolios under ERISA to minimize the risk of large losses. It could be argued that many stable-value portfolios historically did not fulfill this obligation because they were exposed almost entirely to financial services companies, often with large exposures to single issuers. As discussed earlier, defaults in the early 1990s drew attention to the diversification issue, however, and led to the propagation of synthetics.

Prudent diversification standards limit portfolio assets invested in a single issuer to no more than 10%. Most fixed-income practitioners limit holdings of non-U.S. government issues to no more than 5% and broadly diversify among different fixed-income sectors, industries, and security types. A similar result can be achieved in stable-value portfolios by looking through to the securities underlying synthetics. Traditional

GICs/BICs should be viewed as an important sector of the portfolio, but limited by industry diversification guidelines similar to other holdings.

Diversification constraints should be measured according to the net exposure to an individual issuer or sector. For contract issuers, full principal exposure of traditional issues and the difference between the market and book values of their synthetic contracts should be totaled. Likewise, credit exposure is measured for all underlying holdings. A well-diversified stable-value portfolio is portrayed in Exhibits 23.5 and 23.6. As shown, diversification is properly measured at both the aggregate portfolio and underlying security levels.

Maturity Structure

The maturity structure of stable-value portfolios must ensure that liquidity is adequate for meeting participant withdrawals. Generally, a buffer of available cash equal to at least 5% of the portfolio is invested in a stable-value collective fund, a money market fund, or other liquid, short-term instruments. Individual portfolio holdings are then structured with longer maturities to provide funds at regular intervals. Laddering the portfolio in this fashion assures that funds are available to accommodate liquidity needs and reinvest at current market rates. Portfolio maturity structures are typically short, averaging two to three years, with the longest holdings rarely exceeding five to seven years.

EXHIBIT 23.5   Hypothetical Stable-Value Portfolio—Portfolio Level Diversification

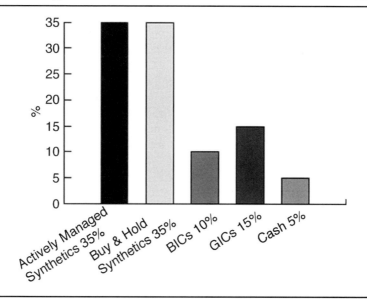

EXHIBIT 23.6   Hypothetical Stable-Value Portfolio—Securities Level Diversification

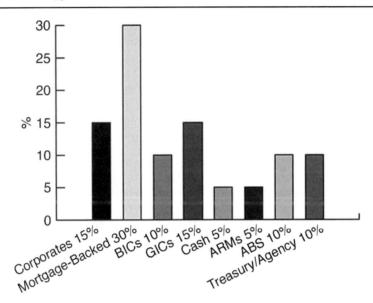

Synthetic contracts, however, have greatly improved the flexibility in portfolio maturity structuring, since the underlying securities are highly marketable. Liquidity may be constrained if the underlying securities' market value is significantly below their book value. When market value is near book value or higher, however, the portfolio manager is more able to meet unusual withdrawal requirements or shift the composition of the portfolio.

When structuring maturities, actively managed synthetics with constant durations must be factored into the equation. The average maturity of each active portfolio may be used as a proxy for the contract's maturity. However, managed contracts neither mature nor provide cash-flow contributions within the broader portfolio structure.

Duration and Convexity

Previously, the exclusive use of traditional GICs precluded the need to understand duration or convexity. However, the use of synthetics requires portfolio managers to track the duration characteristics of the securities underlying synthetics within a stable-value fund. Sophisticated analytical systems are required for this effort. Again, given the principal protection objective of stable-value funds, the volatility of underlying securities should be consistent with a two- to three-year average maturity. Volatility measurement is especially important when securities that possess various cash-flow characteristics, such as mortgage passthrough or mortgage/asset-backed securities are used. Guidelines must be established for active managers to assure that the use of higher-risk mortgage securities is limited. The negative convexity in these instruments can dramatically affect cash flows, which impacts the market value of the underlying portfolio and, thus, the crediting rate of the contract.

Asset Allocation Among Synthetic Structures

Portfolio strategies devised at the aggregate portfolio level must specify the allocation levels for different types of synthetic contracts as well as different issuers. No specific formula for allocation exists, for it depends upon the manager's level of comfort with synthetics, as well as his or her expertise. One approach is, first, to determine allocations to cash and traditional contracts, then allocate remaining assets to synthetic structures with a balance between buy-and-hold and actively managed contracts. The buy-and-hold structures provide cash flow to the broader portfolio and should be structured with portfolio guidelines for credit quality, diversification, and maturity in mind.

Actively managed synthetics are structured to achieve certain return objectives, but must also comply with the aggregate portfolio guidelines. A benchmark is commonly selected and management guidelines are established relative to this bogey. The amount of latitude given to investment managers should be carefully considered. Wrap providers that are liable for the shortfalls incurred when a portfolio's market value drops below book value will typically limit the investment manager's ability to move the portfolio's duration away from its benchmark. Wrap providers also limit, if not ban completely, the use of higher-risk securities, which allows them to quantify potential liabilities and contain risk.

Portfolio Management—Another View

More recently, larger plan sponsors have taken a less traditional approach in managing their stable-value portfolios, choosing to view them in a way that is more similar to their other fixed-income options, only with a book-value wrapper. This allocation strategy involves hiring one or more active fixed-income managers for the fund, each with a particular area of expertise or style, to manage actively all of the assets in the plan option—similar to the way they would structure their marketable bond fund or their defined-benefit plan fixed-income portfolio. The plan sponsor then secures one or more book-value wrapper agreements to provide for portfolio valuations at book.

Each manager must adhere to a set of investment guidelines agreed upon with the plan sponsor and wrap provider. The sponsor may maintain a liquidity reserve for payment of normal plan benefit payments to reduce the likelihood of book-value payments from the active synthetic contracts.

If the plan's cash flow history has consistently been positive, the plan sponsor may retain little or no reserve. But the sponsor will be required by the wrap provider to purchase only experience-rated (participating) contracts, so that any shortfall between the market value of the portfolio and book value in the event of a payout will be recovered from the plan rather than absorbed by the wrap provider.

Contract Considerations

Given that there are no industry standards governing the various types of stable-value contracts, they may vary materially from one issuer to another. As such, a thorough contract review is imperative and should be completed prior to the contract's final execution. All contracts will have terms dealing with the legal representations and warranties of the parties as well as provisions relating to the calculation of the credited rate of interest; contract withdrawals; terminations, including formulae for market-value adjustment; and the hierarchy for withdrawals within the total plan (that is, pro rata or LIFO).

Synthetic contracts are more complex, requiring additional provisions relating to the treatment of any losses realized from the liquidation of the underlying securities in the event of a withdrawal or termination. Synthetic contracts may be experience rated or non-experience rated (also called participating or nonparticpating). If experience rated, any losses realized from security sales to fund a withdrawal would be borne by the plan and recovered through a lower crediting rate of interest to participants. For non-experience-rated contracts, the risk of loss is borne by the issuer. As might be expected, non-experience-rated contracts have a somewhat higher fee than experience-rated contracts to compensate the issuer for the additional risk.

THE FUTURE OF STABLE VALUE

The tremendous change occurring recently in stable-value products, providers, and strategies will continue to reshape the market in coming years. While aggregate industry assets will more than likely experience only modest growth until the long-awaited retirement of baby boomers begins sometime around the year 2007, significant shifts will continue within the market in terms of product use and development, portfolio management strategies, and the players themselves. This section briefly highlights some of the market's major trends and provides some thoughts about the future.

From a product standpoint, pooled funds and actively managed synthetics are likely to continue to experience solid growth at the expense of traditional GICs, the use of which is expected to decline further. Separate account GICs will be utilized, but to a lesser extent than synthetics. Fixed-income managers are the clear beneficiary of the movement to managed synthetics and they will continue to play a bigger and bigger role in the marketplace. Indeed, one of the more interesting developments to watch will be the vanishing distinction between fixed-income managers and stable-value managers.

For the stable-value asset manager, market growth in the immediate future will largely be attained by successfully capturing other segments of the defined-contribution market, such as public deferred compensation plans (457) and retirement plans for tax-exempt organizations (403[b]). These sectors are just beginning to follow the corporate market in offering more diversified stable-value options including synthetic GICs and pooled funds at the expense of bank savings vehicles and fixed annuities.

Product innovations are continuing, as well. The SEC recently registered a stable-value fund for the first time. The mutual fund provides a professionally managed, well diversified fund in a format that is popular with participants, providing them with the ability to track their investments daily in the newspapers together with "portability" at retirement. Innovations continue as well within synthetic structures, including wrapping of specialized fixed-income styles and other asset classes such as high-yield, international bonds, and even equities.

While these newer structures are still a comparatively small part of the market, the quest for higher yields is beginning to manifest itself in riskier strategies. Plan sponsors must take care to understand all of the strategies that are utilized in their stable-value option and make sure they are comfortable that appropriate risk levels are maintained given the objective of principal preservation stated for this investment option.

On the issuer side, wrap fees have continued to plummet as these contracts have virtually become commoditized. Fees for wrapper agreements are averaging 8 to 12 basis points, and many deals have been struck at lower levels. It is likely that continued declines in wrap fees will cause consolidation on the issuer side of the industry, with the emergence of a few very large players.

A final trend that is being promoted within the industry relates to stable value as a distinct asset class, highly efficient in terms of risk and return. With attractive yields and low volatility of returns, many in the industry are beginning to recommend stable value as a substitute in balanced funds for traditional bond portfolios. Given the higher risk-adjusted returns, investors could reduce risk (volatility) in their portfolios by utilizing stable value in place of marketable bonds. Likewise, investors could increase their exposure to equities and improve expected returns while maintaining the same level of return volatility by utilizing stable value in balanced account options.

Whether stable value becomes a staple in balanced account strategies remains to be seen. What is clear is that participants applaud the high-return/low-volatility nature of stable-value investments and will likely continue to allocate a large portion of their fixed-income investments to this asset class in the future.

CHAPTER 24

Investment-Oriented Life Insurance

Frank J. Jones, Ph.D.
Chief Investment Officer
The Guardian Life Insurance Company of America

Insurance and investments are distinct concepts. This distinction leads to the development of various insurance and investment products. In practice, however, there is an overlap between some types of insurance products and investment products. This overlap occurs due partially to specific tax advantages provided to investment-oriented life insurance products. The two major types of investment-oriented life insurance are cash value life insurance and annuities.

This chapter begins with an overview of insurance. The remainder of the chapter considers the major types of investment-oriented life insurance, mainly cash value life insurance and annuities.

INSURANCE

Insurance is defined as a contract whereby one party—the insured—substitutes a small certain cost (the insurance premium) for a large uncertain financial loss based on a future contingent event. Thus, there are two parties to an insurance contract, the *insured*, who pays the premium and receives protection; and the *insurer* (or insurance company), which collects the premium and provides the protection.[1]

---

[1] In concept, an insurance contract is very similar to an option, specifically a put option, which is discussed in Chapter 28. The insured, in effect, buys the put option and the insurer sells the put option. Buying a put option on an individual stock, thus, is equivalent to "insuring" the price of the stock.

Most types of insurance provide for a prespecified payment from the insurer to the insured if and when the contingent insured event occurs and otherwise have no value. This is called *pure insurance*. Other types of insurance have a "cash value" even if the contingent event does not occur. This is called *investment-oriented insurance*. The two types of investment-oriented insurance are discussed later.

The major types of insurance, in general, are:[2]

- Life
- Health
- Disability
- Property (home and automobile)
- Liability

Of these types, only life insurance has a cash value form in addition to pure insurance. Cash value life insurance is a very important type of investment-oriented life insurance. Therefore, let's consider life insurance in more detail.

According to a *pure life insurance* contract, the insurer (the life insurance company) pays the beneficiary of the contract a fixed amount if the insured dies while the life insurance contract is valid. If the insured does not die while the policy is valid, the insurance contract becomes worthless at its expiration. To provide pure life insurance contracts, the insurance company—specifically its actuaries—calculate the probability of the insured dying during the period the contract is valid. Many variables affect this probability, including physical health and whether the person smokes. The most important variable, however, is the insured's age. Specifically, the probability of death increases with age. Actuaries estimate this relationship with some degree of precision.

Obviously the insurance premium charged by the insurance company must cover the average amount paid to all insureds, the administrative and distribution costs, and a profit. The cost of pure insurance to the company depends on the probability of the insured dying during the period which increases with age, as shown in Exhibit 24.1.

Overall, the premium charged to the insured for a pure life insurance contract is shown in Exhibit 24.2, which is determined by the probability of death (the "cost" of paying the death benefit) plus the distribution and administrative costs plus the profits. Pure life insurance is called *term insurance*. It is applicable over the term of the policy.

---

[2] Other types of insurance include long-term care, business interruption, and workers' compensation.

EXHIBIT 24.1   Probability of Dying (U.S. Population, Male)

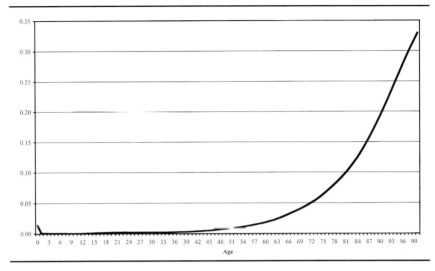

EXHIBIT 24.2   Annual Premium for Yearly Renewable Term Policy

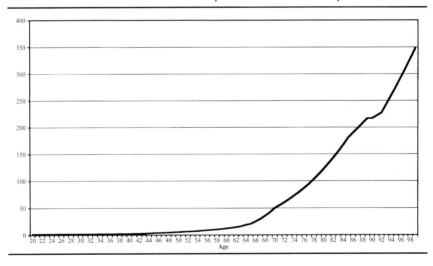

There are three types of term insurance. The most common type is called *annual renewable term*. According to this type, the insured has the right to renew the coverage every year without new underwriting (that is, without a new medical examination). Premiums, however, change; that is, they increase each year and become very expensive at older ages, as indicated below. A second type of term insurance, much less common, does not have the guaranteed renewability feature of the above.

The third type of term insurance is *level-premium term*, wherein the premium is constant during the life of the policy. Its level is higher than for annual renewable term early in the policy. However, the premium does not increase with age and is lower than an annual renewable term policy late in the life of the policy. Typically, policies of ten years or more are written on a level-premium term.

As indicated, for annual renewable term the annual premium increases significantly with age. For example, for a $1 million term policy for a 30-year old non-smoking man, the premium will be approximately $500 for a 20-year level premium policy (which ends when he is 50). At ages 50, 60, and 70, the same man would pay approximately $2,500, $6,000, and $20,000, respectively, for the same type of 20-year of policy.[3] The premiums for these policies vary significantly by issuing company.

Traditional whole life policy premiums are much higher than for term insurance, often ten times higher or more. For example, a non-smoking 40-year old man may pay approximately $16,000 per year for a traditional whole life policy. In this case also, the premiums vary considerably by company.

The costs of non-life types of pure insurance are determined in a similar manner. However, in other types of insurance, factors other than the age of the insured may be the dominant variables. For example, location may be important in home insurance: It costs more to insure against hurricanes in Miami and Galveston than in Chicago and San Francisco. And it costs more for a young male (age is a also a factor here) than a middle-aged female to buy automobile insurance. For both, however, prior driving record is important.

Conceptual Issues in Risk Management

Consider some conceptual issues regarding risk management from the perspective of the insured and the willingness to provide risk coverage from the perspective of the insurer.

From the perspective of the insured, insurance is a mechanism for managing risk. Individuals experience many types of risk and the manner in which they manage the risk depends on the characteristics of the risk. Two important characteristics of the risk are the severity of the risk (the cost) and the frequency of the risk.

There are, in general, also four different ways to manage the risk. Consider specifically these four ways in the context of managing the risk of fire for a house.

---

[3] Karen Hube, "What Kind of Life Insurance Do I Need?" *Wall Street Journal* (January 28, 2002), p. R12.

- *Avoidance:* Avoid the risk-producing activity. For example, do not build a house in a hot, dry area.
- *Reduction:* Reduce the risk of an activity. For example, build a house in a hot dry area, but add a sprinkler system.
- *Retain:* Continue the risk producing activity, but do not insure the risk, that is, self-insure. For example, build a house in a hot, dry area, do not buy insurance, and be prepared to pay for the house yourself if the house burns.
- *Insure:* Engage in an insurance contract on the risk and pay the premium thereon. For example, buy fire insurance on your house. Fire insurance on a house in a hot, dry area will, however, be expensive.

The way in which an individual manages risk will depend on the characteristics of the risk, as summarized in Exhibit 24.3. That is, insurance is most appropriate when the frequency of the insured event is low and the severity is high. Examples of this type of risk might be a serious automobile accident, your house burning down, or the death of a young person. From the perspective of the insurer, the diversification of the risk is important. The essence of insurance is that the financial burden of the losses suffered by a few is shared among many. Suppose it is estimated that in one year, 100 out of 100,000 homeowners will experience losses caused by fire. This is determined based on data assembled about what happened in the past. Instead of those 100 homeowners bearing the entire financial burden of the losses, the burden is shared among the 100,000 homeowners through premiums for homeowners insurance, which includes protection against fire losses. It is necessary to be able to estimate in advance with reasonable accuracy the aggregate losses that will be suffered by the 100,000 homeowners.

EXHIBIT 24.3 Treatment of Risk by Type of Risk

Severity	Frequency	
	High	Low
High[1]	Avoidance or reduction (Insurance is very expensive)[2]	Insurance
Low[3]	Retention or reduction	Retention

[1] When the severity of loss is high, retention is not realistic—another technique is needed.
[2] When the frequency of loss is high and the severity is high, insurance is very expensive.
[3] When the severity of the loss is low, insurance is not needed.

EXHIBIT 24.4   Investment-Oriented Insurance Product

1. Cash Value Life Insurance
   - Whole Life
   - Variable Life
   - Universal Life
   - Variable Universal Life
2. Annuities
   - Variable
   - Fixed
   - GICs

The statistical concept of the "law of large members" is relevant. Considering again life insurance, assume that the probability of death during a 12-month period is 20% for a given age. If only one person of this age is insured, either 0% or 100% of the insureds die, and the insurer experiences either a large loss or a large gain. But if the insurer insures 100 people of this age at an actuarially determined premium, the insurer is likely to have a profit close to the average profit actuarially expected. The law of large numbers says there is more statistical certainty when a large number of insureds (which are diversified) are involved.

The correlation or independence of the individual events is also important. For example, providing hurricane insurance to 100 houses in Galveston, Texas does not benefit from the law of large numbers—either all or none of the houses are likely to experience a hurricane.

In the calculation of premiums, insurers estimate the future based on the past. Insurers need to feel comfortable that their estimates will apply to the future. To calculate the loss component of insurance premiums, insurers multiply their estimates of the probability of future losses times the dollar value of the loss.

Investment-Oriented Life Insurance Products

This chapter does not consider any of the pure insurance products. Rather, it considers only various types of investment-oriented life insurance products. Such products are shown in Exhibit 24.4. Each product is discussed in more detail in this chapter.

There is an important distinction in investment-oriented life insurance with respect to whether the insured or the insurance company bears the investment risk, that is, who gains or loses if the investment experience is greater or less than expected. Exhibit 24.5 segregates the products by who bears the investment risk.

EXHIBIT 24.5   Types of Investment-Oriented Insurance by Risk Bearer

General Account (Insurer Risk)	Separate Account (Insured Risk)
Whole Life Insurance	Variable Life Insurance
Universal Life Insurance	
GICs	Variable Annuities
Fixed Annuities	

EXHIBIT 24.6   Annual Premium for Pure Life Insurance Policy

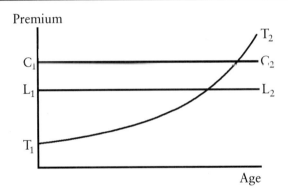

The products in the first column are called "general account products" and those in the second column are called "separate account products." The nature of this distinction is discussed later in this chapter.

In all types of pure insurance, the insurer, that is the insurance company, bears the risk of honoring the contract. That is, it is the obligation of the insurer to deliver the exact amount specified in the insurance contracts. But either the insurance company or the insured may bear the risk of underperforming.

Cash Value Life Insurance

Consider how cash value life insurance relates to the discussion based on Exhibit 24.2 for pure life insurance. The premium for an annual pure life insurance (term insurance) contract is paid each year for a contract that expires after one year and is shown in Exhibit 24.2 which is reproduced in Exhibit 24.6. The annual term insurance premium is denoted by $T_1 T_2$.

This premium, $T_1 T_2$, has two important characteristics:

1. The premium increases each year for a new one-year contract, and increasingly so as age increases; and
2. If the insured does not die during the year, the insurance contract expires worthless at the end of the year (and can be replaced by paying a higher premium the next year).

This consideration provides a transition to cash value life insurance. Suppose the insurance company provided pure life insurance for a period much longer than a year, for example the insured's entire life, but charged a constant, called *level*, premium. In fact, level premium term life insurance is available. In this case, the level premium represents the average premium over the term of the policy. Let L_1L_2 be the level premium of the term life insurance. Such a policy has no cash value.

Second, suppose that the initial (and constant) premium paid is higher than the cost of pure life insurance. This excess premium can be invested and build up cash value during the term of the policy. For example, in Exhibit 24.6 T_1/T_2 represents the initial cost of annual term insurance, L_1/L_2 the cost of level premium term insurance, and C_1/C_2 the level premium of cash value insurance. The excess amount of premium for cash value insurance over annual term, $C_1 - T_1$ at a young age, in addition to potentially covering the deficit between the cost of pure insurance and cash value insurance at an older age (e.g., $T_2 - C_2$), can be entered into an investment account of the insured. This is the essence of cash value life insurance.

Each year's premium is segregated into two components by the insurance company. The first is the amount needed to pay for the pure insurance, which, as indicated, increases each year. The second goes into the insured's investment account, which is the cash value of the life insurance contract. An investment return is earned on this cash value, which further increases the cash value. The buildup of this *cash value* and the ability to borrow against it both have tax advantages, as discussed below. Two important observations can be made here.

First, a common marketing or sales advantage attributed to cash value life insurance is that the higher premium paid will "force" the individuals to save, whereas if they did not pay the higher insurance premium, they would use their income for consumption rather than savings. According to this rationale, the higher insurance premium is, thus, *forced savings*.

Whether or not this first observation has merit, the second observation unequivocally does. The federal government encourages the use of cash value life insurance by providing significant tax advantages. Thus, the second advantage of cash value life insurance is *tax-advantaged* savings.

There are several tax advantages to cash value life insurance. The first and major tax advantage is called *"inside buildup."* This means that the returns on the investment component of the premium, both income and capital gains, are not subject to taxation (income or capital gains) while held in the insurance contract. Inside buildup is a significant advantage to "saving" via a cash value life insurance policy rather than, for example, saving via a mutual fund.

The second tax advantage of a cash value life insurance policy relates to borrowing against the policy. In general, an amount equal to the cash value of the policy can be borrowed. However, there are some tax implications. The taxation of life insurance is covered in more detail in a following section.[4]

Term insurance has become much more of a commodity product and, in fact, there are websites that provide premium quotes for term life insurance for various providers. Cash value life insurance, due to its complexity and multiple features, is not, however, a commodity.

Obviously, the cost of annual term life insurance is much lower than that of whole life insurance, particularly for the young and middle-aged. For example, while there is a wide range of premiums for both term and whole life insurance, for a 35 year old male, the annual cost of $500,000 of annual term insurance may be $400 and the cost of whole life insurance may be $5,000.

The Nature of Insurance Companies

The nature of an insurance company is quite different than that of a traditional manufacturing company. Consider, for a simple comparison, a bread manufacturing company.

The pricing of bread and the calculation of the profits of a bread manufacturing company are quite simple. The bread manufacturer buys flour and other ingredients, produces the bread with its ovens and bakers, and sells the bread soon thereafter. The costs of the inputs are straightforward (the ovens, of course, must be depreciated) and the revenues are received soon after the costs are incurred. Bread prices may be altered as the costs of the inputs vary. Profits can be measured over short periods of time.

The insurance business is much more complex. Premiums—revenues—are determined initially and may be collected once or over a long period of time. The events that trigger an insurance payout are not only deferred but are also contingent on the occurrence of a specified event, for example

---

[4] In addition to the above, the *death benefit*, that is the amount paid to the beneficiary of the life insurance contract at the death of the insured, is exempt from income taxes, although it may be subject to estate taxes. This benefit applies both to cash value and pure life insurance.

death or an automobile accident. Since there is a long and uncertain period between the collection of the premium and the payment of the benefit, the receipts may be invested in the interim and the investment returns represent an important but initially uncertain source of revenue. Insurance company investment practices are not considered in this chapter.

Another important distinction between bread manufacturers and insurance companies is the timing of the claim of the customer on the producing company. The purchaser of a loaf of bread is not concerned about the solvency of the bread manufacturer. The purchaser leaves the store with the bread, that is, the business is "cash and carry."

The purchaser of a life insurance contract, however, has a deferred claim on the life insurance company. This claim may arise decades from the purchase of the life insurance contract. For this reason, the customer is concerned about the long-term solvency of the life insurance company. Rating agencies provide credit ratings on life insurance companies to assist customers in this evaluation. The "claims paying ability," as assessed by these rating agencies, may be an important characteristic to customers in their overall choice of a life insurance company.

In addition, to assure that the insurance company will be able to pay the insurance benefit, if necessary, regulators require that the insurance company retain reserves (in an accounting sense) for the security of future payments. Other accounting complexities are also relevant. Thus, overall, the pricing and measurement of the profits of an insurance company are much more complex than that of a bread manufacturer. And to insure that insurance companies are solvent and pay deferred insurance claims, insurance companies are more regulated than bread manufacturers.

Thus, the fundamental difference between bread manufacturers and life insurance companies is that for bread manufacturers the timing of the costs and revenues is approximately synchronous, while for life insurance companies the timing is potentially very different. There are also significant differences in this regard between annual term insurance and whole life insurance. Companies providing annual term life insurance collect the revenue at the beginning of the year and pay the death benefit by the end of the year, if at all. Companies providing whole life insurance, however, may collect premiums for several years and make a large payment after decades.

Stock and Mutual Insurance Companies

There are two major forms of life insurance companies, stock and mutual. A stock insurance company is similar in structure to any corporation (also called a public company). Shares (of ownership) are owned by independent shareholders and may be traded publicly. The shareholders care only about the performance of their shares, that is the stock appreciation and the dividends over time. Their holding period and, thus, their view may be short term or long term. The insurance policies are simply the products or businesses of the company in which they own shares.

In contrast, mutual insurance companies have no stock and no external owners. Their policyholders are their owners. The owners, that is the policyholders, care primarily or even solely about the performance of their insurance policies, notably the company's ability to eventually pay on the policy and to, in the interim, provide investment returns on the cash value of the policy, if any. Since these payments may occur considerably into the future, the policyholders' view will be long term. Thus, while stock insurance companies have two constituencies, their stockholders and their policyholders, mutual insurance companies only have one, since their policyholders and their owners are the same. Traditionally, the largest insurance companies have been mutual, but recently there have been many demutualizations, that is, conversions by mutual companies to stock companies. Currently several of the largest life insurance companies are stock companies.

The debate on which is the better form of insurance company, stock or mutual, is too involved to be considered in any depth here. However, consider selected comments on this issue. First, consider this issue from the perspective of the policyholder. Mutual holding companies have only one constituency, their policyholder or owner. The liabilities of many types of insurance companies are long term, particularly the writers of whole life insurance. Thus, mutual insurance companies can appropriately have a long time horizon for their strategies and policies. They do not have to make short-term decisions to benefit their shareholders, whose interests are usually short term, via an increase in the stock price or dividend, in a way that might reduce their long-term profitability or the financial strength of the insurance company. In addition, if the insurance company earns a profit, it can pass the profit onto its policyholders via reduced premiums. (Policies that benefit from an increased profitability of the insurance company are called *participating policies*, as discussed in the next section.) These increased profits do not have to accrue to stockholders because there are none.

Finally, mutual insurance companies can adopt a longer time frame in their investments, which will most likely make possible a higher return. Mutual insurance companies, for example, typically hold more common stock in their portfolios than stock companies. However, whereas the long time frame of mutual insurance companies may be construed an advantage over stock companies, it may also be construed as a disadvantage. Rating agencies and others assert that, due to their longer horizon and their long time frame, mutual insurance companies may be less efficient and have higher expenses than stock companies. Empirically, rating agencies and others assert that mutual insurance companies have typically significantly reduced their expenses shortly before and after converting to stock companies.

Overall, it is argued, mutual insurance companies have such long planning horizons that they may not operate efficiently, particularly with respect to expenses. Stock companies, on the other hand, have very short planning horizons and may operate to the long-term disadvantage of their policyholders to satisfy their stockholders in the short run. Recently, however, mutual insurance companies have become more cost conscientious.

Consider now the issue of stock versus mutual companies from the perspective of the insurance company. What have been the motivations of mutual insurance companies to go public (issue stock via an initial public offering [IPO]) in recent years? Several reasons are typically given. First, with the financial industry diversifying, consolidating, and growing, many insurance companies have concluded that they need to acquire other financial companies (including other insurance companies, investment companies, broker/dealers, and banks) to prosper or even survive. To conduct these acquisitions they need capital. Mutual companies cannot, by definition, issue stock and are limited in the amount of public debt they can issue—mutual insurance companies issue public debt via "surplus notes." In addition, internal surplus has been growing slowly for the insurance industry. Thus, many insurance companies have concluded that to expand as quickly as they deem essential, they have to be able to raise equity capital and, thus, go public. Second, some mutual insurance companies and their advisors believe that, at least sometimes, stock is a better "acquisition currency" than cash (typically for reasons of taxes and financial accounting), even if the mutual insurance company has enough cash for the acquisition. Finally, company stock and stock options have become a more important form of incentive compensation in many industries, and many insurance companies have concluded that to attract, retain, and motivate the desired executives, they need to be able to provide public stock in their companies.

Whereas many mutual insurance companies go public for these reasons, other mutual insurance companies continue to prosper as mutuals. And while stock insurance companies can raise capital to acquire other companies, they also become vulnerable to being acquired by other companies. Mutual companies cannot be involuntarily acquired.

General Account versus Separate Account Products

The general account of an insurance company refers to the overall resources of the life insurance company, mainly its investment portfolio. Products "written by the company itself" are said to have a "general account guarantee," that is, they are a liability of the insurance company. When the rating agencies (Moody's, Standard & Poor's, Fitch) provide a credit rating, these ratings are on products written by or guaranteed by the general account, specifically on the "claims-paying ability" of the company. Typical products written by and guaranteed by the general account are whole life, universal life, and fixed annuities (including GICs). Insurance companies must support the guaranteed performance of their general account products to the extent of their solvency. These are called *general account products*.

Other types of insurance products receive no guarantee from the insurance company's general account, and their performance is based, not on the performance of the insurance company's general account, but solely on the performance of an investment account separate from the general account of the insurance company, often an account selected by the policyholder. These products are called *separate account products*. Variable life insurance and variable annuities are separate account products. The policyholder selects specific investment portfolios to support these separate account products. The performance of the insurance product depends almost solely on the performance of the portfolio selected, adjusted for the fees or expenses of the insuring company (which do depend on the insurance company). The performance of the separate account products, thus, is not affected by the performance of the overall insurance company's general account portfolio.

Most general account insurance products, including whole life insurance, participate in the performance of the company's general account performance. For example, whereas a life insurance company provides the guarantee of a minimum dividend on its whole life policies, the policies' actual dividend may be greater if the investment portfolio performs well. This is called the "interest component" of the dividend. (The other two components of the dividend are the expense and mortality components.) Thus, the performance of the insurance policy participates in the overall company's performance. Such a policy is called a *participating policy*, in this case a participating whole life insurance policy.

In addition, the performance of some general account products may not be affected by the performance of the general account portfolio. For example, disability income insurance policies may be written on a general account, and while their payoff depends on the solvency of the general account, the policy performance (for example, its premium) may not participate in the investment performance of the insurance companies' general account investment portfolio.

Both stock and mutual insurance companies write both general and separate account products. However, most participating general account products tend to be written in mutual companies.

Overview of Cash Value Whole Life Insurance

The details of cash value whole life insurance (CVWLI) are very complex. This section provides a simple overview of CVWLI, partially by contrasting it with term life insurance.

As discussed above, in annual term life insurance, the owner of the policy, typically also the insured, pays an annual premium which reflects the actuarial risk of death during the year. The premium, thus, increases each year. If the insured dies during the year, the death benefit is paid to the insurer's beneficiary. If the insured does not die during the year, the term policy has no value at the end of the year.

The construction and performance of CVWLI is quite different. First, the owner of the policy pays a constant premium over their life. This premium is much higher than a term policy for two reasons. First the constant premium must cover the lower insurance risk early in the policy but also the higher insurance risk later in the policy when the insured has a higher age and the annual cost of the pure insurance exceeds the level premium. Second, the premium is also higher than the average of the pure insurance over the life of the policy and this excess builds up a cash value, which represents the investment value of the policy.

Each year the excess of the premium over the pure insurance cost is invested by the insurance company in its general account portfolio. This portfolio generates a return which accrues to the policy owner's cash value. Typically, the insurance company guarantees a minimum increase in cash value, called the *guaranteed cash value buildup*. The insurance company, however, may provide an amount in excess of the guaranteed cash value buildup based on earnings for participating policies. What happens to this excess? Assume that the insurance company has a mutual structure, that is, it is owned by the policyholders. In this case, with no stockholders, the earnings accrue to the policyholders as dividends.

The arithmetic of the development of the cash value in a life insurance contract follows:[5]

> \+ Premium
> − Cost of Insurance (Mortality)
> − Expenses
> \+ Guaranteed (Minimum) Cash Value Buildup
> \+ (Participating) Dividend
> _____
> Increase (Buildup) in Cash Value

---

[5] The overall dividend is calculated from the investment income, the cost of paying the death benefit (the mortality expense denoted by M), and the expense of running the company (denoted by E). The latter two together are called the M&E charges.

If the insurance company is owned by stockholders, some or all of the earnings might go to the stockholders as dividends.

The returns to the insurance company and, therefore, the dividends to the policyholder can increase if: (1) investment returns increase; (2) company expenses decrease; or (3) mortality costs decrease (that is, the life expectancy of the insured increases).

The dividends can be "used" by the policyholder in either of two ways. The first is to decrease the annual premium. In this case, the death benefit remains constant. The second is to increase the death benefit and the cash value of the policy. Such increases are called *"paid up additions"* (PUAs). In this case, the annual premium remains constant. Most policies are written in the second way.

The intended way for the life insurance policy to terminate is for the insured to die and the life insurance company to pay the death benefit to the beneficiary. There are other ways, however. First, the policy can be *lapsed* (alternatively called *forfeited* or *surrendered*). In this case, the owner of the policy withdraws the cash value of the policy and the policy is terminated.

There are also two *non-forfeiture options*—that is methods whereby an insurance policy for the insured remains. The owner can use the cash value of the policy to buy *extended term insurance* (the amount and term of the resulting term insurance policy depends on the cash value). In addition, the cash value of the policy can be used to buy a reduced amount of fully paid (that is, no subsequent premiums are due) whole life insurance—this is called *reduced paid up*.

In addition to the forfeiture option and the two non-forfeiture options of terminating the CVWLI policy, the policy could be left intact and borrowed against. This is called a *policy loan*. An amount equal to the cash value of the policy can be borrowed. There are two effects of the loan on the policy. First, the dividend is paid only on the amount equal to the cash value of the policy minus the loan. Second, the death benefit of the policy paid is the policy death benefit minus the loan.

The taxation of the death benefit payout, a policy lapse, and borrowing against the loan are considered next. For taxation of life insurance, it is important to recall that the insurance premium is paid by the policy owner with after-tax dollars (this is often called the *cost* of the policy). But the cash value is allowed to build up inside the policy with taxes deferred (or usually tax-free), often called the *return* on the policy.

Taxability of Life Insurance

A major attraction of life insurance as an investment product is its taxability. Consider the four major tax advantages of life insurance.

The first tax advantage is that when the death benefit is paid to the beneficiary of the insurance policy, the benefit is free of income tax. If the life insurance policy is properly structured in an estate plan, the benefit is also free of estate taxes.

The second tax advantage is called "inside buildup"—that is, all earnings (interest, dividend, and realized capital gains) are exempt from income and capital gains taxes. Thus, these earnings are tax deferred (and when included in the death benefit become income tax free, and in some cases also estate tax free).

The third relates to the lapse of a policy. When the policy is lapsed, the owner receives the cash value of the policy. The amount taxed is the cash value minus the cost of the policy (the total premiums paid plus the dividends, if paid in cash). That is, the tax basis of the policy is the cost (accumulated premiums) of the policy. The cost, thus, increases the basis and is recovered tax-free. (Remember, however, that these costs were paid with after-tax dollars.) And, the remainder was allowed to accumulate without taxation but is taxed at the time of the lapse.

The fourth tax issue relates to borrowing against the policy—that is, a policy loan. The primary tax issue is the distinction between the cost (accumulated premium) and the excess of the policy cash value over the cost (call it the excess). When a policy loan is made, the cost is deemed to be borrowed first (that is, FIFO [first in-first out] accounting is employed). The amount up to the cash value of the policy can be borrowed and not be subject to the ordinary income tax. (An exception to this practice—for a Modified Endowment Contract—is discussed in the footnote.)[6]

Although CVWLI has both insurance and investment characteristics, Congress provided insurance policies tax advantages because of their insurance, not their investment, characteristics. And Congress does not wish to apply these insurance-directed tax benefits to primarily investment products. In this regard, in the past some activities related to borrowing against insurance policies were considered abuses by Congress and tax law changes were made to moderate these activities. These abuses originated with a product called *single-premium life insurance*. This policy is one in which only a single premium is paid for a whole life insurance policy. The premium creates an immediate cash value. This cash value and the resulting investment income earned are sufficient to pay the policy's benefits. The excess investment income accumulates tax-free.

After the elimination of many tax shelters by the Tax Reform Act of 1986, the sale of single-premium life insurance accelerated significantly because investors found this product to be an attractive tax shelter.

---

[6] If the loan is outstanding at the time of the policy lapse, the loan is treated on a FIFO basis whereby the cost basis is assumed to be borrowed first and is not taxable, and when the cost basis is exhausted by the loan, the remainder of the loan (up to the cash value of the policy) is taxable.

Large amounts could be paid as a premium, the earnings grew tax-free, and the owner could borrow up to the cash value without a tax liability. Single premium life insurance, thus, generated significant tax-sheltered investment income.

In 1988 (via the Technical and Miscellaneous Revenue Act of 1988 [TAMRA]), Congress developed a new policy to discourage the use of life insurance contracts with large premiums as an investment tax shelter. The test embodied in this policy was called the *seven-pay test*. Consider first the effect of not meeting the seven pay test, and then the test itself.

If an insurance policy did not meet the seven-pay test at time of issue, it was deemed to be a Modified Endowment Contract (MEC) and the tax advantages were reduced as follows. MECs have two important tax disadvantages relative to standard life insurance policies (non-MECs). First, policy loans on a MEC are made on a LIFO (last in-first out) basis—that is, the investment earnings, not the cost basis, is borrowed first and is taxable. The remainder of the loan up to the cash value of the policy is the cost basis and not subject to tax. Second, MECs are subject to a 10% penalty on any taxable gains borrowed before age 59½ (similar provisions exist on annuities, as discussed in a later section).

Next consider the seven-pay test for determining whether the policy is a MEC. The seven-pay test is an artificial standard developed by the IRS based on the level premium concept. First, the premium for a level premium seven-year paid policy is calculated. The test or standard for determining whether an insurance policy is a MEC is that the premium actually paid on the policy during the first seven years cannot be greater than the seven-year pay level on a year-by-year basis. For example, if the seven-year pay amount calculated is $1,000 per year for seven years, the premium paid can be no more than $1,000 during the first year; similarly no more than $2,000 during the first two years; and up to $7,000 during the first seven years. If the actual premiums paid are greater than any of these amounts, the policy is a MEC. Whether or not a policy is a MEC should be determined and be divulged to the policy owner before the policy is written.

If a policy is deemed a MEC when it is written, it remains a MEC throughout its life. However, a policy which is initially a non-MEC can be subsequently deemed to be a MEC if premium payments accelerate.

The following illustrates the difference in the taxation of a MEC and a non-MEC.

Cash Value: 100
Premium Paid: 20
Earnings: 80

1. Non-MEC

- Loan up to 100 is non-taxable (that is, neither premium paid nor earnings is taxable)
- Rationale: withdrawal is a loan, not a distribution (i.e., not included in income)

2. MEC

- Borrow earnings (80) first—is taxable
- Then borrow premium paid (20)—is not taxable

The characteristics of MECs and non-MECs are summarized in Exhibit 24.7. It is important to note that MECs have no disadvantage if the policy owner does not borrow against the policy. The MEC condition serves only to disadvantage policy loans in an insurance contract.

INVESTMENT-ORIENTED LIFE INSURANCE

The major investment-oriented insurance products can be divided into two categories—cash value life insurance and annuities. Each has several types, which are listed in Exhibit 24.4. These products are described in the following sections.

EXHIBIT 24.7   Characteristics of Non-MECs and MECs

Non-MEC	MEC
Meets seven-pay test.	Does not meet seven-pay test.
Inside buildup is tax deferred.	Inside buildup is tax deferred.
Can borrow up to cash value of the policy.	Can borrow up to cash value of the policy.
Loans are tax free.	Loans are treated on LIFO basis (investment income is borrowed first).
	Pay income tax on investment income borrowed first (with 10% penalty on earnings if before age 59½); no tax on remainder of loan up to cash value.
	No disadvantage if do not borrow against or surrender the policy.

Cash Value Life Insurance

Cash value life insurance has been introduced above. There are two dimensions of cash value life insurance policies. The first is whether the cash value is *guaranteed* (called whole life) or *variable* (called variable life). The second is whether the required premium payment is *fixed* or *flexible*, that is whether it has a universal (flexible) feature or not. They can be combined in all ways. Thus, there are four combinations, which we discuss next. The broad classification of cash value life insurance, called whole life insurance, in addition to providing pure life insurance (as does term insurance), builds up a cash value or investment value inside the policy.

Traditional cash value life insurance, usually called whole life insurance, has a *guaranteed* buildup of cash value based on the investment returns on the general account portfolio of the insurance company. That is, the cash value in the policy is guaranteed to increase by a specified minimum amount each year. This is called the *cash value buildup*. (The guaranteed cash value buildup of many U.S. CVWLI policies tend to be in the range of 3%–4%.) The cash value may grow by more than this minimum amount if a dividend is paid on the policy. Dividends, however, are not guaranteed. There are two types of dividends, participating and nonparticipating. Participating dividends depend on (that is, participate in) the investment returns of the general account of the insurance company portfolio (the insurance company M&E charges also affect the dividend).

The participating dividend *may be* used to increase the cash value of the policy by more than its guaranteed amount. Actually, there are two potential uses of the dividend. The first is to reduce the annual premium paid on the policy. In this case, while the premium decreases, the cash value of the policy increases by only its guaranteed amount (and the face value the death benefit remains constant).

The second use is to buy more life insurance with the premium (called "paid up additions" [PUA]). In this case, the cash value of the entire policy increases by more than the guaranteed amount on the original policy (and the face value of the current policy is greater than the face value of the original policy).

In either case, the performance of the policy over time may be substantially affected by the participating dividends.

Contrary to the guaranteed or fixed cash value policies based on the general account portfolio of the insurance company, *variable life insurance* polices allow the policyowners to allocate their premium payments to and among several separate investment accounts maintained by the insurance company, and also to be able to shift the policy cash value among these separate accounts. As a result, the amount of the policy cash value depends on the investment results of the separate accounts the policyowners have selected. Thus, there is no guaranteed cash value or death benefit. Both depend on the performance of the selected investment portfolio.

The types of separate account investment options offered in their variable life insurance policies vary by insurance companies. Typically, the insurance company offers a selection of common stock and bond fund investment opportunities, often managed by the company itself and also by other investment managers. If the investment options perform well, the cash value buildup in the policy will be significant. However, if the policyholder selects investment options that perform poorly, the variable life insurance policy will perform poorly. There could be little or no cash value buildup, or, in the worst case, the policy could be terminated because there is not enough value in the contract to pay the mortality charge. This type of cash value life insurance is called variable life insurance. Variable life insurance, mainly their common stock investment options, grew quickly during the stock market rally of the 1990s.

The key element of *universal life* is the flexibility of the premium for the policyowner. The flexible premium concept separates the pure insurance protection (term insurance) from the investment (cash value) element of the policy. The policy cash value is set up as a cash value fund (or accumulation fund) to which the investment income is credited and from which the cost of term insurance for the insured (the mortality charge) is debited. The policy expenses are also debited.

This separation of the cash value from the pure insurance is called the "unbundling" of the traditional life insurance policy. Premium payments for universal life are at the discretion of the policyholder, that is, are flexible with the exceptions that there must be a minimum initial premium to begin the coverage, and there must also be a least enough cash value in the policy each month to cover the mortality charge and other expenses. If not, the policy will lapse. Both guaranteed cash value and variable life can be written on a flexible premium or fixed premium basis.

The universal feature—flexible premiums—can be applied to either guaranteed value whole life (called simply universal life) or to variable life (called variable universal life). These types are summarized in Exhibit 24.8. Variable universal life insurance combines the features of variable life and universal life policies—that is, the choice of separate account investment products and flexible premiums.

Over the last decade, term and variable life insurance have been growing at the expense of whole life insurance. The most common form of variable life is variable universal.

EXHIBIT 24.8   Types of Universal Life

Premium	Guaranteed	Variable
Fixed	Whole Life	Variable Life
Flexible	Universal Life	Variable Universal Life

Most whole life insurance policies are designed to pay death benefits when one specified insured dies. An added dimension of whole life policies is that two people (usually a married couple) are jointly insured, and the policy pays the death benefit not when the first person dies, but when the second person (the "surviving spouse") dies. This is called *survivorship insurance* or *second-to-die insurance*. This survivorship feature can be added to standard cash value whole life, universal life, variable life, and variable universal life policies. Thus, each of the four policies discussed could also be written on a survivorship basis.

In general, the annual premium for a survivorship insurance policy is lower than for a policy on a single person because, by construction, the second of two people to die has a longer life span than the first. Of the total survivorship sales during the first quarter of 2000, 46% was based on variable universal life, 33% on universal life, and 21% on whole life. Survivorship insurance is typically sold for estate planning purposes.

Exhibit 24.9 provides a summary of the various types of cash value life insurance, with (annual renewable) term insurance included for contrast.

Uses of Life Insurance

The standard use of life insurance is to protect the survivors of an income earner. In this case, the insured is the income earner and the survivors are the beneficiaries. This is still a major use of life insurance. For this use, life insurance protects against premature death.

There are, however, many other uses. The life insurance death benefits are used to pay the estate taxes on the deceased's assets in their estate. There are also many business uses of life insurance. Split dollar life insurance, whereby the business pays for a portion or all of the premium on a life insurance policy on the executive, is used as a fringe benefit for its executives. Life insurance policies may also be written on both participants in a partnership to fund the purchase by the surviving partner of the ownership of the deceased partner according to a *buy-sell agreement*. There are also other business uses of life insurance.

EXHIBIT 24.9 Life Insurance Comparison (By Type and Element)

Type	Description	Death Benefit	Premium
Annual Renewable Term	"Pure" life insurance with no cash value; initially, the highest death benefit for the lowest premium; premium increases exponentially.	Fixed, constant	Increases exponentially
Whole Life	Known maximum cost and minimum death benefit; dividends may: reduce premiums; pay-up policy; buy paid-up additions; accumulate at interest; or be paid in cash.	Fixed, constant	Fixed, constant
Variable Life	Whole life contract; choice of investment assets; death benefits depend on investment results.	Guaranteed minimum; can increase based on investment performance	Fixed, constant
Universal Life	Flexible premium, current assumption adjustable death benefit policy; policy elements unbundled.	Adjustable; Two options: 1. like ordinary life; 2. like ordinary life plus term rider equal to cash value.	Flexible at option of policyowner
Variable Universal Life	Features of universal and variable life.	Adjustable	Flexible at option of policyowner

EXHIBIT 24.9 (Continued)

Type	Cash Value (CV)	Advantages to Owner	Disadvantages to Owner
Annual Renewable Term	None	Low premium for coverage	Increasing premium; most term insurance is lapsed
Whole Life	Fixed	Predictable; forced savings and conservative investment	High premiums given death benefit
Variable Life	Based on investment performance; not guaranteed.	Combines life insurance and investments on excess premiums	All investment risk is to the owner
Universal Life	Varies depending on face amount and premium; minimum guaranteed interest; excess increases cash value.	Flexibility	Some investment risk to owner
Universal Variable Life	Varies depending on face amount, premium, and investment performance; not guaranteed.	Flexibility and choice of investments	All investment risk is to owner

Annuities

By definition, an annuity is simply a series of periodic payments. Annuity contracts have been offered by insurance companies and, more recently, by other types of financial institutions such as mutual fund companies.

There are two components to annuities according to cash flows, the accumulation period and the liquidation period. During the accumulation period, the investor is providing funds, or investing. Annuities are considered primarily accumulation products rather than insurance products. During the liquidation period, the investor is withdrawing funds, or liquidating the annuity. One type of liquidation is annuitization, or withdrawal via a series of fixed payments, as discussed below. This method of liquidation is the basis for the name of annuities.

There are several ways to classify annuities. One is the method of paying premiums. Annuities are purchased with *single premiums, fixed periodic premiums,* or *flexible periodic premiums* during the accumulation phase. All three are used in current practice.

A second classification is the time the income payments commence during the liquidation phase. An *immediate annuity* is one in which the first benefit payment is due one payment interval (month, year or other) from the purchasing date. Under a *deferred annuity,* there is a longer period before the benefit period begins. While an immediate annuity is purchased with a single premium, a deferred annuity may be purchased with a single, fixed periodic, or flexible periodic payments, although the flexible periodic payment is most common.

An important basis for annuities is whether they are fixed or variable annuities. Fixed annuities, as discussed in more detail below, are expressed in a fixed number of dollars, while variable annuities are expressed in a fixed number annuity units, each unit of which may have a different and changing market value. Fixed versus variable annuities is the key distinction between annuities currently provided.

Now we will look at the various types of annuities. The most common categories are *variable annuities* and *fixed annuities.*

While cash value life insurance has the appearance of life insurance with an investment feature, annuities, in contrast, have the appearance of an investment product with an insurance feature. The major advantage of an annuity is its inside buildup, that is, its investment earnings are tax deferred. However, unlike life insurance where the death benefit is not subject to income taxes, withdrawals from annuities are taxable. There are also restrictions on withdrawals. Specifically, there are IRS requirements for the taxability of early withdrawals (before age 59½) and required minimum withdrawals (after age 70½). These requirements and the other tax issues of annuities are very complex and considered only briefly here.

The most common types of annuities, variable and fixed annuities, are discussed below.

Variable Annuities

Variable annuities, initiated in the United States during 1952, are, in many ways, similar to mutual funds. Given the above discussion, variable annuities are often considered to be "mutual funds in an insurance wrapper." The return on a variable annuity depends on the return of the underlying portfolio. The returns on annuities are, thus, in a word, "variable." In fact, many investment managers offer similar or identical funds separately in both a mutual fund and an annuity format. Thus, variable annuity offerings are approximately as broad as mutual fund offerings. For example, consider a large capitalization, blended stock fund. The investment manager may offer this fund in both a mutual fund and annuity format. But, of course, the two portfolios are segregated. The portfolios of these two products may be identical and, thus, the portfolio returns will be identical.

Before considering the differences, however, there is one similarity. Investments in both mutual funds and annuities are made with after-tax dollars; that is, taxes are paid on the income before it is invested in either a mutual fund or an annuity.

But there are important differences to investors in these two products. First, all income (dividend and interest) and realized capital gains generated in the mutual fund are taxable, even if the switch is not withdrawn. On the other hand, income and realized capital gains generated in the annuity are not taxable until withdrawn. Thus, annuities benefit from the same *inside buildup* as cash value life insurance.

There is another tax advantage to annuities. If a variable annuity company has a group of annuities in its family (called a "contract"), an investor can switch from one annuity fund to another in the contract (for example from a stock fund to a bond fund) and the switch is not a taxable event. However, if the investor shifts from a stock fund in one annuity company to a bond fund in another annuity company, it is considered a withdrawal and a reinvestment, and the withdrawal is a taxable event (there are exceptions to this, however, as will be discussed). The taxation of annuity withdrawals will also be considered.

While the inside buildup is an advantage of annuities, there are offsetting disadvantages. For comparison, there are no restrictions on withdrawals from (selling shares of) a mutual fund. Of course, withdrawals from a mutual fund are a taxable event and will generate realized capital gains or losses, which will generate long-term or short-term gains or losses and, thus, tax consequences. There are, however, significant restrictions on withdrawals from annuities. First, withdrawals before age 59½ are assessed a 10% penalty (there are, however, some "hardship" exceptions to this). Second, withdrawals must begin by age 70½ according to the IRS required minimum distribution rules (RMD). These mandatory withdrawals are designed to eventually produce tax revenues on annuities to the IRS. Mutual funds have no disadvantages to withdrawing before 59½ nor requirements to withdraw after 70½.

There is an exception to the taxation resulting from a shift of funds from one variable annuity company to another. Under specific circumstances, funds can be so moved without causing a taxable event. Such a shift is called a *1035 exchange* after the IRS rule that permits this transfer.

Another disadvantage of annuities is that all gains on withdrawals, when they occur, are taxed as ordinary income, not capital gains, whether their source was income or capital gains. For many investors, their income tax rate is significantly higher than the long-term capital gains tax rate and this form of taxation is therefore a disadvantage.

The final disadvantage of annuities is that the heirs of a deceased owner receive them with a cost basis equal to the purchase price (which means that the gains are taxed at the heir's ordinary income tax rate) rather than being stepped up to a current market value as with most investments.

Why has the IRS given annuities the same tax advantage of inside buildup that insurance policies have? The answer to this question is that annuities are structured to have some of the characteristics of life insurance, commonly called "features." There are many such features. The most common feature is that the minimum value of an annuity fund that will be paid at the investor's death is the initial amount invested. Thus, if an investor invests $100 in a stock annuity, the stock market declines such that the value of the fund is $90, and the investor dies, the investor's beneficiary will receive $100, not $90. This is a life insurance characteristic of an annuity.

The above feature represents a *death benefit* (DB), commonly called a return of premium. However, new, and often more complicated, death benefits have been introduced, including a periodic lock-in of gains (called a "stepped up" DB); a predetermined annual percentage increase (called a "rising floor" DB); or a percentage of earnings to offset estate taxes and other death expenses (called an "earnings enhancement" DB). In addition to these death benefit features, some *living benefit* features have also been developed, including premium enhancements and minimum accumulation guarantees.

Obviously these features have value to the investor and, as a result, a cost to the provider. The value of a feature depends on its design and can be high or approximately worthless. And the annuity company will charge the investor for the value of these features.

The cost of the features relates to another disadvantage of annuities, specifically their expenses. The insurance company will impose a charge for the potential death benefit payment (called mortality) and other expenses, overall called M&E charges, as discussed previously for insurance policies. These M&E charges will be in addition to the normal investment management, custody, and other expenses experienced by mutual funds. Thus, annuity expenses will exceed mutual fund expenses by the annuity's M&E charges. The annuity investor does, however, receive the value of the insurance feature for the M&E charge.

Thus, the overall tradeoffs between mutual funds and annuities can be summarized as follows. Annuities have the advantages of inside buildup and the particular life insurance features of the specific annuity. But annuities also have the disadvantages of higher taxes on withdrawal (ordinary income versus capital gains), restrictions on withdrawals, and higher expenses. For short holding periods, mutual funds will have a higher after-tax return. For very long holding periods, the value of the inside buildup will dominate and the annuity will have a higher after-tax return.

What is the breakeven holding period, that is, the holding period beyond which annuities have higher after-tax returns? The answer to this question depends on several factors, such as the tax rates (income and capital gains), the excess of the expenses on the annuity, and others. The conventional wisdom is that this breakeven period is currently in the range of 7 to 10 years.[7]

Fixed Annuities

There are several types of fixed annuities but, in general, the invested premiums grow at a rate—the *credited rate*—specified by the insurance company in each. This growth is accrued and added to the cash value of the annuity each year (or more frequently, such as monthly) and is not taxable as long as it remains in the annuity. Upon liquidation, it is taxed as ordinary income (to the extent that is represents previously untaxed income).

The two most common types of fixed annuities are the flexible premium deferred annuity (FPDA) and the single premium deferred annuity (SPDA). The FPDA permits contributions which are flexible in amount and timing. The interest rate paid on these contracts—the credited rate—varies and depends on the insurance company's current interest earnings and its desired competitive position in the market. There are, however, two types of limits on the rate. First, the rate is guaranteed to be no lower than a specified contract guaranteed rate, often in the range 3% to 4%. Second, these contracts often have *bail-out provisions*, which stipulate that if the credited rate decreases below a specified rate, the owner may withdraw all the funds (lapse the contract) without a surrender charge. Bail-out credited rates are often set at 1% to 3% below the current credited rate and are designed to limit the use of a "teaser rate" (or "bait and switch" practices), whereby an insurance company offers a high credited rate to attract new investors and then reduces the credited rate significantly, with the investor limited from withdrawing the funds by the surrender charges.

An initial credited rate, a minimum guaranteed rate, and a bailout rate are set initially on the contract. The initial credited rate, thus, may be changed by the insurance company over time. The *reset* (or renewal)

---

[7] "Variable Annuities and Mutual Fund Investments for Retirement Planning: a Statistical Comparison," Pricewaterhouse Coopers, October 12, 2000.

period must also be specified—this is, the frequency with which the credited rate can be changed.

Another important characteristic of annuities is the basis for the valuation of withdrawals prior to maturity. The traditional method has been book value, that is, withdrawals are paid based on the purchase price of the bonds (bonds rather than stocks are used to fund annuities). Thus, if yields have increased, the insurance company will be paying the withdrawing investor more than the bonds are currently worth. And at this time, there is an incentive for the investor to withdraw and invest in a new higher yielding fixed annuity. Thus, book value fixed annuities provide risk to the insurance company. Surrender charges, discussed next, mitigate this risk. Another way to mitigate this risk is via market value adjusted (MVA) annuities, whereby early withdrawals are paid on the basis of the current market value of the bond portfolio rather than the book value. This practice eliminates the early withdrawal risk to the insurance company. (Obviously, all variable annuities are paid on the basis of market value rather than bonds value.)

While book value annuities were originally the entire fixed annuity market and remain the largest part of the market, MVA annuities have grown considerably in the last decade.[8]

Another characteristic of both variable and fixed annuities relates to one aspect of their sales charges. These charges are very similar for annuities and mutual funds. Mutual funds and annuities were originally provided with front-end loans, that is, sales charges imposed on the initial investment. For example, with a 5% front-end load of a $100 initial investment, $5 would be retained by the firm for itself and the agent, and $95 invested in the fund for the investor.

More recently, back-end loads have been used as an alternative to front-end loads. With a back-end load, the fixed percentage charge is imposed at the time of withdrawal. Currently, the most common form of back-end load is the contingent deferred sales charge (CDSC), also called simply a surrender charge. This approach imposes a load which is gradually declining over time. For example, a common CDSC is a "7%/6%/5%/4%/3%/2%/1%/0%" charge according to which a 7% load is imposed on withdrawals during the first year, 6% during the second year, 5% during the third year, and so forth. There is no charge for withdrawals after the seventh year.

Finally, there are level loads, which impose a constant load (1% for example) every year. Currently on annuities, a front-end load is often used along with a CDSC surrender charge.

---

[8] Eric T. Sondergeld, "Fixed Annuity Sales Hit Record $71.5 Billion in 2001," *National Underwriter* (March 18, 2002), p. 12.

Annuities have become very complex instruments. This section provides only an overview.

GICs

The first major investment-oriented product developed by life insurance companies, and a form of fixed annuity, was the *guaranteed investment contract* (GIC). GICs were used extensively for retirement plans. With a GIC, a life insurance company agrees, in return for a single premium, to pay the principal amount and a predetermined annual crediting rate over the life of the investment, all of which are paid at the maturity date of the GIC. For example, a $10 million five-year GIC with a predetermined crediting rate of 10% means that at the end of five years, the insurance company pays the guaranteed crediting rate and the principal. The return of the principal depends on the ability of the life insurance company to satisfy the obligation, just as in any corporate debt obligation. The risk that the insurer faces is that the rate earned on the portfolio of supporting assets is less than the guaranteed rate.

The maturity of a GIC can vary from 1 year to 20 years. The interest rate guaranteed depends on market conditions and the rating of the life insurance company. The interest rate will be higher than the yield on U.S. Treasury securities of the same maturity. These policies are typically purchased by pension plan sponsors as a pension investment.

A GIC is a liability of the life insurance company issuing the contract. The word guarantee does not mean that there is a guarantor other than the life insurance company. Effectively, a GIC is a zero-coupon bond issued by a life insurance company and, as such, exposes the investor to the same credit risk. This credit risk has been highlighted by the default of several major issuers of GICs. The two most publicized defaults were Mutual Benefit, a New Jersey-based insurer, and Executive Life, a California-based insurer, which were both seized by regulators in 1991.

The basis for these defaults is that fixed annuities are insurance company general account products and variable annuities are separate account products. For fixed annuities, the premiums become part of the insurance company, are invested in the insurance company's general account (which are regulated by state laws), and the payments are the obligations of the insurance company. Variable annuities are separate account products, that is, the premiums are deposited in investment vehicles separate from the insurance company, and are usually selected by the investor. Thus, fixed annuities are general account products and the insurance company bears the investment risk, while variable annuities are separate account products and the investor bears the investment risk.

SPDAs and GICs

SPDAs and GICs with the same maturity and crediting rate have much in common. For example, for each the value of a $1 initial investment with a 5-year maturity and a fixed crediting rate for the five years at $r\%$ would have a value at maturity of $(1 + r)^5$.

However, there are also significant differences. SPDAs have elements of an insurance product and so its inside buildup is not taxed as earned (it is taxed as income at maturity). SPDAs are not qualified products, that is, they must be paid for in after tax-dollars. GICs are not insurance products. GICs, however, are typically put into pension plans (defined benefit or defined contribution), which are qualified. In this case, thus, the GIC investments are paid for in after-tax dollars and receive the tax deferral of inside buildup. SPDAs are also put into qualified plans. Specifically, banks often sell IRAs funded with SPDAs.

Another difference between SPDAs and GICs is that since SPDAs are annuities, they usually have surrender charges, typically the 7%/6%/5%/4%/3%/2%/1%/0%, mentioned previously. Thus, if a 5-year SPDA is withdrawn after three years, there is a 4% surrender charge. GICs do not have surrender charges and can be withdrawn with no penalty (under benefit responsive provisions).

Another feature of SPDAs is the reset period, the period after which the credited rate can be changed by the writer of the product. For example, a 5-year SPDA may have a reset period after three years, at which time the credited rate can also be increased or decreased. For SPDAs, there can also be an interaction between the reset period and the surrender charge. For example, a 5-year SPDA with a 3-year reset period could be liquidated after 3 years due to a lowered crediting rate, but only with a 4% surrender charge. GICs have no reset period, that is, the credited rate is constant throughout the contract's life. Early withdrawals of GICs are at book value; they are interest rate insensitive.

SPDAs typically have a reset period of 1 year but with an initial M-year minimum guarantee (M=1,2,3,5,7,9). SPDAs typically have a maturity based on the age of the annuitant (such as age 90 or 95), not a fixed number of years. Thus, while SPDAs typically have a maturity greater than the guarantee period, for GICs the maturity period equals the guarantee period. Common maturities for GICs and SPDAs are 1, 3, 5, and 7 years.

Annuitization

Strictly speaking, an annuity is a guaranteed (or fixed) amount of periodic income for life. Both are accumulation products rather than income products. Either product can, however, be *annuitized*—that is, converted into a guaranteed lifetime income. Annuitization refers to the liquidation rather than the accumulation period. As a matter of fact, very few—less than 1%—of variable annuities are annuitized.[9] One reason that few investors annuitize is that they fear they will die early and receive very little for the initial investment. On the other hand, the risk to individuals is that they will outlive their savings. Annuitization eliminates this risk. Traditionally, defined benefit retirement plans have provided a lifetime flow of income. But with the decline in defined benefit retirement plans, annuities can fill this vacuum.

Since the fixed payments of an annuity are for life, there is mortality risk for the annuity writer. If the annuitant dies soon, the payout by the annuity writer will be small. However, if the annuitant lives a long life, the payments by the annuity writer will be large. This characteristic introduces an underwriting element to annuities by the annuity writer. Some fixed annuities also have a survivorship feature. That is, when the annuitant dies, the payments will continue and be paid to a named survivor, usually a spouse.

Many variable annuity owners who wish to annuitize elect for a variation on a strict annuity called a *systematic withdrawal plan* (SWP) instead. While there are many types of SWPs, the most common type is based on a specified term rather than lifetime payments in order to assure that the payments last at least a certain amount of time (called a *period-certain payout option*). These plans, thus, do not eliminate the risk of outliving one's savings. Under a SWP, annuity shares are liquidated to pay regular payments that are either a fixed dollar amount or a percentage of the investor's account balance. Thus, unlike annuitization, SWPs cause a continual decline in the investor's account balance. There are also variations of the standard lifetime payout option which include life with a guaranteed period, joint and survivor life, and joint and survivor life with a guaranteed period.

SUMMARY

Fundamentally, insurance and investment products are distinct. Insurance products provide risk protection against a wide variety of risks and have no cash value. Investment products, often called accumulation products, provide returns on an initial investment.

---

[9] Art MacPherson and Lisa Plotnick, "VA Owners Don't Annuitize, But Do Flock to Systematic Withdrawal Plans," *National Underwriter* (January 14, 2002), pp. 17–18.

However, two types of products provide elements of both insurance and investments. These two are cash value life insurance and annuities. Cash value life insurance is a combination of pure life insurance with a buildup of cash value as a result of the higher premium paid relative to a pure life insurance policy. The types of cash value life insurance include whole life and variable life, and universal versions of both of these.

The second type is annuities. There are two types of annuities, variable and fixed. Variable annuities are essentially mutual funds in an insurance wrapper. The insurance elements may include both death benefits and living benefits. The returns on variable annuities depend on the particular type of investment portfolio selected by the investor.

Fixed annuities are a guaranteed yield over an investment term. The return over the term is specified at the time of the investment and is certain. Very few annuities, variable or fixed, are annuitized, that is, converted into a lifetime stream of fixed payments, despite the attractive characteristics of annuitization.

The investment element of these hybrid insurance/investment products benefits from their tax advantages. The major tax advantage of both of these types of investment-oriented insurance products is inside buildup, although the cash value life insurance products also have other significant tax benefits. Congress provided the tax advantages to these products due to their insurance characteristics, not their investment characteristics. There are, as a result, limits on the investment characteristics of these hybrid products to qualify them for the tax advantages.

CHAPTER 25

Hedge Funds

Mark J. P. Anson, CFA, Ph.D., CPA, Esq.
Chief Investment Officer
CalPERS

The term "hedge fund" is a term of art. It is not defined in the Securities Act of 1933 or the Securities Exchange Act of 1934. Additionally, "hedge fund" is not defined by the Investment Company Act of 1940, the Investment Advisers Act of 1940, the Commodity Exchange Act, or, finally, the Bank Holding Company Act. So what is this investment vehicle that every investor seems to know about but for which there is scant regulatory guidance?

As a starting point, we turn to the *American Heritage Dictionary* (third edition) which defines a hedge fund as:

> An investment company that uses high-risk techniques, such as borrowing money and selling short, in an effort to make extraordinary capital gains.

Not a bad start, but we note that hedge funds are not investment companies, for they would be regulated by the Securities and Exchange Commission under the Investment Company Act of 1940.[1] Additionally, some hedge funds, such as market neutral and market timing have con-

---

[1] In fact, hedge funds take great pains to avoid being regulated by the SEC as an investment company. The National Securities Markets Improvement Act of 1996 greatly relieved hedge funds of certain regulatory burdens by allowing an unlimited number of "qualified purchasers" in a hedge fund.

servative risk profiles and do not "swing for the fences" to earn extraordinary gains.

We define hedge funds as:

> A privately organized investment vehicle that manages a concentrated portfolio of public securities and derivative instruments on public securities, that can invest both long and short, and can apply leverage.

Within this definition there are five key elements of hedge funds that distinguish them from their more traditional counterpart, the mutual fund.

First, hedge funds are private investment vehicles that pool the resources of sophisticated investors. One of the ways that hedge funds avoid the regulatory scrutiny of the SEC or the CFTC is that they are available only for high net worth investors. Under SEC rules, hedge funds cannot have more than 100 investors in the fund. Alternatively, hedge funds may accept an unlimited number of "qualified purchasers" in the fund. These are individuals or institutions that have a net worth in excess of $5,000,000.

There is a penalty, however, for the privacy of hedge funds. Although they may escape the regulatory burden of U.S. agencies, they cannot raise funds from investors via a public offering. Additionally, hedge funds may not advertise broadly or engage in a general solicitation for new funds. Instead, their marketing and fundraising efforts must be targeted to a narrow niche of very wealthy individuals and institutions. As a result, the predominant investors in hedge funds are family offices, endowments, and, to a lesser extent, pension funds.

Second, hedge funds tend to have portfolios that are much more concentrated than their mutual fund brethren. Most hedge funds do not have broad securities benchmarks. The reason is that most hedge fund managers claim that their style of investing is "skill-based" and cannot be measured by a market return. Consequently, hedge fund managers are not forced to maintain security holdings relative to a benchmark; they do not need to worry about "benchmark" risk. This allows them to concentrate their portfolio only on those securities that they believe will add value to the portfolio.

Another reason for the concentrated portfolio is that hedge fund managers tend to have narrow investment strategies. These strategies tend to focus on only one sector of the economy or one segment of the market. They can tailor their portfolio to extract the most value from their smaller investment sector or segment.

Third, hedge funds tend to use derivative strategies much more predominately than mutual funds. Indeed, in some strategies, such as convertible arbitrage, the ability to sell or buy options is a key component of executing the arbitrage. The use of derivative strategies may result in non-linear cash flows that may require more sophisticated risk management techniques to control these risks.

Fourth, hedge funds may go both long and short securities. The ability to short public securities and derivative instruments is one of the key distinctions between hedge funds and traditional money managers. Hedge fund managers incorporate their ability to short securities explicitly into their investment strategies. For example, equity long/short hedge funds tend to buy and sell securities within the same industry to maximize their return but also to control their risk. This is very different from traditional money managers that are tied to a long-only securities benchmark.

Finally, hedge funds use leverage, sometimes, large amounts. Mutual funds, for example, are limited in the amount of leverage they can employ; they may borrow up to 33% of their net asset base. Hedge funds do not have this restriction. Consequently, it is not unusual to see some hedge fund strategies that employ leverage up to 10 times their net asset base.

We can see that hedge funds are different than traditional long-only investment managers. We next discuss the history of the hedge fund development.

HEDGE FUND REGULATION

Hedge funds are often referred to as "unregulated" investment vehicles—investment funds that manage to stay outside the reach of the securities laws. The fact is that hedge fund managers take advantage of ready-made exemptions that are part of the securities laws themselves. We briefly summarize how hedge fund managers avail themselves of these regulatory "safe harbors."

The Securities Act of 1933

The Securities Act of 1933 (the "1933 Act") was born out of the Great Depression. With the collapse of the stock market in 1929, and the economic depression that followed, Congress sought to make the financial markets a safer place for investors. The 1933 Act was enacted to regulate the initial sale of securities to investors. Under the 1933 Act, the issuer of securities must file a registration statement with the Securities and Exchange Commission (SEC) and provide investors with a prospectus.

One way to avoid the lengthy registration process is to find an exemption from registration within the 1933 Act. Under the 1933 Act,

Congress provided issuers with an exemption from the registration process titled: "The Rules Governing the Limited Offer and Sale of Securities Without Registration under the Securities Act of 1933." These rules are universally known as "Regulation D." Under Rule 506 of Regulation D, a hedge fund manager can sell its limited partnership interests to an unlimited number of "accredited investors" (essentially sophisticated or high net worth investors), and to no more than 35 non-accredited investors.

The Investment Company Act of 1940

The Investment Company Act of 1940 (the "Company Act") was designed to regulate investment pools. Today, this act primarily regulates the mutual fund industry. Mutual funds are investment companies for purposes of the Company Act and the SEC.

Under Section 3(a) of the Company Act, an investment company:

> Means any issuer which is or holds itself out as being engaged primarily, or proposes to engage primarily, in the business of investing, reinvesting, or trading in securities.

While this definition clearly incorporates mutual funds, it is also broad enough to encompass hedge funds. Hedge funds are investment companies for purposes of the Company Act. Falling within the jurisdiction of the Company Act means that hedge funds must adhere to the same registration requirements under Section 8 of the Company Act as do mutual funds.

However, the Company Act also provides two ready-made safe harbors of which hedge fund managers may take advantage.

First, Section 3(c)(1) of the Company Act states that an investment pool can be offered to any type of investor, sophisticated and unsophisticated, accredited and nonaccredited, provided that the hedge fund manager does not allow more than 100 investors into the fund. For smaller hedge fund managers, the 100-person limit should not be an issue. For larger hedge funds, however, that wish to attract additional capital, the 100-person limit may prove binding.

In 1996, Congress added a new paragraph 7 to Section 3(c) of the Company Act. This paragraph recognizes that an investment pool might contain many investors that are sophisticated, and consequently, might not need the oversight of the SEC.

This new type of fund is often referred to as a "3(c)(7) fund," and it is designed for sophisticated investors. Section 3(c)(7) imposes no limit on the number of investors, provided that the investors are all "Qualified Purchasers" (generally, investors with a net worth of at least $5 million) as defined by the Company Act.

HEDGE FUND STRATEGIES

Hedge funds invest in the same equity and fixed income securities as traditional long-only managers. Therefore, it is not the alternative "assets" in which hedge funds invest that differentiates them from long-only managers, but rather, it is the alternative investment strategies that they pursue.

In this section we review several alternative strategies that hedge funds apply. In general, some hedge funds have considerable exposure to the financial markets. This would be the *long/short, global macro hedge fund or short selling players*. Other hedge funds take little market exposure, but use leverage to magnify the size of their bets. These are the *arbitrage hedge funds*. Last there are hedge fund strategies that take little credit or market risk. These are the *market neutral* and *market timing strategies*.

Equity Long/Short

Equity long/short managers build their portfolios by combining a core group of long stock positions with short sales of stock or stock index options/futures. Their net market exposure of long positions minus short positions tends to have a positive bias. That is, equity long/short managers tend to be long market exposure. The length of their exposure depends on current market conditions. For instance, during the great stock market surge of 1996–1999, these managers tended to be mostly long their equity exposure. However, as the stock market turned into a bear market in 2000, these managers decreased their market exposure as they sold more stock short or sold stock index options and futures.

For example, consider a hedge fund manager in 2000 who had a 100% long exposure to tobacco industry stocks and had a 20% short exposure to semiconductor stocks. The beta of the S&P Tobacco index is 0.5, and for the semiconductor index it is 1.5. The weighted average beta of the portfolio is:

$$[1.0 \times 0.5] + [-0.20 \times 1.5] = 0.20$$

Beta is a well-known measure of market exposure (or systematic risk). A portfolio with a beta of 1.0 is considered to have the same stock market exposure or risk as a broad-based stock index such as the S&P 500.

According to the Capital Asset Pricing Model, the hedge fund manager has a conservative portfolio. The expected return of this portfolio according the model is:[2]

$$6\% + 0.20 \times (-9.5\% - 6\%) = 2.9\%$$

However, in 2000, the total return on the S&P Tobacco Index was 98% while for the semiconductor index it was −31%. This "conservative" hedge fund portfolio would have earned the following return in 2000:

$$[1.0 \times 98\%] + [-0.20 \times -31\%] = 104.20\%$$

This is a much higher return than that predicted by the Capital Asset Pricing Model.

This example serves to highlight two points. First, the ability to go both long and short in the market is a powerful tool for earning excess returns. The ability to fully implement a strategy not only about stocks and sectors that are expected to increase in value but also stocks and sectors that are expected to decrease in value allows the hedge fund manager to maximize the value of his market insights.

Second, the long/short nature of the portfolio can be misleading with respect to the risk exposure. This manager is 80% net long. Additionally, the beta of the combined portfolio is only 0.20. From this an investor might conclude that the hedge fund manager is pursuing a low risk strategy. However, this is not true. What the hedge fund manager has done is to make two explicit bets: that tobacco stocks will appreciate in value and that semiconductor stocks will decline in value.

The Capital Asset Pricing Model assumes that investors hold a well-diversified portfolio. That is not the case with this hedge fund manager. Most hedge fund managers build concentrated rather than highly diversified portfolios. Consequently, traditional models (such as the Capital Asset Pricing Model) and associated risk measures (such as beta) may not apply to hedge fund managers.

Equity long/short hedge funds essentially come in two flavors: fundamental or quantitative. *Fundamental long/short hedge funds* conduct traditional economic analysis on a company's business prospects compared to its competitors and the current economic environment. These manag-

---

[2] The Capital Asset Pricing Model is expressed as:

E(Return on Portfolio) = Risk-free rate + Beta
$\times$ (Return on the Market − Risk-free rate)

In 2000, the return on the market, represented by the S&P 500 was −9.5%, while the risk-free rate was about 6%.

ers will visit with corporate management, talk with Wall Street analysts, contact customers and competitors, and essentially conduct bottom-up analysis. The difference between these hedge funds and long-only managers is that they will short the stocks that they consider to be poor performers and buy those stocks that are expected to outperform the market. In addition, they may leverage their long and short positions.

Fundamental long/short equity hedge funds tend to invest in one economic sector or market segment. For instance, they may specialize in buying and selling internet companies (sector focus) or buying and selling small market capitalization companies (segment focus).

In contrast, *quantitative equity long/short hedge fund managers* tend not to be sector or segment specialists. In fact, quite the reverse. Quantitative hedge fund managers like to cast as broad a net as possible in their analysis.

These managers use mathematical analysis to review past company performance in light of several quantitative factors. For instance, these managers may build regression models to determine the impact of market price to book value (price/book ratio) on companies across the universe of stocks as well as different market segments or economic sectors. Or, they may analyze changes in dividend yields on stock price performance.

Typically, these managers build multifactor models, both linear and quadratic, and then test these models on historical stock price performance. Backtesting involves applying the quantitative model on prior stock price performance to see if there is any predictive power in determining whether the stock of a particular company will rise or fall. If the model proves successful using historical data, the hedge fund manager will then conduct an "out of sample" test of the model. This involves testing the model on a subset of historical data that was not included in the model building phase.

If a hedge fund manager identifies a successful quantitative strategy, it will apply its model mechanically. Buy and sell orders will be generated by the model and submitted to the order desk. In practice, the hedge fund manager will put limits on its model such as the maximum short exposure allowed or the maximum amount of capital that may be committed to any one stock position. In addition, quantitative hedge fund managers usually build in some qualitative oversight to ensure that the model is operating consistently.

In Exhibit 25.1, a graph of a hypothetical investment of $1,000 in an Equity Long/Short fund of funds compared to the S&P 500 is provided. In this chapter, we use data from Hedge Fund Research, Inc. (HFRI), a database of about 1,100 hedge funds.[3] The time period is

---

[3] More information on the HFRI database may be found at www.hfr.com.

1990 through 2000. As can be seen, the returns to this strategy were quite favorable compared to the stock market.

Global Macro

As their name implies, global macro hedge funds take a macroeconomic approach on a global basis in their investment strategy. These are top-down managers who invest opportunistically across financial markets, currencies, national borders, and commodities. They take large positions depending upon the hedge fund manager's forecast of changes in interest rates, currency movements, monetary policies, and macroeconomic indicators.

Global macro managers have the broadest investment universe. They are not limited by market segment or industry sector, nor by geographic region, financial market, or currency. Additionally, global macro managers may invest in commodities. In fact, a fund of global macro hedge funds offers the greatest diversification of investment strategies.

Global macro funds tend to have large amounts of investor capital. This is necessary to execute their macroeconomic strategies. In addition, they may apply leverage to increase the size of their macro bets. As a result, global macro hedge funds tend to receive the greatest attention and publicity in the financial markets.

The best known of these hedge funds was the Quantum Hedge Fund managed by George Soros. It is well documented that this fund made significant gains in 1992 by betting that the British pound would devalue (which it did). This fund was also accused of contributing to the "Asian Contagion" in the fall of 1997 when the government of Thailand devalued its currency, the baht, triggering a domino effect in currency movements throughout southeast Asia.

EXHIBIT 25.1   HFRI Equity Long/Short Index

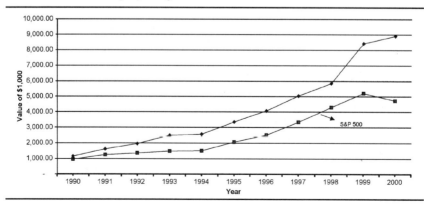

EXHIBIT 25.2   HFRI Global Macro Index

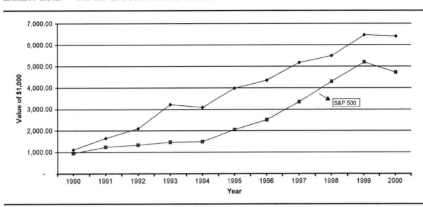

In recent times, however, global macro funds have fallen on hard times.[4] One reason is that many global macro funds were hurt by the Russian bond default in August 1998 and the bursting of the technology bubble in March 2000. These two events caused large losses for the global macro funds.

A second reason, as indicated above, is that global macro hedge funds had the broadest investment mandate of any hedge fund strategy. The ability to invest widely across currencies, financial markets, geographic borders, and commodities is a two-edged sword. On the one hand, it allows global macro funds the widest universe in which to implement their strategies. On the other hand, it lacks focus. As more institutional investors have moved into the hedge fund marketplace, they have demanded greater investment focus as opposed to free investment reign.

Exhibit 25.2 provides a comparison of global macro hedge funds to the S&P 500 over the period 1990–2000. During this time period global macro hedge funds earned favorable returns.

Short Selling

Short selling hedge funds have the opposite exposure of traditional long-only managers. In that sense, their return distribution should be the mirror image of long-only managers: they make money when the stock market is declining and lose money when the stock market is gaining.

These hedge fund managers may be distinguished from equity long/short managers in that they generally maintain a net short exposure to the stock market. However, short selling hedge funds tend to use some form of market timing. That is, they trim their short positions when the

---

[4] See *The New York Times* (May 6, 2000).

stock market is increasing and go fully short when the stock market is declining. When the stock market is gaining, short sellers maintain that portion of their investment capital not committed to short selling in short-term interest rate bearing accounts.

The past 10 years has seen predominantly a strong bull market in the United States. There have been some speed bumps: the short recession of 1990–1991 and the soft landing of 1994. But for the most part, the U.S. equity market has enjoyed strong returns in the 1990s. As a result, short sellers have had to seek other markets such as Japan, or result to more market timing to earn positive results. Later, when we review the distributions of hedge funds, we will see if short sellers have been successful in pursuing other markets or in market timing.

Exhibit 25.3 presents the returns to short selling hedge funds over the period 1990–2000. As might be expected, these hedge funds underperformed the S&P 500.

Convertible Bond Arbitrage

Hedge fund managers tend to use the term "arbitrage" somewhat loosely. Arbitrage is defined simply as riskless profits. It is the purchase of a security for cash at one price and the immediate resale for cash of the same security at a higher price. Alternatively, it may be defined as the simultaneous purchase of security A for cash at one price and the selling of identical security B for cash at a higher price. In both cases, the arbitrageur has no risk. There is no market risk because the holding of the securities is instantaneous. There is no basis risk because the securities are identical, and there is no credit risk because the transaction is conducted in cash.

EXHIBIT 25.3   HFRI Short Selling Index

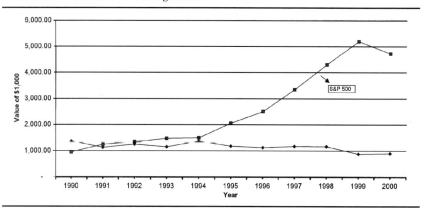

Instead of riskless profits, in the hedge fund world, arbitrage is generally used to mean low risk investments. Instead of the purchase and sale of identical instruments, there is the purchase and sale of similar instruments. Additionally, the securities may not be sold for cash, so there may be credit risk during the collection period. Last, the purchase and sale may not be instantaneous. The arbitrageur may need to hold onto its positions for a period of time, exposing himself to market risk.

Convertible arbitrage funds build long positions of convertible bonds and then hedge the equity component of the bond by selling the underlying stock or options on that stock. Equity risk can be hedged by selling the appropriate ratio of stock underlying the convertible option. This hedge ratio is known as the "delta" and is designed to measure the sensitivity of the convertible bond value to movements in the underlying stock.

Convertible bonds that trade at a low premium to their conversion value tend to be more correlated with the movement of the underlying stock. These convertibles then trade more like stock than they do a bond. Consequently, a high hedge ratio, or delta, is required to hedge the equity risk contained in the convertible bond. Convertible bonds that trade at a premium to their conversion value are highly valued for their bond-like protection. Therefore, a lower delta hedge ratio is necessary.

However, convertible bonds that trade at a high conversion value act more like fixed-income securities and therefore have more interest rate exposure than those with more equity exposure. This risk must be managed by selling interest rate futures, interest rate swaps, or other bonds. Furthermore, it should be noted that the hedging ratios for equity and interest rate risk are not static; they change as the value of the underlying equity changes and as interest rates change. Therefore, the hedge fund manager must continually adjust his or her hedge ratios to ensure that the arbitrage remains intact.

If this all sounds complicated, it is, but that is how hedge fund managers make money. They use sophisticated option pricing models and interest rate models to keep track of the all of moving parts associated with convertible bonds. Hedge fund managers make arbitrage profits by identifying pricing discrepancies between the convertible bond and its component parts, and then continually monitoring these component parts for any change in their relationship.

Consider the following example. A hedge fund manager purchases 10 convertible bonds with a par value of $1,000, a coupon of 7.5%, and a market price of $900. The conversion ratio for the bonds is 20. The conversion ratio is based on the current price of the underlying stock, $45, and the current price of the convertible bond. The delta, or hedge ratio for the bonds is 0.5. Therefore, to hedge the equity exposure in the convertible bond, the hedge fund manager must short the following shares of underlying stock:

10 bonds × 20 conversion ratio × 0.5 hedge ratio = 100 shares of stock

To establish the arbitrage, the hedge fund manager purchases 10 convertible bonds and sells 100 shares of stock. With the equity exposure hedged, the convertible bond is transformed into a traditional fixed income instrument with a 7.5% coupon.

Additionally, the hedge fund manager earns interest on the cash proceeds received from the short sale of stock. This is known as the "short rebate." The cash proceeds remain with the hedge fund manager's prime broker, but the hedge fund manager is entitled to the interest earned on the cash balance from the short sale (a rebate).[5] We assume that the hedge fund manager receives a short rebate of 4.5%. Therefore, if the hedge fund manager holds the convertible arbitrage position for one year, he expects to earn interest not only from his long bond position, but also from his short stock position.

The catch to this arbitrage is that the price of the underlying stock may change as well as the price of the bond. Assume the price of the stock increases to $47 and the price of the convertible bond increases to $920. If the hedge fund manager does not adjust the hedge ratio during the holding period, the total return for this arbitrage will be:

Appreciation of bond price:	10 × ($920 – $900)	=	$200
Appreciation of stock price:	100 × ($45 – $47)	=	–$200
Interest on bonds:	10 × $1,000 × 7.5%	=	$750
Short rebate:	100 × $45 × 4.5%	=	$202.50
Total:			$952.50

If the hedge fund manager paid for the 10 bonds without using any leverage, the holding period return is:

$$\$952.50 \div \$9000 = 10.58\%$$

However, suppose that the hedge fund manager purchased the convertible bonds with $4,500 of initial capital and $4,500 of borrowed money. We suppose that the hedge fund manager borrows the additional investment capital from his prime broker at a prime rate of 6%.

Our analysis of the total return is then:

---

[5] The short rebate is negotiated between the hedge fund manager and the prime broker. Typically, large, well-established hedge fund managers receive a larger short rebate.

Appreciation of bond price:	$10 \times (\$920 - \$900)$	=	$200
Appreciation of stock price:	$100 \times (\$47 - \$45)$	=	-$200
Interest on bonds:	$10 \times \$1,000 \times 7.5\%$	=	$750
Short rebate:	$100 \times \$45 \times 4.5\%$	=	$202.5
Interest on borrowing:	$6\% \times \$4,500$	=	-$270
Total:			$682.5

And the total return on capital is:

$$\$682.5 \div \$4,500 = 15.17\%$$

The amount of leverage used in convertible arbitrage will vary with the size of the long positions and the objectives of the portfolio. Yet, in the above example, we can see how using a conservative leverage ratio of 2:1 in the purchase of the convertible bonds added almost 500 basis points of return to the strategy. It is easy to see why hedge fund manag ers are tempted to use leverage. Hedge fund managers earn incentive fees on every additional basis point of return they earn. Further, even though leverage is a two-edged sword—it can magnify losses as well as gains—hedge fund managers bear no loss if the use of leverage turns against them. In other words, hedge fund manages have everything to gain by applying leverage, but nothing to lose.

Additionally, leverage is inherent in the shorting strategy because the underlying equity stock must be borrowed to be shorted. Convertible arbitrage leverage can range from two to six times the amount of invested capital. This may seem significant, but it is lower than other forms of arbitrage.

Convertible bonds are subject to credit risk. This is the risk that the bonds will default, be downgraded, or that credit spreads will widen. There is also call risk. Last, there is the risk that the underlying company will be acquired or will acquire another company (i.e., event risk), both of which can have a significant impact on the company's stock price and credit rating. These events are only magnified when leverage is applied.

Exhibit 25.4 plots the value of convertible arbitrage strategies versus the S&P 500. Convertible arbitrage earns a consistent return but does not outperform stocks in strong bull equity markets.

Fixed-Income Arbitrage

Fixed-income arbitrage involves purchasing one fixed-income security and simultaneously selling a similar fixed-income security. The sale of the second security is done to hedge the underlying market risk contained in the first security. Typically, the two securities are related either mathematically or economically such that they move similarly with respect to market developments. Generally, the difference in pricing between the two securities is small, and this is what the fixed income arbitrageur hopes to gain. By buying and selling two fixed income securities that are tied together, the hedge fund manager hopes to capture a pricing discrepancy that will cause the prices of the two securities to converge over time.

Fixed income arbitrage does not need to use exotic securities. It can be nothing more than buying and selling U.S. Treasury bonds. In the bond market, the most liquid securities are the *on-the-run* Treasury bonds. These are the most currently issued bonds issued by the U.S. Treasury Department. However, there are other U.S. Treasury bonds outstanding that have very similar characteristics to the on-the-run Treasury bonds. The difference is that *off-the-run* bonds were issued at an earlier date, and are now less liquid than the on-the-run bonds. As a result, price discrepancies occur. The difference in price may be no more than one-half or one quarter of a point ($25) but can increase in times of uncertainty when investor money shifts to the most liquid U.S. Treasury bond.

Nonetheless, when held to maturity, the prices of these two bonds should converge to their par value. Any difference will be eliminated by the time they mature, and any price discrepancy may be captured by the hedge fund manager. Fixed-income arbitrage is not limited to the U.S. Treasury market. It can be used with corporate bonds, municipal bonds, sovereign debt, or mortgage backed securities.

Fixed-income arbitrage may also include trading among fixed-income securities that are close in maturity. This is a form of yield curve arbitrage. These types of trades are usually driven by temporary imbalances in the term structure.

EXHIBIT 25.4   HFRI Convertible Arbitrage Index

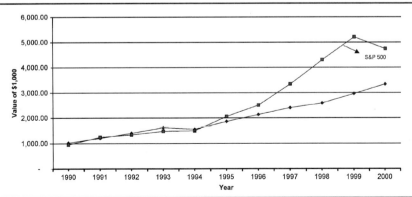

EXHIBIT 25.5   July 2000 Yield Curve

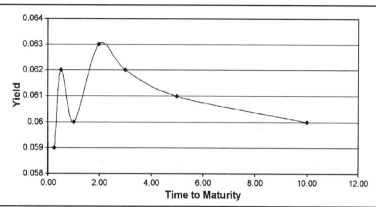

Consider Exhibit 25.5. This was the term structure for U.S. Treasury securities in July 2000. Notice that there are "kinks" in the term structure between the 3-month and the 5-year time horizon. Kinks in the yield curve can happen at any maturity and usually reflect an increase (or decrease) in liquidity demand around the focal point. These kinks provide an opportunity to profit by purchasing and selling Treasury securities that are similar in maturity.

Consider the kink that peaks at the 2-year maturity. The holder of the 2-year Treasury security profits by rolling down the yield curve. In other words, if interest rates remain static, the 2-year Treasury note will age into a lower yielding part of the yield curve. Moving down the yield curve will mean positive price appreciation. Conversely, Treasury notes in the 3- to 5-year range will roll up the yield curve to higher yields. This means that their prices are expected to depreciate.

An arbitrage trade would be to purchase a 2-year Treasury note and short a 3-year note. As the 3-year note rolls up the yield curve, it should decrease in value while the 2-year note should increase in value as it rolls down the yield curve.

This arbitrage trade will work as long as the kink remains in place. However, this trade does have its risks. First, shifts in the yield curve up or down can affect the profitability of the trade because the two securities have different maturities. To counter this problem, the hedge fund manager would need to purchase and sell the securities in the proper proportion to neutralize the differences in duration. Also, liquidity preferences of investors could change. The kink could reverse itself, or flatten out. In either case, the hedge fund manager will lose money. Conversely, the liquidity preference of investors could increase, and the trade will become even more profitable.

A subset of fixed-income arbitrage uses mortgage-backed securities (MBS). MBS represent an ownership interest in an underlying pool of individual mortgage loans. Therefore, an MBS is a fixed-income security with underlying prepayment options. MBS hedge funds seek to capture pricing inefficiencies in the U.S. MBS market.

MBS arbitrage can be between fixed-income markets such as buying MBS and selling U.S. Treasuries. This investment strategy is designed to capture credit spread inefficiencies between U.S. Treasuries and MBS. MBS trade at a credit spread over U.S. Treasuries to reflect the uncertainty of cash flows associated with MBS compared to the certainty of cash flows associated with U.S. Treasury bonds.

As noted previously, during a flight to quality, investors tend to seek out the most liquid markets such as the on-the-run U.S. Treasury market. This may cause credit spreads to temporarily increase beyond what is historically or economically justified. In this case, the MBS market will be priced "cheap" to U.S. Treasuries. The arbitrage strategy would be to buy MBS and sell U.S. Treasury, where the interest rate exposure of both instruments is sufficiently similar so as to eliminate most (if not all) of the market risk between the two securities. The expectation is that the credit spread between MBS and U.S. Treasuries will decline and the MBS position will increase in value relative to U.S. Treasuries.

MBS arbitrage can be quite sophisticated. MBS hedge fund managers use proprietary models to rank the value of MBS by their option-adjusted spread (OAS). The hedge fund manager evaluates the present value of an MBS by explicitly incorporating assumptions about the probability of prepayment options being exercised. In effect, the hedge fund manager calculates the option-adjusted price of the MBS and compares it to its current market price. The OAS reflects the MBS' average spread over U.S. Treasury bonds of a similar maturity, taking into account the fact that the MBS may be liquidated early from the exercise of the prepayment option by the underlying mortgagors.

The MBS that have the best OAS compared to U.S. Treasuries are purchased, and then their interest rate exposure is hedged to zero. Interest rate exposure is neutralized using Treasury bonds, options, swaps, futures, and caps. MBS hedge fund managers seek to maintain a duration of zero. This allows them to concentrate on selecting the MBS that yield the highest OAS.

There are many risks associated with MBS arbitrage. Chief among them are duration, convexity, yield curve rotation, prepayment risk, credit risk (for private label MBS), and liquidity risk. Hedging these risks may require the purchase or sale of other MBS products such as interest-only strips and principal-only strips, inverse floaters, U.S. Treasuries, interest rate futures, swaps, and options.

EXHIBIT 25.6 HFRI Fixed-Income Arbitrage Index

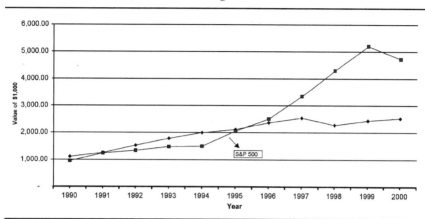

What should be noted about fixed-income arbitrage strategies is that they do not depend on the direction of the general financial markets. Arbitrageurs seek out pricing inefficiencies between two securities instead of making bets on the market. Consequently, we do not expect fixed-income arbitrage strategies to have a high correlation with either stock market returns or bond market returns. Exhibit 25.6 demonstrates that fixed-income arbitrage earns a steady return year after year regardless of the movement of the stock market.

Merger Arbitrage

Merger arbitrage is perhaps the best-known arbitrage among investors and hedge fund managers. Merger arbitrage generally entails buying the stock of the firm that is to be acquired and selling the stock of the firm that is the acquirer. Merger arbitrage managers seek to capture the price spread between the current market prices of the merger partners and the value of those companies upon the successful completion of the merger.

The stock of the target company will usually trade at a discount to the announced merger price. The discount reflects the risk inherent in the deal; other market participants are unwilling to take on the full exposure of the transaction-based risk. Merger arbitrage is then subject to event risk. There is the risk that the two companies will fail to come to terms and call off the deal. There is also the risk that another company will enter into the bidding contest, ruining the initial dynamics of the arbitrage. Last, there is regulatory risk. Various U.S. and foreign regulatory agencies may not allow the merger to take place for antitrust reasons. Merger arbitrageurs specialize in assessing event risk and building a diversified portfolio to spread out this risk.

Merger arbitrageurs conduct significant research on the companies involved in the merger. They will review current and prior financial statements, EDGAR filings, proxy statements, management structures, cost savings from redundant operations, strategic reasons for the merger, regulatory issues, press releases, and competitive position of the combined company within the industries it competes. Merger arbitrageurs will calculate the rate of return that is implicit in the current spread and compare it to the event risk associated with the deal. If the spread is sufficient to compensate for the expected event risk, they will execute the arbitrage.

Once again, the term "arbitrage" is used loosely. As discussed above, there is plenty of event risk associated with a merger announcement. The profits earned from merger arbitrage are not riskless. As an example, consider the announced deal between Tellabs and Ciena in 1998.

Ciena owned technology that allowed fiber optic telephone lines to carry more information. The technology allowed telephone carriers to get more bandwidth out of existing fiber optic lines. Tellabs made digital connecting systems. These systems allowed carriers to connect incoming and outgoing telephonic lines as well as allow many signals to travel over one phone circuit.

Tellabs and Ciena announced their intent to merge on June 3, 1998 in a one for one stock swap. One share of Tellabs would be issued for each share of Ciena. The purpose of the merger was to position the two companies to compete with larger entities such as Lucent Technologies. Additionally, each company expected to leverage their business off of the other's customer base. Tellabs price at the time was about $66 while that of Ciena's was at $57.

Shortly after the announcement, the share price of Tellabs declined to about $64 while that of Ciena's increased to about $60. Still, there was $4 of merger premium to extract from the market if the deal were completed. A merger arbitrage hedge fund manager would employ the following strategy:

Short 1000 shares of Tellabs at $64
Purchase 1000 shares of Ciena at $60

Unfortunately, the deal did not go according to plan. During the summer, Ciena lost two large customers, and it issued a warning that its third quarter profits would decline. Ciena's stock price plummeted to $15 by September. In mid-September the deal fell apart. The shares of Ciena were trading at such a discount to Tellabs' share price that it did not make economic sense to complete the merger, when Ciena's shares could be purchased cheaply on the open market. In addition, Tellabs share price declined to about $42 on earnings concerns.

By the time the merger deal fell through, the hedge fund manager would have to close out his positions:

Buy 1000 shares of Tellabs stock at $42
Sell 1000 shares of Ciena at $15

The total return for the hedge fund manager would be:

Gain on Tellabs shares:	$1000 \times (\$64 - \$42)$	=	$22,000
Loss of Ciena shares:	$1000 \times (\$15 - \$60)$	=	−$45,000
Short rebate on Tellabs:	$4.5\% \times 1000 \times \$64 \times (110/360)$	=	$880
Total:		=	−$22,120

For a total return on invested capital of:

$$-\$22,120 \div \$60,000 = -36.87\%$$

Further, suppose the hedge fund manager had used leverage to initiate this strategy, borrowing one half of the invested capital from his prime broker for the initial purchase of the Ciena shares. The total return would then be:

Gain on Tellabs shares:	$1000 \times (\$64 - \$42)$	=	$22,000
Loss of Ciena shares:	$1000 \times (\$15 - \$60)$	=	−$45,000
Short rebate on Tellabs:	$4.5\% \times 1000 \times \$64 \times (110/360)$	=	$880
Financing cost:	$6\% \times 500 \times \$60 \times (110/360)$	=	−$550
Total:		=	−$22,670

The return on invested capital is now:

$$-\$22,670 \div \$30,000 = -75.57\%$$

On an annualized basis, this is a return of −247%. This example of a failed merger demonstrates the event risk associated with merger arbitrage. When deals fall through, it gets ugly. Furthermore, the event risk is exacerbated by the amount of leverage applied in the strategy. It is estimated that Long Term Capital Management of Greenwich, Connecticut had a 4 million share position in the Tellabs-Ciena merger deal, much of it supported by leverage.

Some merger arbitrage managers only invest in announced deals. However, other hedge fund managers will invest on the basis of rumor or speculation. The deal risk is much greater with this type of strategy, but so too is the merger spread (the premium that can be captured).

EXHIBIT 25.7   HFRI Merger Arbitrage Index

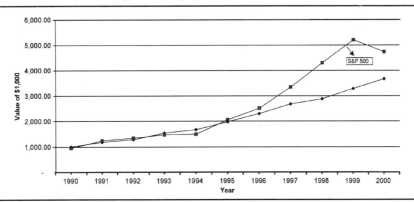

To control for risk, most merger arbitrage hedge fund managers have some risk of loss limit at which they will exit positions. Some hedge fund managers concentrate only in one or two industries, applying their specialized knowledge regarding an economic sector to their advantage. Other merger arbitrage managers maintain a diversified portfolio across several industries to spread out the event risk.

Like fixed income arbitrage, merger arbitrage is deal driven rather than market driven. Merger arbitrage derives its return from the relative value of the stock prices between two companies as opposed to the status of the current market conditions. Consequently, merger arbitrage returns should not be highly correlated with the general stock market. Exhibit 25.7 highlights this point. Similar to fixed income arbitrage, merger arbitrage earns steady returns year after year.

Relative Value Arbitrage

Relative value arbitrage might be better named the smorgasbord of arbitrage. This is because relative value hedge fund managers are catholic in their investment strategies; they invest across the universe of arbitrage strategies. The best known of these managers was Long Term Capital Management (LTCM). Once the story of LTCM unfolded, it was clear that their trading strategies involved merger arbitrage, fixed income arbitrage, volatility arbitrage, stub trading, and convertible arbitrage.

In general, the strategy of relative value managers is to invest in spread trades: the simultaneous purchase of one security and the sale of another when the economic relationship between the two securities (the "spread") has become mispriced. The mispricing may be based on historical averages or mathematical equations. In either case, the relative value arbitrage manager purchases the security that is "cheap" and sells the security that is "rich." It is called relative value arbitrage because the cheapness or richness of a security is determined relative to a second security. Consequently, relative value managers do not take directional bets on the financial markets. Instead, they take focussed bets on the pricing relationship between two securities regardless of the current market conditions.

Relative value managers attempt to remove the influence of the financial markets from their investment strategies. This is made easy by the fact that they simultaneously buy and sell similar securities. Therefore, the market risk embedded in each security should cancel out. Any residual risk can be neutralized through the use of options or futures. What is left is pure security selection: the purchase of those securities that are cheap and the sale of those securities that are rich. Relative value managers earn a profit when the spread between the two securities returns to normal. They then unwind their positions and collect their profit.

We have already discussed merger arbitrage, convertible arbitrage, and fixed income arbitrage. Two other popular forms of relative value arbitrage are stub trading and volatility arbitrage.

Stub trading is an equity-based strategy. Frequently, companies acquire a majority stake in another company, but their stock price does not fully reflect their interest in the acquired company. As an example, consider Company A whose stock is trading at $50. Company A owns a majority stake in Company B, whose remaining outstanding stock, or stub, is trading at $40. The value of Company A should be the combination of its own operations, estimated at $45 a share, plus its majority stake in Company B's operations, estimated at $8 a share. Therefore, Company A's share price is undervalued relative to the value that Company B should contribute to Company A's share price. The share price of Company A should be about $53, but instead, it is trading at $50. The investment strategy would be to purchase Company A's stock and sell the appropriate ratio of Company B's stock.

Let's assume that Company A's ownership in Company B contributes to 20% of Company A's overall revenues. Therefore, the operations of Company B should contribute one fifth to Company A's share price. Therefore, a proper hedging ratio would be four shares of Company A's stock to Company B's stock.

The arbitrage strategy is:

Buy four shares of Company A stock at 4 × $50 = $200
Sell one share of Company B stock at 1 × $40 = $40

The relative value manager is now long Company A stock and hedged against the fluctuation of Company B's stock. Let's assume that

over three months the share price of Company B increases to $42 a
share, the value of Company A's operations remains constant at $45,
but now the shares of Company A correctly reflect the contribution of
Company B's operations. The value of the position will be:

Value of Company A's operations:	4 × $45	= $180
Value of Company B's operations:	4 × $42 × 20%	= $33.6
Loss on short of Company B stock:	1 × ($40 − $42)	= −$2
Short rebate on Company B stock:	1 × $40 × 4.5% × 3/12 =	$0.45
Total:		= $212.05

The initial invested capital was $200 for a gain of $12.05, or 6.02%
over three months. Suppose the stock of Company B had declined to
$30, but Company B's operations were properly valued in Company A's
share price. The position value would be:

Value of Company A's operations:	4 × $45	= $180
Value of Company B's operations:	4 × $30 × 20%	= $24
Gain on short of Company B's stock:	1 × ($40 − $30)	= $10
Short rebate on Company B's stock:	1 × $40 × 4.5% × 3/12 =	$0.045
Total:		= $214.45

The initial invested capital was $200 for a gain of $14.45, or 7.22%
over three months. For stub trading to work there must be some market
catalyst such that the contribution of Company B is properly reflected in
Company A's share price.

Volatility arbitrage involves options and warrant trading. Option
prices contain an *implied* number for volatility. That is, it is possible to
observe the market price of an option and back out the value of volatility implied in the current price using various option pricing models. The
arbitrageur can then compare options on the same underlying stock to
determine if the volatility implied by their prices are the same.

The implied volatility derived from option pricing models should
represent the expected volatility of the underlying stock that will be realized over the life of the option. Therefore, two options on the same
underlying stock should have the same implied volatility. If they do not,
an arbitrage opportunity may be available. Additionally, if the implied
volatility is significantly different from the historical volatility of the
underlying stock, then relative value arbitrageurs expect the implied volatility will revert back to its historical average. This allows hedge fund
managers to determine which options are priced "cheap" versus "rich."
Once again, relative value managers sell those options that are rich based
on the implied volatility *relative* to the historical volatility and buy those
options with cheap volatility relative to historical volatility.

EXHIBIT 25.8   HFRI Relative Value Arbitrage Index

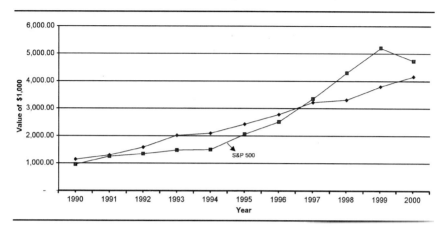

Exhibit 25.8 presents the value of relative value arbitrage compared to the S&P 500. This strategy demonstrates steady returns without much influence from the direction of the stock market.

Event-Driven

Event-driven hedge funds attempt to capture mispricing associated with capital market transactions. These transactions include mergers and acquisitions, spin-offs, tracking stocks, reorganizations, bankruptcies, share buy-backs, special dividends, and any other significant market event.

By their nature, these special events are nonrecurring. Consequently, the market may take time to digest the information associated with these transactions, providing an opportunity for event-driven managers to act quickly and capture a premium in the market. Additionally, some of these events may be subject to certain conditions such as shareholder or regulatory approval. Therefore, there is event risk associated with this strategy. The profitability of this type of strategy is dependent upon the successful completion of the transaction within the expected time frame.

We should not expect event-driven strategies to be influenced by the general stock market, since these are company specific events, not market driven events. However, in Exhibit 25.9 we do see that the value of event-driven strategies does closely parallel that value of the S&P 500. This could be because the strong stock market of 1990s encouraged more capital market transactions.

EXHIBIT 25.9   HFRI Event-Driven Index

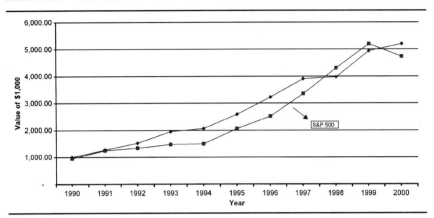

Market Neutral

Our last two categories are different from the previous hedge fund strategies in that they employ little or no leverage and maintain little or no market exposure. In fact, the very nature of their programs is to limit or eliminate market exposure altogether. We start with market neutral hedge funds.

Market neutral hedge funds also go long and short the market. The difference is that they maintain integrated portfolios which are designed to neutralize market risk. This means being neutral to the general stock market as well as having neutral risk exposures across industries. Security selection is all that matters.

Market neutral hedge fund managers generally apply the rule of one alpha.[6] This means that they build an integrated portfolio designed to produce only one source of alpha. This is distinct from equity long/short managers who build two separate portfolios: one long and one short, with two sources of alpha. The idea of integrated portfolio construction is to neutralize market and industry risk and concentrate purely on stock selection. In other words, there is no "beta" risk in the portfolio either with respect to the broad stock market or with respect to any industry. Only stock selection, or alpha, should remain.

Market neutral hedge fund managers generally hold equal positions of long and short stock positions. Therefore, the manager is dollar neutral; there is no net exposure to the market either on the long side or on the short side.

---

[6] See Bruce Jacobs and Kenneth Levy, "The Law of One Alpha," *The Journal of Portfolio Management* (Summer 1995).

Market neutral investors generally apply no leverage because there is no market exposure to leverage. However, some leverage is always inherent when stocks are borrowed and shorted. Nonetheless, the nature of this strategy is that it has minimal credit risk.

Generally, market neutral managers follow a three-step procedure in their strategy. The first step is to build an initial screen of "investable" stocks. These are stocks traded on the manager's local exchange, with sufficient liquidity so as to be able to enter and exit positions quickly, and with sufficient float so that the stock may be borrowed from the hedge fund manager's prime broker for short positions. Additionally, the hedge fund manager may limit his universe to a capitalization segment of the equity universe such as the mid-cap range.

Second, the hedge fund manager typically builds factor models. These are linear and quadratic regression equations designed to identify those economic factors that consistently have an impact on share prices. This process is very similar to that discussed with respect to equity long/short hedge fund manages. Indeed, the two strategies are very similar in their portfolio construction methods. The difference is that equity long/short managers tend to have a net long exposure to the market while market neutral managers have no exposure.

Factor models are used for stock selection. These models are often known as "alpha engines." Their purpose is to find those financial variables that influence stock prices. These are bottom-up models that concentrate solely on corporate financial information as opposed to macroeconomic data. This is the source of the manager's skill—his stock selection ability.

The last step is portfolio construction. The hedge fund manager will use a computer program to construct his portfolio in such a way that it is neutral to the market as well as across industries. The hedge fund manager may use a commercial "optimizer"—computer software designed to measure exposure to the market and produce a trade list for execution based on a manager's desired exposure to the market—or he may use his own computer algorithms to measure and neutralize risk.

Most market neutral managers use optimizers to neutralize market and industry exposure. However, more sophisticated optimizers attempt to keep the portfolio neutral to several risk factors. These include size, book to value, price/earnings ratios, and market price to book value ratios. The idea is to have no intended or unintended risk exposures that might compromise the portfolio's neutrality.

Market neutral programs tend to be labeled "black boxes." This is a term for sophisticated computer algorithms that lack transparency. The lack of transparency associated with these investment strategies comes in two forms. First, hedge fund managers, by nature, are secretive. They are reluctant to reveal their proprietary trading programs. Second, even if a hedge fund manager were to reveal his proprietary computer algorithms, these algorithms are often so sophisticated and complicated that they are difficult to comprehend.

We would expect market neutral hedge fund managers to produce returns independent of the stock market (they are neutral to the stock market). Exhibit 25.10 confirms this expectation.

Market Timers

Market timers, as their name suggests, attempt to time the most propitious moments to be in the market, and invest in cash otherwise. More specifically, they attempt to time the market so that they are fully invested during bull markets, and strictly in cash during bear markets.

Unlike equity long/short strategies or market neutral strategies, market times use a top-down approach as opposed to a bottom-up approach. Market timing hedge fund managers are not stock pickers. They analyze fiscal and monetary policy as well as key macroeconomic indicators to determine whether the economy is gathering or running out of steam.

Macroeconomic variables they may analyze are labor productivity, business investment, purchasing managers' surveys, commodity prices, consumer confidence, housing starts, retail sales, industrial production, balance of payments, current account deficits/surpluses, and durable good orders.

They use this macroeconomic data to forecast the expected gross domestic product (GDP) for the next quarter. Forecasting models typically are based on multifactor linear regressions, taking into account whether a variable is a leading or lagging indicator and whether the variable experiences any seasonal effects.

EXHIBIT 25.10   HFRI Equity Market Neutral Index

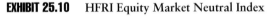
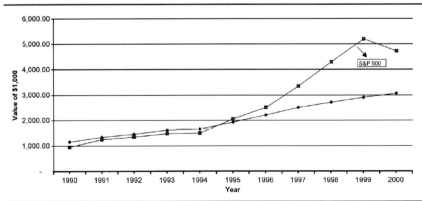

EXHIBIT 25.11   HFRI Market Timing Index

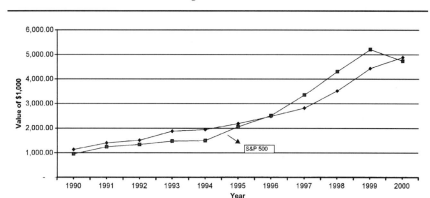

Once market timers have their forecast for the next quarter(s) they position their investment portfolio in the market according to their forecast. Construction of their portfolio is quite simple. They do not need to purchase individual stocks. Instead, they buy or sell stock index futures and options to increase or decrease their exposure to the market as necessary. At all times, contributed capital from investors is kept in short-term, risk-free, interest bearing accounts. Treasury bills are often purchased which not only yield a current risk-free interest rate, but also can be used as margin for the purchase of stock index futures.

When a market timer's forecast is bullish, he may purchase stock index futures with an economic exposure equivalent to the contributed capital. He may apply leverage by purchasing futures contracts that provide an economic exposure to the stock market greater than that of the underlying capital. However, market timers tend to use limited amounts of leverage.

When the hedge fund manager is bearish, he will trim his market exposure by selling futures contracts. If he is completely bearish, he will sell all of his stock index futures and call options and just sit on his cash portfolio. Some market timers may be more aggressive and short stock index futures and buy stock index put options to take advantage of bear markets. In general though, market timers have either long exposure to the market or no exposure. Consequently, this is a conservative hedge fund strategy in the same mode as market neutral programs. Exhibit 25.11 confirms this analysis.

SHOULD HEDGE FUNDS BE PART OF AN INVESTMENT PROGRAM?

A considerable amount of research has been dedicated to examining the return potential of several hedge fund styles. Additionally, a number of studies have considered hedge funds within a portfolio context, i.e., hedge funds blended with other asset classes.

The body of research on hedge funds demonstrates two key qualifications for hedge funds. First, that over the time period of 1989–2000, the returns to hedge funds were positive. The highest returns were achieved by global macro hedge funds, and the lowest returns were achieved by short selling hedge funds. Not all categories of hedge funds beat the S&P 500. However, in many cases, the volatility associated with hedge fund returns was lower than that of the S&P 500, resulting in higher Sharpe Ratios.

Second, the empirical research demonstrates that hedge funds provide good diversification benefits. In other words, hedge funds do, in fact, hedge other financial assets. Correlation coefficients with the S&P 500 range from –0.7 for short selling hedge funds to 0.83 for opportunistic hedge funds investing in the U.S. markets. The less than perfect positive correlation with financial assets indicates that hedge funds can expand the efficient frontier for asset managers.

In summary, the recent research on hedge funds indicates consistent, positive performance with low correlation with traditional asset classes. The conclusion is that hedge funds can expand the investment opportunity set for investors, offering both return enhancement as well as diversification benefits.

IS HEDGE FUND PERFORMANCE PERSISTENT?

This is the age-old question with respect to all asset managers, not just hedge funds: Can the manager repeat her good performance? This issue, though, is particularly acute for the hedge fund marketplace for two reasons. First, hedge fund managers often claim that the source of their returns is "skill-based" rather than dependent upon general financial market conditions. Second, hedge fund managers tend to have shorter track records than traditional money managers.

Unfortunately, the evidence regarding hedge fund performance persistence is mixed. The few empirical studies that have addressed this issue have provided inconclusive evidence whether hedge fund managers can produce enduring results. Part of the reason for the mixed results is the short track records of most hedge fund managers. A 3-year or 5-year track record is too short a period of time to be able to estimate an accurate expected return or risk associated with that manager.

In addition, the skill-based claim of hedge fund managers makes it more difficult to assess their performance relative to a benchmark. Without a benchmark index for comparison, it is difficult to determine whether a hedge fund manager has outperformed or underperformed her performance "bogey." As a result, the persistence of hedge fund manager performance will remain an open issue until manager databases with longer performance track records can be developed.

A HEDGE FUND INVESTMENT STRATEGY

The above discussion demonstrates that hedge funds can expand the investment opportunity set for investors. The question now becomes: What is to be accomplished by the hedge fund investment program? The strategy may be simply a search for an additional source of return. Conversely, it may be for risk management purposes. Whatever its purpose, an investment plan for hedge funds may consider one of four strategies. Hedge funds may be selected on an opportunistic basis, as a hedge fund of funds, as part of a joint venture, or as an absolute return strategy.

Opportunistic Hedge Fund Investing

The term "hedge fund" can be misleading. Hedge funds do not necessarily have to hedge an investment portfolio. Rather, they can be used to expand the investment opportunity set. This is the opportunistic nature of hedge funds—they can provide an investor with new investment opportunities that she cannot otherwise obtain through traditional long only investments.

There are several ways hedge funds can be opportunistic. First, many hedge fund managers can add value to an existing investment portfolio through specialization in a sector or in a market strategy. These managers do not contribute portable alpha. Instead, they contribute above market returns through the application of superior skill or knowledge to a narrow market or strategy.

Consider a portfolio manager whose particular expertise is the biotechnology industry. She has followed this industry for years and has developed a superior information set to identify winners and losers. On the long only side the manager purchases those stocks that she believes will increase in value, and avoids those biotech stocks she believes will decline in value. However, this strategy does not utilize her superior information set to its fullest advantage. The ability to go both long and short biotech stocks in a hedge fund is the only way to maximize the value of the manager's information set. Therefore, a biotech hedge fund provides a new opportunity: the ability to extract value on both the long side and the short side of the biotech market.

The goal of this strategy is to identify the best managers in a specific economic sector or specific market segment that complements the existing investment portfolio. These managers are used to enhance the risk and return profile of an existing portfolio, rather than hedge it.

Opportunistic hedge funds tend to have a benchmark. Take the example of the biotech long/short hedge fund. An appropriate benchmark would be the AMEX Biotech Index that contains 17 biotechnology companies. Alternatively, if the investor believed that the biotech sector will outperform the general stock market, she could use a broad based stock index such as the S&P 500 for the benchmark. The point is that opportunistic hedge funds are not absolute return vehicles (discussed below). Their performance can be measured relative to a benchmark.

As another example, most institutional investors have a broad equity portfolio. This portfolio may include an index fund, external value and growth managers, and possibly, private equity investments. However, along the spectrum of this equity portfolio, there may be gaps in its investment line-up. For instance, many hedge funds combine late stage private investments with public securities. These hybrid funds are a natural extension of an institution's investment portfolio because they bridge the gap between private equity and index funds. Therefore a new opportunity is identified: the ability to blend private equity and public securities within one investment strategy. We will discuss this strategy further in our section on private equity.

Again, we come back to one of our main themes: that alternative "assets" are really alternative investment strategies, and these alternative strategies are used to expand the investment opportunity set rather than hedge it. In summary, hedge funds may be selected not necessarily to reduce the risk of an existing investment portfolio, but instead, to complement its risk and return profile. Opportunistic investing is designed to select hedge fund managers that can enhance certain portions of a broader portfolio.

Another way to consider opportunistic hedge fund investments is that they are finished products because their investment strategy or market segment complements an institutional investor's existing asset allocation. In other words, these hybrid funds can plug the gaps of an existing portfolio. No further work is necessary on the part of the institution because the investment opportunity set has been expanded by the addition of the hybrid product. These "gaps" may be in domestic equity, fixed income, or international investments. Additionally, because opportunistic hedge funds are finished products, it makes it easier to establish performance benchmarks.

Constructing an opportunistic portfolio of hedge funds will depend upon the constraints under which such a program operates. For example, if an investor's hedge fund program is not limited in scope or style, then diversification across a broad range of hedge fund styles would be appropriate. If, however, the hedge fund program is limited in scope to, for instance, expanding the equity investment opportunity set, the choices will be less diversified across strategies. Exhibit 25.12 demonstrates these two choices.

Hedge Fund of Funds

A *hedge fund of funds* is an investment in a group of hedge funds, from five to more than 20. The purpose of a hedge fund of funds is to reduce the idiosyncratic risk of any one hedge fund manager. In other words, there is safety in numbers. This is simply modern portfolio theory (MPT) applied to the hedge fund marketplace. Diversification is one of the founding principles of MPT, and it is as applicable to hedge funds as it is to stocks and bonds.

Joint Venture

As noted in the introduction, the hedge fund market is fragmented with most hedge fund managers controlling a relatively small amount of assets. This provides a good opportunity to enter into a joint venture with an emerging hedge fund manager.

EXHIBIT 25.12 Implementing an Opportunistic Hedge Fund Strategy

Diversified Hedge Fund Portfolio	Equity-Based Hedge Fund Portfolio
Equity Long/Short	Equity Long/Short
Short Selling	Short Selling
Market Neutral	Market Neutral
Merger Arbitrage	Merger Arbitrage
Event-Driven	Event-Driven
Convertible Arbitrage	Convertible Arbitrage
Global Macro	
Fixed-Income Arbitrage	
Relative Value Arbitrage	
Market Timers	

The greatest challenge for any new hedge fund manager is attracting sufficient capital to achieve a critical mass. Park, Brown, and Goetzmann find the attrition rate for hedge funds is about 15% per year, while Brown, Goetzmann, and Ibbotson find that few hedge funds survive more than three years.[7] A large institutional investor can provide the necessary capital along with the stability and the credibility necessary to achieve this critical mass. In such a situation a hedge fund manager receives a much greater benefit than just the fees collected.

In return for these start-up benefits, the institution can ask for reduced fees and a potential equity stake in the manager's revenues. As the hedge fund manager increases its assets under management, the institution will share in this growth. Additionally, the institution can earn excellent returns from its hedge fund investment with a lower fee structure. This form of collaboration can produce good long-term returns for both the institutional investor and the hedge fund manager.

Another new development in the hedge fund marketplace is the hedge fund management company. These are asset management companies that build a stable of hedge fund managers by acquiring equity ownership in the hedge fund manager. This business model is similar to that for mutual fund companies established by traditional money managers.

In the mutual fund industry, a corporation is established that advises each individual mutual fund. The investment adviser registers the mutual fund company with the Securities and Exchange Commission, sells shares of the mutual fund to investors, and performs all of the necessary accounting and operational duties. The fees earned from providing investment advice to the mutual fund flow upward to the advisory company.

Similarly, hedge fund management companies take care of all of the regulatory, operational, and marketing issues for the hedge fund manager, and in return, receive an equity stake in the management and profit sharing fees earned by the hedge fund manager. These hedge fund management companies need investment capital for two reasons.

First, they need working capital to acquire hedge fund managers for their management company. Second, they need investment capital to place with their hedge fund managers. In return, an investor can receive an equity stake in the hedge fund management company, or the individual hedge fund manager and receive the benefit of a hedge fund investment.

---

[7] See James Park, Stephen Brown, and William Goetzmann, "Performance Benchmarks and Survivorship Bias for Hedge Funds and Commodity Trading Advisors," *Hedge Fund News* (August 1999); and Stephen Brown, William Goetzmann, and Roger Ibbotson, "Offshore Hedge Funds: Survival and Performance, 1989–1995," *The Journal of Business*, 1999.

This strategy is a combination of private equity and hedge fund investing, and it offers several advantages. First many institutional investors maintain a private equity staff. Using this staff to enter into another arena in the alternative asset world allows an institution to apply its investment experience in a new venue. This "portable expertise" is analogous to portable alpha in that it can be added to other avenues of the alternative asset market.

Second, private equity investments tend to be structured as funds or pools. This legal structure is similar (but not identical) to that for hedge funds.[8] Consequently, private equity investors tend to have considerable experience sorting through the issues of pooled investors in an alternative asset vehicle.

Lastly, the linking of private equity and hedge fund investing is a natural evolution in alternative asset investing. The expansion of the investment opportunity set need not be done through the selection of discrete pockets of alternative assets; combinations of alternative assets will work just as well.

Absolute Return

Hedge funds are often described as "absolute return" products. This term comes from the skill-based nature of the industry. Hedge fund managers generally claim that their investment returns are derived from their skill at security selection rather than that of broad asset classes. This is due to the fact that most hedge fund managers build concentrated portfolios of relatively few investment positions and do not attempt to track a stock or bond index. The work of Fung and Hsieh shows that hedge funds generate a return distribution that is very different from mutual funds.[9]

Further, given the generally unregulated waters in which hedge fund managers operate, they have greater flexibility in their trading style and execution than traditional long-only managers. This flexibility provides a greater probability that a hedge fund manager will reach his return targets. As a result, hedge funds have often been described as absolute return vehicles that target a specific annual return regardless of what performance might be found among market indices. In other words,

---

[8] For example, private equity funds often offer an incentive fee recapture provision known as a "clawback." Conversely, hedge fund typically offer an incentive fee hurdle rate known as a "high water mark." We will discuss more of these differences in our section on private equity.

[9] See William Fung and David Hsieh, "Empirical Characteristics of Dynamic Trading Strategies: The Case of Hedge Funds," *The Review of Financial Studies* (Summer 1997).

hedge fund managers target an absolute return rather than determine their performance relative to an index.

All traditional long-only managers are benchmarked to some passive index. The nature of benchmarking is such that it forces the manager to focus on his benchmark and his tracking error associated with that benchmark. This focus on benchmarking leads traditional active managers to commit a large portion their portfolios to tracking their benchmark. The necessity to consider the impact of every trade on the portfolio's tracking error relative to its assigned benchmark reduces the flexibility of the investment manager.

In addition, long-only active managers are constrained in their ability to short securities. They may only "go short" a security up to its weight in the benchmark index. If the security is only a small part of the index, the manager's efforts to short the stock will be further constrained. The inability to short a security beyond its benchmark weight deprives an active manager of a significant amount of the mispricing in the marketplace. Furthermore, not only are long-only managers unable to take advantage of overpriced securities, but they also cannot fully take advantage of underpriced securities because they cannot generate the necessary short positions to balance the overweights with respect to underpriced securities.

The flexibility of hedge fund managers allows them to go both long and short without benchmark constraints. This allows them to set a target rate of return or an "absolute return."

Specific parameters must be set for an absolute return program. These parameters will direct how the hedge fund program is constructed and operated and should include risk and return targets as well as the type of hedge fund strategies that may be selected. Absolute return parameters should operate at two levels: that of the individual hedge fund manager and for the overall hedge fund program. The investor sets target return ranges for each hedge fund manager but sets a specific target return level for the absolute return program. The parameters for the individual managers may be different than that for the program. For example, acceptable levels of volatility for individual hedge fund managers may be greater than that for the program.

The program parameters for the hedge fund managers may be based on such factors as volatility, expected return, types of instruments traded, leverage, and historical drawdown. Other qualitative factors may be included such as length of track record, periodic liquidity, minimum investment, and assets under management. Liquidity is particularly important because an investor needs to know with certainty her timeframe for cashing out of an absolute return program if hedge fund returns turn sour.

EXHIBIT 25.13   An Absolute Return Strategy

Absolute Return Portfolio	Individual Hedge Fund Managers
Target Return: 15%	Expected Return: 10% to 25%
Target Risk: 7%	Target Risk: 5% to 15%
Largest Acceptable Drawdown: 10%	Largest Drawdown: 10% to 20%
Liquidity: Semiannual	Liquidity: Semiannual
Hedge Fund Style: Equity-based	Hedge Fund Style: Equity L/S, Market Neutral, Merger Arbitrage, Short Selling, Event-Driven, Convertible Arbitrage
Length of Track Record: 3 years	Minimum Track Record: 3 years

Exhibit 25.13 demonstrates an absolute return program strategy. Notice that the return for the portfolio has a specific target rate of 15%, while for the individual hedge funds, the return range is 10% to 25%. Also, the absolute return portfolio has a target level for risk and drawdowns, while for the individual hedge funds, a range is acceptable.

However, certain parameters are synchronized. Liquidity, for instance, must be the same for both the absolute return portfolio and that of the individual hedge fund managers. The reason is that a range of liquidity is not acceptable if the investor wishes to liquidate her portfolio. She must be able to cash out of each hedge fund within the same timeframe as that established for the portfolio.

SELECTING A HEDGE FUND MANAGER

A considerable amount of research has been dedicated to determining the economic value added of hedge funds. Yet, despite the mounting evidence regarding the value of hedge funds, very little has been written regarding the selection of hedge fund managers. In this chapter we address some practical issues to consider in establishing a hedge fund investment program.

A Graphical Presentation of the Hedge Fund Industry

It should be no surprise to most investors that hedge funds operate differently from traditional long-only investment managers. Long-only managers typically invest in either the equity or bond market, but do not leverage their investment bets. Therefore, their investment programs have considerable market risk exposure, but very little leverage or credit risk exposure.[10]

---

[10] For an excellent and more detailed discussion on this type of classification, see CrossBorder Capital, "TSS(II)-Tactical Style Selection: Integrating Hedge Funds into the Asset Allocation Framework," *Hedge Fund Research* (August 2000).

EXHIBIT 25.14 Long-Only Investments

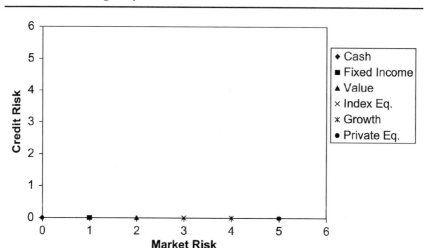

Consider Exhibit 25.14. This exhibit plots market risk versus credit risk for several styles of long-only managers. We use a relative scale of 0 to 5 where 0 represents no exposure to financial market risk and 5 represents the maximum exposure. The same relative scale is applied with respect to credit risk.

As Exhibit 25.14 demonstrates, traditional long-only managers have considerable exposure to market risk but minimal exposure to credit risk. At one end of the scale are money market cash managers. To avoid "breaking the buck" these managers do not take any credit risk or market risk. They invest in the most liquid and creditworthy of short-term financial paper. Typically, this includes high-grade 90-day commercial paper and 90-day U.S. Treasury obligations.

At the other end of the scale are private equity managers. They take no credit risk, but have the greatest exposure to market risk. Most private equity funds, for instance, have lock-up periods between 7 and 10 years. Investments made by private equity funds are in non-public securities for which no readily available market exists. Liquidity is low, and investors are exposed to the long-term prospects of the equity market.

In between the cash managers and the private equity managers, and along the increasing scale of market risk, we find fixed-income managers, value managers, equity index managers, and growth managers.

The graphical analysis changes considerably for hedge fund managers. Exhibit 25.15 demonstrates the market versus credit risk exposures for several major styles of hedge funds. Near the zero axis we find market neutral funds—those hedge funds with no market exposure (market neutral) and low leverage. Market neutral funds use limited amounts of leverage because there is no market exposure to leverage or magnify.

Along the credit risk axis, we see that the exposure to credit risk increases for merger arbitrage, convertible arbitrage, and fixed-income arbitrage. The use of leverage, or credit risk, is a major factor that distinguishes hedge fund managers from traditional long-only managers.

Merger arbitrage, for example, usually applies low leverage, in the range of 2:1. Recall that merger arbitrage involves buying the equity securities of the target company and selling the equity securities of the acquiring company. Although the terms of the merger are announced for all to see, the companies may sell at a discount to the announced price to reflect the uncertainty associated with the completion of the merger. Despite the offsetting positions, there may still be some residual market risk because the two merger partners are corporations whose fortunes depend somewhat on the general market conditions.

Other arbitrage hedge funds, such as convertible arbitrage, have a small market exposure but a large credit exposure. This is because arbitrage funds take small market bets but use leverage (sometimes, considerable amounts) to magnify the size of the market bets.

These types of hedge funds extract their profits from relative value trades. They trade based on relatively small price discrepancies in the market, but use large amounts of leverage to extract the most value from these small discrepancies.

EXHIBIT 25.15   Hedge Funds

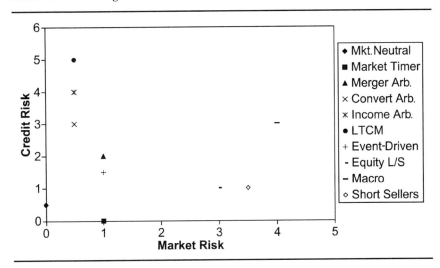

Long Term Capital Management (LTCM) of Greenwich, Connecticut was the best-known example of these relative value/arbitrage players. It has been well documented that LTCM used massive amounts of leverage to extract value from its relatively small market bets.[11] Consequently, we use it to define the upper boundary for credit exposure.

Equity long/short and global macro hedge funds have exposure to both credit risk and market risk. Global macro funds tend to make large bets on the direction of certain currencies, commodities, stock markets, or bond markets. Generally, global macro funds have the ability to invest across the investment spectrum and national borders in the placing of their bets. Consequently, they have a large market exposure. Global macro funds may also use leverage to magnify the size of their bets. George Soros and Julian Robertson were the best known of the macro hedge fund managers.

Long/short equity hedge funds, by their very nature, are exposed to the stock market. Also, this type of hedge fund manager sometimes uses leverage to increase the value of long/short positions.

The main point of Exhibits 25.14 and 25.15 is that hedge fund managers have risk profiles that differ considerably from that of traditional long-only investments. In particular, hedge funds often take considerable credit risk in their investment strategies.

Three Fundamental Questions

The hedge fund industry is still relatively new because it has attracted attention only within the past decade. In fact, most of the academic research on hedge funds was conducted during the 1990s. As a result, for most hedge fund managers, a two- to three-year track record is considered long term. In fact, Park, Brown, and Goetzmann find that the attrition rate in the hedge fund industry is about 15% per year and that the half-life for hedge funds is about 2.5 years. Liang documents an attrition rate of 8.54% per year for hedge funds. Weisman indicates that relying on a hedge fund manager's past performance history can lead to disappointing investment results.[12] Consequently, performance history, while useful, cannot be relied upon solely in selecting a hedge fund manager.

---

[11] See The President's Working Group on Financial Markets, "Hedge Funds, Leverage, and the Lessons of Long Term Capital Management," (April 28, 1999).

[12] See Park, Brown, and Goetzmann, "The Performance Benchmarks and Survivorship Bias of Hedge Funds and Commodity Trading Advisors"; Bing Liang "Hedge Fund Performance: 1990–1999," *Financial Analysts Journal* (January/February 2001), pp. 11–18; and Andrew Weisman, "The Dangers of Historical Hedge Fund Data," working paper (2000).

Beyond performance numbers, there are three fundamental questions that every hedge fund manager should answer during the initial screening process. The answers to these three questions are critical to understanding the nature of the hedge fund manager's investment program. The three questions are:

1. What is the investment objective of the hedge fund?
2. What is the investment process of the hedge fund manager?
3. What makes the hedge fund manager so smart?

A hedge fund manager should have a clear and concise statement of its investment objective. Second, the hedge fund manager should identify its investment process. For instance, is it quantitatively or qualitatively based? Last, the hedge fund manager must demonstrate that he or she is smarter than other money managers.

The questions presented in this chapter are threshold issues. These questions are screening tools designed to reduce an initial universe of hedge fund managers down to a select pool of potential investments. They are not, however, a substitute for a thorough due diligence review. We address that subject later in this chapter. Instead, these questions can identify potential hedge fund candidates for which due diligence is appropriate.

Investment Objective

The question of a hedge fund manager's investment objective can be broken down into three questions:

1. In which markets does the hedge fund manager invest?
2. What is the hedge fund manager's general investment strategy?
3. What is the hedge fund manager's benchmark, if any?

Although these questions may seem straightforward, they are often surprisingly difficult to answer. Consider the following language from a hedge fund disclosure document:

> The principal objective of the Fund is capital appreciation, primarily through the purchase and sale of securities, commodities and other financial instruments including without limitation, stocks, bonds, notes, debentures, and bills issued by corporations, municipalities, sovereign nations or other entities; options, rights, warrants, convertible securities, exchangeable securities, synthetic and/or structured convertible or exchangeable products, participation interests, investment contracts, mortgages, mort-

gage and asset-backed securities, real estate and interests therein; currencies, other futures, commodity options, forward contracts, money market instruments, bank notes, bank guarantees, letters of credit, other forms of bank obligations; other swaps and other derivative instruments; limited partnership interests and other limited partnership securities or instruments; and contracts relating to the foregoing; in each case whether now existing or created in the future.

Let's analyze the above statement in light of our three investment objective questions.

Question 1: In which markets does the hedge fund manager invest?
Answer: In every market known to exist.

By listing every possible financial, commodity, or investment contract currently in existence (or to exist in the future), the hedge fund manager has covered all options, but has left the investor uniformed. Unfortunately, the unlimited nature of the hedge fund manager's potential investment universe does not help to narrow the scope of the manager's investment objective.

Question 2: What is the hedge fund manager's general strategy?
Answer: Capital appreciation.

This answer too, is uninformative. Rarely does any investor invest in a hedge fund for capital *depreciation*. Generally, hedge funds are not used as tax shelters. Furthermore, many institutional investors are tax-exempt so that taxes are not a consideration. Capital appreciation is assumed for most investments, including hedge funds. The above language is far too general to be informative.

Question 3: What is the manager's benchmark, if any?
Answer: There is no effective benchmark. The manager's investment universe is so widespread as to make any benchmark useless.

Unfortunately, the above disclosure language, while very detailed, discloses very little. It does cover all of the manager's legal bases, but it does not inform the investor.

Where does this manager fall within the hedge fund spectrum in Exhibit 25.15? The very broad nature of this hedge fund's investment objective places it in the global macro category. Its investment universe is far too broad to be an arbitrage fund. By the same token, its strategy is too expansive to be considered an equity long/short program. Its only appropriate category is global macro.

By contrast, consider the following language from a second hedge fund disclosure document.

> The Fund's investment objective is to make investments in public securities that generate a long-term return in excess of that generated by the overall U.S. public equity market while reducing the market risk of the portfolio through selective short positions.

This one sentence answers all three investment objective questions. First, the manager identifies that it invests in the U.S. public equity market. Second, the manager discloses that it uses a long/short investment strategy. Lastly, the manager states that its objective is to outperform the overall U.S. equity market. Therefore, a suitable benchmark might be the S&P500, the Russell 1000, or a sector index

From Exhibit 25.15, this hedge fund is clearly identified as an equity long/short strategy. Its primary purpose is to take on market risk, not credit risk.

In summary, long-winded disclosure statements are not necessary. A well-thought-out investment strategy can be summarized in one sentence.

Investment Process

Most investors prefer a well-defined investment process that describes how an investment manager makes its investments. The articulation and documentation of the process can be just as important as the investment results generated by the process. Consider the following language from another hedge fund disclosure document:

> The manager makes extensive use of computer technology in both the formulation and execution of many investment decisions. Buy and sell decisions will, in many cases, be made and executed algorithmically according to quantitative trading strategies embodied in analytical computer software running the manager's computer facilities or on other computers used to support the Fund's trading activities.

This is a "black box." A black box is the algorithmic extension of the hedge fund manager's brain power. Computer algorithms are developed to quantify the manager's skill or investment insight.

For black box managers, the black box itself is the investment process. It is not that the black boxes are bad investments. In fact, the hedge fund research indicates that proprietary quantitative trading strategies can be quite successful.[13] Rather, the issue is whether good performance results justify the lack of a clear investment process.

Black box programs tend to be used in arbitrage or relative value hedge fund programs. From Exhibit 25.15 we can see that these types of programs fall along the credit risk axis. Hedge fund managers use quantitative computer algorithms to seek out pricing discrepancies between similar securities or investment contracts. They then sell the investment that appears to be "expensive" and buy the investment that appears to be "cheap." The very nature of arbitrage programs is to minimize market risk. Leverage is then applied to extract the most value from their small net exposure to market risk.

A black box is just one example of process versus investment results. The hedge fund industry considers itself to be "skill-based." However, it is very difficult to translate manager skill into a process. This is particularly true when the performance of the hedge fund is dependent upon the skill of a specific individual.

Let's consider another, well publicized skill-based investment process. In the spring of 2000, the hedge funds headed by George Soros stumbled leading to the departure of Stanley Druckenmiller, the chief investment strategist for Soros Fund Management. The *Wall Street Journal* documented the concentrated skill-based investment style of this hedge fund group:

> For years, [Soros Fund Management] fostered an entrepreneurial culture, with a cadre of employees battling wits to persuade Mr. Druckenmiller to invest.
>
> "[Mr. Druckenmiller] didn't scream, but he could be very tough. It could be three days or three weeks of battling it out until he's convinced, or you're defeated."[14]

The above statement does not describe an investment process. It is a description of an individual. The hedge fund manager's investment analysis and decision-making is concentrated in one person. This is a pure example of "skill-based" investing. There is no discernible process.

---

[13] See CrossBorder Capital. "Choosing Investment Styles to Reduce Risk," *Hedge Fund Research*, (October 1999); Goldman, Sachs & Co. and Financial Risk Management Ltd., "The Hedge Fund "Industry" and Absolute Return Funds," *The Journal of Alternative Investments* (Spring 1999); and "Hedge Funds Revisited," *Pension and Endowment Forum* (January 2000).

[14] The *Wall Street Journal*, "Shake-Up Continues at Soros's Hedge-Fund Empire," May 1, 2000, page C1.

Instead, all information is filtered through the brain of one individual. In essence, the institutional investor must trust the judgment of one person.

Mr. Druckenmiller compiled an exceptional track record as the manager of the Soros Quantum Fund. However, the concentration of decision-making authority is not an economic risk, it is a process risk.

Investors should accept economic risk but not process risk. Soros Fund Management is a well-known global macro hedge fund manager. From Exhibit 25.15 we can see that fundamental risks of an investment in a global macro fund are credit risk and market risk.

Investors are generally unwilling to bear risks that are not fundamental to their tactical and strategic asset allocations. Process risk is not a fundamental risk. It is an idiosyncratic risk of the hedge fund manager's structure and operations.

Generally, process risk is not a risk that investors wish to bear. Nor is it a risk for which they expect to be compensated. Furthermore, how would an investor go about pricing the process risk of a hedge fund manager? It can't be quantified, and it can't be calibrated. Therefore, there is no way to tell whether an institutional investor is being properly compensated for this risk.[15]

Process risk also raises the ancillary issue of lack of transparency. Skill-based investing usually is opaque. Are the decisions of the key individual quantitatively based? Qualitatively based? There is no way to really tell. This is similar to the problems discussed earlier with respect to black boxes.

To summarize, process risk cannot be quantified and it is not a risk that investors are willing to bear. Process risk also raises issues of transparency. Investors want clarity and definition, not opaqueness and amorphousness.

What Makes the Hedge Fund Manager so Smart?

Before investing money with a hedge fund manager, an investor must determine one of the following. The hedge fund manager must be able to demonstrate that he or she is smarter than the next manager. One way to be smarter than another hedge fund manager is to have superior skill in filtering information. That is, the hedge fund manager must be able to look at the same information set as another manager but be able to glean more investment insight from that data set.

---

[15] See James Park and Jeremy Staum, "Fund of Funds Diversification: How Much is Enough?" *The Journal of Alternative Investments* (Winter 1998). They demonstrate that idiosyncratic process risks can largely be eliminated through a diversified fund of funds program. They indicate that a portfolio of 15 to 20 hedge funds can eliminate much of the idiosyncratic risk associated with hedge fund investments.

Alternatively, if the hedge fund manager is not smarter than the next manager, he must demonstrate that he has a better information set; his competitive advantage is not filtering information, but gathering it. To be successful, a hedge fund manager must demonstrate one or both of these competitive advantages.

Generally speaking, quantitative, computer-driven managers satisfy the first criteria. That is, hedge fund managers that run computer models access the same information set as everyone else, but have better (smarter) algorithms to extract more value per information unit than the next manager. These managers tend to be relative value managers.

Relative value managers extract value by simultaneously comparing the prices of two securities and buying and selling accordingly. This information is available to all investors in the marketplace. However, it is the relative value managers that are able to process the information quickly enough to capture mispricings in the market. These arbitrage strategies fall along the credit risk axis in Exhibit 25.15.

Alternatively, hedge fund managers that confine themselves to a particular market segment or sector generally satisfy the second criteria. They have a larger information set that allows them to gain a competitive edge in their chosen market. Their advantage is a proprietary information set accumulated over time rather than a proprietary data filtering system.

Consider the following statement from a hedge fund disclosure document:

> The Adviser hopes to achieve consistently high returns by focusing on small and mid-cap companies in the biotechnology market.

The competitive advantage of this type of manager is his or her knowledge not only about a particular economic sector (biotechnology), but also, about a particular market segment of that sector (small- and mid-cap). This type of manger tends to take more market risk exposure than credit risk exposure and generally applies equity long/short programs (see Exhibit 25.15).

Identifying the competitive advantage of the hedge fund manager is the key to determining whether the hedge fund manager can sustain performance results. We indicated earlier that the issue of performance persistence is undecided.

Therefore, an investor cannot rely on historical hedge fund performance data as a means of selecting good managers from bad managers. Furthermore, every hedge fund disclosure document contains some variation of the following language:

Past performance is no indication of future results.

Essentially, this statement directs the investor to ignore the hedge fund manager's performance history.

To asses the likelihood of performance persistence, the investor must then determine whether the hedge fund manager is an information gatherer or an information filterer. Consider the following language from a hedge fund disclosure document.

The General Partner will utilize its industry expertise, contacts, and databases developed over the past 11 years to identify ____ company investment ideas outside traditional sources and will analyze these investment opportunities using, among other techniques, many aspects of its proven methodology in determining value.

This hedge fund manager has a superior information set that has been developed over 11 years. It is an information gatherer. Consistent with Exhibit 25.15, this manager applies an equity long/short program within a specific market sector.

Finally, consider the following disclosure language from a merger arbitrage hedge fund manager:

[The] research group [is] staffed by experienced M&A lawyers with detailed knowledge of deal lifecycle, with extensive experience with corporate law of multiple U.S. states, U.S. and foreign securities laws regarding proxy contests, and antitrust laws (both of the U.S. and EU), and who have made relevant filings before regulators and have closed a wide variety of M&A transactions.

This hedge fund manager is an information filterer. Its expertise is sifting through the outstanding legal and regulatory issues associated with a merger and determining the likelihood that the deal will be completed.

To summarize, a good lesson is that successful hedge fund managers know the exact nature of their competitive advantage, and how to exploit it.

DUE DILIGENCE FOR HEDGE FUND MANAGERS

Who should be selected as your hedge fund manager will depend on due diligence. Due diligence starts the initial process of building a relationship with a hedge fund manager. It is an unavoidable task that investors must follow in order to choose a manager. Due diligence is the process of identifying the best and the brightest of the hedge fund managers. This is where the investor must roll up her sleeves and get into the devilish details that can prove to be so elusive with hedge fund managers.

Due diligence consists of seven parts: structure, strategy, performance, risk, administrative, legal, and references. This section reviews each part of the due diligence procedure.

Structural Review

The structural review defines the organization of the hedge fund manager. We start with the basics: how is the fund organized? It is important to remember that the hedge fund manager and the hedge fund are separate legal entities with different legal structures and identities. We then consider the structure of the hedge fund manager, any regulatory registrations, and key personnel.

Fund Organization

The hedge fund manager may invest the hedge fund's assets through an offshore master trust account or fund. An offshore master trust account is often used to take into account the various tax domiciles of the hedge fund's investors. Often, a hedge fund manager will set up two hedge funds, one onshore (U.S.-based) and one offshore. Master trusts are typically established in tax neutral sites such as Bermuda or the Cayman Islands.

The purpose of the master trust is to invest the assets of both the onshore hedge fund and the offshore hedge fund in a consistent (if not identical) manner so that both hedge funds share the benefit of the hedge fund manager's insights. Investors in either fund are not disadvantaged by this structure. Instead, it allows the tax consequences to flow down to the tax code of each investor's domicile country.

Master trusts/funds are often viewed suspiciously as tax evasion vehicles. This is not their purpose. Their purpose is tax neutrality, not evasion. In Bermuda, for example, master trust funds do not pay any corporate income tax. They only pay a corporate licensing fee. Therefore, there are no adverse tax consequences to the hedge fund investors at the master trust level.

Instead, the tax consequences for the investors will depend upon their domicile. Investors in the onshore U.S.-based hedge fund are subject to the U.S. Internal Revenue Code. Investors in the offshore fund are subject to the tax code of their respective domicile. Therefore, master trust vehicles are used to accommodate the different tax domiciles of foreign and domestic investors.

EXHIBIT 25.16 Master Trust Account

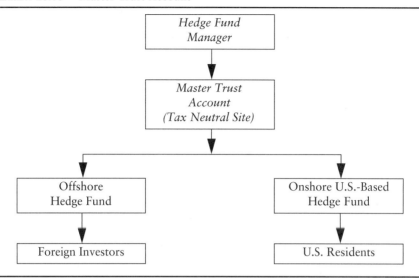

Consider a hedge fund manager who has two investors: one based in the United States and one in France. Where should she locate her hedge fund? If she locates the hedge fund in the United States, the U.S. investor will be happy, but the French investor may have to pay double the income taxes: both in the United States and in France. The best way to resolve this problem is to set up two hedge funds, one onshore and one offshore. In addition, a master trust account is established in a tax neutral site. The hedge fund manager can then invest the assets of both hedge funds through the master trust account and each investor will be liable only for the taxes imposed by the revenue code of their respective countries.[16] Exhibit 25.16 demonstrates the master trust structure.

Hedge fund structures do not have to be as complicated as that presented in Exhibit 25.16. The majority of hedge fund managers in the United States operate only within the United States, have only an onshore hedge fund, and accept only U.S. investors. Nonetheless, the popularity of hedge fund investing has resulted in operating structures that are sometimes as creative as the hedge fund strategies themselves.

Hedge Fund Manager Organization

First, the basics: where is the hedge fund manager located, are there any satellite offices, and where is the nearest office to the investor? These

---

[16] In reality, the United States and France have a tax treaty so the threat of double taxation is minimal. However there are many countries that do not have tax treaties with the United Sates, and the potential for double taxation is a reality.

questions can be very important if the hedge fund manager operates overseas and there are significant time differences between the manager's business hours and that of the investor.

Second, an organization chart is mandatory. Who is the Chief Executive Officer, the Chief Investment Officer, and Chief Operating Officer? A warning: It is not a good business plan if they are all the same person. Hedge fund managers should do what they do best: invest money and leave the operating details to someone else.

Of special importance is the Chief Financial Officer. The CFO will be the investor's most important link with the hedge fund manager after an investment is made because the CFO will be responsible for reporting the hedge fund manager's performance numbers. Consequently, the investor should make certain that the CFO has a strong background in accounting, preferably a Certified Public Accountant, a Chartered Accountant, or another professional accounting designation. Last, the investor must determine who are the senior managers in charge of trading, information systems, marketing, and research and development.

The educational and professional background of all principals should be documented. It should be determined whether they have graduate degrees, whether there are any Chartered Financial Analysts, and what was their prior investment experience before starting a hedge fund.

Another warning: Many equity long/short hedge fund managers were former long-only managers. Yet, shorting stocks is very different than going long stocks. The ability to locate and borrow stock, limit losses in a bull market, and short on the uptick rule are special talents that cannot be developed overnight.

Before investing money with a long/short hedge fund manager, an investor should find out where the hedge fund manager learned to short stocks. If it is a hedge fund manager that previously managed a long-only portfolio, chances are that she might not have much experience with respect to shorting stocks, and therefore, will be learning to short stocks with your money.

Ownership

Ownership of the hedge fund manager must be documented. It is important to know who owns the company that advises the hedge fund. This is important for "key person" provisions of the contractual documentation.

Additionally, ownership is important for ensuring that there is a proper alignment of interests with the hedge fund manager's employees as well as retention of employment. By sharing the ownership of the hedge fund management company with key employees, the hedge fund manager can ensure proper alignment of interests as well as retention of key personnel.

Registrations

The investor should document the regulatory registrations of the hedge fund manager. The hedge fund manager might be registered with the Securities and Exchange Commission as an Investment Adviser under the Investment Adviser's Act of 1940. If so, the hedge fund manager must file annually Form ADV with the SEC that contains important financial and structural information regarding the hedge fund manager.

Alternatively, the hedge fund manager might be registered with the National Futures Association (NFA) and the Commodity Futures Trading Commission (CFTC) as either a Commodity Trading Advisor (CTA) or a Commodity Pool Operator (CPO). The NFA is the self-regulatory organization for the managed futures industry. It is approved by the CFTC to handle all registrations for CTAs and CPOs. Also, the hedge fund manager might be registered with the NFA as an introducing broker or futures commission merchant. If, the hedge fund manager is registered as either a CTA, CPO, introducing broker or futures commission merchant, it must obey the rules and regulations of the NFA and the CFTC.

If the hedge fund manager is registered with either the SEC or the CFTC, the investor should ascertain the date of the original registration, and whether there are any civil, criminal or administrative actions outstanding against the hedge fund manager. This information must be filed with either the NFA (for the managed futures industry) or the SEC (for investment advisers).

Outside Service Providers

The investor must document who is the hedge fund manager's outside auditors, prime broker, and legal counsel. Each of these service providers must be contacted.

First, the investor should receive the hedge fund manager's last annual audited financial statement as well as the most current statement. Any questions regarding the financial statements should be directed to the CFO and the outside auditors. Any opinion from the auditors other than an unqualified opinion must be explained by the outside auditors. Additionally, outside auditors are a good source of information regarding the hedge fund manager's accounting system and operations.

The hedge fund manager's prime broker is responsible for executing the hedge fund manager's trades, lending securities to short, and providing short-term financing for leverage. It is essential that the investor contact the prime broker because the prime broker is in the best position to observe the hedge fund manager's trading positions.

There was an incident on President's Day in 1997 where a prime broker contacted one of its hedge fund manager clients and demanded a margin call. In a margin call the prime broker demands that the hedge fund manager post more cash or collateral to cover either her short positions or her borrowing from the manager.

Margin calls can happen for several reasons. First and foremost, a short position can move against a hedge fund manager creating a large negative balance with the hedge fund manager's prime broker. To protect itself from the credit exposure to the hedge fund manager, the prime broker will make a margin call. In effect, demanding that the hedge fund manager either put up cash or more securities as collateral to cover the prime broker's credit exposure to the hedge fund manager.

Finally, the investor should speak with the hedge fund manager's outside counsel. This is important for two reasons. First, outside counsel is typically responsible for keeping current all regulatory registrations of the hedge fund manager. Second, outside counsel can inform the investor of any criminal, civil, or administrative actions that might be pending against the hedge fund manager. Outside counsel is also responsible for preparing the hedge fund managers offering document. This is with whom the investor will negotiate should an investment be made with the hedge fund manager.

Strategic Review

The second phase of due diligence is a review of the hedge fund manager's investment strategy. This should include a clear statement of the hedge fund manager's style, the markets in which she invests, what competitive advantage the hedge fund manager brings to the table, the source of her investment ideas, and what benchmark, if any, is appropriate for the hedge fund.

Investment Style

Earlier in this chapter, we listed several styles of hedge fund managers. While these are the major hedge fund styles, they are by no means exhaustive. The creativity of hedge fund managers is such that there are as many styles as there are colors of the rainbow.

For instance, relative value arbitrage is a hedge fund style frequently seen. Recall that relative value arbitrage compares two similar securities and buys the security that is "cheap" relative to the other security while selling the security that is relatively "rich." Relative value arbitrage can be subdivided into economic arbitrage and statistical arbitrage. Economic arbitrage compares the pricing fundamentals of two similar securities to determine if the prices set by the market are inconsistent with the fundamentals. If an inconsistency is identified, the "cheap" security is purchased and the "rich" security is sold. The hedge fund manager will hold on to these positions until the market corrects itself and the two security prices are in proper balance. This holding period may be a day, week, or several months. In some cases, it may be necessary to hold the two securities to maturity (in the case of bonds).Conversely, "stat arb" is another form of relative value arbitrage where the trading is based not on economic fundamentals, but rather, on statistical anomalies that temporarily occur in the market. Typically, these anomalies occur only for a moment or for a day at most. Consequently, statistical arbitrage is a very short-term relative value trading program with positions entered and exited within the same trading day.

Additionally, economic relative value or statistical arbitrage can occur in the fixed income, equity, or convertible bond markets. Exhibit 25.17 diagrams how an investment strategy should be documented.

Investment Markets

Next, the investor should document in which markets the hedge fund manager invests. Recall this was one of our basic questions presented earlier in this chapter. For an equity long/short manager, the answer is obvious. Recall the following language:

EXHIBIT 25.17   Documenting a Hedge Fund Investment Strategy

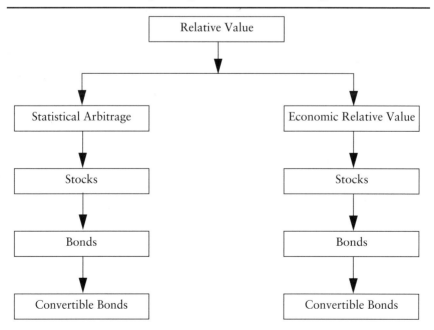

> The Fund's investment objective is to make investments in public securities that generate a long-term return in excess of that generated by the overall U.S. public equity market while reducing the market risk of the portfolio through selective short positions.

From this statement, it is clear that this manager is an equity long/short manager investing in the U.S. equity market.

For other hedge fund managers, however, the answer is not so obvious. For instance, global macro managers typically have the broadest investment mandate possible. They can invest across the world equity, bond, commodity and currency markets. Pinning down a global macro manager may be akin to picking up mercury. Nonetheless, the investor should document as best she can in what markets the hedge fund manager invests. If the hedge fund manager is a global macro manager, the investor may have to accept that the manager can and will invest in whatever market it deems fit.

The investor should also determine the extent to which the hedge fund manager invests in derivative securities. Derivatives are a two-edged sword. On the one hand they can hedge an investment portfolio and reduce risk. On the other hand, they can increase the leverage of the hedge fund and magnify the risks taken by the hedge fund manager.

Investment Securities

Closely related to the investment markets are the types of securities in which the hedge fund manager invests. For some strategies, it will be straightforward. For instance, the sample language provided above indicates that the hedge fund manager will invest in the stock of U.S. companies.

However, other strategies will not be so clear. Recall the language where one hedge fund manager listed every security, futures contract, option, and derivative contract "in each case whether now existing or created in the future." This manager needs to be pinned down, and the due diligence checklist is the place to do it.

Oftentimes, hedge fund disclosure documents are drafted in very broad and expansive terms. The reason is that the hedge fund manager does not want to be legally bound into an investment corner. The purpose of due diligence is not to legally bind the hedge fund manager but to document the types of securities necessary to effect her investment strategy.

It is very important that the investor determine the hedge fund manager's strategy for using derivatives, the type of derivatives used, and in which markets will derivatives be purchased. Of particular concern is the extent to which hedge fund manager may "short volatility."

Shorting volatility is a strategy where hedge fund managers sell out of the money call or put options against their investment portfolio. If the options expire unexercised, the hedge fund manager receives the option premiums and this increases the return for the hedge fund. However, if the options are exercised against the hedge fund manager, significant negative results may occur.

Benchmark

Establishing a benchmark for hedge fund managers is one of the thorniest issues facing the industry. One reason is the skill-based nature of their investment styles. Manager skill cannot be captured by a passive securities benchmark. Skill, in fact, is orthogonal to passive investing.

Second, most hedge fund managers apply investment strategies that cannot be captured by a passive securities index. For instance, it can be argued that a long-only passive equity index is not an appropriate benchmark for derivative instruments, such as options, that have non-linear payout functions. Passive securities indices do not reflect non-linear payout strategies.

Last, hedge fund managers tend to maintain concentrated portfolios. The nature of this concentration makes the investment strategy of the hedge fund manager distinct from a broad-based securities index.

Nonetheless, some performance measure must be established for the hedge fund manager. For instance, if the hedge fund manager runs a long/short equity fund concentrating on the semi-conductor sector of the technology industry, a good benchmark would be the SOX/semi-conductor index maintained by the Philadelphia Stock Exchange.

If the hedge fund manager does not believe that any index is appropriate for his strategy, then a *hurdle rate* must be established. Hurdle rates are most appropriate for absolute return hedge fund managers whose rate of return is not dependent upon the general economic prospects of a sector or a broad-based market index. Generally, these rates are set at the Treasury bill or LIBOR rate plus a spread.

Competitive Advantage

Recall our question posed earlier in this chapter: What makes the hedge fund manager so smart? We made the point that the best hedge fund managers know the exact nature of their competitive advantage, and how to exploit it. This advantage must be documented as part of the due diligence process.

Another way to ask this question, is: What makes the hedge fund manager different from the other managers? For instance, there are many merger arbitrage managers. However, some invest only in announced deals while some speculate on potential deals. Some merger arbitrage funds invest in cross-border deals while others stay strictly within the boundaries of their domicile. Some participate in deals only of a certain market capitalization ranges while others are across the board. And finally, some merger arbitrage funds use options and convertible securities to capture the merger premium while others invest only in the underlying equity.

As another competitive advantage, some merger arbitrage experts develop large in-house legal staffs to review the regulatory (anti-trust) implications of the announced deals. These managers rely on their expert legal analysis to determine whether the existing merger premium is rich or cheap. They exploit the legal issues associated with the merger instead of the economic issues.

Current Portfolio Position

This part of the due diligence is meant to provide a current snapshot of the hedge fund. First, the investor should ascertain the fund's current long versus short exposure. Additionally, the investor should determine the amount of cash that the hedge fund manager is keeping and why. Too much cash indicates an investment strategy that may be stuck in neutral.

The investor should also ascertain how many investments the hedge fund manager currently maintains in the fund. As we have previously discussed, hedge fund managers typically run concentrated exposure. Therefore, the investor is exposed to more stock specific risk than market risk. Again, this is the essence of hedge fund management: hedge fund managers do not take market risk, they take security specific risk. This stock or security specific risk is the source of the hedge fund manager's returns.

Last, the investor should ask the hedge fund manager how she has positioned the hedge fund portfolio in light of current market conditions. This should provide insight not only as to how the hedge fund manager views the current financial markets, but also her investment strategy going forward.

Source of Investment Ideas

What is the source of the hedge fund manager's investment ideas? Does she wait until "it just hits her?" Conversely, is there a rigorous process for sourcing investment ideas. Idea generation is what hedge fund investing is all about. This is the source of the manager's skill.

The source of investment ideas is closely tied in with the nature of competitive advantage. The hedge fund manager's competitive advantage could be her research department that generates investment ideas better or faster than other hedge fund managers. Conversely, some hedge fund managers, such as merger arbitrage managers, wait for deals to be announced in the market.

In addition, the investor should determine in which type of market does the hedge fund manager's ideas work best. Do they work best in bear markets, bull markets, flat markets, or none at all. For instance, an absolute return hedge fund manager (a manager with a hurdle rate for a benchmark) should be agnostic with respect to the direction of the market. Otherwise, an argument could be made that the hedge fund manager's performance should be compared to a market index.

Capacity

A frequent issue with hedge fund managers is the capacity of their investment strategy. Hedge fund manager's have investment strategies that are more narrowly focused than traditional long-only managers. As a consequence, their investment strategies frequently have limited capacity. This is more the case for hedge fund managers that target small sectors of the economy or segments of the financial markets.

For instance, the convertible bond market is much smaller than the U.S. equity market. Consequently, a convertible bond hedge fund manager may have more limited capacity than an equity long/short manager. Global macro hedge fund managers, with their global investment mandate, have the largest capacity. This large capacity is derived from their unlimited ability to invest across financial instruments, currencies, borders, and commodities.

Capacity is an important issue for the investor because the hedge fund manager might dilute her skill by allowing a greater number of investors into the hedge fund than is optimal from an investment standpoint. This may result in too much money chasing too few deals.

PERFORMANCE REVIEW

List of Funds and Assets Under Management

First, the investor should document how many hedge funds the hedge fund manager advises and the assets under management for each fund. The investor should know the size of the hedge fund manager's empire. This is important not only for the collection of performance data, but also it may give the investor some sense of the hedge fund manager's investment capacity.

There are three important questions to ask. How long has the hedge fund manager been actively managing a hedge fund? Have her performance results been consistent over time? Are the investment strategies the same or different for each hedge fund?

We noted earlier that the attrition rate in the hedge fund is very high, up to 15% a year according to one study. Successful hedge fund managers have a long-term track record with consistent results. However, "long-term" in the hedge fund industry is a relative term. For hedge funds, five years is generally sufficient to qualify as long-term.

Additionally, if a hedge fund manager manages more than one hedge fund, the investment strategy and style should be documented for both. If the hedge funds follow the same style, then the issue of trade allocation must be resolved. The investor should determine how the hedge fund manager decides what trades go into which hedge fund.

Drawdowns

Drawdowns are a common phenomenon in the hedge fund industry. Simply defined, a drawdown is a decline in the net asset value of the hedge fund. Drawdowns are not unique to the hedge fund industry, they also occur in the mutual fund industry. However, in the long-only world of mutual funds, drawdowns are often motivated by declines in market indices. This reflects the market risk associated with mutual funds.

The difference with hedge funds is that they eschew market risk in favor of stock specific risk. The amount of stock specific risk in the hedge fund is reflective of the hedge fund manager's skill level of finding overpriced and underpriced securities regardless of the condition of the general financial markets. Therefore, drawdowns in the hedge fund world indicate a lapse of hedge fund manager skill.

Hedge fund managers often claim that their industry is skill-based. This claim is a two-edged sword. On the one hand, it protects hedge fund managers from being compared to a passive long-only index as a benchmark. On the other hand, it also means that when the hedge fund declines in value, the blame rests solely with the hedge fund manager and not with the condition of the financial markets.

Therefore, it is important to measure how much a lapse of hedge fund manager skill cost the fund, and how long it took for the hedge fund manager to regain her skill and recoup the losses. Last, the hedge fund manager should explain her temporary loss of skill.

Statistical Data

This section covers the basic summary information that is expected of all active managers. The average return over the life of the fund as well as the standard deviation (volatility) of returns and the Sharpe ratio.

As an aside, Sharpe ratios can be misleading statistics when measuring hedge fund performance because of the non-linear strategies that hedge fund managers can pursue.

Additionally, if a benchmark can be identified for the hedge fund, then the systematic risk of the hedge fund with that benchmark should be measured. This statistic is known as the beta of the hedge fund and it measures the extent by which the hedge fund returns move in tandem with the benchmark.

Also, if a benchmark is identified, then an Information Ratio (IR) statistic can be calculated. This is the excess return of the hedge fund (the returns to the hedge fund minus the returns to the benchmark) divided by the standard deviation of the excess returns. The IR measures the amount of active return that is earned for each unit of active risk exposure. As a rule of thumb, successful long-only managers generally earn an IR between 0.25 to 0.50. With respect to hedge funds, an investor should expect to receive an IR between 1 and 1.5.

Withdrawals

Withdrawals can be detrimental to fund performance. If a hedge fund manager is fully invested at the time of a redemption request, fund performance will suffer. First, the hedge fund manager must sell securities to fund the withdrawal. This means transaction costs that would not otherwise be incurred will be charged to the fund and will be borne by all investors. Additionally, to the extent that a hedge fund manager cannot liquidate a portion of her investment strategy on a pro rata basis to fund the withdrawal, there may be a loss to the hedge fund from foregone investment opportunities.

Finally, the less liquid the securities in which the hedge fund manager invests, the greater will be these costs. Equity long/short hedge funds usually have the lowest cost associated with a withdrawal because the equity markets are typically the most liquid markets in which to transact. However, more arcane investment strategies and securities such as mortgage-backed arbitrage can have significant costs associated with a withdrawal.

Recall the incident discussed above with respect to a prime broker executing a margin call on President's Day to a mortgage-backed hedge fund manager. The timing of the margin call had severe implications for fund performance. A withdrawal request is similar to a margin call in that a hedge fund investor demands that the hedge fund manager liquidate some of her positions to fund the redemption request. The results, if unexpected, can have a negative impact of fund performance.

RISK REVIEW

Risk Management

Three important questions must be answered: What risks are managed? How is risk measured? How is risk managed?

First, it is important to determine what risks the hedge fund manage monitors. Does she have limits on the percentage of the portfolio that may be invested in any one company or security? Additionally, does the manager monitor her gross long exposure, gross short exposure, and net market exposure? To what extent can the manager be long and to what extent can she be short the market?

Risk can be measured through measures of standard deviation, semi-variance, Sortino measures, by value-at-risk, and by style analysis. The investor must document what type of risk measurement system the hedge fund manager applies.

Last, the investor must determine how the hedge fund manager manages the risk of her positions. As indicated above, one way to control risk is by setting limits on the size of any investment position. This is particularly important because of the concentrated nature of most hedge fund portfolios.

Another way to manage risk is to set an upper boundary on the standard deviation of the hedge fund's returns. Alternatively, the hedge fund manager could set a limit on the amount of *active risk* (the standard deviation of excess returns) in the hedge fund.

Two additional risks that must be discussed are *short volatility risk* and *counterparty risk*. As already mentioned, hedge fund managers can sell options as part of their investment strategy. When a hedge fund manager sells an option, she collects the option premium at the time of the sale. If the option expires unexercised, the hedge fund manager keeps the option premium and the hedge fund's returns will be increased by the amount of the option premium. However, if the option is exercised against the manager, this may have a negative impact on the hedge fund performance.

Additionally, hedge fund managers frequently trade in over-the-counter derivative instruments. These are essentially private contracts between two parties: the hedge fund manager and her counterparty. The counterparty to such trades is often a large Wall Street investment house or large money center bank. Nonetheless, when a hedge fund manager negotiates these custom derivative contracts with a counterparty, the hedge fund manager takes on the credit risk that her counterparty will fulfill its obligations under the derivative contract.

Exchange-traded derivative contracts such as listed futures and options contracts do not have this counterparty risk because the clearinghouse for the exchange will make good on any defaulted contract. However, in the over-the-counter world of derivatives, the hedge fund manager must rely on its counterparty's good faith and credit to perform its obligations under the derivative contract.

In sum, the investor must determine how the hedge fund manager looks at risk, what are the most important risk exposures in the portfolio, and how the hedge fund manager reacts to excess risk.

Leverage

Some hedge fund managers specifically limit the leverage they will employ. This limit is typically set in the limited partnership agreement so that the hedge fund manager is legally bound to stay within a leverage limit. Nonetheless, within the leverage limit the hedge fund manager has considerable flexibility. Also, many hedge fund managers never set a limit on the amount of leverage that they may apply.

If leverage is applied, the investor should document the highest amount of leverage used by the hedge fund manager as well as the average leverage of the fund since inception. As we indicated earlier, one of the reasons for the demise of Long Term Capital Management was the massive amount of leverage employed in its strategy. While leverage can be a successful tool if employed correctly, it will have a significantly detrimental impact on hedge fund performance during periods of minimal liquidity.

Risk Officer

Last, and most important, who monitors risk? The chief investment officer and the chief risk officer should not be the same person. If so, there is a conflict in risk control because risk management should function separately from investment management. Without this independence, there can be no assurance that risk will be properly identified and managed.

Often the chief financial officer serves as the risk officer. This is a good solution as long as the CFO is not also the chief investment officer (rarely is this the case). In the smaller hedge fund shops, this is the usual procedure. However, larger hedge funds have established a chief risk officer who monitors the hedge fund manager's positions across all hedge funds and separate accounts.

If the amount of leverage is not contractually specified in the limited partnership agreement, then the risk manager must set the limit. Even if there is a limit on leverage, the risk manager must monitor the leverage in each hedge fund to ensure that it is consistent with that fund's investment strategy. Finally, the risk manager should establish the position limits for any one investment within a hedge fund portfolio.

ADMINISTRATIVE REVIEW

Civil, Criminal, and Regulatory Actions

The hedge fund manager should fully disclose all civil, criminal and regulatory actions against the hedge fund manager or any of its principals over the past five years. Normally a three-year history is asked for, but five years is also common.

The hedge fund manager may balk at listing civil or criminal actions previously or currently pending against its principals. However, in addition to the expected red flags that legal actions raise, this is necessary information for two more reasons.

First, a history of civil or criminal actions filed against one of the hedge fund manager's principals is a valuable insight into that principal's character. Given the litigious nature of current society, it would not be unusual for a principal to be involved in a civil lawsuit outside the operating business of the hedge fund. However, a pattern of such lawsuits might indicate trouble.

Second, lawsuits are distracting. They take a toll in terms of time, money, and emotions. Such a distraction could impede a principal's performance with respect to the hedge fund.

Employee Turnover

Given the skill-based nature (or claim, thereof) of the hedge fund industry, a hedge fund manager's personnel is its most valuable resource. This is where the skill resides.

A complete list of hired and departing employees is important for three reasons. First, as previously discussed, a good hedge fund manager knows her competitive advantage and how to exploit it. One type of competitive advantage is the people employed by the hedge fund manager. Preserving this workforce may be one of the keys to maintaining her advantage.

Second, similar to lawsuits, turnover is distracting. It takes time, money, and sometimes emotions to recruit new talent. Additionally, new employees take time to come up the learning curve and comprehend all of the nuances of a hedge fund manager's investment strategy.

Last, high employee turnover may be indicative of a volatile Chief Executive Officer. If the employees do not have faith enough in the CEO to remain with the hedge fund manager, why should the investor?

Account Representative

This is very simple. A primary contact person should be designated. This representative will handle issues regarding performance, withdrawals, increased investment, distributions, and meetings. Ideally it should be someone other than the Chief Executive Officer, whose job it is to keep the hedge fund manager on course rather than take client phone calls.

Disaster Planning

Disaster planning was particularly important with the Y2K concerns. However, its import has not been diminished with the passing of the new millennium. Unfortunately, the terrorist attacks of September 11, 2001 demonstrated the continued need for disaster planning. Hedge fund managers employ sophisticated trading models that require considerable computing power. This is especially true for those hedge fund managers that employ quantitative arbitrage models.

The hedge fund manager should have a recovery plan if a natural or other disaster shuts down its trading and investment operations. This plan could be leasing space at a disaster recover site owned by a computer service provider, a back up trading desk at another remote location, or the sharing of facilities with other trading desks.

Consider the simple case of a power "brown-out." How would the hedge fund manager monitor its investment positions? How would it monitor its risks? How would it trade without the use of its analytical computer programs? The hedge fund manager must have a back-up plan to address these questions.

LEGAL REVIEW

Type of Investment

Most hedge fund investments are structured as limited partnerships. Limited partnership units are purchased by the investor where the number of units that the investor owns entitles her to a pro rata share of the returns earned by the hedge fund.

Some hedge fund managers offer separate accounts for their investors. These are individual investment accounts that are dedicated solely to one investor. There are pros and cons of both types of investments.

In a limited partnership structure, the hedge fund manager acts as the general partner, and invests a portion of her own capital in the hedge fund side by side that of the limited partners. This ensures an alignment of interests between the hedge fund manager and her investors.

Also, a limited partnership provides a "financial firewall" for the investor. Limited partnership laws protect the limited partners so that they are at risk only to the extent of their capital committed. Therefore, the limited partner's maximum downside is known with certainty. Any excess risk is borne by the hedge fund manager as the general partner.

Separate accounts do not have the advantages of alignment of interests or financial firewalls. There is more risk associated with this type of investment. However, there are two advantages of a separate account.

First, the investor need only worry about her own motivations. In our section on Performance Review, we discussed how withdrawals of capital from a hedge fund can be detrimental to the fund's performance. Therefore, the withdrawal of capital by one limited partner could disadvantage the remaining investors in the hedge fund. With a separate account, this issue does not exist because there is only one investor per account.

Second, separate accounts facilitate reporting and risk management. In a limited partnership, the investor receives her pro rata share of the fund's return and owns a pro rata share of each individual investment. Reporting these pro rata shares, or aggregating them for risk management purposes, can be cumbersome. However, with a separate account, all gains, losses, and investments are owned 100% by the investor. This simplifies any reporting or risk management requirements.

Fees

The standard in the hedge fund industry is "1 and 20." This means a 1% management fee and a 20% profit sharing or incentive fee. However, this structure is by no means uniform. Some of the larger hedge funds charge up to a 3% management fee and a 30% incentive fee, while some newer hedge funds may charge less than the standard "1 and 20."

In addition to the fee structure, the investor should determine how frequently fees are collected. Typically, management fees are collected on a quarterly basis, but they may also be structured semiannually or annually. Incentive fees are usually collected on an annual basis.

The investor should also determine if there is a "high watermark" or a "clawback" with respect to the incentive fees. A high watermark means that a hedge fund manager cannot collect any incentive fee until she exceeds the highest previous net asset value.

This is particularly important because of the nature of drawdowns. If a hedge fund manager suffers a drawdown, she should not collect any incentive fees while she recoups this lost value. Incentive fees should begin only after the manager has regained the lost fund value and produced new value for her investors. Most hedge funds have high watermarks.

Clawbacks are rare in the hedge fund world. They are much more common in the private equity marketplace. As its name implies, a clawback provision allows the investors in the fund to "claw back" incentive fees previously received by the hedge fund manager. Clawback arrangements generally apply if, over the life of the fund, the hedge fund manager has failed to produce an agreed upon hurdle rate.

Lockups and Redemptions

While lock-up periods are the standard in the private equity world, they are much less common in hedge funds. However, more and more hedge funds are requiring lock-up periods for their investors. A lock-up period is just that: the investors capital is "locked-up" for a designated period. During this time, the investor cannot redeem any part of her investment.

Lock-up periods provide two benefits. First, they give the hedge fund manager time to implement her investment strategy. Imagine how difficult it might be to implement a sophisticated investment strategy while at the same time worrying about how to fund redemption requests.

Second, we have already pointed out that ill-timed withdrawals of capital by one limited partner in a hedge fund can disadvantage the remaining investors. During the lock-up period, this is not an issue. Nervous investors have no choice but to have their capital committed for a specified period of time. Confident investors can be assured that their investment will not be undermined by a fickle limited partner.

Withdrawals and redemptions are specified in the limited partnership agreement. Some hedge funds provide monthly liquidity, but the norm is quarterly or semi-annual redemption rights. Also, limited partners typically must give notice to the hedge fund manager that they intend to redeem. This notice period can be from 30 to 90 days in advance of the redemption. The purpose of the notice is to give the hedge fund manager the ability to position the hedge fund's portfolio to finance the redemption request.

Subscription Amount

All hedge funds have a minimum subscription amount. Generally, this amount is quite high for two reasons. First, the hedge fund manager needs sufficient investment capital to implement his investment strategy. Second, higher capital commitments ensure that only sophisticated investors with a large net worth will subscribe in the hedge fund. Hedge fund investing is not for the average investor. Rather, they are designed for sophisticated investors who can appreciate and accept the risks associated with hedge funds.

Some hedge funds may also have a maximum subscription amount. This is done so that no single investor becomes too large relative to other investors in the fund. Also, the hedge fund manager may have capacity issues that require limits on an investor's capital contribution.

Advisory Committee

Advisory committees serve as a source of objective input for the hedge fund manager. They are comprised of representatives from the hedge fund manager and investors in the hedge fund.

Advisory committees may provide advice on the valuation of certain investments, particularly illiquid investments. The committee may advise the hedge fund manager when it is time to mark down or mark up an illiquid security where objective market prices are not available.

The advisory committee may also advise the hedge fund manager as to whether she should open up the hedge fund for new investors, and how much more capacity the hedge fund manager should take. Before, allowing new investors into the fund, the hedge fund manager may wish to seek the counsel of the advisory committee to see if the existing investors have concerns about capacity or the types of additional investors that may be allowed to invest.

While advisory committees are a useful device for control by the hedge fund limited partners, they are more common in the private equity world than with hedge funds. We will discuss this point further in our chapter on cross over funds.

REFERENCE CHECKS

Service Providers

We indicated previously, in the Structural Review section, the importance of speaking with a hedge fund manager's primary service providers. For instance, with respect to the outside auditors, the investor should ask when the last audit was conducted and whether the auditors issued an unqualified opinion. Additionally, the investor should inquire about any issues that outside auditors have raised with the hedge fund manager over the course of their engagement.

With respect to the prime broker, the investor should inquire how frequently margin calls have been made, the size of the calls, and whether any calls have not been met. Remember that the prime broker is in the best position to evaluate the market value of the hedge fund manager's investments. A discussion with the prime broker should give the investor a reality check whether or not the hedge fund manager is recognizing the proper value of the hedge fund's portfolio.

Legal counsel is important to check on the veracity of any civil, criminal, or regulatory actions against the hedge fund manager or its principals. This conversation should confirm those actions listed by the hedge fund manager under the Administrative Review. Last, the legal counsel can confirm the status of any regulatory registrations under which the hedge fund manager operates.

Existing Clients

Talking to existing clients is a necessary step to check the veracity of the hedge fund manager's statements and to measure his "client responsiveness."

Typical questions to ask are: Have the financial reports been timely? Have the reports been easy to understand? Has the hedge fund manager responded positively to questions about financial performance? Has the hedge fund manager done what she said she would do (maintain her investment strategy)? What concerns does the current investor have regarding the hedge fund manager of the hedge fund's performance? Would the existing client invest more money with the hedge fund manager?

In sum, this is a chance for a prospective investor to ask current investors for their candid opinion of the hedge fund manager. If the prospective investor has any doubts regarding the hedge fund manager, these doubts should be either confirmed or dispelled.

CHAPTER 26

Private Equity

Mark J. P. Anson, CFA, Ph.D., CPA, Esq.
Chief Investment Officer
CalPERS

The private equity sector purchases the private stock or equity-linked securities of non-public companies that are expected to go public or provides the capital for public companies (or their divisions) that may wish to go private. The key component in either case is the private nature of the securities purchased. Private equity, by definition, is not publicly traded. Therefore, investments in private equity are illiquid. Investors in this marketplace must be prepared to invest for the long haul; investment horizons may be as extended as 5 to 10 years.

"Private equity" is a generic term that encompasses four distinct strategies in the market for private investing. First, there is venture capital, the financing of start-up companies. Second, there are leveraged buyouts (LBOs) where public companies repurchase all of their outstanding shares and turn themselves into private companies. Third, there is mezzanine financing, a hybrid of private debt and equity financing. Last, there is distressed debt investing. These are private equity investments in established (as opposed to start-up) but troubled companies.

VENTURE CAPITAL

Venture capital is the supply of equity financing to start-up companies that do not have a sufficient track record to attract investment capital from traditional sources (e.g., the public markets or lending institutions). Entrepreneurs that develop business plans require investment capital to

671

implement those plans. However, these start-up ventures often lack tangible assets that can be used as collateral for a loan. In addition, start-up companies are unlikely to produce positive earnings for several years. Negative cash flows are another reason why banks and other lending institutions as well as the public stock market are unwilling to provide capital to support the business plan.

It is in this uncertain space where nascent companies are born that venture capitalists operate. Venture capitalists finance these high-risk, illiquid, and unproven ideas by purchasing senior equity stakes while the firms are still privately held. The ultimate goal is to make a buck. Venture capitalists are willing to underwrite new ventures with untested products and bear the risk of no liquidity only if they can expect a reasonable return for their efforts. Often, venture capitalists set expected target rates of return of 33% or more to support the risks they bear. Successful start-up companies funded by venture capital money include Cisco Systems, Cray Research, Microsoft, and Genentech.

Initially, ERISA guidelines prohibited pension funds from investing in venture capital funds because of their illiquid and high-risk status. In 1979, the Department of Labor (which oversees ERISA) issued a clarification of the prudent person rule to indicate that venture capital and other high-risk investments should not be considered on a stand-alone basis, but rather on a portfolio basis. In addition, the rule clarified that the prudent person test is based on an investment review process and not on the ultimate outcome of investment results. Therefore, as long as a pension fund investment fiduciary follows sufficient due diligence in considering the portfolio effects of investing in venture capital, the prudent person test is met. The change in the prudent person rule allowed pension funds for the first time to wholly endorse venture capital investing.

Exhibit 26.1 demonstrates the returns to venture capital compared to the S&P 500 over a 1-year, 3-year, 5-year, and 10-year investment horizon (1991–2000). We include the returns for late stage, early stage, and balanced venture capital funds. We can see that over each time horizon, the returns to venture capital dominate those of the S&P 500. This should be expected because investors should be compensated for the risk of start-up companies and the lack of liquidity of their holdings.

The 1-year, 3-year, and 5-year returns to venture capital appear excessive compared to the broader stock market. These returns were fueled by excessively optimistic expectations concerning the ability of new Internet companies to earn extraordinary profits as well as an extraordinarily robust U.S. economy.

A more realistic appraisal of venture capital returns is the 10-year horizon. Over a full economic cycle, venture capital returns should be expected to earn a premium over the public stock market of 5% to 7%.[1] Over the 10-year cycle, for example, balanced and late stage venture capital investments earned a premium over the S&P 500 of 8% and 10%, respectively. Exhibit 26.1 demonstrates this long-term premium.

The new millennium began with a bang, but by the end of its first full year of 2000, ended with a whimper. The Nasdaq stock market, the primary listing ground for private companies going public through IPOs, came crashing down to earth. Throughout the late 1990s, the valuations associated with companies listed on the Nasdaq became inflated compared to companies listed in the S&P 500 and the Dow Jones 30 Industrial Companies. The Nasdaq tracked closely the valuations of the S&P 500 and the Dow Jones until the beginning of 1999. Then valuations began to diverge with the Nasdaq soaring in value compared to the S&P 500 and the Dow Jones. This created a valuation "bubble" fueled by the belief that technology stocks would take over the world. However, the bubble in burst in 2000 when new technology companies failed to produce the earnings and revenue growth forecast by optimistic Wall Street analysts. By the beginning of 2001, these three stock indices had converged back to similar values.

Going forward in the new decade of the 2000s, rational pricing has come back to the stock market as well as the venture capital market. The decline in optimism has reduced the cash flows to venture capital funds. Commitments to venture capital funds in the first six months of 2001 were $21.4 billion, a decline of $27.7 billion from the first six months of 2000. Also, there were only 18 initial public offerings of U.S. companies in the first quarter of 2001, compared to 135 IPOs in the first quarter of 2000.

EXHIBIT 26.1   Returns to Venture Capital

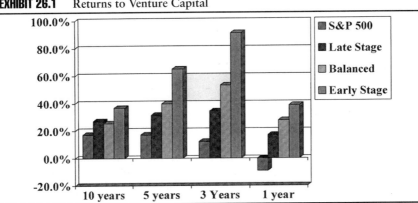

Source: Thomson Financial Venture Economics

---

[1] See Keith Ambachtsheer, "How Should Pension Funds Managed Risk," *Journal of Applied Corporate Finance* (Summer 1998), pp. 1–6.

The Role of a Venture Capitalist

Venture capitalists have two roles within the industry. Raising money from investors is just the first part. The second is to invest that capital with start-up companies.

Venture capitalists are not passive investors. Once they invest in a company, they take an active role either in an advisory capacity or as a director on the board of the company. They monitor the progress of the company, implement incentive plans for the entrepreneurs and management, and establish financial goals for the company.

Besides providing management insight, venture capitalists usually have the right to hire and fire key mangers, including the original entrepreneur. They also provide access to consultants, accountants, lawyers, investment bankers, and most importantly, other business that might purchase the start-up company's product.

In seeking viable start-up companies to finance, venture capitalists focus on certain aspects of the entrepreneur's business opportunity. These are a business plan, intellectual property rights, prior history of the company, prior history of the management team, regulatory matters, and an exit plan.

Business Plans

The most important document upon which a venture capitalist will base her decision to invest in a start-up company is the business plan. The business plan must be comprehensive, coherent, and internally consistent. It must clearly state the business strategy, identify the niche that the new company will fill, and describe the resources needed to fill that niche.

The business plan also reflects the start-up management team's ability to develop and present an intelligent and strategic plan of action. Therefore, the business plan not only describes the business opportunity but also gives the venture capitalist an insight to the viability of the management team.

Last, the business plan must be realistic. One part of every business plan is the assumptions about revenue growth, cash burn rate, additional rounds of capital injection, and expected date of profitability and/or IPO status. The financial goals stated in the business plan must be achievable. Additionally, financial milestones identified in the business plan can become important conditions for the vesting of management equity, the release of deferred investment commitments, and the control of the board of directors.

Intellectual Property Rights

Most start-ups in the technology and other growth sectors base their business opportunity on the claim to proprietary technology. It is very important that a start-up's claim and rights to that intellectual property be absolute. Any intellectual property owned by the company must be clearly and unequivocally assigned to the company by third parties (usually the entrepreneur and management team). A structure where the entrepreneur still owns the intellectual property but licenses it to the start-up company is disfavored by venture capitalists because license agreements can expire or be terminated, leaving the venture capitalist with a shell of a start-up company.

Generally, before a venture capitalist invests with a start-up company, it will conduct patent and trademark searches, seek the opinion of a patent counsel, and possibly ask third parties to confidentially evaluate the technology owned by the start-up company.

Additionally, the venture capitalist may ask key employees to sign non-competition agreements, where they agree not to start another company or join another company operating in the same sector as the start-up for a reasonable period of time. Key employees may also be asked to sign non-disclosure agreements because protecting a start-up company's proprietary technology is an essential element to success.

Prior Operating History

Venture capitalists are not always the first investors in a start-up company. In fact, they may be the third source of financing for a company. Many start-up companies begin by seeking capital from friends, family members, and business associates. Next they may seek a so called "angel investor": a wealthy private individual or an institution that invests capital with the company but does not take an active role in managing or directing the strategy of the company. Then come the venture capitalists.

As a result, a start-up company may already have a prior history before presenting its business plan to a venture capitalist. At this stage, venture capitalists ensure that the start-up company does not have any unusual history such as a prior bankruptcy or failure.

The venture capitalist will also closely review the equity stakes that have been previously provided to family, friends, business associates, and angel investors. These equity stakes should be clearly identified in the business plan and any unusual provisions must be discussed. Equity interests can include common stock, preferred stock, convertible securities, rights, warrants, and stock options. There must still be sufficient equity and upside potential for the venture capitalist to invest. Finally, all prior security issues must be properly documented and must comply with applicable securities laws.

The venture capitalist will also check the company's articles of incorporation to determine whether it is in good legal standing in the state of incorporation. Further, the venture capitalist will examine the company's bylaws, and the minutes of any shareholder and board of directors meetings. The minutes of the meetings can indicate whether the company has a clear sense of direction or whether it is mired in indecision.

The Start-up Management Team

The venture capitalist will closely review the resumes of every member of the management team. Academic backgrounds, professional work history, and references will all be checked. Most important to the venture capitalist will be the professional background of the management team. In particular, a management team that has successfully brought a previous start-up company to the IPO stage will be viewed most favorably.

In general, a great management team with a good business plan will be viewed more favorably than a good management team with a great business plan. The best business plan in the world can still fail from inability to execute. Therefore, a management team that has demonstrated a previous ability to follow and execute a business plan will be given a greater chance of success than an unproven management team with a great business opportunity.

However, this is where a venture capitalist can add value. Recognizing a great business opportunity but a weak management team, the venture capitalist can bring his or her expertise to the start-up company as well as bring in other, more seasoned management professionals. While this often creates some friction with the original entrepreneur, the ultimate goal is to make money. Egos often succumb when there is money to be made.

Last, the management team will need a seasoned chief financial officer (CFO). This will be the person primarily responsible for bringing the start-up company public. The CFO will work with the investment bankers to establish the price of the company's stock at the initial public offering. Since the IPO is often the exit strategy for the venture capitalist as well as some of the founders and key employees, it is critical that the CFO have IPO experience.

Legal and Regulatory Issues

We have already touched on some of the legal issues regarding non-competition agreements, non-disclosure agreements, and proper filings for the issuance of equity and debt securities. In addition, the venture capitalist must also determine if patent protection is needed for the start-up's proprietary intellectual property, and if so, initiate the legal proceedings.

Also, in certain industries, federal regulatory approval is necessary before a product can be sold in the United States. Nowhere is this more important than the biotechnology and healthcare sectors. The business plan for the company must also address the time lag between product development and regulatory approval. Additionally, the venture capitalist must consider the time lag before operating profits will be achieved after regulatory approval of a new healthcare product.

Finally, there should be no litigation associated with the start-up company or its management team. Litigation takes time, money, and emotional wear and tear. It is can be a distraction for the company and its key employees. Outstanding or imminent litigation will raise the hurdle rate even higher before a venture capitalist will invest.

Exit Plan

Eventually, the venture capitalist must liquidate her investment in the start-up company to realize a gain for herself and her investors. When a venture capitalist reviews a business plan she will keep in mind the timing and probability of an exit strategy.

An exit strategy is another way the venture capitalist can add value beyond providing start-up financing. Venture capitalists often have many contacts with established operating companies. An established company may be willing to acquire the start-up company for its technology as part of a strategic expansion of its product line. Alternatively, venture capitalists maintain close ties with investment bankers. These bankers will be necessary if the start-up company decides to seek an IPO. In addition, a venture capitalist may ask other venture capitalists to invest in the start-up company. This helps to spread the risk as well as provide additional sources of contacts with operating companies and investment bankers.

Venture capitalists almost always invest in the convertible preferred stock of the start-up company. There may be several rounds (or series) of financing of preferred stock before a start-up company goes public. Convertible preferred shares are the accepted manner of investment because these shares carry a priority over common stock in terms of dividends, voting rights, and liquidation preferences. Furthermore, venture capitalists have the option to convert their shares to common stock to enjoy the benefits of an IPO.

Other investment structures used by venture capitalists include convertible notes or debentures that provide for the conversion of the principal amount of the note or bond into either common or preferred shares at the option of the venture capitalist. Convertible notes and debentures may also be converted upon the occurrence of an event such as a merger, acquisition, or IPO. Venture capitalists may also be granted warrants to purchase the common equity of the start-up company as well as stock rights in the event of an IPO.

Other exit strategies used by venture capitalists are redemption rights and put options. Usually, these strategies are used as part of a company reorganization. Redemption rights and put options are generally not favored because they do not provide as large a rate of return as an acquisition or IPO. These strategies are often used as a last resort when there are no other viable alternatives. Redemption rights and put options are usually negotiated at the time the venture capitalist makes an investment in the start-up company (often called the Registration Rights Agreement).

Usually, venture capitalists require no less than the minimum return provided for in the liquidation preference of a preferred stock investment. Alternatively, the redemption rights or put option might be established by a common stock equivalent value that is usually determined by an investment banking appraisal. Last redemption rights or put option values may be based on a multiple of sales or earnings. Some redemption rights take the highest of all three valuation methods: the liquidation preference, the appraisal value, or the earnings/sales multiple.

In sum, there are many issues a venture capitalist must sort through before funding a start-up company. These issues range from identifying the business opportunity to sorting through legal and regulatory issues. Along the way, the venture capital must assess the quality of the management team, prior capital infusions, status of proprietary technology, operating history (if any) of the company, and timing and likelihood of an exit strategy.

Venture Capital Investment Vehicles

As the interest for venture capital investments has increased, venture capitalists have responded with new vehicles for venture financing. These include limited partnerships, limited liability companies, and venture capital fund of funds.[2]

Limited Partnerships

The predominant form of venture capital investing in the United States is the limited partnership. Venture capital funds operate either as "3(c)(1)" or "3(c)(7)" funds to avoid registration as an investment company under the Investment Company Act of 1940.

As a limited partnership, all income and capital gains flow through the partnership to the limited partner investors. The partnership itself is not taxed. The appeal of the limited partnership vehicle has increased since 1996 with the "Check the Box" provision of the U.S. tax code.

---

[2] There are also corporate venture funds. However, they do not provide a vehicle for outside investors.

Previously, limited partnerships had to meet several tests to determine if their predominant operating characteristics resembled more a partnership than a corporation. Such characteristics included, for instance, a limited term of existence. Failure to qualify as a limited partnership would mean double taxation for the investment fund; first at the fund level and second, at the investor level.

This changed with the U.S. Internal Revenue Services decision to let entities simply decide their own tax status by checking a box on their annual tax form as to whether they wished to be taxed as a corporation or as a partnership. "Checking the box" greatly encouraged investment funds to establish themselves as a limited partnership.

Limited partnerships are generally formed with an expected life of 7 to 10 years with an option to extend the limited partnership for another 1 to 5 years. The limited partnership is managed by a general partner who has day-to-day responsibility for managing the venture capital fund's investments as well as general liability for any lawsuits that may be brought against the fund. Limited partners, as their name implies, have only a limited (investor) role in the partnership. They do not partake in the management of the fund and they do not bear any liability beyond their committed capital.

All partners in the fund will commit to a specific investment amount at the formation of the limited partnership. However, the limited partners do not contribute money to the fund until it is called down or "taken down" by the general partner. Usually, the general partner will give one to two months notice of when it intends to make additional capital calls on the limited partners. Capital calls are made when the general partner has found a start-up company in which to invest. The general partner can make capital calls up to the amount of the limited partners' initial commitments.

An important element of limited partnership venture funds is that the general partner/venture capitalist has also committed investment capital to the fund. This assures the limited partners of an alignment of interests with the venture capitalist. Typically, limited partnership agreements specify a percentage or dollar amount of capital that the general partner must commit to the partnership.

Limited Liability Companies

A recent phenomenon in the venture capital industry is the limited liability company (LLC). Similar to a limited partnership, all items of net income or loss as well as capital gains are passed through to the shareholders in the LLC. Also, like a limited partnership, an LLC must adhere to the safe harbors of the Investment Company Act of 1940. In addition,

LLCs usually have a life of 7 to 10 years with possible options to extend for another 1 to 5 years.

The managing director of an LLC acts like the general partner of a limited partnership. She has management responsibility for the LLC including the decision to invest in start-up companies the committed capital of the LLC's shareholders. The managing director of the LLC might itself be another LLC or a corporation. The same is true for limited partnerships; the general partner need not be an individual, it can be a legal entity like a corporation.

In sum, LLCs and limited partnerships accomplish the same goal— the pooling of investor capital into a central fund from which to make venture capital investments. The choice is dependent upon the type of investor sought. If the venture capitalist wishes to raise funds from a large number of passive and relatively uninformed investors, the limited partnership vehicle is the preferred venue. However, if the venture capitalist intends to raise capital from a small group of knowledgeable investors, the LLC is preferred.

The reason is twofold. First, LLCs usually have more specific shareholder rights and privileges. These privileges are best utilized with a small group of well-informed investors. Second, an LLC structure provides shareholders with control over the sale of additional shares in the LLC to new shareholders. This provides the shareholders with more power with respect to the twin issues of increasing the LLC's pool of committed capital and from whom that capital will be committed.

Venture Capital Fund of Funds

A venture capital fund of funds is a venture pool of capital that, instead of investing directly in start-up companies, invests in other venture capital funds. The venture capital fund of funds is a relatively new phenomenon in the venture capital industry. The general partner of a fund of funds does not select start-up companies in which to invest. Instead, she selects the best venture capitalists with the expectation that they will find appropriate start-up companies to fund.

A venture capital fund of funds offers several advantages to investors. First, the investor receives broad exposure to a diverse range of venture capitalists, and in turn, a wide range of start-up investing. Second, the investor receives the expertise of the fund of funds manager in selecting the best venture capitalists with whom to invest money. Last, a fund of funds may have better access to popular, well-funded venture capitalists whose funds may be closed to individual investors. In return for these benefits, investors pay a management fee (and, in some cases, an incentive fee) to the fund of funds manager. The management fee can range from 0.5% to 2% of the net assets managed.

Fund of fund investing also offers benefits to the venture capitalists. First, the venture capitalist receives one large investment (from the venture fund of funds) instead of several small investments. This makes fund raising and investor administration more efficient. Second, the venture capitalist interfaces with an experienced fund of funds manager instead of several (potentially inexperienced) investors.

Specialization within the Venture Capital Industry
Like any industry that grows and matures, expansion and maturity lead to specialization. The trend towards specialization in the venture capital industry exists on several levels, by industry, geography, stage of financing, and "special situations." Specialization is the natural by-product of two factors. First, the enormous amount of capital flowing into venture capital funds has encouraged venture capitalists to distinguish themselves from other funds by narrowing their investment focus. Second, the development of many new technologies over the past decade has encouraged venture capitalists to specialize in order to invest most profitably.

Specialization by Industry
Specialization by entrepreneurs is another reason why venture capitalists have tailored their investment domain. Just as entrepreneurs have become more focused in their start-up companies, venture capitalists have followed suit. The biotechnology industry is a good example. Specialized start-up biotech firms have led to specialized venture capital firms.

Specialization by Geography
With the boom in technology companies in Silicon Valley, Los Angeles, and Seattle, it is not surprising to find that many California based venture capital firms concentrate their investments on the west coast of the United States. Not only are there plenty of investment opportunities in this region, it is also easier for the venture capital firms to monitor their investments locally. The same is true for other technology centers in New York, Boston, and Texas.

Regional specialization has the advantage of easier monitoring of invested capital. Also, larger venture capital firms may overlook viable start-up opportunities located in more remote sections of the United States. Regional venture capitalists step in to fill this niche.

The downside of regional specialization is twofold. First, regional concentration may not provide sufficient diversification to a venture capital portfolio. Second, a start-up company in a less-exposed geographic region may have greater difficulty in attracting additional rounds of venture capital financing. This may limit the start-up company's growth potential as well as exit opportunities for the regional venture capitalist.

Stage of Financing

Venture capitalists also distinguish themselves by the point at which they will invest in a start-up company. Some venture capitalists provide first stage, or "seed capital" while others wait to invest in companies that are further along in their development. For a first time entrepreneur, seed financing can be difficult to find. Without a prior track record, most venture capitalists are skeptical of new product ideas.

Seed financing is usually in the range of $500,000 to $3 million. First stage venture capitalists tend to be smaller firms because large venture capital firms cannot afford to spend the endless hours with an entrepreneur for a small investment, usually no greater than $1 to $2 million.

A new development to fill this niche is the venture capital "feeder fund." These have been established where large venture capitalists provide capital to seed venture capitalists in return for the opportunity to make a later stage investment in the start-up company if it is successful.

Most venture capital firms invest either in mid or late stage rounds of equity. Later stage financing provides for a quicker return of capital as well as a lower risk investment. Returns are expected to be lower than that for seed financing. In many cases the start-up company has a viable product by the time a second or third round of venture financing is sought. Also, with the increase flow of money into venture funds, venture capitalists have found that they have larger pools of capital to deploy. Later stage financing provides the most efficacious means to deploy large chunks of investor capital.

Special Situation Venture Capital

In any industry, there are always failures. Not every start-up company makes it to the IPO stage. However, this opens another specialized niche in the venture capital industry: the turnaround venture deal. Turnaround deals are as risky as seed financing because the start-up company may be facing pressure from creditors. The turnaround venture capitalist exists because mainstream venture capitalists may not be sufficiently well-versed in restructuring a turnaround situation.

In summary, the growth of the venture capital industry has created the need for venture capital specialists. The range of new business opportunities is now so diverse that it is simply not possible for a single venture capital firm to stay on top of all opportunities in all industries. Therefore, by necessity, venture capitalists have narrowed their investment domain to concentrate on certain niches within the start-up universe. Specialization also leads to differentiation, which allows venture capitalists to distinguish themselves from other investment funds.

LEVERAGED BUYOUTS

Leveraged buyouts are a way to take a company with publicly traded stock private, or a way to put a company in the hands of the current management (sometimes referred to *management buyouts* or *MBOs*). LBOs use the assets or cash flows of the company to secure debt financing either in bonds issued by the corporation or bank loans, to purchase the outstanding equity of the company. In either case, control of the company is concentrated in the hands of the LBO firm and management, and there is no public stock outstanding.

LBOs represent a mechanism to take advantage of a window of opportunity to increase the value of a corporation. Leverage buyouts can be a way to unlock hidden value or exploit existing but underfunded opportunities.

A Theoretical Example of a Leveraged Buyout

In a perfect world, everyone makes money, and no one is unhappy. We will discuss some spectacular LBO failures below. In the meantime, we describe how a theoretical LBO should work.

Imagine a company that is capitalized with a market value of equity of $500 million and a face value of debt of $100 million. The company generates an EBITDA (earnings before interest and taxes plus depreciation and amortization) of $80 million. EBITDA represents the free cash flow from operations that is available for the owners and debtors of the company. This is a 13.3% return on capital for the company's shareholders and debtholders.

An LBO firm offers $700 million to purchase the equity of the company and to pay off the outstanding debt. The debt is paid off at face value of $100 million and $600 million is offered to the equity holders (a 20% premium over the market value) to entice them to tender their shares to the LBO offer.

The $700 million LBO is financed with $600 million in debt (with a 10% coupon rate) and $100 million in equity. The company must pay yearly debt service of $60 million to meet its interest payment obligations. After the LBO, the management of the company improves its operations, streamlines its expenses, and implements better asset utilization. The result is that the cash flow of the company improves from $80 million a year to $120 million a year.[3] By foregoing dividends and using the free cash flow to pay down the existing debt, the management of the company can own the company free and clear in about seven years.

This means that, after seven years, the LBO firm can claim the annual cash flow of $120 million completely for itself. Using a growth rate of 2% per year and a discount rate of 12%, this cash flow is worth:

$$\$120 \text{ million}/(0.12 - 0.02) = \$1.2 \text{ billion}$$

Therefore, the total return on the investment for the LBO transaction is:

$$[\$1.2 \text{ billion}/\$100 \text{ million}]^{1/7} - 1 = 42.6\%$$

The amount of 42.6% represents the annual compounded return for this investment.

As this example demonstrates, the returns to LBO transactions can be quite large, but the holding period may also be commensurately long. At the end of seven years, the management of the company can reap the $1.2 billion value through one of four methods:

1. The management can sell the company to a competitor or another company that wishes to expand into the industry.
2. Through an initial public offering. Consider the example of Gibson Greetings. This company was purchased from RCA for $81 million with all but $1 million financed by bank loans and real estate lease-backs. When Gibson Greetings went public, the 50% equity interest owned by the LBO firm was worth about $140 million, equal to a compound annual rate of return of over 200%.
3. Another LBO. The management of the company doubled its value from $600 million to $1.2 billion. They can now refinance the company in another LBO deal where debt is reintroduced into the company to compensate management for their equity stake. In fact, the existing management may even remain as the operators of the company with an existing stake in the second LBO transaction, providing them with the opportunity for a second go round of leveraged equity appreciation.
4. Straight refinancing. This is similar to number 3 above, where a company reintroduces debt into its balance sheet to pay out a large cash dividend to its equity owners.

---

[3] Studies of LBOs indicate that coporate cash flows increase 96% from the year before the buyout to three years after the buyout. See Michael Jensen, "The Modern Industrial Revolution, Exit, and the Failure of Internal Control Systems," *The New Corporate Finance*, Second Edition, Donald H. Chew, Jr. (ed.) (New York: Irwin/McGraw Hill, 1999).

How LBOs Create Value

The theoretical example given above is a good starting point for describing an LBO transaction, but there is no standard format for a buyout, each company is different, and every LBO deal has different motivations. However, there are five general categories of LBOs that illuminate how these transactions can create value.[4]

LBOs that Improve Operating Efficiency

A company may be bought out because it is shackled with a non-competitive operating structure. For large public companies with widespread equity ownership, the separation of ownership and management can create agency problems with ineffective control mechanisms. Management may have little incentive to create value because it has a small stake in the company, and monitoring of management's actions by a diverse shareholder base is likely to be just as minimal.

Under these circumstances, management is likely to be compensated based on revenue growth. This may result in excess expansion and operating inefficiencies resulting from too much growth. Safeway Corporation is an example where value creation came not from entrepreneurial input, but rather from greater operating efficiencies.

Unlocking an Entrepreneurial Mindset

Another way an LBO can create value is by helping to free management to concentrate on innovations. Another frequent LBO strategy is the unwanted division. Often an operating division of a conglomerate is chained to its parent company and does not have sufficient freedom to implement its business plan. An LBO can free the operating division as a new company, able to control its own destiny. Duracell Corporation which was taken private in 1988 is an excellent example of an entrepreneurial LBO.

The Overstuffed Corporation

One of the mainstream targets of many LBO firms are conglomerates. Conglomerate corporations consist of many different operating divisions or subsidiaries, often in completely different industries. Wall Street analysts are often reluctant to follow or "cover" conglomerates because they do not fit neatly into any one industrial category. As a result, these companies can be misunderstood by the investing public, and therefore, undervalued. Beatrice Foods (a food processing conglomerate) LBO in 1986 purchased for $6.2 billion is an example.

---

[4] For case illustrations, see Chapter 15 in Mark J.P. Anson, *Handbook of Alternative Assets* (New York: John Wiley & Sons, Inc., 2002).

Buy and Build Strategies

Another LBO value creation strategy involves combining several operating companies or divisions through additional buyouts. The LBO firm begins with one buyout and then acquires more companies and divisions that are strategically aligned with the initial LBO portfolio company. The strategy is that there will be synergies from combining several different companies into one. In some respects, this strategy is the reverse of that for conglomerates. Rather than strip a conglomerate down to its most profitable divisions, this strategy pursues a "buy and build" approach. This type of strategy is also known as a "leveraged build-up."

LBO Turnaround Strategies

With a slowdown in the United States as well as global economies throughout 2000, turnaround LBOs have become increasingly popular. Unlike traditional buyout firms that look for successful, mature companies with low debt to equity ratios and stable management, turnaround LBO funds look for underperforming companies with excessive leverage and poor management. The targets for turnaround LBO specialists come from two primary sources: (1) ailing companies on the brink of Chapter 11 bankruptcy and (2) underperforming companies in another LBO fund's portfolio.

LBO Fund Structures

In this section we discuss how LBO funds are structured as well as discuss their fees. While LBO funds are very similar to venture capital funds in design, they are much more creative in fee generation.

Fund Design

Almost all LBO funds are designed as limited partnerships. This is very similar to the way hedge funds and venture capital funds are established. In fact many LBO funds have the name "partners" in their title.

Every LBO fund is run by a general partner. The general partner is typically the LBO firm, and all investment discretion as well as day to day operations vest with the general partner. Limited partners, as their name applies, have a very limited role in the management of the LBO fund. For the most part, limited partners are passive investors who rely on the general partner to source, analyze, perform due diligence, and invest the committed capital of the fund.

Some LBO funds have advisory boards comprised of the general partner and a select group of limited partners. The duties of the advisory board are to advise the general partner on conflicts of issue that may arise as a result of acquiring a portfolio company or collecting fees, provide input as to when it might be judicious to seek independent valuations of the LBO fund's portfolio companies, and to discuss whether dividend payments for portfolio companies should be in cash or securities.

Fees

If there was ever an investment structure that could have its cake and eat it too, it would be an LBO firm. LBO firms have any number of ways to make their money.

First, consider how LBO firms gather capital. KKR for instance, received in 2000 a $1 billion capital contribution from the State of Oregon pension fund for its newest LBO fund, the Millennium Fund. LBO firms charge a management fee for the capital committed to their investment funds. The management fee generally ranges from 1% to 3% depending on the strength of the LBO firm. On KKR's newest fund, for instance, the management fee offered to some investors is 1% per year. Given that KKR expects to raise between $5 billion and $6 billion, this would indicate an annual management fee in the range of $50 to $60 million a year.

In addition, LBO firms share in the profits of the investment pool. These incentive fees usually range from 20% to 30%. Incentive fees are profit sharing fees. For instance, an incentive fee of 20% means that the LBO firm keeps one dollar out of every five earned on LBO transactions.

LBO firms also may charge fees to the corporation that it is taken private of up to 1% of the total selling price for arranging and negotiating the transaction. As an example, KKR earned $75 million for arranging the buyout of RJR Nabisco, and $60 million for arranging the buyout of Safeway Stores.

Not only do LBO firms earn fees for arranging deals, they can earn break-up fees if a deal craters. Consider the Donaldson, Lufkin & Jenrette LBO of IBP Inc. This $3.8 billion buyout deal, first announced in October, 2000 was subsequently topped by a $4.1 billion takeover bid from Smithfield Foods Inc. in November, 2000. This bid was in turn topped by a $4.3 billion takeover bid from Tyson Foods Inc. in December 2000. Despite losing out on the buyout of IBP, as part of the LBO deal terms, DLJ was due a $66.5 million breakup fee from IBP because it was sold to another bidder.

In addition to earning fees for arranging the buyout of a company or for losing a buyout bid, LBO firms may also charge a divestiture fee for arranging the sale of a division of a private company after the buyout has been completed. Further, a LBO firm may charge director's fees to a buyout company if managing partners of the LBO firm sit on the company's board of directors after the buyout has occurred. In fact there are any number of ways for a LBO firm to make money on a buyout transaction.

RISKS OF LBOs

LBOs have less risk than venture capital deals for several reasons. First, the target corporation is already a seasoned company with public equity outstanding. Indeed, many LBO targets are mature companies with undervalued assets.

Second, the management of the company has an established track record. Therefore, assessment of the key employees is easier than a new team in a venture capital deal.

Third, the LBO target usually has established products or services and a history of earning profits. However, management of the company may not have the freedom to fully pursue their initiatives. An LBO transaction can provide this freedom.

Last, the exit strategy of a new IPO in several years time is much more feasible than a venture capital deal because the company already had publicly traded stock outstanding. A prior history as a public company, demonstrable operating profits, and a proven management team make an IPO for a buyout firm much more feasible than an IPO for a start-up venture.

The obvious risk of LBO transactions is the extreme leverage used. This will leave the company with a high debt to equity ratio and a very large debt service. The high leverage can provide large gains for the equity owners, but it also leaves the margin for error very small. If the company cannot generate enough cash flow to service the coupon and interest payments demanded of its bondholders, it may end up in bankruptcy, with little left over for its equity investors. "Leveraged Fallouts" are an inevitable fact of life in the LBO marketplace.

DEBT AS PRIVATE EQUITY

In this section we discuss two forms of private equity that appear as debt on an issuer's balance sheet. Mezzanine debt is closely linked to the leveraged buyout market, while distressed debt investors pursue companies whose fortunes have taken a turn for the worse. Like venture capital and LBOs, these strategies pursue long-only investing in the securities of target companies, and these strategies can result in a significant equity stake in a target company. In addition, like venture capital and LBOs, these two forms of private equity investing provide alternative investment strategies within the equity asset class.

Since mezzanine debt and distressed debt investors purchase the bonds of a target company, it may seem inappropriate to classify these strategies within the equity asset class. However, we will demonstrate in this chapter that these two strategies derive a considerable amount of return as equity components within a company's balance sheet.

For now, it is important to recognize that mezzanine debt and distressed debt investing can be distinguished from traditional long-only investing. The reason is that these two forms of private equity attempt to capture investment returns from economic sources that are mostly independent of the economy's long-term macroeconomic growth. For instance, the debt of a bankrupt company is more likely to rise and fall with the fortunes of the company and negotiations with other creditors than with the direction of the general stock market. While the direction of the stock market and the health of the overall economy may have some influence on a distressed company, it is more likely that the fortunes of the company will be determined by the hands of its creditors.

Mezzanine Debt

Mezzanine debt is often hard to classify because the distinction between debt and equity can blur at this level of financing. Oftentimes, mezzanine debt represents a hybrid, a combination of debt of equity. Mezzanine financing gets its name because it is inserted into a company's capital structure between the "floor" of equity and the "ceiling" of senior, secured debt. It is from the in between nature of this type of debt that mezzanine derives its name.

Mezzanine financing is not used to provide cash for the day-to-day operations of a company. Instead, it is used during transitional periods in a company's life. Frequently, a company is in a situation where its senior creditors (banks) are unwilling to provide any additional capital and the company does not wish to issue additional stock. Mezzanine financing can fill this void.

Mezzanine Financing to Bridge a Gap in Time

Mezzanine financing has three general purposes. First, it can be financing used to bridge a gap in time. This might be a round of financing to get a private company to the IPO stage. In this case, mezzanine financing can either be subordinated debt convertible into equity, or preferred shares, convertible into common equity upon the completion of a successful IPO.

Examples of this time-gap financing include Extricity, Inc. a platform provider for business-to-business relationship management. In May 2000, Extricity raised $50 million in mezzanine financing from a broad group of corporate and financial investors. Within a matter of days after its mezzanine round, Extricity also filed a registration statement for an IPO, but subsequently withdrew its registration statement as the market for IPOs cooled off. However, the mezzanine round of financing was sufficient to get Extricity through the next 10 months until March 2001, when the company was purchased for $168 million by Peregrine Systems Inc., a business-software maker.

Mezzanine Financing to Bridge a Gap in the Capital Structure

A second and more common use of mezzanine financing is to bridge a gap in the capital structure of a company. In this case, mezzanine financing is used not because of time constraints but rather because of financing constraints between senior debt and equity. Mezzanine financing provides the layer of capital beyond what secured lenders are willing to provide while minimizing the dilution of a company's outstanding equity.

Mezzanine debt is used to fill the gap between senior debt represented by bank loans, mortgages and senior bonds, and equity. Consequently, mezzanine debt is junior, or subordinated, to the debt of the bank loans, and is typically the last component of debt to be retired.

Under this definition, mezzanine financing is used to fund acquisitions, corporate re-capitalizations, or production growth. More generally, mezzanine financing is used whenever the equity component of a transaction is too low to attract senior lenders such as banks and insurance companies. Senior lenders may require a lower debt-to-equity ratio than the borrower is willing to provide. Most borrowers dislike reducing their equity share price through offerings that dilute equity ownership.

Mezzanine Financing to Bridge a Gap in an LBO

The third popular use of mezzanine debt is a tranche of financing in many LBO deals. For instance, LBO target companies may not have the ability to access the bond markets right away, particularly if the target company was an operating division of a larger entity. It may not have a separate financial history to satisfy SEC requirements for a public sale of its bonds. Consequently, a mezzanine tranche may be necessary to complete the financing of the buyout deal. Alternatively, a buyout candidate may not have enough physical assets to provide the necessary collateral in a buyout transaction. Last, bank lenders may be hesitant to lend if there is not sufficient equity committed to the transaction. Mezzanine debt is often the solution to solve these LBO financing problems.

Mezzanine Funds

Mezzanine funds must pay attention to the same securities laws as hedge funds, venture capital funds, and buyout funds. This means that mezzanine funds must ensure that they fall within either the 3(c)(1) or the 3(c)(7) exemptions of the Investment Company Act of 1940. These "safe harbor" provisions ensure that mezzanine funds do not have to adhere to the filing, disclosure, record keeping, and reporting requirements as do mutual funds.

There are two key distinctions between venture capital funds and mezzanine funds. The first is the return expectations. Mezzanine funds seek total rates of return in the 15% to low twenties range. Compare this to LBO funds that seek returns in the mid-to-high twenties and venture capital funds that seek returns in excess of 30%.

For example, senior bank debt in a private equity transaction is usually priced at 200 to 250 basis points over LIBOR, while mezzanine financing usually bears a coupon rate of 400 to 500 basis points over Libor. In addition, mezzanine financing will contain some form of equity appreciation such as warrants or the ability to convert into common stock that raises the total return towards 20%.

Mezzanine financing is the most expensive form of debt because it is the last to be repaid. It ranks at the bottom of the creditor totem pole, just above equity. As a result, it is expected to earn a rate of return only slightly less than common equity.

Second, mezzanine funds are staffed with different expertise than a venture capital fund. Most venture capital funds have staff with heavy technology related experience including former senior executives of software, semiconductor, and Internet companies. In contrast, mezzanine funds tend to have financial professionals, experienced in negotiating "equity kickers" to be added on to the mezzanine debt offering.

Mezzanine funds have not attracted the flow of investor capital compared to venture capital funds or leveraged buyout funds. Part of the reason is that with a robust economy throughout most of the 1990s, mezzanine debt was not a necessary component of many transactions. Second, mezzanine financing tends to be small, generally in the $20 million to $300 million range. Last, mezzanine debt, while it yields greater returns than junk bonds, cannot compete with the returns earned by venture capitalists and leveraged buyout funds.

Mezzanine funds look for businesses that have a high potential for growth and earnings, but do not have a sufficient cash flow to receive full funding from banks or other senior creditors. Banks may be unwilling to lend because of a short operating history or a high debt to equity ratio. Mezzanine funds look for companies that, over the next 4 to 7 years, can repay the mezzanine debt through a debt refinancing, an initial public offering, or an acquisition.

Mezzanine funds are risk lenders. This means that in a liquidation of the company, mezzanine investors expect little or no recovery of their principal. Consequently, mezzanine investors must assess investment opportunities outside of conventional banking parameters. Existing collateral and short-term cash flow are less of a consideration. Instead, mezzanine investors carefully review the management team and its business plan to assess the likelihood that future growth will be achieved by the issuing company. In sum, similar to stockholders, mezzanine debt investors assume the risk of the company's success or failure.

Investors in mezzanine funds are generally pension funds, endowments, and foundations. These investors do not have the internal infrastructure or expertise to invest directly in the mezzanine market. Therefore, they enter this alternative investment strategy as limited partners through a mezzanine fund.

Similar to hedge funds, venture capital funds and LBO funds, mezzanine funds are managed by a general partner who has full investment discretion. Many mezzanine funds are managed by merchant banks who have experience with gap financing or by mezzanine professionals who previously worked in the mezzanine departments of insurance companies and banks.

Advantages of Mezzanine Debt to the Investor

Mezzanine debt is a hybrid. It has debt-like components but usually provides for some form of equity appreciation. This appeals to investors who are more conservative but like to have some spice in their portfolios.

High Equity-Like Returns The high returns to mezzanine debt compared to senior debt appeals to traditional fixed income investors such as insurance companies. Mezzanine debt typically has a coupon rate that is 200 basis points over that of senior secured debt. Additionally, given an insurance company's long-term investment horizon, it may be less concerned with short-term earnings fluctuations.

Further, mezzanine debt often has an equity kicker, typically in the form of warrants. These warrants may have a strike price as low as $0.01 per share. The amount of warrants included is inversely proportional to the coupon rate. The higher the coupon rate, the fewer the warrants that need to be issued.

Nonetheless, the investor receives both a high coupon payment plus participation in the upside of the company should it achieve its growth potential. The equity component can be significant, representing up to 5% to 20% of the outstanding equity of the company. For this reason, mezzanine debt is often viewed as an investment in the company as opposed to a lien on assets.

Priority of Payment Although mezzanine debt is generally not secured by collateral, it still ranks higher than equity and other unsecured creditors. Therefore, mezzanine debt is senior to trade creditors.

Schedule of Repayment   Like senior secured debt, mezzanine debt usually has a repayment schedule. This schedule may not start for several years as senior debt is paid off, but it provides the certainty of when a return of capital is expected.

Board Representation   A subordinated lender generally expects to be considered an equity partner. In some cases, mezzanine lenders may request board observation rights. However, in other cases, the mezzanine lender may take a seat on the board of directors with full voting rights.

Restrictions on the Borrower   Although mezzanine debt is typically unsecured, it still may come with restrictions on the borrower. The mezzanine lender may have the right to approve or disapprove of additional debt, acquisitions made by the borrower, changes in the management team, and the payment of dividends.

Distressed Debt

Distressed debt investing is the practice of purchasing the debt of troubled companies. These companies may have already defaulted on their debt or may be on the brink of default. Additionally, distressed debt may be that of a company seeking bankruptcy protection.

The key to distressed debt investing is to recognize that the term "distressed" has two meanings. First, it means that the issuer of the debt is troubled—its liabilities may exceed its assets—or it may be unable to meet its debt service and interest payments as they become due. Therefore, distressed debt investing almost always means that some workout, turnaround, or bankruptcy solution must be implemented for the bonds to appreciate in value.

Second, "distressed" refers to the price of the bonds. Distressed debt often trades for pennies on the dollar. This affords a savvy investor the opportunity to make a killing if she can identify a company with a viable business plan but a short-term cash flow problem.

Vulture Investors and Hedge Fund Managers

Distressed debt investors are often referred to as "vulture investors," or just "vultures" because they pick the bones of under performing companies. They buy the debt of troubled companies including subordinated debt, junk bonds, bank loans, and obligations to suppliers. Their investment plan is to buy the distressed debt at a fraction of its face value and then seek improvement of the company.

Sometimes this debt is used as a way to gain an equity investment stake in the company as the vultures agree to forgive the debt they own in return for stock in the company. Other times, the vultures may help the troubled company to get on its feet, thus earning a significant return as the value of their distressed debt recovers in value. Still other times distressed debt buyers help impatient creditors to cut their losses and wipe a bad debt off their books. The vulture in return waits patiently for the company to correct itself and for the value of the distressed debt to recover.

There is no standard model for distressed debt investing, each distressed situation requires a unique approach and solution. As a result, distressed debt investing is mostly company selection. There is a low covariance with the general stock market.

The returns for distressed debt investing can be very rewarding. Distressed debt obligations generally trade at levels that yield a total return of 20% or higher. For example, by the beginning of 2001 an estimated 15% to 20% of all leveraged bank debt loans traded at 80 cents on the dollar or less.[5]

Distressed Debt and Bankruptcy

Distressed debt investing and the bankruptcy process are inextricably intertwined. Many distressed debt investors purchase the debt while the borrowing company is currently in the throws of bankruptcy. Other investors purchase the debt before a company enters into bankruptcy proceedings with the expectation of gaining control of the company.

Using Distressed Debt to Recycle Private Equity

LBO firms are a great source for distressed debt. "Leveraged fallouts" occur frequently, leaving large amounts of distressed debt in their wake. However, this provides an opportunity for distressed debt buyers to jump in, purchase cheaply non-performing bank loans and subordinated debt, eliminate the prior private equity investors, and assert their own private equity ownership.

Distressed Buyouts

Even as leveraged buyout firms create distress situations, they also actively invest in this arena. After all, bankruptcy court and creditor workouts provide opportunities to purchase undervalued assets. Often, creditors are sufficiently worried about receiving any recovery that they bail out of their positions when possible, opening up the door for buyout firms to scoop up assets on the cheap.

---

[5] See Riva D. Atlas, "Company in Trouble? They're Waiting," *New York Times* (January 21, 2001).

Converting Distressed Debt to Private Equity in a Pre-Packaged Bankruptcy

In February 2001, Loews Cineplex Entertainment Corp., the largest publicly traded U.S. movie theater chain, and one of the largest movie theater chains in the world, filed for Chapter 11 Bankruptcy. At the same time, it signed a letter of intent with Oaktree Capital Management, LLC and the Onex Corporation to sell Loews Cineplex and its subsidiaries to the investor group. This was a "pre-packaged" bankruptcy where the debtor agrees in advance to a plan of reorganization before formerly filing for Chapter 11 Bankruptcy.

The letter agreement proposed that Onex and Oaktree convert their distressed debt holdings of about $250 million of senior secured bank debt and $180 million of unsecured company bonds into 88% of the equity of the reorganized company. Unsecured creditors, including subordinated debtholders, would receive the other 12% of equity.[6] All existing equity interests would be wiped out by the reorganization. Last, the remaining holders of bank debt would receive new term loans as part of the bankruptcy process equal in recovery to about 98% of the face amount of current debt.

In this prepackaged example, Onex and Oaktree became the majority equity owners of Loews by purchasing its bank and subordinated debt. Furthermore, their bank debt was converted to a private equity stake because all public shares of Loews were wiped out through the bankruptcy proceedings. Loews two largest shareholders, Sony Corporation (40% equity ownership) and Vivendi Universal SA (26%) lost their complete equity stake in Loews. In effect, the bankruptcy proceeding transformed Loews from a public company to a private one.

Distressed Debt as an Undervalued Security

Distressed debt is not always an entrée into private equity; it can simply be an investment in an undervalued security. In this instance, distressed debt investors are less concerned with an equity stake in the troubled company. Instead, they expect to benefit if the company can implement a successful turnaround strategy.

Distressed Debt Arbitrage

If there is any way to skin an arbitrage, hedge fund managers will think of it. While this is not a private equity form of investing, it is a form of equity arbitrage best suited for hedge fund managers.

---

[6] Oaktree Capital also owned about 60% of Loews' senior subordinated notes.

The arbitrage is constructed as follows. A hedge fund manager purchases distressed debt which she believes is undervalued. At the same time, she shorts the company's underlying stock. The idea is that if the bonds are going to decline in value, the company's stock price will decline even more dramatically because equity holders have only a residual claim behind debtholders.

Conversely, if the company's prospects improve, both the distressed debt and equity will appreciate significantly. The difference then will be between the coupon payment on the debt versus dividends paid on the stock. Since a company coming out of a workout or turnaround situation almost always conserves its cash and does not pay cash stock dividends, the hedge fund manager should earn large interest payments on the debt compared to the equity.

Risks of Distressed Debt Investing

There are two main risks associated with distressed debt investing. First, business risk still applies. Just because distressed debt investors can purchase the debt of a company on the cheap does not mean it cannot go lower. This is the greatest risk to distressed debt investing, a troubled company may be worthless and unable to pay off its creditors. While creditors often convert their debt into equity, the company may not be viable as a going concern. If the company cannot develop a successful plan of reorganization, it will only continue its spiral downwards.

It may seem strange, but creditworthiness doesn't apply. The reason is that the debt is already distressed because the company may already be in default and its debt thoroughly discounted. Consequently, failure to pay interest and debt service has already occurred.

Instead, vulture investors consider the business risks of the company. They are concerned not with the short-term payment of interest and debt service, but rather, the ability of the company to execute a viable business plan. From this perspective, it can be said that distressed debt investors are truly equity investors. They view the purchase of distressed debt as an investment in the company as opposed to a lending facility.

The second main risk is the lack of liquidity. The distressed debt arena is a fragmented market, dominated by a few players. Trading out of a distressed debt position may mean selling at a significant discount to the book value of the debt.

In addition, purchasers of distressed debt must have long-term investment horizons. Workout and turnaround situations do not happen overnight. It may be several years before a troubled company can correct its course and appreciate in value.

CHAPTER 27

Real Estate Investment

Susan Hudson-Wilson, CFA
Chief Executive Officer
Property & Portfolio Research, LLC

T his chapter covers the real estate asset class. It focuses on the investment and capital market aspects (the supply of and demand for the investment) and not on the space market aspect (the supply of and demand for space to lease) of real estate.[1] Real estate comprises one-third of the value of global capital assets and represents approximately $10 trillion of value in the United States alone. Of this $10 trillion, approximately $3 to $4 trillion falls into the category of commercial and multifamily investment-grade real estate, which excludes farmland, timber, raw land, hotels, and owner-occupied residential real estate. Hotels, farmland, timber, and raw land are sometimes included and sometimes excluded from institutional investors' definition of real estate, but for simplicity they are not discussed in this chapter. Owner-occupied residential real estate is a separately studied class of investment.

The commercial and rental residential real estate property types covered are as follows:

- *Office buildings*, such as central business district assets, suburban buildings, office parks, and offices attached to mixed-use projects.
- *Retail centers*, including malls, strip centers, big box retail, high street retail, neighborhood centers, and factory outlet projects.
- *Industrial projects*, including both individual buildings and those located in industrial parks, and industrial buildings of all sizes and ceiling clear heights.

---

[1] Jeffrey Fisher, Susan Hudson-Wilson, and Charles Wurtzebach. "Equilibrium in Space and Capital Markets." *The Journal of Portfolio Managemen* t (Summer 1993), pp. 101–107.

EXHIBIT 27.1   Capitalization Shares of Each Quadrant—1982 to 2001 (e)

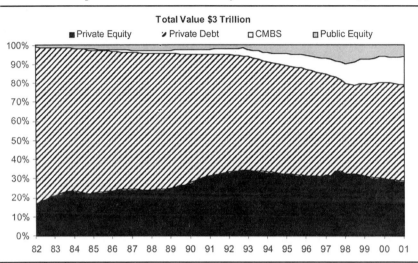

Source: Investment Property & Real Estate Capital Markets Report

■ *Apartment complexes* located in the inner city, suburban garden style units, high-rise high end urban projects, tax exempt buildings, and condominiums converted to rental units.

Real estate investments are characterized by the following structures:

■ *Private commercial real estate equity*, held as individual assets or in commingled vehicles.
■ *Private commercial real estate debt*, held as either directly issued whole loans or commercial mortgages held in funds and/or commingled vehicles.
■ *Public real estate equity* structured as REITs or real estate operating companies (REOCs).
■ *Public commercial real estate debt* structured as commercial mortgage–backed securities (CMBS).

These structures represent the quadrants of the modern real estate investment universe. Exhibit 27.1 shows the approximate value and percentage shares of each quadrant through time. Clearly the real estate investment universe has changed appreciably over the past 20 years. In the past, the private debt and equity markets dominated the real estate investment universe. While public equity had long played a small role in the real estate capitalization structure, the role has grown sharply since the early 1990s when many distressed private owners of real estate turned to the public markets to recapitalize and thereby save their companies from extreme capital shortfalls. Real estate debt markets also turned to the public markets for capital and so the commercial mortgage-backed securities industry developed.

Debt and equity and public and private markets are all covered in the chapter on real estate because while the traditional definition of real estate was limited to private equity, this definition has given way to a more modern and appropriate definition. Prior to the early 1990s, the public debt and equity markets were not of significant size and the private debt market was the province of a handful of the largest insurance companies and, therefore was not routinely considered accessible to an institutional investor.

TWO DISTINGUISHING CHARACTERISTICS OF REAL ESTATE INVESTMENTS

Real estate has two unique characteristics that materially influence its risk and return behaviors. Real estate is a hybrid asset with differing degrees of debt-oriented and equity-oriented investment behaviors and real estate values rarely fall to zero and stay at that level. Each of these distinguishing characteristics is developed below.

Real Estate is a Debt/Equity Hybrid

A mix of debt-like and equity-like behaviors drives every real estate investment's performance. For example, consider the extreme case of a building leased in its entirety on a long-term triple net lease to a credit tenant. The contractually bound fixed-lease payments to the building's owner are analogous to the payments to a bondholder and are not similar in character to the payments to an equity investor. The value of this asset varies in step with the same types of influences to which a mortgage holder or a bondholder is subject; interest rate movements, inflation, and the creditworthiness of the tenant. At the other extreme, the value of a totally vacant building is tied to conditions in the space and capital markets and not nearly as influenced by interest rates and, of course, is not influenced at all by tenant credit. There are no cash flows to equate to bond flows. As the building becomes leased it evolves from pure equity to a debt-equity hybrid, with some of the influences on value elicited from the debt markets and others from the equity markets. If the building is ultimately leased to long-term credit tenants then it becomes more debt-like than equity-like. On the other hand, if the triple net lease building loses its tenant, then it very quickly reverts to a pure equity investment. Equity-oriented value generators like the demand for and the supply of space, local market economic health, the building's location, and other building-specific attributes increase in their influence on value and on volatility, and, therefore, on the investment characteristics of the asset.

Commercial mortgages also exhibit this equity-like and debt-like convolution of behaviors. The creditworthiness of a building that is the collateral underlying a mortgage is dependent upon the lease structure as described above. This creditworthiness can shift on a dime under some conditions. Most commercial mortgages are non-recourse to the borrower, but are recourse to the asset. Thus there are times when a foreclosed mortgage becomes an unintentional (or, as a deliberate strategy, an intentional) equity holding. A CMBS issue is generally comprised of a pool of mortgages, placed on underlying real estate collateral. The cash flows from the mortgages are then carved up to produce high-grade bond cash flows and low-grade or unrated equity-like cash flows from the most subordinated pieces. The tranches between the top and bottom tranches are characterized by varying degrees of equity-like and debt-like behaviors driven largely by the nature of the underlying collateral.

Real Estate Values Rarely Disappear

The second most important characteristic of real estate investments is that the asset is highly likely to have residual value no matter what kind of battering it may have suffered in the space and capital markets. All types of investments in real estate are ultimately grounded upon a physical asset. Real estate is not an "idea" for a business, nor is it a business that is dependent upon the employment of specific people—without whom the enterprise is valueless. Instead, a building is a physical structure that can probably be put to some use in some way over some period of time. This means that only in the rarest of circumstances does the value of an asset go to zero and stay there. This reality alone puts real estate and all of its variants in a distinct class.

Using the Debt-Equity Mix

Given the definition of real estate as a debt-equity hybrid, it only makes sense for the real estate investor to consider real estate an asset for which the debt and equity components can be purposefully weighted to suit the investor's needs. Investors increasingly use all of the quadrants to create a debt-equity mix that exposes them to the influences to which they most wish to be exposed and protects them from undesirable influences. As well, real estate investors can use the public and private trading market to execute arbitrage strategies and to manage liquidity and transactions costs.

THE NATURE OF THE INVESTORS

Who holds these real estate investments? The lion's share of the market has been, and continues to be, controlled by life insurance companies, banks, and private investors. Although the life company holdings as a percent of the total have declined significantly because some have gone public and wanted to purge their asset bases of the less well understood and valued holdings, and also because many experienced a tough cycle in the early 1990s. It is interesting that even in the face of that tough cycle, banks have held their relative position, as have pension funds and private investors. While pension funds look like real players at a 10% share of the institutional real estate market, in fact the portion of the average pension fund portfolio that is comprised of commercial and multifamily debt and equity is only about 4% of their total investment portfolio. Within the pension fund community, many funds have no holdings in real estate, whatsoever. Life companies and banks have always used real estate investing to extract a differential spread on the more debt-like aspects of the investment universe.

Foreign investors' share of the market is likely to expand, as cross-border investing is increasingly a part of all investors' approach to their investment strategy. As domestic investors look offshore and foreign investors look to the large markets of the United States, the foreign investors' share will inevitably rise.

THE INVESTMENT CHARACTERISTICS OF EACH QUADRANT

Exhibit 27.2 presents each quadrant's mean return and standard deviation history.[2]

---

[2] The calculation of the private equity and public debt returns is as follows;
Private Equity
PPR cap-weighted private equity index was used, incorporating returns for all the major metropolitan markets and property types weighted by the true market capitalization in each of those markets.

Public Debt
Public debt returns are measured by the PPR CMBS model which applies typical CMBS structures to a variety of pools of mortgage cash flows and incorporates defaults and prepayments as well as changes in rating, spread, and overall interest rates. Other available CMBS indices, such as the new Lehman Brothers index, are either calculated at the tranche level or are too recent for this study.

EXHIBIT 27.2   Returns for Components of the Real Estate Investment Universe, 1982:1–2000:3

1982:1–2001:3	Private Equity	Private Debt	CMBS	Public Equity
Standard Deviation	5.3%	8.3%	7.2%	15.9%
Historical Mean	7.6%	11.4%	7.0%	13.7%

Sources: PPR; Giliberto-Levy Mortgage Index; NAREIT

Private Equity

Private equity is the least volatile of all of the real estate quadrants. At a mean historic return of 7.6% and a standard deviation of 5.3%, private equity real estate appears to be an effective asset. But is the volatility understated?

The policy of most investors to mark their private assets to market only once each year creates a falsely tame picture of true mark-to-market performance. Certainly, if one were to assess the value of a stock equity only once each year its volatility would diminish significantly. On the other hand, it is reasonable to ask whether the volatility of stock equity is perhaps *over*stated. Doesn't there seem to be a considerable amount of noise around the mean value that cannot be explained by income volatility or by shifts in expectations or perceptions of risk? Thus, while it is likely the case that infrequent valuations do produce a dampening, it is not clear that much greater frequency would generate the truth.

Also, for the most part, private equity real estate investors are "self-policing" and conduct and pay for the valuation exercises themselves. This self-valuation is inherently conflicted and has indeed caused real concern. After the market crash of the late 1980s, there was much discussion and debate around valuation methodology and control and several significant investors took steps to separate themselves from the valuation process of the real estate assets they managed. To address these legitimate concerns, two important steps were taken by an increasing number of institutional investors. First, the valuation process is placed in the control of an independent third-party valuation enterprise and second, the valuations are conducted with greater frequency and timeliness. Both of these changes, especially the one regarding frequency, have made differences, yet we have not observed a radical shift in the volatility of the returns. So, this leads the industry to additional explanations for the low volatility of private real estate equity.

The cash flows emanating from real estate investments are in fact highly stable. Thus the values, based in large part on cash flows, are also relatively stable. Long leases, buildings rented to either single users, or those with many different users on staggered leases generate demonstrably stable cash flows that are not subject to short-lived shifts in the economic environment.

The second explanation for low volatility is that real estate is, by its very nature, a debt-equity hybrid and so each building is essentially a mixed asset portfolio in which the cross-correlation between the two differently driven behaviors operates to reduce overall volatility. Further, we know from studying the performance of different urban area markets and property types within markets that there is a great range of different cycles occurring simultaneously—in part driven by the differences in the degree of debt-like and equity-like behaviors. Thus in real estate, when the buildings and the markets are pooled into indexes, there is room for significant risk mitigation within the index. The cross-correlations among real estate market sectors are quite low. The result is that the volatility for the overall private equity real estate market looks, and may very well be, truly low.

Exhibit 27.3 presents the implied cap rate or yield across the total private equity real estate market and for each of the four major property types—office, industrial, retail, and apartment—based on data from the National Council of Real Estate Investment Fiduciaries (NCREIF) as calculated by PPR. Starting in the late 1970s, real estate values rose and cap rates fell gradually to a value peak in 1989. Retail values showed the greatest rise as caps fell to an unsustainable level of 6%. The second most aggressively priced property type was the office sector, which was briefly valued at a 6% cap rate, also. The recession of the early 1990s certainly had its origins in the real estate sector of the economy and values plummeted—more than 60% in many cases. There were specific situations where values fell by even more (but, again, virtually no values fell to zero and stayed there). Since that great correction, however, values and cap rates have improved and remained fairly stable on growing cash flows. By late 2001, cap rates were back to the kinds of levels sustained prior to the last cycle.

Public Equity

Public equity is a structure applied to a pool of real estate assets that allows them to trade in the public market. The two primary structures (of course, traditional corporate structures are permissible as well) are the Real Estate Investment Trust (REIT), and the Real Estate Operating Company (REOC). The REOC is simply a regular corporation that operates real estate as its primary business activity. The REIT is explained next.

EXHIBIT 27.3 NCREIF Implied Cap Rates

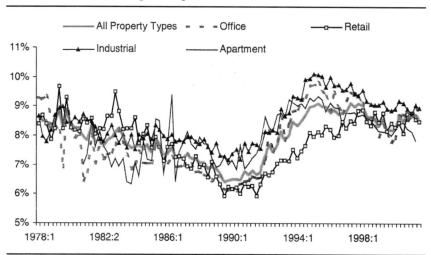

Source: NCREIF

Contrary to its name, a REIT is not a trust—it is a tax election. A REIT is a company that offers shares for trade in the public market and generally acts as a perpetual ownership vehicle of one building or a pool of individual buildings. REITs are subject to certain rules to maintain their special tax status. For example, a REIT is required to pay out at least 90% of its accrual accounting-based earnings generated from the operations of the properties. Until 2000, REITs were encouraged to behave somewhat passively by rules constraining the volume of sales a REIT could execute in a year. These rules have been relaxed somewhat. In exchange for adherence to these rules, the income of the REIT is taxed at the investor level and not at the operating company level.

Most REITs employ leverage at the entity level and, therefore, experience greater volatility than is the case for unlevered private portfolios. The mean return for the all equity National Association of Real Estate Equity Trusts (NAREIT) was 13.7% and the standard deviation was 15.9%. Of course, the REIT also experiences public market price volatility and, therefore, leverage alone does not explain the difference between the volatility of a REIT and that of a pool of private equity. Exhibit 27.4 shows this volatility quite clearly. Total returns for REITs, over the time period shown, have ranged from a high of 50% to a low of less than 20% (excluding hotels, which are not always included in the core definition of real estate).

EXHIBIT 27.4 NAREIT Returns by Property Sector

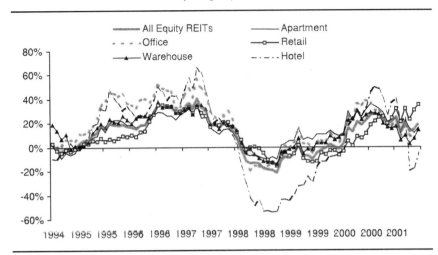

Source: NAREIT

EXHIBIT 27.5 All Equity REITs—Total Return versus Dividend Yield

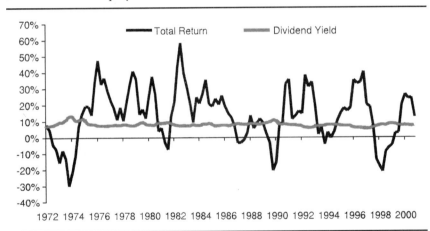

Source: NAREIT

Clearly the volatility comes from how the income is priced and not from the income itself (see Exhibit 27.5). The behavior of the income derived from private equity and that from public real estate equity should be identical. Both income streams are derived from the cash flows obtained from leased buildings. And, in fact, the income streams are identical in character. A study done by Giliberto and Mengden[3] showed that when public equity cash flows were priced using private market cap rates, the performance of the private market was replicated. Analogously, when private market cash flows were priced using public market yields, the performance of the private market was again replicated. So, it's all in the pricing. But which is right? Are REITs real estate or are REITs a creature of the larger stock equity markets with an entirely distinct and overwhelming pricing algorithm? This is an important question to investors who are contemplating using REITS as their sole exposure to the real estate asset class.

The answer to the question can be pursued by examining the correlation between REITs and the S&P 500 through time. Exhibit 27.6 presents this information.

The evidence suggests that while REITs were *not* real estate in the early 1980s up until the real estate market crash of the late 1980s, they were decidedly *not* stock equity in the most recent time period. In between those two extreme periods was a protracted period where REIT issuance was surging and where the correlation between REITs and the general stock market was generally drifting down. So what is the correct view to take on the question of whether or not REITs are real estate? It depends on what is happening in the larger stock equity market and the private real estate market. For example, when both the public stock equity market and the private real estate markets are rising, the correlation is likely to be very high; the two cycles feed one another. When real estate market fundamentals turn down, the divergence will rise. And, as has been the case in the 2000s, when the stock equity market is in bear mode, but property market fundamentals are structurally sound, again, the markets will experience divergent behaviors. The difference between the general stock market and the real estate market will be captured by both the public real estate markets as well as by the private markets. In other words, when the investor needs to see that real estate is real estate, and stock equity is stock equity, the difference asserts itself.

Private Debt—Commercial and Multifamily Mortgages

Private commercial and multifamily mortgages comprise the largest portion of the real estate investment universe and are exactly what they appear to be; loans based on the value of a building for which the underlying building is collateral. These loans are almost universally non-recourse to the borrower and so the influence of the performance of

---

[3] Michael Giliberto and Anne Mengden, "REITs and Real Estate: Two Markets Reexamined," *Real Estate Finance* (Spring 1996), pp. 56–60.

the underlying collateral is of crucial importance to the performance of the loan. These loans can be fixed- or floating-rate, on one building or on a portfolio of buildings, cross-collateralized or not, and amortizing or interest only. Each loan is essentially privately negotiated; there are no standards to guide underwriting, the magnitude of the proceeds, or any other aspect of the loan or the documentation of the loan.

Private debt is largely the province of life insurance companies. The distant second-largest holders of private mortgage debt are the banks and mortgage companies with the S&Ls and mutual savings banks declining in importance through time. From the late 1980s through the early 1990s, many S&Ls and other local lending entities were shut down and their holdings turned over to the Resolution Trust Corporation. The RTC was created to quickly and efficiently remove distressed assets from distressed lenders and to resell the assets at unbelievable discounts to new, presumably healthier holders. The "bad" loans were indeed rehabilitated quickly.

The spreads of ACLI loans over Treasuries are generally quite strong with the period following the real estate crash of the late 1980s posting very high spreads, and at a time when the risk was perhaps the lowest (construction had essentially shut down and the economy was recovering). Real estate markets are not immune from the general, and increasingly the global, capital markets as was evidenced by the great leap in spreads following the Russian default. Towards the end of 2001, spreads again rose as the perception of a new recession became a reality.

EXHIBIT 27.6   Rolling 5-Year Quarterly Correlation: S&P 500 and NAREIT, 1979:4–2001:3

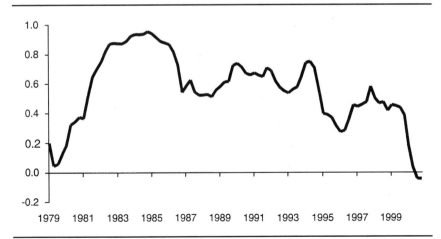

EXHIBIT 27.7   ACLI Commercial Mortgage Delinquency Rates

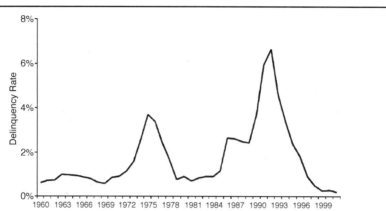

Source: ACLI

The heightened level of spreads is not merited by events in the commercial mortgage sector, as is clearly shown in Exhibit 27.7. While delinquencies through the last recession peaked at over 6%, delinquencies in the
middle of 2001 were steady at one half of one percent. Of course, delinquencies are a lagging indicator of distress and so the final peak for this
cycle is likely to be higher. Seminal research initiated by Snyderman[4] examined cohorts of mortgage originations and found that the year in which a
mortgage is originated has a tremendous impact on the ultimate performance of the mortgage. More recent research executed by Pappadopoulos[5]
suggests that default frequency, severity, and loss can be predicted using a
model that integrates the conditions prevailing when a mortgage is originated and through its life, with the structure of the mortgage.

Commercial Mortgage-Backed Securities (CMBS)

A newly emerged structure for holding commercial and multifamily mortgages is the CMBS. While various small efforts to securitize whole commercial loans emerged through the years preceding the passage of
FIRREA and the creation of the RTC, securitization really is a child of the
RTC. In the early 1990s pools of distressed loans were assembled out of
failed thrifts, S&Ls, and commercial banks, and were sold at auction to
the highest bidders. These pools were sometimes sold as pools of the

---

[4] Mark Snyderman, Howard Esaki, and Steven L'Heureux, "Commercial Mortgage
Defaults: An Update," *Real Estate Finance* (Spring 1999).
[5] George Pappadopoulos, "Benchmarking the Probability of Default for Commercial
Real Estate Mortgages," *RMA Journal* (November 2001).

whole loans, but as time went on it became clear that whole loans were less marketable than portfolios and structured vehicles. The RTC, working closely with Wall Street, began to sell various priorities of claims on the cash flows to meet the specific investment requirements and risk tolerances of buyers. This created a new type of lender—the conduit lender.

The conduit lender is any entity able to originate, underwrite, and securitize loans. The development of the product produced a massive response and new issuance of CMBS surged from a $5–10 billion annual pace to today's $90 billion pace.

Each part of the origination and management process is identified and de-linked, increasingly executed by experts in each area. Originators, servicers, special servicers, master servicers, third-party inspectors, and environmental inspectors abound. Essentially, the whole loan has been decomposed into its dimensions of risk and each dimension is managed and invested in by an appropriate entity. This represents a far more sophisticated reengineering of a real estate investment than does the advent of REITs. REITs are no more than a publicly-traded portfolio of private equities while each tranche of each CMBS is not at all similar in behavior and risk to the underlying mortgage from which it is created. The commercial mortgage-backed security represents a revolution in real estate finance.

CMBS spreads have generally tracked spreads in the whole loan market except that the spreads really widen out for the lower and unrated tranches. Currently, the B pieces trade at 900 basis points over Treasuries while AAAs trade at 150 basis points. As was evident for whole loan spreads, there was a widening that occurred along with the Russian default and a generally heightened level of concern for credit risk in 1998. In fact, just prior to that crisis the spreads had become extremely tight as competition from conduits heated up. Even the spreads on the lowest rated and unrated pieces had tightened.

While ACLI delinquencies are quite low, CMBS delinquencies have begun to rise.[6] Some argue that along with the revolution in issuance, the credit of the whole loans used to create the CMBS has deteriorated. Perhaps a less rigorous job is in fact being done in the underwriting and in the servicing and monitoring of CMBS. If this proves true, it will set the development of the sector back.

Ultimately, however, it is likely that the CMBS market will prosper because it makes a great deal of intuitive sense. Each commercial and multifamily loan is very large, limiting the number of lenders that can offer financing. The possibly excessive spread (at least relative to corporate debt at the same credit levels) could be competed away if there were

---

[6] George Pappadopoulos, "The Impact of Recession on CRE Debt," *RMA Journal* (March 2001), p. 56.

more lenders able to raise capital from smaller and smaller investors, even from individuals, as the securitized pieces can be infinitely divided. Investors in whole loans have to accept the entire return and risk spectrum while investors in CMBS can select exactly where they wish to be in the risk/return hierarchy. From a portfolio management perspective, this structure transforms an unwieldy investment into a precise tool for getting exactly what is needed for a portfolio.

REAL ESTATE IN THE MIXED ASSET PORTFOLIO

There are five primary reasons to consider real estate for inclusion in an investment portfolio:

- Reduce the overall risk of the portfolio by combining asset classes that respond differently to expected and unexpected events
- Achieve a high absolute return
- Hedge against unexpected inflation
- Constitute a part of a portfolio that is a reasonable reflection of the overall investment universe (an indexed, or market-neutral portfolio)
- Deliver strong cash flows to the portfolio

Whether or not real estate can accomplish any of these goals, in the short term as well as over the long haul, has not been an easy question to answer. Two decades of research has yielded little bullet-proof evidence that real estate has a significant role to play in an institutional portfolio. In the analysis in the next section, a cap-weighted index comprised of the components of the real estate investment universe is used to capture the performance of real estate (see Exhibit 27.8). Of course, the cap-weighted index only represents one way to take advantage of the risk mitigation opportunities inherent across the quadrants of the real estate investment universe (all of the cross-correlations within real estate are less than 0.6). Other weighting schemes could be, and are, used by investors.

Real Estate as a Portfolio Diversifier/Risk Reducer

Using the real estate investment universe index (PPR REI), we can calculate the optimal allocation for real estate in a mixed asset class portfolio of stocks, bonds, and cash. The overall bond market is measured by the Lehman Corporate/Government bond index, the stock market is measured by the S&P 500, and cash is measured by the Treasury bill rate. The parameters for the optimization (using quarterly returns from 1987:1

through 2001:3) are shown in Exhibit 27.9 and the results of the optimization are shown in Exhibit 27.10.

The correlations between real estate and stocks, real estate and
bonds, and real estate and cash suggest that real estate can play a significant role in a mixed asset portfolio. Real estate's role extends from the
lowest risk end of the efficient frontier to just past the midpoint of the
mixed asset frontier. This makes sense as real estate is both a low-risk
asset itself and a risk reducer in a stock and bond portfolio. Clearly,
investors who wish to simply go for broke and seek the highest possible
return, regardless of risk, will choose to allocate heavily toward stocks
and will have no allocation to real estate as defined here. This evidence
suggests that real estate is suitable for investors interested in capital preservation and who need to earn a useful rate of return. At one point along
the lower half of the frontier, the model calls for an allocation of 16% to
real estate. This weight drops to zero as one moves up the frontier.

EXHIBIT 27.8   PPR Real Estate Investment Universe Index (PPR REI), 1982:1–2001:3

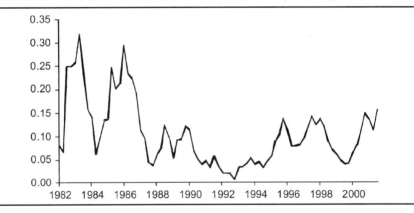

Source: PPR

EXHIBIT 27.9   Real Estate Return and Risk Parameters for Optimization,
1987:1–2001:3

	Return	Risk	PPR REI	Stocks	Bonds	Cash
			Correlations 1987:1–2001:3			
PPR REI	7.5%	3.8%	1.000			
Stocks	15.4%	16.1%	0.395	1.000		
Bonds	7.7%	5.4%	0.763	0.311	1.000	
Cash	5.4%	1.6%	0.487	−0.031	0.481	1.000

Source: PPR

EXHIBIT 27.10   Multiasset Class Efficient Frontier and Example Allocations, 1987:1–2000:3

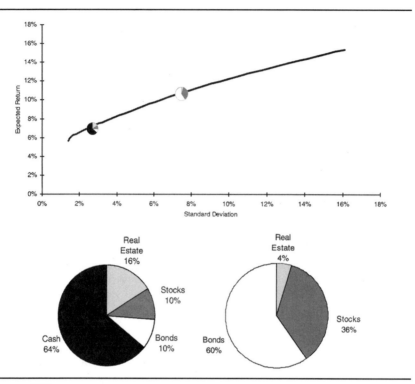

Source: PPR

Real Estate as an Absolute Return Enhancer

The second possible reason to include real estate in an investment portfolio is to bring high absolute and/or risk-adjusted returns to the portfolio. The data in Exhibit 27.9 show that, on average, real estate did not outperform stocks and bonds in absolute terms over the past 15 years. When assessed in terms of total return per unit of risk, real estate outperforms both stocks and bonds. However, employing the more commonly used Sharpe ratio and assuming a risk-free rate of 5.4% (the cash return for the period), real estate fails to outperform stocks on a risk-adjusted basis (see Exhibit 27.11).

Thus, in the aggregate, it would not be justifiable to include real estate in a portfolio for the sole reason of bringing high absolute or risk-adjusted returns to the overall portfolio. There are, however, several other questions to ask about real estate's ability to deliver high absolute and risk-adjusted returns:

EXHIBIT 27.11 Returns and Risk-Adjusted Returns for Major Asset Classes, 1987:1–2001:3

	Return	Risk	Return Per Unit of Risk	Sharpe Ratio
PPR REI	7.5%	3.8%	1.97	0.56
Stocks	15.4%	16.1%	0.96	0.62
Bonds	7.7%	5.4%	1.43	0.44

Source: PPR

■ Did real estate outperform stocks or bonds in *some* quarters? Yes, there are periods in which the full quadrant definition of real estate is able to outperform stocks and bonds (in 2000 and in 2001).

■ Do some *components* of the real estate investment universe outperform stocks or bonds on average over the period? Yes, public equity real estate well outperforms bonds during the period, but none of the components of the real estate index outperform the overall stock average.

■ Do each of the components of real estate outperform stocks or bonds in individual quarters? Yes, each of the four components of the real estate investment universe experienced periods in which the real estate components' returns were above stock or bond returns. There are a good number of quarters when *each* component beats bonds, and even a few quarters in which all four components beat stocks.

The conclusion is that, in its aggregate investment universe form, real estate does not reliably produce high returns relative to the stock and bond investment classes. However, some real estate components provide absolute return benefits and real estate's lower volatility offers the investor some useful protection.

Real Estate as an Inflation Hedge

Conventional wisdom has held that real estate performs as an inflation hedge. This means that if inflation is greater than expected, real estate returns will compensate for the surprise and will help offset the negative response of the other assets in the portfolio. The rationale is important if it is accurate. Real estate returns have a complicated relationship with inflation. Inflation elicits different responses in the different property types through divergent impacts on the income and value components of return, and through variation in the effects of both past and the most recent inflation. Next, we look at the response of private equity to inflation.

Past inflation is partially embedded in rents set previously because every seller of every product, including sellers of rental space, wishes to keep prices level or rising in real terms. Thus current net operating income (NOI) is partly a function of past inflation—rising if past inflation has been greater, and falling (or rising less) if past inflation has been tame. The speed with which such inflation affects NOI, or the time lag necessary to capture inflation's impact on current NOI, depends on the structure of leases, which, in turn, varies with property type. Current office NOI reflects the inflation experience of one to ten years ago while apartment NOI reflects more recent inflation. The impact of past inflation is positive for all four major property types.

Current inflation impacts the levels of current rents and expenses. Current inflation raises NOI by increasing the rental rate on new leases, but lowers NOI by raising all expenses. In the office, warehouse, and apartment markets, current inflation causes NOIs to fall as the rise in current rents associated with recent leases does not fully offset the increase in expenses, which impact the entire asset. However, in the retail sector, current inflation raises NOI, as the impact on rents and percentage rents (which apply to all or much of the square footage in the building) more than offsets the impact on the few expenses that are not passed through. Retail, then, has two characteristics (percentage rents and the generous passthrough of expenses) that render it a very capable transmitter of inflation to asset performance.

Inflation impacts the capital value return in two ways. First, it impacts current NOI, as described above, which feeds through to value via the capitalization rate. This feed is especially strong for retail assets. In addition, inflation affects the cap rate directly by influencing NOI growth expectations and, therefore, investors' demand for real estate investments. The direct capital value impact of inflation is significantly positive for apartment and office properties, but not significantly different from zero for warehouse.

Thus, the empirical assessment shows that private equity real estate is a partial inflation hedge. That said, it is also clear that the degree of inflation-hedging capacity is not uniform across property types.

As with most debt, real estate debt is not a good inflation hedge because unexpected inflation and concomitant increases in nominal interest rates negatively impact the value of outstanding securities (mortgages and CMBS). Publicly traded forms of equity real estate will capture some of the benefits of the inflation hedge but are less successful transmitters of this value than private equity because of links to the stock market, which is generally damaged by inflation. So, if inflation hedging is a key reason why an investor chooses an allocation to real estate, that investor must tilt the portfolio toward private equity.

Real Estate as a Reflection of the Investment Universe

Real estate may have a role in a balanced investment portfolio simply because real estate is an important part of the investment universe. Any portfolio that does *not* include real estate is based on a bet that real estate will perform less well than is implied by the market-driven relative prices. Indeed, any allocation to real estate that does not reflect real estate's overall share in the investment universe implies a different bet from that of an indexed portfolio.

Unfortunately, determining the size of the total real estate investment universe to set the weight for real estate in an indexed portfolio has proven difficult. Using some broadly correct figures for the size of the market and data from the Flow of Funds report from the Federal Reserve Board for the size of the stock, bond, and cash sectors puts real estate at approximately 6% of the current investment universe. Of course, more recent shifts towards continued value growth in real estate and distress in the stock market, all compounded by recession, will cause further shifts in the relative weights.

Strong Cash Flows

An important dimension of the total return derived from a real estate investment is the proportion of that return that is derived from income. On average, real estate produces a long-term average cash yield of about 9% which compares with a cash dividend from stocks that averages about 3% and a yield from bonds that averages almost 8%. If an investor is concerned with the degree of certainty of return and has a need for cash returns, then real estate can serve a useful function.

Relevance to the Investor

It is clear that real estate has more than one role to play and that the investor needs to think about *how* to invest in real estate as well as *whether* to invest. But, in order to reach a conclusion about the role of real estate in a particular investment portfolio, it is important to think through the different types of investors and their needs.

A Risk-Tolerant Investor

Real estate is a risk reducer at low to moderate risk and return levels and so has no role in highly risk-tolerant portfolios. Thus, investors willing and able to seek the greatest return and unconcerned with capital preservation or volatility in returns would not be inclined to allocate any part of their portfolios to real estate as defined in this chapter. Such an investor is not concerned with real estate's size in the context of the overall investment universe and presumably is not concerned about inflation.

While some parts of the real estate universe do periodically outperform equities, on average real estate is not a way to earn the greatest return. Such risk-tolerant investors might include individuals with "money to burn" or extremely overfunded corporate pension funds where the corporation wishes to go for broke as a way to add to earnings.

A final category of investor might be an extremely underfunded pension fund that needs to stretch to achieve full funding (although this behavior would be inconsistent with the risk management mantra of ERISA). There are more fiduciarily responsible ways to achieve this particular objective. There are very few investors in this group because it is somewhat irresponsible to completely disregard risk.

A Risk-Sensitive Investor

The application of real estate as a partial solution to an investor's needs depends on the risk-sensitivity of the investor. If the investor is mostly concerned with capital preservation and has a typical actuarial return requirement, real estate will be an important part of the portfolio. The lower the return requirement and the greater the concern about risk, the greater will be the preferred allocation to real estate, up to the 16% level indicated by the allocations presented earlier in this chapter. As these investors' concern for capital preservation eases somewhat and their need for return rises, they will use less and less real estate until they have crossed the midpoint of the frontier when they will use none. The territory to the left of the midpoint of the frontier is the area relevant to low to moderate risk investors; pension funds with known liabilities and moderate actuarial rates of return, families wishing to ensure that wealth is preserved for future generations, and insurance companies and banks matching liabilities with well-understood cash flows and risk levels.

Risk-sensitive investors also generally prefer to line up with the larger investor community and are therefore interested in the size of the real estate market relative to other asset classes. An allocation that is seriously over- or underweight relative to the true investment universe represents a bet away from an important norm.

Risk-sensitive investors and those who have heavy demands for cash to satisfy liability streams will also have an interest in an asset like real estate with its relatively high yields. Returns derived from capital gains are riskier than those generated in tangible, realized cash. While overall returns might be lower than those for lower-yielding assets such as stocks, the certainty and size of the cash return is greater.

An Inflation-Sensitive Investor

If an investor must pay out a liability stream in real dollars, the inflation-hedging role of real estate is of interest. One of the best examples of such an investor is a defined-benefit pension fund. They are required to pay beneficiaries in real goods and services, not in nominal cash. Clearly, the cost of providing these health and retirement benefits is going to be greatly impacted by the incidence and the level of inflation. Another example would be a foundation or endowment interested in using a part of the cash flow from the investment portfolio to purchase art, provide students with scholarships, or create new physical plant (e.g., museums or educational facilities). All of these uses of the return from the portfolio are measured in real terms and would suffer from erosion in the purchasing power of the cash flows.

Real estate is truly one of the only vehicles able to partially preserve its value during a period of inflation. Inflation-indexed Treasury instruments are an assured way to hedge, but at the cost of lower returns. The time to put a hedge in place is before, not once, inflation occurs, so investors with real liabilities need an exposure to inflation hedges at all times.

LEVERAGE

While owners of residences routinely use leverage as a means to avail themselves of a home, it is less routinely used by institutional investors in real estate. This is because the use of leverage raises some philosophical and operational issues for institutional investors who are invested in multiple asset types. For purposes of this chapter, positive spread leverage at "reasonable" levels is discussed.

Leverage is the simple act of borrowing money based on the value and the security of the underlying collateral, in this case a building. Again the focus is on non-recourse (to the borrower) debt. Because of the non-recourse structure, for the borrower the use of leverage is analogous to short-selling the asset. The borrower takes the proceeds and can "put" the asset to the lender at any time with no further penalties. As mentioned earlier, while it is rare for an asset's value to go to zero and stay there, it is not unheard of for a borrower to be unable to support the mortgage payment through a rough market cycle. Further, it is not unheard of for a lender to lend too much, based on an artificially inflated value. Thus the option value of the put is quite real.

An investor would choose to use leverage to:

- Increase the total return on an asset
- Hedge the downside risk of an asset's value
- Enable a fixed amount of capital to be spread over a larger number of individual investments
- Increase the yield and cash flow generated from a fixed pool of assets
- Reduce exposure to an asset or a pool of assets as a way of reducing exposure to the asset class
- Enhance the ability of real estate to act as a diversifier vis-à-vis the other assets in the mixed asset portfolio

The final reason warrants further exposition. As discussed at the start of this chapter, real estate is a debt-equity hybrid. Thus, applying leverage to a building encumbered by one or more leases is a way of essentially "shorting out" the debt-like aspects of the asset's behavior. This then creates a heightened role for the equity-like aspects of the asset's behavior. This has the additional effect of enhancing the diversification effect of real estate in the context of a mixed asset portfolio; essentially "pure" real estate equity behavior is what remains.

Of course, leverage increases risk as measured by the volatility of the total return of the leveraged asset. This is inescapable. However, volatility has positive and negative dimensions to it. It often makes sense to apply leverage to assets that are, in other ways, less risky than average, thus the application of leverage does not imply that risk rises to unacceptable levels. As well, as was discussed in the section of mortgage debt and delinquency, the condition of the market when the debt is applied will greatly impact the ultimate health of the debt.

For institutional investors investing in multiple asset classes, there are benefits and issues with using leverage on the real estate portfolio. First, the diversification of the real estate portfolio itself can be enhanced with the use of leverage, assuming that appropriate allocations are made with the real estate portfolio. Second, the real estate asset produces enhanced diversification vis-à-vis stocks, bonds, and bills when it is leveraged.

However, the mixed asset investor must also wrestle with the following question—does it ever make logical sense for the same investor to be a borrower and a lender (by making fixed income investments) at the same time? And, even worse, typically the rate at which the borrowing occurs will be greater than the like-credit rate at which the lending occurs. Don't these two approaches essentially neutralize one another while also incurring transaction costs? Of course, in the stock equity world this situation is routine, because most securities are issued by companies that use leverage. The stock investor, however, does not have a choice while the real estate investor (except the REIT investor) does.

So perhaps the fixed income side of an institutional investor could lend to the real estate side? Right up until the moment where there were no problems, there would be no problems, and then the trouble would begin. The two sides of the same investor organization would be conflicted and the situation would be untenable. This would be especially true in a typical situation where the portfolio manager for each asset class is expected to defend his own return and is not accountable for the overall fund level return.

Finally, leverage must be regarded as way for the borrower to raise capital, not to use capital. If a fund is not fully deployed in highly productive investment activities, it is hard to see why leverage would make sense.

Leverage then is a useful portfolio management tool as long as the philosophical issues are put aside and the real estate portfolio manager is judged on his independent performance.

INVESTMENT EXECUTION

In general, real estate is brought into the portfolio via:

- Dedicated portfolios of individual assets executed by an in-house staff or by hiring outside managers, and/or via
- Commingled funds that are either open or closed ended. These funds may be structured as insurance company separate accounts, private REITs, trusts, or public REITs.

Real estate investment carries with it significant execution costs both in terms of the staff required (either in-house or third party) to invest and manage and in terms of the actual costs of executing any transaction. The execution costs include expected costs such as brokerage fees, but also include more subtle ones such as search and underwriting costs. Much effort can be expended on transactions that are ultimately either deemed unworthy or are lost to a competitive bid.

Because of this reality, real estate investing, with the sole exception of investors who invest in public equity, is the province of the institutional player. There are a few commingled open- and closed-end vehicles available to smaller institutional investors, but there is close to nothing available for small institutions, endowments, foundations, and families, and certainly nothing (except REITS) of any magnitude available for individual investors. Given the nature of the investment process—one deal at a time, with large pools of capital required for each investment—real estate is virtually a closed shop.

This will change as the very nature of the institutional investor is changing. As a nation we are rapidly moving from defined-benefit pension plans to defined-contribution plans. The participants in the DC plans will absolutely want to be able to access a risk mitigator like real estate, and over time the investment industry will figure out how to meet their needs. REITs are a good start as they control the same types of assets that are controlled by the private vehicles. CMBS presents another opportunity for the democratization of real estate investing. As baby boomers age and begin to be more interested in cash flow and less interested in the volatility associated with growth, commercial real estate debt investing will take on new interest. But until the nut is cracked, the large institutions will dominate the field and reap the benefits, including real estate, in their portfolios.

OVERVIEW OF ADDITIONAL ISSUES

In this section the important additional issues of private equity valuation and performance measurement and attribution are presented.

Valuation

As alluded to in the discussion of private equity, valuation continues to be an issue, especially for private equity, but then by extension, for any collateral underlying any mortgage or tranche of CMBS. Even with public market pricing in the world of public equity, constant debate exists about the true net asset value of each REIT. While there is no magic bullet for this problem, there are some sensible changes that could be made to the methods used in the valuation industry.

Currently, appraisal professionals exist who use the three methods to estimate an asset's value; the cost approach, the comparables approach, and the income approach. In the world of modern finance only the income approach has any real merit, as it is essentially a discounted cash flow method, exactly as used for other assets. The cost approach can only be interesting to a researcher who might want to know whether values are at or below cost for the purpose of estimating the likelihood of new supply appearing in the market. Clearly, when values exceed the cost of construction, it is likely that new supply will occur. Other than that, there is absolutely no reason why value should bear any short-run relationship to cost. The comparables approach is flawed as it is inherently backward looking and valuation is inherently forward looking. When markets move, this approach is virtually guaranteed to provide an incorrect perspective.

Thus, the industry truly needs to increase the rigor of the income approach. Discount rates should be linked to careful analysis of relative risk, and future rent growth and vacancy scenarios should be better linked to thorough market analysis. The analysis should be rerun as soon as any variable in the cash flow forecast changes. Thus, values would be constantly adjusted as new information is received and there would be less room for judgments and looking over one's shoulder. The deficiency of the valuation system presents a serious challenge for the industry.

Performance Measurement

There are several calculations employed to measure the performance of real estate investments, and several associations collect and disseminate performance statistics on certain dimensions of the real estate investment universe. The National Council of Real Estate Investment Fiduciaries (NCREIF) collects data on the income and capital value returns for a group of private equity assets held by tax-exempt investors. Commercial Mortgage Securitization Association (CMSA) and Lehman Brothers have begun the work of documenting the performance of CMBS. The National Association of Real Estate Investment Trusts (NAREIT) collects and disseminates performance data on the publicly traded REIT industry. A private firm, The John B. Levy Company, produces a modeled statistic on the performance of private debt. Unfortunately, none of these sources is as comprehensive as one would like and so each "benchmark" must be used with a great deal of knowledge of the specific inclusions and limitations of the data.

In real estate, different investors use different calculations to measure performance—the internal rate of return, the time-weighted return, the average annual return, and the since-inception return are some of the measures used. In some cases, investors estimate a value in order to calculate the return and in other cases investors simply look at the cash-on-cash return of an investment. The bottom line is that there is no single standard by which real estate performance is measured.

Attribution analysis is in a very preliminary stage of development in the real estate investment community, partly because the data to support such analysis are weak and partly as a reflection of the generally less analytic predisposition of the investors (although this is changing).

Hold/Sell in the Traditional Private Equity Market

The inverse of the sell decision is the buy decision and any decision not to sell is a decision to re-buy. The criteria for the sell decision are multi-leveled. There are portfolio level considerations—does the market and property type exposure of the asset help or harm the investor's ability to achieve the investment goals of the overall portfolio? There are market level considerations—does the specific market in which the asset resides continue to provide the most effective way to bring the behavior of a desired sector to the portfolio? And there are asset level considerations—is the asset itself able to bring to the market, the sector, and the portfolio the behavior that is required of the asset?

While for other asset classes the hold/sell decision can be based substantially on the criteria presented above, in real estate there is one additional consideration—the cost of selling and redeploying the proceeds of the sale. Costs include staff time, commissions, taxes, and elapsed time. Particularly in the private portions of the real estate capital markets, costs are often significant and can reach levels where it is better to do nothing than it is to rebalance the portfolio.

CONCLUSION

Real estate is an emerging investment class in the context of some institutional portfolios. Pension funds hold very little real estate in general and almost no debt, insurance companies have long used private debt and equity and are using the public debt market increasingly, while banks are decreasing holders of debt and are not generally holders of equity. One of the major issues in real estate investment is the lack of divisible ways to invest in real estate. This causes the largest investors to have greater access to the asset than smaller investors and individuals. Increasing securitization is helping to democratize access to the class.

While real estate has a role in a mixed asset portfolio, real estate is not a reliable outperformer relative to the other major assets. Real estate is a diversifier, an inflation hedge, a good source of cash returns, and a significant segment of the overall investment capital market.

CHAPTER 28

Equity Derivatives

Bruce M. Collins, Ph.D.
Chief Executive Officer
QuantCast

Frank J. Fabozzi, Ph.D., CFA
Adjunct Professor of Finance
School of Management
Yale University

Derivative instruments, or simply derivatives, are contracts that essentially derive their value from the behavior of cash market instruments such as stocks, stock indexes, bonds, currencies, and commodities that underlie the contract. When the underlying for a derivative is a stock or stock index, the contract is called an *equity derivative*. The purpose of this chapter is to explain these instruments, their investment characteristics, and to provide an overview as to how they are priced. The basic features described in this chapter for equity derivatives apply to fixed income derivatives, the subject of the next chapter.

THE ROLE OF DERIVATIVES

Equity derivatives have several properties that provide economic benefits that make them excellent candidates for use in equity portfolio management. These properties are derived from the following four roles that derivatives serve in portfolio management: (1) to modify the risk characteristics of a portfolio (*risk management*); (2) to enhance the expected return of a portfolio (*returns management*); (3) to reduce transaction costs associated with managing a portfolio (*cost management*); and, (4) to achieve efficiency in the presence of legal, tax, or regulatory obstacles (*regulatory management*).

Institutional equity investors have the means to accomplish investment objectives with a host of products and product structures. Pension funds, for example, can structure a product to meet their asset allocation targets, to access foreign markets, or to explicitly manage risk. Products that may meet their needs include listed stock index futures and equity swaps. The choice of an instrument depends on the specific investor needs and circumstances. In each case, the benefits from structuring a derivatives solution to an investment problem either involves cost reduction, risk management, or the management of certain legal or regulatory restrictions.

Equity derivatives give investors more degrees of freedom. In the past, the implementation and management of an investment strategy for pension funds, for example, was a function of management style and was carried out in the cash market. Pension funds managed risk by diversifying among management styles. Prior to the advent of the over-the-counter (OTC) derivatives market in the late 1980s, the first risk management tools available to investors were limited to the listed futures and options markets. Although providing a valuable addition to an investor's risk management tool kit, listed derivatives were limited in application due to their standardized features, limited size, and liquidity constraints. The OTC derivatives market gives investors access to longer-term products that better match their investment horizon and provides flexible structures to meet their exact risk/reward requirements. The number of unique equity derivative structures is essentially unlimited.

EQUITY DERIVATIVES MARKET

The three general categories of derivatives are (1) futures and forwards, (2) options, and (3) swaps. The basic derivative securities are futures/ forward contracts and options. Swaps and other derivative structures with more complicated payoffs are regarded as hybrid securities, which can be shown to be nothing more than portfolios of forwards, options, and cash instruments in varying combinations.

Equity derivatives can also be divided into two categories according to whether they are listed or OTC. The listed market consists of options, warrants, and futures contracts. The principal listed options market consists of exchange-traded options with standardized strike prices, expirations, and payout terms traded on individual stocks, equity indexes, and futures contracts on equity indexes. A FLexible EXchange (FLEX) Option was introduced by the Chicago Board Options Exchange (CBOE) in 1993 that provides the customization feature of the OTC market, but with the guarantee of the exchange. The listed futures market consists of exchange-traded equity index futures with standardized settlement dates and settlement terms.

OTC equity derivatives are not traded on an exchange and have an advantage over listed derivatives because they provide complete flexibility and can be tailored to fit an investment strategy. The OTC equity derivatives market can be divided into three components: OTC options and warrants, equity-linked debt investments, and equity swaps. OTC equity options are customized option contracts that can be applied to any equity index, basket of stocks, or an individual stock. OTC options are privately negotiated agreements between an investor and an issuing dealer. The structure of the option is completely flexible in terms of strike price, expiration, and payout features.

A fundamental difference between listed and OTC derivatives, however, is that listed options and futures contracts are guaranteed by the exchange, while in the OTC market the derivative is the obligation of a non-exchange entity that is the counterparty. Thus, the investor is subject to credit risk or counterparty risk.

LISTED EQUITY OPTIONS

Equity derivative products are either exchange-traded listed derivatives or over-the-counter derivatives. In this section we will look at listed equity options.

An *option* is a contract in which the option seller grants the option buyer the right to enter into a transaction with the seller to either buy or sell an underlying asset at a specified price on or before a specified date. The specified price is called the *strike price* or *exercise price* and the specified date is called the *expiration date*. The option seller grants this right in exchange for a certain amount of money called the *option premium* or *option price*.

The option seller is also known as the option writer, while the option buyer is the option holder. The asset that is the subject of the option is called the *underlying*. The underlying can be an individual stock, a stock index, or another derivative instrument such as a futures contract. The option writer can grant the option holder one of two rights. If the right is to purchase the underlying, the option is a *call option*. If the right is to sell the underlying, the option is a *put option*.

An option can also be categorized according to when it may be exercised by the buyer. This is referred to as the *exercise style*. A *European option* can only be exercised at the expiration date of the contract. An *American option* can be exercised any time on or before the expiration date.

The terms of exchange are represented by the contract unit, which is typically 100 shares for an individual stock and a multiple times an index value for a stock index. The terms of exchange are standard for most contracts. The contract terms for a FLEX option can be customized along four dimensions: underlying asset, strike price, expiration date, and settlement style. These options are discussed further below.

The option holder enters into the contract with an opening transaction. Subsequently, the option holder then has the choice to exercise or to sell the option. The sale of an existing option by the holder is a closing sale.

Listed versus OTC Equity Options

There are three advantages of listed options relative to OTC options. First, the strike price and expiration dates of the contract are standardized. Second, the direct link between buyer and seller is severed after the order is executed because of the fungible nature of listed options. The Options Clearing Corporation (OCC) serves as the intermediary between buyer and seller. Finally, transaction costs are lower for listed options than their OTC counterparts.

There are many situations in which an institutional investor needs a customized option. The higher cost of OTC options reflects this customization. However, some OTC exotic option structures may prove to cost less than the closest standardized option because a more specific payout is being bought.

A significant distinction between a listed option and an OTC option is the presence of credit risk or counterparty risk. Only the option buyer is exposed to counterparty risk. Options traded on exchanges and OTC options traded over a network of market makers have different ways of dealing with the problem of credit risk. Organized exchanges reduce counterparty risk by requiring margin, marking to the market daily, imposing size and price limits, and providing an intermediary that takes both sides of a trade. The clearing process provides three levels of protection: (1) the customer's margin, (2) the member firm's guarantee, and (3) the clearinghouse. The OTC market has incorporated a variety of terms into the contractual agreement between counterparties to address the issue of credit risk and these are described when we discuss OTC derivatives.

For listed options, there are no margin requirements for the buyer of an option once the option price has been paid in full. Because the option price is the maximum amount that the option buyer can lose, no matter how adverse the price movement of the underlying, margin is not necessary. The option writer has agreed to transfer the risk inherent in a position in the underlying from the option buyer to itself. The writer, on the other hand, has certain margin requirements.

Basic Features of Listed Options

The basic features of listed options are summarized in Exhibit 28.1. The exhibit is grouped into four categories with each option category presented in terms of its basic features. These include the type of option, underlying asset, strike price, settlement information, expiration cycle, exercise style, and some trading rules.

EXHIBIT 28.1 Basic Features of Listed Equity Options
Stock Options

Option Type	Call or Put
Option Category	Equity
Underlying Security	Individual stock or ADR
Contract Value	Equity: 100 shares of common stock or ADRs
Strike Price	2½ points when the strike price is between $5 and $25, 10 points when the strike price is over $200. Strikes are adjusted for splits, recapitalizations, etc.
Settlement and Delivery	100 shares of stock
Exercise Style	American
Expiration Cycle	Two near-term months plus two additional months from the January, February, or March quarterly cycles.
Transaction Costs	$1–$3 commissions and ⅛ market impact
Position and Size Limits	Large capitalization stocks have an option position limit of 25,000 contracts (with adjustments for splits, recapitalizations, etc.) on the same side of the market; smaller capitalization stocks have an option position limit of 20,000, 10,500, 7,500, or 4,500 contracts (with adjustments for splits, recapitalizations, etc.) on the same side of the market.

EXHIBIT 28.1 (Continued)

Index Options

Option Type	Call or Put
Option Category	Indexes
Underlying Security	Stock index
Contract Value	Multiplier × index price
Strike Price	Five points. 10-point intervals in the far-term month.
Settlement and Delivery	Cash
Exercise Style	American
Expiration Cycle	Four near-term months.
Transaction Costs	$1–$3 commissions and ⅛ market impact
Position and Size Limits	150,000 contracts on the same side of the market with no more than 100,000 of such contracts in the near-term series.

LEAP Options

Option Type	Call or Put
Option Category	LEAP
Underlying Security	Individual stock or stock index
Contract Value	Equity: 100 shares of common stock or ADRs Index: full or partial value of stock index
Strike Price	Equity: same as equity option Index: Based on full or partial value of index. ⅕ value translates into ⅕ strike price
Settlement and Delivery	Equity: 100 shares of stock or ADR Index: Cash
Exercise Style	American or European
Expiration Cycle	May be up to 39 months from the date of initial listing, January expiration only.
Transaction Costs	$1–$3 commissions and ⅛ market impact
Position and Size Limits	Same as equity options and index options

EXHIBIT 28.1 (Continued)

FLEX Options

Option Type	Call, Put, or Cap
Option Category	Equity: E-FLEX option Index: FLEX option
Underlying Security	Individual stock or index
Contract Value	Equity: 100 shares of common stock or ADRs Index: multiplier × index value
Strike Price	Equity: Calls, same as standard calls Puts, any dollar value or percentage Index: Any index value, percentage, or deviation from index value
Settlement and Delivery	Equity: 100 shares of stock Index: Cash
Exercise Style	Equity: American or European Index: American, European, or Cap
Expiration Cycle	Equity: 1 day to 3 years Index: Up to 5 years
Transaction Costs	$1–$3 commissions and ⅛ market impact
Position and Size Limits	Equity: minimum of 250 contracts to create FLEX Index: $10 million minimum to create FLEX No size or position limits

Stock options refer to listed options on individual stocks or American Depository Receipts (ADRs). The underlying is 100 shares of the designated stock. All listed stock options in the United States may be exercised any time before the expiration date; that is, they are American style options.

Index options are options where the underlying is a stock index rather than an individual stock. An index call option gives the option buyer the right to buy the underlying stock index, while a put option gives the option buyer the right to sell the underlying stock index. Unlike stock options where a stock can be delivered if the option is exercised by the option holder, it would be extremely complicated to settle an index option by delivering all the stocks that constitute the index. Instead, index options are cash settlement contracts. This means that if the option is exercised by the option holder, the option writer pays cash to the option buyer. There is no delivery of any stocks.

The most liquid index options are those on the S&P 100 index (OEX) and the S&P 500 index. Both trade on the CBOE. Index options can be listed as American or European. The S&P 500 index option contract is European, while the OEX is American. Both index option contracts have specific standardized features and contract terms. Moreover, both have short expiration cycles. There are almost 100 stock index option contracts listed across 26 separate exchanges and 20 countries. Among the latest arrivals are options traded on the Dow Jones STOXX 50 and the Dow Jones EURO 50 stock indexes. The indexes are comprised of 50 industrial, commercial, and financial European blue chip companies.

The following mechanics should be noted for index options. The dollar value of the stock index underlying an index option is equal to the current cash index value multiplied by the contract's multiple. That is,

$$\text{Dollar value of the underlying index}$$
$$= \text{Cash index value} \times \text{Contract multiple}$$

For example, if the cash index value for the S&P 100 is 530, then the dollar value of the S&P 100 contract is $530 \times \$100 = \$53,000$.

For a stock option, the price at which the buyer of the option can buy or sell the stock is the strike price. For an index option, the strike index is the index value at which the buyer of the option can buy or sell the underlying stock index. The strike index is converted into a dollar value by multiplying the strike index by the multiple for the contract. For example, if the strike index is 510, the dollar value is $51,000 ($510 × $100). If an investor purchases a call option on the S&P 100 with a strike index of 510, and exercises the option when the index value is 530, then the investor has the right to purchase the index for $51,000 when the market value of the index is $53,000. The buyer of the call option would then receive $2,000 from the option writer.

The other two categories listed in Exhibit 28.1, LEAPS and FLEX options, essentially modify an existing feature of either a stock option, an index option, or both. For example, stock option and index option contracts have short expiration cycles. Long-Term Equity Anticipation Securities (LEAPS) are designed to offer options with longer maturities. These contracts are available on individual stocks and some indexes. Stock option LEAPS are comparable to standard stock options except the maturities can range up to 39 months from the origination date. Index options LEAPS differ in size compared with standard index options having a multiplier of 10 rather than 100.

FLEX options allow users to specify the terms of the option contract for either a stock option or an index option. The value of FLEX options is the ability to customize the terms of the contract along four dimensions: underlying, strike price, expiration date, and settlement style. Moreover, the exchange provides a secondary market to offset or alter positions and an independent daily marking of prices. The development of the FLEX option is a response to the growing OTC market. The exchanges seek to make the FLEX option attractive by providing price discovery through a competitive auction market, an active secondary market, daily price valuations, and the virtual elimination of counterparty risk. The FLEX option represents a link between listed options and OTC products.

Risk and Return Characteristics of Options

Now let's illustrate the risk and return characteristics of the four basic option positions—buying a call option (long a call option), selling a call option (short a call option), buying a put option (long a put option), and selling a put option (short a put option). We will use stock options in our example. The illustrations assume that each option position is held to the expiration date. Also, to simplify the illustrations, we assume that the underlying for each option is for 1 share of stock rather than 100 shares and we ignore transaction costs.

Buying Call Options

Assume that there is a call option on stock XYZ that expires in one month and has a strike price of $100. The option price is $3. Suppose that the current or spot price of stock XYZ is $100. (The *spot price* is the cash market price.) The profit and loss will depend on the price of stock XYZ at the expiration date. The buyer of a call option benefits if the price rises above the strike price. If the price of stock XYZ is equal to $103, the buyer of a call option breaks even. The maximum loss is the option price, and there is substantial upside potential if the stock price rises above $103. Using a graph, Exhibit 28.2 shows the profit/loss profile for the buyer of this call option at the expiration date.

It is worthwhile to compare the profit and loss profile of the call option buyer with that of an investor taking a long position in one share of stock XYZ. The payoff from the position depends on stock XYZ's price at the expiration date. An investor who takes a long position in stock XYZ realizes a profit of $1 for every $1 increase in stock XYZ's price. As stock XYZ's price falls, however, the investor loses, dollar for dollar. If the price drops by more than $3, the long position in stock XYZ results in a loss of more than $3. The long call position, in contrast, limits the loss to only the option price of $3 but retains the upside potential, which will be $3 less than for the long position in stock XYZ. Which alternative is better, buying the call option or buying the stock? The answer depends on what the investor is attempting to achieve.

Writing Call Options

To illustrate the option seller's, or writer's, position, we use the same call option we used to illustrate buying a call option. The profit/loss profile at expiration of the short call position (that is, the position of the call option writer) is the mirror image of the profit and loss profile of the long call position (the position of the call option buyer). That is, the profit of the short call position for any given price for stock XYZ at the expiration date is the same as the loss of the long call position. Consequently, the maximum profit the short call position can produce is the option price. The maximum loss is not limited because it is the highest price reached by stock XYZ on or before the expiration date, less the option price; this price can be indefinitely high. Using a graph, Exhibit 28.2 shows the profit/loss profile for the seller of this call option at the expiration date.

Buying Put Options

To illustrate a long put option position, we assume a hypothetical put option on one share of stock XYZ with one month to maturity and a strike price of $100. Assume that the put option is selling for $2 and the spot price of stock XYZ is $100. The profit or loss for this position at the expiration date depends on the market price of stock XYZ. The buyer of a put option benefits if the price falls. Using a graph, Exhibit 28.3 shows the profit/loss profile for the buyer of this put option at the expiration date.

EXHIBIT 28.2   Profit/Loss Profile at Expiration for a Short Call Position and a Long Call Position

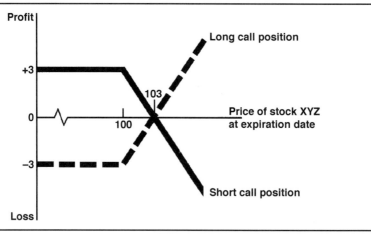

EXHIBIT 28.3   Profit/Loss Profile at Expiration for a Short Put Position and a Long Put Position

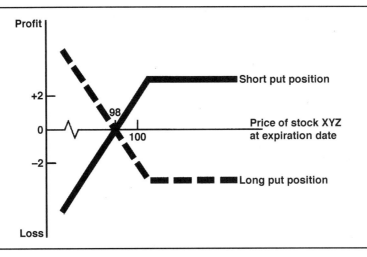

As with all long option positions, the loss is limited to the option price. The profit potential, however, is substantial: the theoretical maximum profit is generated if stock XYZ's price falls to zero. Contrast this profit potential with that of the buyer of a call option. The theoretical maximum profit for a call buyer cannot be determined beforehand because it depends on the highest price that can be reached by stock XYZ before or at the option expiration date.

To see how an option alters the risk/return profile for an investor, we again compare it with a position in stock XYZ. The long put position is compared with a short position in stock XYZ because such a position would also benefit if the price of the stock falls. While the investor taking a short stock position faces all the downside risk as well as the upside potential, an investor taking the long put position faces limited downside risk (equal to the option price) while still maintaining upside potential reduced by an amount equal to the option price.

Writing Put Options

The profit and loss profile for a short put option is the mirror image of the long put option. The maximum profit to be realized from this position is the option price. The theoretical maximum loss can be substantial should the price of the underlying fall; if the price were to fall all the way to zero, the loss would be as large as the strike price less the option price the seller received. Using a graph, Exhibit 28.3 shows the profit/loss profile for the seller of this put option at the expiration date.

The Value of an Option

Now we will look at the basic factors that affect the value of an option and discuss a well-known option pricing model.

Basic Components of the Option Price

The price of an option is a reflection of the option's *intrinsic value* and any additional amount above its intrinsic value. The premium over intrinsic value is often referred to as the *time value* .

Intrinsic Value   The intrinsic value of an option is its economic value if it is exercised immediately. If no positive economic value would result from exercising the option immediately, then the intrinsic value is zero. For a call option, the intrinsic value is positive if the spot price (i.e., cash market price) of the underlying is greater than the strike price. The intrinsic value is then the difference between the two prices. If the strike price of a call option is greater than or equal to the spot price of the underlying, the intrinsic value is zero. For example, if the strike price for a call option is $100 and the spot price of the underlying is $105, the intrinsic value is $5. That is, an option buyer exercising the option and simultaneously selling the underlying would realize $105 from the sale of the underlying, which would be covered by acquiring the underlying from the option writer for $100, thereby netting a $5 gain.

When an option has intrinsic value, it is said to be *in the money* (ITM). When the strike price of a call option exceeds the spot price of the underlying, the call option is said to be *out of the money* (OTM); it has no intrinsic value. An option for which the strike price is equal to the spot price of the underlying is said to be at the money. Both at-the-money and out-of-the-money options have an intrinsic value of zero because they are not profitable to exercise. Our call option with a strike price of $100 would be (1) in the money when the spot price of the underlying is greater than $100, (2) out of the money when the spot price of the underlying is less than $100, and (3) at the money when the spot price of the underlying is equal to $100.

For a put option, the intrinsic value is equal to the amount by which the spot price of the underlying is below the strike price. For example, if the strike price of a put option is $100 and the spot price of the underlying is $92, the intrinsic value is $8. The buyer of the put option who exercises the put option and simultaneously sells the underlying will net $8 by exercising since the underlying will be sold to the writer for $100 and purchased in the market for $92. The intrinsic value is zero if the strike price is less than or equal to the underlying's spot price.

For our put option with a strike price of $100, the option would be (1) in the money when the spot price of the underlying is less than $100, (2) out of the money when the spot price of the underlying exceeds $100, and (3) at the money when the spot price of the underlying is equal to $100.

Time Value   The *time value of an option* is the amount by which the option price exceeds its intrinsic value. The option buyer hopes that, at some time prior to expiration, changes in the market price of the underlying will increase the value of the rights conveyed by the option. For this prospect, the option buyer is willing to pay a premium above the intrinsic value. For example, if the price of a call option with a strike price of $100 is $9 when the spot price of the underlying is $105, the time value of this option is $4 ($9 minus its intrinsic value of $5). Had the current price of the underlying been $90 instead of $105, then the time value of this option would be the entire $9 because the option has no intrinsic value. Other factors being equal, the time value of an option will increase with the amount of time remaining to expiration, since the opportunity for a favorable change in the price of the underlying is greater.

There are two ways in which an option buyer may realize the value of a position taken in an option: the first is to exercise the option, and the second is to sell the option. In the first example above, since the exercise of an option will realize a gain of only $5 and will cause the immediate loss of any time value ($4 in our first example), it is preferable to sell the call. In general, if an option buyer wishes to realize the value of a position, selling will be more economically beneficial than exercising. However, there are circumstances under which it is preferable to exercise prior to the expiration date, depending on whether the total proceeds at the expiration date would be greater by holding the option or by exercising it and reinvesting any cash proceeds received until the expiration date.

Factors That Influence the Option Price

The following six factors influence the option price:

1. Spot price of the underlying
2. Strike price
3. Time to expiration of the option
4. Expected price volatility of the underlying over the life of the option
5. Short-term risk-free rate over the life of the option
6. Anticipated cash dividends on the underlying stock or index over the life of the option

EXHIBIT 28.4 Summary of Factors that Effect the Price of an American Option

Factor	Effect of an Increase of Factor on	
	Call Price	Put Price
Spot price of underlying	increase	decrease
Strike price	decrease	increase
Time to expiration of option	increase	increase
Expected price volatility	increase	increase
Short-term rate	increase	decrease
Anticipated cash dividends	decrease	increase

The impact of each of these factors depends on whether (1) the option is a call or a put and (2) the option is an American option or a European option. A summary of the effects of each factor on American put and call option prices is presented in Exhibit 28.4.

Notice how the expected price volatility of the underlying over the life of the option affects the price of both a put and a call option. All other factors being equal, the greater the expected volatility (as measured by the standard deviation or variance) of the price of the underlying, the more an investor would be willing to pay for the option, and the more an option writer would demand for it. This is because the greater the volatility, the greater the probability that the price of the underlying will move in favor of the option buyer at some time before expiration.

Option Pricing Models

Several models have been developed to determine the theoretical value of an option. The most popular one was developed by Fischer Black and Myron Scholes in 1973 for valuing European call options.[1] Several modifications to their model have followed since then. We discuss this model here to give the reader a feel for the impact of the factors on the price of an option.

By imposing certain assumptions and using arbitrage arguments, the Black-Scholes option pricing model provides the fair (or theoretical) price of a European call option on a non-dividend-paying stock. Basically, the idea behind the arbitrage argument in deriving this and other option pricing models is that if the payoff from owning a call option can be replicated by (1) purchasing the stock underlying the call option and (2) borrowing funds, then the price of the option will be (at most) the cost of creating the replicating strategy.

---

[1] Fischer Black and Myron Scholes, "The Pricing of Corporate Liabilities," *Journal of Political Economy* (May–June 1973), pp. 637–659.

The formula for the Black-Scholes model is

$$C = SN(d_1) - Xe^{-rt} N(d_2)$$

where

$$d_1 = \frac{\ln(S/K) + (r + 0.5s^2)t}{s\sqrt{t}}$$

d_2 = $d_1 - s\sqrt{t}$
ln = natural logarithm
C = call option price
S = price of the underlying
K = strike price
r ■ short term risk free rate
e = 2.718 (natural antilog of 1)
t = time remaining to the expiration date (measured as a fraction of a year)
s = standard deviation of the change in stock price
$N(.)$ = the cumulative probability density[2]

Notice that five of the factors that we said earlier in this chapter influence the price of an option are included in the formula. However, the sixth factor, anticipated cash dividends, is not included because the model is for a non-dividend-paying stock. In the Black-Scholes model, the direction of the influence of each of these factors is the same as stated earlier. Four of the factors—strike price, price of underlying, time to expiration, and risk-free rate—are easily observed. The standard deviation of the price of the underlying must be estimated.

The option price derived from the Black-Scholes model is "fair" in the sense that if any other price existed, it would be possible to earn riskless arbitrage profits by taking an offsetting position in the underlying. That is, if the price of the call option in the market is higher than that derived from the Black-Scholes model, an investor could sell the call option and buy a certain quantity of the underlying. If the reverse is true, that is, the market price of the call option is less than the "fair" price derived from the model, the investor could buy the call option and sell short a certain amount of the underlying. This process of hedging by taking a position in the underlying allows the investor to lock in the

---

[2] The value for $N(.)$ is obtained from a normal distribution function that is tabulated in most statistics textbooks or from spreadsheets that have this built-in function.

riskless arbitrage profit. The number of shares necessary to hedge the position changes as the factors that affect the option price change, so the hedged position must be changed constantly.

To illustrate the Black-Scholes model, assume the following values:

Strike price	= $45
Time remaining to expiration	= 183 days
Spot stock price	= $47
Expected price volatility	= standard deviation = 25%
Risk-free rate	= 10%

In terms of the values in the formula:

$S = 47$
$K = 45$
$t = 0.5$ (183 days/365, rounded)
$s = 0.25$
$r = 0.10$

Substituting these values into the equations presented earlier, we get

$$d_1 = \frac{\ln(47/45) + [0.10 + 0.5(0.25)^2]0.5}{0.25\sqrt{0.5}} = 0.6172$$

$$d_2 = 0.6172 - 0.25\sqrt{0.5} = 0.4404$$

From a normal distribution table:

$$N(0.6172) = 0.7315 \text{ and } N(0.4404) = 0.6702$$

Then:

$$C = 47\,(0.7315) - 45\,(e^{-(0.10)(0.5)})\,(0.6702) = \$5.69$$

Exhibit 28.5 shows the option value as calculated from the Black-Scholes model for different assumptions concerning (1) the standard deviation, (2) the risk-free rate, and (3) the time remaining to expiration. Notice that the option price varies directly with all three factors. That is, (1) the lower (higher) the volatility, the lower (higher) the option price; (2) the lower (higher) the risk-free rate, the lower (higher) the option price; and, (3) the shorter (longer) the time remaining to expiration, the lower (higher) the option price. All of this agrees with what is shown in Exhibit 28.4 about the effect of a change in one of the factors on the price of a call option.

EXHIBIT 28.5   Comparison of Black-Scholes Call Option Price
Varying One Factor at a Time
  Base Case
  Call option:
  Strike price = $45
  Time remaining to expiration = 183 days
  Current stock price = $47
  Expected price volatility = standard deviation = 25%
  Risk-free rate = 10%

Holding All Factors Constant Except Expected Price Volatility

Expected Price Volatility	Call Option Price
15%	4.69
20	5.16
25 (base case)	5.69
30	6.25
35	6.83
40	7.42

Holding All Factors Constant Except the Risk-Free Rate

Risk-Free Interest Rate	Call Option Price
7%	5.27
8	5.41
9	5.55
10 (base case)	5.69
11	5.83
12	5.98
13	6.13

Holding All Factors Constant Except Time Remaining to Expiration

Time Remaining to Expiration	Call Option Price
30 days	2.82
60	3.52
91	4.14
183 (base case)	5.69
273	7.00

How do we determine the value of put options? There is a relationship among the spot price of the underlying, the call option price, and the put option price. This is called the *put-call parity relationship*. If we can calculate the fair value of a call option, the fair value of a put with the same strike price and expiration on the same stock can be calculated from the put-call parity relationship.

Sensitivity of the Option Price to a Change in Factors

In employing options in investment strategies, a manager would like to know how sensitive the price of an option is to a change in any one of the factors that affect its price. Let's discuss the sensitivity of a call option's price to changes in the price of the underlying, the time to expiration, and expected price volatility.

The Call Option Price and the Price of the Underlying   A manager employing options for risk management wants to know how the option position will change as the price of the underlying changes. The measure that estimates this sensitivity is an option's *delta* . This measure indicates the approximate change in the value of an option for a $1 change in the price of the underlying stock.[3] Delta is measured as follows:

$$\text{Delta} = \frac{\text{Change in price of call option}}{\text{Change in price of underlying}}$$

For example, a delta of 0.4 means that a $1 change in the price of the underlying stock will change the price of the call option by approximately $0.40.

The delta for a call option varies from zero (for call options deep out of the money) to 1 (for call options deep in the money). The delta for a call option at the money is approximately 0.5.

The Call Option Price and Time to Expiration   All other factors being constant, the longer the time to expiration, the greater the option price. Since each day the option moves closer to the expiration date, the time to expiration decreases. The *theta* of an option measures the change in the option price as the time to expiration decreases, or equivalently, it is a measure of time decay. Theta is measured as follows:

$$\text{Theta} = \frac{\text{Change in price of option}}{\text{Decrease in time to expiration}}$$

---

[3] The delta of an option is a first approximation to how the price of the option will change if the price of the underlying stock changes. To improve this estimate, a second measure is used and is called the option's *gamma*.

Assuming that the price of the underlying does not change (which means that the intrinsic value of the option does not change), theta measures how quickly the time value of the option changes as the option moves toward expiration. Buyers of options prefer a low theta so that the option price does not decline quickly as it moves toward the expiration date. An option writer benefits from an option that has a high theta.

The Call Option Price and Expected Price Volatility   All other factors being constant, a change in the expected price volatility will change the option price. The vega (also called kappa) of an option measures the dollar price change in the price of the option for a 1% change in the expected price volatility. That is,

$$\text{Vega} = \frac{\text{Change in option price}}{1\% \text{ change in expected price volatility}}$$

FUTURES CONTRACTS

A *futures contract* is an agreement between two parties, a buyer and a seller, where the parties agree to transact with respect to the underlying at a predetermined price at a specified date. Both parties are obligated to perform over the life of the contract, and neither party charges a fee. Once the two parties have consummated the trade, the exchange where the futures contract is traded becomes the counterparty to the trade, thereby severing the relationship between the initial parties.

Each futures contract is accompanied by an exact description of the terms of the contract, including a description of the underlying, the contract size, settlement cycles, trading specifications, and position limits. The fact is that in the case of futures contracts, delivery is not the objective of either party because the contracts are used primarily to manage risk or costs.

The nature of the futures contract specifies a buyer and a seller who agree to buy or sell a standard quantity of the underlying at a designated future date. However, when we speak of buyers and sellers, we are simply adopting the language of the futures market, which refers to parties of the contract in terms of the future obligation they are committing themselves to. The buyer of a futures contract agrees to take delivery of the underlying and is said to be *long futures*. Long futures positions benefit when the price of the underlying rises. Since futures can be considered a substitute for a subsequent transaction in the cash market, a long futures position is comparable to holding the underlying without the financial cost of purchasing the underlying or the income that comes from holding the underlying. The seller, on the other hand, is said to be *short futures* and benefits when the price of the underlying declines.

The designated price at which the parties agree to transact is called the *futures price*. The designated date at which the parties must transact is the *settlement date* or *delivery date*. Unlike options, no money changes hands between buyer and seller at the contract's inception. However, the futures broker and the futures exchange require initial margin as a "good faith" deposit. In addition, a minimum amount of funds referred to as *maintenance margin* is required to be maintained in the corresponding futures account. The initial margin and the maintenance margin can be held in the form of short-term credit instruments.

Futures are marked-to-the-market on a daily basis. This means that daily gains or losses in the investor's position are accounted for immediately and reflected in his or her account. The daily cash flow from a futures position is called *variation margin* and essentially means that the futures contract is settled daily. Thus, the buyer of the futures contract pays when the price of the underlying falls and the seller pays when the price of the underlying rises. Variation margin differs from other forms of margin because outflows must be met with cash.

Futures contracts have a settlement cycle and there may be several contracts trading simultaneously. The contract with the closest settlement is call the *nearby futures contract* and is usually the most liquid. The next futures contract is the one that settles just after the near contract. The contract with the furthest away settlement is called the *most distant futures contract*.

Differences between Options and Futures

The fundamental difference between futures and options is that buyer of an option (the long position) has the right but not the obligation to enter into a transaction. The option writer is obligated to transact if the buyer so desires. In contrast, both parties are obligated to perform in the case of a futures contract. In addition, to establish a position, the party who is long futures does not pay the party who is short futures. In contrast, the party long an option must make a payment to the party who is short the option in order to establish the position. The price paid is the option price.

The payout structure also differs between a futures contract and an options contract. The price of an option contract represents the cost of eliminating or modifying the risk/reward relationship of the underlying. In contrast, the payout for a futures contract is a dollar-for-dollar gain or loss for the buyer and seller. When the futures price rises, the buyer gains at the expense of the seller, while the buyer suffers a dollar-for-dollar loss when the futures price drops.

Thus, futures payout is symmetrical, while the payout for options is skewed. The maximum loss for the option buyer is the option price. The loss to the futures buyer is the full value of the contract. The option buyer has limited downside losses but retains the benefits of an increase in the value in the position of the underlying. The maximum profit that can be realized by the option writer is the option price, which is offset by significant downside exposure. The losses or gains to the buyer and seller of a futures contract are completely symmetrical. Consequently, futures can be used as a hedge against symmetric risk, while options can be used to hedge asymmetric risk.

Features of Futures

The key elements of a futures contract include the futures price, the amount or quantity of the underlying, and the settlement or delivery date. The underlying asset of a stock index futures contract is the portfolio of stocks represented by the index.

The value of the underlying portfolio is the value of the index in a specified currency times a number called a *multiplier*. For example, if the current value of the S&P 500 index is 1100, then the seller of a December S&P 500 futures contract is theoretically obligated to deliver in December a portfolio of the 500 stocks that comprise the index. The multiplier for this contract is 500. The portfolio would have to exactly replicate the index with the weights of the stocks equal to their index weights. The current value of one futures contract is $275,000 (= 1100 × 250).

However, because of the problems associated with delivering a portfolio of 500 stocks that exactly replicate the underlying index, stock index futures substitute cash delivery for physical delivery. At final settlement, the futures price equals the spot price and the value of a futures contract is the actual market value of the underlying replicating portfolio that represents the stock index. The contract is marked-to-market based on the settlement price, which is the spot price, and the contract settles.

Exhibit 28.6 provides a list of selected stock index futures traded in the United States.

Pricing Stock Index Futures

Futures contracts are priced based on the spot price and cost of carry considerations. For equity contracts these include the cost of financing a position in the underlying asset, the dividend yield on the underlying stocks, and the time to settlement of the futures contract. The theoretical futures price is derived from the spot price adjusted for the cost of carry. This can be confirmed using risk-free arbitrage arguments.

EXHIBIT 28.6   Selected Equity Futures Contracts Traded in the United States

Index Futures Contract	Index Description	Exchange	Contract Size
Standard & Poor's 500	500 stocks, Cap weighed	CME	Index × $250
Standard & Poor's Mid-cap	400 stocks, Cap weighted	CME	Index × $500
Russell 2000 Index	2000 stocks, Cap weighted	CME	Index × $500
Nikkei 225 Index	225 stocks, Price weighted	CME	Index × $5
Major Market Index	20 stocks, Price weighted	CME	Index × $500
S&P 500/BARRA Growth Index	100+ stocks, Cap weighted	CME	Index × $250
Standard & Poor's BARRA Value	300+ stocks, Cap weighted	CME	Index × $250
NASDAQ 100 Index	100 stocks, Cap weighted	CME	Index × $100
IPC Stock Index	35 stocks, Cap weighted	CME	Futures × $25
NYSE Composite Index	2600+ stocks, Cap weighted	NYFE	Index × $500

The logic of the pricing model is that the purchase of a futures contract can be looked at as a temporary substitute for a transaction in the cash market at a later date. Moreover, futures contracts are not assets to be purchased and no money changes hands when the agreement is made. Futures contracts are agreements between two parties that establish the terms of a later transaction. It is these facts that lead us to a pricing relationship between futures contracts and the underlying. The seller of a futures contract is ultimately responsible for delivering the underlying and will demand compensation for incurring the cost of holding it. Thus, the futures price will reflect the cost of financing the underlying. However, the buyer of the futures contract does not hold the underlying and therefore does not receive the dividend. The futures price must be adjusted downward to take this into consideration. The adjustment of the yield for the cost of financing is what is called the *net cost of carry*. The futures price is then based on the net cost of carry, which is the cost of financing adjusted for the yield on the underlying. That is,

$$\text{Futures price} = \text{Spot price} + \text{Cost of financing} - \text{Dividend yield}$$

The borrowing or financing rate is an interest rate on a money market instrument and the yield in the case of stock index futures is the dividend yield on a portfolio of stocks that represent the stock index. The theoretical futures price derived from this process is a model of the fair value of the futures contract. It is the price that defines a no-arbitrage condition. The no-arbitrage condition is the futures price at which sellers are prepared to sell and buyers are prepared to buy, but no risk-free profit is possible.

The theoretical futures price expressed mathematically depends on the treatment of dividends. For individual equities with quarterly dividend payout, the theoretical futures price can be expressed as the spot price adjusted for the present value of expected dividends over the life of the contract and the cost of financing. The expression is given below as:

$$F(t,T) = [S(t) - D] \times [1 + R(t,T)]$$

where

$F(t,T)$ = futures price at time t for a contract that settles in the future at time T

$S(t)$ = current spot price

D = present value of dividends expected to be received over the life of the contract

$R(t,T)$ = borrowing rate for a loan with the same time to maturity as the futures settlement date

For example, if the current price of the S&P 500 stock index is 1175, the borrowing rate is 6%, the time to settlement is 60 days, and the index is expected to yield 2.071%. An annualized dividend yield of 2.071% corresponds to 4 index points when the S&P 500 stock index is 1175:

$$1175 \times [0.02071 \times (60/365)] = 4 \text{ index points}$$

The theoretical futures price can be calculated as follows:

$$D = 4/(1 + 0.06)^{60/365} = 3.96$$

$$R = (1 + 0.06)^{60/365} - 1 = 0.009624 \text{ or } 0.9624\%$$

$$F(t,60) = [1175 - 3.96] \times 1.009624 = 1182.31$$

If the actual futures price is above or below 1182.31, then risk-free arbitrage is possible. For actual futures prices greater than fair value, the futures contract is overvalued. Arbitrageurs will sell the futures contract, borrow enough funds to purchase the underlying stock index, and hold the position until fair value is restored or until the settlement date of the futures contract.

If, for example, we assume the actual futures price is 1188, then the following positions would lead to risk-free arbitrage:

- sell the overvalued futures at 1188
- borrow an amount equivalent to 1175
- purchase a stock portfolio that replicates the index for the equivalent of 1175

The position can be unwound at the settlement date in 60 days at no risk to the arbitrageur. At the settlement date, the futures settlement price equals the spot price. Assume the spot price is unchanged at 1175. Then,

- collect 4 in dividends
- settle the short futures position by delivering the index to the buyer for 1175
- repay 1186.31 (1175 × 1.009624) to satisfy the loan (remember the interest rate for the 60 days is 0.9624%)

The net gain is [1188 + 4] − 1186.31 = 5.69. That is, the arbitrageur "earned" 5.69 index points or 48 basis points (5.69/1175) without risk or without making any investment. This activity would continue until the price of the futures converged on fair value.

It does not matter what the settlement price for the index is at the settlement date. This can be clearly shown by treating the futures position and stock position separately. The futures position delivers the difference between the original futures price and the settlement price or 1188 − 1175, which equals 13 index points. The long stock position earned only the dividends and no capital gain. The cost of financing the position in the stock is 11.31 and the net return to the combined short futures and long stock position is 13(futures) + 4(stock) less the 11.31 cost of financing, which is a net return of 5.69. Now consider what happens if the spot price is at any other level at the settlement date. Exhibit 28.7 shows the cash flows associated with the arbitrage. We can see from the results that regardless of the movement of the spot price, the arbitrage profit is preserved.

For actual futures prices less than fair value, the futures contract is undervalued. Arbitrageurs will buy the futures contract, short or sell the underlying, lend the proceeds, and hold the position until fair value is restored or until settlement date of the futures contract. If, for example, we assume the actual futures price is 1180, then the following positions would lead to risk-free arbitrage:

- buy the undervalued futures at 1180
- sell or short the stock index at 1175 and collect the proceeds
- lend the proceeds from the stock transaction at 6%

Once again the position can be unwound at the settlement date at no risk to the arbitrageur. At that time the futures settlement price equals the spot price. Regardless of the settlement price of the index, the arbitrage is preserved in this case as well. Exhibit 28.7 presents a sample of settlement price outcomes. The following process applies to the arbitrage regardless of the direction of the stock market:

- settle the short stock position by taking futures delivery of the stock index
- pay the 4 index points in dividends due the index
- receive the proceeds from the loan (remember the term interest rate is 0.9624%)

EXHIBIT 28.7 Arbitrage Cash Flows
Overvalued Futures[*1]

Futures Stock Index Settlement Price	Futures Cash Flows	Stock Cash Flows	Costs	Profit
1200	1188 − 1200 = −12	25 + 4 = 29	11.31	5.69
1190	1188 − 1190 = −2	15 + 4 = 19	11.31	5.69
1188	1188 − 1188 = 0	13 + 4 = 17	11.31	5.69
1180	1188 − 1180 = 8	5 + 4 = 9	11.31	5.69
1175	1188 − 1175 = 13	0 + 4 = 4	11.31	5.69
1160	1188 − 1160 = 28	−15 + 4 = −11	11.31	5.69

[1] Short futures at 1188

Undervalued Futures[1]

Futures Stock Index Settlement Price	Futures Cash Flows	Stock Cash Flows	Interest Income	Profit
1200	1200 − 1180 = 20	−25 − 4 = −29	11.31	2.31
1190	1190 − 1180 = 10	−15 − 4 = −19	11.31	2.31
1188	1188 − 1180 = 8	−13 − 4 = −17	11.31	2.31
1180	1180 − 1180 = 0	−5 − 4 = −9	11.31	2.31
1175	1175 − 1180 = −5	0 − 4 = −4	11.31	2.31
1160	1160 − 1180 = −20	15 − 4 = 11	11.31	2.31

[1] Buy futures at 1180

In this example, the arbitrageur "earned" 20 basis points (2.31/ 1175) or 2.31 index points without risk or without making any investment. This activity would continue until the price of the futures converged on fair value.

The theoretical futures price can also be expressed mathematically based on a security with a known dividend yield. For equities that pay out a constant dividend over the life of a futures contract, this rendition of the model is appropriate. This may apply to stock index futures contracts where the underlying is an equity index of a large number of stocks. Rather than calculating every dividend, the cumulative dividend payout or the weighted-average dividend produces a constant and known dividend yield. The cost of carry valuation model is modified to reflect the behavior of dividends. This is expressed in the following equation:

$$F(t,T) = S(t) \times [1 + R(t,T) - Y(t,T)]$$

where $Y(t,T)$ is the dividend yield on the underlying over the life of the futures contract and $F(t,T)$, $S(t)$, and $R(t,T)$ are as defined earlier.

For example, if the current price of a stock is 1175, the borrowing rate is 6%, the time to settlement is 60 days, and the annualized dividend yield is 1.38%, the theoretical futures price can be calculated as follows:

$$Y = (1 + 0.0138)^{60/365} - 1 = 0.002256 \text{ or } 0.2256\%$$

$$R = (1 + 0.06)^{60/365} - 1 = 0.009624 \text{ or } 0.9624\%$$

$$F(t,60) = 1175 \times [1 + (0.009624 - 0.002256] = 1183.66$$

In practice, it is important to remember to use the borrowing rate and dividend yield for the term of the contract and not the annual rates. The arbitrage conditions outlined above still hold in this case. The model is specified differently, but the same outcome is possible. When the actual futures price deviates from the theoretical price suggested by the futures pricing model, arbitrage would be possible and likely. The existence of risk-free arbitrage profits will attract arbitrageurs.

In practice, there are several factors that may violate the assumptions of the futures valuation model. Because of these factors, arbitrage must be carried out with some degree of uncertainty and the fair value futures price is not a single price, but actually a range of prices where the upper and lower prices act as boundaries around an arbitrage-free zone. Furthermore, the violation of various assumptions can produce mispricing and risk that reduce arbitrage opportunities.

The futures price ought to gravitate toward fair value when there is a viable and active arbitrage mechanism. Arbitrage activity will only take place beyond the upper and lower limits established by transaction and other costs, uncertain cash flows, and divergent borrowing and lending rates among participants. The variability of the spread between the spot price and futures price, known as the *basis*, is a consequence of mispricing due to changes in the variables that influence the fair value.

The practical aspects of pricing produce a range of prices. This means that the basis can move around without offering a profit motive for arbitrageurs. The perspective of arbitrageurs in the equity futures markets is based on dollar profit but can be viewed in terms of an interest rate. The borrowing or financing rate found in the cost of carry valuation formula assuming borrowing and lending rates are the same. In practice, however, borrowing rates are almost always higher than lending rates. Thus, the model will yield different values depending on the respective borrowing and lending rates facing the user. Every futures price corresponds to an interest rate. We can manipulate the formula and solve for the rate implied by the futures price, which is called the *implied futures rate*. For each market participant there is a theoretical fair value range defined by its respective borrowing and lending rates and transaction costs.

OTC EQUITY DERIVATIVES

An OTC equity derivative can be delivered on a stand-alone basis or as part of a structured product. Structured products involve packaging standard or exotic options, equity swaps, or equity-linked debt into a single product in any combination to meet the risk/return objectives of the investor and may represent an alternative to the cash market even when cash instruments are available.

The three basic components of OTC equity derivatives are OTC options, equity swaps, and equity-linked debt. These components offer an array of product structures that can assist investors in developing and implementing investment strategies that respond to a changing financial world. The rapidly changing investment climate has fundamentally changed investor attitudes toward the use of derivative products. It is no longer a question of what can an investor gain from the use of OTC derivatives, but how much is sacrificed by avoiding this marketplace. OTC derivatives can assist the investor with cost minimization, diversification, hedging, asset allocation, and risk management.

Before we provide a product overview, let's look at counterparty risk. For exchange listed derivative products, counterparty or credit risk is minimal because of the clearing house associated with the exchange. However, for OTC products there is counterparty risk. For parties taking a position where performance of both parties is required, both parties are exposed to counterparty risk. The OTC market has incorporated a variety of terms into the contractual agreement between counterparties to address the issue of credit risk. These include netting arrangements, position limits, the use of collateral, recouponing, credit triggers, and the establishment of Derivatives Product Companies (DPCs).

Netting arrangements between counterparties are used in master agreements specifying that in the event of default, the bottom line is the net payment owed across all contractual agreements between the two counterparties. *Position limits* may be imposed on a particular counterparty according to the cumulative nature of their positions and creditworthiness. As the OTC market has grown, the creditworthiness of customers has become more diverse. Consequently, dealers are requiring some counterparties to furnish collateral in the form of a liquid short-term credit instrument. *Recouponing* involves periodically changing the coupon such that the marked-to-market value of the position is zero. For long-term OTC agreements, a *credit trigger provision* allows the dealer to have the position cash settled if the counterparty's credit rating falls below investment grade. Finally, dealers are establishing DPCs as separate business entities to maintain high credit ratings that are crucial in competitively pricing OTC products.

OTC Options

OTC options can be classified as first generation and second generation options. The latter are called *exotic options*. We describe each type of OTC option in the following sections.

First Generation of OTC Options

The basic type of first generation OTC options either extends the standardized structure of an existing listed option or creates an option on stocks, stock baskets, or stock indexes without listed options or futures. Thus, OTC options were first used to modify one or more of the features of listed options: the strike price, maturity, size, exercise type (American or European), and delivery mechanism. The terms were tailored to the specific needs of the investor. For example, the strike price can be any level; the maturity date at any time; the contract of any size; the exercise type American or European; the underlying can be a stock, a stock portfolio, or an equity index or a foreign equity index; and the settlement can be physical, in cash, or a combination.

An example of how OTC options can differ from listed options is exemplified by an Asian option. Listed options are either European or American in structure relating to the timing of exercise. Asian options are options with a payout that is dependent on the average price of the spot price over the life of the option. Due to the averaging process involved, the volatility of the spot price is reduced. Thus, Asian options are cheaper than similar European or American options.

The first generation of OTC options offered flexible solutions to investment situations that listed options did not. For example, hedging strategies using the OTC market allow the investor to achieve customized total risk protection for a specific time horizon. The first generation of OTC options allow investors to fine tune their traditional equity invest-ment strategies through customizing strike prices and maturities, and choosing any underlying equity security or portfolio of securities. Investors could now improve the management of risk through customized hedging strategies or enhance returns through customized buy writes. In addition, investors could invest in foreign stocks without the need to own them, and profit from an industry downturn without the need to short stocks.

Exotics: Second Generation OTC Options

The second generation of OTC equity options includes a set of products that have more complex payoff characteristics than standard American or European call and put options. These second-generation options are sometimes referred to as "exotic" options and are essentially options with specific rules that govern the payoff.[4] Exotic option structures can be created on a stand-alone basis or as part of a broader financing pack-age such as an attachment to a bond issue.

Some OTC option structures are path dependent, which means that the value of the option to some extent depends on the price pattern of the underlying asset over the life of the option. In fact, the survival of some options, such as barrier options, depends on this price pattern. Other examples of path dependent options include Asian options, look-back options, and reset options. Another group of OTC option struc-tures has properties similar to step functions. They have fixed singular payoffs when a particular condition is met. Examples of this include digital or binary options and contingent options. A third group of options is classified as multivariate because the payoff is related to more than one underlying asset. Examples of this group include a general cat-egory of rainbow options such as spread options and basket options.

---

[4] For a description of exotic options, see Chapter 10 in Bruce M. Collins and Frank J. Fabozzi, *Derivatives and Equity Portfolio Management* (New Hope, PA: Frank J. Fabozzi Associates, 1999).

Competitive market makers are now prepared to offer investors a broad range of derivative products that satisfy the specific requirements of investors. The fastest growing portion of this market pertaining to equities involves products with option-like characteristics on major stock indexes or stock portfolios.

Equity Swaps

Equity swaps are agreements between two counterparties which provide for the periodic exchange of a schedule of cash flows over a specified time period where at least one of the two payments is linked to the performance of an equity index, a basket of stocks, or a single stock. In a standard or plain vanilla equity swap, one counterparty agrees to pay the other the total return to an equity index in exchange for receiving either the total return of another asset or a fixed or floating interest rate. All payments are based on a fixed notional amount and payments are made over a fixed time period.

Equity swap structures are very flexible with maturities ranging from a few months to 10 years. The returns of virtually any asset can be swapped for another without incurring the costs associated with a transaction in the cash market. Payment schedules can be denominated in any currency irrespective of the equity asset and payments can be exchanged monthly, quarterly, annually, or at maturity. The equity asset can be any equity index or portfolio of stocks, and denominated in any currency, hedged or unhedged.

Variations of the plain vanilla equity swap include: international equity swaps where the equity return is linked to an international equity index; currency-hedged swaps where the swap is structured to eliminate currency risk; and call swaps where the equity payment is paid only if the equity index appreciates (depreciation will not result in a payment from the counterparty receiving the equity return to the other counterparty because of call protection).

A basic swap structure is illustrated in Exhibit 28.8. In this case, the investor owns a short-term credit instrument that yields LIBOR plus a spread. The investor then enters into a swap to exchange LIBOR plus the spread for the total return to an equity index. The counterparty pays the total return to the index in exchange for LIBOR plus a spread. Assuming the equity index is the Nikkei 225, a U.S. investor could swap dollar-denominated LIBOR plus a spread for cash flows from the total return to the Nikkei denominated in yen or U.S. dollars. The index could be any foreign or domestic equity index. A swap could also be structured to generate superior returns if the financing instrument in the swap yields a higher return than LIBOR.

EXHIBIT 28.8   Equity Swaps

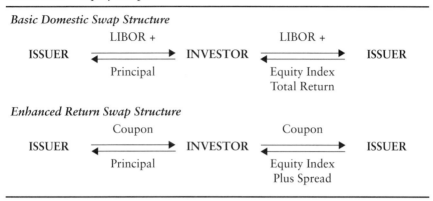

Basic Domestic Swap Structure

Enhanced Return Swap Structure

Equity swaps have a wide variety of applications including asset allocation, accessing international markets, enhancing equity returns, hedging equity exposure, and synthetically shorting stocks.

An example of an equity swap is a 1-year agreement where the counterparty agrees to pay the investor the total return to the S&P 500 Index in exchange for dollar-denominated LIBOR on a quarterly basis. The investor would pay LIBOR plus a spread × 91/360 × notional amount. This type of equity swap is the economic equivalent of financing a long position in the S&P 500 Index at a spread to LIBOR. The advantages of using the swap are no transaction costs, no sales or dividend withholding tax, and no tracking error or basis risk versus the index.

The basic mechanics of equity swaps are the same regardless of the structure. However, the rules governing the exchange of payments may differ. For example, a U.S. investor wanting to diversify internationally can enter into a swap and, depending on the investment objective, exchange payments on a currency-hedged basis. If the investment objective is to reduce U.S. equity exposure and increase Japanese equity exposure, for example, a swap could be structured to exchange the total returns to the S&P 500 Index for the total returns to the Nikkei 225 Index. If, however, the investment objective is to gain access to the Japanese equity market, a swap can be structured to exchange LIBOR plus a spread for the total returns to the Nikkei 225 Index. This is an example of diversifying internationally and the cash flows can be denominated in either yen or dollars. The advantages of entering into an equity swap to obtain international diversification are that the investor exposure is devoid of tracking error, and the investor incurs no sales tax, custodial fees, withholding fees, or market impact associated with entering and exiting a market. This swap is the economic equivalent of being long the Nikkei 225 financed at a spread to LIBOR at a fixed exchange rate.

CHAPTER 29

Interest Rate Derivatives

Frank J. Fabozzi, Ph.D., CFA
Adjunct Professor of Finance
School of Management
Yale University

Steven V. Mann, Ph.D.
Professor of Finance
The Moore School of Business
University of South Carolina

The previous chapter covered the role of derivatives in portfolio management, the different types of derivatives, and the valuation of derivatives. In the description of the types of derivatives, the difference in the risk and return characteristics of futures-type products and option-type products was described, as well as the distinction between exchange-traded products and over-the-counter products. The focus in the previous chapter was on equity derivatives.

In this chapter we look at interest rate derivatives. We will not repeat the fundamental characteristics of derivatives. Instead, we will look at the derivative products available in the market for controlling interest rate risk. The chapter is divided into four sections for each type of derivative: futures/forward contracts, options, swaps, and caps/floors.

INTEREST RATE FUTURES

A futures contract is an agreement that requires each party to the agreement either to buy or sell something at a designated future date at a predetermined price. A forward contract, just like a futures contract, is an agreement for the future delivery of something at a specified price at the end of a designated period of time. Futures contracts are standardized agreements as to the delivery date (or month) and quality of the deliverable, and are traded on organized exchanges. A forward contract differs in that it is usually non-standardized (that is, the terms of each contract are negotiated individually between buyer and seller), there is no clearinghouse, and secondary markets are often non-existent or extremely thin. Unlike a futures contract, which is an exchange-traded product, a forward contract is an over-the-counter instrument.

Futures contracts are marked to market at the end of each trading day. Consequently, futures contracts are subject to interim cash flows as additional margin may be required in the case of adverse price movements, or as cash is withdrawn, in the case of favorable price movements. A forward contract may or may not be marked to market, depending on the wishes of the two parties. For a forward contract that is not marked to market, there are no interim cash flow effects because no additional margin is required.

Finally, the parties in a forward contract are exposed to credit risk because either party may default on its obligation. This risk is called *counterparty risk*. This risk is minimal in the case of futures contracts because the clearinghouse associated with the exchange guarantees the other side of the transaction. In the case of a forward contract, both parties face counterparty risk.

Below we discuss these two types of contracts in which the underlying is a fixed-income security or an interest rate. We begin with interest rate futures contracts, which can be classified by the maturity of their underlying security. Interest rate futures on short-term instruments have an underlying security that matures in one year or less. The maturity of the underlying security of futures contracts on long-term instruments exceeds one year. We then discuss a forward rate agreement. We will discuss another important futures contract, a swap futures, later in this chapter when we cover interest rate swaps.

Interest Rate Futures on Short-Term Instruments

The three interest rate futures contracts on short-term instruments traded in the United States are the U.S. Treasury bill futures contract, the Eurodollar CD futures contract, and the federal funds futures contract. We discuss each in the following sections.

U.S. Treasury Bill Futures

The underlying for the Treasury bill futures contract, traded on the International Monetary Market (IMM) of the Chicago Mercantile Exchange, is a 13-week (3-month) Treasury bill with a face value of $1 million. More specifically, the seller of a Treasury bill futures contract agrees to deliver to the buyer on the settlement date a Treasury bill with 13 weeks remaining to maturity and a face value of $1 million. The Treasury bill delivered can be newly issued or seasoned. The futures price is the price at which the Treasury bill will be sold by the short and purchased by the long. For example, a Treasury bill futures contract that settles in 3 months requires that 3 months from now the short deliver to the long $1 million face value of a Treasury bill with 13 weeks remaining to maturity. The Treasury bill delivered could be a newly issued 13-week Treasury bill or a Treasury bill that was issued six months prior to the settlement date and therefore has only 13 weeks remaining until maturity.

Eurodollar CD Futures

As discussed in Chapter 6, Eurodollar certificates of deposit (CDs) are denominated in dollars but represent the liabilities of banks outside the United States. The contracts are traded on the International Monetary Market of the Chicago Mercantile Exchange and the London International Financial Futures Exchange (LIFFE). The rate paid on Eurodollar CDs is the London interbank offered rate (LIBOR).

The 3-month (90 day) Eurodollar CD is the underlying instrument for the Eurodollar CD futures contract. As with the Treasury bill futures contract, this contract is for $1 million of face value and is traded on an index price basis. The index price basis in which the contract is quoted is equal to 100 minus the annualized futures LIBOR. For example, a Eurodollar CD futures price of 98.00 means a futures 3-month LIBOR of 2%.

The Eurodollar CD futures contract is a cash settlement contract. Specifically, the parties settle in cash for the value of a Eurodollar CD based on LIBOR at the settlement date. The Eurodollar CD futures contract is one of the most heavily traded futures contracts in the world.

The Eurodollar CD futures contract is used frequently to trade the short end of the yield curve and many risk managers believe this contract to be the best hedging vehicle for a wide range of hedging situations.

Fed Funds Futures Contract

When the Federal Reserve formulates and executes monetary policy, the federal funds rate is frequently a significant operating target. Accordingly, the federal funds rate is a key short-term interest rate. The federal funds futures contract is designed for hedgers who have exposure to this rate or speculators who want to make a bet on the direction of U.S. monetary policy. Underlying this contract is the simple average overnight federal funds rate (i.e., the effective rate) for the delivery month. As such, this contract is settled in cash.

Interest Rate Futures on Long-Term Instruments

Interest rate futures on long-term instruments include Treasury bond and note futures, Agency note futures, and long-term municipal bond futures.

Treasury Bond Futures

The Treasury bond futures contract is traded on the Chicago Board of Trade (CBOT). The underlying instrument for a Treasury bond futures contract is $100,000 par value of a hypothetical 20-year, 6% coupon bond. The 6% coupon rate on the hypothetical bond is called the "notional coupon."

We referred to the underlying as a hypothetical Treasury bond. The seller of a Treasury bond futures contract who decides to make delivery rather than liquidate a position by buying back the contract prior to the settlement date must deliver some Treasury bond. But what Treasury bond? The CBOT allows the seller to deliver one of several Treasury bonds that the CBOT specifies are acceptable for delivery. The CBOT makes its determination of the Treasury issues that are acceptable for delivery from all outstanding Treasury issues that have at least 15 years to maturity from the first day of the delivery month. Exhibit 29.1 shows the eligible issues as of August 30, 2001 for the June 2002 Treasury bond futures contract.

It is important to remember that while the underlying Treasury bond for this contract is a hypothetical issue and therefore cannot itself be delivered into the futures contract, the contract is not a cash settlement contract as is the case of the equity index futures and the Eurodollar CD futures. The only way to close out a Treasury bond futures contract is to either initiate an offsetting futures position, or to deliver a Treasury issue that is acceptable for delivery.

Conversion Factors The delivery process for the Treasury bond futures contract makes the contract interesting. At the settlement date, the seller of a futures contract (the short) is required to deliver to the buyer (the long) $100,000 par value of a 6% 20-year Treasury bond. Since no such bond exists, the seller must choose from one of the acceptable deliverable Treasury bonds that the CBOT has specified. Suppose the seller is entitled to deliver $100,000 of a 5% 20-year Treasury bond to settle the futures contract. The value of this bond is less than the value of a 6% 20-year bond. If the seller delivers the 5% 20-year bond, this would be unfair to the buyer of the futures contract who contracted to receive $100,000 of a 6% 20-year Treasury bond. Alternatively, suppose the seller delivers $100,000 of a 7% 20-year Treasury bond. The value of a 7% 20-year Treasury bond is greater than that of a 6% 20-year bond, so this would be a disadvantage to the seller.

EXHIBIT 29.1   Eligible Treasury Bonds (as of August 31, 2001) and
Corresponding Conversion Factors for Settlement
Conversion Factors for Settlement in June 2002

Coupon	Issue Date	Maturity Date	Conversion Factor
5¼	11/16/98	11/15/28	0.9014
5¼	02/16/99	02/15/29	0.9011
5⅜	02/15/01	02/15/31	0.9152
5 _	08/17/98	08/15/28	0.9346
6	02/15/96	02/15/26	1.0000
6⅛	11/17/97	11/15/27	1.0160
6⅛	08/16/99	08/15/29	1.0166
6¼	08/16/93	08/15/23	1.0296
6¼	02/15/00	05/15/30	1.0335
6⅜	08/15/97	08/15/27	1.0482
6 _	11/15/96	11/15/26	1.0633
6⅝	02/18/97	02/15/27	1.0797
6¾	08/15/96	08/15/26	1.0948
6⅞	08/15/95	08/15/25	1.1084
7⅛	02/16/93	02/15/23	1.1317
7¼	08/17/92	08/15/22	1.1445
7 _	08/15/94	11/15/24	1.1828
7⅝	11/15/92	11/15/22	1.1889
7⅝	02/15/95	02/15/25	1.1992
7⅞	02/15/91	02/15/21	1.2078
8	11/15/91	11/15/21	1.2264
8⅛	08/15/89	08/15/19	1.2245
8⅛	05/15/91	05/15/21	1.2371
8⅛	08/15/91	08/15/21	1.2390
8 _	02/15/90	02/15/20	1.2686
8¾	05/15/90	05/15/20	1.2977
8¾	08/15/90	08/15/20	1.3002
8⅞	08/15/87	08/15/17	1.2818
8⅞	02/15/89	02/15/19	1.2985
9	11/22/88	11/15/18	1.3085
9⅛	05/15/88	05/15/18	1.3154

Source: Chicago Board of Trade

To make delivery equitable to both parties, the CBOT uses conversion factors for adjusting the price of each Treasury issue that can be delivered to satisfy the Treasury bond futures contract. Exhibit 29.1 shows for each of the acceptable Treasury issues for the June 2002 futures contract the corresponding conversion factor. The conversion factor is constant throughout the life of the futures contract.

Given the conversion factor for an issue and the futures price, the adjusted price is found by multiplying the conversion factor by the futures price. The adjusted price is called the *converted price*. The price that the buyer must pay the seller when a Treasury bond is delivered is called the *invoice price*. The invoice price is the futures settlement price plus accrued interest. However, as just noted, the seller can deliver one of several acceptable Treasury issues and to make delivery fair to both parties, the invoice price must be adjusted based on the actual Treasury issue delivered. It is the conversion factors that are used to adjust the invoice price. The invoice price is:

$$\text{Invoice price} = \text{Contract size} \times \text{Futures settlement price} \\ \times \text{Conversion factor} + \text{Accrued interest}$$

Cheapest-to-Deliver Issue   In selecting the issue to be delivered, the short will select from among all the deliverable issues the one that will give the largest rate of return from a cash-and-carry trade. A *cash-and-carry trade* is one in which a cash bond that is acceptable for delivery is purchased with borrowed funds and simultaneously the Treasury bond futures contract is sold. The bond purchased can be delivered to satisfy the short futures position. Thus, by buying the Treasury issue that is acceptable for delivery and selling the futures, an investor has effectively sold the bond at the delivery price (i.e., the converted price). A rate of return can be calculated for this trade. This rate of return is referred to as the *implied repo rate*.

Once the implied repo rate is calculated for each deliverable issue, the issue selected will be the one that has the highest implied repo rate (i.e., the issue that gives the maximum return in a cash and carry trade). The issue with the highest return is referred to as the *cheapest-to-deliver issue* and this issue plays a key role in the pricing of a Treasury futures contract. While an issue may be the cheapest-to-deliver issue today, changes in factors may cause some other issue to be the cheapest-to-deliver issue at a future date.

Other Delivery Options   In addition to the choice of which acceptable Treasury issue to deliver—referred to as the *quality option* or *swap option*—the short has at least two more options granted under CBOT delivery guidelines. The short is permitted to decide when in the delivery month delivery actually will take place. This is called the *timing option*. The other option is the right of the short to give notice of intent to deliver up to 8:00 p.m. Chicago time after the closing of the exchange (3:15 p.m. Chicago time) on the date when the futures settlement price has been fixed. This option is referred to as the *wild card option*. The quality option, the timing option, and the wild card option (in sum referred to as the *delivery options*), mean that the long position can never be sure which Treasury bond will be delivered or when it will be delivered.

Treasury Note Futures

There are three Treasury note futures contracts: 10-year, 5-year, and 2-year. All three contracts are modeled after the Treasury bond futures contract and are traded on the CBOT. The underlying instrument for the 10-year Treasury note futures contract is $100,000 par value of a hypothetical 10-year 6% Treasury note. There are several acceptable Treasury issues that may be delivered by the short. An issue is acceptable if the maturity is not less than 6.5 years and not greater than 10 years from the first day of the delivery month. The delivery options are granted to the short position. For the 5-year Treasury note futures contract, the underlying is $100,000 par value of a 6% notional coupon U.S. Treasury note that satisfies the following conditions: (1) an original maturity of not more than five years and three months, (2) a remaining maturity no greater then five years and three months, and (3) a remaining maturity not less than four years and two months. The underlying for the 2-year Treasury note futures contract is $200,000 par value of a 6% notional coupon U.S. Treasury note with a remaining maturity of not more than two years and not less than one year and nine months. Moreover, the original maturity of the note delivered to satisfy the 2-year futures cannot be more than five years and three months.

Agency Note Futures Contract

The CBOT and the Chicago Mercantile Exchange (CME) trade futures contracts in which the underlying is a Fannie Mae or Freddie Mac agency debenture. (As explained in Chapter 9, Fannie Mae and Freddie Mac are government sponsored enterprises.) The underlying for the CBOT 10-year Agency note futures contract is a Fannie Mae Benchmark Note or Freddie Mac Reference Note having a par value of $100,000 and a notional coupon of 6%. As with the Treasury futures contract, there is more than one issue that is deliverable and there is a conversion factor for each eligible issue. Because there are many issues that are deliverable, there is a cheapest-to-deliver issue.

The 10-year Agency note futures contract of the CME is similar to that of the CBOT, but has a notional coupon of 6.5% instead of 6%. For an issue to be deliverable, the CME requires that the original maturity is 10 years and which does not mature for a period of at least 6.5 years from the date of delivery.

The CBOT and the CME also have a 5-year Agency note futures contract. Again, the CBOT's underlying is a 6% notional coupon and the CME's is a 6.5% notional coupon.

Long-Term Municipal Bond Index Futures Contract

The long-term municipal bond index futures contract is traded on the CBOT and is based on the value of the Bond Buyer Index (BBI) which consists of 40 municipal bonds. Unlike the Treasury bond futures contract, where the underlying to be delivered is $100,000 of a hypothetical 6% 20-year Treasury bond, the municipal bond index futures contract does not specify a par amount for the underlying index to be delivered. Instead, the dollar value of a futures contract is equal to the product of the futures price and $1,000. The settlement price on the last day of trading is equal to the product of the Bond Buyer Index value and $1,000. Since delivery on all 40 bonds in the index would be difficult, the contract is a cash settlement contract. This is unlike the Treasury bond futures contract which requires physical delivery of an acceptable Treasury bond issue.

In order to understand this futures contract, it is necessary to understand the nuances of how the BBI is constructed. The BBI consists of 40 actively traded general obligation and revenue bonds. To be included in the BBI, the following criteria must be satisfied: (1) the issue must have a Moody's rating of A or higher and/or an S&P rating of A– or higher, and (2) the size of the term portion of the issue must be at least $50 million ($75 million for housing issues). No more than two bonds of the same issuer may be included in the BBI. In addition, for an issue to be considered, it must meet the following three conditions: (1) have at least 19 years remaining to maturity, (2) have a first call date between 7 and 16 years, and (3) have at least one call at par prior to redemption.

The Bond Buyer serves as the index manager for the contract and prices each issue in the index based on prices received daily from at least four of six dealer-to-dealer brokers. After dropping the highest price and the lowest price obtained for each issue, the average of the remaining prices is computed. This price is then used to calculate the BBI as follows. First, the price for an issue is multiplied by a conversion factor, just as in the case of the Treasury bond futures contract. This gives a converted price for each bond in the BBI. The converted prices for the bonds in the index are then summed and divided by 40, giving an average converted price for the BBI.

Finally, because the BBI is revised bimonthly when newer issues are added and older issues, or issues that no longer meet the criteria for inclusion in the index are dropped, a "smoothing coefficient" is calculated on the index revision date so that the value of the BBI will not change due merely to the change in its composition. The average converted price for the BBI is multiplied by this coefficient to get the value of the BBI for a particular date.

Nuances Associated with the Valuation of Futures Contracts

In the previous chapter, the valuation of stock index futures contracts is explained. Specifically, for stock index futures, the theoretical futures price is

$$\text{Futures price} = \text{Spot price} + \text{Cost of financing} - \text{Dividend yield}$$

For an interest rate futures contract, the first modification is to substitute cash yield on the underlying bond for the dividend yield. That is,

$$\text{Futures price} = \text{Spot price} + \text{Cost of financing} - \text{Cash yield}$$

Further modifications are necessary due to the nuances of specific interest rate futures contracts, particularly those that grant the short various options. Specifically, in deriving the theoretical futures price it is assumed that only one instrument is deliverable. But as explained earlier, the futures contract on Treasury bonds and notes and Agency Notes are designed to allow the short the choice of delivering one of a number of deliverable issues (the quality or swap option). Because there may be more than one deliverable, market participants track the price of each deliverable bond and determine which issue is the cheapest to deliver. The theoretical futures price will then trade in relation to the cheapest-to-deliver issue.

There is the risk that while an issue may be the cheapest to deliver at the time a position in the futures contract is taken, it may not be after that time. A change in the cheapest-to-deliver issue can dramatically alter the futures price. Because the swap option is an option granted by the long to the short, the long will want to pay less for the futures contract.

Therefore, as a result of the swap option, the theoretical futures price must be modified as follows:

$$\text{Futures price} = \text{Spot price} + \text{Cost of financing} - \text{Cash yield} \\ - \text{Value of the swap option}$$

Market participants have employed theoretical models in attempting to estimate the fair value of the swap option.

Moreover, a known delivery date is assumed. As explained earlier, for the Treasury bond and note futures contracts, the short has a timing and wild card option, so the long does not know when the securities will be delivered. The effect of the timing and wild card options on the theoretical futures price is the same as with the swap option. These delivery options result in a theoretical futures price as follows:

$$\text{Futures price} = \text{Spot price} + \text{Cost of financing} - \text{Cash yield} - \text{Value of the delivery options}$$

Forward Rate Agreements

A *forward rate agreement* (FRA) is the over-the-counter equivalent of the exchange-traded futures contracts on short-term rates. Typically, the short-term rate is LIBOR.

The elements of an FRA are the contract rate, reference rate, settlement rate, notional amount, and settlement date. The parties to an FRA agree to buy and sell funds on the settlement date. The contract rate is the rate specified in the FRA at which the buyer of the FRA agrees to pay for funds and the seller of the FRA agrees to receive for investing funds. The reference rate is the interest rate used. The benchmark from which the interest payments are to be calculated is specified in the FRA and is called the *notional amount* (or *notional principal*). This amount is not exchanged between the two parties. The settlement rate is the value of the reference rate at the FRA's settlement date. The source for determining the settlement rate is specified in the FRA.

The buyer of the FRA is agreeing to pay the contract rate, or equivalently, to buy funds on the settlement date at the contract rate; the seller of the FRA is agreeing to receive the contract rate, or equivalently to sell funds on the settlement date at the contract rate. So, for example, if the FRA has a contract rate of 5% for 3-month LIBOR (the reference rate) and the notional amount is $10 million, the buyer is agreeing to pay 5% to buy or borrow $10 million at the settlement date and the seller is agreeing to receive 5% to sell or lend $10 million at the settlement date.

If at the settlement date the settlement rate is greater than the contract rate, the FRA buyer benefits because the buyer can borrow funds at a below-market rate. If the settlement rate is less than the contract rate, this benefits the seller who can lend funds at an above-market rate. If the settlement rate is the same as the contract rate, neither party benefits. This is summarized below:

FRA buyer benefits if settlement rate > contract rate
FRA seller benefits if contract rate > settlement rate
Neither party benefits if settlement rate = contract rate

FRAs are cash settlement contracts. At the settlement date, the party that benefits based on the contract rate and settlement rate must be compensated by the other. Assuming the settlement rate is not equal to the contract rate then:

buyer receives compensation if settlement rate > contract rate
seller receives compensation if contract rate > settlement rate

To determine the amount that one party must compensate the other, the following is first calculated assuming a 360 day-count convention:

If settlement rate > contract rate:

Interest differential = (Settlement rate − Contract rate)
× (Days in contract period/360) × Notional amount

If contract rate > settlement rate:

Interest differential = (Contract rate − Settlement rate)
× (Days in contract period/360) × Notional amount

The amount that must be exchanged at the settlement is not the interest differential. Instead, the present value of the interest differential is exchanged. The discount rate used to calculate the present value of the interest differential is the settlement rate. Thus, the compensation is determined as follows:

$$\text{Compensation} = \frac{\text{Interest differential}}{[1 + \text{Settlement rate} \times (\text{Days to contract period}/360)]}$$

To illustrate, assume the following terms for an FRA: reference rate is 3-month LIBOR, the contract rate is 5%, the notional amount is $10 million, and the number of days to settlement is 91 days. Suppose the settlement rate is 5.5%. This means that the buyer benefits since the buyer can borrow at 5% (the contract rate) when the market rate (the settlement rate) is 5.5%. Then

Interest differential = (0.055 − 0.05) × (91/360) × $10,000,000
= $12,638.89

The compensation or payment that the seller must make to the buyer is:

$$\text{Compensation} = \frac{\$12,638.89}{[1 + 0.055 \times (91/360)]} = \$12,465.58$$

It is important to note the difference as to which party benefits when interest rates move in an FRA and a futures contract. The buyer of an FRA benefits if the reference rate increases and the seller benefits if the reference rate decreases. In a futures contract, the buyer benefits from a falling rate while the seller benefits from a rising rate. This is summarized below

	Interest Rates Decrease		Interest Rates Increase	
Party	FRA	Futures	FRA	Futures
Buyer	Loses	Gains	Gains	Loses
Seller	Gains	Loses	Loses	Gains

This is because the underlying for each of the two contracts is different. In the case of an FRA, the underlying is a rate. The buyer gains if the rate increases and loses if the rate decreases. The opposite occurs for the seller of an FRA. In contrast, in a futures contract the underlying is a fixed-income instrument. The buyer gains if the fixed-income instrument increases in value. This occurs when rates decline. The buyer loses when the fixed-income instrument decreases in value. This occurs when interest rates increase. The opposite occurs for the seller of a futures contract.

The liquid and easily accessible sector of the FRA market is for 3-month and 6-month LIBOR. Rates are widely available for settlement starting one month forward, and settling once every month thereafter out to about six months forward. Thus, for example, on any given day forward rates are available for both 3-month and 6-month LIBOR one month forward, covering, respectively, the interest period starting in one month and ending in four months and the interest period staring in one month and ending in seven months. These contracts are referred to as 1×4 and 1×7 contracts. On the same day, there will be FRAs on 3-month and 6-month LIBOR for settlement two months forward. These are the 2×5 and 2×8 contracts. Similarly, settlements occur three months, four months, five months, and six months forward for both 3-month LIBOR and 6-month LIBOR. These contracts are also denoted by the beginning and ending of the interest period that they cover.

INTEREST RATE OPTIONS

An option is a contract in which the writer of the option grants the buyer of the option the right, but not the obligation, to purchase from or sell to the writer something at a specified price within a specified period of time (or at a specified date). The writer, also referred to as the seller, grants this right to the buyer in exchange for a certain sum of money, which is called the option price or option premium. The price at which the underlying for the contract may be bought or sold is called the exercise or strike price. The date after which an option is void is called the expiration date. Our focus is on options where the "something" underlying the option is a fixed income instrument or an interest rate.

Exchange-traded interest rate options can be written on a fixed income security or an interest rate futures contract. The former options are called *options on physicals*. Options on interest rate futures have been far more popular than options on physicals. However, institutional investors have made increasingly greater use of over-the-counter options.

Exchange-Traded Futures Options

There are futures options on all the interest rate futures contracts mentioned earlier in this chapter. An option on a futures contract, commonly referred to as a *futures option*, gives the buyer the right to buy from or sell to the writer a designated futures contract at the strike price at any time during the life of the option. If the futures option is a call option, the buyer has the right to purchase one designated futures contract at the strike price. That is, the buyer has the right to acquire a long futures position in the underlying futures contract. If the buyer exercises the call option, the writer acquires a corresponding short position in the futures contract.

A put option on a futures contract grants the buyer the right to sell one designated futures contract to the writer at the strike price. That is, the option buyer has the right to acquire a short position in the designated futures contract. If the put option is exercised, the writer acquires a corresponding long position in the designated futures contract.

As the parties to the futures option will establish a position in a futures contract when the option is exercised, the question is: What will the futures price be? That is, at what futures price will the long be required to pay for the instrument underlying the futures contract, and at what futures price will the short be required to sell the instrument underlying the futures contract?

Upon exercise, the futures price for the futures contract will be set equal to the strike price. The position of the two parties is then immediately marked-to-market in terms of the then-current futures price. Thus, the futures position of the two parties will be at the prevailing futures price. At the same time, the option buyer will receive from the option seller the economic benefit from exercising. In the case of a call futures option, the option writer must pay the difference between the current futures price and the strike price to the buyer of the option. In the case of a put futures option, the option writer must pay the option buyer the difference between the strike price and the current futures price.

For example, suppose an investor buys a call option on some futures contract and the strike price is 85. Assume also that the futures price is 95 and that the buyer exercises the call option. Upon exercise, the call buyer is given a long position in the futures contract at 85 and the call writer is assigned the corresponding short position in the futures contract at 85. The futures positions of the buyer and the writer are immediately marked-to-market by the exchange. Because the prevailing futures price is 95 and the strike price is 85, the long futures position (the position of the call buyer) realizes a gain of 10, while the short futures position (the position of the call writer) realizes a loss of 10. The call writer pays the exchange 10 and the call buyer receives from the exchange 10. The call buyer, who now has a long futures position at 95, can either liquidate the futures position at 95 or maintain a long futures position. If the former course of action is taken, the call buyer sells a futures contract at the prevailing futures price of 95. There is no gain or loss from liquidating the position. Overall, the call buyer realizes a gain of 10. The call buyer who elects to hold the long futures position will face the same risk and reward of holding such a position, but still realizes a gain of 10 from the exercise of the call option.

Suppose instead that the futures option is a put rather than a call, and the current futures price is 60 rather than 95. Then if the buyer of this put option exercises it, the buyer would have a short position in the futures contract at 85; the option writer would have a long position in the futures contract at 85. The exchange then marks the position to market at the then-current futures price of 60, resulting in a gain to the put buyer of 25 and a loss to the put writer of the same amount. The put buyer who now has a short futures position at 60 can either liquidate the short futures position by buying a futures contract at the prevailing futures price of 60 or maintain the short futures position. In either case, the put buyer realizes a gain of 25 from exercising the put option.

There are three reasons why futures options on fixed income securities have largely supplanted options on physicals as the options vehicle of choice for institutional investors who want to use exchange-traded options. First, unlike options on fixed income securities, options on Treasury coupon futures do not require payments for accrued interest to be made. Consequently, when a futures option is exercised, the call buyer and the put writer need not compensate the other party for accrued interest. Second, futures options are believed to be "cleaner" instruments because of the reduced likelihood of delivery squeezes. Market participants who must deliver an instrument are concerned that at the time of delivery the instrument to be delivered will be in short supply, resulting in a higher price to acquire the instrument. Because the deliverable supply of futures contracts is more than adequate for futures options currently traded, there is no concern about a delivery squeeze. Finally, in order to price any option, it is imperative to know at all times the price of the underlying instrument. In the bond market, current prices are not as easily available as price information on the futures contract. The reason is that because bonds trade in the over-the-counter market, there is no reporting system with recent price information. Thus, an investor who wanted to purchase an option on a Treasury bond would have to call several dealer firms to obtain a price. In contrast, futures contracts are traded on an exchange and, as a result, price information is reported.

Over-the-Counter Options

Institutional investors who want to purchase an option on a specific Treasury security or a mortgage passthrough security can do so on an over-the-counter basis. There are government and mortgage-backed securities dealers who make a market in options on specific securities. Over-the-counter options, also called dealer options, usually are purchased by institutional investors who want to hedge the risk associated with a specific security. Typically, the maturity of the option coincides with the time period over which the buyer of the option wants to hedge, so the buyer is not concerned with the option's liquidity.

In the absence of a clearinghouse, the parties to any over-the-counter contract are exposed to counterparty risk. In the case of forward contracts where both parties are obligated to perform, both parties face counterparty risk. In contrast, in the case of an option, once the option buyer pays the option price, it has satisfied its obligation. It is only the seller that must perform if the option is exercised. Thus, only the option buyer is exposed to counterparty risk.

OTC options can be customized in any manner sought by an institutional investor. Basically, if a dealer can hedge the risk associated with the opposite side of the option sought, it will create the option desired by a customer. OTC options are not limited to European or American type. An option can be created in which the option can be exercised at several specified dates as well as the expiration date. Such options are referred to as modified American options, Bermuda options, and Atlantic options.

INTEREST RATE SWAPS

Interest rate swaps are over-the-counter instruments. In an interest rate swap, two parties agree to exchange periodic interest payments. The dollar amount of the interest payments exchanged is based on some predetermined dollar principal, the notional principal. The dollar amount each counterparty pays to the other is the agreed-upon periodic interest rate times the notional principal. The only dollars that are exchanged between the parties are the interest payments, not the notional principal.

In the most common type of swap, one party agrees to pay the other party fixed interest payments at designated dates for the life of the contract. This party is referred to as the *fixed-rate payer*. The other party, who agrees to make interest rate payments that float with some reference rate, is referred to as the *fixed-rate receiver*. Such swaps are referred to as *fixed-for-floating rate swaps*. The reference rates that have been used for the floating rate in an interest rate swap arc those on various money market instruments: Treasury bills, the London interbank offered rate, commercial paper, bankers acceptances, certificates of deposit, the federal funds rate, and the prime rate. The most common is LIBOR.

To illustrate an interest rate swap, suppose that for the next five years party X agrees to pay party Y 6% per year, while party Y agrees to pay party X 3-month LIBOR (the reference rate). Party X is the fixed-rate payer, while party Y is the fixed-rate receiver. Assume that the notional principal is $50 million, and that payments are exchanged every three months for the next five years. This means that every three months, party X (the fixed-rate payer) will pay party Y $750,000 (6% times $50 million divided by 4). The amount that party Y (the fixed-rate receiver) will pay party X will be 3-month LIBOR times $50 million divided by 4. If 3-month LIBOR is 4%, party Y will pay party X $500,000 (4% times $50 million divided by 4).

The convention that has evolved for quoting swaps levels is that a swap dealer sets the floating rate equal to the reference rate and then quotes the fixed rate that will apply. The fixed rate is some spread above the Treasury yield curve with the same term to maturity as the swap. The fixed rate is called the *swap rate*. In our illustration above, the swap rate is 6%. The spread over the Treasury yield curve is called the *swap spread*.

The notional principal for the swap need not be the same amount over the life of the swap. That is, the notional principal can change. A swap in which the notional principal decreases over time is called an *amortizing swap*. A swap in which the notional principal increases over time is called an *accreting swap*.

There are swaps where both parties pay a floating interest rate. Such swaps are referred to as *basis swaps*.

Risk/Return Characteristics of an Interest Rate Swap

Because a swap is an OTC instrument, the risk that the two parties take on when they enter into a swap is that the counterparty will fail to fulfill its obligations. That is, each party faces default risk and therefore there is bilateral counterparty risk.

The value of an interest rate swap will change over time. To see how, let's consider our hypothetical swap. Suppose that immediately after parties X and Y enter into the swap, the swap rate changes. First, consider what would happen if the swap rate for a 5-year swap increases from 6% to 8% (i.e., interest rates have increased). If party X (the fixed-rate payer) wants to sell its position to party A, then party A will benefit by having to pay only 6% (the swap rate specified in the contract) rather than 8% (the prevailing swap rate) to receive 3-month LIBOR. Party X will want compensation for this benefit. Consequently, the value of party X's position has increased. Thus, if interest rates increase, the fixed-rate payer will realize a profit and the fixed-rate receiver will realize a loss.

Next, consider what would happen if interest rates decline and the swap rate declines to, say, 5%. Now a 5-year swap would require a fixed-rate payer to pay 5% rather than 6% to receive 3-month LIBOR. If party X wants to sell its position to party B, the latter would demand compensation to take over the position. In other words, if interest rates decline, the fixed-rate payer will realize a loss, while the fixed-rate receiver will realize a profit.

Interpreting a Swap Position

There are two ways that a swap position can be interpreted: (1) a package of forward/futures contracts, and (2) a package of cash flows from buying and selling cash market instruments.

Package of Forward Contracts

Contrast the position of the counterparties in an interest rate swap described previously to the position of the long and short interest rate futures (forward) contract. The long futures position gains if interest rates decline and loses if interest rates rise—this is similar to the risk/return profile for a fixed-rate receiver. The risk/return profile for a fixed-rate payer is similar to that of the short futures position: a gain if interest rates increase and a loss if interest rates decrease. The reason is that an interest rate swap can be viewed as a package of more basic interest rate derivatives, such as forwards. The pricing of an interest rate swap will then depend on the price of a package of forward contracts with the same settlement dates in which the underlying for the forward contract is the same reference rate.

Package of Cash Market Instruments

An interest rate swap is equivalent to a leveraged position in an asset. Specifically, it can be demonstrated that the position of a fixed-rate payer is equivalent to buying a floating-rate asset (i.e., receiving a floating-rate payment) and financing the purchase of that asset by issuing a fixed-rate bond (i.e., making a fixed-rate payment). For a fixed-rate receiver, the cash flow is identical to buying a fixed-rate asset and financing that purchase by issuing a floating-rate bond. That is why the two legs of a swap are referred to as the financing leg and asset leg.

Swaptions

There are options on interest rate swaps. These derivative contracts are called *swaptions* and grant the option buyer the right to enter into an interest rate swap at a future date. The time until expiration of the swap, the term of the swap, and the swap rate are specified. The swap rate is the strike rate for the option.

A *payer's swaption* entitles the option buyer to enter into an interest rate swap in which the buyer of the option pays a fixed rate and receives a floating rate. Suppose that the strike rate is 6.5%, the term of the swap is three years, and the swaption expires in two years. This means that the buyer of this option some time over the next two years has the right to enter into a 3-year interest rate swap where the buyer pays 6.5% (the swap rate which is equal to the strike rate) and receives the reference rate.

In a receiver's swaption the buyer of the option has the right to enter into an interest rate swap to pay a floating rate and receive a fixed rate. For example, if the strike rate is 7%, the swap term is five years, and the option expires in one year, the buyer of a receiver's swaption has the right some time over the next year to enter into a 5-year interest rate swap in which the buyer receives a swap rate of 7% (i.e., the strike rate) and pays the reference rate.

Swap Futures Contract

The CBOT introduced a swap futures contract in late October 2001. The underlying instrument is the notional price of the fixed-rate side of a 10-year interest rate swap that has a notional principal equal to $100,000 and that exchanges semiannual interest payments at a fixed annual rate of 6% for floating interest rate payments based on 3-month LIBOR. This swap futures contract is cash settled with a settlement price determined by the International Swap and Derivatives Dealer (ISDA) benchmark 10-year swap rate on the last day of trading before the contract expires. This benchmark rate is published with a one-day lag in the Federal Reserve Board's statistical release H.15.

INTEREST RATE CAPS AND FLOORS

An interest rate agreement is an agreement between two parties whereby one party for an upfront premium agrees to compensate the other at specific time periods if the reference rate is different from a predetermined level. When one party agrees to pay the other when the reference rate exceeds a predetermined level, the agreement is referred to as an *interest rate cap* . The agreement is referred to as an *interest rate floor* when one party agrees to pay the other when the reference rate falls below a predetermined level. The predetermined level is called the strike rate.

The terms of an interest rate agreement include:

1. The reference rate
2. The strike rate that sets the ceiling or floor
3. The length of the agreement
4. The frequency of settlement
5. The notional principal

For example, suppose that party C buys an interest rate cap from party D with terms as follows:

1. The reference rate is 3-month LIBOR
2. The strike rate is 6%
3. The agreement is for four years
4. Settlement is every three months
5. The notional principal is $20 million

Under this agreement, every three months for the next four years, party D will pay party C whenever 3-month LIBOR exceeds 6% at a settlement date. (Actually the payment is made arrears.). The payment will equal the dollar value of the difference between 3-month LIBOR and 6% times the notional principal divided by 4. For example, if three months from now 3-month LIBOR on a settlement date is 8%, then party D will pay party C 2% (8% minus 6%) times $20 million divided by 4, or $100,000. If 3-month LIBOR is 6% or less, party D does not have to pay anything to party C.

In the case of an interest rate floor, assume the same terms as the interest rate cap we just illustrated. In this case, if 3-month LIBOR is 8%, party C receives nothing from party D, but if 3-month LIBOR is less than 6%, party D compensates party C for the difference. For example, if 3-month LIBOR is 5%, party D will pay party C $50,000 (6% minus 5% times $20 million divided by 4).

Interest rate caps and floors can be combined to create an interest rate collar. This is done by buying an interest rate cap and selling an interest rate floor.

Risk/Return Characteristics

In an interest rate cap or floor, the buyer pays an upfront fee which represents the maximum amount that the buyer can lose and the maximum amount that the seller (writer) can gain. The only party that is required to perform is the seller of the interest rate cap or floor. The buyer of an interest rate cap benefits if the reference rate rises above the strike rate because the seller must compensate the buyer. The buyer of an interest rate floor benefits if the reference rate falls below the strike rate, because the seller must compensate the buyer.

To better understand interest rate caps and interest rate floors, we can look at them as in essence equivalent to a package of interest rate options. Since the buyer benefits if the interest rate rises above the strike rate, an interest rate cap is similar to purchasing a package of call options on the reference rate; the seller of an interest rate cap has effectively sold a package of these options. The buyer of an interest rate floor benefits from a decline in the reference rate below the strike rate. Therefore, the buyer of an interest rate floor has effectively bought a package of put options on the reference rate from the seller. An interest rate collar is equivalent to buying a package of call options and selling a package of put options. Once again, a complex contract can be seen to be a package of basic contracts, options in the case of interest rate agreements.

The seller of an interest rate cap or floor does not face counterparty risk once the buyer pays the fee. In contrast, the buyer faces counterparty risk.

CHAPTER 30

Mortgage Swaps

David Yuen, CFA
Senior Vice President
Portfolio Strategist/Risk Manager
Franklin Templeton Investments

Frank J. Fabozzi, Ph.D., CFA
Adjunct Professor Finance
School of Management
Yale University

As explained in Chapter 14, the market for securities backed by real estate assets is a major part of the investment-grade bond market. An efficient strategy to gain exposure (both risk and reward) to the mortgage market is through a *mortgage swap*. A mortgage swap is a specialized form of interest rate swap developed in the United States. In this chapter we discuss mortgage swaps and other types of swaps (index amortizing swap and total return mortgage swap) that can be used by participants in the mortgage market.

FEATURES OF MORTGAGE SWAPS

As the name implies, a mortgage swap is a swap transaction entered between two counterparties based on the cash flows and performance of a pool of mortgages. It is a synthetic leveraged long position on mortgages. It is economically equivalent to borrowing funds at LIBOR (+/– a spread) and investing in a pool of mortgages or mortgage-backed securities.

As with other generic fixed-to-floating interest rate swaps, it has two legs: the fixed leg and the floating leg. The fixed leg is also referred to as the "mortgage leg" and the floating leg is also referred to as the "funding leg." The mortgage leg replicates the cash flows of a pool of mortgages including the monthly coupon payments, monthly regular principal amortization, monthly irregular principal prepayments, monthly gain (discounts) or loss (premiums) on paydown, and the price appreciation or depreciation on the remaining balance at the end of the holding period. The funding leg replicates the cost of carrying the investment, usually at LIBOR. Since most mortgage swaps are done on 3- to 5-year terms and the reference mortgage pool has 15- or 30-year maturities, a termination price for the swap must be established at the swap expiration to calculate and settle the gain or loss.

A feature of the mortgage swap that makes it unique from other interest rate swaps is that the notional balance of the mortgage swap (both the mortgage leg and the funding leg) amortizes down simultaneously with actual monthly prepayments on the specific pool of reference mortgages. Therefore, the amortization rate is unknown at the inception of the swap. Some market participants enter into amortizing asset swaps with a predetermined amortization schedule to match the sinking fund schedule of the asset, but in that case, the notional balance is fixed and known upfront. Only a mortgage swap and an index amortizing swap (which is a slightly different version of a mortgage swap) have a variable amortizing schedule that both counterparties can agree upon without ambiguity.

Mortgage Swap Structure

A typical mortgage swap structure and its cash flows can best be illustrated using an example with the following structure and terms:

Notional Amount:	$100 million
Term:	3 years
Reference asset:	GNMA 8%, pool#xxxxx or all 1999 production
Initial Price:	103% of notional face
Reference pool WAC:	8.5%
Reference pool WAM:	330 months
Projected prepayment rate:	12% CPR, 1.06% SMM
Initial 1-month LIBOR:	5.50%
Receive:	Fixed coupon of 8% (30/360) on current balances of reference pool
Pay:	LIBOR flat (act/360) on current value (current balance × initial price) of reference pool
Receive:	Principal paydown × discount if initial price is below par

Pay:	Principal paydown × premium if initial price is above par
Payment frequency:	Monthly
Payment dates:	15th of every month to coincide with GNMA payments (25th for FNMA)
Expiration:	Cash settlement on difference between initial price and market price on the remaining balance by polling method (three dealers), or
Physical settlement:	Mortgage leg receiver pays the initial price and takes delivery of mortgage-backed securities of the remaining balance

As the terms indicate, the investor will receive the full economics (coupon income, actual prepayment experience, gain or loss on paydown, and price appreciation or depreciation at the end of the holding period) of owning $100 million of GNMA 8% pool#xxxxx, and will incur the monthly variable cost of funding at LIBOR. This transaction can be replicated by using a dollar roll, a specialized form of repurchase agreement developed for the mortgage market explained in Chapter 14. The difference between "dollar rolling" GNMA 8% on a monthly basis and using a mortgage swap is that the funding cost on the dollar roll is unknown from month to month. With a mortgage swap, the investor is locked into a funding rate for the rest of the term, although unwinding the swap may be more costly than unwinding a dollar roll.

Exhibit 30.1 shows the projected cash flows of the same mortgage swap using 12% CPR as an illustrative prepayment speed and holding LIBOR flat constant at 5.5%. Keep in mind that the balance or pool factor will be determined monthly depending on the actual monthly prepayment rates and LIBOR may also vary monthly.

Prepayment Risk

A feature of MBS, which impacts mortgage swaps, is the borrower's option to refinance or prepay partially or in full. The borrower has that option at any time but is more likely to exercise that option when mortgage rates are low. In a declining rate environment, prepayments would speed up leaving the MBS investor with a lower outstanding balance to realize the price appreciation. The duration[1] of MBS also shortens given the faster prepayment, again limiting upside potential. The prepayment risk and consequently, the negative convexity, get passed through to the

---

[1] Duration is the approximate percentage change in price of a security or a portfolio for a 100-basis-point change in interest rates. See Chapter 2.

mortgage swap receiver also. (By negative convexity it is meant that when interest rates decline a large number of basis points, the price appreciation of a security is less than the price depreciation that would be realized if interest rates increased the same number of basis points.) Unlike a normal fixed-rate receiver in a swap, which has positive convexity, a mortgage swap receiver actually has negative convexity.

EXHIBIT 30.1   Cash Flows of the Hypothetical Mortgage Swap
Structure:

Principal	100	WAC	8.500%	Coupon	8.00%	1-month LIBOR	5.50%
WAM	330	CPR	12.00%	SMM	1.060%	PSA	200%
MBS Price $\Rightarrow$ 103.00		Ending Price $\Rightarrow$ 101		MY	7.349%	BEY	7.463%

Term	Principal Payment	Net Interest	Prepayment	MBS Balance	Principal Settlement	LIBOR Flat	Swaps Cash Flow
1	0.0764	0.6667	1.0588	98.8648	−0.03406	0.4786	0.1540
2	0.0761	0.6591	1.0468	97.7419	−0.03369	0.4732	0.1522
3	0.0759	0.6516	1.0349	96.6311	−0.03332	0.4678	0.1505
4	0.0756	0.6442	1.0231	95.5324	−0.03296	0.4625	0.1487
5	0.0753	0.6369	1.0115	94.4456	−0.03260	0.4573	0.1470
6	0.0750	0.6296	1.0000	93.3706	−0.03225	0.4521	0.1453
7	0.0748	0.6225	0.9886	92.3072	−0.03190	0.4469	0.1437
8	0.0745	0.6154	0.9773	91.2554	−0.03155	0.4418	0.1420
9	0.0742	0.6084	0.9662	90.2149	−0.03121	0.4368	0.1404
10	0.0740	0.6014	0.9552	89.1858	−0.03087	0.4318	0.1388
11	0.0737	0.5946	0.9443	88.1679	−0.03054	0.4269	0.1372
12	0.0734	0.5878	0.9335	87.1609	−0.03021	0.4220	0.1356
13	0.0732	0.5811	0.9228	86.1650	−0.02988	0.4172	0.1340
14	0.0729	0.5744	0.9123	85.1798	−0.02956	0.4124	0.1325
15	0.0727	0.5679	0.9018	84.2053	−0.02923	0.4077	0.1309
16	0.0724	0.5614	0.8915	83.2414	−0.02892	0.4030	0.1294
17	0.0721	0.5549	0.8813	82.2880	−0.02860	0.3984	0.1279
18	0.0719	0.5486	0.8712	81.3449	−0.02829	0.3939	0.1264
19	0.0716	0.5423	0.8612	80.4121	−0.02798	0.3893	0.1250
20	0.0714	0.5361	0.8513	79.4894	−0.02768	0.3849	0.1235
21	0.0711	0.5299	0.8415	78.5768	−0.02738	0.3805	0.1221
22	0.0709	0.5238	0.8319	77.6741	−0.02708	0.3761	0.1207
23	0.0706	0.5178	0.8223	76.7812	−0.02679	0.3718	0.1193
24	0.0703	0.5119	0.8128	75.8980	−0.02650	0.3675	0.1179
25	0.0701	0.5060	0.8035	75.0244	−0.02621	0.3633	0.1165
26	0.0698	0.5002	0.7942	74.1603	−0.02592	0.3591	0.1151
27	0.0696	0.4944	0.7851	73.3056	−0.02564	0.3550	0.1138
28	0.0693	0.4887	0.7760	72.4603	−0.02536	0.3509	0.1125
29	0.0691	0.4831	0.7671	71.6241	−0.02509	0.3468	0.1112
30	0.0688	0.4775	0.7582	70.7970	−0.02481	0.3428	0.1099
31	0.0686	0.4720	0.7495	69.9790	−0.02454	0.3389	0.1086
32	0.0684	0.4665	0.7408	69.1699	−0.02427	0.3349	0.1073
33	0.0681	0.4611	0.7322	68.3695	−0.02401	0.3311	0.1060
34	0.0679	0.4558	0.7237	67.5779	−0.02375	0.3272	0.1048
35	0.0676	0.4505	0.7154	66.7949	−0.02349	0.3235	0.1036
36	0.0674	0.4453	0.7071	66.0205	−1.34364	0.3197	−1.2181

Valuation of Mortgage Swaps

The valuation of mortgage swaps is closely tied to the cash market and the repo market. If the fair market value of GNMA 8% is $103 using the above example and the funding rate is LIBOR flat, the swap at inception has zero value. If the dollar roll market becomes hot after the mortgage swap is put on (meaning the implied funding rate is LIBOR minus a spread in the dollar roll market), then the value of that mortgage swap would be at a discount, or a new mortgage swap can be put on at LIBOR minus a spread. If GNMA 8% market value goes up, the value of that mortgage swap also goes up. If prepayment projection goes up holding everything else constant (i.e., aside from the interest rate induced prepayment), the value of that mortgage swap would go down.

INDEX AMORTIZING SWAP

While a mortgage swap replicates the cash flows of a mortgage pass-through security, an index amortizing swap replicates the cash flows of a collateralized mortgage obligation (CMO) tranche and even a PAC tranche as illustrated in Chapter 14 for hypothetical CMO deal CMO-3. The amortization schedule does not correspond to the underlying prepayment one for one. In fact, it typically has a lock-out period of one year when there is no amortization regardless of the prepayment rates. From year 2 to year 5 (or expiration of the swap), the notional balance of the swap would amortize monthly according to the following schedule depending on the monthly prepayment rate:

If Prepayment of Reference Pool Is	% of Initial Notional Balance Amortized after the One-Year Lock-Out	Average Life of Swap
< 100 PSA	1%	4.53
between 100 PSA and 300 PSA	2%	3.13
between 301 PSA and 500 PSA	4%	2.08
> 501 PSA	8%	1.56

In this example, the index used is the PSA prepayment rate. Other commonly used indices are LIBOR and Constant Treasury Maturity (CMT).

A similar index amortizing swap indexed to 10-year CMT would look like the following:

If 10-Year CMT Rate is	% of Initial Notional Balance Amortized after the One-Year Lock-Out	Average Life of Swap
> 7%	1%	4.53
between 6.5% and 7.0%	2%	3.13
between 6.0% and 6.5%	4%	2.08
< 6%	8%	1.56

The logic is the same here. If rates are high, the prepayment of the reference pool would slow down and the rate of amortization also slows down. If rates are low, the prepayment of the reference pool would speed up and the rate of amortization would also speed up. There are a few implicit assumptions here. One is that the 10-year CMT is highly correlated with mortgage rates. (The R-squared has been 85% in the past 10 years and 77% since 1998.) The second assumption is an implied prepayment model. The prepayment model is implying that when CMT is above 7% (mortgage rate above 8.5%), the prepayment option of the reference pool is out-of-the-money and consequently the prepayment rate would slow to less than 100 PSA. When CMT is between 6.5% and 7.0% (mortgage rate between 8% and 8.5%), refinancing becomes somewhat economical depending on the loan size, loan fees, and all the other costs associated with refinancing, the PSA would fluctuate between 100 and 300. When CMT drops below 6% (implied mortgage rate below 7.5%), the prepayment option is clearly in-the-money and the prepayment rate of the reference pool accelerates beyond 500 PSA. Note that the average life of the swap under various prepayment/interest rate scenarios mirrors that of a typical CMO tranche.

TOTAL RETURN INDEX SWAPS

It is apparent from the economics of a mortgage swap that the cash flows and total return characteristics of the swap mimic the holding period total return of the underlying mortgages financed at LIBOR. This kind of asset swap can be extended to other kinds of assets or indices, for example, Salomon Brothers Mortgage Index, the Mortgage subindex of the Lehman Aggregate Index and the Merrill Lynch Mortgage Index. This type of swap is referred to as a "total return index swap."

A typical total return index swap pays the investor the periodic total return of the reference index while the investor finances it at LIBOR (see Exhibit 30.2). The notional balance of a total return index swap stays constant although the prepayment is already factored into the monthly total return figure (total return = coupon return + price return + paydown return). A total return mortgage index swap is a leveraged exposure to the total mortgage market that is marked to market on a periodic basis. The above illustrated mortgage swap is only a specific type of total return swap with GNMA 8% being the reference index or asset and only marked to market with price settlement at the expiration.

APPLICATIONS OF MORTGAGE AND TOTAL RETURN INDEX SWAPS

In this section we will describe the various applications of mortgage and total return swaps.

Passive Exposure

The most useful application of a mortgage swap and total return index swap is the quick and passive exposure to the mortgage market. Given that the mortgage sector is the largest sector of the investment-grade bond market, it is not surprising that nontraditional mortgage investors would want to gain exposure to the mortgage market. However, an inexperienced mortgage investor (say a traditional corporate investor or a broad investment-grade fixed-income core investor) has to deal with the complexity of mortgage securities—that is, prepayment modeling, valuation modeling, back office to handle monthly cash flows, settlement, and so forth. Proper active management requires specialized expertise and analytical tools. An investor can gain exposure to the broad mortgage market in a passive way through a mortgage swap.

Leverage

As illustrated previously, a mortgage swap is economically equivalent to a synthetic leveraged investment in mortgages with funding at LIBOR (+/– a spread). Although leverage can also be obtained through dollar rolls and mortgage futures, a mortgage swap can lock in a long-term financing spread to LIBOR while short-term implied financing spreads can fluctuate with other alternatives.

EXHIBIT 30.2 Typical Total Return Swap

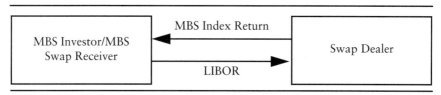

Diversification

Even if the investor has the back office and analytical tools to handle mortgage-backed securities, the size of the portfolio may limit the degree of diversification one wants to achieve. Since specified pools can prepay differently and therefore perform differently than the overall mortgage market, a small portfolio holding small samples of mortgage pools can have volatile performance from one period to another. This is especially problematic for a small new portfolio trying to establish a track record or an index fund that needs to minimize tracking error. Instead of holding small samples of mortgage pools, a small portfolio can enter into a mortgage swap referencing a much bigger portion of the mortgage universe to ensure broad market diversification and consequently broad market type of return.

Hedging

Hedging a portfolio of mortgage-backed securities can be tricky because of the embedded prepayment options. Interest rate futures can hedge out the interest rate (duration) risk but cannot address the negative convexity. Interest rate options can hedge out part of the convexity risk but still leave the risks of mismatch since interest rate options are efficiently exercised but prepayment options are not. Only a mortgage total return swap would have the "true" mortgage characteristics to minimize the basis risk.

Arbitrage

An active mortgage manager or an experienced mortgage specialist who has security selection skills in specific tranches of CMOs or specified pools can "arbitrage" the value differential. For instance, various tranches of CMOs can be assembled to replicate the risk characteristics (i.e., interest rate risk, exposure to interest rate volatility, and prepayment risk) of GNMA 8% while having a higher value. This long CMOs position can be combined with a pay GNMA 8% mortgage swap to have a risk neutral position with a higher value. Specified pools with unique characteristics such as loan-to-value (LTV) ratio, loan balance, regional concentration, and weighted average gross coupon will prepay differently from the generic mortgages. For example, loans with higher LTV prepay slower because of the lack of equity which is required for refinancing. Loans from New York prepay slower than the national average because of the state's transfer tax. Loans with lower balance prepay slower because the fixed portion of refinancing cost becomes a bigger hurdle for low balance loans. Loans from Hawaii prepay slower because of the slow housing market there. A skillful mortgage manager can hold specified premium pools with slower prepayment characteristics given any of the above reasons and enter into an offsetting mortgage swap with generic reference pool thus profiting from the difference in prepayment.

Transferring Alphas

In investment management, "alpha" is a measure of a portfolio manager's performance relative to the manager's benchmark. The alpha in one market can be transferred to another market through the use of a total return index swap. Suppose an experienced mortgage manager has been able to systematically outperform the Lehman Mortgage Index but has little experience in the equity market. The positive alpha of this mortgage manager can be transferred to the equity market by entering into a cross index total return swap paying mortgage index and receiving S&P 500 as shown in Exhibit 30.3. The excess return over the mortgage index becomes an excess return over the S&P index.

The same strategy can be applied to an enhanced indexer. An experienced money market manager who can consistently outperform LIBOR can create an enhanced product with any total return index, or index plus fund. As shown in Exhibit 30.4, the manager can convert his LIBOR plus return into an Index Plus return by entering into a total return index swap paying LIBOR and receiving index return.

EXHIBIT 30.3   Cross Index Total Return Swap for Transferring Alpha

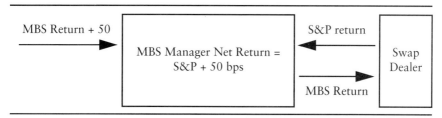

EXHIBIT 30.4   Creating an Enhanced Index Product with a Total Return Index

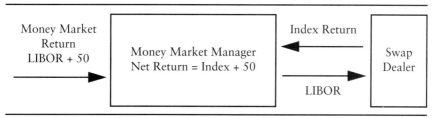

DISADVANTAGES OF MORTGAGE SWAPS

A mortgage swap and total return mortgage index swap have disadvantages. Agency mortgages have little or no credit risks. A swap exposes the investor to swap counterparty credit risk. Liquidity is also a concern in the mortgage swap market while the MBS cash market has become the biggest domestic fixed-income market by size and probably the most liquid only second to the Treasury market. The investor also foregoes the potential to outperform the mortgage index through active management.

CHAPTER 31

Credit Derivatives

Moorad Choudhry*
Senior Fellow
Centre for Mathematical Trading and Finance
City University Business School

With the exception of holders of *default-free* instruments such as U.S. Treasuries or British Gilts, a key risk run by investors in bonds is credit risk, the risk that the bond issuer will default on the debt. To meet the need of investors to hedge this risk, the market uses *credit derivatives* . These are financial instruments originally introduced to protect banks and other institutions against losses arising from *credit events* . As such, they are instruments designed to lay off or take on credit risk. Since their inception, they have been used by portfolio managers to enhance returns, to trade credit, for speculative purposes, and as hedging instruments.

In this chapter we provide a description of the main types of credit derivatives and how they may be used by fixed-income portfolio managers. We also consider how the risks in credit default swaps may sometimes not be fully understood, and how this highlights the need for more awareness on the legal and documentation aspects of such instruments.

CREDIT RISK

Credit derivatives allow investors to manage the credit risk exposure of their portfolios or asset holdings, essentially by providing insurance against

* The author would like to thank Brian Eales at London Guildhall University, Dr. Paul Darbyshire at SOAS, University of London, and Christopher Connelly at JPMorgan for review comments on an earlier draft.

a deterioration in credit quality of the borrowing entity.[1] If there is a technical default by the borrower[2] or an actual default on the loan itself and the bond is marked down in price, the losses suffered by the investor can be recouped in part or in full through the payout made by the credit derivative.

Credit risk is the risk that a borrowing entity will default on a loan, either through inability to maintain the interest servicing or because of bankruptcy or insolvency leading to inability to repay the principal itself. When technical or actual default occurs, bondholders suffer a loss as the value of their asset declines, and the potential greatest loss is that of the entire asset.

The extent of credit risk fluctuates as the fortunes of borrowers change in line with their own economic circumstances and the macro-economic business cycle. The magnitude of risk is described by a firm's credit rating. Rating agencies undertake a formal analysis of the borrower, after which a rating is announced. The issues considered in the rating analysis include:

- the financial position of the firm itself, for example, its balance sheet position and anticipated cash flows and revenues;
- other firm-specific issues such as the quality of the management and succession planning;
- an assessment of the firm's ability to meet scheduled interest and principal payments, both in its domestic and foreign currencies;
- the outlook for the industry as a whole, and competition within it;
- general assessments for the domestic economy.

Another measure of credit risk is the credit risk premium, which is the difference between yields on the same-currency government benchmark bonds and corporate bonds. This premium is the compensation required by investors for holding bonds that are not default-free. The credit premium required will fluctuate as individual firms and sectors are perceived to offer improved or worsening credit risk, and as the general health of the economy improves or worsens.

Credit Risk and Credit Derivatives

Credit derivatives are financial contracts designed to reduce or eliminate credit risk exposure by providing insurance against losses suffered due to credit events. A payout under a credit derivative is triggered by a credit

---

[1] The simplest credit derivative works like an insurance policy, with regular premiums paid by the protection-buyer to the protection-seller, and a payout in the event of a specified credit event.

[2] A technical default is a delay in timely payment of the coupon, or nonpayment of the coupon altogether.

event. As banks define default in different ways, the terms under which a credit derivative is executed usually include a specification of what constitutes a credit event.

The principle behind credit derivatives is straightforward. Investors desire exposure to nondefault-free debt because of the higher returns that this offers. However such exposure brings with it concomitant credit risk. This can be managed with credit derivatives. At the same time, the exposure itself can be taken on synthetically if, for instance, there are compelling reasons why a cash market position cannot be established. The flexibility of credit derivatives provides users with a number of advantages and as they are over-the-counter (OTC) products, they can be designed to meet specific user requirements.

We focus on credit derivatives as instruments that may be used to manage risk exposure inherent in a corporate or non-AAA sovereign bond portfolio. They may also be used to manage the credit risk of commercial loan books. The intense competition amongst commercial banks, combined with rapid disintermediation, has meant that banks have been forced to evaluate their lending policy, with a view to improving profitability and return on capital. The use of credit derivatives assists banks with restructuring their businesses, because they allow banks to repackage and parcel out credit risk, while retaining assets on balance sheet (when required) and thus maintain client relationships.

As the instruments isolate certain aspects of credit risk from the underlying loan or bond and transfer them to another entity, it becomes possible to separate the ownership and management of credit risk from the other features of ownership associated with the assets in question. This means that illiquid assets such as bank loans, and illiquid bonds can have their credit risk exposures transferred; the bank owning the assets can protect against credit loss even if it cannot transfer the assets themselves.

The same principles carry over to the credit risk exposures of portfolio managers. For fixed-income portfolio managers some of the advantages of credit derivatives include the following:

- they can be tailor-made to meet the specific requirements of the entity buying the risk protection, as opposed to the liquidity or term of the underlying reference asset;
- in theory, they can be "sold short" without risk of a liquidity or delivery squeeze, as it is a specific credit risk that is being traded. In the cash market it is not possible to "sell short" a bank loan, for example, but a credit derivative can be used to establish synthetically the economic effect of such a position;

- as they theoretically isolate credit risk from other factors such as client relationships and interest rate risk, credit derivatives introduce a formal pricing mechanism to price credit issues only. This means a market can develop in credit only, allowing more efficient pricing, and it becomes possible to model a term structure of credit rates;
- they are off-balance sheet instruments[3] and, as such, incorporate tremendous flexibility and leverage, exactly like other financial derivatives. For instance, bank loans are not particularly attractive investments for certain investors because of the administration required in managing and servicing a loan portfolio. However an exposure to bank loans and their associated return can be achieved by, say, a total return swap while simultaneously avoiding the administrative costs of actually owning the assets. Hence credit derivatives allow investors access to specific credits while allowing banks access to further distribution for bank loan credit risk.

Thus credit derivatives can be an important instrument for bond portfolio managers as well as commercial banks, who wish to increase the liquidity of their portfolios, gain from the relative value arising from credit pricing anomalies, and enhance portfolio returns. Some key applications are summarized below.

Diversifying the Credit Portfolio

A bank or portfolio manager may wish to take on credit exposure by providing credit protection on assets that it already owns, in return for a fee. This enhances income on their portfolio. They may sell credit derivatives to enable non-financial counterparties to gain credit exposures, if these clients do not wish to purchase the assets directly. In this respect the bank or asset manager performs a credit intermediation role.

Reducing Credit Exposure

A bank can reduce credit exposure either for an individual loan or a sectoral concentration, by buying a credit default swap. This may be desirable for assets in their portfolio that cannot be sold for client relationship or tax reasons. For fixed-income managers a particular asset or collection of assets may be viewed as favorable holdings in the long-term, but is at risk from short-term downward price movement. In this instance a sale would not fit in with long-term objectives, however short-term credit protection can be obtained via a credit swap.

---

[3] When credit derivatives are embedded in certain fixed-income products, such as structured notes and credit-linked notes, they are then off-balance sheet but part of a structure that may have on-balance sheet elements.

Acting as a Credit Derivatives Market Maker

A financial entity may wish to set itself up as a market maker in credit derivatives. In this case it may or may not hold the reference assets directly, and depending on its appetite for risk and the liquidity of the market, it can offset derivative contracts as and when required.

Credit Event

The occurrence of a specified credit event will trigger payment of the default payment by the seller of protection to the buyer of protection. Contracts specify physical or cash settlement. In physical settlement, the protection buyer transfers to the protection seller the deliverable obligation (usually the reference asset or assets), with the total principal outstanding equal to the nominal amount specified in the default swap contract.[4] The protection seller simultaneously pays to the buyer 100% of the nominal. In cash settlement, the protection seller hands to the buyer the difference between the nominal amount of the default swap and the final value for the same nominal amount of the reference asset. This final value is usually determined by means of a poll of dealer banks.

The following may be specified as credit events in the legal documentation between counterparties:

- downgrade in S&P and/or Moody's credit rating below a specified minimum level;
- financial or debt restructuring, for example occasioned under administration or as required under U.S. bankruptcy protection;
- bankruptcy or insolvency of the reference asset obligor;
- default on payment obligations, such as bond coupon and continued nonpayment after a specified time period.
- technical default, for example the nonpayment of interest or coupon when it falls due;
- a change in credit spread payable by the obligor above a specified maximum level.

The 1999 ISDA credit default swap documentation specifies bankruptcy, failure to pay, obligation default, debt moratorium, and restructuring to be credit events. Note that it does not specify a rating downgrade to be a credit event.

---

[4] The term "notional" may also be used to refer to the face value of the credit swap; in some institutions "nominal" and "notional" are used interchangeably.

EXHIBIT 31.1 Credit Default Swap

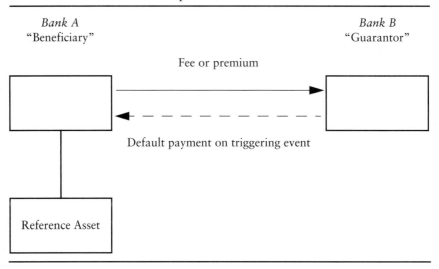

CREDIT DERIVATIVE INSTRUMENTS
═══

We now review some of the more common credit derivative instruments.

Credit Default Swap

The most common credit derivative is the *credit default swap* , *credit swap,* or *default swap* . This is a bilateral contract in which a periodic fixed fee or a one-off premium is paid to a *protection seller* , in return for which the seller will make a payment on the occurrence of a specified credit event. The fee is usually quoted as a basis point multiplier of the nominal value. The swap can refer to a single asset, known as the reference asset or under-lying asset, or a basket of assets. The default payment can be paid in what-ever way suits the protection buyer or both counterparties. For example it may be linked to the change in price of the reference asset or another speci-fied asset, it may be fixed at a predetermined recovery rate, or it may be in the form of actual delivery of the reference asset at a specified price. The basic structure is illustrated at Exhibit 31.1.

The credit default swap enables one party to transfer its credit expo-sure to another party. Banks may use default swaps to trade sovereign and corporate credit spreads without trading the actual assets themselves; for example someone who has gone long a default swap (the protection buyer) will gain if the reference asset obligor suffers a rating downgrade or defaults, and can sell the default swap at a profit if he can find a buyer counterparty. This is because the cost of protection on the reference asset will have increased as a result of the credit event. The original buyer of the default swap need never have owned a bond issued by the reference asset obligor.

The maturity of the credit swap does not have to match the maturity of the reference asset and in most cases does not. On default the swap is terminated and default payment by the protection seller or guarantor is calculated and handed over. The guarantor may have the asset delivered to him and pay the nominal value, or may cash settle the swap contract.

Credit Default Swap Example

XYZ plc credit spreads are currently trading at 120 bps over the benchmark government bond for 5-year maturities and 195 bps over for 10-year maturities. A portfolio manager hedges a $10 million holding of 10-year paper by purchasing the following credit default swap, written on the 5-year bond. This hedge protects for the first five years of the holding, and in the event of XYZ's credit spread widening, will increase in value and may be sold on or before expiry at a profit. The 10-year bond holding also earns 75 bps over the shorter-term paper for the portfolio manager.

Term: 5 years
Reference credit: XYZ plc 5-year bond
Credit event: The business day following occurrence of specified credit event
Default payment: Nominal value of bond × [100 − price of bond after credit event]
Swap premium: 3.35%

Assume that midway into the life of the swap there is a technical default on the XYZ plc 5-year bond, such that its price now stands at $28. Under the terms of the swap the protection buyer delivers the bond to the seller, who pays out $7.2 million to the buyer.

Credit Options

Credit options are also bilateral OTC financial contracts. A credit option is a contract designed to meet specific hedging or speculative requirements of an entity, which may purchase or sell the option to meet its objectives. A credit call option gives the buyer the right without the obligation to purchase the underlying credit-sensitive asset, or a credit spread, at a specified price and specified time (or period of time). A credit put option gives the buyer the right without the obligation to sell the underlying credit-sensitive asset or credit spread. By purchasing credit options banks and other institutions can take a view on credit spread movements for the cost of the option premium only, without recourse to actual loans issued by an obligor. The writer of credit options seeks to earn premium income.

Credit option terms are similar to those used for conventional equity options. A call option written on a stock grants the purchaser the right but not the obligation to purchase a specified amount of the stock at a set price and time. A credit option can be used by bond investors to hedge against a decline in the price of specified bonds, in the event of a credit event such as a ratings downgrade. The investor would purchase an option whose pay-off profile is a function of the credit quality of the bond, so that a loss on the bond position is offset by the payout from the option.

As with conventional options, there are both vanilla credit options and exotic credit options. The vanilla credit option[5] grants the purchaser the right but not the obligation to buy (or sell if a *put* option) an asset or credit spread at a specified price (the *strike* price) for a specified period of time up to the maturity of the option. A credit option allows a market participant to take a view on credit only, and no other exposure such as interest rates. As an example consider an investor who believes that a particular credit spread, which can be that of a specific entity or the average for a sector (such as "all AA-rated sterling corporates"), will widen over the next six months. She can buy a 6-month call option on the relevant credit spread, for which a one-off premium (the price of the option) is paid. If the credit spread indeed does widen beyond the strike price during the six month period, the option will be in-the-money and the investor will gain. If not, the investor's loss is limited to the premium paid.[6]

Exotic credit options are options that have one or more of their parameters changed from the vanilla norm; the same terms are used as in other option markets. Examples include the barrier credit option, which specifies a credit-event that would *trigger* (activate) the option or inactivate it. A digital credit option would have a payout profile that would be fixed, irrespective of how much in-the-money it was on expiry, and a zero payout if it expired out-of-the-money.

Credit-Linked Note

Credit-linked notes exist in a number of forms, but all of them contain a link between the return they pay and the credit-related performance of the underlying reference asset. A standard credit-linked note is a security, usually issued by an investment-graded entity, that has an interest payment and fixed maturity structure similar to a vanilla bond. The performance of the note however, including the maturity value, is linked to the

---

[5] Sometimes referred to as the *standard* credit option.
[6] Depending on whether the option is an American or European one will determine whether it can be exercised before its expiry date or on its expiry date only.

performance of specified underlying assets as well as that of the issuing entity. The notes are often used by borrowers to hedge against credit risk, and by investors to enhance the yield received on their holdings. Essentially credit-linked notes are hybrid instruments that combine a credit derivative with a vanilla bond. The credit-linked note pays regular coupons, however the credit derivative element is usually set to allow the issuer to decrease the principal amount if a credit event occurs.

For example consider an issuer of credit cards that wants to fund its (credit card) loan portfolio via an issue of debt. In order to reduce the credit risk of the loans, it issues a 2-year credit-linked note. The principal amount of the bond is 100% as usual, and it pays a coupon of 7.50%, which is 200 basis points above the 2-year benchmark yield. If, however, the incidence of bad debt amongst credit card holders exceeds 10% then the terms state that note holders will only receive back £85 per £100 nominal. The credit card issuer has in effect purchased a credit option that lowers its liability in the event that it suffers from a specified credit event, which in this case is an above-expected incidence of bad debts. The credit card bank has issued the credit-linked note to reduce its credit exposure, in the form of this particular type of credit insurance. If the incidence of bad debts is low, the note is redeemed at par. However if there a high incidence of such debt, the bank will only have to repay a part of its loan liability.

Investors may wish to purchase the credit-linked note because the coupon paid on it will be above what the credit card bank would pay on a vanilla bond it issued, and higher than other comparable investments in the market. In addition, such notes are usually priced below par on issue. Assuming the notes are eventually redeemed at par, investors will also have realized a substantial capital gain.[7]

The Total Return Swap

A *total return swap* (TRS), sometimes known as a *total rate of return swap* or *TR swap*, is an agreement between two parties to exchange the total return from a financial asset between them. This is designed to transfer the credit risk from one party to the other. It is one of the principal instruments used by banks and other financial instruments to manage their credit risk exposure, and as such, is a credit derivative. One definition of a TRS states that a TRS is a swap agreement in which the *total return* of a bank loan or credit-sensitive security is exchanged for some other cash flow, usually tied to LIBOR or some other loan or credit-sensitive security.[8]

---

[7] For more information on credit-linked notes, see Chapter 4 in Mark J. P. Anson, *Credit Derivatives* (New Hope, PA: Frank J. Fabozzi Associates, 1999).

[8] See, for example, Andrew Kasapi, *Mastering Credit Derivatives* (London: FT Prentice Hall, 1999).

EXHIBIT 31.2   Total Return Swap

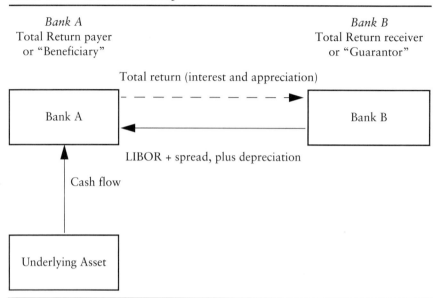

In some versions of a TRS the underlying reference asset is actually sold to the counterparty, with a corresponding swap transaction agreed alongside; in other versions there is no physical change of ownership of the underlying asset. The TRS trade itself can be to any maturity term, that is, it need not match the maturity of the underlying security. In a TRS the total return from the underlying asset is paid over to the counterparty in return for a fixed or floating cash flow. This makes it slightly different to other credit derivatives, as the payments between counterparties to a TRS are connected to changes in the market value of the underlying asset, as well as changes resulting from the occurrence of a credit event.

Exhibit 31.2 illustrates a generic TR swap. The two counterparties are labelled as banks, but the party termed "Bank A" can be any financial institution, including cash-rich fixed income portfolio managers such as insurance companies and hedge funds. In Exhibit 31.2 Bank A has contracted to pay the "total return" on a specified reference asset, while simultaneously receiving a LIBOR-based return from Bank B. The reference or underlying asset can be a bank loan such as a corporate loan or a sovereign or corporate bond. The total return payments from Bank A include the interest payments on the underlying loan as well as any appreciation in the market value of the asset. Bank B will pay the LIBOR-based return; it will also pay any difference if there is a depreciation in the price of the asset. The economic effect is as if Bank B owned the underlying asset, and as such, TR swaps are synthetic loans or securities. A significant feature is that Bank A will usually hold the underlying asset on its balance sheet, so that if this asset was originally on Bank B's balance sheet, this is a means by which the latter can have the asset removed from its balance sheet for the term of the TR swap.[9] If we assume Bank A has access to LIBOR funding, it will receive a spread on this from Bank B. Under the terms of the swap, Bank B will pay the difference between the initial market value and any depreciation, so it is sometimes termed the "guarantor" while Bank A is the "beneficiary."

The total return on the underlying asset is made up of the interest payments and any change in the market value if there is capital appreciation. The value of an appreciation may be cash settled, or alternatively there may be physical delivery of the reference asset on maturity of the swap, in return for a payment of the initial asset value by the total return "receiver." The maturity of the TR swap need not be identical to that of the reference asset, and in fact it is rare for it to be so.

The swap element of the trade will usually pay on a quarterly or semiannual basis, with the underlying asset being revalued or *marked-to-market* on the refixing dates. The asset price is obtained from an independent third-party source such as Bloomberg or Reuters, or as the average of a range of market quotes. If the *obligor* of the reference asset defaults, the swap may be terminated immediately, with a net present value payment changing hands according to what this value is, or it may be continued with each party making appreciation or depreciation payments as appropriate. This second option is only available if there is a market for the asset, which is unlikely in the case of a bank loan. If the swap is terminated, each counterparty will be liable to the other for accrued interest plus any appreciation or depreciation of the asset. Commonly under the terms of the trade, the guarantor bank has the option to purchase the underlying asset from the beneficiary bank, and then deal directly with the loan defaulter.

There are a number of reasons why portfolio managers may wish to enter into TR swap arrangements. One of these is to reduce or remove credit risk. Using TR swaps as a credit derivative instrument, a party can remove exposure to an asset without having to sell it. In a vanilla TR swap, the total return payer retains the rights to the reference asset, although in some cases servicing and voting rights may be transferred. The total return receiver gains an exposure to the reference asset without having to pay out the cash proceeds that would be required to purchase it. As the maturity of the swap rarely matches that of the asset, the swap receiver may gain from the positive funding or *carry* that derives from being able to roll over short-term funding of a longer-term asset.[10] The

---

[9] Although it is common for the receiver of the LIBOR-based payments to have the reference asset on its balance sheet, this is not always the case.

[10] This assumes a positively sloping yield curve.

total return payer on the other hand benefits from protection against market and credit risk for a specified period of time, without having to liquidate the asset itself. On maturity of the swap the total return payer may reinvest the asset if it continues to own it, or it may sell the asset in the open market. Thus the instrument may be considered to be a synthetic repo.[11] A TR swap agreement entered into as a credit derivative is a means by which banks can take on unfunded off-balance sheet credit exposure. Higher-rated banks that have access to LIBID funding can benefit by funding on-balance sheet assets that are credit protected through a credit derivative such as a TR swap, assuming the net spread of asset income over credit protection premium is positive.

A TR swap conducted as a synthetic repo is usually undertaken to effect the temporary removal of assets from the balance sheet. This may be desired for a number of reasons, for example if the institution is due to be analyzed by credit rating agencies or if the annual external audit is due shortly. Another reason a bank may wish to temporarily remove lower credit-quality assets from its balance sheet is if it is in danger of breaching capital limits in between the quarterly return periods. In this case, as the return period approaches, lower quality assets may be removed from the balance sheet by means of a TR swap, which is set to mature after the return period has passed.

Banks have employed a number of methods to price credit derivatives and TR swaps. Space does not permit an in-depth discussion of the different pricing techniques here. Essentially the pricing of credit derivatives is linked to that of other instruments; however the main difference between credit derivatives and other off-balance sheet products such as equity, currency, or bond derivatives is that the latter can be priced and hedged with reference to the underlying asset, which can be problematic when applied to credit derivatives. Credit products pricing uses statistical data on likelihood of default, probability of payout, level of risk tolerance, and a pricing model. With a TR swap the basic concept is that one party "funds" an underlying asset and transfers the total return of the asset to another party, in return for a (usually) floating return that is a spread over LIBOR. This spread is a function of:

- the credit rating of the swap counterparty;
- the amount and value of the reference asset;
- the credit quality of the reference asset;
- the funding costs of the beneficiary bank;

---

[11] This is because in a synthetic repo the economic effects of the TR swap are similar to those in a repurchase agreement. However, a TR swap takes an asset off the balance sheet, unlike a repo transaction.

■ any required profit margin;
■ the capital charge associated with the TR swap.

The TR swap counterparties must consider a number of risk factors associated with the transaction, which include:

■ the probability that the TR beneficiary may default while the reference asset has declined in value, and
■ the reference asset obligor defaults, followed by default of the TR swap receiver before payment of the depreciation has been made to the payer or "provider".

The first risk measure is a function of the probability of default by the TR swap receiver and the market volatility of the reference asset, while the second risk is related to the joint probability of default of both factors as well as the recovery probability of the asset.

APPLICATIONS FOR PORTFOLIO MANAGERS

Credit derivatives have allowed market participants to separate and disaggregate credit risk, and thence to trade this risk in a secondary market.[12] Initially portfolio managers used them to reduce credit exposure; subsequently they have been used in the management of portfolios to enhance portfolio yields and in the structuring of synthetic collateralized debt obligations. We summarize portfolio managers' main uses of credit derivatives next.

Enhancing Portfolio Returns

Asset managers can derive premium income by trading credit exposures in the form of derivatives issued with synthetic structured notes. The multitranching aspect of structured products enables specific credit exposures (credit spreads and outright default), and their expectations to be sold to meet specific areas of demand. By using structured notes such as credit-linked notes tied to the assets in the reference pool of the portfolio manager, the trading of credit exposures is crystallized as added yield on the asset manager's fixed income portfolio. In this way the portfolio manager has enabled other market participants to gain an exposure to the credit risk of a pool of assets but not to any other aspects of the portfolio, and without the need to hold the assets themselves.

---

[12] For example, see Satyajit Das, *Credit Derivatives and Credit Linked Notes*, Second edition (Singapore: John Wiley and Sons Ltd., 2000), Chapters 2–4.

EXHIBIT 31.3   Reducing Credit Exposure

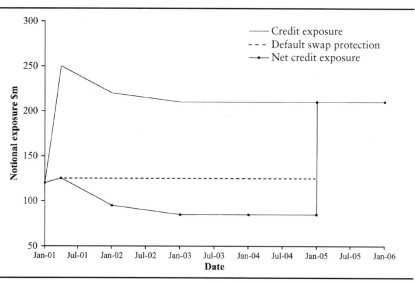

Reducing Credit Exposure

Consider a portfolio manager that holds a large portfolio of bonds issued by a particular sector (say, utilities) and believes that spreads in this sector will widen in the short term. Previously, in order to reduce its credit exposure it would have to sell bonds, however this may crystallize a mark-to-market loss and may conflict with its long-term investment strategy. An alternative approach would be to enter into a credit default swap, purchasing protection for the short term; if spreads do widen these swaps will increase in value and may be sold at a profit in the secondary market. Alternatively the portfolio manager may enter into total return swaps on the desired credits. It pays the counterparty the total return on the reference assets, in return for LIBOR. This transfers the credit exposure of the bonds to the counterparty for the term of the swap, in return for the credit exposure of the counterparty.

Consider now the case of a portfolio manager wishing to mitigate credit risk from a growing portfolio (say, one that has just been launched). Exhibit 31.3 shows an example of an unhedged credit exposure to a hypothetical credit-risky portfolio. It illustrates the manager's expectation of credit risk building up to $250 million as the portfolio is ramped up, and then reducing to a more stable level as the credits become more established. A 3-year credit default swap entered into shortly after provides protection on half of the notional exposure, shown as the broken line. The net exposure to credit events has been reduced by a significant margin.

Credit Switches and Zero-Cost Credit Exposure

Protection buyers utilizing credit default swaps must pay a premium in return for laying off their credit risk exposure. An alternative approach for an asset manager involves the use of credit switches for specific sectors of the portfolio. In a credit switch the portfolio manager purchases credit protection on one reference asset or pool of assets, and simultaneously sells protection on another asset or pool of assets.[13] For example, the portfolio manager would purchase protection for a particular fund and sell protection on another. Typically the entire transaction would be undertaken with one investment bank, which would price the structure so that the net cash flows would be zero. This has the effect of synthetically diversifying the credit exposure of the portfolio manager, enabling the manager to gain and/or reduce exposure to desired sectors.

Exposure to Market Sectors

Investors can use credit derivatives to gain exposure to sectors for which they do not wish to have a cash market exposure. This can be achieved with an *index* swap, which is similar to a TR swap, with one counterparty paying a total return that is linked to an external reference index. The other party pays a LIBOR-linked coupon or the total return of another index. Indices that are used include the government bond index, an high-yield index or a technology stocks index. Assume that an investor believes that the bank loan market will outperform the mortgage-backed bond sector; to reflect this view the investor enters into an index swap in which he pays the total return of the mortgage index and receives the total return of the bank loan index.

Another possibility is synthetic exposure to foreign currency and money markets. Again we assume that an investor has a particular view on an emerging market currency. If he wishes, he can purchase a short-term (say one-year) domestic coupon-bearing note, whose principal redemption is linked to a currency factor. This factor is based on the ratio of the spot value of the foreign currency on issue of the note to the value on maturity. Such currency-linked notes can also be structured so that they provide an exposure to sovereign credit risk. The downside of currency-linked notes is that if the exchange rate goes the other way, the note will have a zero return, in effect a negative return once the investor's funding costs have been taken into account.

Credit Spreads

Credit derivatives can be used to trade credit spreads. Assume that an investor has negative views on a certain emerging market government bond

---

[13] A pool of assets would be concentrated on one sector, such as utility company bonds.

credit spread relative to U.K. gilts. The simplest way to reflect this view would be to go long a credit default swap on the sovereign, paying X basis points. Assuming that the investor's view is correct and the sovereign bonds decrease in price as their credit spread widens, the premium payable on the credit swap will increase. The investor's swap can then be sold into the market at this higher premium.

Application of Total Return Swaps

Total return swaps are widely used by a range of different market participants including bank and repo market makers. We summarize some applications by portfolio managers in this section.

Capital Structure Arbitrage

A capital structure arbitrage describes an arrangement whereby investors exploit mispricing between the yields received on two different loans by the same issuer. Assume that the reference entity has both a commercial bank loan and a subordinated bond issue outstanding, but that the former pays LIBOR plus 330 basis points while the latter pays LIBOR plus 230 basis points. An investor enters into a total return swap in which it effectively is purchasing the bank loan and selling short the bond. The nominal amounts will be at a ratio, for argument's sake let us say 2:1, as the bonds will be more price-sensitive to changes in credit status than the loans.

The trade is illustrated in Exhibit 31.4. The investor receives the "total return" on the bank loan, while simultaneously paying the return on the bond in addition to LIBOR plus 30 basis points, which is the price of the TR swap. The swap generates a net spread of 175 basis points, given by [(100 bps × ½) + 250 bps × ½)].

Synthetic Repo

A portfolio manager believes that a particular bond that it does not hold is about to decline in price. To reflect this view the portfolio manager may do one of the following.

EXHIBIT 31.4   Total Return Swap in Capital Structure Arbitrage

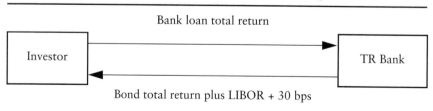

Bank loan total return

Investor   TR Bank

Bond total return plus LIBOR + 30 bps

Sell the Bond in the Market and Cover the Resulting Short Position in Repo The cash flow out is the coupon on the bond, with capital gain if the bond falls in price. Assume that the repo rate is floating, say LIBOR plus a spread. The manager must be aware of the funding costs of the trade, so that unless the bond can be covered in repo at general collateral rates,[14] the funding will be at a loss. The yield on the bond must also be lower than the LIBOR plus spread received in the repo.

As an Alternative, Enter into a TR Swap The portfolio manager pays the total return on the bond and receives LIBOR plus a spread. If the bond yield exceeds the LIBOR spread, the funding will be negative, however the trade will gain if the trader's view is proved correct and the bond falls in price by a sufficient amount. If the breakeven funding cost (which the bond must exceed as it falls in value) is lower in the TR swap, this method will be used rather than the repo approach. This is more likely if the bond is special.

Overview of TR Swap Applications

Total return swaps are increasingly used as synthetic repo instruments, most commonly by investors that wish to purchase the credit exposure of an asset without purchasing the asset itself. This is conceptually similar to what happened when interest-rate swaps were introduced, which enabled banks and other financial institutions to trade interest-rate risk without borrowing or lending cash funds.

Under a TR swap an asset such as a bond position may be removed from the balance sheet. In order to avoid an adverse impact on regular internal and external capital and credit exposure reporting, a bank may use TR swaps to reduce the amount of lower-quality assets on the balance sheet. This can be done by entering into a short-term TR swap with say, a 2-week term that straddles the reporting date. Bonds are removed from the balance sheet if they are part of a sale plus TR swap transaction. This is because legally the bank selling the asset is not required to repurchase bonds from the swap counterparty, nor is the total return payer obliged to sell the bonds back to the counterparty (or indeed sell the bonds at all on maturity of the TR swap).

---

[14] That is, the bond cannot be *special*. A bond is special when the repo rate payable on it is significantly (say, 20 to 30 basis points or more) below the *general collateral* repo rate, so that covering a short position in the bond entails paying a substantial funding premium.

RISKS IN CREDIT DEFAULT SWAPS

As credit derivatives can be tailored to specific requirements in terms of reference exposure, term to maturity, currency, and cash flows, they have enabled market participants to establish exposure to specific entities without the need for them to hold the bond or loan of that entity. This has raised issues of the different risk exposure that this entails compared to the cash equivalent. A Moody's special report highlights the unintended risks of holding credit exposures in the form of default swaps and credit-linked notes.[15] Under certain circumstances it is possible for credit default swaps to create unintended risk exposure for holders, by exposing them to greater frequency and magnitude of losses compared to that suffered by a holder of the underlying reference credit.

In a credit default swap, the payout to a buyer of protection is determined by the occurrence of credit events. The definition of a credit event sets the level of credit risk exposure of the protection seller. A wide definition of "credit event" results in a higher level of risk. To reduce the likelihood of disputes, counterparties can adopt the ISDA Credit Derivatives definitions to govern their dealings. The Moody's report states that the current ISDA definitions do not unequivocally separate and isolate credit risk, and in certain circumstances credit derivatives can expose holders to additional risks. A reading of the report would appear to suggest that differences in definitions can lead to unintended risks being taken on by protection sellers. Two examples from the report are cited next as an illustration.

Extending Loan Maturity

The bank debt of Conseco, a corporate entity, was restructured in August 2000. The restructuring provisions included deferment of the loan maturity by three months, higher coupon, corporate guarantee, and additional covenants. Under the Moody's definition, as lenders received compensation in return for an extension of the debt, the restructuring was not considered to be a "diminished financial obligation," although Conseco's credit rating was downgraded one notch. However under the ISDA definition, the extension of the loan maturity meant that the restructuring was considered to be a credit event, and thus triggered payments on default swaps written on Conseco's bank debt. Hence this was an example of a loss event under ISDA definitions that was not considered by Moody's to be a default.

---

[15] Jeffrey Tolk, "Understanding the Risks in Credit Default Swaps," *Moody's Investors Service Special Report* (March 16, 2001).

Risks of Synthetic Positions and Cash Positions Compared

Consider two investors in XYZ, one of whom owns bonds issued by XYZ while the other holds a credit-linked note (CLN) referenced to XYZ. Following a deterioration in its debt situation, XYZ violates a number of covenants on its bank loans, but its bonds are unaffected. XYZ's bank accelerates the bank loan, but the bonds continue to trade at 85 cents on the dollar, coupons are paid, and the bond is redeemed in full at maturity. However the default swap underlying the CLN cites "obligation acceleration" (of either bond or loan) as a credit event, so the holder of the CLN receives 85% of par in cash settlement and the CLN is terminated. However the cash investor receives all the coupons and the par value of the bonds on maturity.

These two examples illustrate how, as credit default swaps are defined to pay out in the event of a very broad range of definitions of a "credit event," portfolio managers may suffer losses as a result of occurrences that are not captured by one or more of the ratings agencies' rating of the reference asset. This results in a potentially greater risk for the portfolio manager compared to his position were he to actually hold the underlying reference asset. Essentially, therefore, it is important for the range of definitions of a "credit event" to be fully understood by counterparties, so that holders of default swaps are not taking on greater risk than is intended.

CONCLUSIONS

Credit derivatives are well established instruments in the fixed-income markets, and their flexibility mirrors that of an earlier generation of derivatives such as swaps and options. This chapter has highlighted how they may be used both to hedge credit risk exposure as well as to enhance portfolio returns. It is clear though, that users need to be aware of the risks involved in writing credit swaps, such that the legal terms underpinning each contract are clearly defined and communicated.

CHAPTER 32

Managed Futures

Mark J. P. Anson, CFA, Ph.D., CPA, Esq.
Chief Investment Officer
CalPERS

Managed futures refers to the active trading of futures contracts and for-ward contracts on physical commodities, financial assets, and curren-cies. The purpose of the managed futures industry is to enable investors to profit from changes in futures prices. In this chapter managed futures as an investment vehicle are discussed.

INDUSTRY BASICS

The managed futures industry is another skill-based style of investing. Investment managers attempt to use their special knowledge and insight in buying and selling futures and forward contracts to extract a positive return. These futures managers tend to argue that their superior skill is the key ingredient to derive profitable returns from the futures markets.

There are three ways to access the skill-based investing of the man-aged futures industry: public commodity pools, private commodity pools, and individual managed accounts. *Commodity pools* are investment funds that pool the money of several investors for the purpose of invest-ing in the futures markets. They are similar in structure to hedge funds, and are considered a subset of the hedge fund marketplace.

Every commodity pool must be managed by a general partner. Typi-cally, the general partner for the pool must register with the Commodity Futures Trading Commission and the National Futures Association as a

Commodity Pool Operator (CPO). However, there are exceptions to the general rule.

Public commodity pools are open to the general public for investment in much the same way a mutual fund sells its shares to the public. Public commodity pools must file a registration statement with the Securities and Exchange Commission before distributing shares in the pool to investors. An advantage of public commodity pools is the low minimum investment and the frequency of liquidity (the ability to cash out).

Private commodity pools are sold to high net worth investors and institutional investors to avoid the lengthy registration requirements of the SEC and sometimes to avoid the lengthy reporting requirements of the CFTC. Otherwise, their investment objective is the same as a public commodity pool. An advantage of private commodity pools is usually lower brokerage commissions and greater flexibility to implement investment strategies and extract excess return from the futures markets.

Commodity pool operators (for either public or private pools) typically hire one or more Commodity Trading Advisors (CTAs) to manage the money deposited in the pool. CTAs are professional money managers in the futures markets.

Like CPOs, CTAs must register with the Commodity Futures Trading Commission (CFTC) and the National Futures Association (NFA) before managing money for a commodity pool. In some cases a managed futures investment manager is registered as both a CPO and a CTA. In this case, the general partner for a commodity pool may also act as its investment adviser.

Last, wealthy and institutional investors can place their money directly with a CTA in an *individually managed account*. These separate accounts have the advantage of narrowly defined and specific investment objectives as well as full transparency to the investor.

CTAs may invest in both exchange-traded futures contracts and forward contracts. A forward contract has the same economic structure as a futures contract with one difference; it is traded over the counter. Forward contracts are private agreements that do not trade on a futures exchange. Therefore, they can have terms that vary considerably from the standard terms of an exchange-listed futures contracts. Forward contracts accomplish the same economic goal as futures contracts but with the flexibility of custom tailored terms.

HISTORY OF MANAGED FUTURES

Organized futures trading began in the United States in the 1800s with the founding of the Chicago Board of Trade (CBOT) in 1848. It was founded by 82 grain merchants and the first exchange floor was above a flour store. Originally, it was a cash market where grain traders came to buy and sell supplies of flour, timothy seed, and hay.

In 1851, the earliest futures contract in the United States was recorded for the forward delivery of 3,000 bushels of corn, and two years later, the CBOT established the first standard futures contract in corn. Since then, the heart and soul of the CBOT has been its futures contracts on agricultural crops grown primarily in the midwestern states: corn, wheat, and soybeans. Therefore, commodity futures exchanges were founded initially by grain producers and buyers to hedge the price risk associated with the harvest and sale of crops.

Other futures exchanges were established for similar reasons. The Chicago Mercantile Exchange (CME), for example, lists futures contracts on livestock. Chicago was once famous for its stockyards where cattle and hogs were herded to the market. Ranchers and buyers came to the CME to hedge the price risk associated with the purchase and sale of cattle and hogs.

Other exchanges are the New York Mercantile Exchange (NYMEX) where futures contracts on energy products are traded. The Commodity Exchange of New York (now the COMEX division of the NYMEX) lists futures contracts on precious and industrial metals. The New York Coffee, Sugar, and Cocoa Exchange lists futures contracts on (what else?) coffee, sugar, and cocoa. The New York Cotton Exchange lists contracts on cotton and frozen concentrated orange juice.[1] The Kansas City Board of Trade lists futures contracts on wheat and financial products such as the Value Line stock index.

Over the years, certain commodities have risen in prominence while others have faded. For instance, the heating oil futures contract was at one time listed as inactive on the NYMEX for lack of interest. For years, heating oil prices remained stable, and there was little interest or need to hedge the price risk of heating oil. Then along came the Arab Oil Embargo of 1973, and this contract quickly took on a life of its own as did other energy futures contracts.

Conversely, other futures contracts have faded away because of minimal input into the economic engine of the United States. For instance, rye futures traded on the CBOT from 1869 to 1970, and barley futures traded from 1885 to 1940. However, the limited importance of barley and rye in finished food products led to the eventual demise of these futures contracts.

---

[1] The New York Coffee, Sugar, and Cocoa Exchange and the New York Cotton Exchange have merged to form the New York Board of Trade, where each exchange exists as a separate subsidiary of the NYBOT.

As the wealth of America grew, a new type of futures contract has gained importance: financial futures. The futures markets changed dramatically in 1975 when the CBOT introduced the first financial futures contract on Government National Mortgage Association mortgage-backed certificates. This was followed two years later in 1977 with the introduction of a futures contract on the U.S. Treasury Bond. Today this is the most actively traded futures contract in the world.

The creation of a futures contract that was designed to hedge financial risk as opposed to commodity price risk opened up a whole new avenue of asset management for traders, analysts, and portfolio managers. Now, it is more likely that a financial investor will flock to the futures exchanges to hedge her investment portfolio than a grain purchaser will trade to hedge commodity price risk. Since 1975, more and more financial futures contracts have been listed on the futures exchanges. For instance, in 1997 stock index futures and options on the Dow Jones 30 Industrial Companies were first listed on the CBOT. The S&P 500 stock index futures and options (first listed in 1983) are the most heavily traded contracts on the CME. Additionally, currency futures were introduced on the CME in the 1970s (originally listed as part of the International Monetary Market).

With the advent of financial futures contracts more and more managed futures trading strategies were born. However, the history of managed futures products goes back more than 50 years.

The first public futures fund began trading in 1948 and was active until the 1960s. This fund was established before financial futures contracts were invented, and consequently, traded primarily in agricultural commodity futures contracts. The success of this fund spawned other managed futures vehicles, and a new industry was born.

The managed futures industry has grown from just $1 billion under management in 1985 to $35 billion of funds invested in managed futures products in 2000. The stock market's return to more rational pricing in 2000 helped fuel increased interest in managed futures products. Still, managed futures products are a fraction of the estimated size of the hedge fund marketplace of $400 to $500 billion. Yet, issues of capacity are virtually nonexistent in the managed futures industry compared to the hedge fund marketplace where the best hedge funds are closed to new investors.

Similar to hedge funds, CTAs and CPOs charge both management fees and performance fees. The standard "1 and 20" (1% management fee and 20% incentive fee) are equally applicable to the managed futures industry although management fees can range from 0% to 3% and incentive fees from 10% to 35%.

Unfortunately, until the early 1970s, the managed futures industry was largely unregulated. Anyone could advise an investor as to the merits of investing in commodity futures, or form a fund for the purpose of investing in the futures markets. Recognizing the growth of this industry, and the lack of regulation associated with it, in 1974 Congress promulgated the Commodity Exchange Act (CEA) and created the Commodity Futures Trading Commission (CFTC).

Under the CEA, Congress first defined the terms Commodity Pool Operator and Commodity Trading Advisor. Additionally, Congress established standards for financial reporting, offering memorandum disclosure, and bookkeeping. Further, Congress required CTAs and CPOs to register with the CFTC. Last, upon the establishment of the National Futures Association (NFA) as the designated self-regulatory organization for the managed futures industry, Congress required CTAs and CPOs to undergo periodic educational training.

Today, there are four broad classes of managed futures trading; agricultural products, energy products, financial and metal products, and currency products. Before examining these categories we review the prior research on the managed futures industry.

PRIOR EMPIRICAL RESEARCH

There are two key questions with respect to managed futures:

1. Will an investment in managed futures improve the performance of an investment portfolio?
2. Can managed futures products produce consistent returns?

The case for managed futures products as a viable investment is mixed. Elton, Gruber, and Rentzler, in three separate studies, examine the returns to public commodity pools.[2] In their first study, they conclude that publicly offered commodity funds are not attractive either as stand-alone investments or as additions to a portfolio containing stocks and/or bonds. In their second study, they find that the historical return data reported in the prospectuses of publicly offered commodity pools are not indicative of the returns that these funds actually earn once they go public. In fact, they conclude that the performance discrepancies are so large that the prospectus numbers are seriously misleading. In their last study,

---

[2] See Edwin Elton, Martin Gruber, and Joel Rentzler, "Professionally Managed, Publicly Traded Commodity Funds," *Journal of Business*, vol. 60, no. 2 (1987), pp. 175–199; "New Public Offerings, Information, and Investor Rationality: The Case of Publicly Offered Commodity Funds," *Journal of Business*, vol. 62, no. 1 (1989), pp. 1–15; "The Performance of Publicly Offered Commodity Funds," *Financial Analysts Journal* (July–August 1990), pp. 23–30.

they did not find any evidence that would support the addition of commodity pools to a portfolio of stocks and bonds and that commodity funds did not provide an attractive hedge against inflation. Last, they find that the distribution of returns to public commodity pools to be negatively skewed. Therefore, the opportunity for very large negative returns is greater than for large positive returns.

Irwin, Krukemeyer, and Zulaf,[3] Schneeweis, Savanyana, and McCarthy,[4] and Edwards and Park[5] also conclude that public commodity funds offer little value to investors as either stand-alone investments or as an addition to a stock and bond portfolio. However, Irwin and Brorsen find that public commodity funds provide an expanded efficient investment frontier.[6]

For private commodity pools, Edwards and Park find that an equally weighted index of commodity pools have a sufficiently high Sharpe Ratio to justify them as either a stand-alone investment or as part of a diversified portfolio.[7] Conversely, Schneeweis *et al.* conclude that private commodity pools do not have value as stand-alone investments but they are worthwhile additions to a stock and bond portfolio.[8]

With respect to separate accounts managed by CTAs, McCarthy, Schneeweis, and Spurgin[9] find that an allocation to an equally weighted index of CTAs provides valuable diversification benefits to a portfolio of stocks and bonds. In a subsequent study, Schneeweis, Spurgin, and Potter find that a portfolio allocation to a dollar weighted index of CTAs results in a higher portfolio Sharpe ratio.[10] Edwards and Park find that an index

---

[3] See Scott Irwin, Terry Krukemyer, and Carl Zulaf, "Investment Performance of Public Commodity Pools: 1979–1990," *The Journal of Futures Markets*, vol. 13, no. 7 (1993), pp. 799–819.
[4] See Thomas Schneeweis, Uttama Savanayana, and David McCarthy, "Alternative Commodity Trading Vehicles: A Performance Analysis," *The Journal of Futures Markets*, vol. 11, no. 4 (1991), pp. 475–487.
[5] See Franklin Edwards and James Park, "Do Managed Futures Make Good Investments?" *The Journal of Futures Markets*, vol. 16, no. 5 (1996), pp. 475–517.
[6] See Scott Irwin and B. Wade Brorsen, "Public Futures Funds," *The Journal of Futures Markets*, vol. 5, no. 3 (1985), pp. 463–485.
[7] See Edwards and Park, "Do Managed Futures Make Good Investments?"
[8] See Schneeweis, Savanayana, and McCarthy, "Alternative Commodity Trading Vehicles: A Performance Analysis."
[9] See David McCarthy, Thomas Schneeweis, and Richard Spurgin, "Investment Through CTAs: An Alternative Managed Futures Investment," *The Journal of Derivatives* (Summer 1996), pp. 36–47.
[10] See Thomas Schneeweis, Richard Spurgin, and Mark Potter, "Managed Futures and Hedge Fund Investment for Downside Equity Risk Management," in *The Handbook of Managed Futures: Performance, Evaluation, and Analysis*, Carl C. Peters and Ben Warwick, editors, New York: McGraw Hill Companies, Inc., 1997.

of equally weighted CTAs performs well as both a stand-alone investment and as an addition to a diversified portfolio.[11]

An important aspect of any investment is the predictability of returns over time. If returns are predictable, then an investor can select a commodity pool or a CTA with consistently superior performance. Considerable time and effort has been devoted to studying the managed futures industry to determine the predictability and consistency of returns. Unfortunately, the results are not encouraging.

For instance, Edwards and Ma find that once commodity funds go public through a registered public offering, their average returns are negative.[12] They conclude that prior pre-public trading performance for commodity pools is of little use to investors when selecting a public commodity fund as an investment. The lack of predictability in historical managed futures returns is supported by the research of McCarthy, Schneeweis, and Spurgin;[13] Irwin, Zulauf, and Ward;[14] and the three studies by Elton, Gruber, and Renzler.[15] In fact, Irwin *et al* conclude that a strategy of selecting CTAs based on historical good performance is not likely to improve upon a naive strategy of selecting CTAs at random.

In summary, the prior research regarding managed futures is unsettled. There is no evidence that public commodity pools provide any benefits either as a stand-alone investment or as part of a diversified portfolio. However, the evidence does indicate that private commodity pools and CTA managed accounts can be a valuable addition to a diversified portfolio. Nonetheless, the issue of performance persistence in the managed futures industry is unresolved. Currently, there is more evidence against performance persistence than there is to support this conclusion.

In the next section, we begin to analyze the performance in the managed futures industry by examining the return distributions for different CTA investment styles. We then consider the potential for downside risk protection from managed futures.

---

[11] Edwards and Park, "Do Managed Futures Make Good Investments?"

[12] See Franklin Edwards and Cindy Ma, "Commodity Pool Performance: Is the Information Contained in Pool Prospectuses Useful?" *The Journal of Futures Markets* , vol. 8, no. 5 (1988), pp. 589–616.

[13] McCarthy, Schneeweis, and Spurgin, "Investment Through CTAs: An Alternative Managed Futures Investment."

[14] Scott Irwin, Carl Zulauf, and Barry Ward, "The Predictability of Managed Futures Returns," *The Journal of Derivatives* (Winter 1994), pp. 20–27.

[15] Elton, Gruber, and Rentzler, "Professionally Managed, Publicly Traded Commodity Funds," "New Public Offerings, Information, and Investor Rationality: The Case of Publicly Offered Commodity Funds," and "The Performance of Publicly Offered Commodity Funds."

RETURN DISTRIBUTIONS OF MANAGED FUTURES

Similar to our analysis for hedge funds and passive commodity futures, we examine the distribution of returns for managed futures. We use the Barclays Managed Futures Index to determine the pattern of returns associated with several styles of futures investing.

Managed futures products may be good investments if the pattern of their returns is positively skewed. One way to consider this concept is that it is similar to owning a Treasury bill plus a lottery ticket. The investor consistently receives low, but positive returns. However, every once in a while an extreme event occurs and the CTA is able to profit from the movement of futures prices. This would result in a positive skew.

To analyze the distribution of returns associated with managed futures investing, we use the Barclays CTA managed futures indices that divide the CTA universe into four actively traded strategies: (1) CTAs that actively trade in the agricultural commodity futures; (2) CTAs that actively trade in currency futures; (3) CTAs that actively trade in financial and metal futures; and, (4) CTAs that actively trade in energy futures.

Managed futures traders have one goal in mind: to capitalize on price trends. Most CTAs are considered to be trend followers. Typically, they look at various moving averages of commodity prices and attempt to determine whether the price will continue to trend up or down, and then trade accordingly. Therefore, it is not the investment strategy that is the distinguishing factor in the managed futures industry, but rather, the markets in which CTAs and CPOs apply their trend following strategies.[16]

In this chapter we use the Mount Lucas Management Index (MLMI) as a benchmark by which to judge CTA performance. The MLMI is a passive futures index. It applies a mechanical and transparent rule for capitalizing on price trends in the futures markets. It does not represent active trading. Instead, it applies a consistent rule for buying or selling futures contracts depending upon the current price trend in any particular commodity futures market. In addition, the MLMI invests across agricultural, currency, financial, energy, and metal futures contracts. Therefore, it provides a good benchmark by which to examine the four managed futures strategies.

Exhibit 32.1 shows the distribution of returns for the MLMI. The distribution is negatively skewed. Therefore, a simple or naive trend following strategy will produce a distribution of returns that has more neg-

---

[16] In fact, one article has noted that the managed futures industry suffers because too many CTAs are following similar trend following strategies. See Daniel Collins, "A New Life for Managed Futures," *Futures* (April 1, 2001).

ative return observations below the median than positive observations above the median. In reviewing the distribution of returns for managed futures strategies, we keep in mind that the returns are generated from active management. One demonstration of skill is the ability to shift a distribution of returns from a negative skew to a positive skew. Therefore, if CTAs do in fact have skill, we would expect to see distribution of returns with a positive skew.

Further, the passive MLMI strategy produces a distribution of returns with considerable leptokurtosis. This indicates that the tails of the distribution have greater probability mass than a normal, bell-shaped distribution. This indicates that a passive trend following strategy has significant exposure to outlier events. Consequently, we would expect to observe similar leptokurtosis associated with managed futures.

Last, the average return for the MLMI strategy was 0.73% per month. If managed futures strategies can add value, we would expect them to outperform the average monthly return earned by the naive MLMI strategy.

EXHIBIT 32.1   Distribution of Returns for the MLMI

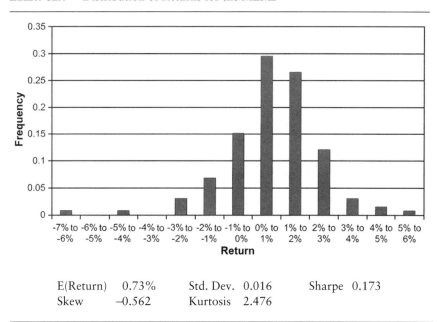

| E(Return) | 0.73% | Std. Dev. | 0.016 | Sharpe | 0.173 |
| Skew | −0.562 | Kurtosis | 2.476 | | |

EXHIBIT 32.2   Barclays Agricultural CTA Returns

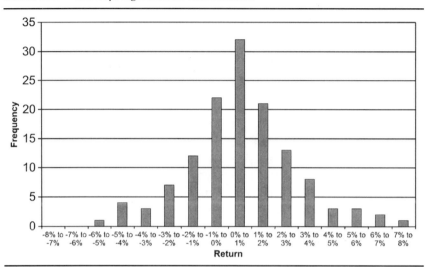

Managed Futures in Agricultural Commodities

In our discussion of commodity futures in Chapter 10, we indicated that commodity prices are more likely to be susceptible to positive price surprises. The reason is that most of the news associated with agricultural products is usually negative. Droughts, floods, storms, and crop freezes are the main news stories. Therefore, new information to the agricultural market tends to result in positive price shocks instead of negative price shocks. (There is not much price reaction to the news that "the crop cycle is progressing normally.") We would expect the CTAs to capture the advantage of these price surprises and any trends that develop from them.

Exhibit 32.2 presents the return distribution for Barclays Agricultural CTA index. We use data over the period 1990–2000. From a quick review of this distribution, it closely resembles a bell curve type of distribution. However, in Exhibit 32.6, we show that this distribution in fact has a positive skew of 0.18. Therefore, compared to the negative skew observed for the passive MLMI, we can conclude that managed futures did add value compared to a passive strategy.

In addition, the value of kurtosis, while still positive at 0.69, is much smaller than that for the MLMI. In fact, the tails of the distribution for the Barclays Agricultural CTA index have probability mass close to that for a normal distribution. Therefore, CTAs were able to shift the distribution of commodity futures returns from a negative skew to a positive skew while reducing the exposure to tail risk.

EXHIBIT 32.3   Barclays Currency CTA Returns

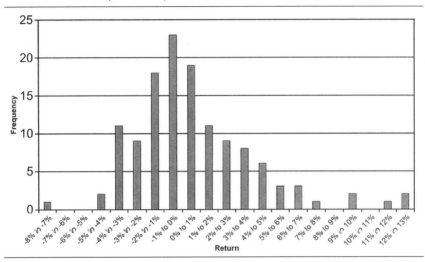

Unfortunately, there is a tradeoff for this skill. The average return to the Barclays Agricultural CTA index of 0.58% per month is less than that for the MLMI index of 0.73%. Additionally, the Sharpe ratio for the managed futures strategy is lower than that for the MLMI. Consequently, the results for managed futures trading in the agriculture markets is mixed. On the one hand, we observe a positive shift to the distribution of returns, but on the other, a reduction in the risk and return tradeoff as measured by the Sharpe ratio.

Managed Futures in Currency Markets

The currency markets are the most liquid and efficient markets in the world. The reason is simple, every other commodity, financial asset, household good, cheeseburger, and so on must be denominated in a currency. As the numeraire, currency is the commodity in which all other commodities and assets are denominated.

Daily trading volume in exchange-listed and forward markets for currency contracts is in the hundreds of billions of dollars. Given the liquidity, depth, and efficiency of the currency markets, we would expect the ability of managed futures traders to derive value to be small.

Exhibit 32.3 provides the distribution of returns for actively managed currency futures. We can see from this graph and later in Exhibit 32.6, that CTAs produced a distribution of returns with a very large positive skew of 1.39. This is considerably greater than that for the MLMI, and presents a strong case for skill. In addition, the average monthly return for CTAs trading in currency futures is 0.8% per month, an improvement of the average monthly return for the MLMI.

Unfortunately, this strategy also provides a higher value of kurtosis, 3.15, indicating significant exposure to outlier events. This higher exposure to outlier events translates into a higher standard deviation of returns for managed currency futures, and a lower Sharpe ratio.

The evidence for skill-based investing in managed currency futures is mixed. On the one hand, CTAs demonstrated an ability to shift the distribution of returns compared to a naive trend following strategy from negative to positive. On the other hand, more risk was incurred through greater exposure to outlier events resulting in a lower Sharpe ratio than that for the MLMI.

Managed Futures in the Financials and Metals Markets

As we discussed, with the advent of the GNMA futures contract in the 1970s, financial futures contracts have enjoyed greater prominence than traditional physical commodity futures. However, considerable liquidity exists in the precious metals markets because gold, silver, and platinum are still purchased and sold primarily as a store of value rather than for any productive input into a manufacturing process. In this fashion, precious metal futures resemble financial assets.

Financial assets tend to have a negative skew of returns during the period 1990–2000 with a reasonably large value of leptokurtosis. Therefore, a demonstration of skill with respect to managed futures is again the ability to shift the distribution of returns to a positive skew.

Exhibits 32.4 and 32.5 demonstrate this positive skew. Managed futures in financial and precious metal futures have a positive skew of 0.58 and a small positive kurtosis of 0.49. Therefore, CTAs were able to shift the distribution of returns to the upside while reducing exposure to outlier returns.

The average monthly return, however, is 0.63%, less than that for the MLMI. Additionally, the Sharpe ratio for this CTA strategy is less than that for the MLMI. Once again, we find mixed evidence that managed futures can add value beyond that presented in a mechanical trend following strategy.

Managed Futures in the Energy Markets

The energy markets are chock full of price shocks associated with news events. These news events tend to be positive for the price of energy related commodities and futures contracts thereon. The Arab Oil Embargo in 1973 and 1977, the Iraq/Iran war of the early 1980s, the Iraqi invasion of Kuwait in 1990, as well as sudden cold snaps, broken pipelines, oil refinery fires and explosions, and oil tanker shipwrecks all tend to increase the price of oil and oil related products.

If there is skill in the managed futures industry with respect to energy futures contracts, we would expect to see a positively skewed distribution with a large expected return. In addition, we would expect to see a large value of kurtosis that reflects the exposure to these outlier events.

EXHIBIT 32.4   Barclays Financial and Metals CTA Returns

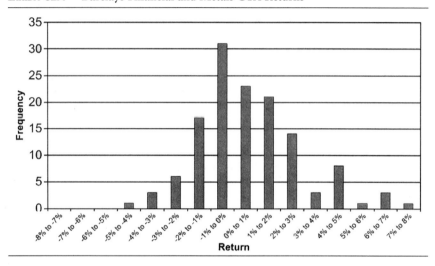

EXHIBIT 32.5   Barclays Energy CTA Returns

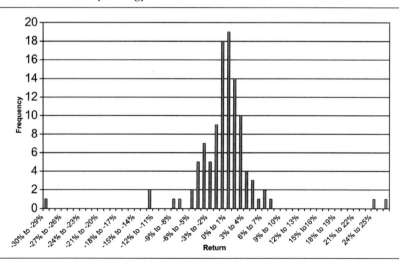

EXHIBIT 32.6   Return Distributions for Managed Futures

	MLMI	CTA Agriculture	CTA Currency	CTA Financial	CTA Energy
Expected Return	0.73%	0.58%	0.80%	0.63%	–0.06%
Standard Deviation	1.61%	2.33%	3.58%	2.21%	5.55%
Sharpe Ratio	0.173	0.055	0.098	0.081	–0.091
Skew	–0.562	0.182	1.394	0.587	0.309
Kurtosis	2.476	0.693	3.147	0.491	14.616

Exhibits 32.5 and 32.6 present the results for managed futures in the energy markets.[17] The results are consistent with our expectations for skew and kurtosis. CTAs did manage to produce a positively skewed distribution of returns. Additionally, a large value of leptokurtosis is observed, consistent with the energy price shocks that affect this market in particular.

Yet, the average return for managed futures in the energy markets is a –0.06% per month. Therefore, even though CTAs are able to shift the distribution of returns to a positive skew, the distribution is centered around a negative mean return. While a positive skew to a distribution is a favorable characteristic of any asset class, it has no utility to an investor if the asset class still loses money. Therefore, we must conclude that managed futures in the energy markets did little to add value for an investor.

Given the mixed and disappointing results observed in Exhibits 32.2 through 32.6, we explore another possible use for managed futures: downside risk protection. We examine this prospect in the next section.

MANAGED FUTURES AS DOWNSIDE RISK PROTECTION FOR STOCKS AND BONDS

The greatest concern for any investor is downside risk. If equity and bond markets are becoming increasingly synchronized, international diversification may not offer the protection sought by investors. The ability to protect the value of an investment portfolio in hostile or turbulent markets is the key to the value of any macroeconomic diversification.

---

[17] Unfortunately, the Barclays Energy CTA index stopped at the end of 1998. This period captures the decline of the energy markets in 1998 due to the world oil glut, but does not include the rebound in energy prices throughout 1999 and 2000.

EXHIBIT 32.7 Frequency Distribution, 60/40 Stocks/Bonds

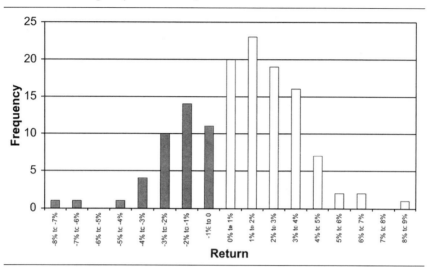

Within this framework, an asset class distinct from financial assets has the potential to diversify and protect an investment portfolio from hostile markets. It is possible that "skill-based" strategies such as managed futures investing can provide the diversification that investors seek. Managed futures strategies might provide diversification for a stock and bond portfolio because the returns are dependent upon the special skill of the CTA rather than any macroeconomic policy decisions made by central bankers or government regimes.

Exhibit 32.7 presents the return distribution for a portfolio that was 60% the S&P 500 and 40% U.S. Treasury bonds. Our concern is the shaded part of the return distribution. This shows where the returns to the stock and bond portfolio were negative. That is, the shaded part of the distribution shows both the size and the frequency with which the combined return of 60% S&P 500 plus 40% U.S. Treasury bonds earned a negative return in a particular month. The average monthly return in the shaded part of the distribution was –2.07%. It is this part of the return distribution that an investor attempts to avoid or limit.

We attempt to protect against the downside of this distribution by making a 10% allocation to managed futures to our initial stock and bond portfolio. Therefore, the new portfolio is a blend of 55% S&P 500, 35% U.S. Treasury bonds, and 10% managed futures. If managed futures can protect against downside risk, we can conclude that it is a valuable addition to a stock and bond portfolio.

EXHIBIT 32.8   55/35/10 Stocks/Bonds/CTA Agriculture

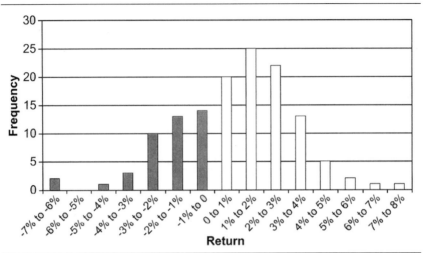

Once again, we use the MLMI as a benchmark to determine if CTAs can improve the downside protection over a passive trend following strategy. The MLMI provided 19 basis points of downside protection for stocks and bonds. Therefore, to demonstrate special skill (and to earn their fees), CTAs in managed futures products must provide greater than 19 basis points of downside risk protection.

Exhibit 32.8 presents the return distribution for a 55/35/10 stock/bond/CTA agriculture portfolio. Exhibit 32.12 presents summary statistics for this portfolio. The average downside return in the shaded part of Exhibit 32.8 is −1.81%. This is an improvement of 26 basis points over the shaded downside area presented in Exhibit 32.7. We can conclude that CTAs managing futures in the agricultural sector did, in fact, exhibit skill by providing additional downside protection beyond that offered by the passive MLMI.

In Exhibit 32.10 we show that this downside protection came at the expense of 3 basis points per month of expected return. Given that, on average, the 60/40 stock/bond portfolio experiences 3.8 downside months per year, the annual expected tradeoff is (26 bp × 3.8) − (3 bp × 12) = 63 basis points.

Exhibit 32.9 presents the return distribution for a 55/35/10 stocks/bonds/CTA currency portfolio. This portfolio also provides downside protection to a stock and bond portfolio. The average monthly downside return is −1.96%. Therefore, currency managed futures provided 0.11% of average monthly downside risk protection. This is less than provided by the MLMI, and consequently, CTAs in this sector did not demonstrate additional skill with respect to downside protection.

In Exhibit 32.10 we present the portfolio return distribution with a 10% allocation to CTA managed futures in financial and metal futures contracts. The average monthly downside return of this portfolio is –1.95%, indicating an improvement of 0.12% per month over the standard stock and bond portfolio. However, again, this is less than the protection offered by the MLMI, and CTA skill is not apparent.

EXHIBIT 32.9   55/35/10 Stocks/Bonds/CTA Currency

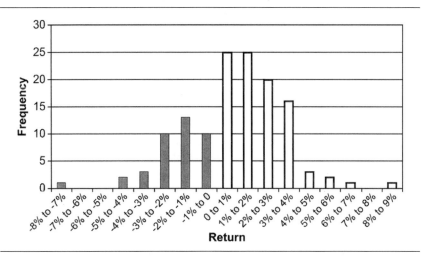

EXHIBIT 32.10   55/35/10 Stocks/Bonds/CTA Financials and Metals

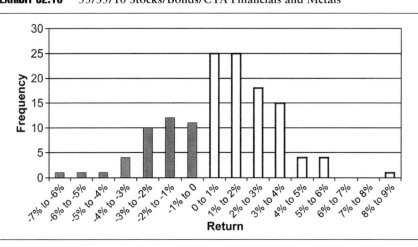

EXHIBIT 32.11   55/35/10 Stocks/Bonds/CTA Energy

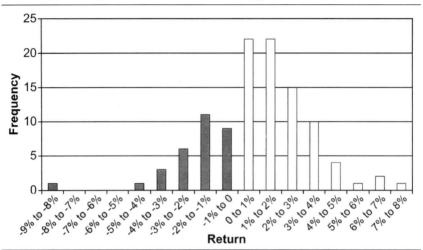

Last, Exhibit 32.11 presents the return distribution for a 55/35/10 stock/bond/CTA energy portfolio. The average monthly downside return in this portfolio is −1.86%, an improvement of 21 basis points over that for stocks and bonds alone. This outperforms the downside risk protection offered by the MLMI.

Once again, we cannot provide firm support for the managed futures industry. Although all managed futures strategies provided downside protection to a stock and bond portfolio, only two strategies (agriculture and energy futures trading) outperformed the downside protection provided by the passive trend following strategy represented by the MLMI. CTAs trading currency and financial products offered less downside protection than that provided by the MLMI. Perhaps currency and financial futures are sufficiently linked to financial assets that they offer less downside protection. In any event, our conclusion regarding the diversification potential of managed futures products is unsettled.

These results are summarized in the first panel of Exhibit 32.12 where we present average downside return compared to the 60/40 stock/bond portfolio as well as the expected returns, standard deviations, and Sharpe ratios for the four portfolios containing managed futures products. We also present the same information for the 55/35/10 stock/bond/MLMI portfolio.

In each case, a portfolio with a 10% allocation to managed futures provided a higher Sharpe ratio than that for the 60/40 stock/bond portfolio. This highlights the concept that managed futures products cannot be analyzed on a stand-alone basis. However, when considered within a portfolio context, some benefit from managed futures products can be achieved.

EXHIBIT 32.12 Downside-Risk Protection (Monthly Returns 1990–2000)

Portfolio Composition	Expected Return	Standard Deviation	Sharpe Ratio	Average Downside	Downside Protection
60/40 U.S. Stocks/U.S. Bonds	0.91%	2.60%	0.177	-2.07%	N/A
55/35/10 Stocks/Bonds/CTA Agriculture	0.88	2.37	0.182	-1.81	0.26%
55/35/10 Stocks/Bonds/CTA Currency	0.90	2.39	0.190	-1.96	0.11
55/35/10 Stocks/Bonds/CTA Financial & Metals	0.89	2.39	0.182	-1.95	0.12
55/35/10 Stocks/Bonds/CTA Energy	0.92	2.38	0.197	-1.86	0.21
55/35/10 Stocks/Bonds/MLMI	0.90	2.33	0.191	-1.88	0.19

Portfolio Composition	Expected Return	Standard Deviation	Sharpe Ratio	Average Downside	Downside Protection
60/40 U.S. Stocks/U.S. Bonds	0.91%	2.60%	0.177	-2.07%	N/A
55/35/10 Stocks/Bonds/GSCI	0.90%	2.39%	0.187	-1.79%	0.28%
55/35/10 Stocks/Bonds/DJ-AIGCI	0.92%	2.30%	0.205	-1.81%	0.26%
55/35/10 Stocks/Bonds/CPCI	0.91%	2.38%	0.192	-1.86%	0.21%
55/35/10 Stocks/Bonds/MLMI	0.90%	2.33%	0.191	-1.88%	0.19%
55/35/10 Stocks/Bonds/EAFE	0.86%	2.66%	0.155	-2.11%	-0.04%

However, in only one case, managed energy futures products, did CTAs provide a Sharpe ratio greater than the passive strategy offered by the MLMI. Even CTA managed agriculture futures did not provide a higher Sharpe ratio than the MLMI. In fact, if we compare the second panel in Exhibit 32.12 to the first panel, it appears that almost all of the passive commodity futures indices outperformed the active CTA strategies in terms of both downside risk protection and Sharpe ratios.

The downside risk protection demonstrated by managed futures products is consistent with the research of Schneeweis, Spurgin, and Potter and Anson.[18] Specifically, they find that a combination of 50% S&P 500 stocks and 50% CTA managed futures outperforms a portfolio comprised of the S&P 500 plus protective put options. Unfortunately, our research indicates that only in limited circumstances do managed futures products offer financial benefits greater than that offered by a passive futures index.

CONCLUSION

In this chapter we examined the benefits of managed futures products. Prior empirical research has not resolved the issue of whether managed futures products can add value either as a stand-alone investment or as part of a diversified portfolio.

On a stand-alone basis, our review indicates that managed futures products fail to outperform a naive trend following index represented by the MLMI. The MLMI is a transparent commodity futures index that mechanically applies a simple price trend following rule for buying or selling commodity futures. We did not find sufficient evidence to conclude that skill-based CTA trading can outperform this passive index of commodity futures.

On a portfolio basis, the results were more encouraging. We found that managed futures products did provide downside risk protection that, on average, ranged from 0.11% to 0.26% per downside month. Unfortunately, only in limited circumstances (energy futures products) did CTA managed products outperform passive commodity futures indices either on a Sharpe ratio basis or with respect to downside risk protection.

---

[18] See Thomas Schneeweis, Richard Spurgin, and Mark Potter, "Managed Futures and Hedge Fund Investment for Downside Equity Risk Protection," *Derivatives Quarterly* (Fall 1996), pp. 62–72. See also Mark Anson, "Managing Downside Risk in Return Distributions Using Hedge Funds, Managed Future and Commodity Futures," working paper (2001).

index